Sources of Japanese Tradition

SECOND EDITION

VOLUME 2, ABRIDGED

PART 2

INTRODUCTION TO ASIAN CIVILIZATIONS

Introduction to Asian Civilizations

WM. THEODORE DE BARY, GENERAL EDITOR

Sources of Japanese Tradition
(1958; vol. 1, 2nd ed., 2001; vol. 2, 2nd ed., 2005; vol. 2, 2nd ed., abr., 2006)

Sources of Indian Tradition
(1958; 2nd ed., 1988)

Sources of Chinese Tradition
(1960; vol. 1, 2nd ed., 1999; vol. 2, 2nd ed., 2000)

Sources of Korean Tradition
(vol. 1, 1997; vol. 2, 2001)

Sources of Japanese Tradition

SECOND EDITION

VOLUME TWO: 1600 TO 2000, ABRIDGED

PART TWO: 1868 TO 2000

*Compiled by Wm. Theodore de Bary, Carol Gluck,
and Arthur E. Tiedemann*

WITH THE COLLABORATION OF

Andrew Barshay, Albert Craig, Brett de Bary, Peter Duus,
Andrew Gordon, Helen Hardacre, James Huffman, Marius Jansen,
Donald Keene, Marlene Mayo, Fred G. Notehelfer, Richard Rubinger

and contributions by

Yŏngho Ch'ŏe, Van Gessel, Ann Stinson, Aida Yuen Wong

COLUMBIA UNIVERSITY PRESS

NEW YORK

Columbia University Press wishes to express its appreciation for assistance given by the Japan Foundation toward the cost of publishing this book.

Columbia University Press
Publishers Since 1893
New York   Chichester, West Sussex

Library of Congress Cataloging-in-Publication Data
Sources of Japanese tradition / compiled by Wm. Theodore de Bary . . . [et al.] ; with the collaboration of Andrew Barshay . . . [et al.] ; and contributions by William Bodiford . . . [et al.]. — 2nd ed.
        p. cm. — (Introduction to Asian civilizations)
    Includes bibliographical references and index.
    Contents: v. 1. From earliest times to 1600
                v. 2. 1600 to 2000
                v. 2, abr., pt. 1. 1600 to 1868
                v. 2, abr., pt. 2. 1868 to 2000
    ISBN 0-231-12138-5 (vol. 1, cloth)   ISBN 0-231-12139-3 (vol. 1, paper)
    ISBN 0-231-12984-X (vol. 2, cloth)
    ISBN 0-231-13916-0 (vol. 2, abr., pt. 1, cloth)   ISBN 0-231-13917-9 (vol. 2, abr., pt. 1, paper)
    ISBN 0-231-13918-7 (vol. 2, abr., pt. 2, cloth)   ISBN 0-231-13919-5 (vol. 2, abr., pt. 2, paper)
    1. Japan—Civilization—Sources.   2. Japan—History—Sources.   I. De Bary, William Theodore, 1919–   II. Bodiford, William M.   III. Series.
    DS821.S68 2001
    952–dc21   00-060181

Acknowledgment is gratefully made for permission to reprint from the following:

Sakai Osugi/*The Autobiography of Osugi Sakae*/© 1992/The Regents of the University of California.

Dedicated to the memory of
Marius Jansen
(1922–2000)

In appreciation of his distinguished contributions to Japanese studies
and of his early collaboration with this project.

CONTENTS

PREFACE

Sources of Japanese Tradition is part of a series introducing the civilizations of India, China, Korea, and Japan to general education, through source readings that tell us what these peoples have thought about themselves, the world they lived in, and the problems they faced living together.

The original *Sources of Japanese Tradition* (1958) was a single volume covering developments from earliest times to the mid-twentieth century. Later this book was divided into two paperback volumes, one from earliest times through the eighteenth century, and the other from the nineteenth to the twentieth century. This division reflected the one prevailing in American education that distinguished modern from traditional primarily on the basis of the encounter with the West in the nineteenth century. The second edition, however, reflects the increasing recognition in both the West and Asia that major factors in the modernization process stemmed from indigenous, pre-nineteenth-century developments. In other words, modernization was not to be understood simply as Westernization. Hence, in their second editions, the Chinese, Korean, and Japanese *Sources* are divided into two volumes, with the second in each case starting from the seventeenth rather than the nineteenth century.

The substantially enlarged volume 2 of the *Japanese Sources* reflects more than just the extended time span from 1600 to 2000. Rather, in this second edition—in volumes 1 and 2 as well as in the abridged parts 1 and 2 of volume 2—educational works have been given particular attention. Instead of focusing on leading thinkers who represented new trends in intellectual or doctrinal thought, we have included basic instructional texts and curricula that helped establish the common terms of educated discourse. Volume 2 also reflects our greater attention to education in both the Tokugawa and Meiji periods as a major factor in the modernization process. Other new developments, covered in part 2, are found in the so-called new religions bridging the dichotomy between traditional and modern.

Even though the early modern period, the subject of part 1, was dominated by Neo-Confucian scholarship and schooling, the warrior ethic continued to play a major role under the military regime of the Tokugawa shogunate, even while the leadership class was being "civilized" by Neo-Confucianism. Buddhism, too, although rejected on intellectual and moral grounds by the Neo-Confucians, persisted on a religious level in ways represented here by a special chapter on the subject. Finally, women's issues (especially education) are included in both parts of volume 2, as they have been in all volumes of the second edition of the East Asian *Sources*.

Since the original edition of *Sources of Japanese Tradition* was published more than forty years ago, many aspects of Japanese (and, indeed, East Asian) studies have undergone substantial development, and we have tried to draw on new studies and expertise wherever possible. Accordingly, the list of collaborators and contributors has expanded greatly, and the compilers are indebted to many distinguished colleagues for their cooperation with this project, a public-service contribution to general education not often recognized.

Marius Jansen was among those collaborators who helped in the planning of this volume, but his untimely death prevented him from contributing to it. This volume is therefore dedicated to him in recognition of his outstanding leadership in Japanese studies and his generous help with both the first and the second editions.

In the final editing of this volume, we have benefited from the extraordinary competence and generous help of Miwa Kai, former curator of the Japanese collection at Columbia University. Others to whom we are indebted for their assistance in producing this volume include Marianna Stiles, Martin Amster, Josephine Vining, and Yuan Zheng. Among our contributors, Tetsuo Najita wishes to acknowledge the collegial assistance of Katsuya Hirano and Yasuko Satō; and Andrew Gordon wishes to thank John Campbell, Sheldon Garon, Timothy Gordon, Laura Hein, Simon Partner, Robert Pekkanen, Ken Ruoff, Mark Selden, M. William Steele, William Tsutsui, and Professors Nakamura Masanori and Hashizume Daizaburō.

EXPLANATORY NOTE

The consonants of Japanese words or names are read as they are in English (with g always hard) and the vowels as in Italian. There are no silent letters. The name Abe, for instance, is pronounced "Ah-bay." The long vowels ō and ū are indicated except in the names of cities already well known in the West, such as Tokyo and Kyoto, and in the words familiar enough to be included in *Webster's Collegiate Dictionary*. All romanized terms have been standardized according to the Hepburn system. Chinese philosophical terms used in Japanese texts are given in their Japanese readings (e.g., *ri* instead of *li* for "principle," "reason") except where attention is specifically drawn to the Chinese original, in which case the *pin-yin* system is followed. Sanskrit words appearing in italics follow the standard system of transliteration found in Louis Renou's *Grammair sanskrite* (Paris: Adrien-Maisoneuve, 1930), pp. xi–xiii. Sanskrit terms and names appearing in roman letters follow *Webster's New International Dictionary*, second edition unabridged, except that a macron is used to indicate long vowels and the Sanskrit symbols for ś (ç) are uniformly transcribed as *sh* in the text itself. Personal names also are spelled in this manner except when they occur in the titles of works.

Japanese names are given in their Japanese order, with the family name first and the personal name last. The dates given after personal names are those of birth and death except in the case of rulers, whose reign dates are preceded by "r." Generally, the name by which a person was most commonly known in

Japanese tradition is the one used in the text. Since this book is intended for general readers rather than specialists, we have not burdened the text with the alternative names or titles usually accompanying biographical references to a scholar that are found in Chinese or Japanese historical works. For the same reason, the sources of translations given at the end of each selection are as concise as possible. There is a complete bibliography at the end of the book.

The name following the chapter title in the table of contents refers to the writer of all the introductory material in that chapter unless otherwise noted. The initials following the source at the end of each selection are those of the translator or compiler. Excerpts from existing translations have often been adapted and edited to suit our purposes. In particular, we have removed unnecessary brackets and footnotes and have inserted essential commentary in the text whenever possible instead of putting it in a footnote. Those interested in the full text and annotations may, of course, refer to the original translation cited with each excerpt. As sources for our own translations, we have tried to use standard editions that would be available to other scholars.

W. T. de B.

CHRONOLOGY

Meiji Period (1868–1911)

1868   Meiji Restoration begins, and the Charter Oath is written. Edo is renamed Tokyo.

1869   Tokugawa status hierarchy is abolished, and Tokyo becomes the capital of Japan.

1871   Feudal domains are abolished by imperial decree, and prefectures are established. Former outcasts are emancipated. Samuel Smiles's *Self-Help* is published in Japanese translation. The Iwakura Mission departs for the West.

1872   Conscription ordinance and Fundamental Code of Education (Gakusei) are proclaimed.

1873   Land tax reforms are passed. A forceful "opening" of Korea (Seikanron) is debated. The ban against Christianity is lifted.

1877   Satsuma Rebellion takes place.

1881   Ōkuma Shigenobu memorializes the throne, demanding a national assembly; a parliament is promised for 1890.

1882   Fukuzawa Yukichi founds the newspaper *Jiji shinpō*.

1885   Japan's first cabinet is formed, with Itō Hirobumi as prime minister.

1889   Meiji constitution is promulgated.

1890	First Diet is convened. The Imperial Rescript on Education (Kyōiku chokugo) is issued.
1894–1895	Sino-Japanese War is fought.
1898	Meiji Civil Code is written, legally redefining gender and family roles.
1900	Imperial ordnance is passed, stipulating that war and navy ministers be generals or admirals on the active list. The Boxer Rebellion takes place.
1902	Anglo-Japanese Alliance is signed.
1904–1905	Russo-Japanese War is fought.
1910	Korea is annexed. Kōtoku Shūsui allegedly plots to assassinate the emperor.
1911	*Bluestocking* magazine is founded: "In the beginning, woman was the sun."

Taishō Period (1912–1926)

1912	Emperor Meiji (1852–1912) dies.
1914–1918	World War I is fought.
1915	Twenty-one Demands are issued to China.
1918	Siberian expedition takes place. Japan's first party cabinet, with Hara Takashi as premier, is formed.
1921	Hara Takashi (1856–1921) is assassinated.
1923	Great Kantō Earthquake shakes Japan.

Shōwa Period (1926–1989)

1925	Universal manhood suffrage is passed.
1930	London Naval Treaty is signed.
1931	Manchurian "incident" takes place.
1932	Manchukuo is formed.
1936	Rightist coup d'état is attempted on February 26 (February 26 incident).
1937	China "incident" commences total war against China.
1940	Axis alliance among Rome, Berlin, and Tokyo is formed.
1941–1945	Japanese attack on Pearl Harbor, Hawaii, in 1941 leads to Pacific War (World War II).
1945	United States drops atomic bombs on Hiroshima and Nagasaki, leading to Japan's unconditional surrender. Allied Occupation begins.
1947	"Peace constitution" goes into effect.
1946–1947, 1948–1954	Yoshida Shigeru serves as prime minister.
1948	Verdicts of Tokyo war crimes tribunal are handed down.
1950–1953	Korean War is fought.

1951	San Francisco peace treaty and U.S.–Japanese security treaty are signed.
1952	Japan regains its independence, and military occupation by Allied forces ends.
1953	Japan's Self-Defense Forces are established.
1959	Crown Prince Akihito marries a commoner.
1960	Demonstrations are held against the renewal of the U.S.–Japanese security treaty.
1960s	Era of "high growth" commences.
1964	Summer Olympics are held in Tokyo.
1965	Korea–Japan treaty is concluded.
1968	Japan's GDP is the world's third highest, after those of the United States and the Soviet Union. Kawabata Yasunari receives Japan's first Nobel Prize in Literature. Centennial of the Meiji Restoration is celebrated.
1971–1973	Japan experiences the "Nixon shock" and the first oil shock. Minamata and other pollution tragedies are uncovered.
1972	Okinawa is returned to Japan, and diplomatic relations are established with China.
1982–1987	Nakasone Yasuhiro serves as prime minister. Japan is first labeled an "economic superpower," leading to frictions with the United States.
1989	Emperor Hirohito (1901–1989) dies, and Emperor Akihito (b. 1933) succeeds him.

Heisei Period (1989–)

1990–1992	Japan's "bubble economy" bursts.
1993	Liberal Democratic Party ends thirty-eight-year monopoly of power.
1994	Ōe Kenzaburō receives Nobel Prize in Literature.
1995	Big earthquake shakes Kobe. Aum shinrikyō cult attacks Tokyo subway with sarin gas. Fiftieth anniversary of the end of the Pacific War is commemorated.
1996	Liberal Democratic Party regains power in coalition government.

CONTRIBUTORS

AB   Andrew Barshay, University of California, Berkeley
AC   Albert Craig, Harvard University
AET   Arthur E. Tiedemann, Columbia University
AG   Andrew Gordon, Harvard University
AS   Ann Stinson, Columbia University
AYW   Aida Yuen Wong, Vassar College
BdB   Brett de Bary, Cornell University
CG   Carol Gluck, Columbia University
DK   Donald Keene, Columbia University
FN   Fred G. Notehelfer, University of California, Los Angeles
HH   Helen Hardacre, Harvard University
JH   James Huffman, Wittenberg University
MJ   Marius Jansen, Princeton University
MM   Marlene Mayo, University of Maryland
PD   Peter Duus, Stanford University
RR   Richard Rubinger, Indiana University
VG   Van Gessel, Brigham Young University
YC   Yŏngho Ch'ŏe, University of Hawai'i

Sources of Japanese Tradition

SECOND EDITION

VOLUME 2, ABRIDGED

PART 2

PART V

Japan, Asia, and the West

Part V, covering the period from 1868 to 1945, begins with the so-called Restoration (*ishin*) of 1868 and ends with the devastation and surrender of Japan at the end of World War II in 1945. The Japanese term *ishin* has connotations of both "restoration" and "renovation." As the restoration of imperial rule, the events of 1868 marked the end of the military regimes that had dominated Japan since the twelfth century. This outcome, however, left an open question of whether the military might still play as great a role in the expected "Renovation" as it did in the Restoration itself. For much of the late nineteenth and early twentieth century, that role was still a major one. Yet after the military's eclipse in 1945, the civil (*bun*) aspects of the Renovation, starting with the Meiji "enlightenment," emerged from the shadow of the military (*bu*) with greater significance for Japan's future.

In historical perspective, the "civilizing" aspects of the Renovation had already begun with the spread of Neo-Confucianism under the Tokugawa, especially with the increasing propagation of meritocratic values through the extension of schooling, literacy, and a literate culture that was already, from the seventeenth century, beginning to assimilate Western learning in the form of "Dutch learning" (*rangaku*).

As a long-term trend, the aims of this civilizing process were expressed in the Meiji emperor's Charter Oath of 1868, which, in sum, set as its goals:

1. Deliberative assemblies to decide all matters by means of public discussion.
2. The participation of all classes in government.
3. The abolition of hereditary status and occupation.
4. The discarding of past evil customs.
5. A search for knowledge throughout the world to strengthen the foundations of imperial rule.

The following chapters illustrate the ways in which these civilizational goals were to be pursued: by sending cultural missions abroad; establishing a new, Westernized education and national school system, new state and private universities, and new publication media to disseminate information and promote public discussion; creating new cultural associations and political parties to advocate liberal and even radical causes; drawing up a constitution to provide for parliamentary rule; and making the most of the economic and social developments that accompanied these political and cultural changes.

Many of these developments are recognizable as characteristic of a modern civil society and arguably can be seen as extending the original consensus-building consultation processes envisaged in Prince Shōtoku's early Seventeen-Article Constitution of the seventh century c.e. But the Meiji constitution of 1889 (like Shōtoku's) also incorporated authoritarian elements that could be used by a ruling oligarchy to strengthen its hold on power. Moreover, a strong undercurrent of radical nationalism, agitating against parliamentarism and party politics, used violence and terror to pressure the political process in a rightward direction and toward a policy that asserted Japan's own economic growth as inseparable from, and indeed demanding, military expansion in Asia.

The idea that Japan could assume the leadership of a resurgent Asia gained some plausibility from the rapid advances it had made in many aspects of modernization, compared with the seeming backwardness or fractiousness of other Asian countries unable to cope with the challenge from the West. Thus the ideology of the national polity or essence (*kokutai*), combining imperial rule with a new state-centered version of popular loyalty, aspired to more than just the conversion of local, feudal loyalties into a powerful state nationalism and even threatened to become charged with a world imperialistic (though ostensibly modernizing, civilizing) mission.

In the disastrous outcome of this ambition, there was plenty of complicity and blame among Japanese elites of all kinds. The national habit of consensus formation and feeling for solidarity tended toward political conformity, which obviated the more intense repression and liquidation of all opposition characteristic of the Nazis and Communists in Europe. But historically there had always been strong individuals who resisted the consensus, and after the war, some leadership groups survived, relatively unscathed from the ordeal, to carry on. Thus, despite the disaster of war and the unprecedented destruction it brought to Japan, the period from 1868 to 1945 should be seen as a time of lively, spirited activity on many levels of Japanese society and substantial advances made, despite their sometimes high cost and great setbacks.

Chapter 35

THE MEIJI RESTORATION

The Meiji Restoration, like the Taika Reform of the mid-sixth century, was a major turning point in Japanese history. Just as the Taika Reform opened Japan to the incorporation of new ideas and institutions from China, which led to a profound restructuring of the Japanese polity and society, so the Meiji Restoration opened Japan to similar influences from the West. While most scholars agree that the Meiji Restoration ushered in Japan's modern age by creating the political, economic, and social institutions that governed Japanese lives until World War II, both the nature and the interpretation of this event remain controversial. Was the Restoration a simple coup d'état in which one part of Japan's feudal elite replaced another? Was it a revolution? If a revolution, what kind of a revolution was it? Did the Restoration reflect class interests or ideology? Did the Restoration leaders have clear plans? Was the Restoration the product of internal changes that reflected the social and economic transformation of late Tokugawa Japan? Or was it largely foreign induced? Such questions continue to be debated by students of modern Japan and are still of great interest to historians. What is generally agreed, however, is that in its broad sense, the Meiji Restoration transformed Japan in less than forty years from a backward feudal nation into one of the world's great powers.

EDICT TO SUBJUGATE THE SHOGUN TOKUGAWA YOSHINOBU

In a narrow sense, the Meiji Restoration consisted of a coup d'état that was announced on January 3, 1868, when troops from Satsuma and Chōshū seized the Imperial Palace in Kyoto and declared an "imperial restoration." Two months earlier, on November 9, 1867, in response to a request made by Ōkubo Toshimichi, Satsuma and Chōshū had obtained a secret imperial rescript to overthrow the shogunate. Its harsh language leaves it open to question, although it appears that Iwakura Tomomi vouched for its veracity.

Minamoto Yoshinobu [Tokugawa Yoshinobu, the last shogun], borrowing the authority of successive generations and depending on the strength of his pack of bandits, has wantonly impaired the loyal and the good, and has frequently disobeyed imperial commands. In the end, not fearing to distort the edicts of the late emperor, and not caring that he has plunged the populace into an abyss, his all-pervasive evil threatens to overturn the Land of the Gods. We are father and mother of the people. If We fail to strike down this traitor, what excuse shall We have to offer to the spirit of the late emperor? How shall We make Our profound amends to the people? This is the cause of Our grief and indignation. It is unavoidable that the period of mourning be disregarded. Implement the wishes of Our heart by slaughtering the traitorous subject Yoshinobu. When you have speedily accomplished this great deed to save the nation, you will enable the people to enjoy the lasting peace of the mountains. This is Our wish. See to it that you are prompt in carrying it out.

[Ishii, *Boshin senso ron*, pp. 66–67; trans. in Keene, *Emperor of Japan*, p. 115]

LETTER OF RESIGNATION OF THE LAST SHOGUN

Despite Yoshinobu's decision to restore political rule to the emperor on the same day (November 9, 1867), thereby formally terminating the Tokugawa shogunate, and despite efforts by moderates from Tosa such as Sakamoto Ryōma and Gotō Shōjirō to create a plan of government that would have included the Tokugawa in a new shared administration with other domains, the Satsuma and Chōshū loyalists decided to pursue the subjugation order and plunged the nation into the Boshin civil war, which lasted until the summer of 1869. Yoshinobu's willingness to submit to imperial authority and to surrender Edo Castle with minimal resistance can be attributed in part to his consciousness that in the background stood the aggressive Western powers that had already pressured Japan into signing the unequal treaties and appeared to be seeking further concessions. Even the last shogun was fully aware that Japan would have to become a centralized state in order to defend itself against the outside world, as his letter of resignation notes.

My ancestor [Tokugawa Ieyasu] received more confidence and favor from the Court than any of his predecessors, and his descendants have succeeded him for more than two hundred years. Though I fill the same office, almost all the acts of the administration are far from perfect, and I confess it with shame that the present unsatisfactory condition of affairs is due to my shortcomings and incompetence. Now that foreign intercourse becomes daily more extensive, unless the government is directed from one central authority, the foundations of the state will fall to pieces. If, however, the old order of things be changed, and the administrative authority be restored to the Imperial Court, and if national deliberations be conducted on an extensive scale, and the Imperial decision be secured, and if the empire be supported by the efforts of the whole people, then the empire will be able to maintain its rank and dignity among the nations of the earth.

[*Hōrei zensho*, 1867, p. 1; McLaren, *Japanese Government Documents*, pp. 2–3]

EDICT TO FOREIGN DIPLOMATS

While the legitimacy of the new government was being contested on the battlefield, the Meiji leaders were quick to indicate to both domestic and foreign audiences the role and position of the emperor, Mutsuhito, who was still only a boy of sixteen. On February 3, 1868, the emperor issued the following edict.

The Emperor of Japan announces to the sovereigns of all Foreign countries and to their subjects that permission has been granted to the Shogun Tokugawa Yoshinobu to return the governing power in accordance with his own request. We shall henceforward exercise supreme authority in all the internal and external affairs of the country. Consequently the title of Emperor must be substituted for that of Tycoon, in which the treaties have been made. Officers are being appointed by us to the conduct of foreign affairs. It is desirable that the representatives of the treaty powers recognize this announcement.

[Satow, *Diplomat in Japan*, p. 324]

THE CHARTER OATH

Placing the emperor squarely at the heart of the new polity, the Meiji leaders acted quickly to consolidate their rule. The Charter Oath of April 1868 is one of the most important and intriguing documents that was issued in the name of the young Meiji emperor by the men who carried out the Restoration. The oath is usually viewed as expressing the progressive side of the Restoration. It also has been interpreted as underscoring the generally hostile attitudes of the samurai from the western clans toward the old order and their eagerness to make room for a new leadership group. While many historians have seen the Restoration as a top–down event in which one segment of the samurai class replaced another segment of that class in what T. C. Smith labeled "Japan's aristocratic revolution," more recent scholarship has come to view the Restoration not simply as a narrow political event and internal power shift but as a broader change in which new intellectual, economic, and social forces were at work in a way that included considerable bottom–up participation. The ferment of late Tokugawa society is now perceived not only through the lenses of the discontented samurai who, in the name of loyalty to the throne and antiforeignism, wanted to create a new Japan but also through the social strife, discontent, and disorder expressed in new religions, millenarian movements, mass pilgrimages, urban riots, and peasant uprisings. As George Wilson noted, "The samurai elite and the popular movements were simultaneously groping for a new and stable order in Japan."[1] There can be no question that the Charter Oath was designed as a general policy pronouncement intended to rally the greatest degree of popular support behind the Restoration. Its vagueness allowed it to be interpreted later along diverse lines, but it was equally difficult to overlook the strong focus on the public and popular concerns. This indicates that the new administration was not unaware of the broader changes apparent in late Tokugawa socioeconomic life.

By this oath, we set up as our aim the establishment of the national weal on a broad basis and the framing of a constitution and laws.

1. Deliberative assemblies shall be widely established and all matters decided by public discussion.
2. All classes, high and low, shall unite in vigorously carrying out the administration of affairs of state.
3. The common people, no less than the civil and military officials, shall each be allowed to pursue his own calling so that there may be no discontent.
4. Evil customs of the past shall be broken off and everything based upon the just laws of Nature.
5. Knowledge shall be sought throughout the world so as to strengthen the foundations of imperial rule.

[*Meiji boshin*, pp. 81–82; McLaren, *Japanese Government Documents*, p. 8]

THE CONSTITUTION OF 1868

The constitution of June 1868 was promulgated in the emperor's name to confirm the original intentions of the Restoration leadership. Article I of the constitution reiterates

---

1. Wilson, *Patriots and Redeemers in Japan*, p. 80.

the Charter Oath, and the rest of the document was designed to flesh out the original policy lines outlined in the earlier document. Articles II, III, V, and IX indicate that the writers of this document were influenced by Western concepts of representative government and attempted to implement the idea of the separation of powers. At the same time, the constitution shows that the Restoration leaders had to walk a fine line between asserting new prerogatives for the throne and court and avoiding an open attack on established feudal authority. The document provides further insights into the dual nature of the Restoration. It clearly shows the Meiji leaders considering Western constitutional ideas and democratic principles while simultaneously implementing a system of formal government structures based on the earlier centralized system borrowed from China in the seventh century. The administrative structure spelled out in the appendices of this document, which are not reproduced here, reveal that the Restoration leaders sought from the outset a strong government that would be administered by a ruling oligarchy. At the same time, they also felt compelled to cater to the new political forces that wanted greater public participation in government and a more popular system that might implement such participation. These elements, the search for top–down control and the desire for bottom–up participation in government, constituted the fundamental and often contradictory forces that shaped Japanese politics well into the twentieth century.

I. (Restates the Charter Oath)

II. All power and authority in the empire shall be vested in a Council of State, and thus the grievances of divided government shall be done away with. The power and authority of the Council of State shall be threefold, legislative, executive, and judicial. Thus the imbalance of authority among the different branches of government shall be avoided.

III. The legislative organ shall not be permitted to perform executive functions, nor shall the executive organ be permitted to perform legislative functions. However, on extraordinary occasions the legislative organ may still perform such functions as tours of inspection of cities and the conduct of foreign affairs.

IV. Attainment to offices of the first rank shall be limited to princes of the blood, court nobles, and territorial lords, and shall be by virtue of [the sovereign's] intimate trust in the great ministers of state. A law governing ministers summoned from the provinces (*chōshi*) shall be adopted, clan officials of whatever status may attain offices of the second rank on the basis of worth and talent.

V. Each great city, clan, and imperial prefecture shall furnish qualified men to be members of the Assembly. A deliberative body shall be instituted so that the views of the people may be discussed openly.

VI. A system of official ranks shall be instituted so that each [official] may know the importance of his office and not dare to hold it in contempt.

VII. Princes of the blood, court nobles, and territorial lords shall be accompanied by [no more than] six two-sworded men and three commoners, and persons of lower rank by [no more than] two two-sworded men and one commoner, so that the appearance of pomp and grandeur may be done away with and the evils of class barriers may be avoided.

VIII. Officers shall not discuss the affairs of the government in their own houses with unofficial persons. If any person desire interviews with them for the purpose of giving expression to their own opinions, they shall be sent to the office of the appropriate department and the matter shall be discussed openly.

IX. All officials shall be changed after four years' service. They shall be selected by means of public balloting. However, at the first expiration of terms hereafter, half of the officials shall retain office for two additional years, after which their terms shall expire, so that [the government] may be caused to continue without interruption. Those whose relief is undesirable because they enjoy the approval of the people may be retained for an additional period of years.

X. A system shall be established for levying taxes on territorial lords, farmers, artisans, and merchants, so that government revenue may be supplemented, military installations strengthened, and public security maintained. For this purpose, even persons with rank or office shall have taxes levied upon them equivalent to one-thirtieth of their income or salaries.

XI. Each large city, clan, and imperial prefecture shall promulgate regulations, and these shall comply with the Charter Oath. The laws peculiar to one locality shall not be generalized to apply to other localities. There shall be no private conferral of titles or rank, no private coinage, no private employment of foreigners, and no conclusion of alliances with neighboring clans or with foreign countries, lest inferior authorities be confounded with superior and the government be thrown into confusion.

[*Meiji boshin*, pp. 87–89; McLaren, *Japanese Government Documents*, pp. 8–10]

THE ABOLITION OF FEUDALISM AND THE CENTRALIZATION OF THE MEIJI STATE

The Restoration leaders were fully conscious of the need to create a newly centralized nation-state that could compete with the Western powers. To achieve this end, they realized that Japan would have to move beyond the decentralized feudal system, with its more than 250 separate feudal domains that had marked the Tokugawa age. Several crucial steps were taken to move ahead with the abolition of feudalism.

MEMORIAL ON THE PROPOSAL TO RETURN THE REGISTERS

In 1869 the lords of four of the most important feudal domains—Chōshū, Satsuma, Hizen, and Tosa—agreed to return their lands to the emperor and sent a memorial to the throne to that effect. The Return of the Domain Registers, as this act was called, was followed by new administrative regulations to govern the *fu* (urban districts) and *ken* (prefectures).

Your servants again venture to address Your Majesty with profound reverence. Two things are essential to the Imperial administration. There must be one central body of government, and one sovereign authority which must be preserved intact. Since the time when your Majesty's ancestors founded this country and established a basis of government, all things in the wide expanse of heaven and all things on earth to its furthest limits, have belonged to the Emperor from generation to generation. This is what is known as "one central government." And the sole power of giving and of taking away, which renders it impossible for the nobles to hold the people in subjection in virtue of their land, or to deal with the smallest piece of ground at their pleasure, or to seize and treat despotically any individual of the humbler classes, this is what is understood by the term "one sovereign authority."

The administration of the Emperors was conducted entirely on this principle. They conducted the government in their own persons, the name and reality of power were combined, and consequently the nation was tranquil and contented. But from the time of the middle ages the administration became lax, and the authority of the Emperors came to be a plaything. . . . Everywhere men of influence, but of unprincipled character, took advantage of the existing disorder to promote their own interests, and the weak became food for the strong. . . . Finally the Mikado's [emperor's] government lost all real authority and was entirely dependent upon the will of the shogunate. The boundless despotism of the shogunate lasted for over six hundred years, and during this interval violent dealings with land and with the people were carried out by stealth under pretense of the Imperial authority. . . .

When the Tokugawa family rose to power, half the country was held by them and their relatives. In addition new families rose up. These houses took no heed of the question of whether their lands and subjects had been received in grant from the Imperial court. It was commonly said by members of these houses: "Our possessions were gained by the military power of our ancestors." But there is little doubt that those ancestors had originally raised forces, plundered the Imperial storehouses, and laid forcible hands on the treasures they contained and had braved the penalty of death in the execution of their designs. Those who break into storehouses are commonly termed robbers, but no suspicion was attached by the nation to those who seized upon the land and people. This confusion between right and wrong is terrible indeed.

Now that we seek to establish an entirely new form of government, it is incumbent on us to take care to preserve intact both one central body of government and one sovereign authority. The land in which your servants live is the land of the Emperor, and the people whom they govern are his subjects. Neither the one, nor the other can belong to us. We entreat Your Majesty to issue such Imperial Decrees as may be deemed necessary to deal with the lands and the people of the four clans represented in this memorial, and to make such changes as Your Majesty may think proper. We also beg that all laws, decrees, and military regulations, extending even to military dress and accouterments, may be issued by the Central government, so that all matters of state may be decided by one and the same authority. In this way both name and reality will be secured, and this country will be placed upon a footing of equality with foreign powers. . . .

[Hōrei zensho, 1869, p. 42; McLaren, Japanese Government Documents, pp. 29–32]

IMPERIAL RESCRIPT ON THE ABOLITION OF THE *HAN*

On August 29, 1871, an imperial rescript formally disbanded the feudal domains (*han*) and promulgated the prefectural system across the nation. In effect, this spelled the end of feudalism in Japan.

We are of the opinion that in a time of radical reform like the present, if We desire by its means to give protection and tranquillity to the people at home and to maintain equality with foreign powers abroad, words must be made to mean in reality what they claim to signify, and the government of the country must center in a single authority.

Some time ago We gave Our sanction to the scheme by which all the clans restored to Us their registers; We appointed governors for the first time, each to perform the duties of his office.

But owing to the lengthened endurance of the old system during several hundred years, there have been cases where the word only was pronounced and the reality not performed. How is it possible for Us, under such circumstances, to give protection and tranquillity to the people, and to maintain equality with foreign nations?

Profoundly regretting this condition of affairs, We now completely abolish the Clans (*han*) and convert them into Prefectures (*ken*), with the object of diligently retrenching expenditure and of arriving at convenience of working, or getting rid of the unreality of names and of abolishing the disease of government proceeding from multiple centers.

Do ye, Our assembled servants, take well to heart this Our will.

[Hōrei zensho, 1871, p. 283; McLaren, Japanese Government Documents, pp. 32–33]

THE LEADERS AND THEIR VISION

The leaders of the Restoration who came to power in 1868 were largely young and low- to middle-ranking samurai from the four domains of Satsuma, Chōshū, Tosa, and Hizen, plus a few courtiers, like Iwakura Tomomi, who surrounded the emperor. Most of these men initially harbored strong antiforeign biases that emerged from the combination of loyalism and xenophobia that had fueled the Restoration. But in the early Meiji years, such sentiments were quickly jettisoned. Talented, young, and ambitious, they were determined to create a new, viable Japan. With few ties to the past, they were prepared to move in new directions. The abolition of feudalism and the centralization of the new Meiji state were among their highest priorities. At the same time imbued with a strong national-istic sentiment, they were equally concerned with maintaining sovereignty against the threat of the Western powers. As the foregoing documents show, the men who were directing the transformation of Japan were less concerned with pro-tecting tradition than with learning the secrets of Western wealth and power in order to strengthen Japan. The goal that most of these men agreed on was that Japan had to penetrate the opponents' camp, master the West's civilization, in-cluding its weapons, and use them to protect the national interest. While the West played an important role in this process, it was never an end in itself. As the Charter Oath noted, Japan would seek knowledge from around the world, but the goal was to shore up the foundations of imperial rule. Although the ends were clear, the means to those ends often elicited serious debate. What kind of culture should Japan develop? What should lie at the core of that culture? How were Japanese peasants to be transformed into citizens of the modern state?

In the 1870s, such debates raged both inside and outside government circles. At the same time, a group of reform bureaucrats consolidated their position within the administration. They included men like Ōkubo Toshimichi from Satsuma and Kido Takayoshi and Itō Hirobumi from Chōshū. Their priority was to preserve stability and order within Japan while maintaining national sovereignty abroad. For leaders such as Kido, Ōkubo, and Itō, the main question remained how to steer a middle course between the liberal influences of West-ern political structures and the essential despotism of the Japanese emperor system, which they identified with the Japanese national polity. What they searched for was a way to "civilize" and "Westernize" Japan without harming the prerogatives of the throne.

THE IWAKURA MISSION

The Iwakura Mission (1871–1873) played a key role in shaping the views of the Restoration leaders. The mission took half the leadership group—including Ōkubo Toshimichi, Kido Takayoshi, and Itō Hirobumi—as well as fifty students, to the United States and Europe for two years. This sojourn abroad played a crucial part in transforming the vision of the men who created modern Japan. Ostensibly, it was a mission designed to renegotiate the unequal treaties and was led by the court noble Iwakura Tomomi. But it served as an eye-opening experience for most of its members. Faced with Western wealth and power, these men realized that Japan would require significant reforms in its economy, social system, and political institutions before it could achieve equality with the West. In the process, Westernization became a central theme of the Restoration.

KIDO TAKAYOSHI'S OBSERVATIONS OF EDUCATION IN THE UNITED STATES

Although in historical perspective, the Meiji leaders are often regarded as conservative, they also were quite innovative. As we can see in the following letter written by Kido Takayoshi from the United States, they were concerned not only with shoring up their own and the emperor's authority but also with dealing with broader issues such as education and the need to transform Japan socially and culturally to meet the demands of modernity. Clearly, the issue for Kido was that Japan could not become a modern state if it did not have an educated and enlightened citizenry. While education could serve as a means of control, it also retained, as men like Fukuzawa Yukichi recognized, the potential for liberating the citizens from state authority.

When it comes to things like schools and factories, it is impossible to tell you everything, for it defies description. From now on, unless we pay a great deal of attention to the children, the preservation of order in our country in the future will be impossible. . . . Maintaining a stable state will be difficult unless we consider social conditions and pay attention to social evils. Nothing is more important than schools for improving social conditions and uprooting social evils. The civilization we have in our country today is not a true civilization, and our enlightenment is not true enlightenment. To prevent trouble ten years from now, there is only one thing to do, and that is to establish schools worthy of the name. A long-range program for the stability of our country will never be carried out if we have only a small number of able people; we have to have universal adherence to the moral principles of loyalty, justice, humanity, and decorum. Unless we establish an unshakable national foundation, we will not be able to elevate our country's prestige in a thousand years. The creation of such public morals and the establishment of such a national foundation depend entirely on people. And the supply of such people in endless numbers over a long period of time clearly depends on education, and on education alone. Our people are no different from Americans or Europeans of today: it is all a matter of education or the lack of education.

[Kido Takayoshi to Sugiyama Takatoshi, January 26, 1872,
in *Kido Takayoshi monjo*, vol. 4, p. 320; trans. adapted from Irokawa,
The Culture of the Meiji Period, pp. 54–55]

KIDO ON THE NEED FOR CONSTITUTIONAL GOVERNMENT

As one of the drafters of the Charter Oath, Kido is said to have insisted on Article IV: "Evil customs of the past shall be broken off and everything based upon the just laws of Nature." While on the Iwakura Mission, he became an early supporter of constitutional government for Japan. On March 1, 1872, he wrote the following.

In the first year of the Restoration, we worked out the five-article Charter Oath hastily and had it accepted by the leaders, daimyo, and court nobles, setting out the direction for the people's future. But now it is time for us to have an unshakable fundamental law. Therefore, from now on I want to concentrate my attention on matters such as the basic laws and governmental structures of other countries.

[*Kido Takayoshi nikki*, vol. 2, p. 142; Irokawa, *The Culture of the Meiji Period*, p. 56]

KUME KUNITAKE'S ASSESSMENT OF EUROPEAN WEALTH AND POWER

The official chronicle of the Iwakura Mission was produced by Kume Kunitake, Iwakura's chief secretary. Like the other members of the embassy, Kume was a careful observer. As the following suggests, he, too, believed that through cautious planning, Japan could catch up with the West. Impressed by the European nations' wealth and power, he noted that much of this was the product of recent history. After going to an exposition in London, Kume wrote the following, whose implications for further reforms in Japan are obvious.

Most of the countries in Europe shine with the light of civilization and abound in wealth and power. Their trade is prosperous, their technology is superior, and they greatly enjoy the pleasures and comforts of life. When one observes such conditions, one is apt to think that these countries have always been like this, but this is not the case—the wealth and prosperity one sees now in Europe dates to an appreciable degree from the period after 1800. It has taken scarcely forty years to produce such conditions. . . . How different the Europe of today is from the Europe of forty years ago can be imagined easily. There were no trains running on the land; there were no steamships operating on the water. There was no transmission of news by telegraph. Small ships plied navigable rivers; sailing ships crossed the high seas, horse-drawn carriages trod the roads, letter carriers ran between stations. Soldiers, using copper cannon or flint rifles, fought within a restricted battle area. Woolen cloth was the finery of the wealthy. Cotton was a rare good from across the seas. . . . Although the fashions of France were the shining example for all of Europe, England was the first to break away and create out of its traditions the crafts and customs appropriate to itself. England had gradually stimulated other nations to produce what they can do best. At present, the crafts of Europe vie in beauty with each other. It is just as if a variety of trees and flowers were growing profusely giving off a fragrance.

These were our thoughts after seeing the Kensington Exposition. Those who read this record should reflect upon the lesson to be drawn for Japan.

[Kume Kunitake, *Tokumei*, vol. 2, pp. 58–59; MM]

KIDO'S OBSERVATIONS ON RETURNING FROM THE WEST

The following statement by Kido shows the evolution of his ideas after returning to Japan from the United States and Europe in 1873. Like other Meiji leaders, he was concerned about the institutionalization of authority, which was initially exercised by individuals under the emperor. As Kido saw it, such an arbitrary exercise of power should be replaced by the rule of law. In this sense, he remained true to the progressive impulses of the Restoration and was a herald of the constitutional movement that blossomed in the late 1870s and 1880s. What struck Kido most about the West were the constitutional processes limiting those in power and providing a sound basis for orderly change. Indeed, in a long preamble to the passage quoted here, he asserts as a universal law of history that the rise and fall of nations are determined by their fidelity to constitutional order. Kido praised the so-called constitution established under the Charter Oath but expanded the need for a more popularly based governmental structure. His analysis confirms at the same time both his firm commitment to greater popular participation in government and the gradualist approach toward change that marked the nature of early Meiji reforms. The heart of his argument reads as follows.

In enlightened countries, though there may be a sovereign, still he does not hold sway in an arbitrary fashion. The people of the whole country give expression to their united and harmonious wishes, and the business of the State is arranged accordingly, a department (styled the government) being charged with the execution of their judgments, and officials appointed to transact business. For this reason all who hold office respect the wishes of the whole nation and serve their country under a deep sense of responsibility, so that even in extraordinary crises, they take no arbitrary step contrary to the people's will. The strictness [of the constitution] of these governments is such as I have just described, but as [an] additional check upon illegal acts, the people have parliamentary representatives whose duty it is to inspect everything that is done and to check arbitrary proceedings on the part of officials. Herein lies the best quality of these governments. But if the people are not yet sufficiently enlightened, it becomes necessary, at least for a time, that the Sovereign should by his superior discernment anticipate their unanimous wishes and act for them in arranging the affairs of State and in entrusting to officials the execution of their wishes. By this means he will gradually lead them forward in the path of enlightenment. Such a course is consonant with natural principles, and I am inclined to believe that the thought of the Emperor when he inaugurated by an oath his energetic policy was based on this idea. My belief is that although

Japan is not yet ready for parliamentary inspection of the affairs of state, in the importance of its laws and the magnitude of its affairs it is no different from those countries of Europe and America the conduct of whose governments embodies the will of the people. It is important that our officials should not be forgetful of their responsibility and should take as their model our five-clause Constitution. . . .

Every citizen's object in life is to preserve his natural liberty by exercising his rights, and to assist in carrying on the government by sharing its obligations. Therefore, [these rights and obligations] are specified exactly in writing and men bind themselves by a solemn promise to permit no infringement of them, but to act as mutual checks on each other in maintaining them. These writings are what we call laws. The laws grow out of the Constitution, for the Constitution is the root of every part of the government, and there is nothing which does not branch out from it. For this reason, every country, when the time comes for changing its constitution, bestows on it the greatest care and the ripest consideration and ascertains to the full the general wishes. No new measures are put in force unless they are imperatively called for by the circumstances, [nor are any adopted] lightly or hastily. In a country whose sovereign generously decides to meet the wishes of the people the greatest care must be taken to ascertain them with accuracy, the internal conditions of the country must be profoundly studied, what the people produce must be taken into account, and, most important of all, policies must be suited to the degree of civilization of the people.

Again, in ordering the affairs of a nation, its strength must be taken into account. If not, one good will be converted into a hundred evils. The poor man's son who tries to rival the son of the rich man ruins his property and his house, and in the end does not make a show equal to his rival. Those who order the affairs of a nation should remember before taking action, to consider the due sequence of measures, and should proceed by gradual steps in nourishing its strength, for no nation ever attained to a perfect state of civilization in a single morning.

[Kido Takayoshi, *Shōgiku Kido-kō den,* vol. 2, pp. 1563–68; McLaren, *Japanese Government Documents,* pp. 571–75]

CONSEQUENCES OF THE IWAKURA MISSION: SAIGŌ AND ŌKUBO ON KOREA

The Iwakura Mission determined the course of the Restoration. The leaders who had gone abroad came back convinced not only that the political renovation of Japan would have to advance and move in the direction of a constitutional system but also that national education, large-scale factories and industrialization, and the development of a modern military system should be

Japan's highest priorities. There were additional implications. The first was that Westernization would be needed to achieve these goals. The second was that Japan was still a weak and backward nation and that any aggressive military adventures should be curtailed until further reforms were carried out at home.

Kido Takayoshi and Ōkubo Toshimichi, who along with Saigō Takamori, represented the three leading figures of the Meiji government in the 1870s, came home impressed by the scope of Western wealth and power. Their experiences confirmed their conviction that Japan's future, including its military potential, depended on its successful renovation. At the same time, they continued to be committed to a program of gradualist reforms that sought change while preserving social stability and the imperial prerogative. In this, they faced considerable challenges. More than ever convinced that wealth and power were linked, they faced the need to industrialize Japan. They also realized that a new military structure based on conscription would have to be implemented. The last vestiges of feudal privileges would also have to be eliminated, and a new tax structure established to provide state revenues. Finally, both education and information would be needed to prepare the Japanese citizens for an expanded role in government and the establishment of a future constitutional order.

The initial challenge that Ōkubo rushed home to meet, however, was more immediate and pressing. It stemmed from a proposed expedition against Korea that was being spearheaded by Saigō Takamori. A samurai and military leader from Satsuma, Saigō had long been closely allied with Kido and Ōkubo. Perhaps the most charismatic figure of the Restoration, he was a giant of a Japanese, almost six feet tall and weighing two hundred pounds. He had enormous shoulders, a bull neck with a collar size of nineteen and a half, and large piercing eyes under big bushy eyebrows. So commanding was he in appearance that it is said almost everyone introduced to him "bowed his head in spite of himself." But he was known less for his fearsome appearance than for his heartiness, which attracted young men to him in great numbers, and for his magnanimity and forbearance, which, when he was chief of staff of the imperial armies at Edo, caused him to spare the shogunal capital from the final ravages of war. The quintessential samurai, Saigō's charisma was clearly attached to the old order, and he was one of the few Meiji leaders who never visited the West.

By the early 1870s, Saigō enjoyed great popularity and the unique rank of field marshal, but he proved to have less influence in government councils than did those who urged rapid changes in Japanese society, to which he was opposed. Especially disturbed by the treatment of the old warrior class and by the process of Westernization, which he felt would undermine traditional values, he wished to strengthen the position and spirit of the samurai by employing them to improve Japan's military situation. Japan could not resist the West, he was convinced, unless it had Korea and China at its side. Fearing Russia particularly, he believed that Korea had to be won over quickly, by force if necessary. In the face of obvious hostility from the Korean government, however,

Saigō favored first sending an ambassador whose certain execution by the contemptuous Koreans would provide ample pretext for war. As the emissary who would thus meet death, he offered himself.

When his plan was rejected in favor of Ōkubo's policy of peace and internal reform, Saigō withdrew from the government along with other prominent Restoration leaders, such as Itagaki Taisuke, Gotō Shōjirō, and Etō Shinpei. Having earlier suffered patiently in exile for his loyalist convictions and activities, he was prepared to retire quietly to Satsuma and bide his time. Nevertheless, when his more hot-blooded followers openly resisted government forces, his sense of loyalty and comradeship impelled him to join them in the Satsuma Rebellion. When the rebellion was crushed in 1877, the life that Saigō was prepared to offer his country was lost for his friends. But his death, like that of Yoshida Shōin, made him a hero to future generations of Japanese patriots. Moreover, the failure of his rebellion marked the last stand of feudal opposition to the Restoration and confirmed the path of modernization that Kido and the others had adopted.

LETTERS FROM SAIGŌ TAKAMORI TO ITAGAKI TAISUKE ON THE KOREAN QUESTION

In the summer of 1873, Saigō wrote eight letters to his friend Itagaki Taisuke on the Korean question. Three of these follow. All show Saigō's sincerity and straightforward simplicity.

July 29 [1873]

Thank you so much for coming all the way to visit me the other day.

Has any decision been made on Korea, now that Soejima is back? If the meeting has yet to take place, I should like to be present despite my illness if I am informed of what day I may attend. Please let me know.

When a decision is at last reached, what will it involve if we send troops first? The Koreans will unquestionably demand their withdrawal, and a refusal on our part will lead to war. We shall then have fomented a war in a manner very different from the one you originally had in mind. Wouldn't it be better therefore to send an envoy first? It is clear that if we did so, the Koreans would resort to violence and would certainly give us an excuse for attacking them.

In the event that it is decided to send troops first, difficulties may arise in the future [elsewhere]. Russia has fortified Sakhalin and other islands, and there have already been frequent incidents of violence. I am convinced that we should send troops to defend these places before we send them to Korea.

If it is decided to send an envoy officially, I feel sure that he will be murdered. I therefore beseech you to send me. I cannot claim to make as splendid an envoy as Soejima, but if it is a question of dying, that, I assure you, I am prepared to do.

August 14 [1873]

Should there be any hesitation at your place with reference to my being sent, it will mean further and further delays. I ask you therefore please to cut short the deliberations and to speak out in favor of my being sent. If we fail to seize this chance to bring us into war, it will be very difficult to find another. By enticing the Koreans with such a gentle approach, we will certainly cause them to give us an opportunity for war. But this plan is doomed to fail if you feel it would be unfortunate for me to die before the war or if you have any thoughts of temporizing. The only difference is whether [my death comes] before or after the event. I shall be deeply grateful to you, even after death, if you exert yourself now on my behalf with the warm friendship you have always shown me.

August 17 [1873]

Last evening I visited the prime minister's residence and discussed my plan with him in great detail. . . . However, I could not help feeling uneasy when he said that he would wait until the return of the [Iwakura] mission. I have never meant to suggest an immediate outbreak of hostilities. War is the second step. Even under the present circumstances, grounds for starting a conflict might be found from an examination of international law, but they would be entirely a pretext, and the people of the nation would not accept them. But if we sent an envoy to tell the Koreans that we have never to this day harbored hostile intentions and to reproach them for weakening the relations between our countries, at the same time asking them to correct their arrogance of the past and strive for improved relations in the future, I am sure that the contemptuous attitude of the Koreans will reveal itself. They are absolutely certain, moreover, to kill the envoy. This will bring home to the entire nation the necessity of punishing their crimes. This is the situation that we must bring to pass if our plan is to succeed. I need hardly say that it is, at the same time, a far-reaching scheme that will divert abroad the attention of those who desire civil strife and thereby benefit the country. The [adherents of the] former government will lose the opportunity to act and, having to refrain from creating any internal disturbance, will lose the country once and for all.

[*Dai Saigō zenshū*, vol. 2, pp. 736–38, 751–52, 754–56; FN]

ŌKUBO TOSHIMICHI'S REASONS FOR OPPOSING THE KOREAN EXPEDITION

Although he had been a boyhood friend of Saigō Takamori, Ōkubo Toshimichi was less devoted to upholding the former samurai values and preserving the old system. He was also more a politician than a military figure and thus saw the threat to Japan in terms different from Saigō's. If Saigō was the quintessential samurai, Ōkubo, by comparison, can be seen as the quintessential bureaucrat. Ōkubo's consuming passion was internal order and systematic progress, which contrasted with Saigō's more immediate concerns for directing Japanese energies abroad. Ōkubo shared Kido Takayoshi's long-range vision and possessed a tenacity to pursue that vision over time. He also was capable of transcending domain loyalties and attracted to his side talented young men from other domains, such as Itō Hirobumi from Chōshū and Ōkuma Shigenobu from Hizen. Although he was the chief architect and driving force behind the transformation of Japan along modern lines in the 1870s, Ōkubo's bold rejection of Saigō's planned Korean expedition and firm commitment to eliminate all feudal privileges, both of which led to the Satsuma Rebellion, ultimately cost him his life. In 1878, with the course of the Restoration clearly established, Ōkubo was assassinated by six former samurai. Indeed, all three of the major Restoration leaders—Ōkubo, Kido, and Saigō—died within a year of one another in 1877/1878, leaving the completion of the Restoration to their understudies, like Itō and Ōkuma. In 1873 it was Ōkubo's cold, clear logic that won the day in the council of state over Saigō's impetuous and dramatic appeal for a war with Korea.

The most mature consideration and forethought are essential to govern the nation and to protect the land and the people. Every action, whether progressive or conservative, should be taken in response to the occasion and, if it develops unfavorably, should be abandoned. This may entail shame, but it is to be endured; justice may be with us, but we are not to choose that course. We must act as our greatest needs dictate, taking into account the importance of any problem and examining the exigencies. We have here the problem of dispatching an envoy to Korea. The reasons why I am in no great haste to subscribe to the proposal come from much careful and earnest reflection on the problem. The gist of my arguments is as follows:

1. Because of His Majesty's supreme virtue, sovereignty has been restored, and extraordinary achievements have been made to bring about today's prosperity. However, His Majesty's reign is still young, and its foundations are not yet firmly laid. The sudden abolition of feudal fiefs and the establishment of prefectures are indeed a drastic change unusual in history. A look at the situation in the capital seems to indicate that the change has been accomplished. But in the remote sections of the country there are not a few who have lost their homes and property and who are extremely bitter and restless because of this measure. . . . Within the last two years, how many scenes of bloodshed have taken place unavoidably? Owing to their misunderstanding of public proclamations or their misgivings about rising taxes, the ignorant, uninformed people of the remote areas have become easy victims of agitation and have started riots. A careful consideration of these facts is the first argument against any hasty action regarding Korea.

2. Government expenditure today is already tremendous, and there is the difficulty of matching the annual revenues with the annual expenditures. To start a war and to send tens of thousands of troops abroad would raise expenditures by the day to colossal figures; and should war be prolonged, expenditures would continue to soar so as to necessitate heavy taxes or a foreign loan, with no prospect of repayment, or the issuance of paper notes with no hope of redemption. . . . Our loans from foreign countries now exceed 5 million [yen], but we have no definite plan for their repayment. Even if a definite plan is evolved, the undertaking of the Korean venture would, in all likelihood, lead to a considerable deviation from our plans. It would be so disastrous as to preclude any chance of salvation. This is my second reason against any hasty action regarding Korea.

3. The government's present undertakings intended to enrich and strengthen the country must await many years for their fulfillment. These projects, in the areas of the army, navy, education, justice, industry, and colonization, are matters that cannot be expected to produce results overnight. To launch a meaningless war now and waste the government's efforts and attention needlessly, increase annual expenditures to enormous figures, suffer the loss of countless lives, and add to the suffering of the people so as to allow no time for other matters will lead to the abandonment of the government's undertakings before their completion. In order to resume these undertakings, they would have to be started anew. . . . This is the third reason against the hasty commencement of a Korean war.

4. In looking at the sum total of our country's exports and imports, there is an annual shortage of exports of approximately 1 million [yen]. This deficit must be made up in gold. If gold in such quantity leaves the country, there will be a corresponding decrease in the country's gold reserves. At the present time the currency in use in the country consists of gold and paper. If gold is reduced, it will, in itself, impair the credit of the government, reduce the value of the paper notes, and cause considerable hardship to the people. It will produce a situation for which there may be no remedy later. . . . Now, without examining the wealth or poverty of our country or without clarifying the strength or weakness of our army, if we should hastily launch a war, our able-bodied youths would be subjected to hardships both at home and abroad, and their parents, out of worry and trouble, would lose their will to be thrifty or to work hard. . . . It would inevitably lead to the impoverishment of our country. Such a state of affairs would be a matter of serious concern, which is the fourth reason against any hasty venture in Korea.

5. Turning to foreign relations, we note that for our country, Russia and England occupy the position of foremost and greatest importance. Russia, situated in the north, could send its troops southward to Sakhalin and could, with one blow, strike south. . . . Thus, if we crossed arms with Korea and became

like the two water birds fighting over a fish, Russia would be the fisherman standing by to snare the fish. This is a matter of constant vigilance and is the fifth reason against a hasty venture in Korea.

6. England's influence is particularly strong in Asia. It has occupied land everywhere and has settled its people and stationed its troops [in those places]. Its warships are poised for any emergency, keeping a silent, vigilant watch, and are ready to jump at a moment's notice. However, our country has been largely dependent on England for its foreign loans. If our country becomes involved in an unexpected misfortune, causing our stores to be depleted and our people reduced to poverty, our inability to repay our debts to England will become its pretext for interfering in our internal affairs, which would lead to baneful consequences beyond description. . . . This is the sixth reason against hasty action in Korea.

7. The treaties that our country has concluded with the countries of Europe and America are not equal, as they contain many terms that impair the dignity of an independent nation. The restraints they impose may bring some benefit, but these treaties also contain harmful elements. England and France, for example, on the pretext that our country's internal administration is not yet in order and that it cannot protect their subjects, have built barracks and stationed troops in our land as if our country were a territory of theirs. Externally, from the standpoint of foreign relations, is this not as much a disgrace as it is internally, from the standpoint of our nation's sovereignty? The time to revise the treaties is close at hand. The ministers in the current government, through their zealous and thorough attention, must find a way to rid the country of its bondage and to secure for our country the dignity of an independent nation. This is an urgent matter of the moment which provides the seventh reason why a hasty venture in Korea should not be undertaken.

I have argued in the foregoing paragraphs that a hasty Korean war should not be precipitated. . . . Before dispatching an envoy, the question of whether or not to embark on a war should be settled. Should the decision be to wage war, then more than a hundred thousand men for the campaign abroad and for the defense of the country should be raised. Moreover, additional tens of thousands of men should be called to escort the envoy. Although it is difficult to estimate in advance the enormous cost of ammunition, weapons, warships, transports, and other expenses, it may well reach into tens of thousands daily. Even if the campaign makes a favorable start, it is unlikely that the gains made will ever pay for the losses incurred. What would happen if the campaign dragged on for months and years? Suppose total victory is gained, the entire country occupied, and the Koreans permitted to sue for peace and to indemnify us. Still, for many years, we would have to man garrisons to defend vital areas and to prevent any breach of the treaty's terms. When the entire country is occupied, it is certain that there will be many discontented people who will cause disturbances everywhere, making it almost impossible for us to hold the country. In considering the cost of the campaign, and the occupation and defense of Korea, it is unlikely that it could be met by the products of the entire country of Korea. Then there is Russia, and there is China. Although it is argued, on the basis of one or two conversations among officials or on the tacit understanding of officials, that Russia and China would not interfere in the Korean affair, there is no actual document to confirm it. Even if such a document existed, who can say that the governments of these two countries would not plot and take advantage of the opportunity to bring about a sudden and unexpected calamity? It is certainly not difficult to find an excuse to break an earlier promise. If we permit the initiation of such a great venture, blithely and with no consideration for such an eventuality, we shall in all probability have cause for much regret in the future. . . .

Some argue that Korea's arrogance toward our country is intolerable. But as far as I can see, the reasons for sending an envoy extraordinary seem to be to look for a positive excuse for war by having him treated arrogantly and discourteously. We would then dispatch troops to punish them. If this is the case, it is clear that this venture is to be undertaken, not because the situation makes it unavoidable or because there is no other way, but rather because the honor of the country will have been sullied and our sovereignty humiliated. I consider such a venture entirely beyond comprehension, as it completely disregards the safety of our nation and ignores the interest of the people. It would be an incident occasioned by the whims of individuals who have not seriously evaluated the eventualities or implications. These are the reasons why I cannot accept the arguments for undertaking this venture.

[Kiyosawa, *Gaiseika to shite Ōkubo Toshimichi*, pp. 28–31; FN]

THE MEIJI EMPEROR

The Restoration was carried out in the name of the Meiji emperor, Mutsuhito, who in 1868 was a mere boy of sixteen. With time, he grew into a formidable figure, perhaps one of the greatest individuals to occupy the Japanese throne since Emperor Tenchi, who was responsible for the Taika Reform of 645. Asukai Masamichi, a late-twentieth-century biographer of the emperor, referred to him as "Meiji the Great," in the way that Peter the Great and Frederick the Great were seen in Russia and Germany. And yet unlike Queen Victoria, who was his contemporary, Meiji never kept a diary and wrote almost no letters. As Donald Keene noted in his biography of the Meiji emperor, there is hardly anything now extant in the emperor's handwriting. Even very few photographs, perhaps no more than three, exist of him in an age when most Meiji leaders were widely photographed. Instead, what knowledge we have of the emperor comes largely from the men who worked with him and who venerated him as the leader of the circle dedicated to transforming the country into a modern state. With time, the emperor became increasingly shrouded in mystery as the Meiji leaders used him to structure the ideology of the imperial state. This was particularly true after the 1890s, but earlier he seems to have functioned more as part of the group that set Japan on its new course. He worked closely with Kido Takayoshi, Ōkubo Toshimichi, and Saigō Takamori. His respect for Saigō was such that even after his death as a "rebel" in 1877, the emperor subsequently pardoned him in view of his earlier contributions to the Restoration. Many of the edicts issued in the Meiji emperor's name—such as the Charter Oath, the Imperial Rescript to Soldiers and Sailors, and the Imperial Rescript on Education—were composed by his advisers, but it seems unlikely that they could have been issued without his sanction. Keene also noted that the one remaining clue to the emperor's personal feelings can be found in the more than 100,000 poems he composed during his lifetime. But here, too, the majority were transcribed by others. In short, the Meiji emperor remains largely an enigmatic figure; his official presence was clearly larger than life, and for many Japanese he came to symbolize the whole era of renovation and reform that covered his lengthy reign from 1868 to 1912.

LETTER FROM THE MEIJI EMPEROR TO HIS PEOPLE, APRIL 7, 1868

On the day the Charter Oath was promulgated, another letter was presented by the emperor to his subjects. The content of this letter suggests that the court realized that in creating the modern state, the relationship of the emperor to his people was of paramount importance. At the same time, few Japanese had any notion of who the emperor was. When peasants were asked whether they knew of the emperor's existence, they replied in the negative and shrewdly added that if there was such a being, their taxes would be higher. The task of the emperor's advisers, therefore, was to make him known to the public through the imperial "progresses," which took the emperor to virtually every part of Japan in the first half of the Meiji period. As the following letter suggests, the emperor was himself concerned about the gap that had grown between the court and the public and hoped to remedy the situation.

Ever since, quite unexpectedly, We succeeded to the throne, young and weak though We are, We have been unable to control Our apprehension, day and night, over how We are to remain faithful to Our ancestors when dealing with foreign countries. It is Our belief that when the authority of the court declined in the middle ages and the military seized power, they maintained on the surface worshipful respect of the court, but in reality their respect intentionally isolated the court, making it impossible for the court, as the father and mother of the entire people, to know the people's feelings. In the end, the emperor became the sovereign of the multitude in name only. This is how it happens that although awe of the court today is greater than ever before, the prestige of the court has diminished correspondingly, and the separation between those above and those below is as great as that between heaven and earth. Under these conditions, how are We to reign over the country? Now, at a time of renovation of rule of the country, if even one of the millions of people in this country is unable to find his place in society, this will be entirely Our fault. Accordingly, We have personally exerted Our physical and spiritual powers to confront the crisis. It is only by stepping into the shoes Our ancestors wore in ancient times and throwing Ourself into governing the country that We fulfill Our Heaven-sent mission and do not violate Our duty as the ruler of the hundred millions.

In ancient times Our ancestors personally disposed of all state affairs. If anyone behaved in a manner inappropriate in a subject, they themselves would punish the guilty. The administration of the court was simple in every respect, and because the emperor was not held in awe, as he is today, emperor and subjects were close; those above and those below loved each other; the blessings of heaven pervaded the land; and the majesty of the country shone brightly abroad. In recent times the world has become much more civilized. At a time when every other country is progressing in all directions, only our country, being unfamiliar with the situation prevailing in the world, stubbornly maintains old customs and does not seek the fruits of change. It fills Us with dread to think that if We were idly to spend a peaceful existence in the palace, enjoying the tranquillity of each day and forgetful of the hundred years of grief, Our country would in the end be subject to the contempt of all others, bringing shame to Our ancestors and hardship to the people. For this reason We have sworn, along with many officials and daimyos, to continue the glorious work of Our ancestors. Regardless of the pain and suffering it may entail, We intend personally to rule over the entire country, to comfort you, the numberless people, and in the end to open up the ten thousand leagues of ocean waves, to proclaim the glory of our country to the world and bring to the land the unshakable security of Mount Fuji. You of countless numbers have become accustomed to the evils inherited from the past and to think of the court only as a place to be held in awe. Not knowing the acute danger threatening the Land of the Gods, you manifest extreme surprise when We bestir Us, and this has given rise to doubts of every kind. The people are confused, but if a time should come when they prevent Us from carrying out Our plans, this would mean not only that We had wandered from the Way of the ruler but that they had caused Us to lose Our ancestral patrimony. You of countless numbers give due consideration to Our aspirations and join with Us. Cast away private thoughts and choose the general good. Help Us in Our work and ensure the safety of the Land of the Gods. If We can comfort the spirits of my ancestors, this will be the greatest happiness of Our life.

[*Meiji tennō ki*, vol. 1, pp. 649–52; trans. in Keene,
Emperor of Japan, pp. 140–41]

COMMENTS FROM THE IMPERIAL PROGRESS OF 1878

The imperial progresses were important in two respects. On the one hand, they provided the emperor with a better idea of the condition of his people. On the other, it gave his subjects a chance to observe their ruler. Often these trips were less than pleasant for the sovereign, but he faithfully followed the course laid out for him by his advisers. The progress of 1878 was particularly difficult for the emperor. The route took him to Urawa, Maebashi, and then through Nagano Prefecture to the Japan Sea coast. Day after day, it rained and the roads were deep in mud. Often the emperor had to get out and walk because the paths were too clogged and impassable for his palanquin. His accommodations were also surprisingly rustic. When he spent the night at Izumozaki, his quarters were not only cramped but also invaded by swarms of mosquitoes. When his chamberlains tried to persuade him to take refuge under a mosquito net they had set up for him, he replied:

The whole purpose of this journey is to observe the suffering of the people. If I did not myself experience their pains, how could I understand their condition? I do not in the least mind the mosquitoes. . . . Years later (in 1899) the emperor recalled the journey in this *tanka* [poem]:

natsu samuki	It's now long ago
Koshi no yamaji wo	Since I traveled mountain roads
samidare ni	Soaked by the spring rains
nurete koeshi mo	In Koshi, where it is cold
mukashi narikeri	Even in the summertime.

[*Meiji tennō ki*, vol. 4, pp. 490, 528; trans. in Keene, *Emperor of Japan*, pp. 300–301]

A GLIMPSE OF THE MEIJI EMPEROR IN 1872
BY TAKASHIMA TOMONOSUKE

While we know little about the Meiji emperor's personal feelings and attitudes from his own hand, occasionally we are given glimpses of his more human side by those who worked with him. We know, for example, that he was a formidable drinker, although he rarely drank to excess. At the same time, he was thoroughly dedicated to his official duties. The following portrait of the emperor, composed by his chamberlain Takashima Tomonosuke in 1872, gives such a view.

He was a heavy drinker, and sometimes he would assemble his favorites among the chamberlains to have a drinking party. (I can't take much saké, so I generally escaped.) Men like Yamaoka Tesshō and Major Counselor Nakayama [Tadasu] were heavy drinkers who never refused saké, no matter how huge the quantities. They were his drinking partners. The saké cup His Majesty used at that time was not the usual small size but a big cup, as big as the cups from which the lower classes drink tea, and he would have it filled to the brim before he drank.

His diligence was extraordinary. Every morning he would rise early and go to his office, not retiring to his private quarters until five or six in the afternoon. Sometimes he did not leave even then but would command, "This evening let's have a party in my office." He would talk for hours, until late at night. Then, when it was time for His Majesty to go to bed, people would at once bring bedding from the back palace. It was by no means unusual for us chamberlains to spend the night in the corridors on night duty.

[Asukai, *Meiji taitei*, p. 148; trans. in Keene, *Emperor of Japan*, p. 174]

CHARLES LANMAN'S DESCRIPTION OF THE MEIJI EMPEROR IN 1882

Foreign diplomats and dignitaries also were able to interact with the emperor and empress, and some commented on the emperor as they saw him in comparison with other sovereigns they had met. Charles Lanman, who served as secretary to the Japanese legation in Washington, provides us with the following assessment.

Unlike many of the princes and royal personages of Europe, he is not addicted to self-indulgence, but takes delight in cultivating his mind; sparing no pains nor personal inconvenience to acquire knowledge. Although still young he frequently presides at the meetings of his Privy Councillors. . . . He often visits his executive departments, and attends at all the public services where the Imperial presence is desirable. While prosecuting his literary as well as scientific pursuits, he subjects himself to the strictest rules, having certain hours for special studies, to which he rigidly conforms. In his character he is said to be sagacious, determined, progressive and aspiring; and from the beginning of his reign he has carefully surrounded himself with the wisest statesmen in his Empire, and these have naturally assisted in his own development; so that it is almost certain that the crown of Japan has been worn in this century by one who was worthy of the great honor.

[Lanman, *Leading Men of Japan*, p. 18]

THE MEIJI EMPEROR'S CONVERSATION WITH HIJIKATA HISAMOTO ON THE OUTBREAK OF THE SINO-JAPANESE WAR

Although Japan fought two major foreign wars, the Sino-Japanese War (1894/1895) and the Russo-Japanese War (1904/1905), during the Meiji emperor's reign, he seems to have been reluctant to go to war in both instances. In 1894, asked by the imperial household minister, Hijikata Hisamoto, whom to send as an envoy to report the outbreak of war to the Ise Shrines and the tomb of his father, Emperor Kōmei, he is reported to have replied in the following outspoken manner that shows he did not always agree with his ministers (although he later did send the requested envoy).

Imperial Household Minister Hijikata Hisamoto visited the emperor to ask which envoys he wished sent to Ise and the tomb of Emperor Kōmei [his father]. The emperor answered, "Don't send anybody. I have not been in favor of this war from the start. It was only because cabinet ministers informed me that war was inevitable that I permitted it. It is very painful for me to report what has happened to the Ise Shrine and the tomb of the previous emperor." Hijikata, astonished by these remarks, admonished the emperor, "But Your Majesty has already issued a declaration of war. I wonder if Your Majesty might not be mistaken in giving me such a command." The emperor flew into a rage and said, "Not another word out of you. I don't wish to see you again." Hijikata withdrew in fear and trepidation.

[*Meiji tennō ki*, vol. 8, p. 481; trans. in Keene, *Emperor of Japan*, pp. 482–83]

A POEM BY THE MEIJI EMPEROR ON THE EVE OF THE RUSSO-JAPANESE WAR

The emperor's ambivalence about going to war was also suggested at the time of the Russo-Japanese conflict. Despite the immense public outcry for war with Russia, the emperor left behind a poem that suggests he felt troubled about going to war. This poem was later read by his grandson, Hirohito, before the policy conference that led to the attack on Pearl Harbor in 1941. One of the great ironies of the Meiji period can be seen in the emperor's personal commitment to peace and the expansive imperialist policies pursued by his advisers, who on several occasions took the country to war in his name.

Yomo no umi	On all four seas
Mina harakara to	I thought all men were brothers
Omou yo ni	Yet in this world
Nado namikaze no	Why do winds and waves
Tachisawaguran	Now rise and stir?

[*Kodansha Encyclopedia of Japan*, vol. 5, p. 153]

Chapter 36

CIVILIZATION AND ENLIGHTENMENT

The Civilization and Enlightenment movement, which began during the late 1860s and continued into the early 1880s, was composed of samurai "intellectuals" who advocated the introduction of Western ideas, values, and institutions into Japan. Many were government officials. As perceived by its members, its goal was to raise Japan to the level of wealth and power that had been attained in the United States and the advanced nations of Europe. To reach this goal, they called for sweeping reforms in education as well as fundamental changes in many areas of government and society.

The movement was partly an offshoot of the new Meiji government's program of Westernizing reforms, which provided Western-style weapons and uniforms for its soldiers; adopted the Gregorian calendar; promoted the consumption of Western foods; and encouraged samurai to cut their topknots, abandon their swords, and wear Western clothing. It also established telegraph and postal services; began the construction of railways, ports, and bridges; inaugurated a new educational system; and implemented a multitude of other Westernizing reforms. But the movement went beyond the government's actions in its consideration and even advocacy of such issues as the natural rights of freedom and equality, popularly elected representative bodies, and radical reforms of marriage and family.

The movement was notable for the breadth of its influence. While it would be a mistake to say that there had been no public opinion in the Tokugawa era, the movement shaped a nationwide public opinion for the first time after the 1868 Meiji Restoration. Although the core of the movement may have been samurai thinkers living in Tokyo, the ideas it espoused reached the educated in other cities and castle towns and penetrated social strata that hitherto had been almost entirely isolated from questions of national politics.

Since the ideas of the Civilization and Enlightenment movement differed so markedly from those that had prevailed in Japan only a few years earlier, some consideration of its origins will help explain why it emerged so suddenly. One background factor was Japan's confrontation with Western powers during the 1850s and the political turbulence that ensued. Japanese already knew something about Europe and had learned about China's defeat in the Opium War. Still, the arrival of Commodore Matthew Perry and his ships in 1853 and 1854 was a rude shock. In the face of steam-powered warships with cannon vastly superior to their own, the Japanese were forced to abandon their hallowed policy of seclusion and sign a treaty of friendship in 1854 and a commercial treaty in 1858. The shock was all the greater since during the preceding centuries of seclusion the Japanese had regarded themselves, along with the Chinese and Koreans, as civilized and the world beyond, as barbarian. The weakness of the *bakufu* vis-à-vis the foreigners led to criticism and to the movement to "revere the emperor and repel the barbarian." Although the politics of the pre-Restoration era were exceedingly complex, in the end a handful of domains overthrew the *bakufu* and established a new government. One reason they could do so was their purchase of weapons from foreign merchants and the formation of "Western-style" rifle companies, which set a precedent for the far-ranging Westernizing reforms of the Meiji era.

Another background element was Dutch studies, which had developed to the point that by the early nineteenth century, schools of Dutch language and medicine had opened in several domains and large cities. Dutch studies was a small current within an educational establishment predominantly oriented toward Chinese learning, but it had produced a few dozen scholars who could read a Western language.

The incursion of the Western powers during the 1850s led to a demand for scholars knowledgeable about the West. Some Dutch studies graduates, who earlier would have become doctors, were now hired by the *bakufu* or the domains as Western specialists. As the new career path opened up, Dutch studies changed in two important respects. First, the emphasis shifted from Dutch to other Western languages, especially English. For example, in 1858 or 1859, Fukuzawa Yukichi, who had studied Dutch since 1855, visited the treaty port of Yokohama and was chagrined to find that he could neither read the signs nor understand a word that was spoken. He thereupon dropped Dutch and began to study English. The second change was a shift in content from medicine and its associated natural sciences to history, politics, economics, and geography. With these developments, *rangaku*, or "Dutch studies," gradually became *yōgaku*, or "Western studies."

Many of the scholars who were proficient in Western languages were hired by two *bakufu* offices: the Gaikokugata, a foreign ministry of sorts, and the Bansho shirabesho (Office for the Study of Barbarian Books), which in 1862 became the Yōsho shirabesho (Office for the Study of Western Books). Those hired were almost entirely domain samurai, not *bakufu* retainers. Among them were Fukuzawa Yukichi, Mori Arinori, Katō Hiroyuki, Nishi Amane, Mitsukuri Genpo, Tsuda Mamichi, and Nakamura Masanao. After the Restoration, they went on to become translators of Western books and the principal pamphleteers of the Civilization and Enlightenment movement.

FUKUZAWA YUKICHI

Foremost among these scholars in terms of his contribution to the movement was Fukuzawa Yukichi (1835–1901). A samurai from a minor, middle-size domain, he studied Dutch at the Ogata school in Osaka and in 1860 was hired as a translator by the Gaikokugata. He excelled at his official duties of translating diplomatic correspondence and foreign newspapers but apparently was not overworked, for he also found time to read English and American histories, geographies, gazetteers, biographies, and entries in various reference works. As a student of Dutch in Osaka, he had become convinced of the greater efficacy of Western medicine and of the truth of Western science. Now, as a scholar-translator in Edo, he became convinced of the truth of Western views of human nature and society.

A part of this newly discovered "truth" was a view of human progress almost universally accepted in the mid-nineteenth-century West, which regarded history as a gradual progression from savagery, the rudest human condition. According to this schema, many backward areas of the world were still mired in savagery or barbarism, whereas others, including Japan, had advanced to a half-barbarous and half-civilized condition. Only western Europe and the United States had become fully civilized or, beyond that, "enlightened," in the eighteenth-century sense of the term.

Fukuzawa presented these and other ideas in his most influential works of translation: *Conditions in the West* (*Seiyō jijō*), published in three volumes in 1866, 1868, and 1870, and *All the Countries of the World* (*Sekai kunizukushi*), published in 1869. He further refined these ideas and explicated their meaning for Japan in his earliest original works: *An Encouragement of Learning* (*Gakumon no susume*), published from 1872 to 1876, and *An Outline of a Theory of Civilization* (*Bunmeiron no gairyaku*), published in 1875. The Civilization and Enlightenment movement took its name from the term (*bunmei kaika*) that Fukuzawa used to denote this highest stage of human advance.

During the 1870s, the Civilization and Enlightenment movement was propelled by a variety of developments. Sweeping government reforms contributed to what some Japanese writers referred to as the "spirit of the age." New schools taught Western languages, geography, and science. Newspapers appeared. Books were translated and brought out by newly established publishing houses. Several became best-sellers, such as those by Fukuzawa and Nakamura Masanao's 1871 translation of Samuel Smiles's *Self-Help*.

One important center of intellectual activity was the Meiji Six Society (Meirokusha). Proposed in 1873 (the sixth year of the Meiji era) by Mori Arinori, a Satsuma samurai, diplomat, and later minister of education, the society formally began in 1874. Its purpose was to promote civilization and enlightenment through public lectures and a journal: *Meiji Six Magazine* (*Meiroku zasshi*). Members met regularly, presented papers, and debated a wide range of the topics of the day. Some of the issues treated were the role of scholars, freedom and human rights, religion, wives and concubines, national finance, currency and specie, the trade balance, the nature of society, the national character, types of political systems, rewards and punishments, torture, and the death penalty. Most members of the society were officials in the new government; a few, most notably Fukuzawa, remained outside. The magazine ceased publication in November 1875 after the government passed its Press Ordinance and Libel Laws, but the society continued to meet until the end of the century.

Members of the Meiji Six Society had much in common. They all agreed on the validity of science and the need for a new system of education based on Western learning. Most accepted some version of natural rights, at least during the early 1870s. Most felt that Japan would eventually have a constitution and a popularly elected national assembly. But from the start, there were differences of approach and temperament among the members. For instance, Nakamura emphasized the spiritual and moral underpinnings of the Western nations' economic and military strength. Besides Smiles, he translated John Stuart Mill's *On Liberty*, and he became a Christian in 1874. Fukuzawa, in contrast, saw Christianity much as he saw Buddhism, as a source of morality for those unable to comprehend philosophy. He advocated freedom, equality, and other natural rights but felt that Japan was not ready for an elected national assembly. During the late 1870s, he gradually shifted to a more tough-minded position on rights but also came to favor a national assembly. Katō Hiroyuki was an early advocate of natural rights and eventual constitutional government. But after reading Herbert Spencer, Ernst Haeckel, Henry Buckle, and Charles Darwin, he repudiated his earlier thought in 1882 and argued in his *New Theory of Human Rights* (*Jinken shinsetsu*) that rights did not exist in nature but rested on the civil law of an organically evolving state. Katō introduced German studies in Japan, served twice as the president of Tokyo Imperial University, and became a member of the House of Peers.

These small differences of position within the movement became more pronounced in the late 1870s and early 1880s as its adherents arrived at a better understanding of the different strands within Western thought. As a result, the movement broke up into several schools of thought supported by separate interest groups. In some measure, it was a victim of its own success. The Freedom and People's Rights (*jiyū minken*) movement, for example, had formed during the mid-1870s, based on one set of ideas within the Civilization and Enlightenment movement. By the late 1870s, it had become a separate, organized political movement. Some of its leaders were influenced by Fukuzawa's moderate, British-style constitutionalism, and they welcomed to their ranks graduates of Fukuzawa's school, Keiō gijuku. Other thinkers in the movement were influenced by newer currents of thought. Nakae Chōmin (1857–1901), for example, was never a member of the Meiji Six Society. He studied French in Nagasaki, became an interpreter for the French minister Léon Roches in Edo, and, after the Restoration, studied for three years in France. After returning to Japan, he opened a private academy, helped found a newspaper, translated Jean-Jacques Rousseau's *Social Contract* in 1882, and became a spokesman for the radical wing of the Freedom and People's Rights movement. To counter such ideas, the government commissioned a translation of the conservative writings of Edmund Burke.

FUKUZAWA YUKICHI'S VIEW OF CIVILIZATION

Throughout the Tokugawa era, Japanese accepted a Confucian view of civilization—that China, Japan, and Korea were civilized and the rest of the world was barbarian. Fukuzawa took in Western ideas that stood this Confucian view on its head, and in two highly influential works of the mid-1870s, *An Outline of a Theory of Civilization* and *An Encouragement of Learning*, he applied the ideas to fit Japanese circumstances.

AN OUTLINE OF A THEORY OF CIVILIZATION
(*BUNMEIRON NO GAIRYAKU*)

Early in this work, Fukuzawa Yukichi asks about the role of thinkers in society. He defines them as persons who challenge orthodox thought and holds that such challenges lead to advances in knowledge. His answer is that these thinkers are responsible for advances in knowledge.

Consider if you will how, since ancient times, progressive steps in civilization were always unorthodox at the time they were first proposed. When Adam Smith first expounded his economic theory, did not everyone condemn it as heresy? Was not Galileo punished as a heretic when he articulated his theory of the earth's rotation? Yet with the passage of time the mass of "common men," guided by the intellectuals, were, before they knew it, drawn over to the side of these "heresies"; as a result, at our present stage of civilization even school-children entertain no doubts about the theories of modern economics and the earth's revolution. Doubt these theories? We have reached a point where anyone who questioned them would be regarded as a fool! To take a more proximate example: just ten years ago our solidly entrenched feudal system, in which three hundred daimyo each governed independently and held the power of life and death over his subjects by reason of a clear distinction between lord and vassal, high and low, was thought to be a thing that would endure forever. Yet in an instant it crumbled and was replaced by the present imperial system. Today no one considers this new system strange, but if ten years ago a warrior within a *han* had proposed such measures as the abolition of the *han* and the establish-ment of prefectures, do you think for an instant the *han* would have debated the matter? Why, the man's very life would have been in immediate jeopardy!

Thus the unorthodox theories of the past become the commonly accepted ideas of the present; yesterday's eccentric notions become today's common knowledge. Therefore the unorthodox views of today will most certainly become the common ideas and theories of the future. Without fear of public opinion or charges of heresy, scholars should boldly espouse what they believe. Even when another's thesis does not square with your own, try to understand his intention and accept those points which can be accepted. Let those points which do not merit acceptance run their course, and wait for the day when both positions can be reconciled, the day when the basis of argumentation will be the same. Do not try to pressure others into your own way of thinking, nor try to induce conformity in every discussion, everywhere. [pp. 10–11]

Fukuzawa next discusses world history and the lessons it provides for the Japan of his day. His didactic conclusion, modified only slightly by the notion that even Western civilization is less than perfect, is that Japan must learn from the West. Note in the following passage that "semideveloped" refers to the stage of society that is half-civilized and half-barbarous.

In the preceding chapter I argued that such designations as light and heavy and good and bad are relative. Now, the concept of "civilization and enlight-enment" (*bunmei kaika*) is also a relative one. When we are talking about civilization in the world today, the nations of Europe and the United States of America are the most highly civilized, while the Asian countries, such as Tur-key, China, and Japan, may be called semideveloped countries, and Africa and Australia are to be counted as still primitive lands. These designations are com-mon currency all over the world. While the citizens of the nations of the West are the only ones to boast of civilization, the citizens of the semideveloped and primitive lands submit to being designated as such. They rest content with being branded semideveloped or primitive, and there is not one who would take pride in his own country or consider it on a par with nations of the West. This attitude is bad enough. What is worse, though, those with some intelligence start to realize, the more they find out what is happening, the true condition of their native lands; the more they come to realize this, the more they awaken to the distance separating them from the nations of the West. They groan, they grieve; some are for learning from the West and imitating it, others are for going it alone and opposing the West. The overriding anxiety of Asian intellectuals today is this one problem to the exclusion of all others. At any rate, the designations "civilized," "semideveloped," and "primitive" have been universally accepted by people all over the globe. Why does everybody accept them? Clearly because the facts are demonstrable and irrefutable. I shall explain this point further below. For there are stages through which mankind must pass. These may be termed the stages of civilization.

First, there is the stage in which neither dwellings nor supplies of food are stable. Men form communal groups as temporary convenience demands; when that convenience ceases, they pull up stakes and scatter to the four winds. Or even if they settle in a certain region and engage in farming and fishing, they may have enough food and clothing, but they do not yet know how to make tools. And though they are not without writing, they produce no literature. At this stage man is still unable to be master of his own situation; he cowers before the forces of nature and is dependent upon arbitrary human favor or accidental blessings. This is called the stage of primitive man. It is still far from civilization.

Secondly, there is the stage of civilization wherein daily necessities are not lacking, since agriculture has been started on a large scale. Men build houses, form communities, and create the outward semblance of a state. But within this facade there remain very many defects. Though literature flourishes, there are few who devote themselves to practical studies. Though in human relations sentiments of suspicion and jealousy run deep, when it comes to discussing the nature of things men lack the courage to raise doubts and ask questions. Men are adept at imitative craftsmanship, but there is a dearth of original production. They know how to cultivate the old, but not how to improve it. There are accepted rules governing human intercourse, and slaves of custom that they are, they never alter those rules. This is called the semideveloped stage. It is not yet civilization in the full sense.

Thirdly, there is the stage in which men subsume the things of the universe within a general structure, but the structure does not bind them. Their spirits enjoy free play and do not adhere to old customs blindly. They act autonomously and do not have to depend upon the arbitrary favors of others. They cultivate their own virtue and refine their own knowledge. They neither yearn for the old nor become complacent about the new. Not resting with small gains, they plan great accomplishments for the future and commit themselves whole-heartedly to their realization. Their path of learning is not vacuous; it has, indeed, invented the principle of invention itself. Their business ventures prosper day by day to increase the sources of human welfare. Today's wisdom overflows to create the plans of tomorrow. This is what is meant by modern civilization. It has been a leap far beyond the primitive or semideveloped stages.

Now, if we make the above threefold distinction, the differences between civilization, semidevelopment, and the primitive stage should be clear. However, since these designations are essentially relative, there is nothing to prevent someone who has not seen civilization from thinking that semidevelopment is the summit of man's development. And while civilization is civilization relative to the semideveloped stage, the latter, in its turn, can be called civilization relative to the primitive stage. Thus, for example, present-day China has to be called semideveloped in comparison with Western countries. But if we compare China with countries of South Africa, or, to take an example more at hand, if we compare the Japanese people with the Ezo, then both China and Japan can be called civilized. Moreover, although we call the nations of the West civilized, they can correctly be honored with this designation only in modern history. And many of them, if we were to be more precise, would fall well short of this designation.

For example, there is no greater calamity in the world than war, and yet the nations of the West are always at war. Robbery and murder are the worst of human crimes; but in the West there are robbers and murderers. There are those who form cliques to vie for the reins of power and who, when deprived of that power, decry the injustice of it all. Even worse, international diplomacy is really based on the art of deception. Surveying the situation as a whole, all we can say is that there is a general prevalence of good over bad, but we can hardly call the situation perfect. When, several thousand years hence, the levels of knowledge and virtue of the peoples of the world will have made great progress (to the point of becoming utopian), the present condition of the nations of the West will surely seem a pitifully primitive stage. Seen in this light, civilization is an open-ended process. We cannot be satisfied with the present level of attainment of the West.

Yes, we cannot be satisfied with the level of civilization attained by the West. But shall we therefore conclude that Japan should reject it? If we did, what other criterion would we have? We cannot rest content with the stage of semidevelopment; even less can the primitive stage suffice. Since these latter alternatives are to be rejected, we must look elsewhere. But to look to some far-off utopian world thousands of years hence is mere daydreaming. Besides, civilization is not a dead thing; it is something vital and moving. As such, it must pass through sequences and stages; primitive people advance to semideveloped forms, the semideveloped advance to civilization, and civilization itself is even now in the process of advancing forward. Europe also had to pass through these phases in its evolution to its present level. Hence present-day Europe can only be called the highest level that human intelligence has been able to attain at this juncture in history. Since this is true, in all countries of the world, be they primitive or semideveloped, those who are to give thought to their country's progress in civilization must necessarily take European civilization as the basis of discussion and must weigh the pros and cons of the problem in the light of it. My own criterion throughout this book will be that of Western civilization, and it will be in terms of it that I describe something as good or bad, in terms of it that I find things beneficial or harmful. Therefore let scholars make no mistake about my orientation. [pp. 13–15]

After describing the several stages of human progress, Fukuzawa attempts to define more precisely the nature of civilization. In the end, he resorts to metaphor.

Now civilization is a relative thing, and it has no limits. It is a gradual progression from the primitive level. Man is by nature a social animal. A man in isolation cannot develop his innate talents and intelligence. The community of the family does not exhaust the possibilities of human intercourse. The more social intercourse there is, the more citizens of a nation meet one another; the more human relationships broaden and their patterns evolve, so much the more will human nature become civilized and human intelligence develop. Hence the term "civilization" in English. It derives from the Latin *civitas*, which means "nation." "Civilization" thus describes the process by which human relations gradually change for the better and take on a definite shape. It is a concept of a unified nation in contrast to a state of primitive isolation and lawlessness.

Civilization is all-important; it is the goal of all human endeavors. We can discuss civilization in terms of its various aspects, such as institutions, literature, commerce, industry, war, government, and law; but when taking all of these together and discussing their relative values, what criteria are we to use? The only criterion we have is that what advances civilization is beneficial and what retards it is harmful. [pp. 35–36]

As Fukuzawa sees it, on the great stage of civilization, all members of a society are actors, and accordingly, the stage of any civilization reflects the level of knowledge and virtue of an entire people. It cannot be discussed in terms of a handful of leaders.

Though we here describe the Western nations as civilized and Asian countries as only semicivilized, if we were to take only two or three individuals as samples, then there would be boorish and stupid people in the West, too, and outstandingly wise and virtuous men in Asia, too. To say that the West is civilized and Asia uncivilized means that in the West the very stupid cannot give free rein to their stupidity and that in Asia the very outstanding cannot give free rein to their knowledge and virtue. This is because civilization is not a matter of the knowledge or ignorance of individuals but of the spirit of entire nations. Thus we can only judge a nation civilized by considering the spirit which pervades the whole land. This "spirit" is a manifestation of the knowledge and virtue of the entire population. It goes through cycles of change and is the source of national vitality at any given moment. Once we have been able to determine the presence of this spirit, the degree of civilization of the whole nation will become clear, and it will be easy to evaluate and discuss its merits and demerits, easier even than fishing a thing from one's pocket. [p. 47]

Since it is the spirit of an entire nation that counts, Fukuzawa downplays the role of great men in history.

The independence of the United States of America was not achieved in the eighteenth century as a result of anything done by the forty-eight leaders, nor was it due to the victories of Washington. The forty-eight leaders merely gave expression to the spirit of independence spread among the people in the thirteen colonies, and Washington only channeled that spirit onto the battle-field. American independence, therefore, was not some miraculous, "once in a thousand years" event. Even had the American people been defeated and temporarily set back, they would have produced 480 great leaders and ten George Washingtons. Eventually they would have been sure to win their independence. . . .

. . . For the outcome of a war does not depend on generals or weaponry but entirely on the spirit of a people. If a defeat is suffered by a large army of valiant warriors, the fault does not lie with the troops in the field but in the lack of expertise of the officers, who have interfered with the troops' own momentum and been unable to channel their fighting spirit properly.

Let me give another example. The present Meiji government thinks it is not being entirely successful because the various head officials are not able men; even with a great deal of shuffling of offices and functions the results always end up the same. Because of the dearth of personnel, foreigners are being employed as teachers or advisers, but the affairs of government still show no improvement. It would seem from the lack of improvement that the officials are all incompetent, and the foreigners hired as teachers and advisers are all fools. Yet the present government officials are among the most talented men in the country, and the foreigners selected are no fools. There must, then, be another reason for the failure of the government to improve, something that makes it impossible for government policies to be implemented.

That something is extremely hard to describe, but as the saying goes, "The feeble few are no match for the mighty many." The reason why government policies fail is that the feeble few are always being hindered by the mighty many. Government heads are not unaware of the failure of their policies, but what can they do about it? They are the feeble few; public opinion is the mighty many; and the few are helpless. Try to trace the origins of public opinion and you will find it an impossible task; it seems to come out of nowhere, yet it has the power to control the affairs of government. The reason the government cannot handle its affairs is not some fault of a handful of officials, but this public opinion. When the mass of society is in error, one should not put the blame on the policies of officials. The ancients felt the necessity of first recti-fying the ruler's mind, but my idea is different. The most urgent national task is to rectify the ills of public opinion. Since officials are the ones who have closest contact with national problems, they should naturally have the strongest concern for the country and be sufficiently worried about public opinion to seek ways to rectify this opinion. This is not what happens, however. Instead, officials sometimes themselves become proponents of these popular ideas or at least become enamored of them and tend to favor them. These men are in a position where they are supposed to worry about the people under them, but instead they do things which cause people to worry about them. The blunders of government, which often seem as if the very same people are tearing down what they built up, are the doings of such people.

Under such distressing circumstances, it is imperative that scholars who are concerned about the state of the country advocate a theory of civilization, try to rescue all men, both in government and in private circles, who are subject to blind attachment to false ideas, and correct the flow of public opinion. The tide of public opinion sweeps everything before it. Why should scholars pick on the government? Why should they find fault with every little act of officials? Of its very nature, government will change its course in line with public opin-ion. Therefore, I say, the scholars should not blame the government but should be concerned about the errant ways of public opinion. [pp. 60–61]

A nation's civilization thus is determined by the level of virtue and knowledge it has attained. But which of these is more important? In which area is Japan deficient? Fu-kuzawa discusses the question in terms of cows and cats.

. . . Everyone will grant that Japan's civilization is not equal to that of the countries of the West. If this is so, it means that here people are deficient in knowledge and virtue; these are the two things Japan must seek in order to attain civilization. . . .

Now, a person does not have to be very smart to see that in Japan there is no dearth of morality, whereas there is no surplus of intelligence, either. Any number of instances could be adduced to prove this, but there is no need to list them all here. Let me give just one or two by way of illustration.

The moral teaching current in Japan derives from Shintoism, Confucianism, and Buddhism, whereas in the West it derives from Christianity. All of these do not teach exactly the same thing, yet they are not all that different in their general definitions of good and evil. . . .

My main concern here is not to discuss which side is better, but I might point out that we Japanese also have ethical values we live by. Hence, when discussing the question of who has how much private virtue, no one should conclude that we are necessarily second to the West. For if we go from theory to reality, we might find more morally superior individuals among us unenlightened Japanese than we should find in the West. Therefore, though a survey of the amount of virtue in our country as a whole may show we are relatively deficient in it, the deficiency clearly has not reached crisis proportions.

The question of intelligence, however, is something completely different. If we compare the levels of intelligence of Japanese and Westerners, in literature, the arts, commerce, or industry, from the biggest things to the least, in a thousand cases or in one, there is not a single area in which the other side is not superior to us. We can compete with the West in nothing, and no one even thinks about competing with the West. Only the most ignorant thinks that Japan's learning, arts, commerce, or industry is on a par with that of the West. . . . While we regard Japan as the sacrosanct islands of the gods, they have raced around the world, discovering new lands and founding new nations. Many of their political, commercial, and legal institutions are more admirable than anything we have. In all these things there is nothing about our present situation that we can be proud of before them. The only things we Japanese boast of are our natural products or our scenic landscapes, but we never talk about anything made by man. We feel no urge to compete with them, nor they with us. . . . [pp. 98–99]

[Fukuzawa, *An Outline of a Theory of Civilization*, trans. Dilworth and Hurst, pp. 10–11, 13–15, 35–36, 47, 60–61, 98–99]

AN ENCOURAGEMENT OF LEARNING
(*GAKUMON NO SUSUME*)

Fukuzawa was a patriot. In writing *An Outline of a Theory of Civilization*, his goal was to strengthen Japan and preserve its independence. Nonetheless, he was attacked for his uncompromising advocacy of Westernization. Perhaps to defend himself against these charges, the following year (1876) he wrote a satirical passage in *An Encouragement of Learning* about those "masters of enlightenment" who praised even the defects of the West and criticized even the virtues of Japan. The following is from a section entitled "Methodic Doubt and Selective Judgment."

"Methodic Doubt and Selective Judgment"

Now, the superiority of Western over Japanese civilization is certainly very great, but Western civilization is hardly perfect. I could never begin to enumerate all its defects. Its ways and customs are not all beautiful and believable; our customs are not all ugly and open to question. . . .

Let us imagine that Westerners bathed every day, while the Japanese barely once or twice a month; the teachers of enlightenment would exclaim that the people who are civilized and enlightened are always clean, stimulate their skin, maintain the laws of hygiene, etc., but the uncivilized Japanese do not understand these principles! If the Japanese kept a small chamber pot in their bedrooms at night or did not wash after going to the bathroom, while the Westerners rose even in the middle of the night to go to the toilet and each time washed their hands, the proponents of enlightenment would declare that the enlightened Westerners place a high value on cleanliness, while the unenlightened Japanese do not know the meaning of the word, that they are like infants who are still too immature to distinguish cleanliness from filth. They will declare that the Japanese will imitate the beautiful customs of the West once they advance to the level of modern Western civilization. . . . If *miso* soup was brought on foreign vessels, it would not be thought of so lightly, as it is now. If tofu [bean curd] was also found on the tables of the Westerners, its reputation would increase tenfold. Such dishes as baked eel or *chawanmushi* [custard] would be praised as among the world's superlative dishes. There would be no end if I enumerated these things. But let me go on to the more elegant matter of religious teachings. . . .

I myself have entertained doubts about these things for a long time. But I still am not sure I have grasped the real causes of the great differences between the religions of East and West. When I ponder the matter privately, the following kind of questions come to my mind. Although Christianity preached in Japan and Buddhism in the West are similar in nature, is it that when practiced in a barbarous land they promote the spirit of killing, but create a spirit of tolerance in an enlightened country? Or do they differ in essence from the start? Or did Luther, the founder of the Japanese Reformation, and Shinran of the West differ greatly in the attainments of their virtue? The proponents of the enlightenment would say that these questions are not to be recklessly and superficially decided, but await the judgment of the scholars of future generations.

[Fukuzawa, *An Encouragement of Learning*, trans. Dilworth and Hirano, pp. 95–99]

ENLIGHTENMENT THINKERS OF THE MEIROKUSHA: ON MARRIAGE

Of the many topics discussed by members of the Meiji Six Society (Meiroku-sha), none aroused greater interest and controversy than their proposals concerning the institution of marriage. In discussing this issue, all writers took the West as their model in one way or another, although they differed in their approaches and conclusions.

MORI ARINORI

Mori Arinori (1847–1889), who started Western studies in the Satsuma domain, extended his horizons through travel and service in England and America. As chargé d'affaires in Washington in 1871/1872, he published works in English on religious freedom and education in Japan. On returning to Japan, he became a leading figure in the Meiji Six Society, writing especially on the condition of women. Later he served as the first minister of education in the Meiji government (see chap. 38).

ON WIVES AND CONCUBINES

The relation between man and wife is the fundamental of human morals. The moral path will be achieved by establishing this fundamental, and the country will only be firmly based if the moral path is realized. When people marry, rights and obligations emerge between them so that neither can take advantage of the other. If you ask what these rights and obligations are, they may be described as the paths of mutual assistance and mutual protection. That is, the husband has the right to demand assistance from the wife while he shoulders the obligation to protect her. And, conversely, the wife has the right to demand protection from the husband while she bears the obligation to assist him. Unless the marriage is strictly according to these principles, it cannot be recognized as human marriage. Looking at marriage customs in our country today, the husband treats the wife as he pleases, and there is still no national legislation [protecting the wife] against arbitrary divorce by the husband simply because she does not please him. Since husbands and wives cannot mutually honor their rights and obligations and since, even though persons are husbands and wives in name, they are far from such in actuality, I would affirm that our country has not yet established the fundamental of human morals.

There have hitherto been a variety of marriage practices [in our country]. Persons married through the agency of a go-between (*nakōdo*) are known as husband and wife, and the woman in such a union is recognized as the wife. The woman is called a concubine in a union not arranged by a go-between. Sometimes there may be one or even several concubines in addition to the wife, and sometimes a concubine may become the wife. Sometimes the wife and the concubines live in the same establishment. Sometimes they are separated, and the concubine is the favored one while the wife is neglected. Moreover, marriages are negotiated by the respective parents, it sometimes being only necessary to obtain their consent.

Taking a concubine is by arbitrary decision of the man and with acquiescence of the concubine's family. The arrangement, known as *ukedashi*, is made by paying money to the family of the concubine. This means, in other words, that concubines are bought with money. Since concubines are generally geisha and prostitutes patronized by rich men and nobles, many descendants in the rich and noble houses are the children of bought women. Even though the wife is superior to the concubine in households where they live together, there is commonly jealousy and hatred between them because the husband generally favors the concubine. Therefore, there are numerous instances when, the wife and the concubines being scattered in separate establishments, the husband repairs to the abode of the one with whom he is infatuated and willfully resorts to scandalous conduct.

In extreme cases, those who take concubines boast of their affluence and are disdainful of those who abstain from the practice. The national law regards wives and concubines as equals and accords equal rights to their offspring. Thus, I have here explained that our country has not yet established the fundamentals of human morality, and I hope later to discuss how this situation injures our customs and obstructs enlightenment.

[Braisted, *Meiroku Zasshi*, pp. 104–5]

KATŌ HIROYUKI

Katō Hiroyuki (1836–1916), a student of military science and Dutch, became an instructor at the shogunate's research center, Bansho shirabesho, in 1860 and, after the Restoration, was an early advocate of representative government. Later he became increasingly conservative. Eventually he became president of Tokyo Imperial University and a privy councillor. While he was a participant in the Meiji Six Society, he was known as an advocate of human rights, but with reservations of the kind expressed in the following.

ABUSES OF EQUAL RIGHTS FOR MEN AND WOMEN

As the true principles regarding married couples have been gradually clarified in public since the appearance of the discussion on equal rights for husbands and wives by Mori [Arinori] and Fukuzawa [Yukichi], the ugly custom of keeping concubines promiscuously and the bad practice by which the husband holds his wife in contempt will gradually be destroyed, and we shall consequently reach the point where equality between husband and wife is truly observed. Are not the achievements of these two gentlemen indeed wonderful?

It is my opinion, however, that, even though the system of near equality between husband and wife in modern Europe conforms with Heaven's Reason, the rights of the wife seem rather to surpass those of the husband in present-day society. This evil, after all, arises from a misunderstanding of the principle of equal rights. There is not time to enumerate all the abuses, but the following are a few examples.

When husband and wife pass through a door, the wife goes first and the husband follows. When they are seated, the wife occupies the highest seat; the husband, the next best seat. When others call on the couple, they greet the wife before the husband. When they address the couple, they place the wife's name first, the husband's later. If men are seated with the ladies, they are especially discreet in speech, and they do not smoke without first securing permission from the ladies. The extent of women's rights is really surprising. Although it appears that Westerners cannot actually understand the impropriety of their ways since they have been soaked in them for a long time, I must say that the customs are indeed strange from the point of view of East Asians. How can they be called equal rights of husband and wife? . . .

Although such a question [as the right to smoke in the presence of women] is really a small matter, it clearly misrepresents the principle of equality between men and women, and it is also clearly an evil that has arisen from the infatuation with which men court the favor of women with flattery. It is an unbearable but natural outcome that in Europe one often hears of adulterous scandals even about women reputed to be noble ladies. How dreadful this is! At present, when we are putting into practice in our country the principle of equal rights for men and women, we shall finally reach the point at which we are unable to control the injury of excessive women's rights if men of intelligence, fully recognizing this danger, do not prevent it in advance. What do my friends make of this?

[Braisted, *Meiroku Zasshi*, pp. 376-77]

FUKUZAWA YUKICHI

THE EQUAL NUMBERS OF MEN AND WOMEN

Fukuzawa Yukichi wrote on civilization, but he also applied his enlightened general schemas to a variety of specific topics. He was an early and outspoken advocate of women's rights. Here, in tongue-in-cheek fashion, he uses numbers in a question that, he realizes, has little to do with mathematics.

One does not know who is right in the recent noisy discussion of equal rights for men and women. Now when a person discusses anything, he will not grasp the matter unless he first closely examines its character. Therefore, we should take up even this discussion of equal rights for men and women only after we have first considered the nature of men and women and become well informed on what rights are. If to the contrary we set forth our opinions at will according to our individual viewpoints, conjecturing on the nature of men and women and speculating on the word "right," we shall be reduced to limitless futile argument. When equal seating for men and women is taken up, for example, giving precedence in seating to ladies is veneration for those who call it veneration and helping for those who call it helping. Even though some may not become angry when they think of the practice as helping, they may also gnash their teeth if they regard it as completely dedicated, sincere veneration.

Since public discussion has generally sunk to this level rather than become embroiled in a noisy discussion of the merits of equal rights, I would direct attention only to an aspect that anyone can easily understand after we have taken up a simple point that is close at hand. This simple point is neither religious nor theoretical but rather a mathematical computation on the *soroban* [abacus] of the equal number of men and women that anyone can readily grasp.

First, since the number of men and women in the world [is] roughly equal, the calculation will show that one man should marry one woman. If, contrary to this, an excessive number of women [are] taken into one house, there must be scarcity in another. If the phrase "eight suitors for one daughter" on the *iroha* [Japanese "alphabet"] card is unfair, it is also unreasonable for one man to take eight concubines. Today, setting aside the difficult discussion of equal rights, I only say that for one man to take several wives is not right, as it does not conform to computations on the *soroban*. We may then take this as the first step toward equal rights and decide to postpone other discussion of the matter until scholarship has progressed. If anyone feels that even this theory is too advanced, we shall tacitly allow him to keep concubines or take geisha. But these practices must be hidden from others as private affairs. Hiding from others is the beginning of shame, and being ashamed naturally is the beginning of voluntary abstention. Once we thus introduce the first step toward equal rights, the present futile arguments somehow can also be resolved in a few years.

[Braisted, *Meiroku Zasshi*, pp. 385–86]

SAKATANI SHIROSHI

Sakatani Shiroshi (1822–1881) received his early education in the school run by Ōshio Heihachirō (see chap. 32) but later turned to the Zhu Xi school. Generally on the conservative side in the Meiji Six Society debates, he later became active in efforts to revive Confucian ethics.

ON CONCUBINES

The wise men of Japan, China, and the West are agreed in holding that marriage is the foundation from which the fine qualities of nations emerge, since it is the basis of morality and the source of propriety as well as the institution upon which the conduct of the people rests. Even though secular ethical teachings (*seikyō*) are the source of the morals of marriage, the damage to customs from the concubine system is great, and the vice of concubines is rife in modern society. I am not resorting to idle theory apart from human feelings. Yet some will smile without becoming angry and think me impractical and unenlightened when I discuss concubines. Extreme persons claim boastfully and without shame that they are emulating Western ways when they ride with their concubines in the same carriage shoulder to shoulder and hand in hand, or when they walk with these ladies down the main streets in broad daylight.

Ah, how can the concubine system be attributed to the West? It is false to the West to ascribe such ugly and barbaric conduct to Western tutelage. Fortunately, however, distinguished scholars in Western studies are advocating reform [in this area]. Mori [Arinori]'s discourses on wives and concubines are clear and just, while Fukuzawa [Yukichi] is equally instructive to society when he felicitously calls even a lofty mansion the hut of beasts [if it is a house of but one father and many mothers]. Both gentlemen have washed out the eyes and ears of the pseudo-enlightened and left them speechless. . . .

When husband and wife enjoy equal rights, it would seem that the wife should also have the right to take additional mates if her husband keeps concubines. A woman is also a person. Women are by nature strong and weak, some being able to live without husbands all their lives, while others are not satisfied with several men. Morality is destroyed when men and women alike become so lustfully dissipated that they are no more than beasts. Thus the advocates of equal rights for men and women promote the establishment of morality by employing these rights to impose mutual restraints. Yet men stand above women, and husbands are above wives. Women are weak; men strong. The husband deals with the outside world while the wife manages domestic matters. Such occasional exceptions as the queen of England notwithstanding, it is generally the invariable custom throughout the five continents that men are above women. The true principle of equal rights, therefore, appears to be limited only to the prevention of sexual license by establishing mutual restraints in the bedchamber. . . .

What we should honor are the enlightened ideas of Europe and America according to which husband and wife equally love and help each other. Even though the European and American customs contain the reasonable intention that the weak female shall be protected by the strong male like a child, however, I must deplore the prevailing ugly way in which their men have practically all become slaves to women. This is exactly the same as the ugly situation in which wives are oppressed by the husband's rights in China and Japan. Looked at reasonably, even though it is naturally proper for the strong man to protect the woman, it is also right for the woman obediently to serve the man.

The words "equal rights," therefore, should not establish equality in life generally, although they may provide equality in the bedchamber. If today we establish this equality between the sexes in all aspects of life, we shall reach the point where the men will strive to oppress the women while the women attempt to oppress the men. In America, women's parties have gained the right to agitate for prohibition of drinking by men. Even though their intentions may be fine, how are their acts fine? How is such conduct for the benefit of those [women] who should obediently receive protection? Such women probably resemble the wives in the back streets of Tokyo. In sum, the word "rights" includes evil. There is a tendency for the advocacy of rights to generate opposing power. This was never the intention of the wise men of Europe and America, and the translation [of the word "right" as *ken*] is not appropriate. Instead, it would be well to speak of preserving the spheres of men and women (*danjo shubun*) or of the harmonious bodies of husband and wife (*fūfu dōtai*). Further, from the point of view of rights, the man should stand slightly above the woman, just as elder brother takes precedence before younger brother. We naturally cannot discuss as typical a case such as England in which the husband's rights are necessarily inferior to those of the wife, who is queen and empress. Such a situation thus should not be regarded as the normal shape of things.

[Braisted, *Meiroku Zasshi*, pp. 392–96]

TSUDA MAMICHI

Tsuda Mamichi (1829–1903), a student of Sakuma Shōzan (see chap. 34), went to Holland to study law and on his return taught at the Kaisei school (predecessor of Tokyo Imperial University). Later active in the Meiji government in both foreign affairs and parliamentary matters, he was notable in his early contributions to the *Meiji Six Magazine* for his advocacy of Western liberal and humanitarian ideals.

DISTINGUISHING THE EQUAL RIGHTS OF HUSBANDS AND WIVES

Why is it that the phrase "the equal rights of husbands and wives" (*fūfu dōken*), having recently come into circulation, is scattered through the press as well as mistakenly uttered by accomplished gentlemen? Now "the equal rights of men and women" (*danjo dōken*) are words that previously have been intoned quite often in the countries of Europe and America, and they correspond exactly to the position of Western men and women from the point of view of civil rights (*minken*). For example, there is absolutely no discrimination or differentiation between the rights of men and women when one consults the stipulations in Western civil codes that establish personal rights, property rights, and the rights and duties of contract. Yet there are naturally distinctions between the public rights of men and women that relate to national political affairs. After all, women are unable to share these public rights as they have been customarily monopolized by men. This is for the reason that women have not yet participated in the three great rights of legislation, justice, and administration. Even though there have been suggestions that women should also share in these public rights, this has not yet actually been practiced.

On the other hand, there has been absolutely no provision even in civil law for what might be called "the equal rights of husbands and wives." This is because the husband is the person who controls the family's affairs as head of the household. A woman possessed of a husband, being a wife, is not allowed by civil law to manage the family's affairs except under extraordinary circumstances. Not only this, a wife also has not the right to manage even her private property, and a woman possessed of a husband does not have the right to institute civil suits in her own name. These are areas in which the provision of Western civil codes differentiate between the rights of husbands and wives. This ought to be entirely understandable from one reading of the writings of Westerners on civil law. I am incredulous, therefore, when I hear references from time to time to "the equal rights of husbands and wives."

Even though husbands and wives do not possess the same rights under the law, they are naturally equal without distinction as to high or low in their traditional marital intercourse. After all, none doubt that husbands and wives should employ the proprieties of equals as was indeed the case in our ancient Japanese customs. Asians, however, debased womanhood to such an extreme degree that they do not enjoy what is called equal rights of men and women even under civil law. Especially, there is the evil among the Chinese in which wives, like criminals, are all shut up in their courtyards and forbidden any contact with outsiders. This is an extremely outrageous custom. Without appreciating this [great evil], gentlemen in society vainly discuss the minor abuse in which the frailty of wives is protected under Western custom. I also fail to understand the reason for this. How do [these gentlemen] hope to overtake the far higher level of European and American civilization and enlightenment? After all, this not being their intent, they have finally fallen to the evil of capricious progress. Let us reflect on what in the final analysis will be their situation if they are moved to attempt the establishment of a popularly elected assembly? Undoubtedly, uneducated and unskilled fellows, with tumultuous clamor, will want to do things that have not yet been done in the countries of Europe and America. How will this achieve happiness for the people and the nation? As the proverb goes, "Superficial tactics are the source of great wounds." I would just say that superficial enlightenment is the cause of rebellion. Should we not be prudent? As I fear that I have reached the point of redundancy in elucidating the error of "equal rights of husbands and wives," I beg your kind indulgence.

[Braisted, *Meiroku Zasshi*, pp. 435–36]

NAKAMURA MASANAO: CHINA SHOULD NOT BE DESPISED

The repudiation of old, largely Chinese, learning and the ardent embrace of new, Western, learning was the hallmark of the Civilization and Enlightenment movement. But studies of the movement usually ignore or gloss over the fact that all thinkers in the movement had been educated in their youth in Chinese philosophy and history. Indeed, the platform on which they stood to reach out for Western ideas was, in large part, this earlier education. Had their minds been blank, had they lacked the sophistication of Chinese learning, they would not have been able to understand the thought of the modern West. When we read their enlightenment writings in the original Japanese, the debt to Chinese philosophy is clear. It was the source of much of the vocabulary they drew on to translate such Western concepts as "nature," "human nature," and "reason." Of course, they also realized that they were using such terms in ways that departed from their original meanings. An early acknowledgment of certain aspects of the debt to China can be seen in the following passage, written by Nakamura Masanao (1832–1891) in 1875 at the crest of the Civilization and Enlightenment movement.

JAPAN'S DEBT TO CHINA

As may be seen by referring to history, China has produced numerous outstanding men, turning out sages, superior men, and heroes one after another. Should you desire their names recited in their entirety, they could not be exhausted even if you relieve me with an assistant. This is the first reason why China should not be despised. China can probably take first place in the East in the abundance of her writings. Furthermore, being tasteful, her prose can readily convey men's intentions. And having strict grammatical rules, it is also convenient for translating foreign materials. Even in daily communications, we must invariably use Chinese words when dealing with important matters. The Chinese seem to have a particular genius for contriving ideographs. As their own writing possesses some grace, they do not easily change to horizontal script or yearn for Western literary styles. Yet since China is a country skilled in letters, young Chinese studying abroad may emerge one after another within a few years to advance their [Western] studies to a high level. This is the second reason why China should not be despised.

Being now under a Tartar house, even the public-spirited men of China are disinclined to exert their natural vigor, and her people are seemingly in a drugged condition unable to move their arms and feet. If they throw off the poison of the Tartar drug and awake from their stupor, however, a Han Gaozu may emerge from the village headmen of Si Shui or a Ming Taizu may come forth from the monks of Huangque Si. . . . If from among the leading families of China proper that bear the name of Li or Liu there emerges a great hero who destroys the Manchu-Qing dynasty and who by resolute decree directs the use of the arts and sciences of Europe and America, he can quickly introduce steamships, trains, telegraph, fortifications, and warships the great distances

between the eighteen provinces and the two capitals notwithstanding. Moreover, he will face an extremely serious situation should [China] then establish
a popularly elected assembly and attempt to avenge the shame of defeat. This
is the third reason why China should not be despised.

That China produces many raw materials is entirely natural since she is a
large country. Even in manufactures, however, her exports to Japan of ink,
paper, and books alone have been extremely large for more than a century.
Maki Ryōko[1] states that it should be appreciated that the Japanese craftsmen
are clumsy at producing writing brushes. The Chinese in ancient times made
useful skills of mathematics and astronomy in which they were extremely proficient. Our country employed Chinese texts on medicine and horticulture
until twenty years ago. In addition, this country has not matched China in the
large number of useful instruments that the Chinese have invented. In the
words of an English friend, "The Chinese people are good, but their government is bad." If the above statement proves correct, once her government is
reformed, China will necessarily progress since her people are really of a good
type. This is the fourth reason why China should not be despised. . . .

Enlightenment in our country is now being fostered by foreigners rather
than advanced by our own efforts. The situation is one in which, rather than
using foreigners, we are being used by them. We have reached the point where
[officials] within the various ministries are shifting their burdens to foreigners
hired at exorbitant salaries. We cannot know whether the Chinese will cease
admiring the foreigners once China has been induced to study Europe and
America and surpassed the West in knowledge. If we disparage China, feeling
that we have acquired a part of Western culture, we shall be scorned by intellectuals as this is just like the person who looks down on a man in rags after
donning beautiful clothes borrowed from another. This is the seventh reason
why China should not be despised. As the old proverb goes, "An individual
should clean away the snow from before his own gate before he inquires into
the frost on his neighbor's roof." We shall not have much time to reflect on
others if we hereafter assiduously cultivate ourselves by devoting our attention
to our nation's affairs and appreciating its inadequacies. Still less will we presume to despise other countries!

[Braisted, *Meiroku Zasshi*, pp. 425–28]

---

1. Maki Ryōko (1777–1843) was a famous Japanese calligrapher.

Chapter 37

POPULAR RIGHTS AND CONSTITUTIONALISM

During the first years of the Meiji era, Japan's political leaders were dogged by issues of every sort: the divisiveness of old class distinctions; the danger that regional power conflicts would pull the country apart; a dire shortage of revenues; the lack of efficient economic, military, and educational systems; a fear of being overwhelmed by Western imperialism. The historian Tōyama Shigeki says of the 1870s that "there was a real danger that Japan would become a colony"; the educator-journalist Fukuzawa Yukichi observed at the time that Japan was "a government, not a nation." Among all the issues, none dominated the public discourse of the 1870s and 1880s more than the question of what shape the state system should take. What should the relationship between the emperor and his subjects be? What role should the "people" play in the political system? Should Japan have a national legislature? Who should be in it? When should it be convened? Above all, what kind of constitution should Japan have? At the core of these debates was a consensus that the new system must balance the family-like, emperor-centered approach of Japanese tradition and myth with the contemporary world's insistence on popular representation and "rational" state systems.

The debates over state structures hardly were new. Political discourse in the Tokugawa era had been sophisticated and continual. By the early nineteenth century, influential scholars, conscious of the declining effectiveness of the *bakufu* system, were advocating everything from the restoration of imperial rule to participation in international trade, from nativism to republicanism. What was new after the Meiji Restoration in 1868 was the volume, as well as the intensity, of the state philosophy debates. Released from the restraints of the Tokugawa system, Japan's thinkers unleashed a deluge of debate in these years, drawing on both East Asian and European theorists: Confucius from China, Aizawa Seishisai from Japan, John Stuart Mill from Great Britain, Jean-Jacques Rousseau from France. They also used new avenues for discussion: debating societies, public lectures, newspapers, and magazines. And the debates reached new corners of society, including the mountain village commons as well as the public thoroughfare.

The other thing that was new in these discussions was the focus on constitutionalism, a concept adapted from the West. Increasingly, after the mid-1870s, the debaters talked about what kind of constitution Japan should have and what institutional structures the constitution should support. The constitutional arguments spanned three general periods: 1873 to 1875, when discussion centered on the creation of a national legislature; 1876 to 1883, when the focus was on what kind of a constitution Japan needed; and 1884 to 1889, when the constitution was drawn up and promulgated.

DEBATING A NATIONAL ASSEMBLY, 1873–1875

The leaders of the Meiji state adopted one new structure after another in the first Meiji years, trying to find an administrative system adequate to the world that now challenged them. Although there was no cabinet, key ministries such as justice, foreign affairs, and finance emerged, as did a council of state. The early debates about these evolving structures were carried out largely within government circles, among the insiders who had overthrown the Tokugawa. That insider approach to discussion changed, however, late in 1873, after a small coterie, led by Saigō Takamori and Itagaki Taisuke, left office to protest Japan's policies toward Korea. When Itagaki and eight others sent a memorial to the throne the next January, urging the early creation of a national legislature, a storm of public debate ensued over when such an assembly should be created and what shape it should take. The fact that Japan's first daily newspapers had sprung into existence barely two years before gave the debate wider circulation than had been possible earlier—and led to the emergence of what was called "public opinion" (*kōron*), an arena in which issues could be discussed outside the inner circles. The debates also prompted the creation of Japan's first political associations and led to the rise of the Freedom and People's Rights (*jiyū minken*) movement. The following documents trace the contours of these early discussions.

ITAGAKI TAISUKE

MEMORIAL ON THE ESTABLISHMENT OF A
REPRESENTATIVE ASSEMBLY

Itagaki Taisuke and eight others submitted this memorial to the throne on January 17, 1874. Despite being heralded by some as "democrats," they had a limited vision, seeking representation for only their own samurai class. The implications of their ideas, however, drew supporters from much broader segments of society.

When we humbly reflect upon the quarter in which the governing power lies, we find that it is not the Imperial House above, nor the people below, but the officials alone. We do not deny that the officials revere the Imperial House, nor that they protect the people. Yet, the manifold decrees of the government appear in the morning and are changed in the evening, the administration is influenced by private considerations, rewards and punishments depend on personal favor or disfavor, the channel by which the people should communicate with the government is blocked, and they cannot state their grievances. . . . We fear, therefore, that if a reform is not effected the state will be ruined. Unable to resist the promptings of our patriotic feelings, we have sought to devise a means of rescuing it from this danger. We find this means to consist in developing public discussion in the empire. The means of developing public discussion is the establishment of a council-chamber chosen by the people. Then a limit will be placed on the power of the officials, and high and low will obtain peace and prosperity. We ask leave then to make some remarks on this subject.

The people whose duty it is to pay taxes to the government have the right of sharing in their government's affairs and of approving or condemning. Since this is a universally acknowledged principle, it is not necessary to waste words in discussing it. . . .

We are informed that the present officials . . . are generally averse to progress and call those who advocate reforms "rash progressives." . . . If "rash progress" means measures which are heedlessly initiated, then a council chamber chosen by the people will remedy this heedlessness. Does it mean the want of harmony between the different branches of the administration, and in times of change, the postponement of urgent matters in favor of those less urgent, so that the measures carried out are wanting in unity of plan? Then the cause of this is the want of a fixed law in the country and the fact that the officials act in accordance with their own inclinations. These two facts suffice to show why it is necessary to establish a council chamber chosen by the people. Progress is the most beautiful thing in the world, and is the law of all things moral and physical. Men actuated by principle cannot condemn this word "progress," so their condemnation must be intended for the word "rash," but the word "rash" has no application to a council chamber chosen by the people. . . .

Another argument of the officials is that the council chambers now existing in European and American states were not formed in a day, but were only brought into their present state by gradual progress, and therefore we cannot today copy them suddenly. But is this true only of council chambers? It is the same with all branches of knowledge, science, and mechanical arts. The reason why [foreigners] developed them only after the lapse of centuries is that no examples existed previously and they had to be discovered by actual experience. If we can select from among their examples, why can we not apply them successfully? If we were to postpone using steam engines until we had discovered for ourselves the principles of steam, or postpone laying telegraph lines until we had discovered the principles of electricity, the government should by the same token never set to work.

[Itagaki, *Jiyūtō shi*, vol. 1, pp. 86–89; McLaren, *Japanese Government Documents*, pp. 426–32]

NAKAMURA MASANAO

ON CHANGING THE CHARACTER OF THE PEOPLE

Whereas Itagaki Taisuke's supporters demanded the early creation of an upper-class representative assembly, his opponents, who called themselves "gradualists," also favored an assembly but said that it should include commoners (*heimin*), who needed political education before they could participate. The opening, they said, should be delayed until the *heimin* were ready. A representative of this group was the scholar Nakamura Masanao, who advocated incremental changes rooted in Japan's earlier political and social traditions. On February 16, 1875, he made this argument to the Meiji Six Society (Meirokusha), a discussion society of influential young intellectuals, most of whom had close ties to the government.

The people are like water, while the political system is like a vessel into which one pours water. If you pour water into a round vessel, it becomes round; into a square vessel, square. The character of the water does not change, even though the vessel is changed for another of different shape. The people, after all, remain as before even though the vessel into which they have been placed since 1868 may have a better shape than the old one.

They are the people rooted in servitude, the people who are arrogant toward their inferiors and flattering toward their superiors, the ignorant and uneducated people, the people who love saké and sex, the people who do not like reading, the people who do not reflect on their duties and who know not the laws of Heaven, the people of shallow wisdom and limited capacity, the people who avoid toil and do not endure hardships, the egocentric people who practice cheap tricks, the people without perseverance and diligence in character, the frivolous and shallow people who are without principles in their hearts, the people who like to rely on others as they are without a spirit of independence, the people who are poor in their powers of thought and perception, the people who know not the value of money, the people who break promises without honoring loyalty, the people who are unable to act together and have but a slim capacity for friendship, and the people who do not strive for new inventions. People are generally of such types even though there naturally are not a few who are able to escape from the above injuries.

If we desire to change the people's character and thereby encourage elevated conduct and virtuous feelings, we will accomplish absolutely nothing if we only reform the political structure, which is only changing round containers for hexagonal or octagonal vessels without altering the character of the water within. Rather than changing the political structure, therefore, we should aspire instead to change the character of the people, more and more rooting out the old habits and achieving "renewal" with each new day.

We should welcome as a good omen the recent public clamor for a popularly elected assembly. Such an assembly, of course, will undoubtedly contribute to a renewal of the public mind since it will develop the will to possess and to defend the country among the people themselves, change the attitudes of those who have relied on government officials, daily reduce the spirit of subservience, enable talented men to emerge from all quarters in large numbers, and gradually halt the evil of selecting leaders from a single source.

There is one point, however, to which we should here give our attention. Even though the rulers may share a part of the political power with the people through the establishment of a popularly elected assembly, since the people still remain as before, there will be no major effect in the direction of changing the people's character from the fact that only the political structure has been somewhat changed. Should you ask how to change the character of the people, there are but two approaches—through religious and moral education and through education in the arts and sciences. Through the mutual assistance of these two acting together, like the wheels of a cart or the wings of a bird, we shall guide human lives to happiness. . . . If there is any other method to change the character of the people and to elevate them to the level of the most advanced peoples of Europe and America, I shall welcome your advice.

[Braisted, *Meiroku Zasshi*, pp. 372–74]

REPRESENTATIVE ASSEMBLIES AND NATIONAL PROGRESS, FEBRUARY 1879

In response to the demands for representation, the government set up city and provincial (*fu* and *ken*) assemblies. The assemblies' powers were criticized widely as ineffectual, but they helped promote the Freedom and People's Rights (*jiyū minken*) movement and prompt even more calls for a national assembly.

EDITORIAL FROM *CHŌYA SHINBUN*

This editorial from the Tokyo newspaper *Chōya shinbun*, a stronghold of prodemocratic thought, was reprinted in the *Tokio Times* on March 1, 1879.

The local assemblies which have just sprung up are the most delicate subjects to deal with. The experiment of establishing them is, as it were, like setting a prairie on fire. There is a story of a bear's cub which a hunter caught in the mountains and sold to a person of the town, who fed it on fish and grain and carefully reared it. The animal grew up very mild and tame, and played with dogs and cats. One day it happened that its master fed it on pork, and at the first taste of raw flesh it at once became possessed of its natural ferocity, attacking the people and resisting all control. Now the reason why so vicious an animal associated contentedly with dogs and cats was because it had never tasted blood and did not therefore know anything about it. So it is with the people and with political rights. The masses have hitherto been ruled according to the will of the government, which they have submitted to tranquilly because they had not tasted any political rights, but when they begin to do so, their desire to obtain more will be the same as that of the bear, after its first meal of raw flesh. The inhabitants of Japan, up to the eleventh year of Meiji, were like the bear before its change of diet, and the establishment of the *fu* and *ken* assemblies is their first introduction to a stimulating regimen. Are our countrymen likely to rest contented after that taste of political rights? By all means not. They will stretch out their claws and open their mouths and ask for more and more, until they obtain a national parliament. Should the government, after sanctioning the *fu* and *ken* assemblies, refuse to grant the larger representative institution, what will be the result? . . .

Would the foundation of despotic sway be thereby permanently laid? Not so, for the tide of the time and the progress of popular intelligence is like a stream running down from the mountains, and can be checked by no human power. If the ministry take[s] measures by which these initial legislatures are abolished, and in this manner defer[s] indefinitely the establishment of a national assembly, we can hardly foretell the catastrophe that may result therefrom. Japan is a country in which, hundred of years past, nothing but autocracy existed on the side of the rulers, and blind submission on the side of the people. That within ten years from the time when the despotic system was in fullest force, the inhabitants should enjoy a popular representation in every district, appears strange; yet such is the effect of the spirit of progress, and for a few men in power to try to oppose it would be the same as trying to stop a flood with a few grains of sand. It is impossible.

At the time of the Restoration, His Majesty the Emperor, in the presence of the nobility of the land—the daimyo and princes—took five oaths; and one of them was that the government should be administered according to the will of the people. This oath is the foundation upon which the form of a limited monarchy is to be built up, for its words mean that the laws of the nation shall be made by the representatives of the community.

[*Tokio Times*, March 1, 1879]

DEFINING THE CONSTITUTIONAL STATE, 1876–1883

Responding to both the popular debate and the rulers' sense of what the international environment required, the emperor asked each councillor (*sangi*) early in 1879 to prepare a memorial on what form a constitution should take. That fact, added to a corruption scandal in the summer of 1881 over insider sales of government lands in Hokkaido, precipitated a lively public discussion of constitutional issues. The officials prepared their own gradualist constitutional opinions; newspaper editorialists wrote draft constitutions and argued whether sovereignty should reside in the emperor or in the people; even mountain villagers debated constitutionalism. The Freedom and People's Rights movement supported Itagaki Taisuke and the progovernment journalist Fukuchi Gen'ichirō. Spurring all the discussions was an imperial announcement on October 12, 1881, accompanying the ouster of Finance Minister Ōkuma Shigenobu, that a constitution would be granted within a decade.

The major issues that propelled the discussions were how quickly Japan should move toward a constitutional system and what form the system should take. Everyone agreed on two points: the imperial institution should remain inviolate, and there should be an assembly. On other points, the disagreement was wide. The gradualists continued to argue that it would require several years to determine the way to legislative rule and that the legislature's powers should, as in Germany, be sharply limited. They also emphasized the need for a system consonant with Japan's "national essence" (*kokutai*). None of them wanted political party government. Conversely, Ōkuma and the popular rights forces first called an assembly to be convened quickly; then, after the emperor's promise of a legislature by 1890, they focused on the kind of system Japan needed, most of them advocating a British-style democracy with a powerful bicameral assembly and a cabinet responsible to political parties. The parties declined and the debate cooled in the mid-1880s, but not before both the parties and the discussions had laid a foundation for the eventual constitutional state.

ITŌ HIROBUMI

MEMORIAL ON CONSTITUTIONAL GOVERNMENT, DECEMBER 1880

The central official developing a constitution was Itō Hirobumi, a moderate conservative who talked often about the need to maintain Japan's traditions even as the country kept pace with international trends. As this response to the emperor's call for constitutional opinions shows, he was willing to move toward broader representation in that government, but only deliberately, so that the orderly flow of society would not be disrupted. After arguing that the discontent of the former samurai and the changing world situation demanded a new system, he proposed revisions in current structures rather than radical change.

I, for one, am convinced that now is the time to make unprecedented reforms and that conditions are already ripe for them. However, we must not follow the increasing thoughtless opinions; at the same time, it will be difficult to maintain old practices unconditionally. In politics, it is best to adopt methods that fit changing circumstances. Unless we take suitable measures and advance properly as well as gradually, how can we hope to lay the foundations of lasting peace? . . .

1. I ask that we enlarge the Genrōin (Senate) and select its members from among the nobles (*kazoku*).

I say that we should not establish a parliament hastily. This does not mean that we, the ruling group, want to remain at the helm of state and occupy the highest posts as long as possible. Although it is very desirable to establish limited monarchy by convoking a parliament, we must not do anything that would seriously modify our national polity. We should first make the footings firm, then erect the foundation posts, and finally raise the house. This must be done in an orderly fashion. Needless to say, the above is clearly known to the intelligent mind of the Emperor. . . .

The Genrōin was established in 1875, actually the result of the Emperor's intention to advance gradually toward constitutional government. . . . Now is the time to enlarge it and extend its functions, and make it live up to its name. At present, viewing the quality of our people, we find that the ex-samurai (*shizoku*) are the only ones who can manage national affairs and who are the most enlightened. Thus, the ex-samurai must be considered as one part of the nobility, though actually they rank just below the nobles. The members of the Genrōin should be selected from among the nobles and ex-samurai as well as from among those persons who are eminent for their services to the country or for their scholarship. There should be one hundred members of the Genrōin, and each member should be paid. We should convene the Genrōin each year for a definite length of time. If the drafts of all laws are submitted for discussion to the Genrōin, the following results will be obtained:

1. We can employ ex-samurai in posts of honor, thereby enabling them to function through many ages as guardians of the imperial family.
2. We can provide a ground on which equilibrium will be maintained between the two houses of parliament in the future.
3. Through the Genrōin, we can establish and maintain harmony between the government and the people.
4. Thus we can continue the fine results of the past eight years, and following the plans of our forerunners, we will tread the path of gradual progress.

2. I ask that we establish an extra board of auditors.

I think that in addition to broadening public opinion by selecting Genrōin members from among the nobles and ex-samurai, we should select members of the prefectural assemblies to fill positions as extra auditor-representatives who will discuss finance publicly. This will be the initial step toward constitutional government. It is observed in every country that some people despise their government and its officials because they suspect that a great deal of money raised by heavy taxation is spent wastefully. So it is considered to be most important in all constitutional states to permit the people to participate in the management of national finance. . . .

An extra board of auditors should be established with its members selected from among the members of the prefectural assemblies. . . . Together with the regular auditors, they should engage in the business of auditing finances. However, their power should be limited only to auditing, and they should not be permitted to interfere in general financial policies. By this method, for one thing, we can pave the way for public discussion of finance and second, we can acquaint the people with the actual state of affairs and give them experience. . . .

3. I ask that Your Imperial Majesty declare the aims of the nation.

If we do not decide the aims of the nation, what will stop popular sentiments from drifting? At present, there are persons who are stirring up the disorderly elements in town and country in the name of public opinion. If we fail to check such public sentiment by clearly revealing the will of the Emperor, based on some firm proposal, the people will unite to make disturbances, rising here and there like rivers overflowing their banks. Once violence bursts out like this, I fear that in the end an adjustment cannot be made. . . . Resentful persons would distort the Charter Oath and the Imperial Rescript of 1875 in support of their views. This is why the government should inform the people of its intentions and make them aware of actual conditions. . . .

Your Majesty should kindly make up his mind and show his utmost sincerity by an imperial edict. I beg that you inform the people that the nation should advance gradually, and make your plans clear to them. How to share the legislative power with the people is without doubt a matter that comes under the supreme power of the Emperor and which is beyond the right of discussion by his humble subjects. Moreover, the timing of the decision is left to the discretion of the Emperor, and the people are not permitted to make disturbances or put on pressure. . . . If an imperial rescript is issued explaining that this policy is just, those persons who are loyal to the imperial family will be reminded of the direction in which they should turn their sentiments. On the other hand, unenlightened people will avoid being led astray to acts of violence.

[Beckmann, *The Making of the Meiji Constitution*, pp. 131–35]

ŌKUMA SHIGENOBU

MEMORIAL ON A NATIONAL ASSEMBLY

Longtime Finance Minister Ōkuma Shigenobu, a member of the government's mainstream until 1881, was slow to turn in his constitutional opinion. When he finally delivered it in March of that year, he took a "radical" stance, calling for legislative representatives to be elected the very next year and for political parties to be encouraged. This position, in addition to his role in leaking information about the corrupt Hokkaido land sales, led to his expulsion from the government in October. It also gave him a lifelong reputation as a "man of the people."

1. The date for the establishment of a parliament should be promulgated. . . .

2. High officials should be appointed on the basis of the support of the people. . . . In constitutional government, the place where the will of the people can be indicated is indeed the parliament. What do I mean by "will of the people"? It is the will of more than half of the parliamentary representatives. Who commands this will? It is the leader of the political party that has a majority in parliament. . . . A constitutional form of government produces an excellent arena where the Emperor can easily recognize such a man. Not only does he avoid actually making the selection himself, but he keeps the nation blessed with tranquillity. Because a person who is appointed in this way has a majority in parliament where the people participate in government, he has the power to control the legislature. And because he has his position in the government with the favor of the Emperor, . . . he also has the power to control the administration. Thus, there is no clash between the legislature and the administration.

3. The distinction between political party officials and permanent officials: . . . The various party officials . . . are councillors (*sangi*), ministers, vice-ministers, bureau chiefs, the imperial tutor, and the grand chamberlain. These party officials will be for the most part persons who hold seats in the upper or lower house. (In general, this is based on the example of England. . . .) The

... permanent officials, with the exception of heads of government offices, vice-ministers, and bureau chiefs, . . . will be officials below imperial appointment (*sōnin*) rank and petty officials. . . .

4. With imperial approval, we should establish a constitution. . . .

5. We should elect representatives by the end of 1882 and convoke parliament at the beginning of 1883. . . . Constitutional government is party government, and the struggles between parties are the struggles of principles. When its principles are supported by more than half of the people, a party wins control of the government. When the opposite is true, it loses control. This is the operation of genuine constitutional government.

[Beckmann, *The Making of the Meiji Constitution*, pp. 136–42]

CHIBA TAKASABURŌ

"THE WAY OF THE KING"
(ŌDŌ)

The urban intellectual elites were not the only participants in the political conversations of the early 1880s. People across Japan took up the topic, too, often quite fervently and usually on the popular rights side. "The Way of the King," an essay written in 1882 by a schoolteacher in present-day Itsukaichi in the mountains west of Tokyo, illustrates the political sophistication of many provincial citizens. Chiba refined his thoughts during meetings of a local discussion group that included doctors, farmers, and lumbermen. Drawing on Western and Confucian ideas (the kingly Way of Mencius), these excerpts from his eight-chapter "Way of the King" discuss both the divine origins of the concept of law and the limits that must be placed on the ruler. Chiba also wrote his own draft constitution.

1. All governments, whether they be dictatorships, aristocracies, or republics, must be in accordance with the Way of the King if they are faithful to the nation. It is the very foundation of a government's or monarch's qualification to rule. If it is absent, the qualifications to be a nation are lacking. In the Way of the King, harmony, stability, flexibility, and justice predominate. . . .

Those who manifest the following signs believe in the Way of the King. They want to establish constitutional government—and that constitution is a national contract. They want to open a parliament. They want to maintain the esteem for the crown and secure the welfare of all the people. They want to see the hopes of all the classes for constitutional government realized, and they observe the spirit [of the Charter Oath]—"unite in carrying out vigorously the administration of affairs of state." Finally, they will be untiring in the performance of government. You men in our country who are loyal subjects of His Majesty and truly cherish the people as brothers should accept this theory and accomplish in your own lives the Way of the King. . . .

Without exception those who bring about the decline of the Way of the King disdain the people and destroy the people's liberties. Such instances are not confined to China and Japan, but have occurred in a number of European countries as well. The reason is that when the monarch destroys the people's liberties, he first abandons and disregards the imperial prerogatives. He exercises unlimited sovereignty, ignoring virtue and proper rule. He makes the nation his household and the people his slaves. Consequently, when the people rise up against oppression, they do not care for virtue and rule, and it often happens that they start a rebellion and scheme a violent and odious disturbance to overthrow the government.

It is reported that in former times Louis XIV professed to be a person of the highest nobility and abused the unlimited rights which he claimed. [He declared:] "The State is I; I am the State." This assertion can be considered the source of the calamity that overtook Louis XVI. The following appears in the *Analects*: "Is there a single sentence that can ruin a country?" The above assertion of Louis XIV is such a single sentence. His words served only to heighten and aggravate the anger of the people. The people said in turn: "Government consists of the people, the people are the Government." The monarch and the people thus clashed. The people brought the monarch to the block and disgraced him by executing him with a blunt sword. This is precisely what is meant by the proverb [quoted] by Mencius: "What proceeds from you, will return to you again." This certainly hits the mark. A monarch dares not abuse his authority and mistreat his people because the constitution imposes limits on his authority. Just as King Louis found it easy to abuse his authority and thus mistreat his people, so the people in their turn found it easy to rely on their own power to slight their ruler.

Therefore, if the monarch establishes imperial prerogatives and has the people likewise establish their liberties, this will be not only for the benefit of the people but also for the continuance of the Imperial House for untold generations to come. The first step in the implementation of the Way of the King is the establishment of the monarch's prerogatives, but this is dependent on the establishment of the people's liberties. . . . When both the imperial prerogatives and the people's liberties are simultaneously operative and neither is infringed upon, then the Way of the King will be manifest and visible to all. . . .

You may well ask why I have written this essay on the Way of the King. Perhaps it is because I am a little deranged, or perhaps I did it just for amusement. Quite possibly I am one of those outdated Chinese classicists who knows of antiquity but are ignorant of what is going on today. Or perhaps I am one of those National Learning [*kokugaku*] scholars who fail to understand politics; they know only the existence of the Imperial House and ignore the existence of the people. In fact, there are scholars of the National Learning school who do not realize that a constitution and a parliament, long desired by the Emperor Meiji, conform to the Way of the King even in this day and age. Thoughtlessly and fearlessly they reject and obstruct this concept and thus end up being offenders against the imperial decree. These people are to be pitied and it was for them that this essay was written. Those who do not know what constitutional government, a constitution, or a parliament really mean, should read this essay carefully and then they will be able to speak of the Way of the King and understand the times we live in. I hope that this essay will serve as a ship to carry them to the shores of understanding.

[Devine, "The Way of the King," pp. 63–72]

NAKAE CHŌMIN

A DISCOURSE BY THREE DRUNKARDS ON GOVERNMENT

Few people better illustrate the intellectual complexity and vitality of the Freedom and People's Rights (*jiyū minken*) movement than Nakae Chōmin, a native of Kōchi Prefecture in Shikoku who studied in France as a youth, worked a time for the government, gained renown as a journalist, and later was successful in politics. Sometimes called the "Rousseau of the Orient," Nakae drew on the major thinkers of Europe, China, and Japan. He advocated a strong Japan, the rejection of militarism, and the expansion of representative government. The following selections from *A Discourse by Three Drunkards on Government* (1887), one of Japan's classic pieces of political literature, relate host Nankai's comments to two alcohol-saturated guests on issues relevant to the constitutional debate.

Master Nankai loves drinking and discussing politics. When he drinks only one or two small bottles of saké, he is pleasantly intoxicated—his spirits are high and he feels as if he were flying through the universe. Everything he sees and hears delights him; it seems unthinkable that there should be suffering in the world.

When he drinks two or three more bottles, his spirits suddenly soar even higher, and ideas spring up, unrestrained. Although his body remains in his small room, his eyes scan the world. . . .

"Do kings and noblemen possess larger and heavier brains than we? Do they have more gastric juices and blood cells? . . . Both we common people and the aristocrats are lumps of flesh made of a combination of a few chemical elements. And yet when we meet, *this* lump of flesh bows low with clasped hands, while *that* lump of flesh remains standing, with only a slight nod of the head. When we talk, *this* lump of flesh shows respect to *that* lump of flesh by calling it 'Sir,' which means 'lord,' or 'monseigneur,' which also means 'lord.' But what do you think? . . . Is this not an extreme affront? Is it not an unbearable shame? . . .

"All enterprises of human society are like alcohol, and liberty is the yeast. If you try to brew wine or beer without yeast, all the other ingredients, no matter how good they are, will sink to the bottom of the barrel, and your efforts will be in vain. Life in a despotic country is like a brew without ferment: sediments at the bottom of a barrel. Consider, for example, the literature of a despotic country. Occasionally some work appears to be noteworthy, but closer scrutiny reveals that nothing new is produced in a thousand years, nothing unique among ten thousand works. The kinds of phenomena that would ordinarily appeal to an author's sight and hearing are, in these societies, merely sediments at the bottom of a barrel, and the author copies these phenomena with a spirit which is also a sediment. Isn't it only natural then, that there should be no change in the arts? . . .

"O, law of evolution! Law of evolution! Ceaseless progress is your true nature. Once you drove your children out of the wilderness of chaos and disorder into the narrow valley of despotism, where you let them rest for a while until they gained strength. After that, you drove your children out of the valley and made them climb up to the top of the wide hill of constitutionalism, where you let them dry their eyes and breathe freely. When they turn their eyes upward, they see the green trees soaring into the sky, a trailing mist of clouds, and birds singing harmoniously. This is the high peak of democracy, with a view unparalleled in the world. Later, I shall explain more fully the superior vistas of this peak. . . .

"Constitutionalism is not bad, but democracy is better. Constitutionalism is spring with a faint touch of frost or snow; democracy is summer with no trace of frost or snow. As the Chinese might put it, constitutionalism is a wise man, but democracy is a holy man. Or in the phrasing of India, constitutionalism is a Bodhisattva, but democracy is a Buddha. Constitutionalism is to be respected, but democracy loved. Constitutionalism is an inn from which we have to depart sooner or later. It is only the weak or crippled who cannot leave. Democracy is a final home. What a restful feeling to return home after a long journey."

[Nakae, *Discourse by Three Drunkards on Government*, trans. Tsukui, pp. 47–76]

THE EMERGENCE OF POLITICAL PARTIES

Japan's first political parties were formed after the emperor promised to give Japan a constitution and legislature: Itagaki Taisuke's Liberal Party (Jiyūtō) in October 1881, Fukuchi Gen'ichirō's Constitutional Imperial Party (Rikken tei-seitō) in March 1882, and Ōkuma Shigenobu's Constitutional Reform Party (Rikken kaishintō) in April 1882. The Jiyūtō and Kaishintō were tied to the popular rights movement, while the smaller Teiseitō spoke for the government's grad-ualist philosophy. The parties went into eclipse during 1883, and then two of them, the Jiyūtō and the Kaishintō, were revived as the basis for the parliamen-tary opposition when national elections were held in 1890. The following documents—a speech delivered in 1882 by Itagaki on liberty, which shows his Confucian regard for unity as much as his belief in freedom; the Teiseitō plat-form of 1882, which posits power in an absolutist emperor; and a speech on reform by Ōkuma to members of the Kaishintō—reflect the distinctions among the parties.

ITAGAKI TAISUKE

"ON LIBERTY"

Gentlemen: Our Liberal Party is not yet thoroughly established as a political organization, and therefore what I am now about to say, in deference to your request, must not be considered as a political exposition but as a private enun-ciation. I mention this, because I have good hopes for the future formation of a strong political association, and I beg you to bear this in mind. . . .

In the Middle Ages the system of governing divided everyone into two classes, the samurai and the people. The samurai occupied the position of rulers, while the people were the ones whom they ruled. Hereditary tradi-tion creates common custom. Power was vested solely in the rulers, and the samurai made it their business to participate in the affairs of state, so they were well versed in political theory; the people, on the other hand, accepted being ruled as their lot, and had nothing to do with affairs of state, so they were deficient in political theory. Since this system of government was fostered for so many years, the ignorant masses declined in the knowledge of political theory, and in the end had none at all. Though it has been said that the people of our country never developed political thought, this is true only of the ig-norant masses. The political thought of the informed classes developed to a very high level. Truly the difference in the appreciation of politics between our informed and ignorant classes is as wide as the distance between heaven and earth. To maintain balance and harmony between them is most dif-ficult, for as the wise add to their wisdom the foolish progress in their ignorance . . .

In Western nations political parties contend with one another, and each one tests its principles thoroughly. Often the intensity of party strife is conducive to party welfare, but this is because these parties are well established and mature. Since our party is newly organized and immature, we must not follow their example. It would be a great mistake for our new, immature party to thrash out its principles thoroughly and thus fall into disputes over trifles. . . .

The object of our union is to institute a form of government wherein the people shall have a voice in public affairs. Public opinion is the axis around which government policy should revolve. On its prosperity or decay depends the prosperity or decay of the government. For its promotion and a simultaneous inauguration of a beneficial policy we must educate the people in politics. The means by which good government and the happiness of the people can be assured is for the governed to control their rulers through the force of public opinion and prevent them from using their power arbitrarily. If those who are governed lack political knowledge and are ignorant of the technique by which public opinion can be made to control their rulers, even a good government and just laws can suddenly degenerate into despotism and oppression, and the people will be deprived of their just benefits.

Good governments depend on good people. Therefore, to reform the government and ensure lasting benefits from it, we should reform the national character and foster good people. We cannot hope for reform of the national character so long as the educated and the ignorant classes are so far apart in their understanding of politics as to lack a feeling of concord with each other. Therefore, our party should help the educated lead the ignorant and the ignorant to follow the educated onward, and thus spread political understanding and establish the welfare of the people on a sound foundation. . . .

Our party desires a liberal, not an interfering, government. The interference of a government with the private affairs of the people is due to its ignorance of the distinction between politics and religion or between public and personal matters. Government interference means the loss of independence. Our party should discriminate between politics and religion and oppose government interference with private affairs. Propagation of liberal principles by our party is a public, not a private, venture. Those who agree with us in public matters are good friends of liberty, and although they may not be in harmony with us in private affairs, we can still be in perfect accord with them otherwise. On the other hand, those who, no matter how intimate they may be with us privately, oppose the cause of liberty, cannot tread the same road with us.

[Itagaki, *Jiyūtō shi*, vol. 2, pp. 442–48; McLaren, *Japanese Government Documents*, pp. 605–13]

FUKUCHI GEN'ICHIRŌ

TEISEITŌ PLATFORM

Neither adhering to conservatism nor disputing with radicalism, we seek both reform and the preservation of national tranquillity through a continuous search for progress and order. It is to this end that we establish these basic principles of our party.

1. It has been made clear by imperial order that a national assembly will be convened in 1890. Our party will serve the emperor's will; we will not discuss any alteration of those plans.
2. It has been made clear by imperial order that a constitution will be granted by the emperor. Our party will observe the emperor's will; we will not violate the rule of the authorized constitution.
3. Sovereign power in the empire resides, indisputably, in the sole control of the emperor. The application of his will shall be regulated by the constitution.
4. We seek the establishment of two branches in the national assembly.
5. We seek to restrict the parliamentary electorate by basing the requirements on social standing.
6. We believe that the national assembly should be granted authority to enact laws for promulgation throughout the land.
7. The emperor should have the authority to approve or disapprove of the national assembly's decisions.
8. We maintain that naval and army men should not take part in government or politics.
9. We seek the independence of judicial officials in order to maintain the purity of our legal system.
10. We support freedom of speech and assembly as long as it does not interfere with national peace and order; we also seek freedom of public lectures, newspapers, and publication, within the limits of law.
11. We maintain that today's inconvertible paper money should be changed gradually into convertible paper money by a reform of the monetary system.

[*Tōkyō nichi nichi shinbun*, March 18, 1882; JH]

ŌKUMA SHIGENOBU

TO MEMBERS OF THE KAISHINTŌ, MARCH 14, 1882

I was one of those who labored in support of the glorious work of the Restoration in order that the monopoly of the empire's political power by the few families might be destroyed, and I do not imagine that my adherence to these principles will change in the future. No, I hope always to work with an ever firmer resolve for the achievement of the glorious work of the Restoration; for the laying of a foundation for our empire, which will last through all eternity; and for the everlasting preservation of the dignity and prosperity of the imperial household and the happiness of the people.

Some people, though they style themselves the party of "respect for the emperor" and wear the trappings of that virtue, actually are seeking mainly to establish a few families as the bulwark of the imperial household or else to protect the imperial household with troops. The extremists of this group would push the sovereign to the very forefront and make him bear directly the brunt of the administration. They would, by their support of the imperial household, place it in a position of danger.

Is it actually possible to promote the dignity and prosperity of the imperial household by such means? No. . . . The tides of the progress from abroad reach us unhindered, and their strength is enormous. Today, when public opinion is universally inclined toward progress, any attempt to reverse this trend should be dismissed with scorn. Indeed, an examination of natural principles shows that reform and progress are the invariable law of all creation. Consider any objects, whatever their species, and you will see that every one advances from crude to refined and from coarse to pure; each improves without cease from day to day and progresses from month to month. To resist these forces stubbornly or to attempt to oppose the grand scheme of nature is surely a mistake. . . .

Political reform and progress are the unanimous wish of our party and have always been my abiding purpose. They must, however, be achieved by sound and proper means. . . . Some, the spiritual descendants of Rousseau, would seek their ultimate objectives by means of direct action, but such endeavors would upset the social order and end by actually impeding political reform. Our party entertains no such desire. We seek political reform and progress by sound and proper means and hope to reach our objectives step by step. Because we desire reform and progress by such means, if any among you follow Rousseau and would reenact the violent drama of the Jacobins in the hope of achieving precipitous changes, I reject your support and have no wish to travel further with you. And while I am emphatic in my rejection of precipitous changes, I feel it is important to distinguish our party from those that mask their real conservatism by pretending to stand for gradual progress.

Our party is the party that stands for political progress. By sound and proper means, we wish to achieve political reform and progress as complete as possible. We differ categorically from those parties that fail to act when the occasion demands it and that, under the guise of working for gradual progress, seek private advantage through deliberate procrastination.

[Watanabe, *Ōkuma Shigenobu*, pp. 92–95; JH]

OZAKI YUKIO

FACTIONS AND PARTIES

The significance of Itagaki Taisuke's address to the Liberal Party, presented earlier in this chapter, may be more readily appreciated in the light of observations on Japanese party politics made later, in 1918, by the veteran progressive leader Ozaki Yukio. Ozaki's critique of factionalism could well apply to party politics almost the world over, but it was especially pertinent to the politics of Japan in the early twenty-first century.

Here in the Orient we have had the conception of a faction, but none of a public party. A political party is an association of people having for its exclusive object the discussion of public affairs of state and the enforcement of their views thereon. But when political parties are transplanted into the East, they at once partake of the nature of factions, pursuing private and personal interests instead of the interests of the state—as witnessed by the fact of their joining hands by turn with the clan cliques or using the construction of railways, ports and harbors, and schools, etc., as means for extending party influence. Besides, the customs and usages of feudal times are so deeply impressed upon the minds of men here that even the idea of political parties, as soon as it enters the brains of our countrymen, germinates and grows according to feudal notions. Such being the case, even political parties, which should be based and dissolved solely on principle and political views, are really affairs of personal connections and sentiments, the relations between the leader and the members of a party being similar to those which subsisted between a feudal lord and his liegemen, or to those between a "boss" of gamblers and his followers in this country. A politician scrupulous enough to join or desert a party for the sake of principle is denounced as a political traitor or renegade. That political faith should be kept not vis-à-vis its leader or its officers but vis-à-vis its principles and views is not understood. They foolishly think that the proverb "A faithful servant never serves two masters; a chaste wife never sees two husbands" is equally applicable to the members of a political party. In their erroneous opinion, it is a loyal act on the part of a member of a party to change his principles and views in accordance with orders from headquarters, while in the event of headquarters changing their views it is unfaithful to desert them.

[Ozaki, *The Voice of Japanese Democracy*, pp. 93–94]

BESTOWING THE CONSTITUTION ON THE PEOPLE, 1884–1889

Barely a week after the emperor promised the constitution in 1881, an office was established, with Itō Hirobumi as chair, to start the drafting process. The next spring, Itō led a group to Europe for an eighteen-month study of constitutional systems, particularly that of Germany. The drafters drew heavily on the advice of German legal scholars Herman Roessler and Lorenz von Stein, as well as the Japanese scholar-official Inoue Kowashi. Although the drafters cast their nets broadly in the search for ideas, they focused on systems that made the emperor absolute and limited the powers of the legislature. At the institutional level, they spent the mid-1880s creating the structures necessary to support a modern constitutional monarchy: a peerage (1884), from which an upper house would be drawn; a cabinet (1885) to replace the Council of State (Dajōkan); and a privy council (1889) to ratify the constitution and consult with the emperor and the government. The Freedom and People's Rights (*jiyū minken*) forces were relatively quiet until the latter years of this period, partly because the parties were unable to sustain enthusiasm over a decade without elections, and partly because the government used harsh new laws to suppress political activity, even removing hundreds of political adversaries from the Tokyo region in 1887. The constitution was given to the Japanese people on February 11, 1889. It established the emperor's sovereignty and made the cabinet responsible to the emperor rather than to the legislature, even as it created the long-desired, if fairly weak, assembly. Although it is a conservative document, the Meiji constitution placed Japan in the mainstream of the world's leading constitutional governments, and the voting rights it granted to the people, along with the budgetary powers it gave to the Diet (parliament), set precedents that eventually led to universal male suffrage and a government dominated by the political parties.

ITŌ HIROBUMI

REMINISCENCES OF THE DRAFTING OF THE NEW CONSTITUTION

Looking back from 1908, Ito Hirobumi saw the constitutional drafting process as a balancing exercise, with the traditional emphases on harmony and submission preventing excesses in freedom and democracy. His self-portrait as the one who held together the center differs from pictures painted by his critics and most historians, who saw him as leaning in an absolutist direction toward a state in which the emperor and his advisers ruled with only restricted input from the "people." After a lengthy introduction in which Itō argues "that what was lacking in our countrymen of the feudal era was not mental or moral fiber but the scientific, technical, and materialistic side of modern civilization," he explains the "features of national life" that had to be taken into account in preparing the draft.

It was in the month of March 1882 that His Majesty ordered me to work out a draft of a constitution to be submitted for his approval. No time was to be lost, so I started on the fifteenth of the same month for an extended journey to different constitutional countries to make as thorough a study as possible of the actual workings of different systems of constitutional government, of their various provisions, as well as of theories and opinions actually entertained by influential persons on the actual stage itself of constitutional life. I took young men with me, who all belonged to the elite of the rising generation, to assist and to cooperate with me in my studies. I sojourned about a year and a half in Europe, and having gathered the necessary materials, insofar as it was possible in so short a space of time, I returned home in September 1883. Immediately after my return I set to work to draw up the Constitution. . . .

Peculiar Features of the National Life

It was evident from the outset that mere imitation of foreign models would not suffice, for there were historical peculiarities of our country which had to be taken into consideration. For example, the Crown was, with us, an institution far more deeply rooted in the national sentiment and in our history than in other countries. . . . At the same time, it was also evident that any form of constitutional regime was impossible without full and extended protection of honor, liberty, property, and personal security of citizens, entailing necessarily many important restrictions on the powers of the Crown.

Emotional Elements in Social Life of People

On the other hand, there was one peculiarity of our social conditions that is without parallel in any other civilized country. Homogeneous in race, language, religion, and sentiments, so long secluded from the outside world, with the centuries-long traditions and inertia of the feudal system, in which the family and quasi-family ties permeated and formed the essence of every social organization, and moreover with such moral and religious tenets as laid undue stress on duties of fraternal aid and mutual succor, we had during the course of our seclusion unconsciously become a vast village community where cold intellect and calculation of public events were always restrained and even often hindered by warm emotions between man and man. . . . It must, of course, be admitted that this social peculiarity is not without beneficial influences. It mitigates the conflict, serves as the lubricator of social organisms, and tends generally to act as a powerful lever for the practical application of the moral principle of mutual assistance between fellow citizens. But unless curbed and held in restraint, it too may exercise baneful influences on society, for in a village community, where feelings and emotions hold a higher place than intellect, free discussion is apt to be smothered, attainment and transference of power liable to become a family question of a powerful oligarchy, and the realization of such a regime as constitutional monarchy to become an impossibility, simply because in any representative regime free discussion is a matter of prime necessity. . . . The good side of this social peculiarity had to be retained as much as possible, while its baneful influences had to be safeguarded.

Conflict Between the Old and New Thoughts

Another difficulty equally grave had to be taken into consideration. We were just then in an age of transition. The opinions prevailing in the country were extremely heterogeneous, and often diametrically opposed to each other. We had survivors of former generations who were still full of theocratic ideas and who believed that any attempt to restrict an imperial prerogative amounted to something like high treason. On the other hand, there was a large and powerful body of the younger generation educated at the time when the Manchester theory was in vogue, and who in consequence were ultraradical in their ideas of freedom. Members of the bureaucracy were prone to lend willing ears to the German doctrinaires of the reactionary period, while, on the other hand, the educated politicians among the people, having not yet tasted the bitter significance of administrative responsibility, were liable to be more influenced by the dazzling words and lucid theories of Montesquieu, Rousseau, and other similar French writers. A work entitled *History of Civilization [in England]*, by Buckle, which denounced every form of government as an unnecessary evil, became the great favorite of students of all the higher schools, including the Imperial University. On the other hand, these same students would not have dared to expound the theories of Buckle before their own conservative fathers. At that time we had not yet arrived at the stage of distinguishing clearly between political opposition, on the one hand, and treason to the established order of things, on the other. The virtues necessary for the smooth working of any constitution, such as love of freedom of speech, love of publicity of proceedings, the spirit of tolerance for opinions opposed to one's own, etc., had yet to be learned by long experience.

Draft of the Constitution Completed

It was under these circumstances that the first draft of the constitution was made and submitted to his Majesty, after which it was handed over to the mature deliberation of the Privy Council.

[Ōkuma, *Fifty Years of New Japan*, vol. 1, pp. 127–31]

CONTROLLING THE FREEDOM AND PEOPLE'S RIGHTS MOVEMENT

The quiescence of the Freedom and People's Rights (*jiyū minken*) movement in the 1880s did not relax the government's determination to curb speech that might stir up conflict. The first document illustrates both that fact and the emergence of women as public figures. Fukuda Hideko was one of several women who wrote and spoke in the movement (sometimes over the objections of male movement leaders) for expanded popular participation in the national life, for greater equality between the sexes, and even for women's suffrage. The excerpt, from Fukuda's autobiography, describes the official roadblocks that popular rights advocates had to overcome. The second document is excerpted from newspaper accounts in 1887 of how, in accordance with the Peace Preservation Law, the police removed 570 potential political dissidents from Tokyo. The law was issued in response to agitation by the Freedom and People's Rights movement against weak official efforts to revise Japan's unequal treaties. Those arrested included Nakae Chōmin and Ozaki Yukio, the future mayor of Tokyo.

FUKUDA HIDEKO

MY LIFE THUS FAR
(HANSHŌGAI)

That summer [1884], some Liberal Party members decided to gather along the Asahi River one evening, when it had cooled down. When they invited the women's social group to join in the excursion, I talked to our senior members, Mrs. Takeuchi and Mrs. Tsuge. They agreed, and we all took a boat out on the Asahi River. The party members sang freedom songs, accompanied by musical instruments, and even now, I am struck with the timeless feelings that overwhelmed me as those melancholy tunes wafted across the water. Just then, we heard a voice from another boat. A Liberal Party member was standing on shipboard, making a speech. People were getting worked into a frenzy; it made you shudder. If we had been in town, we surely would have been banned by the authorities. But there was no one out here, on the water, to prevent our anarchist camaraderie; so people just went on making more and more heated speeches. There was a fiery, yet somehow sad, feeling about it.

Suddenly, right there on the Asahi River, some men appeared in the water. Looking like sea goblins, they ordered the group to break up. We could hardly believe that some wretched policemen would hide in the water, suspicious of our boat excursion, and check up on us. The merrymaking on the boats had reached a peak by now, so the people began jostling about, shouting out: "Kill the water sprites (kappa)!" "We'll beat them to death!" Then, on the advice of some of our elders, we went away quietly. Fortunately, it did not turn into a serious episode. The next day, however, my school received the following decree from Mr. Takasaki, the prefectural governor: "There will be no further investigation." What did they mean, no further investigation? I sought out the authorities and asked why there would be no more questioning. My elder sister's husband, a member of the prefectural assembly's permanent standing committee, was told that it was because I had gone along on the Liberal Party's river excursion. Even he was reprimanded for it, although he was not, in the end, confined.

[Fukuda, *Warawa no hanshōgai*, p. 16; JH]

NEWSPAPER ACCOUNTS OF ARRESTS UNDER THE PEACE PRESERVATION LAW

Ozaki Yukio . . . nonchalantly approached the gate to his home, and someone nearby asked him to identify himself. He replied: "I am Ozaki Yukio. Is there anything suspicious about Yukio returning to Yukio's home?" The man responded that it was precisely Yukio for whom he was looking; he showed him a subpoena and told him to accompany him to the police station. Ozaki offered no resistance and was taken to the station, where he first passed through a small, clean waiting room.

After a wait, Ozaki was called in and given his deportation sentence, which left him completely stunned. He insisted on being told the reason for the sentence. Since the police could give him no explanation, he decided to go to Metropolitan Police Headquarters and demand an explanation there. His inquiry was equally futile at police headquarters. . . . Discouraged about ever receiving an explanation for his sentence, . . . he joked that he must write something about this mess.

Yagihara Shigetomi, who also received a deportation notice, left Tokyo for Yokohama the day before yesterday accompanied by a police escort. When Yagihara started to buy a first-class ticket at Shinbashi Station, his police escort stopped him and said that unfortunately he himself had only enough money for a second-class ticket. It would be difficult to guard Mr. Yagihara from a different section of the train, the officer said , . . . so Mr. Yagihara agreed to ride second class.

At one point, sixty-six deportees from the Kōchi area were all staying at the Matsui Inn at 5 Honchō Street. With a ratio of one policeman for each deportee, the inn was virtually surrounded by police. Whenever a deportee left the inn, he was followed by a policeman. There also were seven policemen assigned to duty inside each inn on the street.

An honest and simple farmer from Kōchi Prefecture by the name of Okimoto decided that rather than spend the rest of his life as a farmer, he would set out for the capital and look for a manservant's position. Unfamiliar with city life, he decided first to work for someone from his home prefecture and was hired as a servant by Takeuchi Kō. Okimoto later found the manservant's position he had wanted with Matsuoka Yōjirō, a dealer in products from Hokkaido, but shortly thereafter he suddenly received a police summons. An honest man, he appeared trembling at the police station and inquired about the summons, only to learn that he had been ordered deported. Dazed, Okimoto went to Yokohama with his police escort. He returned home to his life as a farmer, determined that life here was preferable to the frightful capital.

One man (name unknown) was given a three- to four-day reprieve before being exiled. Realizing that the next several years would offer few opportunities to partake in the pleasures of beautiful women, he told his police escort that he would like to spend the evening with one of the "flowers of Yoshiwara," where-upon they called two rickshaws and set out for the famous pleasure quarters. The man went first to establishments where he was known, but even the courtesans who knew him were terrified when they saw the policemen and rejected his hapless entreaties. At other area brothels, where he was not known at all, he was politely refused entrance. After what amounted to a thorough tour of the area, he decided to try his luck at Nezu; he set out toward the southwest only to be courteously turned down by the brothels there, too. The man's efforts were to no avail. He returned home after a most uneventful night.

[*Jiji shinpō*, in *Meiji nyūsu jiten*, vol. 3, pp. 704–7; JH]

THE MEIJI CONSTITUTION

February 11, 1889, was a huge news day in Japan. Education Minister Mori Arinori was assassinated by an ultranationalist; the influential newspaper *Nihon* was launched; and the Meiji constitution was promulgated. The preamble re-flects the near-total power given to the emperor and his cabinet. He bestowed the constitution on the people; he was the repository of state sovereignty; only he could initiate constitutional amendments; the ministers of state were re-sponsible to him alone. The Diet, however, was given veto power over all laws (article 37) and the annual budget (article 64), responsibilities that soon trans-lated into enough power to shape national debates and topple governments. The Meiji constitution remained in effect until 1947.

THE CONSTITUTION OF THE EMPIRE OF JAPAN

Preamble

Having, by virtue of the glories of Our Ancestors, ascended the Throne of a lineal succession unbroken for ages eternal; desiring to promote the welfare of, and to give development to the moral and intellectual faculties of Our beloved subjects, the very same that have been favored with the benevolent care and affectionate vigilance of Our Ancestors; and hoping to maintain the prosperity of the State, in concert with Our people and with their support, We hereby promulgate, in pursuance of Our Imperial Rescript of the twelfth day of the tenth month of the fourteenth year of Meiji, a fundamental law of State, to exhibit the principles, by which We are to be guided in Our conduct, and to point out to what Our descendants and Our subjects and their descendants are forever to conform.

The rights of sovereignty of the State, We have inherited from Our Ancestors, and We shall bequeath them to Our descendants. Neither We nor they shall in future fail to wield them, in accordance with the provisions of the Constitution hereby granted.

We now declare to respect and protect the security of the rights and of the property of Our people, and to secure to them the complete enjoyment of the same, in the extent of the provisions of the present Constitution and of the law.

The Imperial Diet shall first be convoked for the twenty-third year of Meiji and the time of its opening shall be the date when the present Constitution comes into force.

When in the future it may become necessary to amend any of the provisions of the present Constitution, We or Our successors shall assume the initiative right, and submit a project for the same to the Imperial Diet. The Imperial Diet shall pass its vote upon it, according to the conditions imposed by the present Constitution, and in no otherwise shall Our descendants or Our subjects be permitted to attempt any alteration thereof.

Our Ministers of State, on Our behalf, shall be held responsible for the carrying out of the present Constitution, and Our present and future subjects shall forever assume the duty of allegiance to the present Constitution.

Chapter I: The Emperor

Article 1. The Empire of Japan shall be reigned over and governed by a line of Emperors unbroken for ages eternal.

Article 2. The Imperial Throne shall be succeeded to by Imperial male descendants, according to the provisions of the Imperial House Law.

Article 3. The Emperor is sacred and inviolable.

Article 4. The Emperor is the head of the Empire, combining in Himself the rights of sovereignty, and exercises them, according to the provisions of the present Constitution.

Article 5. The Emperor exercises the legislative power with the consent of the Imperial Diet.

Article 6. The Emperor gives sanction to laws, and orders them to be promulgated and executed.

Article 7. The Emperor convokes the Imperial Diet, opens, closes, and prorogues it, and dissolves the House of Representatives.

Article 11. The Emperor has the supreme command of the Army and Navy.

Chapter II: Rights and Duties of Subjects

Article 22. Japanese subjects shall have the liberty of abode and of changing the same within the limits of the law.

Article 23. No Japanese subject shall be arrested, detained, tried or punished, unless according to law.

Article 26. Except in the cases mentioned in the law, the secrecy of the letters of every Japanese subject shall remain inviolate.

Article 27. The right of property of every Japanese subject shall remain inviolate. . . .

Article 28. Japanese subjects shall, within limits not prejudicial to peace and order, and not antagonistic to their duties as subjects, enjoy freedom of religious belief.

Article 29. Japanese subjects shall, within the limits of law, enjoy the liberty of speech, writing, publication, public meetings and associations.

Chapter III: The Imperial Diet

Article 33. The Imperial Diet shall consist of two Houses, a House of Peers and a House of Representatives.

Article 34. The House of Peers shall, in accordance with the ordinance concerning the House of Peers, be composed of the members of the Imperial Family, of the orders of nobility, and of those who have been nominated thereto by the Emperor.

Article 35. The House of Representatives shall be composed of members elected by the people, according to the provisions of the law of Election.

Article 38. Both Houses shall vote upon projects of law submitted to it by the Government, and may respectively initiate projects of law.

Chapter VI: Finance

Article 62. The imposition of a new tax or the modification of the rates (of an existing one) shall be determined by law.

Article 63. The taxes levied at present shall, in so far as they are not remodeled by a new law, be collected according to the old system.

Article 64. The expenditure and revenue of the State require the consent of the Imperial Diet by means of an annual Budget.

Article 67. Those already fixed expenditures based by the Constitution upon the powers appertaining to the Emperor, and such expenditures as may have arisen by the effect of law, or that appertain to the legal obligations of the Government, shall be neither rejected nor reduced by the Imperial Diet, without the concurrence of the Government.

Article 71. When the Imperial Diet has not voted on the Budget, or when the Budget has not been brought into actual existence, the Government shall carry out the Budget of the preceding year.

[Tiedemann, *Modern Japan*, pp. 114–23]

UBUKATA TOSHIRŌ

"THE PROMULGATION OF THE CONSTITUTION"
(KENPŌ HAPPU)

In "The Promulgation of the Constitution," written in 1926, the journalist Ubukata Toshirō recalls both the sense of excitement that pervaded Japan, even in its mountainous recesses, when the Meiji constitution was promulgated and the disillusionment of his fellow Gunma villagers when the constitution did not live up to its promise. The pride lay in two factors: the opening up of government to the people, and Japan's role as Asia's first constitutional state. Japan, said one provincial paper, was now "worthy of being called a nation." The cynicism arose from the fact that very few people were allowed to vote and from the domination of politics by wealthy elites.

The promulgation of the constitution was the first epochal event of my childhood. I was in kindergarten then, ready to enter first grade that spring. What did I know about the significance of the constitution? We lived in the north, and if I recall correctly, it snowed that day—not all that much, perhaps four or five inches. The roads and rooftops were completely white. Every street corner in my small village was beautifully decorated. My friends and I went to see the ornaments at the cocoon market a block or two from home. They had piled up soy sauce barrels, not a spectacular sight to the eyes of a child, I suppose. I heard that various meetings had been planned but had to be called off because of the snowfall. We celebrated at home by cooking special rice. These things were not as much fun as the festivals we had every summer, yet somehow the event engraved itself vividly on my young mind.

My father, a great supporter of the constitution, had gone to Tokyo for the celebrations. He took my older brother with him, so it was lonely at home. Father liked me and might have taken me along, but he had taken me to Tokyo on a spring sightseeing trip two years earlier, when I was six. They returned two or three days later, bringing me a little book of magic tricks and a toy as souvenirs. . . . I remember that all the adults were talking about the promulgation of the constitution. The people in my village were much more interested in politics than people are today. Our region long had been a stronghold of the Liberal Party (Jiyūtō). . . . My uncle especially loved politics, and from the time when I was a child, [he] would talk to me about [important political figures]. I also heard my father and his friends talk often about local politicians. . . .

One of my recollections from those childhood days is that the promulgation of the constitution did not really bring about much change in the provincial people. It fell short of their expectations; they felt betrayed by it. Not until the Sino-Japanese War did the provincial people really come to trust, or submit to, the new Meiji government. Even three years after the promulgation, my townsmen still were as insubordinate as they had been in earlier years. They did not create disturbances, but neither did they trust the government. At least that was my impression as a young child. The people in my area harbored antipathy toward the new government. They still sympathized with the rebel Saigō Takamori and talked from time to time about the possibility that even now, he was living on a mountain somewhere. . . .

Surprisingly, provincial political enthusiasm faded quickly once representative government was established. At a Meiji Gakuin alumni meeting held at San'entei this spring [1926], one of my older classmates recollected a song that was popular in the dormitory back then. It went: "May three things occur. May the school burn down. May Mr. M— die of cholera. May the national assembly open." Mr. M— was a stern dormitory superintendent. Everyone had been calling for a national assembly back then. How ignorant we were not to realize that our calls would lead to such a farce, to the meaningless assembly of fools that we have today. . . . The popular movement to create a national assembly was not, in truth, a movement of all Japanese. It was a movement of ex-samurai alone, men who were dissatisfied with the Satsuma–Chōshū regime: failed politicians like Ōkuma and Itagaki who had been expelled from the government, along with rich merchants and prosperous farmers in the bourgeois class— nothing more than that. . . . The Popular Election Theater attracted patrons by promising wealth for the nation and happiness for the people. All its actors did, however, was to stuff the pockets of the rich class.

[Ubukata, "Kenpō happu to Nisshin sensō," pp. 80–87; JH]

Chapter 38

EDUCATION IN MEIJI JAPAN

Education in Meiji Japan (1868–1912) was both more and less than what it had been before. It was more in that the national school system eventually came to include nearly every child in the nation; the system had a central authority that provided uniform standards across the country; attendance became compulsory, seriously revising the lifestyles of children and parents throughout the country; teachers were trained at state-run facilities; and textbooks were authorized and even published by central authorities. By the end of the Meiji period, almost every school-age child was attending school, and very large numbers were staying for the full six years of compulsory elementary schooling. By 1912, a significant number of children were beginning to move beyond the elementary levels into the middle and upper levels and even into the two imperial universities, Kyoto Imperial University having been added to Tokyo Imperial University in 1897. In effect, the country had succeeded in bringing all children into a centrally controlled system and in training them in the basic rudiments of literacy as well as civic virtue, considered essential to make a competitive global power out of what had been a decentralized jumble of feudal domains only a few decades earlier.

Education in the Meiji period was also, in some ways, less. Although it had succeeded in bringing large numbers of children into its net, it had, out of necessity, standardized the teaching methods, subject matter, and goals and had homogenized what had been a diverse, if limited, educational universe. In the

Tokugawa period (1603–1868), education had been essentially class based, with segregated schools for the samurai class and a wide variety of autonomous and ad hoc institutions for the common classes: merchants, farmers, artisans, and assorted others. For most, education was largely a family endeavor, with decisions about what school to go to, how long to stay, and so forth being private matters. Teachers taught whatever pleased them, and the variety was impressive. There is no evidence of daimyo or *bakufu* authorities closing down a school because of the subject matter taught, with the sole exception of institutions known to be bent on sedition. But the constituency of official schools was limited to samurai, who required Confucian-based schooling as the leaders of society and in order to perform effectively as urban bureaucrats in the castle towns. Merchants, who required book knowledge and numbers to do business, and the leaders of the farming class, who were responsible for administering Japan's sixty thousand or so villages for their feudal overseers, picked up the basics of literacy at writing schools or continued on to one of the various private academies.

The major accomplishment of education in the Meiji period was centralization and standardization across the entire population. This did not happen at once, nor did it proceed smoothly, because education in Meiji Japan was one of the most contentious areas of national life, bearing on the interests of parents, children, political authorities, educational professionals, and ideologues of every stripe who sought conformity to their own view of a model citizenry. Education involved not only questions about standards, control, and educational outcomes but also issues of the citizens' relation to the government bureaucracy and the imperial state and of the way such things should be expressed and taught to the young. The policy debates and decisions made about national educational policy as well as the public responses to and criticisms of it reveal much about the people, politics, cultural values, and ideologies of the time.

The early Meiji leaders agreed on the need to create a national system of education in order to develop the people's talents and to consolidate a national citizenry responsive to the goals of the central regime. They did not agree, however, on the means to accomplish these objectives. The serpentine twists and turns as the process unfolded reflected the conflicts and confusions of the Meiji years as a whole. There was little question that the government's first priority was to establish a system of higher education that would attract the best talent in the country to the leadership. Despite the Western themes in the imperial Charter Oath of April 6, 1868, such as "Knowledge shall be sought throughout the world" and "The common people, no less than the civil and military officials, shall each be allowed to pursue his own calling," the new government's first educational initiative was to open the Peers' School (Gakushūin) for the court nobility in Kyoto. Not unexpectedly, the philosophy defin-

ing the curriculum of the Meiji government's first school was imperial resto-
rationist Shinto.

This philosophy led to three years of bitter conflict among specialists of
Confucian studies (the entrenched leaders of higher education), Shintoists
(guardians of nativist thought), and adherents of Western studies as to who
would determine the content and goals of education. There was also conflict
between the authorities in Kyoto (the traditional seat of higher education) and
Tokyo (the new capital) over the location of the new university. The outcome
of such basic educational matters was determined by the consolidation of political and military power in a group of young oligarchs who looked to the West
as the model for building a modern state. As the state grew, fewer concessions
were made to the traditional holders of power—court nobles, Confucian scholars, and Shintoists. In the spring of 1869, when the emperor's residence moved
from Kyoto to Tokyo, plans to divide the new university into Kyoto and Tokyo
branches were dropped in favor of a single institution in Tokyo. By the summer
of 1870, when the new regime had full political and military control, plans for
integrating Confucian, Shinto, and Western learning programs in the new university were set aside. The growing influence of Westernizing pragmatists like
Itō Hirobumi and Kido Takayoshi at the center of power ended the Confucian
domination of higher education, and Western scholars took uncontested control
of the new Tokyo Imperial University. This became the government's central
institution for assimilating the advanced and practical knowledge of the West.

With the university in place, in the summer of 1871 the government turned
its attention to creating a national system of public elementary schools. A central
office of education (Monbushō), which became the Ministry of Education in
1886, was established on September 2, 1871, and a committee was appointed to
draft a national plan. A year later, on September 5, 1872, all schools in the
country were ordered closed, in order to reopen according to provisions of a
new national plan called Gakusei (literally, School System, but often called the
Fundamental Code of Education). The Preamble to the new code, strongly
utilitarian in spirit and clearly reflecting the ideas of Westernizers like Fukuzawa
Yukichi, made it clear that under the new system the goals of education would
be quite different from the mostly Confucian goals of loyalty and filial piety
that had defined official schools during the Tokugawa period. Instead, self-
improvement, training for individual success in life, and equality of opportunity
for all people were made the explicit goals of public education in Japan.

The new school plan provided the first comprehensive national school system for Japan, with the entire country divided into university, middle school,
and elementary school districts. Although compulsory education was set at four
years, it was not strictly enforced in many regions, and adherence to the plan's
many provisions was scattershot and ineffectual in some areas. Nevertheless,
the Fundamental Code of Education (Gakusei) announced that henceforth

education in Japan was to be a central government enterprise; it established a focal point around which public views on education could form as the Japanese wrestled with the complicated issues surrounding the goals and structures for national education.

The immediate response to the new plan was frustration and disappointment because it had vastly overestimated what was realistically possible in a short time. Although enrollment went up, it varied greatly around the country, and in many areas, the enrollment of girls trailed that of boys by a significant margin. A crescendo of complaints arose from parents because they had to bear almost the entire cost and because most of the textbooks were filled with translations from American textbooks, which they saw as useless. The new Education Law (Kyōikurei) of 1879 was intended to address these complaints by turning over more control to local authorities and reducing the compulsory attendance requirement from eight years to four months each year for four years. The result was a general slackening of effort down the line, and the perceived weakening of central authority led to flight from the system. The Westernizing spirit of the 1879 law was met head-on by no less than the emperor himself. Having returned from a trip to the provinces and disturbed by what he had observed in schools, the emperor issued an imperial proclamation, the Imperial Rescript on Education (Kyōgaku taishi), actually written by his Confucian adviser, Motoda Eifu, that called for a return to traditional values in education. This, in turn, was rebutted by Itō Hirobumi, who viewed the spiritual malaise among people as related more to rapid social change than Western notions of individual self-fulfillment.

Efforts to reform the educational system toward greater support for the state culminated in 1886 in a series of school ordinances designed and implemented by Mori Arinori. The fundamental principle behind the school ordinances expressed by Mori, as the first minister of education, was that education should primarily serve the interests of the state. He repeatedly emphasized this statist philosophy of national education in order to shift the goals of the state system away from the more individualistic philosophy embodied in the Preamble to the Fundamental Code of Education and other legislation of the 1870s. Mori's plan called for a "dual structure" of schools. At the bottom, elementary schools, locally financed and teaching basic literacy and numeracy, were redirected to inculcate proper character and patriotic loyalty; pupils would be guided by teachers trained in teacher-training schools run along military lines, complete with uniforms and military-style drills, which Mori believed to be essential to moral cultivation. At the top, the newly designed imperial university, which was nationally financed and trained elites for government service, provided relative academic freedom, although within parameters defined by the national interest.

This structure was shaped like a dumbbell, with the higher and elementary institutions at either end and the middle schools (somewhat later in development) in between, functioning as an elite sorting mechanism. The middle schools themselves had a dual structure: a terminal course for training mid-level specialists and teachers and a university preparatory course, later separated as higher schools (*kōtō gakkō*), providing direct access to the imperial university. Each prefecture was to concentrate public funds on only one middle school, thereby putting it far out of reach of girls and the majority of boys. It was not until the Middle School Ordinance of 1889 was enacted that middle schools were finally made part of the overall structure, but it was Mori, earlier, who first unequivocally proclaimed secondary education to be the privilege of the few and not the prerogative of the many. Nevertheless, despite these elitist intentions, the existence of middle schools provided access upward for all. By 1890, the proportion of non-samurai families in middle schools climbed above 50 percent for the first time and continued to rise. The path may have been narrow, but some upward mobility was possible, and the system was no longer primarily class based.

With Mori Arinori's school ordinances of 1886, a distinctive Japanese organization of schools had taken shape and remained in place until 1945. To be sure, the system was not yet fully formed. School attendance did not reach nearly universal levels until the end of the Meiji period, and even then, in some localities where factory work and baby-sitting were viewed as more practical alternatives, many girls dropped out. Movement upward through the system remained limited during the Meiji period, and there was only one recognized university until 1897, when Kyoto Imperial University was added to Tokyo Imperial University.

Throughout the process of building a modern educational system, two major issues continued to be hotly contested: (1) new values (largely derived from the West) versus traditional Confucian morality and (2) central government control of education versus local authority. Mori himself did not advocate the narrow, emperor-centered nationalism that took over the educational system in later years, nor did he try to impose a national creed on children through morals courses in schools. He did not believe in the central control of all educational matters, preferring some local initiative, for example, in the selection of text-books. The battles over these matters intensified in 1889 when a new constitution was promulgated and in 1890 with the Imperial Rescript on Education. The Meiji constitution created a new parliament composed partly of elected members who were eager to enter the ideological debates to represent the views of their constituents. The Imperial Rescript on Education, which was supposed to bring closure to the disagreements both inside and outside the government over the ethical content of national education, had the effect of stirring up more debate.

The Imperial Rescript on Education was not, as is frequently alleged, just a triumph of Confucian reactionaries over Western reformers. Rather, its broad conceptual sweep and ambiguous language allowed all sides of the ideological struggles to claim it as their own. It linked Confucian notions of loyalty and filial piety; nativist ideas of a unique national essence (*kokutai*), with the emperor as the source of virtue; and Western traditions of civil obedience, respect for law, and sacrifice for the national good. The document itself was distributed to every school and displayed along with the portrait of the emperor. Principals were instructed to read from the rescript on appropriate occasions, and students were required to study the text for moral lessons. To the extent that it became a civic icon, it brought on abuses because traditionalists could exert control merely by invoking its aura. In the name of the rescript, in 1891 traditionalists attacked Uchimura Kanzō (1861–1930), a Christian teacher at the First Higher Normal School in Tokyo, for alleged disrespect to the emperor. They denounced Professor Kume Kunitake (1839–1931) of Tokyo Imperial University for suggesting that Shinto was outmoded. This, in turn, led the other side to criticize the increasing uniformity, rigidity, and formality of Japanese education as it was developed under bureaucratic leadership. Later, the rescript became the pretext for an increasingly virulent form of nationalism that focused narrowly on a mythic imperial cause.

It would be a mistake, however, to view the national leadership as stridently nationalistic at the end of the nineteenth century. On the contrary, the upsurge of nationalism among the public (including teachers) that followed the Sino-Japanese War (1894/1895) put bureaucratic leaders on the defensive. Saionji Kinmochi (1849–1940), who served as the minister of education from 1894 to 1896 (also in 1898 and again early in 1906), tried to turn the educational tide away from a focus on the unique character of the Japanese spirit toward more pragmatic and global considerations. Minister of Education Kabayama Sukenori (1837–1922), serving in the cabinet of General Yamagata Aritomo from 1898 to 1900, appointed to various bureaus progressive young bureaucrats like Sawayanagi Masatarō (1865–1927), who drew up a set of policies uniquely enlightened for a cabinet and a ministry headed by military men. The Revised Elementary School Ordinance of August 1900 abolished elementary school tuition, making schools free for the first time; included a one-year extension to compulsory education; reduced the number of hours of instruction; standardized the Japanese syllabary, leading to a jump in literacy among children; limited the number of Chinese characters to be taught; and abolished the examination system.

During the Meiji period, much of the debate over local autonomy, as opposed to central control of education, focused on textbooks. Although ministry certification had been required since Mori's school ordinances of 1886, publication had remained under the control of private firms, and choices among competing texts could be made at the local level. Beginning in 1901 with newspaper reports, public concern was raised by a graft case involving more than two hundred local officials accused of accepting bribes from publishers interested in securing government approval for privately compiled school textbooks.

The "textbook scandal" of 1903, coming at the end of the term of Minister of Education Kikuchi Dairoku (1855–1917), opened the door to parliamentary action. Demands for action came originally not from Ministry of Education officials seeking control but from opposition politicians and educators. There were two main reasons: (1) to reduce the cost of compulsory education by eliminating bribery associated with textbook approval and (2) to achieve national unity in the area of popular morality, which conservative forces in politics and many educators felt had been undermined by the spread of individualism and capitalism. In the end, parliament gave the Ministry of Education an exclusive mandate to commission and publish all school textbooks. Local selection options were abolished, and all elementary schools were required to adopt identical state-approved textbooks. From then until the end of World War II, Japanese elementary school textbooks were written, published, and distributed by the Ministry of Education.

Unlike the Sino-Japanese War, the Russo-Japanese War (1904/1905) made huge demands on the educational system. Funds to support compulsory education diminished, and educational activities generally were cut back. The number of teachers had to be reduced despite the expansion of enrollment brought on by the patriotic frenzy surrounding the war. Hostility toward the enemy reached such a fever pitch that the Ministry of Education felt compelled to warn teachers about excesses of patriotic zeal. Once the popular reaction to the government's perceived weakness in the Portsmouth Treaty negotiations ending the war had subsided, attention was quickly redirected to maintaining and advancing the international position to which military victory had suddenly elevated Japan. A progressive educational theory even prospered for several years after the war before a conservative reaction to the rise of socialism swung the pendulum back to traditional ideology and tightened the morals curriculum around the virtues of duty to the family, respect for the gods, and reverence for the emperor.

By the end of the Meiji period, educational reformers had carried out a revolution in education. In terms of school attendance, Japan entered the twentieth century on a par with the advanced nations of the West. Virtually the entire male and female populations were entering modern schools, and about half the male population was completing elementary school. Secondary and tertiary education were less impressive, as were the opportunities for women, but compared with forty years earlier, it was a different world. Just as Japan's success in its wars with China and Russia earned it a measure of acceptance by the Western powers, schoolchildren in Japan now had a vastly superior knowledge of world affairs.

More significantly, Japanese leaders had committed themselves to learning and borrowing from abroad while preserving essential traditions. The battles between traditional and modern values had yielded an eclectic mix, with both sides having to answer powerful critics both inside and outside government.

The debate over central versus local control of education had swung to the former, following the public's pressure on the Ministry of Education to take over textbook selection, but local authorities continued to be heard on a wide range of issues. The multilayered web of Meiji educational thought and practice left a decidedly mixed and ambiguous legacy. Thus it could be argued that the progressive experimentation in education during the brief Taishō period (1912–1926), the rise of ultranationalism and the military takeover of the schools afterward, and the assimilation of American-inspired reforms after World War II all owed something to different strands from the Meiji legacy in education.

VIEWS IN THE EARLY MEIJI PERIOD

IWAKURA TOMOMI AND ARISTOCRATIC EDUCATION

Although education during the first decade of the Meiji period (1868–1912) is often characterized as "Western dominated," the very first initiative by the emerging leadership group with respect to education was to advocate training for the imperial aristocracy. Iwakura Tomomi (1825–1883), the most influential member of the nobility and a powerful government leader during the transition years between the Tokugawa and Meiji periods, was the leading force behind a traditional education for court aristocrats. Iwakura was convinced that a true restoration required a return to the ancient imperial polity that had existed before the ascendancy of the military class, the samurai (*bushi*). If that polity was to be restored, then it was essential to train the nobles to be as capable of leadership as the samurai were.

"ADMONITIONS TO COURT NOBLES"

In his "Admonitions to Court Nobles," written in 1866, two years before the Restoration coup, Iwakura Tomomi tried to stir the long dormant nobility to action. Two years later, shortly after the overthrow of the shogunal regime, Iwakura, believing that the time for the courtiers had come, again admonished the Kyoto aristocracy, urging on it the necessity for education.

The reason our imperial land lost its martial vigor is that the imperial court abandoned its military prerogative, and this happened because the nobility was arrogant and lazy. The responsibility for the failure to restore the country's former glory therefore must be shouldered by the nobles themselves. How, then, can we blame the samurai alone? In this time of crisis, it is of the utmost importance for the court to take the initiative in putting the country in order and external pressures under control. If that is to be achieved, above all the nobility must cooperate wholeheartedly and participate in the imperial design, thus setting an example for the *bushi*.

[*Iwakura Tomomi kankei monjo*, vol. 1, pp. 224–25; trans. adapted from Motoyama, *Proliferating Talent*, p. 86]

"FURTHER ADMONITIONS"

Orders to pursue and smite the bandits shall at length make imperial authority flourish. All the nobility—from imperial princes and the highest nobles down to titular officials not ranked as chamberlains—should be inspired to the most strenuous efforts, ready to give their lives in loyal service to the cause of the imperial court. Some, however, remain uninvolved spectators of events and expect to receive stipends for doing nothing. . . . The times demand that hereditary stipends be decreased, not increased. If someone performs distinguished service, he may then be given an individual, not a heritable, increase in stipend. Insofar as offices and ranks are concerned, the traditional social hierarchy also will be reformed: instead of hereditary family status, appointments will be made on the basis of talent. Keeping this in mind, all should earnestly devote themselves to the study of arms and arts. . . . It is intended that those who, studying night and day, reach a level of accomplishment shall be rewarded with an official appointment commensurate with their talents. Do not be remiss; persist in your endeavor!

[*Iwakura Kō jikki*, vol. 1, p. 1009; trans. adapted from Motoyama, *Proliferating Talent*, pp. 86–87]

KIDO TAKAYOSHI AND ITŌ HIROBUMI ON UNIVERSAL EDUCATION

Kido Takayoshi (Kōin, 1833–1877) and Itō Hirobumi (1841–1909) were the first of the influential early Meiji statesmen to enunciate ideas of universal public education directed at training every child and not just elites. In contrast to Iwakura Tomomi's early views that it was the members of the court aristocracy who needed to be trained, Kido and Itō, whose views eventually won the day, concentrated on a mass public-education system intended to educate the entire population of the country.

During his short career, Kido, best known for his drafting of the Charter Oath and his work on establishing the prefectural system, took an active interest in educational matters. Itō, as the first prime minister and the chief architect of the Meiji constitution of 1890, played a key role in guiding Japan in its formative years as a modern nation. He also understood the importance of education in that process. About a month after Kido submitted his proposal urging universal education, Itō, who at the time (early 1869) was the governor of Hyōgo Prefecture, submitted an even more reformist view in "Principles of National Policy."

Itō was convinced that education had played an important role in securing the foundations of a modern state, and he believed that developing every person's intellectual ability would naturally lead to a Western type of "civilization and enlightenment" (*bunmei kaika*). Rejecting both the dualism that characterized the feudal age, when one type of education was provided for the ruling classes and another for the ruled, and the conventional view that schools were meant primarily to enhance national strength and prosperity, Itō linked education to the activation and enhancement of the individual's natural capacity for knowledge.

KIDO TAKAYOSHI: DRAFT MEMORIAL FOR THE IMMEDIATE PROMOTION OF UNIVERSAL EDUCATION

With reverence I, Jun'ichirō (changed to Takayoshi later in 1869), submit this memorial. Not a year has passed since the restoration of imperial governance and the Tōhoku insurgents have completely capitulated. Following your majesty's wishes we endeavor to relieve the lingering resistance of the previous military government. Domestically we shall carry out the policies of governing equitably among the citizenry while externally we strive to cope with the rich and powerful nations of the West. I have no doubt that these are your wishes.

I have long obeyed the august imperial will and, although unworthy, have exhausted my energies deliberating on the future state of affairs. If the people remain ignorant and poor and are unable to improve themselves, even if a few exemplary men provide support for imperial governance, it will not be sufficient to make the country wealthy and strong. The restoration government will inevitably fall prey to despotism and the expectations of the imperial restoration will falter. The strength and prosperity of a country lie in the strength and prosperity of its people. If ordinary people are held back by ignorance and poverty, the beautiful phrase "imperial restoration" has no meaning, and the effort of keeping up with the leading countries of the world must fail.

Therefore, we should strive for advancement in knowledge of all the people. We must select knowledge from the civilized nations, promote schools throughout the country, and cause education to be spread widely. This is a matter of utmost urgency. Even if we start right away, it stands to reason that it will take time to accomplish. It would not be wise to copy hastily from the advanced nations. On the contrary, I believe that expedient and superficial knowledge would foment incalculable discontent among our people. I humbly request that a timely decision be rendered.

> *With awe and reverence, I remain your humble servant,*
> Kido Jun'ichirō [Takayoshi]
> Boshin 12.2 (January 14, 1869)

[Katō et al., *Kido Takayoshi*, in NKST, vol. 6, p. 13; trans. Charles Andrews]

ITŌ HIROBUMI: "PRINCIPLES OF NATIONAL POLICY" (KOKUZE KŌMOKU)

The human body is endowed with eyes, ears, nose, and mouth, and each of these must be used in accordance with its function. If, while knowing how the nose and mouth perform their functions, we then fail to realize how to apply the eyes and ears to theirs, that would be the same as not having eyes or ears. Today, the world situation has changed dramatically. Engaged in intercourse with all the world, men vie with each other to keep their ears and eyes open, gaining information that spreads as from one person to another and eventually reaches ten thousand. Accordingly, we have initiated a policy of civilization and enlightenment. Now is our millennial opportunity to reform the bad old habits that have been followed in our imperial land for centuries and to open up the eyes and ears of the people of our realm. If, at this juncture, we fail to act quickly and make our people broadly pursue useful knowledge from throughout the world, we will in the end reduce them to a backward folk without eyes and ears. We must therefore establish new universities and change our old, conventional style of learning. A university should be founded in each of the capital cities, Kyoto and Tokyo, and elementary schools should be opened in every locality, from metropolitan districts, domains, and prefectures on down to every district and village. Pursuant to each university's charter, people of city and country alike shall be brought to the light and to knowledge.

[*Itō Hirobumi den*, vol. 1, p. 423; Motoyama, *Proliferating Talent*, pp. 117–18]

FUKUZAWA YUKICHI AND EDUCATION

Fukuzawa Yukichi (1835–1901) was one of the most influential proponents of both public and private education and a strong supporter of learning from the West (see chaps. 34 and 36). He also was a writer, a publicist, an educator, and a journalist. As a young man, he rejected traditional learning and gravitated to the new ideas coming from the West. His private school, Keiō gijuku, founded as a school of Western learning before the Meiji Restoration, later became one of Japan's great private universities. In the following excerpt from

An Encouragement of Learning (*Gakumon no susume*), his most popular and widely quoted essay on education, Fukuzawa gives his view of the importance of education in general, attacks the traditional learning of the past, supports practical learning, and makes the case for studying the West and the rest of the world.

AN ENCOURAGEMENT OF LEARNING
(*GAKUMON NO SUSUME*)

An Encouragement of Learning was begun in 1872 and finished in 1876, and its first edition sold 200,000 copies. It eventually went through seventeen printings, a total of 3.4 million copies during Fukuzawa Yukichi's lifetime, making it one of the best-selling and most influential works of the Meiji period. The entire work consists of seventeen sections. Section 1, from which an extended excerpt follows, was used widely as an ethics text in the 1870s but was banned in 1881 as part of the government's reaction to the Freedom and People's Rights movement and Western influences in education.

It is said that heaven does not create one person above or below another person. This means that when people are born from heaven, they all are equal. There is no innate distinction between high and low. It means that people can freely and independently use the myriad things of the world to satisfy their daily needs through the labors of their own bodies and minds and that, as long as they do not infringe on the rights of others, may pass their days in happiness. Nevertheless, as we broadly survey the human scene, there are the wise and the stupid, the rich and poor, the noble and lowly, whose conditions seem to differ as greatly as the clouds and the mud. . . .

Moreover, there are difficult and easy professions in society. The person who performs difficult work is regarded as an individual of high station. One who performs easy work is called a person of low station. Work involving intellectual effort is considered more difficult than work done through one's own physical strength. Consequently, such persons as doctors, scholars, government officials, merchants who manage large businesses, [and] farmers who employ many hands are considered noble and of high station. Being such, their households are naturally wealthy, and they seem to tower above and out of reach of the lower levels of society. But when we inquire into the reason for this, we find that these differences are entirely the result of whether they have or do not have the powers that learning brings. It is not because of some decree of heaven. As the proverb says: Heaven does not give riches and dignity to man himself but to his labors. Therefore, as I said above, there are no innate status distinctions separating the noble and base, the rich and the poor. It is only the person who has studied diligently, so that he has a mastery over things and events, who becomes noble and rich, while his opposite becomes base and poor.

Learning does not consist essentially of such impractical pursuits as studying obscure Chinese characters, reading ancient texts that are difficult to make out, or enjoying and writing poetry. These kinds of interests may be useful diversions, but they should not be esteemed as highly as the Confucian and Japanese Learning scholars have esteemed them since ancient times. Among the Chinese Learning scholars, those who have been skilled in practical matters have been few indeed. Rare also has been the merchant who, if well versed in poetry, was also successful in business. Consequently, we observe that when they see their own children concentrating on books, thoughtful merchants and peasants fear as good parents that they will eventually bring the family fortune to ruin. This is not without reason. And it proves that such forms of learning are ultimately without practical value and will not serve daily needs.

Such impractical studies thus should be relegated to a secondary position. The object of one's primary efforts should be practical learning that is closer to ordinary human needs. For example, a person should learn the forty-seven-*kana* syllabary, methods of letter writing and of accounting, the practice of the abacus, the way to handle weights and measures, and the like. And there are many additional things to be learned. Geography is the guide to the climates of not only Japan but also the many countries of the world. Physics is the science that investigates the properties and functions of the myriad things of the universe. Histories are books that study the condition of the countries of the past and present through a detailed chronicling of the historical ages. Economics explains the financial management of self, family, and the state. Ethics expounds the natural principles of personal moral cultivation and of social intercourse.

To study each of these areas, a person should investigate translations of Western books. A boy who is talented in letters should be taught to read Western languages. By grasping the practical matters of each science, which vary in subject matter and content, he can search for the truth of things and make them serve his present purposes. . . .

To learn, it is necessary that each person knows his capacity. There are no innate bonds around human beings. They are born free and unrestricted and become free adult men and women. Nevertheless, many will become selfish and fall into dissipation if they assert only their own freedom and do not know their place. "Place," or capacity, means to achieve one's own personal freedom without infringing on that of others, based on natural principle and in harmony with human feeling. The borderline between freedom and selfishness lies at the point where one does or does not infringe on the freedom of others. . . .

Since the Meiji Restoration, the ways of the Japanese government have greatly improved. In foreign affairs, we have regular relations with foreign nations in accord with international law. Internally, the government has explained the meaning of independence to the people and has already allowed the use of family names and horse riding to the commoners. These changes are among the most commendable since the founding of the Japanese empire. It can be said that the state is now grounded on the principle that all people are socially equal. Therefore, from the present day forward, there will be no such thing as hereditary class rank among the Japanese people. Individuals will have rank only by dint of their talents, virtues, and accomplishments.

For example, it is natural that we show deference to a government official. But this is not because of the dignity of that person's status. He is accorded that respect only because he performs that important role through his talent and virtues and because he deals with important laws for the sake of the people. It is the laws that have dignity, not the person. . . .

Now that the basis of equality of all classes has been established, each citizen can enjoy peace and do his own work to his own liking in accord with natural principle. However, since every person has his own place, each person must also have the virtues and talents appropriate to it. It is necessary to know the principles of things in order to possess such talents and virtues. It is necessary to study in order to learn the principles of things. This is the reason for the urgency I have placed on learning. . . .

The important thing is to let each person conduct himself correctly on the basis of human nature, then to diligently pursue learning and broaden his knowledge and develop abilities appropriate to his station in life. Thus, the government will be able to rule easily, and the people will accept its rule agreeably, each functioning in his proper capacity to preserve the peace of the nation. The encouragement of learning that I advocate has this sole end in view.

[Adapted from Fukuzawa, *An Encouragement of Learning*, trans. Dilworth and Hirano, pp. 1–6]

THE FIRST MEIJI SCHOOL SYSTEM

The Gakusei (or School System, also referred to as the Fundamental Code of Education) was the first comprehensive legislation regarding national education in Japan following the Meiji Restoration. Sent to local officials throughout the country on September 5, 1872, the Gakusei consisted of 109 articles (expanded to 213 by 1873) that for the first time provided a comprehensive outline of a national school system. Japan was to be divided into university, middle school, and elementary school districts, with 8 universities, 256 middle schools, and 53,760 elementary schools. Compulsory education was set at four years, and local supervisors were appointed to enforce attendance, construct new schools, and oversee the distribution of public funds.

The Preamble (Ōseidasaresho) was issued by the Dajōkan (the government's central administrative organ at the time) on September 4, 1872, the day before the Gakusei was issued. The Preamble indicated that the goals of education under the new system would be quite different from the emphasis on Confucian morality as represented by the samurai elite. Strongly reflecting Western influences, and particularly Fukuzawa Yukichi's arguments in *An Encouragement of Learning*, the document emphasized individual goals, equality among classes, and education in practical affairs of a Western type. It called on citizens, regardless of gender or status, to study widely in areas of practical arts and sciences in order to create independent citizens as the foundation of a strong nation. At the same time, it built on the Confucian love of learning widely diffused in the Tokugawa period.

PREAMBLE (ŌSEIDASARESHO) TO THE
FUNDAMENTAL CODE OF EDUCATION
(GAKUSEI)

It is only by building up their characters, developing their minds, and cultivating their talents that people may make their ways in the world, employ their wealth wisely, make their businesses prosper, and thus attain the goals of life. But people cannot build up their characters, develop their minds, or cultivate their talents without education. That is the reason for the establishment of schools. Beginning with speech, writing, and arithmetic in everyday life and extending to military affairs, government, agriculture, trade, law, politics, astronomy, and medicine, there is not a single phase of human activity that is not based on learning. Only by pursuing the path of his natural talents can individuals prosper in their undertakings, accumulate wealth, and succeed in life.

Learning is the key to success in life, and no one can afford to neglect it. It is ignorance that leads people astray, makes them destitute, disrupts their families, and in the end ruins their lives. Centuries have passed since schools were first established, but people have gone off in the wrong direction. Because learning was viewed as the exclusive prerogative of the samurai and courtiers, others—farmers, artisans, merchants, and women—have neglected it completely and have no idea what it is. Even those few samurai and courtiers who did pursue learning were apt to claim that it was for the state, not knowing that it was the very foundation of success in life. They indulged in poetry, empty reasoning, and idle discussions, and their dissertations, while not lacking in elegance, were seldom applicable to life. This was due to our evil traditions and, in turn, was the very cause that impeded the spread of culture, hampered the development of talent and accomplishments, and sowed the seeds of poverty, bankruptcy, and disrupted homes. Everyone should therefore pursue learning, and in so doing they should not misconstrue its purpose.

Accordingly, the Office of Education will soon establish an educational system and will revise the regulations related to it from time to time so that in the future, there shall be no village with an uneducated family or a family with an uneducated person. Every guardian, acting in accordance with this, shall bring up his or her children with care and see to it that they attend school. (While advanced learning should be left to the ability and means of the individual, any guardian will be considered negligent if he or she fails to send a young child, whether boy or girl, to elementary school.)

Heretofore, the evil tradition that looked on learning as the privilege of the samurai and courtiers and as being solely for the benefit of the state, caused many to depend on the government for the expenses of education, even including food and clothing; and failing to receive such support, many wasted their lives by not going to school. Hereafter, such errors must be corrected, and everyone shall, of his own accord, subordinate all other matters to the education of his children.

[Adapted from Passin, *Society and Education in Japan*, pp. 210–11]

THE CONFUCIAN CRITIQUE

MOTODA EIFU AND EMPEROR-CENTERED EDUCATION

Motoda Eifu (or Nagazane, 1818–1891) was born to a samurai family in Kumamoto and became a student of Yokoi Shōnan's pragmatic school of Confucianism. In 1871 he became tutor to the Meiji emperor, through whose support he became a court adviser in 1886. As the leader of the court's conservative faction, Motoda helped establish an educational ideology for the new Meiji government centering on the values of traditional Japan and reverence for the emperor. His ideas were especially influential in drafting the Imperial Rescript on Education in 1890. Among Motoda's most important writings was *Great Principles of Education* (*Kyōgaku taishi*), written in 1879.

GREAT PRINCIPLES OF EDUCATION (*KYŌGAKU TAISHI*)

In the summer of 1878, Emperor Meiji took a tour of schools in the Tōkai and Hokuriku regions. He was disturbed by the overwhelming influences of Western "enlightenment" thought in the schools and asked his Confucian tutor, Motoda Eifu, to summarize his views. As the first imperial statement on education, this is an important historical document that had the effect of bringing educational policy into intense national debate. Clearly in evidence is criticism of the overemphasis on intellectual training and a call for greater stress on moral cultivation, both of which became important elements in the conservative critique of Meiji education.

The essence of education, our traditional national aim, and a watchword for all men, is to make clear the ways of benevolence, justice, loyalty, and filial piety, and to master knowledge and skill and, through these, to pursue the Way of Man. In recent days, people have been going to extremes. They take unto themselves a foreign civilization whose only values are fact-gathering and technique, thus violating the rules of good manners and bringing harm to our customary ways. Although we set out to take in the best features of the West and bring in new things in order to achieve the high aims of the Meiji Restoration — abandonment of the undesirable practices of the past and learning from the outside world — this procedure had a serious defect: It reduced benevolence, justice, loyalty, and filial piety to a secondary position. The danger of indiscriminate emulation of Western ways is that in the end our people will forget the great principles governing the relations between ruler and subject, and father and son. Our aim, based on our ancestral teachings, is solely the clarification of benevolence, justice, loyalty, and filial piety.

For morality, the study of Confucius is the best guide. People should cultivate sincerity and moral conduct, and after that they should turn to the cultivation of the various subjects of learning in accordance with their ability. In this way, morality and technical knowledge will fall into their proper places. When our education comes to be grounded on Justice and the Doctrine of the Mean, we shall be able to show ourselves proudly throughout the world as a nation of independent spirit.

Two Notes on Elementary Education

1. All men are by nature benevolent, just, loyal, and filial. But unless these virtues are cultivated early, other matters will take precedence, making later attempts to teach them futile. Since the practice has developed recently of displaying pictures in classrooms, we must see to it that portraits of loyal subjects, righteous warriors, filial children, and virtuous women are utilized, so that when the pupils enter the school, they will immediately feel in their hearts the significance of loyalty and filial piety. Only if this is done first and then other subjects taught later will they develop in the spirit of loyalty and filial piety and not mistake the means for the end in their other studies.

2. While making a tour of schools and closely observing the pupils studying last autumn, it was noted that farmers' and merchants' sons were advocating high-sounding ideas and empty theories and that many of the commonly used foreign words could not be translated into our own language. Such people would not be able to carry on their own occupations even if they some day returned home, and with their high-sounding ideas, they would make useless civil servants. Moreover, many of them brag about their knowledge, slight their elders, and disturb prefectural officers. All these evil effects come from an education that is off its proper course. It is hoped, therefore, that the educational system will be less high flown and more practical. Agricultural and commercial subjects should be studied by the children of farmers and merchants so that

they return to their own occupations when they have finished school and prosper even more in their proper work.

[Passin, *Society and Education in Japan*, pp. 226–28]

TANI TATEKI'S CRITIQUE OF THE WEST

One of the most effective critics of the overreliance on Western culture and values in education and elsewhere was Tani Tateki (1837–1911). An army officer and head of the Army Academy, Tani was active in conservative politics and served in the first cabinet of Itō Hirobumi as the minister of agriculture and commerce. Tani's thought blended ideas on nationalism, derived from a trip to Europe, with ethical concerns regarding the lives of ordinary people. He espoused the Confucian political idea of "humane government and loving the people" to combat what he saw as the Meiji government's despotic policies of Westernization. The conservative intellectual strain represented by Tani transcended mere traditionalism. For him, Confucianism did not function simply as an ideology in support of the emperor system and state power, as Motoda Eifu's often did; rather, it could also constrain autocracy and oblige the government to serve the people.

OPINION ON REFORM OF ARMY PENSION LAW
(ONKYŪREI KAISEI NO IKEN)

In our country, when we set up teachings, we make loyalty and filial piety their basis. This goes a long way back. Therefore, when somebody is loyal in serving his lord, the officials commend him and the people praise him. Loyalty, propriety, and filial piety are the exquisite virtues of the human race and the most famous product of the East. Since intercourse with foreign nations began, the various systems and institutions have changed greatly; there are those that have gained and those that have lost as a consequence. They who fawn upon the fashions of the day, only imitating Western ways, denigrate and diminish even those sterling qualities of our mind and nature in which we excel and the foreigners fall short. . . . But even if the systems and institutions of our country have changed greatly, one thing remains unaltered from former days: loyalty and filial piety are obligations implied in the human condition. Therefore, when parents raise their children, there is not one who does not desire them to be loyal subjects and pious children. How much more does this apply to those who make soldiering their profession! Since from the beginning death is their lot—how loyal, how pious are they who die when they must die! Nowadays the surviving parents of someone who has died for the state cannot enjoy the same rights as his widow or his children. How then can we say that the balance is kept even? When privately I reflect on the Army Pension Regulations, I note that there is a statute regarding the support of the widow but provisions for the support of the parents are lacking. Thus I know for sure that the regulations are based on the Western system and that it is not a matter of their being carelessly composed. What to do, however, with the fact that they are not in accord with the teachings or the human feelings of our country?

[Boot, in Motoyama, *Proliferating Talent*, pp. 203–4]

NAKAMURA MASANAO'S SYNTHESIS OF EAST AND WEST

Nakamura Masanao (or Keiu, 1832–1891), an active contributor to the enlightenment debates in the *Meiji Six Magazine* (*Meiroku zasshi*), was distinguished among the many promoters of the Civilization and Enlightenment movement by his early serious study of Neo-Confucianism under Satō Issai at the shogunal school, the Shōheikō. Issai reflected the current trend toward synthesis of the Zhu Xi and Wang Yangming schools (already seen in Sakuma Shōzan and Yoshida Shōin). The strong emphasis in this synthesis on the morally responsible self and dedicated activism may help explain why Nakamura was attracted to Protestant Christianity and became a translator of Samuel Smiles's *Self-Help* as well as of John Stuart Mill's *On Liberty*, both of which were widely influential in promoting modern Western ideas in Meiji Japan.

No doubt still influenced by his early Neo-Confucian training, Nakamura saw many similarities between the Confucian tradition and the modern Western values he came to espouse. This contrasted with the early thinking of Fukuzawa Yukichi, whose advocacy of Western civilization, progress, and modernization implied a strong break with tradition.

Thus the two were often seen as at opposite poles. Although his familiarity with Western civilization was mostly with the post-Reformation and Enlightenment movements in Europe, Nakamura saw himself as basically looking for common human ground on which to reconcile Western and Confucian values.

"PAST–PRESENT, EAST–WEST: ONE MORALITY" (KOKIN TŌZAI ITCHI)

This document is not one of the *Meiji Six Magazine* articles but comes from a speech presented by Nakamura Masanao in April 1890. It offers reflections on East–West values that can be interpreted as long-term tendencies, predisposing him both to accept new ideas and to see in them confirmation of underlying human values common to China, Japan, and the West.

In discussing similarities and differences among things, each is a distinct case. In comparing them, there is the objective of acknowledging the points they have in common—for example, when one says that even though men and women are different, they are alike as humans, one is speaking in recognition of the similarities. When one says that even though both men and women are human, still their natures differ in regard to firmness and softness, our objective is to acknowledge the differences.

Thus there are times when one acknowledges similarities using generalizations and synthesis and other times when one recognizes differences using analysis. In teaching, even though a thousand similarities and ten thousand differences could be cited, in order to lead all people to the good, one emphasizes the similarities and talks in generalizations. . . .

What I will discuss today is the essential unity of East and West in basic morality. It is a case of what I have called acknowledging similarities and achieving synthesis. In such a discussion, however, there are times when one must also compare and analyze and one cannot simply generalize. But today my aim is to set aside small differences and stress large similarities, to do away with a narrow view and approach the large view of those of consummate achievement.

When there was Heaven-and-earth, only then were the myriad things born;[1] with the myriad things, man and woman come into being; with man and woman, the [relation of] husband and wife follows; with husband and wife [the relation of] parent and child follows; with parent and child, there is the relation of ruler and minister. There is no such thing as people who can separate themselves from society and live by themselves. In China, Yao appointed Qi minister of education to expound human relations.[2] He taught that between father and child there is affection; between ruler and minister there is rightness; between husband and wife there is differentiation; between senior and junior there is the order of precedence; and between friends there is trust. This then is the moral Way of human relationships. . . .

The main principles of this Chinese morality, that is to say, the teachings of Confucius and Mencius or, in other words, the Way of the Confucian scholar, we Japanese have also had since the beginning of the Ōnin era (1467–1469) until now. Sometimes flourishing, sometimes in decline, not always consistently observed, this Way has nevertheless reached from ministers at court down to commoners in the villages and lanes/harbors. . . .

. . . Because of this, Japan has had an unwritten constitution that has allowed it to mature quickly and that has provided the basis of its national unity. Of course, although Japan has its own unique character and its own unique teachings of the gods—which it did not need to borrow from others—China's classics, histories, the hundred philosophers, and the teachings of Shakyamuni have also joined to shape one moral body among high and low. . . .

---

1. *Yijing*, "Ordering the Hexagrams" (Xu gua).
2. *Mencius* 3A–4C.

Moral virtue inheres in people naturally. It is a natural endowment from Heaven. From this naturally good knowledge and ability[3] in the people comes good conduct. In other words, it is the same as a person's body; just as we are born with five senses, four limbs, and one hundred joints, so the moral virtues are innate in us. They are not added after we are born. Therefore regardless of whether it is past or present, East or West, North or South, in all times, all places—this inherent moral virtue and basis of moral conduct is common to all. There is overall great similarity and little difference [among humankind]. . . .

Careful judgments of the trends of the times and the hearts of people today reveals that all-under-Heaven is in a great uproar.

In this survival of the fittest situation, force becomes inevitable. It is as if morality and humaneness are being swept away like dust from the face of the earth, and rather than emphasizing morality, people think they should display military might and assert themselves by force. . . .

When generalizing about the various countries of the West today, it is a mistake to say that they are immoral. When generalizing about the various countries of the West today, it is a mistake to say they are hellish realms, full of bloodshed and fighting. Overall, it is a mistake to say that the countries of the West are ruled by force. When looking at the various countries of the West today, can we not say they are prosperous and have strong armies? And can we not say they have great power to overwhelm Asia? Is this prosperity and strength accidental? There is a cause; if we examine this closely we will surely know that [in the various Western countries] there is a base of morality, a trunk of wisdom, and a flowering of learning. Today the prosperity and strength they have harvested are the fruits of this. . . .

It is not possible to look at one person and generalize about the whole country or to observe one hand or foot and know the entire body. In the same way, great mistakes are bound to arise when making generalizations about the various countries of the West with respect to their feelings and customs, on the basis of observations we make in contact only with Westerners living in Asia. . . .

In the West, the individual (independent self) and sociality (human relations) are the two main pillars standing together. Around these two elements one's life is built. This sociality of human relations is a characteristic unique to mankind. We associate with others, sharing joys and sorrows, sharing fortune and misfortunes. Nevertheless, this is secondary. The independent self within each person is the basis of morality, that is to say, the self is to be regarded as fundamental. . . . Since the choice of accepting or disregarding the good and evil in them is up to the freedom of each individual, the words or actions of

---

3. *Mencius* 7A:15.

the heart and mind all belong to the individual. Because they are based on the self, the responsibility for them also unavoidably reverts to the self. Again, the response to or retribution for moral goodness or sin is something that returns to each individual. This then is the way of the principle of freedom. One will surely be able to see the resultant prosperity and peace in a society or a country that gathers together the good virtues of independent individuals to create a society. . . .

As far as individual morality is concerned, regardless of past and present, East or West, in the end, the main principle is one thing called self-governance. . . .

In this discussion, there is no freedom to be found apart from the moral person, and without freedom one is unable to choose goodness. Without freedom one cannot be resolute and at ease. To enlarge on this discussion, [I will use the ideas of a] Western scholar who states that this thing called freedom means to be the master of oneself. This closely resembles the earlier teaching in China that one should "be discriminating, keep to oneness and hold to the Mean."[4] Moreover, this corresponds to the Song Confucian understanding that emphasized the mind of the Way as master and the mind of man, which is to obey Heaven's imperative [in the mind of the Way].[5] . . . Is it not the kind of freedom that involves choosing the good, such as was said of Yan Hui: "Yan Hui [only had] a handful of rice, a gourdful of water, lived in a humble lane [and yet was] not depressed."[6] If this is not the freedom to choose the good, as in "choosing the Mean and obtaining the one good,"[7] then what is it? . . .

To sum this up in a few words, the true meaning of the Western philosophy of freedom, in Chinese terms, is to gain freedom by making the mind of the Way [Heaven's principles] one's master and not being a slave to the human mind [human desire]. This thing, freedom, is actually the basis of self-cultivation, that is, the root of self-governance. It is precisely in this that the origin of well-being lies, as well as the foundation of family and state. This is one preeminent aspect of the view that the morality of past and present, East and West is one.

What I want to do next is bring together the Chinese view that human nature is basically good, the ancient Greek wisdom, and the modern Western philos-

---

4. Part of the "sixteen-character formula."

5. Reference to Zhu Xi's explanation of the sixteen-character formula in his preface to the Mean: "If one applies oneself to this without any interruption, making sure that the mind of the Way is the master of one's self and that the human mind always listens to its commands, then the precariousness and the insecurity will yield to peace and security, and what is subtle and barely perceptible will become clearly manifest" (de Bary and Bloom, eds., *Sources of Chinese Tradition*, 2nd ed., vol. 1, pp. 732–33).

6. *Analects* 7:11.

7. *Mean* 8.

ophers' view of the goodness of human nature. Aristotle said, "Only humans, among all living beings, are able to discern right from wrong." He also asked, "Is not good also what we expect to be the goal of various skills and people's conduct and exercise of choice?" The view that human nature is basically good started with Mencius. What is referred to as the mind of the Way was something handed down by Yao and Shun and the rulers of the Three Dynasties. What is called the "Way of the mind-and-heart," "the Mean," the *Great Learning*'s "luminous virtue and utmost goodness," and the *Mean*'s "bright-goodness, sincere person," are they all not part of the theory of the goodness of human nature? . . .

The reason why moral learning is different from the other types of learning is that all the others, such as physics, botany, psychology, arithmetic, geography, statistics, and history inquire into things as they actually exist. Conversely, moral learning inquires into things as they ought to be. The sense that such things ought to be done or ought not to be done is not something that inheres in the material world. The origin of this concept is nothing other than the fact that humans have a good heart and mind (moral sense), can distinguish between good and evil, and can be masters of their own actions. People must take responsibility for their actions. . . .

People do not just feel the pleasures and pains of their own body and mind— they perceive other people's pleasure and pain and share in them. This feeling in English called "sympathy" can be translated as "feeling the same emotions," "compassion," or "affection" and arises out of the sentiment between parent and child. Sympathy, "being stirred by shared emotions" or "compassion," is the most basic element in the many aspects of human relations. . . .

One's conscience and loving feeling, being rooted in human nature, are the main basis of morality as understood in past and present, East and West—what we have referred to as largely one and the same, with large similarities and small differences. . . .

[Nakamura, "Kokin tōzai itchi," pp. 326–33; AS]

MORI ARINORI AND THE
LATER MEIJI SCHOOL SYSTEM

Mori Arinori (or Yūrei, 1847–1889) was born into a samurai family in Satsuma domain (now Kagoshima Prefecture) and in 1865 was secretly sent abroad for study by domain authorities. After studying naval surveying, mathematics, and physics for two years in Britain, in 1867 he went to America, where he spent a year with the Brotherhood of the New Life, a spartan religious colony in Brocton, New York, run by the former Swedenborgian spiritualist and sexual mystic Thomas Lake Harris (1823–1906). Mori returned to Japan in 1868 to join the new Meiji government in a variety of important administrative posts. Mori was

Japan's ambassador to the United States (1871–1873), to China (1876–1877), and to England (1880–1884). An ardent nationalist and advocate of enlightenment, he helped found, with Fukuzawa Yukichi and others, the Meirokusha in 1873. He also founded Japan's first commercial college, the forerunner of Hitotsu-bashi University.

Mori was an early advocate of religious freedom, of abandoning the Japanese language in favor of English, and of the social emancipation of women. His suggestions for a more centralized, state-oriented educational system fit the constitutional plans of Itō Hirobumi, who took Mori into his cabinet in 1886 as Japan's first minister of education. Within three months of his appointment, Mori had set in place a series of educational ordinances that consolidated Meiji schools under national control and were to define the basic structure of Japa-nese education from the spring of 1886 until 1945. His strong support for mod-ernization and ties to the West led to his assassination at the age of forty-two by a radical nationalist on February 11, 1889, the day the Meiji constitution went into effect.

"ESSENTIALS OF EDUCATIONAL ADMINISTRATION" (GAKUSEI YŌRYŌ)

Despite Mori Arinori's overwhelming personal imprint on Meiji schools, he never articulated his educational philosophy in a single coherent statement. The best sum-mary of his ideas can be found in "Essentials of Educational Administration" (Gakusei yōryō), in which he briefly outlines the essential points of his national system: statist goals (the interests of the nation taking priority over those of the individual), the dual system (higher learning for a small elite and basic education for all), the importance of the moral purposes of school education, the high priority given to proper teacher training, and the principle of local finance for local schools. This was written in the form of a memorandum, and although the date is unknown, it is thought to be 1885, shortly before Mori became minister of education.

Section 1: Policy

Item: The national school system (schools established at state or public expense) is the predominant element in the school system and should be administered in accordance with the principle of enhancing the national economy (wealth and power of the state).

Item: The good of the individual and the good of the state are to be promoted equally.

Item: It is essential that those who learn foreign languages become leaders and take control of affairs of state. For this purpose we must immediately provide appropriate education, before any harm is incurred.

Section 2: Higher Learning

Item: Higher learning should be divided into pure science and applied science. Both are essential to the interests of the state. The former has limited applicability and focus, whereas the latter has far broader applications.

Item: Pure science involves research that penetrates deeply to the essence of matter. Pure science will contribute to the long-range benefit of Japan and of the world in general and should be engaged in by only the most qualified scholars.

Item: Applied science (something like professional education) involves the training of those with specialized knowledge in fields that have immediate practical social applications (business, engineering, law, commerce, medicine). People in these fields are professionals who do practical things to benefit people and meet national requirements. This includes providing appropriate training for those able to qualify as government officials.

Section 3: Basic Education

Item: The purpose of elementary education is to provide training sufficient for children to understand their duties as Japanese subjects, to conduct themselves in an ethical fashion, and to secure their own individual well-being.

Item: The most urgent task of all is to train enough teachers for every elementary school. The prefectures will take responsibility for this, and the central government will provide general oversight.

Item: The character of pupils must first be trained and rectified so that they can make proper use of their studies.

Section 4: School Fees

Item: Expenses for national schools will be paid by local school taxes. When necessary these will be supplemented by national taxes. This will be in accord with local conditions and regulations pertaining to the national economy.

Item: A system of local school taxes will be established separate from other local taxes. While the central government will have oversight, the details will be handled by local authorities.

[Adapted from Hall, *Mori Arinori*, pp. 409–12]

MILITARY-STYLE PHYSICAL TRAINING (*HEISHIKI TAISŌ*)

Aside from determining the structure of a comprehensive national school system, Mori's greatest legacy was probably the introduction of military-style physical training into the Meiji period's normal schools. Mori did not have training soldiers in mind; in fact, even the health-building function was secondary. Rather, it was moral discipline that the training was supposed to instill. *Military-Style Physical Training* (1885) was intended to produce not only a new generation of teachers but also a whole new disciplinary framework for everyday school life.

Mori believed that the new teacher should display three essential traits of character: obedience (*jūjun*) toward superiors, friendship (*yūjō*) toward equals, and dignity (*igi*) toward inferiors. By obedience, Mori had in mind conforming to school regulations and following teachers' commands. By friendship, he meant a spirit of mutual assistance, which Mori believed to be the foundation of public morality and the measure of a civilized nation. And by dignity, he was referring to self-assurance or composure in speech and manners. Mori viewed the relationship between military exercise and character building in the following terms in a speech he delivered at an elementary teachers' training school, three days before he became minister of education.

This military-style physical training is something to be used entirely as a means for promoting the three qualities of character I have just mentioned, as a tool for hammering them into shape. We are not adding it to the curriculum with the thought of producing officers and enlisted men for the defense of our country, on the chance that the nation might someday find itself in need of soldiers. The things we hope to achieve by means of this training are three: first, to instill—with the sense of urgency possessed by actual soldiers—those habits of obedience which are appropriate in the classroom. Secondly, as you know, soldiers are always formed into squads, each squad possessing its own leader who devotes himself, heart and mind and soul, to the welfare of his group. And thirdly, every company has its commanding officer who controls and supervises it, and who must comport himself with dignity. By the same token our students, by trading off the roles of common soldier, squad leader and commanding officer, will build up the traits of character appropriate to each of these three roles.

[Hall, *Mori Arinori*, p. 427]

INOUE KOWASHI AND PATRIOTIC TRAINING

After Mori Arinori's death in 1889, Inoue Kowashi (1844–1895) became a pivotal figure in completing the basic Meiji educational structure, by providing a technical/vocational track and enhanced facilities for women. Inoue successfully walked the line between the statist politicians like Mori and Itō Hirobumi and the traditionalists like Motoda Eifu. He worked with Itō on drafts of the Meiji constitution and the Imperial Household Laws, with Mori on educational policy, and with Motoda on the Imperial Rescript on Education of 1890. In 1893 Inoue was appointed minister of education in the second Itō cabinet, and although he served for only a year and five months, his influence on education was greater than this abbreviated term would suggest.

Whereas Mori had promoted a national education that primarily served the interests of the state, Inoue did not favor a national creed or ideology imposed from above. Rather, he went beyond Mori in this respect and took an important step toward what would later become education in the service of ultranationalistic ends.

PUBLIC EDUCATION AND THE NATIONAL SUBSTANCE
(*KOKUTAI KYŌIKU*)

Because Japan did not have a state religion that could unite people, Inoue Kowashi believed that the notion of "national substance" (*kokutai*), including both form and spirit, could act as a similar principle of unity for educating the young. For Inoue, loyalty to the emperor as the living symbol of the *kokutai* should become the first principle of educational goals. In *Public Education and the National Substance*, written in 1889, shortly after Mori Arinori was assassinated, Inoue summarizes his own views on a national creed.

The fundamental principle of Mori's educational policy was education based on the *kokutai*. Education does not mean merely collecting and explaining the materials of textbooks. The most important thing in education is to build up the character and orient the students by showing them the spiritual way. This is an extremely difficult task. The education that was practiced two thousand years ago during Shun's reign cannot be used today. Europe has a religion that serves to confirm the spirit of the young. There is no such creed in our country. I think that it is very difficult to achieve a sense of unity among the people through education. Fortunately, in our country we have a beautiful treasure that cannot be compared with that of any other country. This is the *kokutai* based on the imperial line unbroken for ages eternal. Nothing but the *kokutai* can be the keynote of education. No other country has a history like ours: our people have been loyal to the emperors of an unbroken line from the beginning of the country, and they will be loyal to all future emperors as long as the national land continues to exist. Therefore we should make the *kokutai* the first principle of our education. Nothing else can be the basis of our educational system, and this was the first principle of the late Mori.

[Adapted from Pittau, "Inoue Kowashi," pp. 101–2]

"PLAN TO DEFEND THE NATIONAL INTEREST"
(RIEKISEN BŌGO NO KEIKAKU)

In "Plan to Defend the National Interest," a famous speech drafted by Inoue for Yamagata Aritomo in 1890, Inoue assigns a central place to patriotic education in the promotion of Japan's foreign policy.

There are two indispensable elements in the field of foreign policy: the armed forces first and education second. If the Japanese people are not imbued with patriotic spirit, the nation cannot be strong, no matter how many laws are issued. . . . Patriotism can be instilled only through education. Every powerful nation in Europe strives to foster through compulsory education a deep sense of patriotism, together with the knowledge of the national language, history, and other subjects. Patriotism becomes a second nature. Because of such an education, the minds of the people become one in the defense of the national interest even if they have different opinions in other matters. Therefore I think it is vitally important to improve the patriotic spirit among the Japanese people, because the very survival of the nation depends on it. The two things mentioned earlier are indispensable to make a nation fully independent.

[Adapted from Pittau, "Inoue Kowashi," p. 103]

THE IMPERIAL RESCRIPT ON EDUCATION

The Imperial Rescript on Education (Kyōiku chokugo), the product of a complex institutional and ideological sorting out that followed the educational reforms of the 1870s, preceded the establishment of a new political system in the 1890s. Frequently described as the outcome of a successful campaign by conservative moralists to reassert traditional values against the influences of an insurgent progressivism, it actually emerged from a process of consultation and contestation among Confucian advisers to the throne (principally Motoda Eifu and Nishimura Shigeki), Western-oriented educators, conservatives, progressives, cabinet members under Yamagata Aritomo, and prefectural governors concerned about the erosion of public morality on both the local and the national level. The resulting mix contained a core of simple, homespun ethical precepts (which could be interpreted as either "Confucian" or "universal human" values, as one preferred) combined with elements of a new imperial ideology centered on the concept of "national polity" (*kokutai*).

This document was labeled as a "rescript" because it was meant to function not as formal law but as instruction from on high, couched in the succinct, aphoristic style of the "classic" and the portentous language of sacred utterance.

THE OPENING

Know ye, Our subjects:

Our Imperial Ancestors (*waga kōso kōsō*) founded our empire on a basis broad and everlasting and have deeply and firmly planted virtue; Our subjects, ever united in loyalty (*chū*) and filial piety (*kō*), have, from generation to generation, illustrated the beauty thereof. This is the glory of the fundamental character of Our Nation (*kokutai no seika*), and herein also lies the source of Our education (*kyōiku no engen*). Ye, Our subjects, be filial to your parents, affectionate to your brothers and sisters; as husbands and wives be harmonious, as friends true; bear yourselves in modesty and moderation; extend your benevolence to all; pursue learning and cultivate the arts and thereby develop intellectual faculties and perfect moral powers; furthermore, advance public good and promote common interests; always respect the constitution and observe the laws; should emergency arise, offer yourselves courageously to the state (*giyū ko ni hōshi*); and thus guard and maintain the prosperity of our imperial throne coeval with heaven and earth. So shall ye not only be our good and faithful subjects (*chūryō no shinmin*), but render illustrious the best traditions of your forefathers.

The Way here set forth is indeed the teaching bequeathed by our imperial ancestors, to be observed alike by their descendants and the subjects, infallible for all ages and true in all places. It is our wish to lay it to heart in all reverence, in common with you, our subjects, that we all thus attain to the same virtue.

The 30th day of the 10th month of the 23rd year of Meiji (1890)

The middle portion of the text (and its ethical core) is indeed traditional and has a long history. It comes originally from Zhu Xi's precepts for village instruction and community compacts, which by a long, circuitous process became staples in Tokugawa-period village and family instruction (see chap. 25). Zhu Xi's original instructions, however, emphasized filial piety, respect for elders, brotherliness, vocational commitment, and learning—virtues applicable to all members of a family or community, irrespective of class or status, to which hardly anyone would object. Significantly, Zhu Xi made no reference whatever to ruler, state, or "loyalty" as a supposed Confucian virtue. These elements were incorporated into the original precepts only later when Zhu Xi's formulation was co-opted by the founding emperor of the Ming and later amended by Qing rulers for their own imperial purposes, focusing more on the state than on the local community.[8] In this late Meiji version, the original core has become encased in a new Japanese imperial ideology.

As a combination of familiar ethical platitudes and patriotic sentiments, this consensus document won acceptance from many sides in the 1890s, as well as resistance from some independents like Uchimura Kanzō. It was given a strong nationalist twist by the widely disseminated commentary of Inoue Tetsujirō (1856–1944), a prominent proponent of Confucian philosophy and a critic of Western liberal influences. His interpretations were cast in the standard Neo-Confucian genre of "extended meaning" (engi), long associated with adaptations of Zhu Xi's original six precepts (see chap. 25). Inoue's "extended meaning" was a modernized and Japanized interpretation incorporating Western concepts of the organic state and survival of the fittest.

---

8. See de Bary and Bloom, eds., *Sources of Chinese Tradition*, 2nd ed., vol. 1, chap. 21; and de Bary and Lufrano, eds., *Sources of Chinese Tradition*, 2nd ed., vol. 2, chap. 25.

THE EXTENDED MEANING OF THE RESCRIPT

In the world today, Europe and America are, of course, great powers, and all the countries settled by the Europeans have prospered as well. Now only the countries of the East are capable of competing with the progress of these nations. Yet India, Egypt, Burma, and Annam have already lost their independence; Siam, Tibet, and Korea are extremely weak and will find it difficult to establish their autonomy. Thus in the Orient today, Japan and China alone have an independence stable enough to vie for rights with the powers. But China clings to the classics and lacks the spirit of progress. Only in Japan does the idea of progress flourish, and Japan has it within its means to anticipate a glorious civilization in the future.

Japan, however, is a small country. Since there are now those that swallow countries with impunity, we must consider the whole world our enemy. Although we should always endeavor to conduct friendly relations with the powers, foreign enemies are watching for any lapse on our part, and then we can rely only on our 40 million fellow countrymen. Thus any true Japanese must have a sense of public duty by which he values his life lightly as dust, advances spiritedly, and is ready to sacrifice himself for the sake of the nation.

But we must encourage this spirit before an emergency occurs. "Making a rope to catch a thief only after he shows up" is obviously foolish. The purpose of the rescript is to strengthen the basis of the nation by cultivating the virtues of filiality and fraternal love, loyalty and sincerity (*kōtei chūshin*) and to prepare for any emergency by nurturing the spirit of collective patriotism (*kyōdō aikoku*). If all Japanese establish themselves by these principles, we can be assured of uniting the hearts of the people.

[Adapted from Gluck, *Japan's Modern Myths*, pp. 129–30]

TEACHERS AND REFORM FROM BELOW

Officials of the national government were not the only interested parties enunciating new goals and practices for national education during the Meiji period. As early as the 1870s, teachers, too, were actively organizing and promoting their own views, sometimes in opposition to national policy. Advocates of "developmental education" (*kaihatsu shugi*), for example, eschewed traditional methods of "pouring in" information and advocated cultivating innate abilities according to a child's capacities. Strongly influenced by Pestalozzian and other Western theories of child development, they put children at the center of the educational process and gave teachers the authority to guide them. They repudiated traditional methods and saw children as active agents, not passive receptacles, of knowledge. They challenged the role of the state in determining the content, methods, and texts for primary education. Centered at Tokyo Normal School, this group had its heyday from the 1870s to 1895 when changing circumstances, internal squabbling, and a powerful conservative response led the group to weaken its antistatist positions.

"REDUCING INTERFERENCE IN TEXTBOOK SELECTION" (KYŌKASHO NO SENTAKU NI WA KANSHŌ NO USUKI O NOZOMU)

For a time, in their journal *Educational Review* (*Kyōiku jiron*), the advocates of developmental education spearheaded grassroots efforts by teachers to reform Japanese education from below, often in the face of intractable, conservative administrators who favored the status quo. The antibureaucratic legacy of the movement and its contributions to the profession of teaching in Japan are apparent in later educational discourses and reform movements. Although on the whole *Educational Review* supported Mori Arinori's administration, its view of where the real authority over educational matters ought to lie is made clear in the following editorial, published on February 25, 1886.

There are probably some who believe that ministry officials are the most knowledgeable about education and who think it only natural that they should assume the responsibility for examining [textbooks]. But ministry officials are not gods. What guarantee is there that they are superior [in knowledge] to the countless educators throughout the country? And even if the knowledge [possessed by] the nation's educators [still] is shallow, does that necessarily mean it is inferior to the knowledge that ministry officials have? The same goes for prefectural officials, who are no more knowledgeable than the educators within their jurisdictions.

The qualities necessary for selecting textbooks—learning (*gakumon*) and experience—reside with those who have experience teaching ordinary students, not with the petty officials who handle the administrative affairs pertaining to general education. Why, then, should complete authority over the selection of textbooks rest with educational officials in the prefectures and with ministry bureaucrats? It is best to assemble the educators in each prefecture or each school district and let them handle it.

> ["Kyōkasho no sentaku ni wa kanshō no usuki o nozomu," trans. adapted from Lincicome, *Principle, Praxis*, p. 194]

STATE CONTROL OVER TEXTBOOKS

KIKUCHI DAIROKU AND THE TEXTBOOK SCANDAL OF 1903

Kikuchi Dairoku (1855–1917), who was the minister of education when the state took over compiling and authorizing textbooks in the early twentieth century, was a liberal Westernizer by background and predisposition. A tireless promoter of mathematics education in Japan, his 1881 elementary geometry textbook became the standard text until the end of World War II. Kikuchi was the president of Tokyo Imperial University from 1898 to 1901. Late in his term as minister of education (1901–1903), the state stepped up efforts to centralize its control of texts in response to pressures from opposition politicians and educators. Kikuchi's explanation of the textbook case is excerpted from his book, *Japanese Education*, published in English in 1909.

JAPANESE EDUCATION

In 1886, along with other reforms in educational matters generally, a regular system of textbook inspection was introduced. Textbooks in normal schools were to be determined by the minister himself, while those to be used in elementary schools and middle schools had to be chosen from among those that had been previously examined and approved by the minister of education. Textbooks in middle schools were to be chosen by the directors of respective schools with the approval of prefects. For elementary schools, the choice was to be made in each prefecture by a committee specially nominated for the purpose and composed of the director and teachers of the normal school of that prefecture, education officials of the prefectural bureau, teachers of elementary schools, and all elementary schools throughout that prefecture for a term of four years. At the end of [this time] a revision might be made if deemed advisable, but those children who began with one series of textbooks were to continue with the same series until the end of their four years' ordinary elementary course. This system of selection of textbooks continued until 1903, although during that time there were several changes in the composition of the committee, as a means of remedying abuses that arose, as stated below.

At the same time (1886), the Ministry of Education itself began compiling a set of readers and other textbooks for elementary schools, which, being far superior to those in use up to this time, raised the general standard of textbooks very much higher than what it had been up to that time. The ministry likewise had textbooks for use in normal and middle schools prepared by those specially fitted for the task by their knowledge and experience, some of which [textbooks] continue to be used even up to the present day.

It can be easily seen that once chosen for a prefecture, if textbooks for elementary schools were assured of being used for four years in all the schools in that prefecture, they would be a source of very great profit to the publishers whose books were so adopted. This naturally gave rise to very keen competition among publishers of textbooks. Although this competition was beneficial in that the textbooks were very much improved in regard to their contents, otherwise the system caused many great and serious abuses. Having secured a monopoly in prefectures, the publishers gradually lowered the quality of the paper, printing, and binding so as to make a greater profit. They often neglected to supply the necessary number of books, especially in remoter districts, to which transportation was expensive, so that children had often to be without textbooks for some time at the beginning of a session or term.

These, however, were not the only abuses, nor were they the worst. The publishers began to tamper with members of the textbook selection committees, using all sorts of illegal and immoral means. Their agents forced presents, even of money, upon them. Whether or not the members accepted them, agents reported them so to their principals, thereby damaging the reputation of members of the committees with or without cause. All sorts of influence were brought to bear upon them; every means of temptation and even of coercion was resorted to. Representations were made in both houses of the Imperial Diet that textbooks should be compiled and published by the state. How to deal with the elementary school textbook question was one of the problems with successive ministers of education. Changes were made in the composition of the committee, and several punitive clauses were inserted in the regulations, all to no effect. Rumors true or otherwise, but in either case having a very bad effect on education, continued to be spread. Finally in 1903, several of the members of committees of different prefectures and others besides were brought to trial on charges of corruption. Some were found guilty, and others were acquitted. But this event made some decisive steps necessary and facilitated the introduction of the state textbooks system, which had been regarded by the Ministry of Education as the only solution to the question, but which could not be carried out for various reasons. By the Imperial Ordinance of April 1903, however, the present regulations regarding elementary school textbooks were adopted, which I will explain briefly.

According to [the regulations], all textbooks to be used in elementary schools must be those whose copyrights belong to the Ministry of Education—that is to say, books compiled by either the official compilers in the ministry or private persons at the request of the ministry but in all cases copyrighted by the ministry so that no private persons shall have any interest in them from a business point of view. However, with the exception of the textbooks for ethics, Japanese history, geography, and the readers, the minister of education may grant permission to elementary schools to use textbooks whose copyright does not belong to the ministry but that have been examined and approved by the ministry. The above four [subjects] were exempted, as they form an essential part of the moral and civic education imparted in elementary schools, so it was thought advisable to reserve their compilation for the state. There was another reason, namely, that because of their importance and number, they were the most likely to result in abuses. At present, besides these four, textbooks on arithmetic and writing, and drawing copybooks also are exempted. . . .

If there are more than one set of textbooks to choose from, the choice is to be made by the prefect for each prefecture. Once chosen, a series of textbooks must not be changed for four years, and then only beginning with the lowest class, so that a child can complete his course with books of the same series.

As for printing and publishing those textbooks, the simplest way would have been for the ministry to undertake it. But because this could not be done under the circumstances, great pains have been taken to allow them to be published by private firms to make sure that the quality of paper, printing, and binding are kept up to the standard determined by the ministry, that the price of books shall never, under any circumstances, be above a certain fixed sum, and, last but not least, that the supply shall be regular and evenly distributed throughout the country, lest children in the remotest parts of the country be unable to obtain books at the beginning of the term, as happened frequently under the old system.

Textbooks published in accordance with these reforms began to be used at the beginning of the school year 1904/1905. Although it was with great difficulty that these changes could be made, as there was scarcely a year between the promulgation of the Imperial Ordinance and the beginning of the year, it was felt that the iron must strike while it was hot; otherwise publishers whose monopoly had been thus abolished would do their best to prevent the reform from being carried out—in fact, they did do their utmost to prevent it, but they did not succeed.

The advantages of the new books or, rather, of the new system, which became evident at once, was the great reduction in the price of books, in some cases being as great as 70 percent of the former price [that is, the price of new books was sometimes less than one-third of that of similar books under the old system], a very much superior quality of paper, printing, and binding, and the regularity of supply, notwithstanding that the transportation was in an awkward condition on account of the war [Russo-Japanese War of 1904/1905].

About the contents of those books I have spoken in my lectures on elementary education, but here I may remark that not only are the official compilers in the ministry charged with the task of continually revising them so as to improve them and keep them up to date, but teachers in normal schools and those actually using them in their classes are ordered to send any suggestions that may occur to them with the same end in view. A committee has been appointed by the minister of education specially for the purpose of a complete revision, so that in April 1908, when according to regulations new series may be introduced, there may be a thoroughly revised and improved series of textbooks ready. [This was not done, owing to objections to the reformed spelling proposed for the new readers and textbooks. A committee was appointed in May 1908 to discuss and decide on the spelling to be used in them.]

Textbooks for normal, middle, and girls' high schools remain subject to the same rules as before; that is, they must be those previously examined by textbook inspectors of the Ministry of Education and approved of by the minister. With this restriction, the choice is left to the director of each school, subject to the approval of the prefect. In certain cases, books that have not yet been examined may be used provisionally with the permission of the minister until they have been examined.

[Adapted from Kikuchi, *Japanese Education*, pp. 325–30]

THE EDUCATION OF WOMEN IN THE MEIJI PERIOD

Even though the Fundamental Code of Education (Gakusei) of 1872 called for equal education for both boys and girls, attendance at elementary schools by girls lagged behind that of boys until the end of the Meiji period. It was at the secondary level, however, where the distinctions became most apparent. Secondary schools were considered male institutions. Indeed, the Education Act of 1880 formally excluded girls from public middle schools. Accordingly, secondary and higher education for women developed primarily in the private sector, where Christian missionary schools and the efforts of individual promoters like Tsuda Umeko (1865–1929) and Naruse Jinzō (1858–1919) helped fill the void. Notwithstanding the advanced ideas of some educators, like Fukuzawa Yukichi, the official view persisted that beyond primary schooling, the purpose of female education was training women to be "good wives and wise mothers" (*ryōsai kenbo*), not independent professionals. This expression, coined by Nakamura Masanao, derived from the nineteenth-century European ideal of womanhood. When the Meiji government required each prefecture in 1898 to provide at least one high school for women, it was in order to create "good wives and wise mothers" and not to provide academic education leading to advanced study.

PROGRESS OF FEMALE EDUCATION IN MEIJI

The limitations and lingering biases among educational leaders that prevented the vast majority of Meiji women from obtaining a full education can be seen in the following, particularly the final paragraph, written by the minister of education, Kikuchi Dairoku, in 1909.

Notwithstanding the encouragement given to female education, it is only quite recently that people in general have begun to perceive its importance. In 1873, out of a total of 1,145,800 attending elementary schools; 879,200, or 77 percent, were boys; and only 266,600, or 23 percent, were girls. In 1883, the total number had increased to 3,238,000, but the ratio was 68 percent boys to 32 percent girls, showing that while education had spread pretty rapidly during those ten years, girls' education was still very much neglected. The statistics of 1893 show no very great advance either in the number (3,338,000) or in the ratio of boys to girls (68 to 32, or, if we take the ordinary elementary course only, 66 to 34). In 1906 the total number of boys and girls had increased to 5,515,000, showing the enormous strides that have been made in elementary education in the ten years after the China War; the ratio of boys to girls shows the same satisfactory progress, being 52 to 48 in the ordinary and 68 to 32 in the higher elementary course, or 56 to 44 taking the whole elementary course.

If we take secondary education into consideration, we observe the same thing. Provisions for the education of girls after they have finished the elementary course were very few, and what there were [were] not of a very high order, being confined chiefly to the teaching of reading and arithmetic, etc., only a little advanced beyond the standard of the elementary course, with special attention paid to sewing. In 1883, there were 7 girls' high schools (all public), with 350 girls. It should be remarked, however, that these were not the only provisions, for there were schools, not classed as high schools, which gave some sort of secondary education to girls. In 1893 the number had increased to 28 (of which 8 were public), with 3,020 girls. In those days there was no separate Imperial Ordinance for girls' high schools; they were merely mentioned in that on middle schools as a sort of middle school, there were no regulations even about the subjects to be taught and their standard up to 1895. The first Imperial Ordinance on Girls' High Schools, which is now in force was issued in 1899, and the revised regulations in 1901. Provisions in the ordinance and in the regulations about the establishment, closure, organization, admittance, promotion, graduation, terms, holidays, qualifications, and number of teachers, etc., are similar to those of middle schools.

There is one distinction which is worth mentioning, that is, that marks are to be given, not by examinations, but as the result of ordinary daily work, except in a few specified subjects, the reason being that girls are very emotional, and excitement caused by examinations is prejudicial to their moral and physical development; for the same reason, in many schools the order of pupils is not made known to them, but simply whether they are promoted or not. (I note that in the revised regulations issued in May 1908, examination is permitted generally, although the rule is still that marks shall be given by daily work.)

[Kikuchi, *Japanese Education*, pp. 271–73]

Chapter 39

NATIONALISM AND PAN-ASIANISM

Nationalism as an element in Japanese tradition had been evident since ancient times in many forms: for instance, in the hegemonic claims of the early Yamato state; in the writings of Kitabatake Chikafusa; in medieval Shinto; in the imperialist ambitions of Toyotomi Hideyoshi;[1] in the popular literature of the seventeenth and eighteenth centuries (especially Chikamatsu's *Coxinga*); and in the National Learning and Mito schools of the late Tokugawa period. We also encountered nationalism as a major component of the modernization movements in the Meiji period.

In this chapter, we address two new forms of nationalism that appeared with the rise of the modern, Western-style nation-state. One is the formal incorporation of Shinto as an adjunct of the new state administration, overriding the local and particularistic associations of traditional Shinto. Despite the reversal of many institutional arrangements identified with it, and the formal disestablishment of State Shinto in 1945, the issue of the state's endorsement of and the prime minister's engagement in religious practices at Shinto shrines remains a subject of great political controversy. It has roots in tradition but acquired a specific modern form at new shrines associated with State Shinto.

---

1. See de Bary et al., eds., *Sources of Japanese Tradition*, 2nd ed., vol. 1, chaps. 11, 15, 19.

The second form is cultural nationalism, which had both internationalist and imperialist forms. Here we see it as a Pan-Asianism, initially defined in Japanese terms. Although it sought common religious and aesthetic grounds with other Asian cultures, it also was exploited by Japanese colonialism. The protest against colonialism, recorded here by Yanagi Muneyoshi, who genuinely respected both the similarities and the differences of Asian cultures and courageously defended both, illustrates the point. Yanagi's view contrasts with the Japanese colonialists' establishment of Shinto shrines in Taiwan and Korea, where they had no local roots or native links.

STATE SHINTO

The term "State Shinto" describes the state's financial support of, and selective ideological appropriation of, Shinto in the modern period, from the beginning of the Meiji period (1868–1912) until it was dissolved by the Allied Occupation with the "Shinto Directive" of 1945. State Shinto encompasses diverse phenomena: the government's funding and regulation of shrines and priests, the emperor's religious roles, the state's creation of Shinto doctrines and rituals, the construction of shrines in imperial Japan's colonies, the compulsory participation in shrine rites, the teaching of Shinto myth as history, and the suppression of other religions that contradicted some aspect of Shinto. Because the term designates a political use of Shinto during the formation of the modern Japanese state until the end of World War II, State Shinto is not considered a "natural" evolution of Shinto itself. In this sense, State Shinto is not strictly a religion, and many Japanese who participated in it did so under pressure rather than from personal belief.

When seen from the perspective of secular scholars taking a critical attitude toward the prewar and wartime Japanese political regime, State Shinto appears as a blueprint for the intellectual and spiritual engineering of a loyal and obedient populace. Using State Shinto as an analytic concept to show how the state's aims were presented as sacred, and opposition as traitorous, it is possible to explain why the regime encountered so little popular resistance. This perspective bears little relation, however, to that of Shinto priests and scholars, who see Shinto's modern history as a checkered picture of erratic, always insufficient, government financing; selective political adoption of some Shinto ideas, but not all; and insufficient public support for making Shinto a suprareligious ritual order that all Japanese, regardless of religious belief, would willingly embrace. For them, Shinto's most significant influence came at the beginning of the Meiji period, with the government's establishment of the Department of Divinity (Jingikan), but soon faded with the failure of the Great Promulgation Campaign (1870–1884). Shinto's influence was not regained until the reestablishment of the Bureau of Divinity (Jingiin) in 1940, and then only partially. Shinto received strong support until 1945, but it was swept aside thereafter. From this point of view, the idea of State Shinto is largely a fiction, and its postwar treatment by the Occupation, an egregious example of victor's justice. That these two incommensurate perspectives of State Shinto cannot be reconciled even at the beginning of the twenty-first century illustrates the continuing controversy regarding questions of Shinto's modern history.

Between 1870 and 1884, Shinto bureaucrats attempted to make a state religion out of Shinto through the Great Promulgation Campaign. A small number in the National Learning movement, mainly from Hirata Atsutane's faction, held office in the early Meiji government. Bureaucrats composed an official creed loosely based on Shinto and authorized Shinto priests to create a network of preachers to spread it to the populace. But because the creed had no basis in popular religious life and because it was composed of platitudes about obeying authority and revering the emperor (who previously had played no role in popular religious life), the people found it incomprehensible and its priests ludicrous. As Fukuzawa Yukichi wrote,

> Shinto has not yet established a body of doctrine. While some identify "restorationism" (*fukko*) with Shinto, Shinto has always been the puppet of Buddhism, and for hundreds of years it has failed to show its true colors. . . . It is only an insignificant movement trying to make headway by taking advantage of the imperial house at a time of political change.[2]

As this passage shows, intellectuals regarded the Great Promulgation Campaign as a dismal failure and Shinto as a "puppet."

When the campaign failed, Shinto bureaucrats fell out of favor, and the state's support for Shinto declined. Meanwhile, the shrines were drawn into a national hierarchy and a unified annual ritual calendar centering on imperial rituals and on new, national holidays, with newly created national symbols, such as a flag and an anthem. This gave the shrines a national focus for the first time. In many cases, new deities with national or patriotic associations, but no historical connection to the shrines in question, were assigned to shrines, considerably altering the character of local religious life. The cult of the war dead was institutionalized with the construction in 1879 of the Yasukuni Shrine in Tokyo and an associated network of provincial shrines for the war dead. Dying in battle was upheld as the highest possible honor for a Japanese subject, since the emperor personally visited the Yasukuni Shrine to honor the spirits enshrined there. From about 1880 to 1905, the Shinto priests gradually organized themselves nationally to respond to what they regarded as a deplorable lack of state support. A national association of shrine priests was established in 1900.

---

2. Quoted in Hardacre, "Creating State Shintō," p. 29.

Part of the Meiji debate on Shinto concerned whether it should be considered a religion. As suggested by Fukuzawa's remarks, intellectuals regarded it as an incompletely developed religion, or a religion stunted in its intellectual development owing to centuries of being overshadowed by Buddhism. Shinto ideologues agreed that Shinto was not a religion. For them, Shinto was much more than a religion; it was "suprareligious" in that, first, it transcended the beliefs of a mortal founder and, second, it embodied the essence of the Japanese nation, its divine creation, and the divinity of imperial rule. According to this view, it was theoretically possible both to recognize the limited rights of religious freedom granted under the Meiji constitution and to require subjects to participate in shrine rites. Shrines were viewed as national facilities for the expression of patriotic sentiment, which all subjects could be expected to nurture, whatever their religious beliefs.

Japan's victory in the Russo-Japanese War in 1905 stimulated a great expansion of Shinto's influence. The dead from this war and the preceding Sino-Japanese War of 1894/1895 were enshrined at the Yasukuni Shrine, bringing many ordinary people to Tokyo to pay their respects to the spirits of their loved ones. The annexation of Korea in 1910 and the colonization of Manchuria led to a heightened mood of patriotism and to energetic shrine construction in the colonies. The state increased its support of Shinto and financed the training of shrine priests. Shrine priests of a certain rank became teachers in the public schools, where they promoted the teaching of Shinto mythology as history. Rites to revere the imperial portrait and ceremonial recitations of the Imperial Rescript on Education were established as regular school observances, along with visits to shrines by schoolchildren. The observance of shrine rites in local communities began to assume a semiobligatory character, and families were expected to keep a talisman of the Ise Shrine in their home altars for the gods (kami). As a part of Shinto's transformation to facilitate the unification of the populace, thousands of shrines were merged, in order to produce one shrine per village, with a patriotic meaning attached to the remaining shrine. There was considerable local opposition to this policy.

Popular religious life also was influenced by state suppression and intimidation using Shinto elements. Most striking was the suppression of the new religion Ōmoto in 1921 and 1935. Other religions were suppressed on charges of lèse-majesté if their doctrines conflicted with Shinto mythology. In 1932, when Christian students at Sophia University refused to pay tribute at the Yasukuni Shrine, Christianity as a whole was accused of being unpatriotic.

In 1940 the Bureau of Divinity (Jingiin) was established within the government, marking a further expansion of Shinto's influence. State appropriations for training priests and administering shrines continued at a high level. During World War II, Shinto priests served as military chaplains, and local shrine parishes were mobilized to support the war effort.

State Shinto came to an end in 1945 with the Allied Occupation's promulgation of the Shinto Directive. Remaining in force until the end of the Occupation, this directive prohibited all state support for and patronage of Shinto and ordered that all Shinto influences be removed from the public schools. All bureaucratic mechanisms for administering shrines were dismantled, and many Shinto figures were purged. The priesthood as a whole suffered an immediate loss of prestige. This document was issued "in order to free the Japanese people from direct or indirect compulsion to believe or profess to believe in a religion or cult officially designated by the state, and . . . in order to prevent a recurrence of the perversion of Shinto theory and beliefs into militaristic and ultranationalistic propaganda."[3]

Because State Shinto was not a naturally occurring religion—indeed, some of those most closely associated with it denied that Shinto was or could be a religion of personal faith—it had no sacred texts. Instead, such pronouncements as the Imperial Rescript on Education and the Imperial Rescript to Soldiers and Sailors functioned as sacred writings when they were ceremonially read before an assembly of schoolchildren or military personnel standing with bowed heads and receiving the words as divine. Similarly, when ultranationalist texts like *Fundamentals of Our National Polity* (*Kokutai no hongi*) (see chap. 42) and the myths of the *Kojiki* (*Record of Ancient Matters*) were reproduced in school textbooks as part of the national history, those nationalist sentiments and stories of the nation's creation by the gods, or the entrusting of the god's will to the first emperor, came to play a role in national life similar to the role of sacred writings in a religion.

THE UNITY OF RITES AND RULE

Central to the construction of the modern Japanese nation was the presentation of the emperor as a sacred ruler who rules through rituals for his divine ancestors. The ideal of a union of ritual and rulership was called *saisei itchi*, an idea that was expounded in various edicts. The following from 1870 is representative.

We solemnly announce: The Heavenly Deities and the Great Ancestress [Amaterasu Ōmikami] established the throne and made the succession secure. The line of Emperors in unbroken succession entered into possession thereof and handed it on. Religious ceremonies and government were one and the same (*saisei itchi*), and the innumerable subjects were united. Government and education were clear to those above, while below them the manners and

---

3. Quoted in Hardacre, *Shintō and the State*, p. 167.

customs of the people were beautiful. Beginning with the Middle Ages, however, there were sometimes seasons of decay alternating with seasons of progress. Sometimes the Way was plain, sometimes, darkened; and the period in which government and education failed to flourish was long.

Now in the cycle of fate, all things have become new. Polity and education must be made clear to the nation, and the Great Way of obedience to the gods must be promulgated. Therefore we newly appoint propagandists (the National Teachers of the Great Promulgation Campaign, *kyōdōshoku*) to proclaim this to the nation. Do you our subjects keep this commandment in mind?

[Holtom, *Modern Japan and Shintō Nationalism*, p. 6]

THE IDEA OF SHINTO AS A NATIONAL TEACHING

Texts associated with State Shinto sometimes have taken the form of memorials presented to the state. The following memorial of 1874, the period of the Great Promulgation Campaign, promotes the idea of Shinto as a National Teaching and tries to distinguish it from religion.

MEMORIAL

National Teaching (*kokkyō*) is teaching the codes of national government to the people without error. Japan is called the divine land because it is ruled by the heavenly deities' descendants, who consolidate the work of the deities. The Way of such consolidation and rule by divine descendants is called Shinto. . . . The Way of humanity in the age of the gods is nothing other than Shinto in the world of humanity. Ultimately, Shinto means a unity of government and teaching. . . . The National Teaching of the imperial house is not a religion, because religions are the theories of their founders. The National Teaching consists of the traditions of the imperial house, beginning in the age of the gods and continuing throughout history. Teaching and consolidating these traditions for the masses is inseparable from government, related as the two wheels of a cart or the wings of a bird. The National Teaching is Shinto . . . and Shinto is nothing other than the national Teaching.

[Hardacre, "The Shintō Priesthood," p. 303]

THE DIVINITY OF THE EMPEROR

The idea of the emperor's divinity was a hallmark of State Shinto. This notion inevitably followed from articles 1 and 3 of the Meiji constitution of 1889, which stated, "The Empire of Japan shall be reigned over and governed by a line of

emperors unbroken for ages eternal" and "The Emperor is sacred and inviolable." The idea of the emperor's divinity was promulgated in many other forms,
and while many Japanese rejected it, it pervasively influenced Japanese society
and culture until the emperor renounced it in 1946.

The divinity of the emperor was understood to mean, among other things,
that the emperor was above the law, a theme taken up by Itō Hirobumi in
Commentaries on the Constitution (1889).

FROM ARTICLE 3 OF THE MEIJI CONSTITUTION

The sacred Throne was established at the time when the heavens and the earth
became separated. The Emperor is Heaven-descended, divine and sacred; He
is preeminent above all his subjects. He must be reverenced and is inviolable.
He has indeed to pay due respect to the law, but the law has no power to hold
him accountable to it. Not only shall there be no irreverence for the Emperor's
person, but also He shall not be made a topic of derogatory comment nor one
of discussion.

[Holtom, *Modern Japan and Shintō Nationalism*, p. 9]

KATŌ GENCHI: "MIKADOISM"

Katō Genchi, one of the most prominent Shinto scholars of the first half of the twentieth century, identified the divinity of the emperor as the essence of Shinto, offering
the term "Mikadoism" for the idea of worshiping the emperor as a living god (*aki-
tsukami*, literally, "manifest deity").

Shinto . . . has culminated in Mikadoism or the worship of the Mikado or
Japanese Emperor as a divinity, during his lifetime as well as after his
death. . . . Herein lies even at the present day, in my opinion, the essence or
life of Shinto, inseparably connected with the national ideals of the Japanese
people. Japanese patriotism or loyalty, as you might call it, really is not simple
patriotism or mere loyalty as understood in the ordinary sense of the words, that
is, in the mere ethical sense of the term. It is more—it is the lofty self-denying
enthusiastic sentiment of the Japanese people toward their august Ruler, believed to be something divine, rendering them capable of offering up anything
and everything, all dearest to them, willingly, that is, of their own free will; of
sacrificing not only their wealth or property, but their own life itself, for the
sake of their divinely gracious sovereign. . . . All this is nothing but the actual
manifestation of the religious consciousness of the Japanese people.

[Katō, *Study of Shinto*, pp. 206–7]

THE PATRIOTIC MEANING OF SHRINES

Shrines provided the facilities to revere the emperor and to experience the associated sentiments of patriotism. The attribution of a patriotic significance to shrines and worship at shrines transformed them from religious institutions with a mainly local influence to facilities of national importance. However, since the shrines originated in limited local contexts, their objects of worship ranged from natural phenomena, to deified heroes, to local tutelary spirits. In the Meiji period, other shrines were dedicated to imperial ancestors. How to unify this diversity and thus produce a national sentiment was a problem for State Shinto. The solution was to give all the shrines a patriotic meaning through a focus on the emperor. These ideas were not merely promulgated by the state, the shrines, or the Shinto priesthood but also expounded in the popular press, as in the following essay, "A Policy for the Unification of the National Faith," which appeared in a national newspaper, the *Yomiuri shinbun*, on May 26, 1940.

"A POLICY FOR THE UNIFICATION OF THE NATIONAL FAITH"

At some of the shrines of our country, the ancestors of the Imperial Family are worshiped; at others, the spirits of loyal subjects who have contributed meritorious service to the state; and at still others, manifestations of nature, such as mountains, rivers, plants, and animals. The enshrined objects are exceedingly complex and diversified. Much thought has been given to the problem of how to coordinate and standardize these many deities so as to bring unity to the national faith. No matter how sound the historical origins or how exalted the personages of the enshrined deities may be, if the attitudes and motives of the people who worship them are impure and sordid and scattered in many directions, the unification of the national faith is hardly to be expected. On the other hand, if the attitudes and beliefs of the people who revere and worship these many deities are pure and noble and systematized, then the national faith attains spontaneous unification.

For example, if when we worship before the sanctuaries where the ancestors of the Imperial Family are enshrined, we bear in mind that the sacred spirits of the great ancestors are even now living in the mighty will of the Emperor, then mediated through these shrines, we do reverence to the Emperor's will. If, again, when we worship at the shrines dedicated to national heroes, we bear in mind that the great work of the Emperor in ruling over the state is exalted by these heroes, then in the same way, mediated through these shrines, we are revering the will of the Emperor. And if, again, when we worship before the shrines dedicated to the manifestations of the natural world such as mountains, rivers, animals, and plants, we bear in mind that these various manifestations offer up their manifold power and thereby sustain the imperial destiny, then in the same way, mediated through these shrines, we worship the will of the Emperor.

In this manner, no matter what may be the nature of the enshrined deity, if mediated through them all in a single line, the great heart of the Emperor alone is revered, then the faith of the nation is completely unified and the greater the number of deities worshiped, the more does this single faith attain depth and loftiness.

[Holtom, *Modern Japan and Shintō Nationalism*, pp. 43–44]

STATE SHINTO IN THE COLONIES OF IMPERIAL JAPAN

Shrines were constructed in all of Japan's colonies, but their use to discipline colonial subjects was the most severe in Korea. Nearly four hundred Shinto shrines were erected in Korea as part of the effort to "Japanize" Korean colonial subjects, who were required to worship at them, a stricter obligation than existed in Japan proper. Koreans were not permitted to question the idea that Shinto was not a religion, nor could religious schools be excused from shrine worship on religious grounds. In 1936 the Japanese head of the Home Office in a Korean province issued the following statement on shrines.

ON THE REFUSAL TO WORSHIP AT SHRINES (JINJA FUSANPAI NI TSUITE)

The shrines are public agencies whereby the ancestors of the Imperial Family and people who have rendered distinguished service to the state are enshrined, and where the subjects of the state may offer true reverence and commemorate their meritorious deeds forever. Thus the fundamental idea differs from that of religion. That is to say, from ancient times down to the present the shrines have been national institutions expressive of the very center and essence of our national structure. Thus they have an existence totally distinct from religion, and worship at the shrines is an act of patriotism and loyalty, the basic moral virtues of our nation.

Schools, whether or not they are founded by governmental or private agencies, and regardless of whether or not they are supported by religious groups, all without exception have their primary significance in the cultivation of national character. It is, accordingly, entirely proper that educational institutions which are charged with the important duty of developing Japanese subjects, should carry out worship at the shrines for educational reasons. It is on no

grounds permissible that school principals and teachers who unite their educational functions with those of religious propagandists, should confuse religion
and education and be deficient in an understanding of the system of laws and
ordinances which the state has established because of the requirements of national education, and oppose orders and fail to perform worship at the shrines.

In the matter of the national interpretation of the shrines and of national
necessity, all people, both from the point of view of their relation as subjects of
the Empire and from that of the education of the people of the nation, should
yield obedience. Such things as the advocacy of the individualistic and arbitrary
interpretation that the shrines are religious in nature, and in particular the
opposition to orders concerning educational administration, are not to be permitted.

[Holtom, *Modern Japan and Shintō Nationalism*, p. 167]

THE EMPEROR'S RENUNCIATION OF HIS DIVINITY

Emperor Hirohito renounced the idea of his divinity in a rescript on January 1, 1946,
his New Year greeting to the people for that year. This action probably had more
influence on public opinion than did the Shinto Directive, which brought State
Shinto to an end.

The devastation of war inflicted upon our cities, the miseries of the destitute,
the stagnation of trade, shortage of food, and the great and growing number
of the unemployed are indeed heart-rending. But if the nation is firmly united
in its resolve to face the present ordeal and to seek civilization consistently in
peace, a bright future will undoubtedly be ours, not only for our country, but
for the whole humanity.

Love of the family and love of the country are especially strong in this country. With more of this devotion should we now work toward love of mankind.

We feel deeply concerned to note that consequent upon the protracted war
which ended in our defeat, our people are liable to grow restless and to fall into
the Slough of Despond. Radical tendencies in excess are gradually spreading
and the sense of morality tends to lose its hold on the people, with the result
that there are signs of confusion of thoughts.

We stand by the people and We wish always to share with them in their
moments of joys and sorrows. The ties between Us and Our people have always
stood upon mutual trust and affection. They do not depend upon mere legends
and myths. They are not predicated on the false conception that the Emperor
is divine (*akitsu mikami*) and that the Japanese people are superior to other
races and fated to rule the world.

[Woodward, *The Allied Occupation of Japan*, p. 316]

TOKUTOMI SOHŌ: A JAPANESE NATIONALIST'S VIEW OF THE WEST AND ASIA

Few Japanese in the modern period reflected more clearly the changing attitudes toward the West and Asia than the historian, journalist, and publicist Tokutomi Sohō (or Iichirō). Born in 1863, five years before the Meiji Restoration, and dying in 1957, after Japan's defeat in the Pacific War, Tokutomi had a career as a social commentator and spokesman for popular and national ideals that spanned the entire century of Japan's emergence as a modern state. Intellectually, he also traversed a wide expanse from an early fascination with popular democracy and Western-oriented democratic reforms, to support for the centralized imperial state and imperialistic expansion, and, in his later years, to a form of ultranationalistic chauvinism that included strong support for Japan's mission to rid Asia of Western influence and create a "new order" for all Asians under Japanese leadership.

Born the son of a village headman and raised in a typical "rich peasant" (*gōnō*) household, Tokutomi was initially trained in the Chinese classics and exposed to the reform ideas of Yokoi Shōnan. After the Restoration, he attended the Kumamoto School for Western Learning run by Captain L. L. Janes and, for a short time, was converted to Christianity. In the mid-1870s, Tokutomi joined other members of the Kumamoto Band and pursued his education at Dōshisha College in Kyoto. Although Tokutomi abandoned Christianity and left Dōshisha in 1880, he remained strongly influenced by Western liberal ideas. In the 1880s, he established himself as both a teacher and one of Japan's most important journalists and publishers. His early writings are of particular interest because they combine ideas rooted in his well-to-do peasant background with elements of democratic reformism that fueled the Freedom and People's Rights movement. Tokutomi labeled his version of popular democracy *heiminshugi* (commonerism or populism). Borrowing the ideas of Herbert Spencer, Tokutomi argued that the process of evolution for all nations moved through similar stages. Influenced by Spencer and the Manchester school, he believed that commercial economic development would replace the military, or feudal, stage. Commercial, or financial, power would replace military force. Indeed, he thought that this is what had taken place in the late Tokugawa period. At the same time, like many of his compatriots, he was preoccupied with the question of how Japan could become modern, wealthy, and strong. For the early Tokutomi (no doubt under the influence of Yokoi Shōnan), the quest for wealth and power was based less on demonstrating military might than on breaking the fetters of the past and releasing the energies of the younger generation, advancing commercial and industrial output, and supporting trade. By the late 1890s, Tokutomi had abandoned his earlier populist ideas in favor of an expanding imperial state, military power, and colonialism. Events such as the Triple Intervention of 1895 and the discrimination against Japanese in the United States (California Alien Land Acts, 1913 and 1920) played significant roles in his "transformation." Indeed, by the 1920s and 1930s, Tokutomi had become increasingly anti-Western and believed, as his support of the Pacific War revealed, that Japan should expel the West from Asia. Tokutomi was arrested as a class-A war criminal by the Occupation in 1945 and spent two years under house arrest. Despite being purged from public life, he remained stubbornly independent and refused to retract any of the ideas and ideals he had espoused for modern Japan.

THE EARLY MEIJI VISION

Tokutomi Sohō's influence on what Kenneth B. Pyle calls "the new generation" of Meiji Japan was immense. In 1886 he published his first best-seller, *The Future Japan* (*Shōrai no Nihon*), and in 1887 another immensely popular book, *Youth of New Japan* (*Shin Nihon no seinen*). Also in 1887, when he was just twenty-four, he founded the Min'yūsha (Society of the People's Friends). For the next decade, he published and edited the Meiji period's most significant journal, *Kokumin no tomo* (*The Nation's Friend*). It was through another book, also entitled *The Nation's Friend* (*Kokumin no tomo*), and the *Kokumin shinbun*, a newspaper he founded in 1890, that Tokutomi introduced young Japanese to Western political and economic ideas, particularly those of Herbert Spencer, John Stuart Mill, and Jean-Jacques Rousseau as well as Richard Cobden, John Bright, and the Manchester school. The early Tokutomi wanted to place Japan in world history and to give the youthful generation a sense of where Japan was going. Like other early Meiji thinkers, such as Fukuzawa Yukichi, he saw the break with the past—that is, the Meiji Restoration—as a liberating event.

The present transformation is a progressive and not a retrogressive one. The field on which we now do battle is not the last, but the first; the present departure is not one of despair but of hope. . . . Today, if the rotted and withered old trees were to be blown down in a typhoon, there would still remain young shoots which with proper nurture would soon rise loftily to the heavens. This age is one of hope. For this reason we should call this not the Transformation of Japan but rather, more appropriately, the Resurrection of Japan. For the old Japan has already died, and what exists in the present day is the new Japan. The question remains: what of Japan's future?

[Tokutomi, *Shōrai no Nihon*; Kōsaka, ed., and Abosch, trans.,
Japanese Thought in the Meiji Era, p. 202]

ON WEALTH AND POWER

Sharing the belief expressed in the Charter Oath that Japan had to rid itself of the "evil customs of the past," Tokutomi urged the youth of the new Japan to reject Japan's feudal past, which he identified with a passing military age, and move ahead on the course of evolutionary progress that would lead to commercial development and economic growth. Revealing his confidence in the power of economic change and the shift in power relations that stemmed from it, he observed the following about the Restoration.

Peace was the servant of wealth; wealth progressed, indeed, made extraordinary progress. This wealth, however, was all outside the compass of the feudal warrior class. Peace not only contributed to the "production of wealth," it brought the "joys of wealth." And not these alone, but also the "worship of wealth." There- fore, the social structure, which was centered on the feudal samurai, could not but tend to focus on the attainment of wealth. . . . Conditions of society being like this, even without the irruption of the problems of foreign affairs, revolution could not have been avoided.

[Tokutomi, *Shōrai no Nihon*; Kōsaka, ed., and Abosch, trans.,
Japanese Thought in the Meiji Era, p. 204]

YOUTH AND REVOLUTION

While the early Tokutomi regarded the Meiji Restoration as a revolution, he also believed that it was an incomplete revolution that had to be completed by the young people of Meiji Japan. In the 1880s, Tokutomi was a fervent advocate of a "second revolution." For him, all great historical changes were spurred by clashes between classes and generations.

Everybody knows passively the power of wealth; nobody reflects on the force of the desire for wealth. Everybody knows the force of power; nobody reflects on the force of the lust for power. To have experience is to have power, but in not having experience there is also power. Those without experience . . . can act impulsively, without reflecting. Rank is a source of power, not to have rank is also a source of power. . . . At the same time that we admit the importance of wealth, strength, learning, authority, in political affairs, we must also admit that there are other important resources. This is what is meant by the phrase "to be inexhaustible through possessing nothing." This quality of inexhaustible re- sources is limited to youth alone. Youth is naturally endowed with populist, reforming, and progressive tendencies. It is always this class that is drawn upon when it becomes necessary to cleanse society of corruption.

[Tokutomi, *Shōrai no Nihon*; Kōsaka, ed., and Abosch, trans.,
Japanese Thought in the Meiji Era, p. 206]

ON ECONOMIC VERSUS MILITARY POWER

The early Tokutomi was a fervent believer in the power of democracy and the emergence of a middle class that he identified with men like his father and other "rural gentlemen," or *inaka shinshi*, who possessed a bourgeois consciousness. Indeed, in his early years, as John D. Pierson noted, Tokutomi thought that "the *inaka shinshi* were gradually replacing the old warrior aristocracy as the dominant class, as the controlling social and political force in the new society."[4] Tokutomi was convinced that the first victory for democracy had occurred when military force was replaced by the rule of wealth. At the same time, he possessed a social consciousness that saw this change as presenting new challenges. It is no accident that later socialists, such as Kōtoku Shūsui and Ishikawa Sanshirō, saw in the early Tokutomi and the Min'yūsha the origins of their movement.

The limiting of military power by wealth constitutes the first victory for democracy in the world. To limit wealth by labor would be the second victory for democracy in the world. The first victory has already been partially attained in the nineteenth century. Though there are not too many signs as yet of the second victory, it is certain that these will appear in the future.

What are the great societal changes that we can speak of for the period comprising the end of the nineteenth and the beginning of the twentieth centuries? . . . The limiting of military power by wealth following the emergence of the middle-classes which developed commerce and industry.

I used the word *limiting*, not *destruction*. . . . When we think of a country like Russia, proud of her military power, yet, humbly floating loans from republican France, or a country like England, her ironclads all over the world, yet having her power of taxation vested in the Lower House of Parliament, may we not conclude that wealth limits military power? . . . Similarly wealth will be limited by labor. The present power of wealth penetrates to the very marrow of society. Can this power be easily destroyed? To destroy this is never the way to foster the progress of society. Therefore, I speak of limiting, not destroying. What does limiting mean in this regard? It means for the power of labor to transcend the power of wealth. And though wealth now has power, the power of labor will be triumphant. Where does the power of labor come from? From the lower classes, from those who earn their bread by the sweat of their brows.

[Tokutomi, *Shōrai no Nihon*; Kōsaka, ed., and Abosch, trans.,
Japanese Thought in the Meiji Era, p. 204]

ADVOCATE OF FREEDOM AND PEOPLE'S RIGHTS

Given Tokutomi's subsequent support for the ideology of the imperial state and ultra-nationalism, it is interesting to read the early Tokutomi on the importance of freedom

---

4. Pierson, *Tokutomi Sohō*, p. 192.

and the rights of free expression. Teaching at the Ōe gijuku, his school in Kumamoto, in the early 1880s, Tokutomi fiercely resisted the conservative inclinations of the Ministry of Education to control all aspects of education, including the choice of appropriate textbooks, arguing that the highest degree of freedom was needed to produce the modern state and productive citizens. In the following passage from Tokutomi's book *Freedom, Morality, and Confucianism* (*Jiyū dōtoku oyobi jukyōshugi*), we can also see the search for economic rights and freedoms that were essential to the interests of the rural elite in the Restoration.

That Westerners, with [their] wealth, literature, military, science, and legal systems, predominate in the universe and are the leaders of the world is because Western people have put freedom into practice. That Orientals are losing their rights to independence, are regarded as barbarians, are ridiculed, hang their heads in but one corner of the earth . . . and are cowed into silence is because Oriental people have neglected freedom.

If we make our system a free system, reform the economy . . . secure the rights of the people, emancipate all occupations, leaving this to the free [choice of the] people, eliminate all traces of [state] protectionism and interventionism, deepen our harbors, reduce our tariffs, there is absolutely no doubt but that our nation's industries will prosper. . . . At once we will become like a great wharf in the Pacific, a great city of the Orient, a wholesaler of international commerce and the sun will be darkened by the smoke rising from thousands of smokestacks. . . . And all this will come just because there is this precious freedom.

I say, give [us] freedom. Give [the people] freedom quickly. Then the nation will instantly prosper. . . . And morality will be encouraged. . . . I am not satisfied with gaining just political liberties. I want to protect our civil liberties, protect our personages and protect our rights. . . . Proceeding from this we must sweep away the bad habits and evil practices of [the feudal] society, eliminate and level all artificial class distinctions, eliminate the oppression of prejudice, making the whole society replete with the atmosphere of freedom. And proceeding even farther, we must cut the chains that bind the minds of the people and develop human intellect, making all the people [really] free. . . . The ultimate objective of mankind is to become civilized. . . . Once having received freedom we must then use it, and I wish, encouraged by this freedom, to travel the route to civilization.

[Tokutomi, *Jiyū dōtoku oyobi jukyōshugi*; Pierson, *Tokutomi Sohō*, p. 114]

NATIONALISM

Even though the early Tokutomi espoused liberal ideals, he also was a nationalist. The preservation of national sovereignty was his ultimate goal. Believing that the nineteenth century demonstrated that an age of peace and democracy was at hand, Tokutomi rejected military expansion in *The Future Japan* in favor of pacifism, but he retained certain doubts about the degree to which the forces of peace had the upper hand against military might. The West, he admitted, still approached Asia with force.

The present-day world is one in which civilized people tyrannically destroy primitive people. . . . The European countries stand at the very pinnacle of violence and base themselves on the doctrine of force. . . . India, alas, has been destroyed, Annam has been destroyed, Burma will be next. The remaining countries will be independent in name only. . . . What is the outlook for Persia? For China? Korea? And even Japan? The future will be extremely critical. This, I feel, is unbearable.

[Tokutomi, *Shōrai no Nihon*; Kōsaka, ed., and Abosch, trans.,
Japanese Thought in the Meiji Era, p. 209]

SUPPORTING THE IMPERIAL STATE AND MILITARY EXPANSION

In the late 1890s, Tokutomi underwent a major transformation, which was shaped by two forces. One was the demise of the middle class of country gentlemen that he had idealized in his early writings. With the Matsukata deflation, the majority of these progressively inclined rural leaders, who had been moving away from agriculture, were once again transformed into land-lords. Moreover, they now headed an unruly and unhappy countryside in which the majority of Japan's independent farmers had been turned into ten-ants. In short, the very class that had carried him to prominence and that he felt would replace Japan's samurai aristocracy as the leaders of the country was now in trouble. To protect itself, it needed the police and military power of the former samurai who controlled the center. The very men who had struggled against the central government through the Freedom and People's Rights movement now had decided to join the center in order to preserve domestic stability. Thus by the middle of the 1890s, not only was the Free-dom and People's Rights movement dead, but the progressive men for whom Tokutomi spoke had turned conservative. He was not alone in sensing this change, which also influenced Fukuzawa Yukichi, the other leading voice for this class. Both men were influenced as well by the wave of aggressive Western imperial expansion that took place in the late 1890s, which they felt threatened Japan. Tokutomi's shift to statism, his support for Japanese mili-tary expansion, and his increasingly nationalistic vision should be seen in this context.

REJOICING OVER VICTORY IN THE SINO-JAPANESE WAR

The Sino-Japanese War of 1894/1895 strongly influenced Tokutomi. Shortly after Japan's victory he rejoiced.

We are no longer ashamed to stand before the world as Japanese. . . . The name "Japanese," like the names Satsuma and Chōshū after the Boshin [Restoration] War, like the name of Wellington after Waterloo, now signifies honor, glory, courage, triumph, and victory. Before we did not know ourselves, and the world did not yet know us. But now that we have tested our strength, we know ourselves and we are known by the world. Moreover, we know that we are known by the world!

[Hayakawa, *Tokutomi Sohō*, p. 176; Pierson, *Tokutomi Sohō*, p. 236]

RESENTMENT RESULTING FROM THE TRIPLE INTERVENTION

At the time of the Triple Intervention in 1895, Tokutomi was on the Liaodong Peninsula, the territory that Japan had taken from China and that France, Germany, and Russia had forced it to return. Like many Japanese, the joy of victory suddenly soured for him when Japan was forced to give in to Western demands. He stated that he was "vexed beyond tears" and quickly returned to Japan, picking up a handful of gravel from the beach at Port Arthur, which he tied in his handkerchief. For years, he kept this gravel in a box on his desk as a reminder of Japan's humiliation. In 1896 he expressed his views on Japan's new Asian mission, which emerged from the hostility and resentment he now felt for the West.

The countries of the Far East falling prey to the great powers of Europe is something that our nation will not stand for. East Asia becoming a mire of disorder is something that our nation will not tolerate. We have a duty to radiate the light of civilization beyond our shores and bring the benefits of civilization to our neighbors. We have the duty to guide backward countries to the point of being able to govern themselves. We have the duty to maintain peace in East Asia for this purpose. As a man has his calling, so too does a nation have its mission.

[Tokutomi, "Jishuteki gaikō no igi," *Kokumin no tomo*, February 8, 1896; Pierson, *Tokutomi Sohō*, p. 241]

SUPPORT FOR THE IMPERIAL STATE, CRITICISM OF TAISHŌ SOCIETY

Tokutomi's nationalism expanded in the first decades of the twentieth century. He was now firmly committed to the Japanese empire under military domination as well as critical of the self-indulgence of the Taishō period (1912–1926).

In the Taishō period [the nation] lost its ideals and became intoxicated only with the present. . . . Those who did not succumb to this tendency fell into foreign ways and heretical ideologies [becoming] radical socialists, communists, and bolsheviks. . . . A world in which man has no ideals other than materialistic avarice is a world of mammonism. A world of mammonism is a world of lust and hedonism. People say the world of politics is degenerate. But why is it degenerate? Is it not ultimately because ideals have been lost? People say the world of bureaucrats is degenerate. And why is it degenerate: is it not ultimately because ideals have been lost? People say the society at large is degenerate. Why is it degenerate? Is it not ultimately because of the loss of ideals? The loss of ideals is no small matter; it emasculates both man and society alike. . . . Those of our people who have not lost the spirit of being Japanese and who are not leading empty, vain lives are really rare!

[Tokutomi, *Shōwa ishin ron*, pp. 30–31; Pierson, *Tokutomi Sohō*, p. 356]

WORSHIP OF THE IMPERIAL HOUSE

Tokutomi tried to counter Taishō hedonism by a new spiritual revolution focusing on loyalty to the emperor. In 1927 he wrote the following in his call for a new "Shōwa Restoration."

Nothing is more urgent for the long-term future of Imperial Japan than cultivating in the hearts of the people the idea of loyalty to the Imperial House as being central to all things. . . . There must be encouragement of worship of the Imperial House and the nurturing of a spirit of loyalty to the sovereign and love of the country.

[Tokutomi, *Shōwa ishin ron*, p. 51; Pierson, *Tokutomi Sohō*, p. 357]

REJECTING THE WEST AND WITHDRAWING FROM THE
LEAGUE OF NATIONS

As the Triple Intervention showed, Tokutomi was often unhappy with Western responses to Japanese accomplishments. These concerns expanded in the 1920s and 1930s as Tokutomi began viewing the West in increasingly critical terms. He also felt that Europeans and Americans were hypocritical and often attacked Japan for acts they themselves engaged in. By the 1930s, Tokutomi had come full circle and rejected the form of Westernism that he had advocated in the early Meiji years. Instead, he now strongly backed what he called the "Imperial Way," which included Japan's expansion on the Asian continent. When Japan withdrew from the League of Nations in 1933, Tokutomi wrote the following in a newspaper article.

We are by no means withdrawing from the League simply because there is no purpose to our continued membership. We withdraw to proclaim our beliefs to the world. We withdraw in order to protest the tyranny of the League of Nations. . . . By our withdrawal from the League we give the wayward gentlemen of Europe and America an object lesson. That is, we awaken them to the existence in Asia also of a strong-willed people. Moreover, we promote the awareness among the races of Asia that, like Asian peoples, Westerners are also human [and therefore vulnerable]. Our withdrawal is therefore not just a matter of fulfilling our own aspirations, but it teaches Europeans and Americans that the world is not a place for them to monopolize, and it also shows Asians that they can be free from domination by Europeans and Americans. Our aims are . . . self-government for Asia, autonomy for Asia.

[Tokutomi, in *Ōsaka mainichi shinbun*, February 25, 1933; Pierson, *Tokutomi Sohō*, p. 371]

JUSTIFICATION FOR THE CHINA WAR

By the outbreak of the China War in 1937, Tokutomi had added anti-Communism to Japan's role in Asia, an approach to the China conflict that was shared by other Japanese intellectuals.

It is a serious mistake to view this war as a fight between Japan and China. Japan has not from the beginning regarded China as the enemy; and Japan holds no malice toward China. . . . Japan's concern with regard to China is not focused on China but upon the Soviet Union, which stands behind China. The Soviet Union is now attempting to expand and waits for an opportunity to eliminate Japanese influence from Manchuria. The influence of the Soviet Union encompasses nearly 70 percent of the Asian continent . . . and the fact is that the Soviet Union is now attempting to bring China and Manchuria into its fold. Both China and Manchuria are now very much threatened. Manchuria is a nation inseparably united with Japan and cannot be allowed to be touched by the Soviet Union. . . . If China should come under Soviet influence, it would be a serious threat to our country. . . . Our national policy is to promote the Imperial Way in Asia. . . . If communism grows in China, and China comes under the control of the Comintern, then Japan's position in Asia will be lost . . . and Japan itself will be endangered. Given this situation, it is the natural duty of Japan to use all of its strength, material and spiritual, to save China from communism, not only for the sake of China but for the defense of Japan itself. For these reasons, we regard this war not as a war between Japan and China but as a war against the Comintern . . . a war with communism.

[Tokutomi, *Senji gaigen*, pp. 10–12; Pierson, *Tokutomi Sohō*, p. 372]

AMERICAN–JAPANESE RELATIONS IN 1941

On the eve of the outbreak of hostilities between Japan and the United States, Tokutomi presented what he thought was the Japanese case for a righteous war.

America, which eighty-eight years ago pressured us into opening the country with its warships and cannon, is now blockading us with the ABCD encirclement, abrogation of the commercial treaty, freezing of assets, and other such policies. . . . If this process continues along its present course, we can only suffer the grief of being contained at the mercy of America. Japan's goodwill toward America has been exhausted. Japan has exhausted every possible means of working to achieve an understanding with America. . . . America is tightening the knot of encirclement and strangling us day by day. . . . I give but one example: Oil is essential to our life. If we do not have oil, we cannot live for even a day. . . . The policy [of an oil embargo] is clearly a hostile act against Japan! Even worse is the instance of blockading the shipment of Dutch East Indies oil to us. . . . Patience has its limits. . . . Japan cannot sit idly by and be resigned to the fate of confinement while being strangled to death. It is entirely appropriate for us as a nation to act freely in order to live. No matter how easygoing the Japanese may be, we are not ones to sit by meekly and stab our backs with the left hand while suffocating ourselves with the right hand. Japanese people! Strengthen your resolve for self-defense quickly!

> [Tokutomi, in *Ōsaka mainichi shinbun*, November 4, 1941;
> Pierson, *Tokutomi Sohō*, p. 375]

COMMENTS ON THE IMPERIAL RESCRIPT FOR WAR WITH GREAT BRITAIN AND THE UNITED STATES

Japan declared war on the United States and Great Britain by means of an imperial rescript that went point by point through Japan's grievances and argued that it had no alternative but to go to war. Shortly after this official proclamation, Tokutomi wrote an extensive commentary on the rescript. Exhorting Japan to become the Leader and Light of Asia, Tokutomi reveals the degree to which he now espoused the ideology of imperial Japan and the sacred imperial institution. As Tokutomi saw it, the war was clearly a moral campaign waged by the "moral" Japanese against the "immoral" West.

The Basis of the Imperial Way

The virtue of sincerity is represented by the Mirror, the virtue of love is represented by the Jewels, and the virtue of intelligence is represented by the Sword. . . . Then, it is not wrong to liken the Three Sacred Treasures to the three virtues of intelligence, love, and courage by saying that the Mirror represents the intelligence which reflects everything, the Jewel, the love which embraces everything, and the Sword the courage which judges between justice and injustice, honesty and dishonesty.

In any case, the basis of the Imperial Way lies in truth, in sincerity, and in justice. Its range is wide and there is nothing it does not embrace. It expels evil, subjugates injustice, absolutely maintains the tenets of justice, and itself occupies a position which can never be violated. The August virtue of the divine imperial lineage has not a single instance when it did not arise from these three virtues. In other words, they form the national character of Nippon, and at the same time the national trait of the people of Nippon. Combining them all, we call it the Imperial Way.

The phrase "the three virtues of intelligence, love, and courage" may sound very much like a common ethical teaching, but when considered realistically, it gives us the reason why our country, under whatever circumstances, has never resorted to arms for the sake of arms alone.

Three Qualifications of the Leader of Greater East Asia

Now that we have risen up in arms, we must accomplish our aim to the last. Herein lies the core of our theory. In Nippon resides a destiny to become the Light of Greater East Asia and to become ultimately the Light of the World. However, in order to become the Light of Greater East Asia, we must have three qualifications. The first is, as mentioned previously, strength. In other words, we must expel Anglo-Saxon influence from East Asia with our strength.

To speak the truth, the various races of east Asia look upon the British and Americans as superior to the Nippon race. They look upon Britain and the United States as more powerful nations than Nippon. Therefore, we must show our real strength before all our fellow-races of East Asia. We must show them an object lesson. It is not a lesson in words. It should be a lesson in facts.

In other words, before we can expel the Anglo-Saxons and make them remove all their traces from East Asia, we must annihilate them. In this way only will the various fellow-races of Greater East Asia look upon us as their leader. I believe that the lesson which we must first show to our fellow-races in Greater East Asia is this lesson of cold reality.

The second qualification is benevolence. Nippon must develop the various resources of East Asia and distribute them fairly to all the races within the East Asia Co-Prosperity Sphere to make them share in the benefits. In other words, Nippon should not monopolize the benefits, but should distribute them for the mutual prosperity of Greater East Asia.

We must show to the races of East Asia that the order, tranquillity, peace, happiness, and contentment of East Asia can be gained only by eradicating the evil precedent of the encroachment and extortion of the Anglo-Saxons in East Asia, by effecting the real aim of the co-prosperity of East Asia, and making Nippon the leader of East Asia.

The third qualification is virtue. East Asia embraces various races. Its religions are different. Moreover, there has practically been no occasion when these have mutually united to work for a combined aim. It was the favorite policy of the Anglo-Saxons to make the various races of East Asia compete and fight each other and make them mutually small and powerless. We must, therefore, console them, bring friendship among them, and make them all live in peace with a boundlessly embracing virtue.

In short, the first is the Grace of the Sacred Sword, the second, the Grace of the Sacred Mirror, and the third, the Grace of the Sacred Jewels. If we should express it in other words, we must have courage, knowledge and benevolence. If Nippon should lack even one of the above three, it will not be able to become the Light of Asia.

[IMTFE, International Prosecution Section, document 2402B, exhibit 1336 (Draft of Basic Plan for Establishment of Greater East Asia Co-Prosperity Sphere)]

ANALYZING DEFEAT

With the country he loved in ruins and personally under house arrest for his part in supporting the war, Tokutomi reexamined modern Japan's development.

All the moves of the Japanese Government, the people, or rather the entire nation since the Meiji Restoration were motivated primarily by self-survival. That is, the Japanese people began moving out of their country in search of livelihood—food and clothing. The second motive was self-defense. These moves were aimed at achieving complete independence, maintaining her prestige as an independent country, and safe-guarding such independence from foreign influences. . . . A third motive was self-respect, that is, a protest as a result of an explosion of dissatisfaction and discontentment with the unfair treatment the World Powers accorded Japan as an independent state. . . .

Suppose that the moves of Japan had been tainted with imperialism, who were they that taught the Japanese what imperialism is? They were the World Powers, I do not hesitate to say so openly. The history of Japan from the latter half of the nineteenth century to the early half of the twentieth century was not of her own [making] but closely interwoven with that of the world. It shows that Japan was constantly imitating what the senior powers had done, though she might have been clumsy in playing her part compared with the other powers. There is a Japanese saying, "People ruin themselves by trying to ape their betters." This saying may be applied to Japan, with this reservation that what the "ruined people" aped was not of their invention but of "their betters." The World Powers, if I may compare them to cormorants, dived into the water and caught fishes big and small. Japan followed suit but failed to catch any fish and drowned herself. The folly of the Japanese is indeed unsurpassed.

[Defense document 632, pp. 40–41; Pierson, *Tokutomi Sohō*, pp. 386–87]

FINAL ASSESSMENT

Tokutomi's final assessment was blunt and direct and was as much a judgment of himself as of his fellow Japanese.

If the Japanese are to be blamed, they should be for their misjudgment of China, the Anglo-American Powers, the U.S.S.R., Germany, Italy, and most of all Japan herself. The Japanese, as Sunzi said, "knew neither others nor themselves." This is the cause of the present disaster. Thus the Japanese have nobody to blame but themselves.

[Defense document 632, p. 42; Pierson, *Tokutomi Sohō*, p. 387]

OKAKURA KAKUZŌ: AESTHETIC PAN-ASIANISM

Okakura Kakuzō (1862–1913), later known as Tenshin, was the son of an Echizen samurai turned merchant in the treaty port of Yokohama. There, as a youth, Okakura profited from an excellent Western-style education which he later used to promote Japanese art, first as the distinctive expression of a Japanese spiritual culture and then as the quintessence as well as synthesis of Asian art as a whole—thus qualifying Japan to serve as the leader of Asia in resisting Western military and cultural imperialism.

Some of Okakura's basic ideas came from his teacher in the school that became Tokyo Imperial University, Ernest Fenollosa, who championed traditional Japanese art and its spiritual qualities over decadent Western art and the crass materialism of the modern West. In this, both Okakura and Fenollosa reacted against the "wholesale" Westernization of Japan in the 1870s and 1880s. Increasingly, however, with the rising tide of nationalism following the Sino-Japanese (1894/1895) and Russo-Japanese (1904/1905) Wars, Okakura's celebration of Japanese cultural superiority and its civilizing mission to the world lent itself to the service of a Pan-Asianism that, whether he recognized it or not, also served a growing Japanese imperialism claiming to defend Asia against the West.

Okakura's professional career was a checkered one, complicated by serious personal problems—drink, sex, and money—that led him to escape abroad and exploit his eloquence in English. In India, he found in Rabindranath Tagore a natural ally for his Pan-Asian views, and in America, as a curator at the Museum of Fine Arts in Boston, he gained a strong following among American collectors and art critics.

After returning from India in 1902, Okakura completed *The Ideals of the East, with Special Reference to the Art of Japan*, which opens with the aphorism "Asia is one." This book was followed by three others in English. *The Awakening of Japan* (1904, coinciding with the Russo-Japanese War) stresses the need for the Japanese to overcome their passivity and take a more active lead in defending Asia from Western militarism. *The Book of Tea* (1906) celebrates the tea ceremony and the "Zen" aesthetic of fifteenth-century Muromachi Japan and enjoyed a great vogue in the West. The third book, *The Awakening of the East*, originally written in 1902, was published posthumously in 1938.

As a curator at the Museum of Fine Arts from 1910 to his death in 1913, Okakura helped the museum acquire a number of important artworks and propagated a new myth of Asia that meshed comfortably with the romanticized view of Eastern culture that was becoming prevalent in Europe and America at the time, emphasizing the spiritual and peaceful nature of Asia, especially of Japan, which he portrayed as among all Asian nations the one most in tune with the noble and refined spirit of the East. Although Okakura did not live to witness the two world wars, his thinking foreshadowed some of the imperialistic rhetoric of wartime Japan. The concept of the Greater East Asia Co-Prosperity Sphere, which served to legitimize Japan's expansionism, was also predicated on the idea that "Asia is one," with Japan as its destined leader.

THE IDEALS OF THE EAST

In fifteen chapters, Okakura Kakuzō offers a chronological account of Japanese art history from antiquity to the Meiji period. His aim was not so much to explain stylistic developments as to elevate the status of Japanese art and, with it, that of the Japanese nation. In the late nineteenth and early twentieth centuries, many Westerners saw Japanese art as no more than pretty objects, products of craft and industry and devoid of higher meaning. Okakura tried to change this view by constructing an elaborate network of geographical, religious, and historical relationships. In chapter 1, he iden-tifies Japan as part of a much larger geocultural sphere that includes China, India, Persia, and other regions in Asia. He also claims it as the repository of all the best traditions born of this sphere. The book is replete with characterizations of Japan that emphasize its unique superiority. Indeed, he more than matches the condescending tone of some Western "Orientalists" in this regard.

Japan Is a Museum of Asiatic Civilization

Asia is one. The Himalayas divide, only to accentuate, two mighty civilizations, the Chinese with its communism of Confucius, and the Indian with its indi-vidualism of the Vedas. But not even the snowy barriers can interrupt for one moment that broad expanse of love for the Ultimate and the Universal, which is the common thought-inheritance of every Asiatic race, enabling them to produce all the great religions of the world, and distinguishing them from those maritime peoples of the Mediterranean and the Baltic, who love to dwell on the Particular, and to search out the Means, not the end, of life. . . .

For if Asia be one, it is also true that the Asiatic races form a single mighty web. We forget, in an age of classification, that types are after all but shining points of distinctness in an ocean of approximations, false gods deliberately set up to be worshiped, for the sake of mental convenience, but having no more ultimate or mutually exclusive validity than the separate existence of two interchangeable sciences. If the history of Delhi represents the Tartar's imposition of himself upon a Mohammedan world, it must also be remembered that the story of Baghdad and her great Saracenic culture is equally significant of the power of Semitic peoples to demonstrate Chinese, as well as Persian, civilization and art, in the face of the Frankish nations of the Mediterranean coast. Arab chivalry, Persian poetry, Chinese ethics, and Indian thought, all speak of a single Asiatic peace, in which there grew up a common life, bearing in different regions different characteristic blossoms, but nowhere capable of a hard and fast dividing-line. Islam itself may be described as Confucianism on horseback, sword in hand. For it is quite possible to distinguish, in the hoary communism of the Yellow Valley, the traces of a purely pastoral element, such as we see abstracted and self-realized in the Mussulman races.

Or, to turn again to eastern Asia from the West, Buddhism—that great ocean of idealism, in which merge all the river-systems of Eastern Asiatic thought—is colored not only with the pure water of the Ganges, for the Tartaric nations that joined it made their genius also tributary, bringing new symbolism, new organization, new powers of devotion, to add to the treasures of faith.

It has been, however, the great privilege of Japan to realize this unity-in-complexity with a special clearness. The Indo-Tartaric blood of this race was in itself a heritage which qualified it to imbibe from the two sources, and so mirror the whole of Asiatic consciousness. The unique blessing of unbroken sovereignty, the proud self-reliance of an unconquered race, and the insular isolation which protected ancestral ideas and instincts at the cost of expansion, made Japan the real repository of the trust of Asiatic thought and culture. Dynastic upheavals, the inroads of Tartar horsemen, the carnage and devastation of furious mobs—all these things, sweeping over her again and again, have left to China no landmarks, save her literature and her ruins, to recall the glory of the Tang emperors or the refinement of Song society.

The grandeur of Asoka[5]—the ideal type of Asiatic monarch, whose edicts dictated terms to the sovereigns of Antioch and Alexandria—is almost forgotten among the crumbling stones of Bharhut[6] and Buddha Gaya.[7] The jeweled court of Vikramaditya is but a lost dream, which even the poetry of Kalidasa fails to

---

5. Aśoka (r. ca. 265–238 or ca. 273–232 B.C.E.) was the last major emperor in the Mauryan dynasty of India. His vigorous patronage of Buddhism in the third century B.C.E. spread the religion throughout India and beyond.

6. Bharhut, a village in north central India, is known for a stupa (architectural reliquary) that dates to the time of Aśoka, with sculptural decorations that are among the earliest and most elegant specimens of Indian Buddhist art.

7. Buddha Gayā, also spelled Buddh Gaya or Bodh Gayā, is the Buddhist holy site in northeastern India where Siddhartha is said to have attained enlightenment.

evoke.[8] The sublime attainments of Indian art, almost effaced as they have been by the rough-handedness of the Hunas [Huns], the fanatical iconoclasm of the Mussulman, and the unconscious vandalism of mercenary Europe, leave us to seek only a past glory in the moldy walls of Ajanta,[9] the tortured sculptures of Ellora,[10] the silent protests of rock-cut Orissa,[11] and finally in the domestic utensils of the present day, where beauty sadly clings to religion in the midst of an exquisite home-life.

It is in Japan alone that the historic wealth of Asiatic culture can be consecutively studied through its treasured specimens. The Imperial collection, the Shinto temples, and the opened dolmens, reveal the subtle curves of Hang [sic] workmanship.[12] The temples of Nara are rich in representations of Tang culture, and of that Indian art, then in its splendor, which so much influenced the creations of the classic period—natural heirlooms of a nation which has preserved the music, pronunciation, ceremony, and costumes, not to speak of the religious rites and philosophy, of so remarkable an age, intact.

The treasure-stores of the daimyos, again, abound in works of art and manuscripts belonging to the Song and Mongol dynasties, and as in China itself the former were lost during the Mongol conquest, and the latter in the age of the reactionary Ming, this fact animates some Chinese scholars of the present day to seek in Japan the fountain-head of their own ancient knowledge.

Thus Japan is a museum of Asiatic civilization; and yet more than a museum, because the singular genius of the race leads it to dwell on all phases of the ideals of the past, in that spirit of living Advaitism which welcomes the new without losing the old. The Shinto [believer] still adheres to his old pre-Buddhist rites of ancestor worship; and the Buddhists themselves cling to each various school of religious development which had come in its natural order to enrich the soil. . . .

Art with us, as elsewhere, is the expression of the highest and noblest of our national culture, so that, in order to understand it, we must pass in review the various phases of Confucian philosophy; the different ideals which the Buddhist mind has from time to time revealed; those mighty political cycles which have one after another unfurled the banner of nationality; the reflection in patriotic

---

8. Kālidāsa, a master of Sanskrit, was a poet and dramatist of the fifth century, sometimes considered one of the "nine gems" of King Vikramaditya (r. ca. 380–ca. 415) of Ujjian in northern India.

9. Ajanta is a site in western India with Buddhist cave temples built between the first century B.C.E. and the seventh century C.E., celebrated for their painted murals.

10. Ellora is a site in western India famous for temples hewn out of rock cliffs during the Gupta period (sixth to eighth century C.E.), best known for the erotically decorated Kailasanatha Temple, dedicated to the Hindu god Siva.

11. Orissa was a thriving eastern kingdom in the time of the historic Buddha; in subsequent eras, it developed a rich artistic heritage exhibiting a broad array of techniques, styles, and media.

12. Probably a reference to Han or Chinese workmanship in general.

thought of the lights of poetry and the shadows of heroic characters; and the echoes, alike of the wailing of a multitude, and of the mad-seeming merriment of the laughter of a race.

Any history of Japanese art-ideals is, then, almost an impossibility, as long as the Western world remains so unaware of the varied environment and interrelated social phenomena into which that art is set, as if it were a jewel. Definition is limitation. The beauty of a cloud or a flower lies in its unconscious unfolding of itself, and the silent eloquence of the masterpieces of each epoch must tell their story better than any epitome of necessary half-truths. My poor attempts are merely an indication, not a narrative.

[Okakura, *The Ideals of the East*, pp. 1–10; AYW]

TEA, THE CUP OF HUMANITY

The Book of Tea focuses on the peacefulness of the Japanese aesthetic spirituality and the serenity of their classic art while minimizing the violence that in those days attended the growing cult of the samurai and ferocity of the Way of the warrior (*bushidō*).[13]

The philosophy of tea is not mere aestheticism in the ordinary acceptance of the term, for it expresses conjointly with ethics and religion our whole point of view about man and nature.

It is hygiene, for it enforces cleanliness; it is economics, for it shows comfort in simplicity rather than in the complex and costly; it is moral geometry, inasmuch as it defines our sense of proportion to the universe. It represents the true spirit of Eastern democracy by making all its votaries aristocrats in taste. . . .

Those who cannot feel the littleness of great things in themselves are apt to overlook the greatness of little things in others. The average Westerner, in his sleek complacency, will see in the tea ceremony yet another instance of the thousand and one oddities that constitute the quaintness and childishness of the East to him. He was wont to regard Japan as barbarous while she indulged in the gentle arts of peace: he calls her civilized since she began to commit wholesale slaughter on Manchurian battlefields. Much comment has been given lately to the Code of the Samurai—the Art of Death that makes our soldiers exult in self-sacrifice; but scarcely any attention has been drawn to Teaism, which represents so much of our Art of Life. Fain would we remain barbarians if our claim to civilization were to be based on the gruesome glory of war. Fain would we await the time when due respect shall be paid to our art and ideals. . . .

---

13. See de Bary et al., eds., *Sources of Japanese Tradition*, 2nd ed., vol. 1, chaps. 12, 18; vol. 2, abr., chaps. 20, 29, 43.

So much harm has been done already by the mutual misunderstanding of the New World and the Old, that one need not apologize for contributing his tithe to the furtherance of a better understanding. The beginning of the twentieth century would have been spared the spectacle of sanguinary warfare if Russia had condescended to know Japan better. What dire consequences to humanity lie in the contemptuous ignoring of Eastern problems! European imperialism, which does not disdain to raise the absurd cry of the Yellow Peril, fails to realize that Asia may also awaken to the cruel sense of the White Disaster. . . .

The heaven of modern humanity is indeed shattered in the Cyclopean struggle for wealth and power. The world is groping in the shadow of egotism and vulgarity. Knowledge is bought through a bad conscience; benevolence practiced for the sake of utility. The East and West, like two dragons tossed in a sea of ferment, in vain strive to regain the jewel of life. . . . Meanwhile, let us have a sip of tea. The afternoon glow is brightening the bamboos; the fountains are bubbling with delight; the soughing of the pines is heard in our kettle. Let us dream of evanescence, and linger in the beautiful foolishness of things.

[Adapted from Okakura, *The Book of Tea*, pp. 1–7, 13–14]

YANAGI MUNEYOSHI AND THE KWANGHWA GATE IN SEOUL, KOREA

While Okakura Kakuzō was meditating on tea as "the Cup of Humanity," celebrating the common aesthetic bonds among India, China, and Japan, the Japanese in Korea were engaged in a takeover of the country (following the Russo-Japanese War) that was increasingly subjugating the Koreans and their culture to the Japanese—even to the point of the latter's establishing the shrines of State Shinto in Seoul. When, however, this process threatened the destruction of a historic gate before the Korean royal palace, it brought an anguished protest from a young Japanese whose career followed closely Okakura's, although almost a generation later.

A graduate of the Peers' School (Gakushūin) and Tokyo Imperial University, Yanagi Muneyoshi (1889–1961), also known literarily as Sōetsu, became the founder and a leader of Japan's folkcraft (*mingei*) movement and, in 1936, established the Japan Folkcraft Museum (Mingeikan) in Tokyo. A member of the literary group Shirakaba, Yanagi was also a noted art critic. After several visits to Korea, first in 1916, Yanagi developed a profound attachment to and appreciation of Korea's artistic tradition and wrote extensively on Korean arts and folkcraft. He was one of very few Japanese whom Koreans loved and respected as true friends of Korea during Japan's colonial rule. Yanagi also did much to promote the appreciation of Okinawan arts and crafts.

When Japan began to build the massive Government General's office in front of the main audience hall (Kŭnjŏngjŏn) of the Kyŏngbok Palace in 1916, the Kwanghwa Gate was slated to be destroyed to make way for the new Western-style building. The Kyŏngbok Palace and its main front entrance, the Kwanghwa Gate, were originally constructed in 1395, at the outset of the Chosŏn dynasty, but were destroyed during Toyotomi Hideyoshi's invasion in 1592. Then in 1867, they were rebuilt as a part of the Taewŏngun's efforts to revitalize the country. These structures thus symbolized Korea's past glory. The planned demolition of the Kwanghwa Gate was seen by most Koreans as a wrecking of Korea's heart and soul. But because of Japan's tight control over Korea, no one in Korea dared to speak out against the Japanese move. Faced with this situation, Yanagi published an article in the form of a personal letter to the Kwanghwa Gate, lamenting its impending death; the letter brought tears to the eyes of many grateful Koreans.

Yanagi's letter touches on at least three main points. First, he expresses his sincere sympathy with and respect for the Korean people, who were about to lose one of their cherished monuments; thus he is obliquely criticizing Japan's mistreatment of Korea. Second is his sympathy for the preservation of Asian arts. For him, the Kwanghwa Gate was a rare artistic treasure of Asia that should be preserved at all costs, transcending any political considerations. Third is his deploring of the destruction of natural surroundings and aesthetic harmony as a consequence of the demolition of the Kwanghwa Gate and the imposition of a massive Western-style building in its place.

First published in the September 1922 issue of the journal *Kaizō*, this letter led to the Japanese authorities' listing Yanagi as "a dangerous person," and for a time he was secretly followed by police detectives. Largely in response to criticism like Yanagi's, the Japanese authorities refrained from destroying the Kwanghwa Gate but in 1926 moved it to another location, east of the Kyŏngbok Palace. In 1968, it was restored to the original site, while the former Government General's building on that site was demolished in 1995 as part of the commemoration of the fiftieth anniversary of Korea's liberation from Japanese rule.

Yanagi's case is a reminder that in the midst of strong authoritarian, ultra-nationalist, and imperialist trends, there were independent voices among Japanese scholars and writers who spoke for cultural values that should be defended and preserved from both Western and Japanese hegemonism.

FOR A KOREAN ARCHITECTURE ABOUT TO BE LOST

The text of this letter is preceded by a parenthetical explanation of Yanagi's public statement.

(I think the time has come for me to make this letter public. I feel my heart is being strangled when I think about the senseless destruction about to take place against an example of old Asian architecture. Perhaps those who have never visited the Kyŏngbok Palace in Seoul, Korea's capital may have no feeling about the destruction of the Kwanghwa Gate, the magnificent main entrance to that palace. I am, however, inclined to believe that all readers of this letter possess a heart that loves the artworks of Asia. Even if what happens in Korea may not stir any feelings in the readers' hearts directly, I wish you to read this letter on behalf of an old Asian artwork that is facing extinction. I am writing a mournful epitaph to the fate of an artwork that must not be lost and yet is about to be destroyed. At the same time, I am expressing my deep sympathies for a people who are compelled to watch with their own eyes the destruction of a work of art they had built! . . .)

The Public Letter

Kwanghwa Gate, Kwanghwa Gate, your life is about to end in a matter of days. The memory of your existence in this world is about to be coldly wiped out forever. What shall I do? I am at a loss. There are not many days left before the cruel chisels and the heartless hammers start to destroy your body, piece by piece. There must be many people who feel pain in their hearts over this. No one, however, can save you now. Unfortunately, those who are in a position to save you are people who do not mourn your fate. . . .

Everyone is hesitant to speak out. But the misery in my heart is much too great to let you go in silence. Therefore, in place of those who cannot speak out, I am writing this letter in order to let the world know of your existence once more before your impending death. . . .

Oh, Kwanghwa Gate, Kwanghwa Gate, magnificent is thy appearance! . . . Anyone who sees it cannot help but be struck by its tranquil beauty and dignity, and it amply deserves to be the main gate to the largest palace of a nation. . . . In Kwanghwa Gate, one looks at the epitome of beauty of the Chosŏn dynasty. How simple and tranquil does it stand on the ground! All those who have passed through that gate have become awestruck by its commanding stature. Truly, it befits a monument that demonstrates the dignity of a dynasty. . . .

My brethren, love and respect the pure architectures of Asia. Isn't it true that we are no longer capable of building architectures that can match [their beauty]? We should not throw away artistic works lightly simply because they have no use in our daily life today. Art transcends egotistic interest. We must preserve whatever we find with beauty in it. Especially, we must love with zeal the pure Asian works for the sake of our own glory and pride. To preserve and protect them under whatever conditions is the true way of respecting our ancestors and appreciating the arts. Although Kwanghwa Gate was built in modern times, it is one of the rare examples of architecture in Asia. It is one of the five most distinguished gates in Korea. . . . No other structure in Korea can match this palace in its form and grandeur. It is the best representative, an exemplary model, of the spirit of Chosŏn dynasty architecture.

Politics must not be insensible to art. One must refrain from infringing on art in the exercise of power. . . .

[Kwanghwa Gate] enhances its beauty twofold as its architecture was designed carefully in consideration of the nature that surrounds it. The natural surroundings protect the architecture while the architecture adorns the natural surroundings, and men should not destroy their organic relationship. However, for unknown reasons, this harmony between nature and human work is about to be destroyed by those who do not understand such relationships. . . .

. . . A Western building totally devoid of creative beauty is now abruptly desecrating the sacred site in its place. . . .

Why have we been led to the point of thinking of destroying the Kwanghwa Gate? . . . Where in the world can we find a positive excuse to justify its destruction? . . .

I recall what Jesus said on the cross: "They know not what they do." If they had known what they are doing, they would not have committed the foolish sin of doing what they ought not to do.

Kwanghwa Gate, your life originally was meant to be long lasting, but fate is such that you are about to end with a short life. Surely, you must feel pain and sorrow. I will cross the sea to meet you one more time while you are still in a healthy condition. Please wait for me. But before that, I wish to write this letter. The people who produced you and are dear to you have been under order to be cautious with their words. Therefore, I wish to let you know before your death that there is someone in this world who loves and mourns you in their place. Anxious to do this, I am sending out these words to the general public. How pleased I will be if these words induce thoughtful people to reflect on your existence once more! And, if this letter helps the perpetuation of your memory, that will please you also. How delighted I will be if this is the case!

(Written on July 4, 1922, in Tokyo)

["Chōsen to sono geijutsu," in *Yanagi Muneyoshi senshū*, pp. 200–216; YC]

Chapter 40

THE HIGH TIDE OF PREWAR LIBERALISM

The prewar Japanese liberal movement reached its height in the 1920s, when, for a time, it appeared that the principles espoused by that movement had become the guiding light of Japanese political life. These principles might be roughly stated as follows:

1. The government should be conducted by party cabinets responsible to the majority in the lower house of the Diet (legislature).
2. The lower house should be elected by universal manhood suffrage.
3. The people should be guaranteed the full exercise of their civil liberties.
4. Japan should abandon its policy of force and aggression in China and do no more than maintain the rights it already possessed in Manchuria.
5. Japan should follow a policy of international cooperation, particularly with regard to disarmament.

The movement's main vocal support came from five groups: party politicians, businessmen, journalists, educators, and certain diplomats. Of course, not all these principles received equal support from each of these groups. The party politicians insisted strongly on the principle of party cabinets, but they were not so enthusiastic about the other four principles. Indeed, when the opposition of the Privy Council and the House of Peers to universal manhood suffrage suddenly evaporated, the party politicians displayed a surprising reluctance to enact the measure into law. To them, it merely meant further complications in the business of getting elected, a point not lost on the Peers, who seem to have been reasoning along much the same lines followed by Benjamin Disraeli when he extended the vote to English labor.

The liberal businessmen were concerned primarily with the first, fourth, and fifth principles. They favored party cabinets for the simple reason that they seemed to offer them a way to influence the government's economic and social policies, although the businessmen also had mechanisms through which they could work directly with bureaucrats to shape policy. In addition, those businessmen who traded with China or produced either for the China trade or in China felt they had suffered great losses from the boycotts that Japanese aggression had sparked. Consequently, they were eager for a more conciliatory policy to be adopted toward China. Japanese financiers also believed that Japan had to cooperate with the Western powers if it wished to retain access to international short-term credits and investment funds. For this reason, they wanted to have Japan demonstrate its peaceful intentions by entering into disarmament agreements.

The business world in general as well as agricultural interests also backed these agreements in the hope that the military budget, and therefore the tax burden, would be reduced. In their support of these international policies, they were joined by diplomats such as Baron Shidehara Kijūrō, whose study of the international situation in general and of the China situation in particular had led them to conclude that these were the only feasible policies for Japan. Although Shidehara was well known for his liberal position on international affairs, he never publicly expressed a correspondingly liberal view with regard to domestic politics.

The only persons who can be said to have given unqualified support to the whole liberal creed were the liberal journalists and educators. The journalists were the shock troops of the movement, and at several critical moments in its history they helped carry the day by using the news and editorial columns of their newspapers to arouse public opinion. The educators, particularly university professors like Yoshino Sakuzō and Minobe Tatsukichi, provided the intellectual foundations for Japanese liberalism and, in their writings, showed how the democratic ideal could be adapted to Japan. They also planted liberal ideas in the minds of their students, frequently taking the initiative in helping organize student groups dedicated to the spread and implementation of these ideas. During and after World War I, a number of these students, mostly the sons of wealthy landlord-, business-, or professional-class families, entered politics and contributed greatly to the attempt to establish responsible parliamentary government. They constituted the only group of politicians who were seriously concerned with the civil rights issue.

We have not included organized labor among the groups supporting the liberal movement. Organized labor did accept many of the principles of Japanese liberalism and was willing to cooperate with the liberals to achieve common objectives—for example, in the universal manhood suffrage movement. But Japanese liberalism was not much concerned about social and economic reforms, which were important to the labor movement. In fact, in these areas the thinking of most liberals tended toward a kind of paternalism that differed very little from that of the conservatives and the reactionaries, and they seem to have believed that universal suffrage would somehow solve all other problems. Consequently, organized labor devoted most of its political energies to the left-wing political movement, particularly after the achievement of universal manhood suffrage. In addition, because of their social programs, many of the ultranationalist groups also appealed much more to the lower orders than did liberalism. This failure to win labor's backing was a serious weakness of the liberal movement, which needed all the support it could muster in its struggle to reshape Japan's political life.

Japanese liberalism had to struggle against many unfavorable circumstances. First, the men who fashioned the Japanese constitution placed the Diet in a very weak position: it had neither the legal means to hold a cabinet accountable for its actions nor any effective financial controls over the cabinet. Moreover, what little power the Diet did possess, the elected House of Representatives had to share equally with the nonelected House of Peers. The popularly elected house was confronted with other well-established centers of power: the bureaucracy, the Privy Council, the military services, the informal council of elder statesmen (genrō), and the Imperial Household officials. Since most of these other centers of power had a legal veto over any attempt to curtail their prerogatives by law or by constitutional amendment, liberals had to work to establish within the existing framework extralegal customs that would give Japan the substance, if not the form, of a parliamentary democracy. They could do this only if they rallied the mass of the Japanese people behind their program. Yet the diffusion of liberal ideals among the people was trammeled by primary and secondary education systems that had been deliberately designed to foster a spirit uncongenial to the values usually associated with a democratic society. And the operations of most Japanese social groups did not engender the sense of individualism, personal responsibility, and self-confidence essential to the proper functioning of representative government.

The weaknesses that we have so far discussed might be regarded as due to environmental or external factors, but the liberal movement also was plagued by a number of internal failings. Of these flaws, the most important were those that impaired the strength of the political parties, for it was they that were responsible for proving the worth and viability of parliamentary government.

The party politicians' gravest defect was their opportunism. They rarely were ready to suspend their differences and unite to defend parliamentary principles.

If a party cabinet became involved in jurisdictional or policy disputes with one of the other centers of power, the opposing political party was more than willing to side with the latter in the hope that the occasion might be used to drive its opponents from office. They never seem to have cared that the ultimate result of these petty maneuvers would be to weaken the political party movement as a whole. In fact, there were only two instances in which united fronts were organized to defend the principle of party government (the third Katsura cabinet and the Kiyoura Keigo cabinet), and both times a substantial number of party members gave their allegiance to the antiparliamentarian forces. Undoubtedly, it was this niggling concern for office that persuaded party politicians to welcome into positions of party leadership Itō Hirobumi, Katsura Tarō, Katō Takaaki, Tanaka Giichi, and many other products of the civil or military bureaucracy. These men were able to assume party presidencies on virtually dictatorial terms, since the parties, convinced that the *genrō* would entrust office only to such leaders, believed this to be the one means by which even a modicum of political power might be achieved.

This type of leadership had an unfortunate effect on the character of Japanese political parties. No serious effort was made to reform the institutional obstacles to responsible party government (e.g., the House of Peers, the Privy Council, military independence, educational indoctrination). Party administration was bureaucratized, and policies were handed down from above on a take-it-or-get-out basis. Each party came to be held together by a panting eagerness for the crumbs of office rather than by a firm foundation of common principle. As a result, they had little to offer to the wider public and therefore never became mass parties but remained primarily aggregations of legislators and their immediate backers. Even if the principles had been followed, it is doubtful that the parties could have developed mass support, for the leaders were reserved men and seldom appeared before mass audiences. Moreover, when they did speak, they seemed incapable of articulating liberal ideas. Indeed, it is difficult to find among their cold speeches any stirring expressions of their credo. The most momentous occasions, such as the passage of the Universal Manhood Suffrage Law—a wonderful opportunity for publicizing parliamentary principles—brought forth only perfunctory and jejune phrases. Japan's party leaders thus must be charged with neglecting to educate the Japanese citizenry in the principles of parliamentary government. It matters little whether the failure was caused by a distaste for mass movements or by a feeling that the best way to advance the liberal cause was to go about one's business silently and thus avoid arousing the active opposition of the conservatives and reactionaries. The end result was the same: when the crisis came, the party politicians were generals without armies.

The public came to look on the politicians as men not only without principles but also without morals. It was a rare candidate for office who felt he could win on his own merits and did not have to spend thousands of yen buying votes through professional "election brokers." Indeed, this practice was so wide-spread that only the most obtuse voter could have been ignorant of it. Faced with the need for huge campaign funds, a Diet member was glad to sell what-ever influence he had for whatever price he could get. Those who could not obtain enough through their own efforts badgered the party headquarters for money. The party headquarters, in turn, accepted donations from businessmen who hoped to receive favors when and if the party formed a cabinet. Although great bribery scandals were continually coming to light and undermining the public's confidence in the parties, it is only fair to note that there were just as many scandals involving civil and military bureaucrats. In fact, widespread cor-ruption among Diet members first appeared when Yamagata's political lieuten-ants, finding that they could not control the Diet through either violence or dissolution, turned to systematic bribery. Those who gave bribes were usually smaller businessmen who were not themselves powerful enough to command favorable treatment from the government. The greatest source of political do-nations—as distinct from bribes—was popularly supposed to be the *zaibatsu* (financial groups), with the Mitsui supporting the Seiyūkai (party) and the Mit-subishi, the Minseitō (party). These ties have never really been documented, but this hardly matters. The important thing is that it would have been difficult to find a Japanese who did not believe that these connections existed and that government by party cabinet therefore meant government in the interests of one or another of the *zaibatsu*.

There was another respect in which party cabinets—when they did come to power—proved a great disappointment to Japanese liberals. In their disregard of civil liberties, they were unsurpassed by any of the bureaucratic cabinets of the past. Under them, books and other publications continued to be rigorously censored. The cabinets of Hara Takashi and Hamaguchi Yūkō were formally charged by the newspaper profession with prohibiting the press's mention of more news items than any of their predecessors had. The Higher Special Police were regularly used to spy on the activities of political opponents. The home ministers of two party cabinets were forced to leave office as a result of their flagrant interference in general elections (1915, 1928). The greatest mass arrests of nonconformist thinkers in Japanese history were conducted under Minseitō and Seiyūkai cabinets. They also began the process of rooting out "dangerous thought" from the nation's school systems, and of course it was under a coalition party cabinet that the Peace Preservation Law of 1925 was enacted. This law made it a crime to advocate any change in either the national polity or the capitalist system. It was officially interpreted to mean that the public could not even discuss a constitutional amendment. By expansive interpretation, this law became the basis for developing an elaborate system of repression. Ironically, the very same Diet that passed this law also passed the Universal Manhood Suffrage Law. At the highest moment of the tide of Taishō democracy, the ebb had begun.

Perhaps this attitude toward civil rights was only to be expected of the party cabinets, for from its very beginning the political party movement contained a strong element of ultranationalism. Whether from conviction or cunning, the founders of the early Meiji political societies (the Aikoku kōtō and the Risshisha) had argued that a parliament would strengthen the state in its task of national defense and expansion abroad. They had exalted the emperor's sovereignty and asserted that a parliament would unify the nation and so facilitate the execution of the imperial will. In the 1890s, the party politicians constantly berated the bureaucratic cabinets for not being aggressive enough in their foreign policy, and one of the shrillest voices was that of the liberal Ozaki Yukio. Nor should we forget that it was the liberal Katō Takaaki, serving as foreign minister under the liberal Ōkuma Shigenobu, who, against the objections of the conservative Yamagata, presented the infamous Twenty-one Demands to China. On some occasions in the early 1930s, the Japanese government was able, through the Achilles' heel of patriotism, to induce some prominent liberals to present in foreign venues a good face for Japanese aggression in East Asia. To all this must be added the prominent role played by politicians of every party in such ultranationalist organizations as the Kokusuikai, the Kokuhonsha, and the Seinendan. In view of these facts, it is not surprising that the political parties offered such ineffectual resistance to the militarists in the 1930s.

We should make three more points about Japanese liberals. First, although liberal ideologues believed that responsible parliamentary government required political parties and were always ready with advice for them, they themselves usually declined to join parties and participate in the hurly-burly of party life, fearing perhaps that it would compromise their objectivity as critics. Second, although they preached that government should be conducted in accordance with the will of the people, they did not trust the people to make the correct decisions on their own and therefore believed that means should be devised through which "wise men" like themselves could subtly and unobtrusively guide the people to the proper outcomes. Third, the liberals, with a few exceptions like Kawai Eijirō, never developed a philosophical or theoretical foundation on which to base their arguments for adopting liberal principles of government. Usually they simply contended that this was the trend of the world and that Japan had better not be out of step.

It is obvious, then, that the Japanese liberal movement was beset with great difficulties, and yet its failure was by no means a foregone conclusion. In the 1920s a new crop of younger politicians appeared who had come to maturity during the great upsurge of liberalism that had characterized the war and postwar period. These younger men had wholeheartedly accepted liberal principles and dedicated themselves to creating a true parliamentary government in Japan. They were not shy about asserting the supremacy of the House of Representatives and attacking as anachronisms the House of Peers, the Privy Council, and the independence of the military services. They even found some kindred spirits among reform-minded bureaucrats (e.g., in the Social Bureau of the Home Ministry) with whom cooperation for social and economic reform was possible. If the world envisaged by the idealists of 1919 had come into being and achieved a degree of permanence, these younger politicians in time might have brought around the majority of the nation to their view, for the Japanese are a people given to searching out and adjusting to what they conceive to be the trend of world developments. As World War I ended, the signs seemed to read "democracy and peace": the victory of the Western democracies over German militarism; the fall of the czarist autocracy; the international enthusiasm for Wilsonian democracy; the war to end all wars and bring an era of peaceful international cooperation; the League of Nations; the spontaneous rice riots in 1918, which had toppled a reactionary cabinet and brought in a political party cabinet; and the creation of a large, white-collar middle class and a large, blue-collar labor class as a result of economic expansion during the war. All this was of inestimable help to the liberal movement. Unfortunately, by the early 1930s, world political and economic events had produced a situation that was, both objectively and psychologically, unfavorable to the further progress of Japanese liberalism.

DEMOCRACY AT HOME

MINOBE TATSUKICHI: THE LEGAL FOUNDATION FOR LIBERAL GOVERNMENT

Minobe Tatsukichi (1873–1948) graduated from Tokyo Imperial University in 1897 and entered the university's graduate program in law. In 1899 he was ordered to study for three years in Germany, England, and France. While he was away, he was appointed professor of comparative legal systems and, on his return in 1903, took up his duties. In 1920 a second chair in constitutional law was created for him. The first chair was held by Hozumi Yatsuka, who was succeeded on his retirement by his disciple Uesugi Shinkichi, both of whom were opponents of Minobe's theories. In 1934 at the customary age, he retired, having been appointed to the House of Peers two years earlier. In the summer of 1911, Minobe had been invited by the Ministry of Education to deliver a series of lectures on the Japanese constitution to an audience of administrators and teachers from schools of education and middle schools who were attending a summer short course sponsored by the ministry. In these lectures, he summed up ideas that he had been broaching in articles in scholarly journals over the previous decade. As a law professor, he, of course, covered in great detail all the technicalities of constitutional law. But he also gave an interpretive twist to the Meiji constitution, demonstrating that its spirit not only did not preclude but rather led ineluctably to responsible party cabinet government. In 1913 these lectures appeared in book form under the title *Lectures on the Constitution* (*Kenpō kōwa*).

LECTURES ON THE CONSTITUTION
(*KENPŌ KŌWA*)

Preface

It is almost beyond imagination that although some twenty years have passed since constitutional government was put into effect in Japan, there as yet has been no general dissemination of knowledge about constitutional government. Even among persons who discuss the constitution as scholarly specialists, we hear opinions that are still trying to advocate an absolutist ideology, under the cloak of "national polity," to suppress the people's rights and demand their absolute submission, and, under the guise of constitutional government, to carry on a despotic government. As a student of constitutional law I have for many years deplored this situation. If there had been an opportunity, I would have wished to write a book that, on behalf of the education of our people, clearly describes the essentials of our constitution. However, because of the press of official duties, I never had the leisure for this, something I have always regretted. That I have obtained the opportunity to lecture you gentlemen . . . on the elements of our constitution has enabled me to fulfill a portion of my ever present hope. . . . Above all, it will be my earnest endeavor to clarify the fundamental spirit of the constitution and thereby eradicate the advocacy of disguised despotism which prevails in certain quarters. [p. 33]

A constitutional form of government must always have a parliament consisting of representatives of the people. All the people must participate in governing the nation through a parliament. It is an expression seldom used today, but formerly we used the phrase *kunmin dōchi* government [joint governance by the monarch and the people] to express the idea of constitutional government. It expresses quite simply the distinguishing characteristic of constitutional government, that is, that we the people are not only the governed but are at the same time members of the governing group. While we submit to the authority of the state, at the same time we ourselves participate in the governance of the nation. Of course, not all the people themselves participate in these consultations. However, because the parliament, as representatives of the people, participates in governance, the people indirectly participate. When the monarch and the people jointly exercise state authority, a true constitutional monarchy exists. [pp. 36–37]

To say in a legal sense that the monarch is the one who possesses the governmental power means that the governmental power belongs to the monarch as his personal right. To have a right expresses legally the idea that the right exists for that person's benefit. If one says that the monarch is the person who possesses the governmental power, it implies it is a right that exists for the monarch's personal benefit. To say that the monarch exercises the governmental power for his own benefit truly is contrary to our own history since ancient times and is most contrary to our present form of government. It is a salient historical fact that in our long history, successive emperors have always made the people's well-being their own well-being. Gracious imperial edicts have said, more than once, that to enrich the people was to enrich the monarch. If it were understood that the monarch was the person who possessed the governmental power, it would mean . . . the governmental power did not exist for the group's common objectives but only for the monarch's own objectives. The objectives of the monarch and the people could be completely different. Thus it would be incompatible with the idea that the nation was a single entity. In traditional Japanese thought about the state and especially in modern thought about the state, the governmental power exists for the benefit of the collective goals of the whole nation. . . . [All things] are planned for the benefit of the whole country; [all things are done] to advance the nation's interests and the people's welfare, not simply for the benefit of the monarch. . . .

Saying that the state is the holder of the governmental power and that the monarch is an organ of the state merely expresses this idea. Not only is it not offensive to our sense of reverence for the emperor, but on the contrary, it makes that sense of reverence more evident.

Therefore, from the viewpoint of legal theory, I believe it is a very mistaken idea to say the monarch is the possessor of the governmental power. . . . Still, the highest source of the empire's state authority is undoubtedly the emperor. [pp. 66–68]

The general principle for the emperor's prerogative is laid down in article 4 of the constitution. Although articles 5 through 16 stipulate its more important functions, the emperor's prerogative is not exhausted by those functions listed in the constitution. Those listed are only the most important ones. . . .

However . . . a theory very different from this has been widely adopted. . . . According to this theory, the emperor's prerogative is limited to those items enumerated in the constitution. . . . [According to this theory,] absolutely no interference by the parliament is allowed in connection with these items; that is, it is not permissible to decide any matter connected with these items by a law [passed by the Diet]. Second, this theory holds that matters [falling under these items] must be dealt with by the emperor personally and cannot be delegated to administrative officials. . . .

This is a theory that has been widely discussed and that my senior colleague, Dr. Hozumi, has been advocating especially zealously. However, I cannot believe that this theory has any basis. First, nowhere in the constitution can be found the view that it is not permitted to make decisions in connection with these items by means of a law [passed by the Diet]. The purport of the constitution goes no further than that it is all right if these items are not always dealt by means of a law [passed by the Diet]. There is not the slightest implication that they cannot be handled by laws. . . . Laws also come into existence with the approval of the emperor, so even if matters of administrative organization were to have been decided by laws, there should not be the least objection to seeing this as the emperor's having made the decision.

The second point, that the emperor must personally decide everything with regard to prerogative items and is not permitted to delegate these matters to administrative officials, is, I believe, a theory with no basis. All administrative officials have been delegated a portion of [his] prerogatives by the emperor. Their authority is nothing more than the emperor's prerogative: administrative officials have no authority of their own. [pp. 88–91]

Our imperial house maintains a dignity unparalleled in the world, and the people's feeling of reverence and loyalty for the emperor will not be in the least shaken, no matter what political changes occur. One reason for this is that in fact in our form of government from ancient times the emperor has not personally undertaken the governance of the country. Of course, this was so in the Fujiwara period and in the period of military rule. However, even in the [ancient] period of direct imperial rule, the emperor did not personally conduct the government at his own discretion. There always were ministers to assist him, and he conducted the government in accordance with this advice. This is truly our national polity (*kokutai*), and through this system the dignity of the national polity is preserved. From this same motive it has also developed in our present system that the imperial family do not occupy positions of accountability. [pp. 96–97]

In our country there have always been persons equivalent to [modern] ministers and prime ministers at the side of the emperor who advised him. . . . In a [modern] constitutional state, if the emperor's official acts are, without exception, not based on a minister's advice, they have no legal validity. The constitution stipulates that the emperor's exercise of his prerogative must unfailingly be based on a minister's advice. It is absolutely impossible for the emperor to administer the country by personal acts not based on ministerial advice. . . .

No state business can be effected on the sole decision of His Majesty himself. . . .

The minister bears the responsibility for matters on which he has advised the emperor. . . .

No matter what the situation, the minister cannot escape his responsibility by pleading an order from the emperor. . . . Even if the emperor were to command something, if the minister thinks the command violates the constitution or the laws or is disadvantageous to the interests of the state, the minister must strongly remonstrate with the emperor. . . . If despite his remonstration the emperor commands him to countersign something that the minister believes is against the interests of the state, he must resign as minister on the grounds the emperor has no confidence in him. If he does not resign but does

what the emperor is commanding . . . then the minister must bear the responsibility for the act. [pp. 129–37, passim]

Some persons say that each minister may independently offer advice to the
emperor without the necessity of consulting with other ministers or without
having to go through the prime minister. However, this [idea] is a terrible
mistake. . . . Whether it is diplomatic matters, military matters, financial matters, educational matters, or, in general, any matter of domestic administration,
no important matter can be settled by only the minister within whose competence it falls. It must be settled by discussions of the entire cabinet.

The only exception to this is matters of military secrecy. In such matters the
army minister and the navy minister may directly approach the emperor and
seek his consent without discussions with [the rest of] the cabinet. This is
generally referred to as the right of supreme command (*iaku jōsō*). And it is the
sole exception. . . .

Since the imperial approval of all important state business is sought only
after lengthy discussion by the whole cabinet, all the ministers must bear responsibility for acts that the cabinet has discussed. [pp. 132–35, passim]

With regard to ministerial responsibility, the Japanese constitution says only
that the minister of state shall advise the emperor and be responsible for his
advice. Since it does not stipulate that the minister will be responsible to the
parliament for his advice, there are a number of different opinions on this point.
Some persons say that according to the Japanese constitution, ministers are not
responsible to the parliament but are responsible solely to the emperor. However, I believe that this is a big mistake. Even if it is said a minister is responsible
to the parliament, this does not mean that the parliament can in any way make
the minister retire from his position or that because of a resolution by parliament, the minister must, as a matter of law without fail, give up his position. It
goes without saying the power to appoint and dismiss ministers resides exclusively with the monarch. To say that a minister is responsible to parliament
means no more than it is possible for the parliament to raise questions about
the minister's responsibility. . . .

According to Japan's constitution, the parliament can memorialize [the em-
peror] against a minister's malfeasance in his official duty and request his dismissal, or it can pass a resolution of no confidence, or it can interpellate a
minister, or it can seek explanations from a minister. Especially in regard to
this questioning of a minister and seeking explanations is the premise that a
minister has a responsibility [to the parliament]. . . . [However, these] acts do
not directly have any legal effects: because of them, a minister is not legally
obligated to resign his position. What consequences, then, do these acts have?
It becomes simply a practical [political] problem: the minister may resign; the
parliament may be dissolved or prorogued; or there may be mutual concessions
and compromise.

In sum, even according to the Japanese constitution, it is not open to question that ministers are responsible to parliament. Ministers are, of course, responsible to the emperor . . . but this is the same responsibility that all officials have to the emperor. Only the ministers have a special responsibility to the parliament. The parliament's right to question ministers, its right to vote ex-post facto approval or disapproval [of emergency measures by ministers], [and] its right to memorialize the emperor [regarding a minister's action] all are proof that Japan's constitution acknowledges this special responsibility [of the minister to the parliament]. [pp. 145–48]

In a constitutional government, it is impossible to maintain for long a cabinet that ignores the parties. There is an unavoidable natural tendency to gradually approach the parliamentary cabinet or party cabinet [system]. I think the main reason that a pure parliamentary cabinet has not yet appeared in Japan is that the strength of the political parties is largely confined to the House of Representatives and does not extend to the House of Peers; and there is absent in the House of Peers any sense of deference to the decisions of the House of Representatives as expressing the people's will. Furthermore, in Japan's present system, the army and the navy ministers must, without fail, be chosen from army generals and navy admirals. For this reason . . . they always have been appointed from outside the political parties and . . . are frequently carried over [from one cabinet to the next]. . . . This is one of the circumstances that hinders the establishment of a pure parliamentary cabinet government. . . . [But] the development of party cabinets is an inevitable tendency once constitutional government is in effect. [pp. 155–56]

Since the parliament represents all the people, it naturally follows that all or at least a portion of the parliament should be elected from among the people. . . . If all the people had equal ability and equal qualifications, the fairest thing would be to give equal voting rights to all the people. . . . But in reality the people are by no means equal. In their lineage, property, education, experience, and moral repute, people are infinite in their variety and actually are very unequal. To disregard their real inequalities, to treat all people as equal and give them equal voting rights, to publicly elect all representatives equally from among the whole people is not the way to obtain suitable representatives of the people. . . .

It is correct to say that the world trend is toward universal [manhood] suffrage. . . .

Today no one doubts that the theory of natural rights was completely wrong. The right to vote is certainly not a natural right of human beings. [The adoption of] universal [manhood] suffrage is not based on the unfounded fanciful idea that voting is a natural right. It was adopted because in today's general social situation the adoption of universal suffrage has become an unavoidable necessity. In a word, the main cause is the social condition of the working class and their advancement in self-awareness. All political systems must keep in step with actual social forces. . . .

In Japan also it is certain that as the people's self-awareness spreads generally to the lower reaches of society, it will be necessary to expand the suffrage. . . . [pp. 166, 196, 199–202]

In Japan, since the inauguration of the constitution, there has not yet been a single instance of the emperor's declining to approve [a law passed by the parliament]. Since the parliament represents the mind of a nation's people, a law passed by the parliament represents, in my opinion, what the people desire. I humbly conjecture that this reflects an imperial wish to accede as far as possible to the people's will and sanction those laws that the people desire. [p. 226]

Constitutional government is government by the common people. In order to practice constitutional government smoothly, it is indispensable that the people's political thought develop and the people be aware of their own political responsibilities. [p.364]

None of the administrative operations [of the state] are absolutely free and unlimited. All are legally subject to various limits. If you look at the law textbooks currently on the market, you will often find them saying that the state has an absolute and unlimited authority, that it can freely order subjects to do anything whatsoever, and that the subjects must obey. This, it must be said, is an egregious error. The authority of the state is, by law, subject to definite limits and can function only within those limits. Laws are, of course, made by the state itself. Once a law exists, even the state cannot violate it. . . . [p. 408]

Limiting the people's liberties by an administrative act must be in circumstances in which it is permitted by law. . . . When there is no such provision in law or regulations, it is completely impermissible to use an administrative act to impose a duty on subjects or to restrain the liberties of subjects. . . . The constitution lists a variety of liberties, such as the freedom of speech and publication and the freedom to change residence, and it stipulates that these liberties cannot be infringed except by law. Constitutional countries also generally recognize as a natural basic rule that all freedoms beyond those listed in the constitution also cannot be infringed except in accordance with law. . . . The liberties of the subject are not necessarily only those enumerated in the constitution. Beyond those listed are various liberties, not all of which can be listed. For example, freedom of marriage, freedom of contract, freedom of occupation, freedom to engage in business, freedom of education, academic freedom, inviolability of one's body—none of these are listed in the constitution. . . .

No liberties of the subject, whether or not listed in the constitution, can be arbitrarily infringed by administrative acts. This is one of the most important basic rules in modern constitutional countries. . . . What we call a law-governed country is based on this fundamental principle. As a basic rule we have the right to do whatever pleases us. We can also safely possess and enjoy our lives, our persons, our property, our honor and all other rights and advantages. [pp. 410–12]

Some persons say the state is all-powerful and can freely make any kind of law it wants to. This is an egregious error. . . . If people are ordered to do something that does not basically conform to our ordinary ideas of social life, this law cannot be effective as a law. . . . A law carried out as a law is based on the social conviction of us ordinary people. A law that completely contradicts these convictions, even though it is the will of the state, basically can have no power as a law.

For this reason it is a great mistake to say law is the command of the sovereign or law is the will of the state. . . . [pp. 485, 497]

[Minobe, *Kenpō kōwa*, pp. 33–497; see also Miller,
Minobe Tatsukichi, pp. 64, 133; AET]

The power of the state exists in order to advance the interests of the state and the people. It does not exist in order to suppress the people. If the government abuses its power in order to suppress the people, there cannot be any greater misfortune for the state and the people. . . . Constitutional government is government that rests on respect for the will of the people. There must be an opportunity for the will of the people to be freely expressed. That is the essence of the constitutional system. . . . If power is used arbitrarily, if the expression of the people's will is muzzled, and if from the first the people are denied any opportunity to declare their will, that is an abuse of power, and the basis of constitutional government is endangered. We regret very much that we have seen at the termination of the Russo-Japanese War that kind of abuse of power. In order to repress the people's will, which opposed the government's diplomatic policy, the government prohibited meetings, limited speech, revived the suspension of newspaper publications, and, on the first day of peace, placed the capital under martial law.

[Minobe, "Kenryoku no ranyō to kore ni hankō"; text from Ienaga,
Minobe Tatsukichi, pp. 203–4; AET]

Freedom of speech is both the basis of social progress and a source of social disturbance. . . . [But it is] discontent with society that constitutes the chief threat to the peace and order of society. If the discontent mounts steadily and all society is consumed by it, then to limit free discussion in an effort to maintain social order will, on the contrary, strike at the very basis of order. Furthermore, since social progress usually results from the stimulus of a variety of ideas, if the expression of ideas is restricted, very likely social progress will be checked. A society that does not have freedom of speech . . . is a dead society. . . . [Under the present law] penalties are fixed for persons who publish articles that are disrespectful of the imperial household. It is unnecessary and dangerous that there should be additional sections fixing penalties on persons responsible for articles that disturb the public order. Since men differ according to their individual positions on what constitutes a disturbance of public order . . . it is very disquieting to find such a matter left to the discretion of the police. Some people will say that those who advocate democracy endanger public order; others will say that the supporters of Shinto and the defenders of national polity are a threat to public order. . . . To put the question in the hands of a police court with power to impose a prison sentence of up to six months means that no one can take up a pen in peace.

> [Minobe, "Shinbunshi hō kaisei mondai"; trans. adapted from Miller, *Minobe Tatsukichi*, p. 152]

The principle of monarchical sovereignty and the principle of popular sovereignty are really only constitutional principles, merely differences in the form of government. Regardless of either, governmental power is a right always vested in the state, and only the state possesses that power. Under popular sovereignty the people govern as an organ of the state, and even under monarchical sovereignty it is as an organ of the state that the monarch is the highest source of governmental power. . . . The [term] "sovereignty" means, strictly speaking, "the highest organ." . . .

In our constitution the principle of monarchical sovereignty must be construed in this manner, meaning that the monarch is the highest source of governmental power as chief of state and its highest organ.

Constitutional government rejects oligarchical government. Because constitutional government is conducted with the assistance of the people, it is the basic principle of constitutional government that the cabinet, which is responsible for the governance of the state, must always have the confidence of the people. Thus even though legally the designation of the prime minister rests with the free choice of the sovereign, politically it is not based on the sovereign's personal confidence but always must have the confidence of the people as the criterion for selection. Since under constitutional government the institution that represents the people's opinion is the parliament and especially the House of Representatives, the political basis for the cabinet's existence must always be the confidence of the parliament and particularly of the House of Representatives.

> [Minobe, *Chikujō kenpō seigi*, pp. 17–18, 535–36; trans. adapted from Miller, *Minobe Tatsukichi*, pp. 84, 131–32]

To view the military authorities and the military as identical, to consider criticism of the military authorities' attitude as a direct attack on the military, and to allow no outsider criticism of the proceedings of the military authorities, all must be termed a manifestation of a . . . (censored) [way of] thinking and is an egregious restraint of [freedom of] expression.

The following was written in response to the army's pamphlet *On the Basic Meaning of National Defense* (*Kokubō no hongi*).

[How can an army publication] use such expressions as "to root out individualism, liberalism, and internationalism"! Since the Meiji Restoration, individualism and liberalism have been our empire's fundamental national policy . . . the establishment of the constitution proclaimed these two things as basic constitutional principles. . . . Our country's rapid development since the Meiji Restoration, a development that has astonished the world, is principally nothing but the fruit of this individualism and liberalism. How could it have been possible to bring about such a speedy cultural development if our people had been constrained in a life of slavish obedience? Truly individual freedom is itself the father of creation and the mother of culture. It is actually because of this that the articles of chapter II of the constitution guarantee the liberties of the individual. If the talk about the necessity of eliminating individualism and liberalism is to be taken literally, then it is nothing less than a real attempt to destroy the constitution.

> [Minobe, "Dai rokujūgo gikai no kaiko" and "Rikugun happyō no kokubōron o miru"; text from Ienaga, *Minobe Tatsukichi*, pp. 212–13; AET]

In that work [*Nihon kenpo*, vol. 1], Minobe recognized that the modern state was responsible for positively developing a society's culture. However, he held, this cannot be used to construe that the state can engage without limits in whatever function it cares to. Despite the state's cultural responsibilities, there must certainly be definite limits. In the field of scholarship, the arts, religion, and other intellectual aspects of culture, development can occur only through the free investigation of individual persons. The state's function in this regard is the negative one of eliminating external obstacles that would interfere with such investigations. Its positive function is limited only to protecting and encouraging this development. Any attempt to use the state's power to decide the direction of these intellectual aspects of culture must be said to be an instance of the state's exceeding its responsibilities.

> [Minobe, *Nihon kenpō*, vol. 1; quoted in Ienaga, *Ichi rekishigakusha no ayumi*, pp. 69–71; AET]

YOSHINO SAKUZŌ: DEMOCRACY AS MINPON SHUGI

Yoshino Sakuzō (1878–1933) graduated from Tokyo Imperial University in 1904. In 1906 he went to China as the private tutor of the eldest son of Yuan Shikai, then the dominant political figure in China. In 1909 Yoshino returned to Japan and became a professor of political history and theory in the Faculty of Law at Tokyo Imperial University, a post he held until his resignation in 1924. In 1910, he was sent abroad to study in Germany, England, and the United States. On his return in 1913, he began to write articles analyzing the problems of democratic government. For a number of years, these articles appeared periodically in *Chūō kōron*, an important journal of opinion. "On the Meaning of Constitutional Government," one of the most significant of these articles, was published in January 1916. It was a powerful reaffirmation of faith in the inevitable triumph of democracy and represented a reaction against the belief current in certain Japanese circles that Germany's successes had proved the superiority of the Prussian pattern. Yoshino describes what he believes to be the most important characteristics of democracy. He demonstrates that democracy is fully compatible with the concept of the emperor's sovereignty, a principle that had become so sacrosanct as to be unchallengeable. Yoshino considers the special problems confronting democracy in Japan and suggests ways to resolve them. All the problems he touches on were extremely important at the time he wrote: political corruption, nonparty cabinets, the rise of a plutocracy, universal suffrage, the need for popular education in the ways of democracy, and so on.

"ON THE MEANING OF CONSTITUTIONAL GOVERNMENT AND THE METHODS BY WHICH IT CAN BE PERFECTED" (KENSEI NO HONGI O TOITE SONO YŪSHŪ NO BI O SEISU NO TO O RONZU)

Preface

Whether or not constitutional government will work well is partly a question of its structure and procedures, but it is also very much a question of the general level of the people's knowledge and virtue. Only when the level is rather mature can a constitutional government be set up. . . . However, since the trend toward constitutional government is worldwide and can no longer be resisted, advanced thinkers must try to establish it firmly. They should voluntarily assume the responsibility, without delay, of instructing the people so as to train them in its workings. If they do not, constitutional government can never function perfectly, however complete it may be in form. Therefore, the fundamental prerequisite for perfecting constitutional government, especially in politically backward nations, is the cultivation of knowledge and virtue among the general population. This is not a task that can be accomplished in a day. Think of the situation in our own country. We instituted constitutional government before the people were prepared for it. As a result there have been many failures, failures that have caused those with high aspirations for government to feel that we have accomplished very little. Still, it is impossible to reverse course and return to the old absolutism, so there is nothing for us to do but cheerfully take the road of reform and progress. Consequently, it is extremely important not to rely on politicians alone but to use the cooperative efforts of educators, religious leaders, and thinkers in all areas of society.

The United States and Mexico illustrate how two countries with equally well developed forms of constitutional government may be at opposite ends of the scale in their operation, in accordance with the different levels of knowledge and virtue attained by their people. [pp. 4–6]

I. What Is Constitutional Government?

The word "constitution" invariably means a nation's fundamental laws. However, when used as a modern political term, it has certain additional connotations. . . .

First, one usually assigns to a constitution greater force than to ordinary laws. . . . Since a nation's fundamental laws are of great importance, the idea has persisted from antiquity that there should be a distinction between them and ordinary laws. However, there is another reason why modern nations give such special weight to constitutions. The intention is to prevent the reckless infringement, at some later time, of the rights that [constitutions] describe with great care. Whatever they ostensibly may be, modern constitutions have in fact appeared as a result of the long struggle for popular rights that was waged against those who in the past monopolized political power, those rightly called the privileged classes. [pp. 13–15]

Second, a constitution must include as an important part of its contents the following three provisions: (1) guarantees of civil liberties, (2) the principle of the separation of the three branches of government, and (3) a popularly elected legislature. . . .

1. The fifteen articles of chapter II of the Japanese constitution concern the "Rights and Duties of Subjects." As the title indicates, some of these articles prescribe duties, but most of them enumerate those rights and liberties that are indispensable to the people's material and spiritual happiness and progress. . . . They clearly state that these rights and liberties may not be arbitrarily restricted by the government but can be limited only by law, in whose enactment the Diet participates. [pp. 16–17]

2. If it is defined theoretically, the principle of separation of powers becomes a very troublesome problem. Generally speaking, it means that the executive, judicial, and legislative powers are exercised by separate organs of the government. . . . It is true for all countries, without exception, that the intention of the principle . . . is best shown in the area of judicial independence. However, nowadays its application to relations between the executive and legislative branches differs substantially from country to country. Of course, the executive and the legislative branches should be independent of each other, but if there

is no provision at all for negotiations between the two, constitutional government cannot be expected to function smoothly. [pp. 18–19]

3. More than any other factor, [provision for a popularly elected legislature] . . . is regarded by the public as the most important characteristic of a constitution. Indeed, many people think of it as the only essential characteristic of a constitution. . . . Why is this provision so important? Because the popularly elected legislature is the only branch of government in whose composition the people have a direct voice. The members of the other two branches are experts appointed by the government. The people have almost no direct concern in naming them. With the legislature it is just the opposite. Its members are directly elected by the people. Naturally, the people can influence it and thereby make it express the popular will. . . .

These are the [three] indispensable elements of a modern constitution. . . . If they are present, then there is a constitution. When such a constitution exists and is the guiding principle of political life, we have a constitutional government. [pp. 21–22]

II. What Is Meant by the Perfection of Constitutional Government?

Living as we do under a constitutional government, we must work all the harder for its perfection. But we must not work blindly. The task requires a strenuous effort based on the same . . . ideology that originally brought about the establishment of the constitution and on the fundamental spirit concealed in its innermost depths. . . .

What, then, is the spirit of a constitution? No generalization is possible, for it varies from one country to another. . . . In some countries the privileged classes survive as relics of a bygone age and still continue to exercise their influence. Where this is so, even though the pressure of world trends has forced the promulgation of a constitution, many people try to implement it so as not to injure their antiquated political ideology. These people stridently emphasize the principle that their nation's constitution has nothing in common with that of any other but instead has its own peculiar traits. We frequently see this in our country, where there is a tendency in constitutional theory to assert as the basis for the political structure a peculiar national morality of our own, attempting in this way to avoid interpreting the constitution in accordance with Western constitutional ideas. . . . Of course, each country's constitution reflects that country's peculiar characteristics. It would be difficult to summarize the unique qualities of each country's constitution, but it is possible to infer from the history of modern world civilization the spiritual basis common to them all. . . . The common spiritual basis that I discover in all constitutions is democracy. [pp. 26–28]

III. The Spiritual Basis of Constitutional Government: Democracy

The Japanese word *minpon shugi* (democracy) (people as the basic principle) is of very recent use. Previously, *minshu shugi* (people's rule principle) seems to have been generally favored, and even *minshū shugi* and *heimin shugi* have been used. However, *minshu shugi* is likely to be understood as referring to the theory held by the social democratic parties that "the sovereignty of the nation resides in the people." *Heimin shugi* implies an opposition between the common people (*heimin*) and the nobility, and it risks being misunderstood to mean that the nobility is the enemy and the common people are the friendly forces. By themselves, the words *minshū shugi* are not open to such a misinterpretation, but they represent an overemphasis on the masses (*minshū*). Since . . . the basis of constitutional government is a universally accepted political principle that emphasizes the people at large but does not differentiate between nobles and commoners or distinguish between a monarchical and a republican national polity, I suspect that the comparatively new term *minpon shugi* is the most suitable. [pp. 28–29]

I think [the Western word] "democracy," as used in the fields of law and political science, has at least two distinct meanings. In one sense it means that "in law the sovereignty of the nation resides in the people." In the other it is used to mean that "in politics the fundamental end of the exercise of the nation's sovereignty should be the people." . . . I would like to use *minshu shugi* and *minpon shugi*, respectively, as the suitable translations for these two senses of "democracy." [pp. 30–31]

In our country many people are prevented by the "popular sovereignty" aspect of *minshu shugi* from properly understanding democracy. This has unavoidably led to a prejudice that has noticeably retarded the development of democracy. Consequently, I believe that in order to have the people strive for the advancement of a constitutional government with a correct understanding of democracy, it is extremely important to clarify the distinction between the two meanings of the word.[1] [pp. 31–32]

IV. The Distinction Between Popular Sovereignty and Democracy

Even "popular sovereignty," if we examine it closely, is seen to be of two kinds. . . .

The first has been set forth in the following form: In the corporate body known as the nation the original and natural locus of sovereignty must be the people as a whole. This I call absolute or philosophic popular sovereignty. . . .

---

1. From here on, *minshu shugi* will be translated as "popular sovereignty" to distinguish it from *minpon shugi*, the term that Yoshino prefers for "democracy."

The second kind is set forth in the following form: In a specific country it has been decided by interpretation of the constitution that the sovereignty resides in the people. This I call popular sovereignty by mutual consent or by interpretation. . . . Both types, however, concern the legal location of the nation's sovereignty. Consequently, there cannot be the slightest doubt that the words "popular sovereignty" are inappropriate to a country like ours, which from the beginning has been unmistakably monarchical. Therefore, I believe it is very clear that while "popular sovereignty" and "democracy" may seem similar, they differ a great deal in substance, for "democracy" raises no question of republicanism or monarchism and constitutes the fundamental spirit common to the constitutions of all modern countries. [pp. 32–38]

V. Misinterpretations of Democracy

Democracy is not contingent on where legal theory locates sovereignty. It merely implies that in the exercise of this sovereignty, the sovereign should always make it his policy to value the well-being and opinions of the people. . . . There is no doubt that even in a monarchy this principle can be honored without contravening the established system in the slightest degree. . . . Nevertheless, many people think that democracy and the monarchical system are completely incompatible. This is a serious misconception. [pp. 38–39]

Most of the misconceptions about democracy arise from emotional arguments that have no theoretical basis. This is especially true of the small class that up to now has possessed special privileges and monopolized political power. . . . In the past the system made them rulers of the common people. In the new age they must yield this formal dominance to the people and be content with the substance of moral leadership. . . . As long as they alter neither their attitudes nor their motives to accord with the change in the times, no true progress can be expected in constitutional government. The public is prone to say that constitutional government has failed to develop as we had hoped because the thought of the people has not developed. But whether the people's thought develops is really determined by whether advanced thinkers properly guide it. When the small class of leaders holds to its narrow-minded views, it is impossible to implant in the hearts of the common people sound constitutional ideas, no matter how much the necessity of spreading constitutional thought is preached. In this connection I must turn to the small enlightened intellectual class in the upper ranks of society and express the hope that they themselves reach a true understanding of constitutional ideas and become conscious of their duty to guide the common people. [pp. 39–41]

In addition to misinterpretations based on emotional arguments, there also are criticisms of democracy that have a somewhat theoretical basis, or what would outwardly appear to be such. First, some persons confuse democracy with popular sovereignty and see no clear difference between them. They therefore think that democracy is opposed in theory to the principle of the sovereignty of the emperor. . . . Second, some persons look at the history of democracy's development, see that it has invariably gone hand in hand with popular sovereignty, and conclude from this that it is incompatible with the monarchical system. . . . Up to a point, this theory is true. Indeed, if we look at the history of the development of constitutional governments, we see that for the most part they have passed through a revolutionary stage. . . . But it would be a mistake to conclude that because constitutional government originated in revolutionary democratic thought, it must always be dangerous. This is as illogical as it is to argue that since man is descended from the monkeys, he will always have the monkey's inferior characteristics. . . .

If we hesitate for fear of possible evil effects, progress and development will never be achieved. If something is necessary for the advancement of the nation and society, we must quickly search for a method to attain it. And we must strive greatly to prevent the abuses that we fear may result. We should not live in inaction, bound by our old established ways. Progress requires strenuous effort. As a people with constitutional government, we must willingly throw open our doors to world trends and actively seek the greatest progress and development for our nation and society. Yet at the same time, we must resolve to reject and fight to overcome whatever harm may accompany this. This is truly the glorious responsibility borne by the advanced thinkers in a constitutionally governed country. As long as they are determined not to shirk it, I believe we need have no fear whatsoever for the future of the nation under democracy. [pp. 41–44]

VI. The Substance of Democracy: Political Objectives

Earlier I defined democracy as the policy in exercising political power of valuing the profit, happiness, and opinions of the people. On the face of it, this definition reveals two aspects of democracy. First, the object of the exercise of political power . . . must be the people's welfare. Second, the policies that determine how political power is exercised . . . are settled in accordance with the people's opinions. . . .

The first requirement of democracy, then, is that the ultimate end of the exercise of political power be the good of the people. . . . In ancient times the objective of government was the survival and prosperity of a small number of powerful persons or the preservation of their authority; it was never the well-being of the people as a whole. . . . To the feudal mind, the land and people of a country were no more than the personal property of the royal family. But in the feudal period it became quite clear that land and people were the foundation on which the royal family stood, so the people gradually came to be valued. . . . In general, international competition further deepened the ruling classes' feeling of dependence on the people. . . . Accordingly, the feudal state came to treat the people with a great deal of consideration. . . . From our point of view today, the people were, in the final analysis, like servants happy under a kindhearted master. They were not permitted to claim consideration for themselves as a matter of right. . . . Our democracy is opposed to placing the people in such a position. It demands that the ultimate goal of government must change and become the welfare of the people. It further demands that . . . [their welfare] absolutely never be used as a means to some other end. In modern politics it is certainly not permissible to sacrifice the general welfare to the interests of a small number. [pp. 44–48]

Some people still may denounce democracy as contravening the idea of loyalty to the emperor, a sentiment dating from the founding of our country. . . . Some people may ask whether democracy would oppose setting aside the people's welfare even if this were to be done in the interest of the imperial family. In my answer to these criticisms I would make the following two points. First, there is absolutely no contradiction nowadays between the "interest of the imperial family" and the interest of the nation, [an interest] standing at the very top of the people's well-being. . . . Since the imperial family is the unique head of the national family, it is utterly unthinkable that it should become necessary, "in the interest of the imperial family," to disregard the interest of the people. Consequently, I believe the interest of the imperial family and the interest of the people can never conflict with each other. Second, let us yield the point and suppose such a conflict to have arisen between the two. Since democracy relates to the sovereign's way of using his powers, there is nothing to prevent him from establishing the basic principle that he will not arbitrarily disregard the welfare of the people. . . . It is the determination of the Japanese people to willingly go through fire and water for the sake of the emperor. However, if the state systematically exploited this devotion to secure the people's acceptance of acts that disregarded the people's welfare, might not a certain cheerlessness come to characterize the subjects' spirit of loyalty? I would therefore like to make it a principle that whenever the state demands from the people sacrifices beyond a certain level, the choice of whether or not they are to comply should be left entirely to their moral judgment. . . . Our loyal people will never, for fear of their own safety, hesitate to strive for their emperor and country. Loyalty to the emperor is a spirit dating from the founding of our country; it is the essence of our national polity. Reinforcing it by erecting it into a system would, I believe, lead to many evils but bring no advantage. [pp. 48–50]

Democracy does not permit the welfare of the people to be sacrificed for any purpose whatsoever. However, if we ask whether today this point has been completely realized in every country, [the answer is] most assuredly no. . . .

In our own country, unhappily, the people do not yet comprehend this problem and have not progressed to the point of insisting on [the principle]. Conversely, although in general the privileged classes have, little by little, come to understand the demands of the people and thus may be considered to be aware of how to meet them, there still are narrow-minded persons in these classes who value themselves highly and are condescending to the people. . . . In order that the place of these classes in a democracy be peacefully settled and a trend toward a healthy development of society thereby created, it is necessary that on the one hand we work for the development of the people's knowledge and that on the other we urge the upper classes seriously to search their hearts. [pp. 51–53]

In recent times there has been a trend in our country and others for certain new privileged classes to appear in addition to the historic ones. Chief among these is the plutocracy. . . . It is contrary to the objective of democracy for economically superior and inferior classes to develop and, as a consequence, for profits to become the monopoly of a single class. Therefore, without touching on the fundamental problem of whether the organization of society should be basically reconstructed, it has recently been considered necessary in government to resort temporarily to moderate measures directed against these economically privileged classes. . . . To consider now the situation in our own country, in recent times capitalists have gained strength and with their huge financial power are finally on the point of wrongfully trampling on the public interest. It is true that this tendency is not so strong [in Japan] as it is in America and Europe, but recently the influence of the capitalists has increased markedly. After the Sino-Japanese War and the Russo-Japanese War, their power grew especially quickly. Wealth has never lacked a certain degree of power, but before the Sino-Japanese War the money power was in fact completely under the control of the political power. In the early years of the Meiji period, wealth bent its knee at the door of political power and under the latter's shelter worked by degrees to increase financial power   The Sino-Japanese War forced, for the first time, political power to beg aid from wealth. In this way wealth first achieved a position of equality with political power. With the Russo-Japanese War, the government of Prince Katsura kowtowed to the capitalists in all matters and sought their financial aid. Consequently, in one jump, wealth became strong enough to control political power. The bestowal of peerages on rich men dates from this time. . . . In this way the wealthy put pressure on political power and, for the profit of their own class, demanded the passage of various unfair laws. As a result, various kinds of financial legislation are in force today that are very disadvantageous to the general public and serve only the interests of the capitalist class. Thus in our country, a new privileged class has recently appeared whose interests are unfairly protected by law. In the future, this kind of privileged class will conflict with the demands of democracy; how the two will be harmonized is a matter that engages our most anxious attention. Since the moneyed class is concerned with material things, they do not readily listen to the ordinary people. Consequently, if there are great difficulties in solving problems in the area of [constitutional government], will they not in all likelihood arise from this problem of the financially privileged class? If the plutocracy were by some chance to make common cause with the traditional privileged classes in confronting democracy, there could be no greater misfortune for the nation. In this connection I must incessantly arouse the attention of the intellectuals and entreat the reflection of the nobility and plutocrats who are flouting the affections of the nation. [pp. 53–55]

VII. The Substance of Democracy: Determination of Policies

Democracy not only implies that the purpose of government is the welfare of the people but also demands that in the final determination of policies, the people's opinions must be valued highly. This certainly does not mean that in each individual case the opinions of each individual person must be heard. It is an overall principle according to which nothing is done in opposition to the views of the people and no political action is undertaken without their general approval—expressed or tacit. [p. 56]

This second essential [purpose] of democracy is strongly criticized. If we examine these criticisms closely, [we will find,] I think, that they are of three kinds.

The first is the idea that democracy is opposed constitutionally to the principle of imperial sovereignty. . . . Yet, democracy is a theory of politics, not of law. From a legal standpoint, sovereignty resides in the emperor. Democracy comes in when one asks what principle should guide the emperor in the exercise of his sovereignty. It is in no way inconsistent with monarchy. Of course, I too agree that in order to protect the imperial institution, we should reject the dangerous theory of popular sovereignty. But opposition on this account to the advance of democracy—so similar in name to popular sovereignty but so different from it in substance—is a serious problem for the future of constitutional government. [pp. 57–58]

Another criticism is the notion that, even conceding democracy to be a political concept, if in the exercise of his power the sovereign must by custom always take into account the general will of the people, his sovereignty is thereby limited and the free exercise of his authority is prevented. However, those who believe this ignore the fact that in a constitutional country the sovereignty of the ruler is always limited in some way. It is because the word "limitation" is used that this impression is produced; how would it be if the word "Way"[2] were used in its place? Assume that constitutional government is a system under which a sovereign rules not by arbitrary whim but in accordance with the "Way." Is not this "Way" a sort of limitation on the free exercise of sovereignty? Well, the "Way" manifests itself both legally and politically; in other words,

---

2. Yoshino is using the Confucian concept of the "Way."

constitutional countries make it a rule to limit the power of the sovereign in both legal theory and political practice. . . . Practically speaking, there is no country in the world today in which the sovereign decides all the policies of state by himself. . . . [Thus] the real problem is what kind of limitations there should be on the ruler's authority. Should he be limited by concern for the will of the people generally or by the opinions of two or three of his confidants? Concern for the will of the people may or may not limit the ruler's sovereignty, but I find it a one-sided argument not to admit that other limitations exist even when there is no such concern. Let us assume, for example, that the cabinet has changed and that custom demands that the responsibility for forming a successor cabinet be left to the leader of the political party that commands a majority in the parliament. It is objected that this practice imposes limitations on the ruler's sovereignty. . . . The ruler's complete freedom of action, if applied literally on such an occasion, would imply that without consulting anyone else, he alone could decide who was to be the prime minister. . . . Yet whether or not such a method would be practical, in fact the usual practice is for him to consult with two or three of the experienced persons of his court. . . . As I see it, both the appointment of ministers according to party majorities in parliament and their appointment on the advice of elder statesmen are limitations of the ruler's authority. . . . The question that arises here is *which* sort of limitation should the ruler accept? Should he consult a small number of people, or should he consult at large with great numbers of people? Consequently, it is improper to reject democracy on the grounds that it limits the emperor's sovereignty and is therefore bad. If one wishes to reject democracy validly, one must go a step further and clearly demonstrate that it is always bad to take counsel with many men and always good to take counsel with a few men. In Japan since early Meiji, however, it has been the fundamental national policy to take counsel with large numbers of persons. His Majesty, the Meiji emperor, decreed at the beginning of the Restoration that deliberative assemblies should be widely established and all matters decided by public discussion. Thus the spirit of democracy, which consists of the just and equitable conduct of government in consultation with the majority of the people, has been our national policy since early in the Meiji [period]. Those who today deny this and advocate the principle of minority advice are moving against the general trend of political evolution. [pp. 58–61]

It is said that the enlightened are always likely to be a minority; that therefore the best government must be government by the minority; and that conversely, majority rule deteriorates into mob rule. This . . . is partly true. However, we must not forget that minority rule is always government in a dark chamber. However splendid a person's character may be, when others do not observe him, he is likely to commit excesses. . . . Some point to the corruption of the Diet and its members and say that there are bound to be evils in majority rule. . . . But in general, since government by the minority is secret government, many of its evils never come to the attention of the country, while since majority government is open government, there is a tendency to magnify its most minute deficiencies. [pp. 65–66]

It may be mistakenly thought that majority government makes no use at all of the enlightened minority, but this is absolutely not so. . . . [This minority] can best fulfill their function as truly enlightened people when they modestly identify themselves with the majority, ostensibly following the majority will and yet, as the spiritual leaders of the majority, quietly working for the public good. . . . In all formal respects, the majority forms the basis for the exercise of governmental power, and they must be the political rulers, but within their ranks they in fact need spiritual leaders. . . . If the enlightened minority are truly to serve the national society, they must resolve to use their wisdom to guide the masses spiritually. At the same time they must resolve to enlist themselves in the service of the masses and, by making their own influence prevail, work for the public good. . . . Only when these two groups work together can a constitutional government develop perfectly. Seen politically, this cooperation means that the country is ruled by the will of the majority, but seen spiritually, it means that the country is guided by the enlightened minority. . . . It is government by the people, but in one sense it can also be called government by the best. Thus one can claim that constitutional government reaches its most splendid perfection when there is a harmonious reconciliation of political democracy with spiritual aristocracy. . . . In this respect, I am thoroughly disgusted with the attitude of Japan's elder statesmen and other bureaucratic statesmen. Although they enjoy the special favor of the imperial house and the esteem of the nation, they sometimes use their exalted position to interfere irresponsibly in political affairs. They will not reach down from their eminent position to establish contact with the masses but instead take a hostile attitude toward democratic influences. It is regrettable that they thus fail to understand the true meaning of modern political life, but one must say it is especially unfortunate for the nation that they neglect the social function of the enlightened minority by not assuming the responsibility of popular leadership. After all, surprisingly enough, the ordinary people actually pay excessive respect to honors and titles. When the aristocrats who inherit historical and social authority are at the same time highly capable in point of actual ability and jointly undertake the leadership of the people, the people gladly submit to this leadership. For the sake of the healthy development of constitutional government, nay, say rather for the sake of the future success of our society and nation, I beg the enlightened minority to reflect deeply on this. We must hope that the aristocrats and plutocrats will respond to the handsome treatment they have received from the nation, not only by giving great thought to how they should conduct themselves, but also by giving serious attention to the education of their children and younger brothers. [pp. 67–70]

VIII. Representative Government

In this section, Yoshino argues the merits of representative government against those who claim that it does not go far enough toward meeting the demands of true democracy. Syndicalism and the popular referendum, he notes, have been the two methods most commonly advanced for achieving more direct popular government, but both of them, he believes, are impractical and unnecessary.

IX. The Relation of the People to the Legislators

The most important point regarding the relation between the people and the legislators is that the people always occupy the position of master of the house, while the legislators are necessarily transients. The proper maintenance of this relationship is absolutely essential to the functioning of constitutional government. The abuses of constitutional government generally stem from the inversion of this relationship. And it is not just a question of the relation between the people and the legislators. The same truth holds as between legislators and the government. Whenever the legislators, who should supervise the government, are puppets of the government, many evils arise. Likewise, whenever the people, who should supervise the legislators, are instead manipulated by them, the operation of constitutional government is replete with innumerable scandals and corruption. If the government seduces legislators with offers of gain [and] if legislators also lead the people astray with offers of gain, then the proper relationships will be inverted, and the structure of constitutional government will be filled with abuses. If we wish to clean up political life and see a normal evolution of constitutional government, the first thing we must do is to pay strict attention to rectifying the relationship between the people and the legislators. There are at least three measures that must be adopted in order to accomplish this. [p. 87]

1. Inculcation of election ethics. . . . I do not think that the ethics of the Japanese are, broadly speaking, especially low. But because elections are a new experience for them, they have, regrettably, greatly ignored morality in conducting them. I feel it is necessary for us to inculcate the principles of election ethics in the people of the nation.

This being the case, what points should the people be made to understand especially? One of them is that although a single vote seems to be of very little importance, it actually is of great consequence to the fate of the nation. It is too sacred to be subject to influence by bribes or intimidation. A second point is that one votes in the interest of the nation, not for the profit of a single locality. To vote with only local interests in mind is likely more often than not to result in sacrificing the interests of the whole nation. A third point is that voting is our prerogative, not something to be done at the solicitation of the candidates. It is up to us to recommend proper candidates to the nation. Nowadays it is extremely important to drive these three points deep into the minds of the people. [pp. 88–89]

2. The necessity of adopting and enforcing strict election regulations. When legislators manipulate the people, invariably corruption and bad government flourish. Only when the people control their legislators does the operation of constitutional government follow the proper course. Therefore, it is especially important to impose strict penalties on the corrupt practices that may be carried on between the legislators and the people. . . . In this respect, a rather strict election law has been adopted in Japan; the only thing to be regretted is that it has not been rigorously enough enforced and that the government tends to be lax in dealing with the activities of its own party. [pp. 91–92]

3. The necessity of extending the suffrage as widely as possible. If the suffrage is limited, corruption will be rampant. When the suffrage is extended as far as possible, there can be absolutely no distribution of bribes and the like. Moreover, only when it has become absolutely impossible for candidates to fight one another with money and things of value will they compete by sincerely and frankly presenting their views and personal qualifications to the people. Consequently, the people will have an opportunity of receiving a political education through this means. When suffrage is limited, as it is today, there is a chance of winning a contest without presenting one's views and qualifications. Therefore the political parties pay little heed to the political education of the people. . . . There is no doubt that Diet members truly represent politically all the people of the country. Therefore, they should not be the representatives of only one class. It is logical, then, that the scope of the electorate should be as broad as possible. . . . Today, as in the past, the basic political consideration is to hold elections that result essentially in representing the overall interests of the people generally. We think it proper on this ground that the suffrage should be extended as widely as possible. Naturally this is not to say that suffrage should be unlimited. We must admit that from the standpoint of necessity and convenience, several kinds of limitations should be set if the objectives of elections are to be achieved. To begin with, we must probably exclude infants, the insane, criminals, persons on public relief, bankrupts, and so forth. . . . Whether or not women should be excluded is, in the final analysis, a problem for the future. Today, suffrage is generally the exclusive possession of men. Of course, some countries do extend political rights to women. [pp. 93–95]

Most of the world's civilized countries have seen fit to adopt universal [manhood] suffrage. The only civilized countries . . . that impose comparatively great limitations on suffrage are Russia and Japan. In all other civilized countries, universal suffrage is already a settled issue and no longer comes up for political discussion. In Japan the agitation for extending the suffrage has recently increased, but apparently it will take a long time before the idea becomes generally accepted. . . . As a consequence of our present suffrage limitations, no more than 3 percent of all Japanese are enfranchised. In the general elections in March of last year [1915], only 1,544,725 persons had the right to vote. [pp. 102–3]

Thus, the extension of the suffrage and the strict enforcement of electoral laws are the most pressing matters facing Japan. The history of other countries shows that these two actions have often effected a cleanup of political life. If they are neglected, the ideal of constitutional government cannot be realized, no matter how much one preaches about election ethics and prods the conscience of the people. The argument for extending suffrage is a subject that we must study most earnestly, and we must henceforth advocate it most fervently. Insofar as the public has misconceptions, we must, on the one hand, appeal to the intellectuals to reconsider the issue and, on the other, dispel the confusions of the political world. We must work diligently at these two things so that in the near future, universal suffrage may become a reality. [p. 104]

X. The Relation of Parliament to the Government

It is the government that takes direct charge of state affairs. Only when parliament oversees the government can there be just and equitable administration. But since the government wields real power, it is likely to use its position to control and manipulate the legislators, thereby reversing matters and ordering about as it pleases the very persons by whom, properly speaking, it should be supervised. Many hidden evils spring from such a situation. . . . Therefore, it is essential to the healthy functioning of constitutional government that the government be kept in a state of strict subordination to the parliament. [pp. 107–8]

Hence we consider it necessary to sharpen the moral conscience of office-holders as much as possible. . . . Fidelity to conscience and regard for integrity are the very life and soul of a politician. For a politician there is no greater crime than to change his opinion for the sake of dishonest gain. It is surprising that such affairs should be problems in a constitutional country. It is more than surprising; it is shameful. Under constitutional government, worthless individuals should not become legislators in the first place. Government is fundamentally a very exalted calling, one that can be undertaken well only by persons of high cultivation. Therefore is it not an insult to a politician merely to investigate his character? It is the practice in Western countries that men about whose character there is some doubt are never accepted as politicians in the first place. . . . The frequent occurrence of corrupt behavior among legislators is probably a peculiarity of Japan. With such a state of affairs it is absolutely impossible for constitutional government to progress in Japan. To prevent [corruption], as I have said again and again, it is necessary to keep the people from committing errors at the very start in the elections. Moreover, it is necessary that the people inflict the severest punishments on representatives who defile their offices. By means of the law, we must not only sternly punish any representatives who defile their offices; we must also resolve to use the power of public opinion to bury them in political oblivion.

In this regard, one point I wish to emphasize is that the offense of one who tempts [an official] is far more serious than that of the one who is tempted. [pp. 109–10]

Making the legislators morally independent of the government is only the first step. If we are to persuade the legislators to discharge their supervisory responsibility and thoroughly inquire into the government's transgressions, it also is necessary that the government be made to fulfill its political responsibility to the parliament. . . . If the principle of responsible cabinets has not been firmly established in political institutions or usage, it is impossible to achieve the proper relationship between government and the parliament. Consequently, the requisites for democracy cannot be fully met.

In contrast to the responsible cabinet system, there is also the principle of the nonparty cabinet. According to this idea, the cabinet should rise above the wishes of parliament and occupy a position of absolute independence. Under this system, no matter how much the government is opposed by parliament, no matter even if there occasionally are votes of no confidence [in parliament], the government unconcernedly continues in office. To put the theory in its worst light, it is a pretext that enables the government freely to commit any kind of arbitrary misrule. Thus it is inconsistent with the principle that final decisions on policy should depend on the views of the people generally. Therefore, the nonparty cabinet system is decidedly not the normal rule in constitutional government. Of course, under our constitution, theoretically the ministers of state are responsible to the sovereign alone, so it is not absolutely necessary for them immediately and as a matter of course to resign their posts when the Diet opposes them. That is to say, [this practice] cannot be called unconstitutional. However, it is clear from the foregoing that it is contrary to the spirit of constitutional government. [p. 112]

The usual method used nowadays for calling the responsibility [of the government] into account is the parliamentary cabinet system. In most countries it has recently become the practice for the government to be formed by the leader of the political party that has a majority in parliament. In this sense most governments are today party cabinets. . . . In countries that have just two major parties, this system works well, but in those that have many small parties, it does not. . . . In order that the wisdom of the party cabinet system may be demonstrated, it is absolutely necessary to encourage the establishment of two major parties. The establishment of two major parties, however, is a matter determined by the course of events and cannot very well be controlled by a constitution's theory. As a result, the workability of the party cabinet system always varies from one country to another. Hence the problem arises as to whether party government can really work smoothly in Japan. . . .

I have explained why we must have a fully responsible cabinet system if constitutional government is to reach its most perfect development. In the West this matter was settled long ago and is hardly an issue any more. If there were a place where this became an issue today, that place would be unexpectedly showing itself to be far behind the times in the development of constitutional government. [pp. 113–20]

As I see it, Japan is generally on the right track in this respect. Although we do not yet have a responsible cabinet system, today everyone seems to believe firmly that a vote of no confidence in the Diet would inevitably result in the cabinet's resignation. Consequently it has become the practice for the government always to dissolve the Diet as soon as it sees that a no-confidence motion is about to be passed. Since December 1885, when Count Itō first instituted the present cabinet system, there have been about twenty cabinet changes. The great majority of them resulted from clashes with the Diet. Even in the beginning, when the principle of nonparty cabinets was asserted, no cabinet could maintain its position in the face of parliamentary opposition. . . . At that time, a nonparty cabinet seems to have meant a cabinet that stood apart from the political parties in the Diet; it does not seem to have meant a cabinet uninfluenced by Diet decisions. Halfway through this thirty-year period, Katsura and [Kinmochi] Saionji began the custom of alternating with each other as prime minister. Since that time, although the principle of party cabinets has not yet been fully implemented, it has become impossible for anyone to enter the cabinet without allying himself in some fashion or other with the majority forces in the Diet. We should try to promote this tendency and more thoroughly enforce [the idea of a] party government. From this point of view, I believe that even though good results might temporarily be achieved with a national unity cabinet, such as has been advocated from time to time, or with the cabinet of "talents" that some schemers have occasionally dreamed of, we must firmly reject these for the sake of the progress of constitutional government. Therefore in this area today, we must struggle and contend on an even larger scale. If we are to have the Diet adequately supervise the government and thereby make the Diet in fact the central force in government, I believe it is absolutely essential that we eradicate the bigoted views [of party cabinets that prevail].

It is essential to the operation of constitutional government that parliament be the central force in government. This is why we have preached the principle of responsible cabinets. Yet the West has gone ahead to a still further stage of development. Namely, in one or two countries it is no longer the government that is the powerful obstruction to making parliament, especially the popularly elected house, the central political force. If there is anything today that still somewhat stands in the way of the political supremacy of the popularly elected house, it is the upper house. Hence it now is advocated that the lower house be made supreme over the upper house. . . . Originally the upper house [was established as a body whose] duty it was to give further consideration to the decisions of the lower house because it was felt that the people, whom the lower house represents, were not yet sufficiently well informed. Some among the masses today, however, are extremely advanced. Accordingly, from the practical point of view, no great harm would come if the restraining powers of the upper house were eliminated and the supremacy of the lower house were recognized. [pp. 122–24]

The advanced nations of the West believe the popularly elected house is extremely important to the functioning of constitutional government. They believe this because the essence of constitutional government is, after all, democracy; and the complete realization of democracy, presupposing as it does the various reforms I have mentioned, ultimately consists of making the lower house the central political force. Thus intellectuals in all countries are extremely anxious to give the lower house, in both form and fact, a position of supremacy over the upper house and the government. In Japan, the meaning of a responsible cabinet is only now becoming clear. Although this is cause for rejoicing, we must at the same time regret very much that the authority of the lower house, which directly represents the power of the people. is not very important. This is partly because the legislators who comprise it are not yet endowed with knowledge and dignity. No matter how important the lower house ought to be in the governmental system, the authority of the nation will never be vested in it if those who actually make up its membership consist solely of mediocre, unprincipled fools. Because able men are not attracted to it, it lacks the authority to deal with the upper house; and when a cabinet is formed, the unseemly truth is that at the very least the prime minister must be sought outside the lower house. As long as the lower house lacks able men, it will lack power; as long as it lacks power, men of promise will seek careers elsewhere. In this vicious circle, the wisdom of the responsible cabinet system cannot be fully demonstrated. Under the present circumstances, it is useless for the lower house to assume an air of importance. Screaming that the lower house should be respected will not give it any actual power. In this matter, on the one hand, we must earnestly seek self-respect and strenuous effort from the legislators; on the other, we must ardently hope that the people will not go astray in elections and that they will not neglect to spur on, indirectly and directly, the legislators whom they have chosen. In regard to the elder statesmen and other upper-class politicians, we must earnestly hope that they do not assume an attitude of detached loftiness, of useless disparagement of the lower house, and of disdain for the power of the people's representatives. We must earnestly hope that as Japanese, they too will, like us, cooperate for the sake of the nation in the task of strengthening the lower house. [pp. 128–30]

[Yoshino, *Minpon shugi ron*, pp. 4–130; AET]

ISHIBASHI TANZAN: A LIBERAL
BUSINESS JOURNALIST

Ishibashi Tanzan (1884–1973) graduated from Waseda University in 1907. At Waseda he was strongly influenced by his teacher, the liberal Tanaka Ōdō, who had studied with John Dewey at the University of Chicago in the 1890s. Ishibashi first took a job as a reporter for the *Mainichi shinbun*, but in 1911 he joined the staff of the *Tōyō keizai shinpō* (*Oriental Economist*), a business journal with strong Waseda connections that was considered a bastion of ultraliberalism. By 1924, Ishibashi had risen to editor in chief, a position he held until the end of World War II. During the years of his editorship, almost every important event or problem evoked a trenchant, liberal comment from him. Although well known as a liberal, Ishibashi was so highly regarded by the government authorities for his economic expertise that even as the repression intensified and war came, they frequently called on him to serve in various advisory capacities. After the war, he entered party politics and played a major role in reconstructing the Japanese economy. He was finance minister from May 1946 to May 1947 and minister of international trade and industry from December 1954 through December 1956. In December 1956, he became prime minister but had to resign two months later because of ill health. Nevertheless, until his death he continued to help shape policy.

The postwar Japan that ultimately emerged was very like the Japan that Ishibashi envisaged in the following selection. In a July 13, 1921, editorial discussing the policy that Japan should adopt at the forthcoming Washington Conference, Ishibashi confused his readers by suggesting that Japan should announce to the conference that it was going to give up all its overseas possessions and spheres of influence. Shortly thereafter, he wrote the following essay to explain in detail why he saw that course as Japan's best possible future.

"THE FANTASY OF GREATER JAPANISM"
(DAI NIHONSHUGI NO GENSŌ)

Part 1: Discard Korea, Taiwan, and Sakhalin!
Stop Interfering in China and Siberia!

The following two arguments will probably be offered by persons who oppose my proposal actually advocating making these slogans the basis of our policy toward the Pacific Conference:

1. If our country does not securely maintain control of these places, it will be impossible for us to be economically and militarily independent. At the very least we will risk jeopardizing our economic and military independence.

2. All the powers possess vast overseas colonies. In the case of America, where this is not so, the homeland itself is extensive. Also, the powers have put up walls around their vast resource-rich territories and do not allow in persons from other countries. In view of these facts, it is unfair that only Japan should discard its overseas possessions and spheres of influence.

To these counter arguments, I offer the following responses: the first argument is a fantasy; the second argument is the captive of small ambitions and displays ignorance of the path to accomplishing great ambitions.

To argue the first point, is it really advantageous for our country to continue to control Korea, Taiwan, and Sakhalin and to meddle in China and Siberia? I will divide "advantageous" into economic advantages and military advantages. First, looking at it from the economic viewpoint, how much economic profit do these lands contribute to our country? The quickest way to answer that is to look at the trade figures. Now for 1920 the trade of Korea, Taiwan, and Kwantung with Japan proper and Sakhalin were as follows:

	Exports	Imports	Total[a]
Korea	169,381	143,112	312,493
Taiwan	180,816	112,041	292,857
Kwantung	196,863	113,686	310,549
Total	547,060	368,839	915,899

[a] 1,000 yen units.

Source: Governments General of Korea and Taiwan; for Kwantung, Japan Monthly Trade Figures.

Together, these three lands had trade with Japan proper and Sakhalin of only 900 million yen. That same year, trade with America totaled 1.438 billion yen; with India, 587 million yen; and with England, 330 million yen.

If we look at either Korea or Taiwan or Kwantung, our trade with any one of them is less even than our trade with England. If we turn to America our trade there is more than 520 million yen more than with all three of these countries combined. In regard to trade figures, we have a greater economic advantage with America than we do with Korea, Taiwan, and Kwantung combined. With India and Britain, respectively, compared with any one of the trio, we have a superior economic advantage. If we speak of economic independence, we must say that America by itself, India by itself, and England by itself are countries indispensable to our economic independence.

A case might be made that though the overall amount of trade is limited, the goods produced in these lands are indispensably important to our industry or to our people's daily life, and in that respect, the trade has a special economic advantage. However, happily or unhappily, there are no such products in Korea,

Taiwan, or Kwantung. The most important raw material for our industry is cotton, which comes entirely from India and America. In the food category the most important item is rice, which comes almost entirely from French Indo-China, Siam, and places like that. As for other important items—coal, oil, iron, wood—for the supply of not one of them can we look solely to Korea or Taiwan or Kwantung. For instance, last year we imported 57 million *kin*[3] of iron from Kwantung. However, that same year our imports of iron exceeded 2 billion *kin*. Compared with that, 57 million *kin* is insignificant. Even with rice, Korea and Taiwan together can barely supply us with 2 million or 3 million *koku*.[4] For these amounts of imports why should our people hang on to Korea or Taiwan or Kwantung? . . .

The preceding has been about Korea, Taiwan, and Kwantung. We do not need a detailed explanation of Sakhalin. Everybody knows that after more than ten plus years [*sic*] of occupation, it has not been possible to produce any economic gain. For the northern part of Sakhalin [Russian territory occupied by Japan] there are said to be considerable hopes, and for that reason we have occupied the port of Nikolaevsk [on the Siberian mainland]. However, I fear it is probably rhetorical hype like the publicity ten years ago about great hopes for southern Sakhalin. What now remains to be discussed are the China and Siberian questions.

From an economic point of view, our policy of meddling in China and Siberia has undoubtedly been very disadvantageous for us. The Chinese and Russian peoples' antipathy toward our country is a great obstacle hindering our economic expansion in those lands. So long as we do not end our policy of meddling in those lands, our country cannot eliminate this antipathy. There may, of course, be some partially advantageous results from our meddling. For example, it stops the Chinese from raising the import tariff on [our] cotton yarn, and to that extent our export of cotton yarn to China has been made easier. However, if we were to ask how much our meddling has helped us successfully develop our overall trade, the increase over the last ten years has been only about one-third the increase of our trade with America. . . . What results will come of meddling in Siberia is a question for the future. If it is worse than the Chinese precedent, it clearly will not be good.

Well, the theory is that possessing Korea, Taiwan, and Sakhalin; having a leasehold in Kwantung; and meddling in China and Siberia all are indispensable to our economic independence. This theory, as just explained, is absolutely untenable. The economic relations of these lands with our country are, in both amount and character, below those we have with America and England. To think that because we maintain control over these lands we will reap great

---

3. One *kin* equals 1.323 pounds.
4. One *koku* equals about five bushels.

profits is only a fantasy that has arisen because the realities are not clearly understood. This being so, what about the point that these lands are militarily essential to our country?

Nowadays, various theories are in vogue concerning armaments. However, in my opinion the necessity of preparing armaments arises in only two situations:

1. Are you invading another country?
2. Are you afraid of being invaded by another country?

If you have no intention of invading another country or if you have no fear of being invaded by another country, there is absolutely no use for a military force beyond the police—both land and sea. Now if that is so, what circumstances are anticipated in which our country would prepare armaments? Politicians, military men, and journalists unanimously say that the objective of our armaments is definitely not to invade other countries. And [since they say it is so,] that, of course, is the way it must be. I also certainly do not think our armaments have been accumulated with the objective of invading other countries. Now, at this point what always becomes a question is if we do not have the objective of invading another country and if we do not fear being invaded by another country, then should our country have any need to accumulate armaments? In heaven's name, by what country do we fear being invaded? Previously, it was said to be Russia. Now it seems to be America. It is this case I would like to inquire about further. Whether it is America or some other country, if they attack our country, what area of it will they try to conquer? To my mind, there is not a person who would answer that they will come and seize a part of Japan proper. Even if you just simply made a present of it, there is probably no country that would accept [the gift]. Consequently, whether America or some other country, there is no fear of an attack on Japan proper. The attack would in all probability be against our overseas possessions. But even those territories would probably not be the problem. The greatest danger of an outbreak of war is probably with respect to China or Siberia. If our country tries to do as it pleases in China or Siberia, America will try to prevent this. Or if America tried to spread its influence in China or Siberia, our country would probably try to restrain America. If war comes, war will break out there. However, out of this will come the danger that our overseas possessions and Japan proper will also be attacked by enemy forces. If we rid ourselves of the ambition of trying to make China or Siberia our sphere of influence and if we adopted the attitude that we had no need for Manchuria, Taiwan, Korea, and Sakhalin, then absolutely no war would occur. Consequently, our country would definitely not be invaded by another country. Some argue that keeping these lands as our possessions and maintaining our sphere of influence are necessary from the standpoint of national defense. In reality, keeping these lands or trying to keep them is itself what gives rise to the necessity for a national defense. Possessing them is the reason that armaments are necessary. The necessity of possessing them does not arise from the needs of a national defense.

Thus people confuse the cause and effect. They think that Taiwan, China, Korea, Siberia, and Sakhalin are our national defense fence. But can this be so? This fence itself is in fact a dangerous barrier consisting of combustible grass. Yet in order to protect this "fence," our people are diligently preparing a so-called passive national defense. As I have explained, if we discarded the fence, there would be no need for a national defense. Some say that if our country discarded these lands, other countries would probably seize them. . . . However, if these are lands no longer necessary economically for our country to hold, is it not all right for some other country to take them? In reality, however, it would be absolutely impossible for a country to seize China from the Chinese or Siberia from the Russians. If Japan discarded Korea and Taiwan, there is definitely no country that in place of Japan could seize these lands from the Koreans and the Taiwanese. People say that because Japan has been militarily strong, China has been saved from being divided up among the powers, and thus peace has been maintained in the Far East. Perhaps in the past there was that connection, but now the situation is rather different. Now because Japan is militarily strong and has ambitions in China and seems to act as if it owns the Far East, the powers, which cannot afford to lose out, are keeping a keen eye on China and the Far East.

Part 2

As I explained previously . . . Greater Japanism, that is, the policy of trying to expand possessions and spheres of influence outside Japan, has no merit economically or militarily. Yet some people may say that my argument . . . is short of proof. For example, the amount of trade with Japan proper may be comparatively small. However, in addition to trade there are the Japanese who have migrated from the homeland and are making a living in these regions. Critics say that even though [their] trade with Japan proper is small, we cannot speak of these regions as having no economic value. To the extent that there is a relation to the solution of the population problem about which our people are so apprehensive, I think many people reasonably emphasize this point. However, here again, I argue, is a fantasy that does not clearly see the reality. Let us look at the figures. According to recent research, 149,000 Japanese from Japan proper are living in Taiwan; 337,000 in Korea; 78,000 in Sakhalin; 181,000 in all Manchuria (including Kwantung); 8,000 in Russian Asia; [and] 32,000 in China proper, a grand total of around 800,000. From 1905 . . . to the end of 1918, our population increased by 9.45 million. Assuming that all the Japanese living abroad moved there after 1905, 800,000 is about 8.6 percent of 9.45 million. Of course, it can be said that even if only one person was sent abroad, the population problem has to that extent been solved. However, if you consider how many tangible and intangible sacrifices have been paid, there is probably another road that should have been chosen [to relieve the population problem]. The [number of] persons living in the other lands amount to 800,000; persons living in Japan proper amount to 60 million. In my opinion, it is important not for the sake of 800,000 to forget the well-being of 60 million.

Good God, it is a mistake to try to solve Japan's economic and population problems simply by sending large numbers of human beings abroad. If you send human beings abroad in large numbers, somehow or other, ordinary working people will end up being sent. In today's enterprise system, whatever the country to which workers are sent, their incomes will be very small. They cannot possibly earn a lot for the mother country. Usually the workers receive barely enough for their food. Thus whether it is to a foreign country or one of our possessions it is foolish to rely on methods like these to use other lands for our economy. A special case is when the indigenous population is small and there are no local workers to use. When this is not the case, the workers used for Japanese enterprises abroad should be the inhabitants of the other lands. [Japanese] should go bringing only capital, technology, and entrepreneurial know-how. . . . To put it in the worst terms, bring capital, technology, and entrepreneurial skills and exploit native labor. . . .

If sending a great many human beings abroad is accepted as useless, then the economic profits yielded by overseas possessions and spheres of influence should be generally reckoned in the amount and character of the trade [with them]. For . . . no matter what enterprise we carry on in those lands, the outcome must unfailingly come to be directly or indirectly expressed in trade. That is why previously I held back on a general exposition and relied on trade figures to explain the worthlessness of adhering to Greater Japanism. . . .

Some people may say, "Your argument is all based on present-day conditions. Whether it is Taiwan, Korea, or Kwantung, may they not develop greatly in the future?" If the materials I presented previously had been studied seriously, this kind of doubt should not arise.

I will simply say this. Taiwan has been in our possession for twenty-five years, and Korea and Kwantung have been under our power for fifteen years. In that time our people have expended very great efforts on these regions. . . . After all the great effort, our trade with none of these areas has reached even the level of increase with India. Doesn't this imply that predictions about future trade development with these areas are problematical?

Well, the preceding is the gist of my argument that Greater Japanism has no value. But despite this discussion, perhaps some of the public do not accept my theory. In all probability, without any clear reasoning or calculation, they simply yearn for an expansion of the nation's territory. They probably assume all that I have explained was a mistake on my part. They probably imagine Greater Japanism is very profitable for us. However, for the sake of those persons who are fixated on expanding [into other nations'] territories, let me once more try to explain how they can be mistaken. Although they blindly believe Greater Japanism to be a profitable policy for us, the fact is that from now on and for a long time to come, such a policy would be confronted by circumstances under which it would be extremely difficult to carry it out. In the old days when England and others were eagerly expanding overseas, the inhabitants of the lands being invaded were not yet awake to the sentiment of national independence. Consequently, it was comparatively easy for England to do as it pleased in such lands. However, after that period this [kind of behavior] has not gone very well. With the development of world transportation and communication facilities, the air of civilization has penetrated to even the remotest places and taught the inhabitants the rights that they must assert. That is why their condition has become difficult for people in India, Ireland, and other places to bear. I believe that henceforth no matter what the land, it will be absolutely impossible to make new agreements by which people of different ethnicities or nationalities are annexed and subjected to the rule of another nation. And where such annexations have been carried out in the past, it probably is inevitable that the subject peoples will gradually be liberated and given independence or self-government. In Ireland that time has already been reached. In India there is a question of how long the present condition will continue. Confronting such an age, how will just our country alone maintain in perpetuity the present state of affairs in Korea and Taiwan? How can our nation keep up its obstruction of autonomy in China and Russia? The Korean Independence movement, the Movement for a Taiwanese Parliament, [and] the anti-Japanism in China and Siberia all already bespeak changes in the future. I maintain these movements will never be kept down by police and military interference and oppression, just as it has not been possible by interference and oppression to repress the workers' movement against capitalism.

The peoples will not end these movements until in one form or another they finally achieve the satisfaction of autonomy. They will, without fail, have a day when they achieve satisfaction. Consequently, for those who are oppressing them, the only difference is whether we will voluntarily give them autonomy today or whether autonomy will be wrested from us by them tomorrow. No matter how much profit Greater Japanism may offer us, we cannot pursue it for long. That being the case, to vainly persist [in this policy], to squander public monies, to be regarded as an enemy by four neighboring peoples of different ethnicities and nationalities—this situation, it must be said, is the old story of not seeing what is before one's eyes. If one is fated to be required to discard something anyway, then it is wise to throw it away quickly. I think that whether it is Taiwan, Korea, or China, if Japan adopts a policy of liberation and freedom, these people will never be estranged from Japan. In all likelihood, they will surely look up [to Japan] and make Japan their leader. They will continue an economic and political intimacy with Japan, an intimacy as close as if we were all one and the same people. The feelings of the Chinese, the Taiwanese, and the Koreans are surely these. They are angered only because Japan has assumed the position of the whites, is imitating the whites, is oppressing [its Asian neighbors], and is constantly trying to make them prey for its eating. They hope that the Japanese will somehow change their attitude and treat them as brothers and friends. If this were so, they would be happy and follow Japan's orders. "He among you who wishes to become great must serve you— he who wishes to become head among you must become your servant." Surely, today that must be the attitude that Japan should adopt toward its four neighbors. . . .

If our country does not do this but persists in the present attitude for any length of time, then the day may not be far off when we completely lose the hearts of our four neighbors. . . . At that time, regrets will be useless. The wise policy is to liberate Korea and Taiwan in any way and as quickly as possible and to adopt the principle of peace with China and Russia, thus gaining the moral support of our four neighbors. With this kind of beginning, our country's economy will be able to fully utilize the raw materials and markets of the East. With this kind of beginning, our nation's national defense will be perfectly secure. . . . Here I have reached my conclusion about the value of Greater Japanism.

To sum it up, as I see it, Greater Japanism fails to advance our economic interests, and in addition we have no hope [of sustaining] this policy in the future. To persist in this policy and thereby throw away the profits and preeminent position that can be obtained from the very nature of things and, for its sake, to make even greater sacrifices; that is decidedly not a step our people should take. Also, from a military point of view, if we persist in Greater Japanism, [greater] armament will be necessary. If we discard this policy, [greater] armament will be unnecessary. To say that Korea and Manchuria are necessary for our national defense is to completely confuse cause and effect. . . .

Part 3

The second point made in the argument against my proposal was this: It is unfair for the powers to possess vast colonial territories or vast home territories while Japan is cooped up in a very small homeland. According to the explanation I already gave, I believe that the reader can surmise that my advocating that our country discard Greater Japanism does not at all mean a small Japan should be cooped up in its homeland. On the contrary, I am saying that we must discard Greater Japanism so that our Japanese people can make the whole world their homeland and be active [worldwide]. My suggestion is in no way a proposal to make our homeland small. Just the opposite. It is a proposal to widen it to include the whole world. . . . [In presenting a racial equality clause at Versailles,] our country was proposing something that it itself did not do and yet wished to press on others. Therefore the resolution was opposed by England and America, but from China and other quarters sincere support could not be secured. If it had gained heartfelt support from such countries, I believe that the proposal would definitely have not been so sadly defeated.

Some will probably say: Even if all the powers liberated their overseas possessions, there would still be countries like America whose own homeland is immense. Also, all the various liberated countries might close their borders and not allow persons from other countries to enter. What can be done about that? To which I answer as follows: America does not allow Japanese or Chinese into its vast land. But that restriction applies only to immigrants. There is no obstacle of any kind to merchants doing business in America. As explained previously, 800 million yen, or 900 million yen worth of goods annually come to our country from America. This is matched by goods from our country [to America]. In our trade statistics, America is actually our number-one trading partner. Why is it constantly said America excludes our people? When we look at it from the point of ordinary economic relations, the idea has absolutely no factual basis. It is only with regard to immigrants that complaints of one kind or another can be made. If one looks at immigration from the viewpoint of the people of the other country, it is not an unreasonable policy. In our country also, manners, customs, and languages are different. Imagine if large numbers of very uncultured foreign workers formed villages here. A great deal of annoyance would be felt. . . . Our country, thinking only from its own point of view, sends workers to foreign countries as immigrants and has them compete against the foreign workers with our workers' low standard of living as their sole weapon. . . . This behavior is never profitable, nor is it honorable. . . .

For these reasons, I assert that giving up Greater Japanism will not be a disadvantage at all to our country. On the contrary, not only will it not be a disadvantage; it will bring us great gains. If we give up lands like Korea, Taiwan, Sakhalin, and Manchuria and if we make vast China a friend, then of their own volition the whole Far East and all the weak and small countries of the world will become our moral supporters. . . . The quintessence of strategy is harmony. No matter how much armament one or two arrogant nations have, our country—the leader of the free and liberated world and backed by the hearts of the Far East and the whole world—could not possibly be defeated in this war. If in the future our country goes to war, it must be exactly this kind of war. Moreover, if our country resolutely moves ahead and gives up all small ambitions, perhaps even without war the arrogant countries will come to ruin. This present Pacific Conference is truly the great stage on which our country ought to try out this great policy.

[*Ishibashi Tanzan hyōronshū*, pp. 101–21; AET]

"BEFORE DEMANDING THE ABOLITION OF
RACIAL DISCRIMINATION"
(JINSHUTEKI SABETSU TEPPAI YŌKYŪ NO MAE NI)

On February 5 [1919] more than five hundred public-spirited persons representing more than thirty organizations gathered in the Seiyōken [restaurant] in
Ueno Park and adopted the following resolution: "The Japanese People resolve
that at the Peace Conference the racially discriminatory treatment up to now
practiced internationally be abolished." The text of this resolution was cabled
to our ambassadors extraordinary at Paris and to Clemenceau, the chairman of
the Peace Conference.

In this resolution were brought together public-spirited persons from the
various political parties . . . and the army and navy reservist associations, journalists, and representatives from other influential organizations. By this action,
the strength of our people's feeling about the demand for the abolition of racial
discrimination was amply displayed. The people of Japan, Chinese persons,
Indian persons, and others do not receive the same treatment as whites do in
North America, Canada, Australia, Africa, and other places. About this discrimination instituted by whites in the treatment of people of color, the resolution
said: "Not only does this violate the noble cause of liberty and equality, but it
also preserves into the future this evil root of dissension. If this is allowed to
continue unchanged, though a hundred thousand treaties be piled one on the
other, it will be like a tower built on sand. Universal world peace will be absolutely impossible to attain." From my innermost heart, I also think the same
thing. Therefore I advocate more strongly than anyone that this racial discrimination be ended without the loss of a single day.

However, when I look at how our own people are behaving, I think it is
shameful, and I must regretfully speak out about it. What's going on here? This
racial discrimination that these public-spirited persons have powerfully criticized and rejected, . . . this racial discrimination that is an evil root that will
destroy peace, this very racial discrimination is practiced by our own country
both at home and abroad.

First, by its regulations on the entry of foreigners into Japan, our country
. . . has in fact prohibited the use of Chinese workers in Japan. Actual examples
occurred in Kyushu and Kobe in 1907 when Chinese coolies were prohibited
from entering. Without being aware of the existing regulations, the Chūgoku
Ironworks . . . imported two hundred Chinese coolies. . . . Later they discovered
the ban existed and . . . they had wasted 50,000 yen. . . . Is it not clear that our
country has instituted discrimination in its treatment of the Chinese? . . .

There are, of course, other examples: our government has adopted a permit
system with regard to the entry into Japan of Koreans and Taiwanese, persons
who have the status of inhabitants of Japanese national territory: foreigners are
prohibited from owning land, [and] foreigners cannot conduct coastal trade.

There are many such examples of discriminatory treatment of foreigners and Japanese subjects. While we smugly practice discriminatory treatment of our brethren, what authority can there be in these public-spirited persons passing and cabling to the Paris Conference a resolution to abolish whites' discriminatory treatment of people of color? The resolution will earn only a derisive smile directed toward those who are unaware of their own failings. . . .

[*Ishibashi Tanzan chosakushū*, vol. 3, pp. 37–39; AET]

"THE ONLY METHOD FOR PROPER GUIDANCE OF THOUGHT IS TO ALLOW ABSOLUTE FREEDOM OF SPEECH" (GENRON O ZETTAI JIYŪ NARASHIMURU HOKA SHISŌ O ZENDŌ SURU HŌHŌ WA NAI)

The Fourth Japan Communist Party roundup [in 1932], recently revealed to the public, was on an astonishingly massive scale. It reached the large number of 2,200 persons throughout the country and, in Tokyo alone, 687 persons, of whom 107 were women. From what we have heard, the authorities seem to have intended by this sweep to have thoroughly smashed the Communist Party in our country. . . . However, to this reporter's way of thinking, the idea that this effort has destroyed the Japanese Communist Party will not last very long. At least that would seem to be so from past history. If we call this the fourth sweep, the mass arrests in 1928 were the first (March 15), the mass arrests in 1929 were the second (April 16), and the mass arrests in 1930 were the third (February 24). In the case of each of these three prior mass arrests, the authorities, of course, believed at the time that they had thoroughly rooted out the nests of Communist Party members. Nevertheless, their expectations were mistaken, and after each mass arrest, the Communist Party's activities, contrary to expectations, expanded and became more virulent. . . .

To a certain degree this [failure of the government's efforts] has already been recognized even by the government. In a speech to the Diet the other day Prime Minister Saitō [Makoto] confessed that "prevention" is "very difficult." This being so, if we ask what policies other than suppression the government has, [the answer is that] there are no plans other than suppression. One thing that is easily cranked out is the incantation "Proper Guidance of Thought." A number of agencies have operated along these lines, but to absolutely no effect. In the speech just quoted, Prime Minister Saitō explained, "I think I would like to aim at the extirpation of this scandalous matter by henceforth striving more and more for proper guidance of thought in politics, education, and every other area." Among our people there is probably not a one who feels any real conviction behind the prime minister's words.

Why are both repression and the proper guidance of thought ineffective? To this reporter, the answer is very clear. It is because in today's society, as the

Communists are pointing out, there undeniably are certain shortcomings. Many persons who abhor Communism know only the petty talk and actions of the rank-and-file Communists and make the hasty judgment that this is Communism. However, it is the way of the world that if many human beings are engaged in some activity, among them will necessarily be persons of inferior quality and also persons who are needlessly extremist. Even in the Meiji Restoration movement, the rightness of which is not doubted by any of our people today, there were in fact some very questionable characters on the prowl among the heroes. In no school of thought whatsoever is there absolute perfection. Without fail, each will run to some extreme. That is because the life of human beings is arranged in such a way that thought is channeled in this direction by the real necessities of life. Therefore no matter what sort of persons may have entered among today's Communists and no matter how extreme their style of thought may be, it is a mistake on those grounds to reject the whole out of hand. Why do our people not display their liberality by listening calmly to what the Communists say [and] from out of that adopt what they can accept and thereby rectify the defects of our society? . . . Be it Communism, fascism, militarism, pacifism, or any other type of thought, it is good to allow all to freely discuss their ideas just as they are. By means of natural selection, society will accept the correct and discard the mistaken. . . .

John Stuart Mill offered the following three reasons for absolute freedom of speech:

1. If the opinion is correct and society is wrong, by not allowing the expression of this opinion, society has lost the opportunity to discard the false and move to the true.
2. If the opinion is wrong, by not allowing the expression of this opinion, society has lost the opportunity to further improve a truth held by society, as well as to clarify and deepen its meaning.
3. However, in most cases neither of the two preceding situations arises. Usually it is a situation in which several conflicting opinions exist and each of them includes some truth and some error. Only when free speech is allowed is it possible to discover the error in each opinion and unify into one the truths that exist in each opinion only separately.

These reasons, as they stand, are also true today.

If in our country today this absolute freedom of speech were permitted and protected (of course, suppression of speech by nongovernmental forces must be eliminated), 80 or 90 percent of today's political and social darkness would probably be cleared away. In an open society, bad thought cannot thrive. The number one condition for making a society open is absolute freedom of speech.

[*Ishibashi Tanzan hyōron senshū*, pp. 280–83; AET]

KIYOSAWA KIYOSHI: WHY LIBERALISM?

Kiyosawa Kiyoshi (1890–1945) had an unusual background for a Japanese intellectual. After finishing elementary school in rural Nagano Prefecture, he attended for two years a small private school with a strong Christian flavor operated by a disciple of Uchimura Kanzō. In 1906, at age sixteen, Kiyosawa emigrated to Washington State. While supporting himself with odd jobs, he graduated from Tacoma High School. He also attended courses at Whitworth College and the University of Washington, although he did not graduate from either institution. Meanwhile, he had begun a career as a reporter for a number of Japanese newspapers that had started publishing on the Pacific coast. In 1920 Kiyosawa returned permanently to Japan, where he had a position as foreign affairs reporter for the *Chūgai shōgyō shinpō* (*Journal of Foreign and Domestic Commerce*; the present-day *Nihon keizai shinbun*, Japan's preeminent business newspaper). In 1927 he became deputy chief of the Planning Section at *Tōkyō Asahi shinbun*. However, in 1929 he had to resign this position as a result of ultranationalist attacks for having published an imagined dialogue between the anarchist Ōsugi Sakae and his murderer, Gendarmerie Captain Amakasu, which reveals that they are brethren under the skin. By this time, Kiyosawa had gained a reputation as an astute observer of and commentator on foreign affairs as well as of the political and social scene. Consequently, he was able to become a well-paid freelance writer. As such, he often traveled to the United States, Europe, and East Asia and conducted numerous interviews with important leaders. As the repression of freedom of speech tightened during the 1930s, Kiyosawa switched to writing diplomatic history, mostly by commission from the *Tōyō keizai shinpō* (*Oriental Economist*), which had appointed him as adviser in 1938 and whose editor in chief, Ishibashi Tanzan, had become his very close friend. Kiyosawa died just before World War II ended. During the war, he kept a very detailed diary recording his impressions of events and drawing lessons that he hoped would be useful in constructing a better Japan in the postwar period. The diary was published in Japan in 1970 to 1973, and in 1999 an English translation appeared.

PRESENT-DAY JAPAN
(GENDAI NIHON RON)

Introduction

Although I was born and raised in Japan and every day for some forty years have been closely studying the state of Japan, few enigmas are as difficult for me to penetrate as Japan. Occasionally when one has settled on what one thinks the answer is, it slips away in an instant, like an eel grasped in your hand.

It is said that the Japanese are a progressive people. A people who have progressed so much in such a short time must be progressive. Because the Japanese are progressive, they have been responsive to foreign cultures and influences. Walking the streets of Tokyo, we are conscious above all that here, more than in any other capital city, is centered the world's vanguard.

For all that, this progressive Japan is at the same time a startlingly conservative Japan. By way of experiment, open any newspaper convenient to hand and read its political section, its social section, and then its foreign affairs section. Instead of the date 1935 on each page, insert the date 1866. Would you be able to detect any great differences? Seeing the phenomena on the one side of an issue does not warrant rejecting the phenomena on the other side: Japan is both conservative and at the same time progressive. . . .

[O]ur Japan has, as the Japanese people, an ancient culture. We can even take pride that only in case of necessity have we taken sustenance from other worlds. We pray that by this ancient culture's putting on the attire of a new age, the rising eastern sun will brightly illuminate the world.

Yet at the same time this hard-core native culture has not coalesced with Western culture, and we must be cautious that the native culture does not somehow break through the veneer and appear in its old form. When the old form appears on the home scene, it becomes a feudalistic reaction; when it appears on the foreign scene, it becomes a mistaken foreign policy out of touch with the times. If such an outbreak is not now subjected to the white light of criticism, it is a sign that our Japan is about to be driven into danger.

Today, what is most wanting in Japan is self-criticism. Everyone assembles, sits around in a circle, praises one another, drinks self-congratulatory saké, and then parts. That is the present situation. As a result, the scene is inevitably dominated by the dogmatism and shortsighted views of those with an exaggerated and unrealistic idea of their own abilities. We fear that only this dull, vulgar dogmatism will enter the heads of the active masses, the university students, and the children and will become the received wisdom of our Japan. If both individuals and society as a whole fall into the habit of emphasizing one side of a problem and forgetting the other side, then their psychological attitude will be impaired and unavoidably crippled. As a result, everything will be dealt with only halfway and will lack the insight that comes from looking at the whole. In other words, the critical attitude will be lost, and conceptual blindness will become the norm for actions. Isn't this harmful practice to be seen in present-day Japan?

This book has been written in order to restore some measure of criticism in a Japan where criticism has been lost. . . .

This book probably expresses a minority view. However, my hopes will be fulfilled if I gain company among patriots who think that to develop a country on a grand scale, the quickest path is a roundabout way using methods approved by the peoples of the world.

Early summer 1935.

[Kiyosawa, *Gendai Nihon ron*, pp. 1–6; AET]

WHY LIBERALISM?
(*NANIYUE NI JIYŪSHUGI DE ARU KA?*)

Let us first try to advance our conversation by considering what our aims in life are. . . .

For me the most important thing is living. I think agreement has been gained on the point that material stability is required in order to make life happy. Looking at this socially, the inequities and abuses in society show up most frequently in connection with wealth. As I will explain later, I do not regard wealth as wholly evil so long as one is not blinded by one's own social special privileges. I think that one cannot doubt that an ideal society is one in which, as Bernard Shaw said, the daughter of the local carpenter can marry the son of the neighboring great landowner. However, experience up to now has made clear the uselessness for attaining such a society of a system that produces and distributes in pursuit of private profits only. In times when the world is still in difficulty because of inadequate production, a system is appropriate that allows the individual's desire for profits to operate freely. And more than anything it is capitalism that has brought about our present civilization. However, we now have come to understand that this anachronistic chaos [of capitalism] will not maintain forever the well-being of humanity. . . .

Concretely speaking, the world we are envisaging is a world without private profit, a world in which all production and consumption and wealth are used for the social community, a world in which no matter how much is produced, there is no oversupply. In this world, production will, of course, be consumed, share and share alike by all. No longer will individual persons be able to use vast wealth to control other people's lives. If great accumulations of wealth do not exist, social inequities will probably diminish somewhat. . . .

How do we bring forth the ideal society without discarding what we presently have and with the least possible sacrifice of human beings? . . . The first necessity is developing the new age in consonance with the national character. Regardless of their origins and beginnings, the national characters of the various nations that we see before our eyes all are different. Therefore we do not think that something suitable to Russia is valid for China or something fit for Japan is perfectly adaptable to France.

On this point we differ from the Marxists. They think that economic considerations transcend races and national boundaries. They think the proletariat and bourgeoisie unite and cooperate laterally across such boundaries with other proletariats and bourgeoisies. They think that the workers fail to be liberated only because of their chains. Consequently, by discarding all things like patriotism and nationalism, the same class in each country will unite across borders with one another. In general, it is their point of view that economic laws operate unconditionally throughout the world. But we do not believe this. When it comes to ethnic differences derived from history and tradition, we do not think the world is divided only laterally [by class].

If the question is, do you think, as do conservatives in every country, that the law of nature common to all peoples ceases to operate in your country alone, [the answer] is, of course, no, [the law of nature operates everywhere]. We cannot stop laughing at our ultranationalists who place Japan, and only Japan, completely outside the law of evolution. To think that something applicable to the West, some intellectual theory bred in the West is entirely unsuitable to Japan, is, I think, an error equivalent to thinking it is correct to apply a principle worldwide and unconditionally.

On the one hand, we oppose Marxism's formulism, and on the other, we oppose our right-wing ideologues with their nativistic supremacist absolutism that emphasizes Japan's exceptionalism. While we recognize this strength of tradition and history, we nevertheless acknowledge the laws that are common to all humanity. We will advance adhering to this line and using it as the path to progress. We will pursue the well-being and progress of humanity with eyes that never see national boundaries. At the same time, we intend not to distance ourselves from the existing conditions of the masses, who, as a result of a mistaken education, are illiberal, dogmatic, and thoughtless to an extent almost the same as in the *bakumatsu* [last days of the Tokugawa] period. . . .

If all the abuses of the present day have come from capitalism, it is thought that it would be good if capitalism were overthrown. And since Marxism has such an extraordinary passion for overthrowing capitalism, it would be fine if Marxism alone were adopted. However, I do not believe this. Compared with the earlier view of history, which gave importance only to the human, Marxism was certainly insightful to have called attention to the importance of economic necessity. But to attribute all causation to economics alone is, I think, really a stretch.

It is necessary that we overcome feudalism [reactionary thought] with the same ardent force applied to overcoming capitalism. If a Marxist opens his mouth, he says that the task of overcoming feudalism has been left to be shouldered by the bourgeoisie. For all that, do Marxists have the kind of qualities required to overcome feudalism? As we see it, we think that believers in feudalism are ultimately the same as Marxists. . . .

Take a look at how adherents of feudalism and Marxism resemble each other. In order to accomplish their wills, both approve the appeal to violent revolution. Both also advocate dictatorial rule by a minority. They believe in the absolute nature of the state and society and advocate the extreme suppression of the individual. The left wing and the right wing similarly approve the abandonment of the individual rights embodied in the constitution. Furthermore, they both are the same in making liberalism their enemy. . . . The difference lies in this point: the left wing uses the dialectical theory to clarify its ideology, and the right wing makes a weapon of historical sentiment. Consequently, it is not rational to use the same thing to overcome the same thing. It is liberalism alone that can overcome both the right and the left. . . .

Even though we recognize the abuses in modern society and hate capitalism, we nevertheless cannot favor using violence to bring them down. At present it cannot be said that the danger of such an eventuality is entirely absent. If the present educational policy and the present politics continue, we think it very possible that there could be such a danger. We think we must expend every effort to avoid paying the great sacrifice of human life entailed in such an event. . . .

The number-one reason is this: although a new system can be established by means of a revolution, there is no guarantee it will be a better system than the existing one. Of course, in a violent revolution, capitalism will probably disappear. But as I explained before, the abuses of the present do not come from capitalism alone. Both the dominant class that governs and the people who are governed are the same [human] material. Do you think that because the economic organization has changed . . . the extremists . . . will disappear? No. The temptation [for corruption] of the governing classes will become proportionately greater and greater as their power grows greater. Nowadays there are outlets for public opinion, media that will publicize and complain about such things, but in that [new] epoch you must be prepared for the fact that speech attacking the ruling class will absolutely not be allowed. . . . I do not know about the distant future, but if there is someone who believes there will be a left-wing victory in the near future, I would think this was a person blinded by formulism who cannot look squarely at the facts. What about the intelligentsia who are predominantly left wing? Well, think about what has happened in Germany which is *the* place in the world where Communism has flourished the most. Third, if today there is a social revolution, it is not Communism and it is not socialism. It is a turning back to barbarism. . . .

My opposition to the means used by the right wing and the left wing does not end with what I have just said. There is a somewhat more fundamental reason [for my opposition], and that is my view of the matter as it relates to the progress of humanity and society.

I think the progress of humanity is the product of education and research. Freedom of speech ought to be looked at from that point of view: in itself, freedom of speech is not sacred. On behalf of the general progress of society, of course, the individual's interests have to be sacrificed. In civilized societies, freedom of speech has been purchased at a high price simply because it is believed to be necessary for social progress.

However, whatever else you may get under either right-wing or left-wing dictatorships, there is not the least freedom of speech or research. Because Einstein is a Jew, his theory of relativity is not considered valid in Germany. Recently, a thirty-seven-year-old scholar was appointed rector of Berlin University. His specialty was veterinary medicine, and up to now he has been a completely unknown person. He is not a good scholar, but he is a Nazi. Any number of similar examples can be given.

It is quite unnecessary to seek such examples at a distance. Recently, in our present period of national emergency, has not a scholarly theory of long standing been easily junked?[5] If this . . . [censored] trend becomes strong, we must be prepared for the phenomena that will appear.

However, it is not fair to make the right wing bear the sole responsibility for the repression of freedom of speech. On that score, the left wing is [equally responsible]. Can anyone possibly assert that in the Soviet Union there is freedom of speech? . . .

If we are honest about it, the intellectual class always tends to be more sympathetic to the left wing than to the right wing. It is a fact that compared with our vehement criticism of the conduct of the right wing, we tend to pass over the conduct of the left wing. In this respect, the world's intellectuals have a double standard. The problem is that to that extent we are frittering away the value of our judgment on the point of which of these two groups in its ultimate ideal is rational and better. . . .

If it is assumed that you accept the argument that free inquiry and discussion give rise to the progress of the world, then you can no longer go to either the left wing or the right wing. The only way for you is to come straight to liberalism. At present, other than liberalism, there is no ideology that tolerates arguments and theories opposed to itself.

Finally, let me once again reiterate why I am a liberal and what liberalism is.

First, I believe that the mission that capitalism had to perform is over and that in a new society a new structure is needed. In that new society, the means of production naturally cannot be as it is at present; that is, it cannot exist for the profits of individuals. Therefore, socialism is to be desired.

Second, just as capitalism must be ended, it is, speaking from the present state of affairs, as likely as not that we must go far beyond that and overcome feudalistic [reactionary] principles. However, as [I] explained earlier, the tendencies in Marxism are the same as in feudalistic thinking, so it is impossible for Marxism to fight against feudalistic thinking. Only liberalism can overcome it. This is why in every country whatsoever, resistance to the extreme right wing is the liberals and not the Marxists.

Third, liberalism opposes Marxists. Liberals who do not want to lose the cultural privileges they currently hold, of course, oppose Marxism, an ideology

---

5. Reference to the Minobe incident.

that rushes into risky adventures, whose outcome is not clear. As some people say, liberals are people who try to reconstruct the railway station while the trains are running. They are opposed to stopping the operation of the trains in order to reconstruct the station.

Fourth, liberalism does not make . . . [censored] things. Marxists do not admit the slightest error in Marx. Liberals have no doubt that at least in some places Marx got it wrong. Right-wing ideologues also absolutely cannot think that their nation can make a mistake. Liberals hazard the thought that since human beings run their country, sometimes they can make mistakes. At the same time, liberals do not think they have a monopoly on patriotism. They recognize that among persons who differ in thought from liberals there are many who have an equal love for their country.

When one thing alone is believed to be the absolute truth, there is no progress there. Discovery and improvement come from recognizing there can be defects and striving to achieve perfection. Freedom to investigate is therefore significant. For liberals, all things are relative. Liberals do not fashion idols, as do both the right wing and the left wing.

Fifth, liberals love peace. Some have said the best war is worse than the worst peace. Although liberals dislike such grandiloquent words, the liberal rejection of the left wing and the right wing lies in the point that the left wing wages "war" domestically and the right wing continually wages "war" against foreign countries. Because liberals are peaceful, they tend toward self-examination. They oppose persons who always trace causes to foreign sources and do not reflect on their own responsibility and their own country's responsibility. However, even though liberals are pacifistic, they are not, of course, passive. They are inferior to no one in fighting with enthusiastic vigor for what they believe to be true.

Sixth, liberals think that other than liberalism, there are no strong working principles for carrying on practical governance. Until the dictatorship of the proletariat has arrived, Marxism has no policy other than simply obstruction and destruction. Fascism brushes aside the constitution that was bought with blood and sweat. They have no plan other than restoring some sort of ancient spirit. If we return to the spirit of such an age, for what purpose have we, raised in the glorious Meiji period, done our best to get where we are? Which period should be the one to whose spirit we return?

That aside, sandwiched as we are between the right wing and the left wing, the single practical principal of operation can only be moderate progressivism. From a historical perspective, this plainly and clearly will advance the age's program.

[Kiyosawa, *Gendai Nihon ron*, pp. 1–24; AET]

IENAGA SABURŌ: THE FORMATION OF A LIBERAL

Ienaga Saburō (1913–2002) was one of postwar Japan's most distinguished historians. He was also, by any test, a liberal. To the general public he was best known for bringing a lawsuit against the Ministry of Education in 1965 challenging as unconstitutional the ministry's practice of reviewing all textbooks and denying permission for use in schools to any considered to contain objectionable material. Ienaga also sued in connection with a history of Japan he submitted that the ministry refused to approve because he would not make some three hundred changes that it had demanded. The case dragged on for many years and became a cause around which many intellectuals rallied.

Ienaga graduated from Tokyo Imperial University in 1937 and immediately was engaged as a researcher in the university's Historiographical Institute. In 1941 he left the institute for a teaching post in Niigata. In 1943 he returned to Tokyo and became an editor for an Imperial Academy–sponsored history of the imperial household system, of which the chief editor was Minobe Tatsukichi. In 1944 Ienaga was appointed professor at the Tokyo Higher School of Education, where he remained for many years.

A HISTORIAN'S PROGRESS, STEP BY STEP
(ICHI REKISHIGAKUSHA NO AYUMI)

One of the most interesting things about Ienaga Saburō is that this postwar liberal went through a school system aimed at indoctrinating him with all the shibboleths of the official prewar ideology, and yet his own experience controverted this indoctrination. The following passages are from Ienaga's autobiography.[6]

1. A Taishō Classroom

[Mr. Okano] had only recently graduated from Aoyama Teachers School, and as might be expected of a young man in the middle of the Taishō period, the education [he gave us] was rich in personal peculiarities.

Mr. Okano announced that the morals textbook had nothing but worthless things written in it, and therefore we need not read it. We did not use the morals textbook even once. . . .

Mr. Okano's not using a morals textbook was an excellent idea. That was not all he did. He also told us that it was not necessary to buy the science textbook. His reason was that science was something you studied by experiment and observation and that reading a book was not studying science. This must also be said to have been an excellent view.

Mr. Okano undertook to explain the word "democracy" to us second-year elementary school students. Because of this memory, the scholarly phrase "Taishō democracy" is for me not simply an objective historical term. The definition he gave was simply treating everyone fairly and without partiality,

---

6. For a complete English translation of this work, see Ienaga, *Japan's Past, Japan's Future*.

and equality before the law. It did not include the principle of the people's sovereignty. However, you can understand the atmosphere of that time from the fact that in any event the word "democracy" was taught to second-year elementary school children.

Something like the following also occurred. Once Mr. Okano fired this question at us students: "What on earth is the goal for which you people are studying?" Some of my classmates suggested such answers as "because life would be difficult if when they became adults they were illiterate," or "because they would be inconvenienced if they could not handle their money accounts." Mr. Okano summed up such answers by saying, "In the end, the idea is that you are studying for your own sake." Perhaps because I was a little conceited and around that time had embraced a nationalistic feeling, I answered, "For the sake of Japan." However, Mr. Okano said even that was wrong and finally expressed his own conclusion. This was that a person studied on behalf of the world. If all the people of the world studied very hard and became wise, foolish things like war would be lessened, and the world would be at peace. That is the way Mr. Okano settled the discussion.

Looking back from today when our peace constitution has been established and world peace has been elevated as the ideal of our people, I cannot but be deeply impressed when I recall that in the late Taishō period there was a teacher who taught children in this kind of spirit. . . .

For the time the Meiji constitution was in force, even though the age of Taishō democracy was an exceptionally liberal period, elementary school education . . . was tightly controlled by the state authorities. The education I received—viewed in the total picture—was probably an absolutely most rare exception.

Mr. Okano gave us a liberal education similar to that of today, but our education in history was drawn from the required textbook. . . . [W]e just learned Japanese history from the official textbook called *Elementary School National History*. . . .

Looking back at it today, how did we accept with no doubts at all the myths . . . which in common sense could not be? Even I myself do not understand the psychological state of that time. At least among my friends there were none who doubted these "truths."

Right after I entered middle school, I read Dr. Nishimura Shinji's *The Yamato Period*. I remember with what great surprise I learned for the first time the vast difference between the history learned in school and objective history. For persons like me, by reading a book such as this it was possible to free myself comparatively quickly from the unscientific history education received in school. But didn't the large majority of our people become adults without any opportunity like mine and thus no alternative to believing what they had been taught in school? . . .

[With regard to the prewar history textbook] . . . it can only be thought that a policy had been adopted of teaching nothing about domestic political problems coming after the promulgation of the [Meiji] constitution. From today's perspective, at the mention of "the Taishō period," the first thing that comes to mind is Taishō democracy and immediately in association with that such things as the maturation of the capitalist economy, the evolution of the labor movement, the rise of party politics, and the development of constitutional government. Not a single line appears about such things. Just seeing this probably makes one understand how distorted the prewar history education was. . . .

Nevertheless, thinking back, I was after all truly fortunate to have received . . . a most valuable elementary school education. At least in the later process of the formation of myself as a human being, I have been able to get to the present without being swallowed up in a fanatical myth-rooted ideology. Wasn't this thanks to the fact that at that starting point—although there were limitations—I received what for that time was the maximum liberal education? [pp. 19–29]

2. A Middle School Student Discovers Minobe

While still in middle school, Ienaga came across and read Minobe Tatsukichi's *Constitutional Handbook* (*Kenpō satsuyō*), a textbook that his older brother was using in a course taught by Minobe.

I was attracted by Dr. Minobe's logical clarity. But it cannot be said that it necessarily went so far as to my being influenced by the intellectual concept of Dr. Minobe's theory of the state as a juridical person or the emperor as an organ of the state. However, there is no doubt that at least Dr. Minobe's thought on constitutionalism entered my mind without resistance. For that reason, although in my mind I was loyal to the *tennōsei* [emperor system], a brake was at once installed that checked my falling into a fanatical *tennōsei* ideology based on the divinity of the emperor. Although it was an outcome based on fortuitous circumstances, my being able as early as my first year in middle school to come into contact with Dr. Minobe's book must be said to be the lucky event of my life.

However, Dr. Minobe's influence cannot have been advantageous for me in every respect. Even though from a legal point of view Dr. Minobe considered the emperor as an agent [organ] of the state and clearly stated that there were limits to the emperor's prerogative, he, on the other hand, recognized the existence of the concept of the polity as a historical and moral idea, and he chose to shut the concept of the polity out of the world of legal theory as a means of trying to protect the constitutionalism of the emperor-as-agent [organ] doctrine. Thus as a legal theorist Dr. Minobe displayed a very constitutionalist—in today's terms, democratic—attitude. At the same time psychologically he had a side of him in which in his heart he was a loyal upholder of the *tennōsei* ideology. Affecting me in this way, on the one hand he planted in me a critical awareness toward the divinity-based *tennōsei* ideology. On the other hand he created a disadvantage in that it was not possible for me to have an objective and totally critical attitude . . . for a few decades. Thus for a long time this materially delayed my seizing opportunities for opening my eyes to a correct view of the true nature of the *tennōsei*.

In any event, in middle school, I was blessed by an opportunity to learn a bit about the limitations of the orthodox morality, but in spite of this I finished the final year of middle school and advanced to higher school continuing as usual to, on the whole, believe with no doubts the orthodox morality. [pp. 57–58]

3. "A College Student Defends Minobe"

The following is an essay published by Ienaga in November 1935 in his middle school's alumni journal, *Dai ichi chūgakkō no dōsōkai zasshi* (*Journal of the First Tokyo Middle School Alumni Association*).

When it comes to the emperor organ theory problem, we are more than indignant: we are totally disgusted. I am by no means a supporter of Minobe's theory. Nevertheless, it must be emphatically said that it is absolutely impermissible to use power and force, under the guise of morality, to suppress another person's convictions. To hand down narrow-minded, pernicious, and arbitrary interpretations of the "national polity," and then when others differ in the slightest from these interpretations to say that they are traitors guilty of lèse-majesté, that is an attempt to inflict a cowardly persecution. To do this is to take the "national polity," which is revered by all the people of Japan, and make it one's private possession. Under the guise of the sacred it gives free rein to bias. Moreover, when one listens to what is being said, none of it goes beyond the theory of imperial sovereignty. Although they say it is bad to discuss the "national polity" from the standpoint of rights and obligations, whatever is sovereignty? Furthermore, for them to attack the juridical person theory found in state law and to consider the state simply as an abstraction entails the glaring contradiction of falling unknowingly into the very individualism that they attack. They say that the organ theory is a direct import from Western scholarship. But on that score, the same is true of the theory of sovereignty. If you go into the real particulars of the substance [of their ideas], it is in the end nothing but a disguised absolutism.

There are those who regard Japan's national polity as identical with the absolute monarchies of China and the West. (Among them are even persons who glorify the book burning by China's first emperor.) They are persons who end up protecting a ruling class that inserts itself between the imperial house and the people and that thereby obstructs the everlasting development of our empire. It is this kind of conduct itself that threatens the national polity. It is an attitude that should be rigorously curbed. When I think about the exalted tradition of our country, I feel extremely blessed to be born on Japan's soil. I cannot remember being in any manner carried away by the elaborate language in which they devise their schemes. That is because what they say is all withered and ossified sophism without any roots in the sincere living sentiments of the people. These exalted persons hurl abuse in the speech of street hooligans, thus advertising the vulgarity of their own character.

There are words in the last half of this essay that extol Japan's national polity. That is because at that time I really thought that way. They are not at all the "words of a slave." Still, even I, who had such a viewpoint, could not tolerate the persecution of Dr. Minobe.

To continue with this article, I included a strong criticism of the idea of rejecting Western thought, a rejection that was beginning to become fashionable at that time and ended up as follows:

Even if the intellectual basis of the recent ultranationalist trend is an error, it has brought about the stimulation of research into Japanese culture, a gratifying phenomenon for us who specialize in that field. The strange thing is that simultaneously from these same quarters come various affronts to the Japanese classics. These persons find fault with *The Tale of Genji* (*Genji monogatari*), try to meddle with St. Hōnen's writings, forbid instruction in nō chants, etc. . . . Their contempt for the classics, which are the very things transmitted to the present as . . . the glorious heritage of our ancestors and the crystallization of Japan's spirit, that contempt for the classics belittles our ancestors and destroys the Japanese spirit. . . . [pp. 80–82]

4. Questioning the Official Accounts of Early Japanese History

In my shifts in thought, I was always influenced by the old behind-the-times thought of the period immediately preceding [the one I was currently in], rather than by the newly minted fashionable thought of the moment. Is not there reflected in this an obtuse personality that cannot be at the leading edge of a period?

Conversely, was it not for this very reason that I was not influenced during the war by the ultrafashionable militaristic thought, that I held fast to anachronistic liberalism and thus was able to escape engaging in any shameful opportunistic conduct. . . .

By chance about the time [I was reading Nishimura's book], Kitagawa Saburō's translation of H. G. Wells's *The Outline of History* was published. Reading these two books was instrumental in greatly changing my view of history.

Wells's history of world culture begins with the coming into existence of the universe and then takes up in order the formation of the earth, the evolution of living things, the appearance of human beings, and the evolution of civilization. Dr. Nishimura's *The Yamato Period* . . . begins with the coming into being of the universe and the appearance of human beings and then advances from the Jōmon period to the formation of the Japanese state. . . .

When I read *The Yamato Period* I first learned that Japan's history did not begin with the Age of the Gods but that one had to take as a starting point the life of the Stone Age. Dr. Nishimura had borrowed from the critical research on the *Kojiki* (*Record of Ancient Matters*) and the *Nihon shoki* (*Chronicle of Japan*) by Dr. Tsuda Sōkichi. At that time I had not read the actual works of Dr. Tsuda, and basically I could not grasp the true nature of the *Kojiki* and the *Nihon shoki* as revealed by Dr. Tsuda's studies. However, at least I knew for the first time that a history of Japan that began with Amaterasu Ōmikami, as taught in school, was not an objective history of Japan. To have been able already in the first year of middle school to understand the beginnings of scientific history must be said to have been a great good fortune for me.

Still, I knew only that the stories of the Age of the Gods were not objective historical fact. At this stage it did not yet enter my head to criticize overall the moral thought involved in the concept of national polity, a concept that had been solidly constructed on the foundation of these stories of the Age of the Gods. The orthodox morality of the people under the *tennōsei* as before had great authority for me. I was such a loyal supporter of the *tennōsei* that I thought of becoming a historian precisely to defend it. . . .

[In 1932] I began to read the German Southwest school of philosophy.[7] At that time I was very fond of reading Rickert's *Der Gegenstand der Erkenntnis*. That does not necessarily mean that I got this or that specifically from this one book. But inasmuch as the German Southwest school of *sollen* philosophy was a world to which I had up to [then] never stretched my thinking, its influence was decisive. The concept of *sollen*, which was not *sein* but rather was in opposition to *sein*, was somehow a thought that was fresh and attractive.

The concept of "national polity" (*kokutai*), which had been drummed into us from infancy until middle school, rested on the logic that the Japanese state was a national polity unique in the world and had the blessing of being ruled from time immemorial by one imperial line. In sum, it had a logical structure that through past history justified a present-day system. Therefore historical fact was the basis of "what should be" (*sollen*), and it became an arrangement by which the norms of behavior were deduced from the facts. The German Southwest school of philosophy, which argued that "what is" and value were to be sharply distinguished and that there was a well-defined break between them,

---

7. The Southwest school was a school of Neo-Kantian philosophy exemplified by Wilhelm Windelband and Heinrich Rickert. Its basis was a dualism that sharply distinguished between "what is" (*sein*) and "what ought to be"(*sollen*) and advocated an approach stressing value as the source of the normative power of *sollen*. It was a philosophy widely favored in Japanese philosophical circles during the Taishō period.

was useful in thoroughly destroying this logic of from fact to *sollen*, from history to [current] practice. . . .

This philosophy had the power to destroy thoroughly the orthodox morality that over many years had controlled my mind. Through this *sollen* philosophy I was able to be spiritually reborn. Through the mediation of the philosophy of the German Southwest school, I was able to bury the traditional Japanism-centered state morality and began to walk the path of a new life as a liberal. The history of my mind can be sharply divided into two parts: before and after 1932.

Although it is true to say that I became a liberal, it was, looking back from today, nothing more than a revision of traditional nationalistic beliefs. However, at any rate I was completely saved from the danger of sinking into fascism, and yet I did not join up with Marxism. It was possible for me to stand in an independent position of my own. For this reason, 1932 is a point in time that has a very important significance in my life. . . .

The influence on me of Dr. Tsuda [Sōkichi]'s criticism of the *Kojiki* and the *Nihon shoki* as well as his research in intellectual history was immense. His . . . four-volume work, *Studies on the Thought of Our People as Expressed in Literature* (*Bungaku ni arawaretaru waga kokumin shisō no kenkyū*), which I read after graduating from Tōdai (Tokyo University), was especially a shock beyond description. I had the impression that my view of the world changed completely after I had read this work. . . . [pp. 50, 54–56, 67–69, 94]

5. Saved by a Diversion to Religion

Early on I gave great attention to the state. I accepted without resistance the orthodox morality. But this was not simply because it was poured into me by an external authority through the "pipe" of education. The groundwork was already there because I myself had the habit of always thinking about matters with the thought in mind that the state was superior to the individual. . . . From my youth my mind was inclined toward nationalism. This meant that . . . my thinking about the individual began not from [the point of view of] the internal and individual problem but from thinking about things on the level of the state and society. . . .

As a person who entered the life of intellectual speculation with my discovery of the Neo-Kantian school of philosophy, I did not at first think that a theoretical worldview was to be found outside Western philosophy. To have learned [upon my discovery of the thought of Shōtoku and Shinran] that such a superior type of thinking existed even in Japanese thought opened new mental horizons for me.

Through both Shinran and the Bible I came to grapple seriously with the question of religion. This was the background for my deep appreciation of Shōtoku's words: "The world is illusion. Only Buddha is true." . . .

I gradually became absorbed in religious problems and little by little lost any great interest in the problems of the state and society. This [kind of] stance I still continued for several years after graduating from university [March 1937]. . . . [In the meantime] the Japanese intellectual world became more and more deeply right wing. It became so extreme that if you were not a supporter of Japanism you were considered to be a traitor. Because I had by chance become diverted from the problem of state and society, I was able to escape being entangled in these kinds of developments. That occurred because of circumstances . . . and not because my intellectual convictions were especially firm. It is not a story to be too proud of. . . . My obtuseness always led me to follow anachronistic thought out of sync with the fashion of the current period. Thus contrariwise I did not jump on the bandwagon when the whole nation was turning to the right. That certainly must be called an irony of fate. [pp. 87, 90–92]

6. "Self-Censorship"

Under Tsuda's influence, Ienaga wrote an article on a topic drawn from the *Nihon shoki* and submitted it to a journal edited by his colleagues in the Historiographical Institute.

If I put things together from subsequent events, on seeing the title the editors undoubtedly were frightened. But the editorial board sent it just as it was to the printer, and it reached the proofs stage. At that point the editors, apparently concerned that publication might be prohibited if the article were printed as it stood, sought a change in the title. The ostensible reason for this was that the present title would be too conspicuous [and attract the censor's attention.] Thinking I could not avoid making at least this much of a compromise, I changed the title . . . and thought that would do the trick. At this point, the editors seemed to become increasingly worried, and after consulting with our seniors they finally asked me to withdraw the article. I had to face squarely my first ordeal of deciding whether to fight for academic freedom or to compromise. . . .

The younger members of the Historiographical Institute all agreed that it should not be published. One senior colleague said to me, "You have written an article that commits lèse-majesté, haven't you?" Another said, "Even if you don't publish this article, there are lots of other research subjects." These things gave [me] insight into the nature of the scholarship of the historians in the Historiographical Institute. . . . I did not really take seriously the possibility of what I had written becoming a problem. Even if I received some punishment, I had secretly determined to resign myself to it. However, depending on how the problem developed, responsibility could spread not only to the writer [me] but to everyone involved in publishing the article. Even though whatever happened to me was all right, I thought I must, after all, not cause trouble for my colleagues. So I swallowed my pride and withdrew the article. This manuscript, which was to have been printed as my first scholarly work, was in the end buried in galley proofs, and until the end of the war I could do nothing but preserve it with great care.

In my first step in my life as a scholarly researcher, this is the experience I went through. Isn't it possible that this became one of the formative experiences shaping my behavior today? At the time I had a low level of awareness, and I was not so seriously conscious of the necessity of guarding academic freedom. However, in that first step in my academic research life, I was made personally aware of how severe under the Meiji constitution the control of academic freedom and freedom of expression was. . . .

When all is said and done, the most painful thing in my scholarly life was that [my] freedom of learning and freedom of expression had been taken away. This was truly a great problem for me, who was specializing in Japanese history, a field over which there was severe scholarly and intellectual control. [pp. 103–5]

[Ienaga, *Ichi rekishigakusha no ayumi*, pp. 19–29, 50, 54–56, 57–58, 67–69, 80–82, 87, 90–92, 94, 103–5; AET]

PEACEFUL COOPERATION ABROAD

SHIDEHARA KIJŪRŌ: CONCILIATORY DIPLOMACY

Shidehara Kijūrō (1872–1951) is so closely identified with the peaceful and cooperative policies that Japan usually followed in the 1920s that they have come to be designated as "Shidehara diplomacy." From 1915 to 1919, he was the vice minister of foreign affairs. In 1921 and 1922, he was the chief delegate to the Washington Conference, a gathering whose outcome typifies his diplomacy, since it provided for naval disarmament, security in the Pacific through international agreement, and conciliation with China by settling the Shandong question. From 1924 to 1927 and again from 1929 to 1931, Shidehara held the post of foreign minister in the Kenseikai and Minseitō cabinets. Largely as a result of the high regard in which he was held by foreign opinion, Shidehara played a prominent role in Japan's political life after World War II, serving as prime minister in 1945/1946.

A RAPPROCHEMENT WITH CHINA

The following is an extract from a policy statement that Shidehara Kijūrō presented to the Diet on January 21, 1930. It is a good illustration of his conciliatory attitude toward China and his sympathetic regard for the problem created by the Nationalist revolution.

We in Japan have only to look forward with sympathy and patience to the achievement of their task by those who have been devoting their attention and energy to composing China's existing difficulties. We cannot, however, dismiss from our mind an apprehension borne out by various instances in history that in any country faced with similar troubles, the temptation may grow strong for men in power to resort to an adventurous foreign policy with a view to diverting the minds of the people from internal to external affairs. It would be needless to point out that in our modern world, a policy repugnant to all sense of reason and moderation can scarcely tend to enhance the prestige of a nation or to serve the purpose for which it is intended. I sincerely trust that the responsible statesmen of China will avoid all such temptations and will proceed to work out their own country's destiny by steady and measured steps.

The future of Sino-Japanese relations is variously viewed in this country. There are pessimists who maintain that however fair and liberal a course Japan may steer, China will never meet us halfway but will be swayed by considerations of domestic politics and assume toward us an attitude more wanton than ever, which would only be calculated to aggravate the situation. Others entertain a more optimistic view. They hold that all the suspicion and mistrust which the Chinese people have hitherto harbored toward Japan rest on no substantial grounds and that with better understanding on China's part of our real motives, there must come a better relationship between the two peoples. They further anticipate that the stabilization of the internal political status of the Chinese government will be followed by a reorientation of China's foreign policies upon more moderate and normal lines.

I am not here to pass judgment either way upon these conflicting views. In any case, whatever response we may receive at the hands of the Chinese, we are determined to exert our best efforts to regulate our relations with China on a basis which we believe to be just and fair. Our peculiarly close relations with China, and more especially the complexity and variety of their ramifications, are naturally bound to give rise to questions from time to time calling for diplomatic treatment and tending to excite the feelings either of the Japanese or of the Chinese people.

If, however, one takes a broader view of the future well-being of both China and Japan, one will be satisfied that there is no other course open to the two nations than to pursue the path of mutual accord and cooperation in all their relations, political and economic. Their real and lasting interests, which in no way conflict but have much in common with each other, ought to be a significant assurance of their growing rapprochement. If the Chinese people awaken to these facts and show themselves responsive to the policy so outlined, nothing will more conduce to the mutual welfare of both nations. Should they, on the contrary, fail to understand us and seek trouble with us, we can at least rest assured of our strong position in the public opinion of the world.

[*Documents on International Affairs*, 1930, pp. 181–82]

YAMAMURO SŌBUN: CALL FOR A PEACEFUL JAPAN

The following is from a speech delivered in December 1929 by Yamamuro Sōbun (1880–1950), an important Mitsubishi executive who was at that time the president of the Mitsubishi Trust Company. It indicates one important source of support for Shidehara Kijūrō's policies and the reasons for that support. Shidehara was married to a member of the family that owned the Mitsubishi enterprises, and the Minseitō was popularly believed to receive a substantial part of its funds from Mitsubishi.

SPEECH

When we consider [the state] of Japan's national economy, when we think of our scarcity of natural resources, when we reflect on today's international situation, [the solution to our problems might seem to lie in] either the seizure of dependencies under a policy of aggression or the establishment of a Monroe Doctrine. Nevertheless, there is absolutely no place in Japan's future for [these policies]. Japan can remain a going concern only through international cooperation. Under this policy of international cooperation we can get along by producing goods of the highest possible quality at the lowest possible price, thereby expanding our foreign markets to the greatest [extent] possible. A country as deficient in natural resources as Japan buys raw materials from foreign countries at low prices and processes [these materials] at a low cost. Of course, circumstances peculiar to Japan have [modified] our development. For example, silk has been an important item. However, in addition to encouraging the expansion of this industry, we must endeavor through a policy of international cooperation to establish our country as an international industrial producer of international commodities. To that end we must do our best to create an amicable atmosphere in international relations. If we have the reputation of liking war or of being militarists, [a policy of] international cooperation will be impossible. We must resolutely follow a policy of peace. It is essential to make all foreigners feel that the Japanese have been converted from their old religion and have become advocates of peace. For that reason we must, as far as possible, eliminate international barriers. In that sense, a commercial treaty with China is probably necessary. For this same purpose, the abolition of unnecessary tariffs is also required. I wonder if the best way to manage the post-resumption[8] financial world isn't to eliminate the various international barriers [and] to adopt a viewpoint as similar as possible to that of the foreigner and to maintain close cooperation with foreigners.

[Yamamuro, *Waga kuni keizai oyobi kin'yū*, pp. 292–93; AET]

---

8. That is, after Japan returned to the gold standard, in January 1930.

Chapter 41

SOCIALISM AND THE LEFT

"There is no way," wrote the Marxist economist Uno Kōzō, "to industrialize in the abstract."[1] In Uno's day, as in ours, the dominant mode of industrialization was capitalist. Capitalist industrialization, however, has occurred in various and complex ways. Timing and location are crucial, as is speed: the rapidity or compressed character of the transition reflects the urgent choice by some national elites to attempt industrialization without completely transforming the existing structure of society. Thus whether a nation came "early" or "late" to capitalism and where it was situated—within whose sphere of influence, and in what broader sociohistorical sense—formed its destiny in important ways.

Modern socialism is a product and a critique of capitalism, but not necessarily of industrialization. It is—or was—held to be the antithesis of capitalism. No society, Japan's included, that has tried to industrialize in the capitalist mode has failed to generate an indigenous socialist movement. Whether Christian or guild socialist, anarchist or revolutionary Marxist in character, vernacular socialisms have always and everywhere been part of a self-consciously international workers' movement. In their formative years, they draw on their predecessor and contemporary movements for models of discourse, organization, and

---

1. Uno, "Shihonshugi no seiritsu to nōson bunkai no katei," *Chūō kōron* (November 1935), in *Uno Kōzō chosakushū*, vol. 8, p. 38.

action. At the same time, as an indigenous movement, socialism naturally and inevitably borrows traditional (precapitalist) sentiments, concepts, practices, and protocols of social criticism and protest, which then are selectively assimilated into and help define the particular national variant of the "socialism." It is the specific interplay of universalist and local, or vernacular, elements in the movement to realize a vision of society permanently freed from capitalist exploitation that defined socialism.

Japan's forcible introduction to the international economy and system of national states came amid the onset of imperialism. It was impossible, therefore, that along with its denunciation of capitalism, Japanese socialism should not at the same time have retained traces of anti-imperialist nationalism. This dual perspective endured even as Japan itself emerged as an imperialist power, leaving a legacy of argument and political conflict within the movement over the question of "the nation" versus "class and party." The story is similar to that of the Second International, with its collapse in 1914. But the phasing in Japan was different: there, many of these struggles came after 1918, playing out through the 1920s, with the decisive political and organizational failures following the Great Depression and the invasion of Manchuria in 1931. In the end, the nation triumphed over all other solidarities, only to bring catastrophe in its wake.

The following selections are intended to illustrate both the universal and the particular aspects of the Japanese socialist movement—and, more broadly, of the Japanese left—from its beginning in the 1890s through the end of the Pacific War in 1945, and to indicate some of the forces influencing it. The socialist movement's later fate—and still unknown future—while adumbrated in a number of the selections, must await fuller treatment elsewhere.

THE EARLY SOCIALIST MOVEMENT

In the movement's early phases, and depending on who was counting, Japanese socialists numbered from the low hundreds to a figure approaching fourteen thousand.[2] In any case, it was an exceedingly small and harassed minority, often drawn to Christian socialist ideas, for whom the problem of capitalism was first and foremost its moral destructiveness. Also much in evidence was a critical Confucian perspective: witness the early writings, for example, of both Katayama Sen (1859–1933), a Christian and later official of the Comintern, and Kōtoku Shūsui (1871–1911), Japan's first major modern anarchist. In addition, the early movement claimed the mantle of the vanquished Freedom and People's Rights

---

2. Peter Duus and Irwin Scheiner, "Socialism, Liberalism, and Marxism," in *Modern Japanese Thought*, ed. Bob Tadashi Wakabayashi (Cambridge: Cambridge University Press, 1988), p. 162, n. 26.

movement (1874–1884), which had appropriated the task of completing the "revolutionary Restoration" of 1868. The Restoration, it was claimed, had been derailed and subverted by Satsuma–Chōshū despotism. From the first, Japanese socialism demonstrated a strong "trade-unionist" consciousness and appeal that linked it, ideologically at least, to the American Federation of Labor under Samuel Gompers. While in some ways a movement of intellectuals, Japanese socialism genuinely tried to appeal to workers. The extent to which socialists were harassed, even persecuted, suggests that this appeal was probably greater than is sometimes claimed in historical retrospect. There can be no doubt that Japan's fervent embrace of imperialism, its official neotraditionalism, and the emergence of concentrated capital and a large and growing working class created the conditions for the movement's radicalization. In this process, the Russo-Japanese War was, by all accounts, the critical turning point. The early movement definitively ended with the Great Treason incident of 1910, in which Kōtoku Shūsui, at the head of a group of twenty-four defendants, was tried for having plotted to assassinate the emperor. Its grim resolution—the execution early in 1911 of Kōtoku and eleven others—ushered in the "winter years" of the Japanese socialist movement.

KATAYAMA SEN

A SUMMONS TO THE WORKERS
(SHOKKŌ SHOKUN NI YOSU)

This summons, dating to 1887, appeals less to the workers as members of a class-conscious proletariat with a revolutionary mission than it does to their traditional Japanese attitudes, such as the fear of foreign domination and exploitation, the desire for self-improvement and the preservation of family life, their generally law-abiding character, and, finally, their sense of social cohesion and responsibility.

The year 1899 will see Japan really opened to foreign intercourse. It will be a time when foreign capitalists will enter our country and attempt to amass millions in profits by exploiting our cheap labor and our clever workers. In such a situation, these foreign capitalists, who are not only different in character, manners, and customs but who are also notorious for their cruel treatment of workers, will try to become your masters within the next three years. In the light of this situation, you workers must soon start preparing yourselves, or you will not be able to avoid suffering the same abuses as the workers of Europe and America. Considering recent developments, moreover, the relations between the workers and employers of our country, in the same way as in Europe and America, will change each day as factories and plants increase in number.

Considerations of profit alone will prevail. The strong will be triumphant, and the weak will be destroyed. Since the superior are heading for days of prosperity, and the inferior, for times of ruin, it will not be easy to conquer and to flourish in the coming days. Moreover, when the foreigners do enter our country, it will be vitally necessary for you to double your resolution and to devise moderate means to protect your position on the field of struggle, without getting involved in disputes on their behalf.

You workers, like others before you, are people without capital who provide a living for others than yourselves. One of your arms and one of your legs are, so to speak, devoted to the support of society. When you meet with some misfortune and are disabled or when you become infirm with age and can no longer work, you will immediately be deprived of the means of earning a living and are turned out into the street. Should death overtake you, your wife and children will be hard put to stay alive. In this state of affairs you are really as helpless as a candle in the wind. Unless you workers heed the precept of the ancients and prepare for adversity while you are able, and make it your practice to provide for ways to cope with future difficulties while you are strong and sound of body, it will be hard for you to avoid violating the fundamental obligations of a human being, a husband, or a parent. This matter demands sober consideration.

In this day and age, our country is still not enlightened. In the olden days, when there were no machines, your wife and children stayed at home and worked and helped earn a living. But with the rise of factories and mills your wife, who should be looking after the home, went off to work in the factories. And since even innocent children work at the machines, the life of the home is thrown into confusion. At times the lives of children are endangered, when machines, which should be of benefit to man, function improperly and present the astounding spectacle of harming him. In some factories children with delicate bodies are made to work hours that would be too long even for adults. The lifeblood of those who are little more than infants is squeezed out with impartiality, and for their parents this is indeed unbearable. It should be evident that you must first and foremost take vigorous action and devise ways and means of coping with the situation. You must put your homes in order and protect the lives of your women and children. Do not forget, you workers, that those who take the lives of men do not do so only with the lethal instruments of murderers and criminals.

It is evident that when wives who should be caring for the home and children who should be in school are working in factories, an extremely unnatural state of affairs exists. If we seek the reason for this, we will find that because of the cheapness of labor, a man with only one pair of hands cannot support a wife and children. This is truly most deplorable. If you are a husband, you will want to give your wife a comfortable life. If you are a parent, you will want to have your children educated. These must, of course, be your feelings, and if you would only once rouse yourself, you would in the end find a way to correct this unnatural state of affairs and, by so doing, preserve your dignity.

One more matter that should be mentioned concerns your behavior. If you are an honest man earning a living by selling your labor power and if you make no mistakes in your work and conduct, you need not fear anything under the sun. But if you once do something dishonest or improper, your reputation as an upright man will thereby be destroyed, and your life itself will be ruined. The saying that honesty prevails in the end is known to all of us. The way to protect yourself lies in this. Furthermore, men who are in the unfortunate position that you are in will find it difficult to obtain completely satisfactory results if, in attempting to improve their position, they are the least bit indiscreet in their behavior. Accordingly, it is necessary for you to strive to advance and extend your position and interests and, at the same time, to be courageous enough to follow a righteous course. Why should you workers not try to improve yourselves and mend your ways and pursue your ends in an open and above-board fashion? You should know that the most heartless person will not prevail before your righteousness.

How you workers are to perform the necessary acts of resolution and preparation, which have been indicated previously, will understandably raise questions in your minds. Some of you will say: "Matters have by now gone beyond the stage of talking. The rich are becoming richer, and the poor are becoming poorer. The injustices and ruined circumstances that are the workers' lot are indeed cause for bitterness. Only through a revolution that corrects this situation may the differences in wealth be equalized." This argument is truly attractive, and it would be splendid if you were able to achieve complete reform by the revolution advocated by its proponents. But the affairs of the world are not so simple as these men believe. Unexpected developments occur, making it impossible to realize original objectives, and great disorders are not infrequent.

You workers should think twice before accepting these arguments. The advances of society have always been at a leisurely and orderly pace. Revolutionists are opposed to the supporters of order, and when the former make haste and recklessness a prime factor, the actions of the two groups become diametrically opposed. As far as equalization of economic differences is concerned, since not all men are equally wise, inequalities in the amount of property individually possessed are inevitable. Proposals for eliminating differences between rich and poor are more easily stated than achieved.

In view of this, You workers should firmly and resolutely reject ideas of revolution and acts of radicalism. To advance a mile, you must go forward by steps. You should thus spurn the counsel of the economic levelers.

We thus would recommend that you workers establish trade unions based on the feelings common to men engaged in the same work and possessed of kindred sentiments. These trade unions, moreover, should be organized on a nationwide cooperative basis. In carefully viewing your past actions, it is evident that you have refrained from joining together, that you have struggled with one another, and that you have achieved no unity. Thus, even if some of you, with laborious effort and after countless appeals, have finally secured an increase in wages, others remain satisfied with their outrageously low wages. Some want to reprove your unworthy fellow workers, but also [others] want to protect them. The spectacle of some men building and other men destroying, of kindred people engaged in mutual strife, is really cause for regret.

Your internecine strife, the contempt in which the foreigners hold you, and the position in which you find yourselves today all may to a large extent be attributed to you workers' failure to act as one.

[Katayama and Nishikawa, *Nihon no rōdō undō*, pp. 18–22; AB]

ANARCHISM

From its very beginning, the twentieth century in Japan was marked by a more or less unremitting official campaign against socialism that included antiso-cialist legislation, the establishment of the Special Higher Police, the suppres-sion of attempts to organize political parties, waves of arrests, and constant harassment. Socialists, as Carol Gluck put it, became Japan's "metaphorical foreigners." Under these circumstances, it is not surprising that "economism" and a parliamentary strategy began to seem, at best, inadequate. For a significant number of people, the repressive power of the state was by far the greatest target for the movement's revolutionary energies, and anarchism was the most com-pelling framework for action. To be sure, anarchism was not a single doctrine. But in the sense that the removal of the state as such—and not simply of a given regime—was accepted as necessary for society and its constituent groups to flourish, anarchism diverged sharply from its Christian socialist predecessors. Such views also separated it from Marxism, its great antagonist within the so-cialist tradition and movement. Related to this divergence was the inherently centrifugal character of anarchist notions of political organization. But as the appeal of anarchosyndicalism in the labor movement through the 1920s dem-onstrates, anarchism could indeed serve as the ideological framework for rev-olutionary action without the benefit of a centralized party or a strategy focused on seizing state power. Of considerable importance to the appeal of anarchism and its legacy was its elevation of collective spontaneity (on the part of the proletariat) and the unfettered realization of individual freedom as a supreme value. At the level of political practice, such attitudes could lead to strategies of violent "direct action" that could call on the movement the even heavier hand of state power. The same attitudes nurtured a leadership of powerful, even charismatic, personalities, most notably Kōtoku Shūsui and Ōsugi Sakae, but also a number of women: Kanno Suga, Itō Noe, and Kaneko Fumiko, among others.

KŌTOKU SHŪSUI

The trade-union movement and an equally young socialist movement, which emerged during the last years of the nineteenth century, did not last long. In 1900, fearful of social unrest, the Japanese government passed the Public Peace Preservation Law which legally hamstrung radical social movements for more than two decades. One of the principal effects of this legislation was the constriction of radical expression, which tended to become increasingly theoretical, intellectual, and polemical. But with the gradual strengthening of parliamentary government and the extension of suffrage, many radicals were encouraged to think that their objectives could be achieved through the ballot box.

It was in this atmosphere that Kōtoku Denjirō (1871–1911), better known by his pen name Shūsui, and his anarchist philosophy appeared. Few, if any, intellectuals in modern Japanese history have wielded a more trenchant pen than Kōtoku did. A fearless and outspoken foe of established institutions, he was still a young man when he was executed in 1911 for allegedly having plotted against the emperor's life. Just four years earlier, at a meeting of the Socialist Party in Tokyo, Kōtoku proclaimed his break with parliamentarianism and his newfound conviction in direct action. With the passage of the years, the fame of the man, rather than of his ideas, has continued to grow. To all radicals, he has been a symbol of opposition to oppression.

"THE CHANGE IN MY THOUGHT" (ON UNIVERSAL SUFFRAGE)
(WAGA SHISŌ NO HENKA)

I

I want to make an honest confession. My views of the methods and policy to be adopted by the socialist movement started to change a little from the time that I went into prison a couple of years ago.[3] Then during my travels last year,[4] they changed dramatically. If I recall how I was a few years back, I get the feeling that I am now almost like a different person.

Because of this change in my ideas, I have had heated discussions with Sakai [Toshihiko, 1871–1933] on dozens of occasions and have also frequently tried

---

3. Kōtoku was imprisoned for an offense against the Press Law from February to July 1905.

4. Kōtoku was away from Japan, living in the United States, from November 1905 to June 1906.

talking things over with a few of my other friends, too. Then again, since I have from time to time put down some of my ideas in articles in *Hikari*,[5] some people may already have grasped the gist of what I have been thinking. All the same, for want of a suitable organ[6] and also because my illness has made writing difficult,[7] until now I have not been able to address all the comrades and explain my basic ideas. But now the opportunity has come, for I certainly would not be true to my principles if I kept silent indefinitely.

For these reasons, I want—as I said before—to make an honest confession. If I were to put in a nutshell the way I think now, it would be along the following lines: "A real social revolution cannot possibly be achieved by means of universal suffrage and a parliamentary policy. There is no way to reach our goal of socialism other than by the direct action of the workers, united as one."

II

Previously I listened to the theories of the German socialists and those in the same current and put far too much emphasis on the effectiveness of votes and of parliament. I used to think: "If universal suffrage is achieved, then surely a majority of our comrades will be elected. And if a majority of the seats in parliament are occupied by our comrades, then socialism can be put into effect by means of a parliamentary resolution." It is true, of course, that I recognized at the same time the urgent need for workers' solidarity, but still I believed that at least the first priority for the social movement in Japan was universal suffrage. My speeches and articles were full of this, but I now think of it as an extremely childish and naive idea.

To go into a little more detail, one cannot promote the happiness of the majority under today's so-called representative system. The representatives are first elected from a morass of candidates, supporters, henchmen, newspapers, deception, threats, banquets, and corruption. It makes one wonder whether there really are any who are seriously thinking about either the state or the people. Yet even if, for the sake of argument, we assume that competent people were elected, what then? People change with their circumstances, and as MPs they would by no means be the same individuals as when they first put themselves forward as candidates. As politicians living in the capital, they would be different again from the public-spirited people they first were when still in their

5. *Hikari* (*Light*) was a socialist newspaper that was published from November 20, 1905, to December 15, 1906. Kōtoku was an irregular contributor.

6. Kōtoku's words "for want of a suitable organ" refer to the situation that had existed for some time before the daily *Heimin shinbun* (*Common People's Newspaper*) appeared, when no single journal was recognized by all sections of Japan's socialist movement. The daily, though, was published only from January 15 to April 14, 1907. This article appeared in the February 5 issue.

7. By this stage, Kōtoku was a semi-invalid suffering from chronic intestinal tuberculosis.

home districts. One wonders whether there really can be any who genuinely remain true to the values they held before they were elected. Isn't prestige what invariably comes first in the lives of all MPs (or, at any rate, the vast majority of them)? And next comes power, followed by profit. Isn't their field of vision restricted to themselves, their families, or, at most—and even this applies to only the very best among them—to their parties? . . .

So you could say that not a parliament anywhere in the world until now, in the strict sense of the word, has represented the will of the people. The fact that even under universal suffrage, parliament is unable to fully represent the will of the people is recognized these days by a majority of scholars throughout the world. . . . The fact is that at present, parliament is constituted from the bourgeoisie, the very class that regards the working class with hostility and uses it as a stepping-stone. . . .

Perhaps MPs do not only have to be of bourgeois origin. If universal suffrage is achieved, many working-class MPs might be elected. Indeed, already in Britain fifty workers were elected last year.[8] But no sooner are these MPs elected than immediately most of them lose their working-class frame of mind, develop a taste for fine clothes and fine food in the bourgeois style, and give themselves airs and graces. And aren't they the butt of bitter condemnation because of this? . . .

III

. . . But the day will come when socialism is a force to be reckoned with, and when it gains a majority in the electoral arena, what will happen then? Under those circumstances, many of the candidates who have campaigned professing to be socialists will not be anything like the sincere men and women of today. On the contrary, they will have joined the Socialist Party in order to acquire honor, power, and profit for themselves—or simply in order to win a seat in parliament. . . .

At the time when the old Jiyūtō (Liberal Party) was struggling against the stream, all the party members were patriots burning with righteous indignation. And when we think of their spirit and élan, it was far superior to that of the socialists today. Yet no sooner had they become a force in parliament than, instead of putting the interests of the people first, they became preoccupied with maintaining their own strength in parliament, defending their seats, and advancing their own interests. . . . But what if the Socialist Party, too, were to be dazzled and seduced by the type of worldly power that comes with winning a majority of votes and occupying a majority of seats in parliament? If [the party] made this its first priority, its fate would be no different from the sorry

8. Reference to the British general election of 1906.

end of the Jiyūtō, and one would have to say that the way ahead was fraught with danger. . . .

IV

Even if I were to concede everything and we were to assume that elections really were conducted fairly, that suitable MPs could be elected, and that on the whole those MPs faithfully represented the will of the people, could we still in fact achieve socialism by these means? Let us take Germany—the country of both Marx and Lassalle—as an example. When the first comrades were elected there under universal suffrage, there were only two of them. After that it took more than thirty years, struggling day by day, to reach a total of eighty-one MPs. And the fruit of those more than thirty years of hard fighting and bitter struggle was that they were sent packing by a piddling imperial proclamation ordering parliament to dissolve and were unable to put up any resistance whatsoever. Doesn't this illustrate just how fragile . . . an electoral majority is? . . .

And when this turn of events occurs, there is nothing else to do but to rely on the strength of the united working class. Yes!—There is nothing else to do but to rely on the direct action of the united workers. But the question is whether it will be possible to immediately resort to direct action as soon as it is required unless effort has already been expended on training the ordinary working class itself to acquire solidarity? . . .

But being a member of a party in the sense that one votes for it and being a conscious member are [completely] different. Even if one does have three million people trained [to conduct] an election, they are useless for conducting a revolution. . . . [W]hen the workers are told, "Now is the revolution! Rise up!" they are flabbergasted and, seeing that the ballot is worthless, have to rethink their ideas all over again. Thus we can see that, to the extent that a parliamentary policy takes hold, the revolutionary movement is emasculated. . . .

V

A majority of socialists in Europe today have become disillusioned with the poor results that parliamentary power has to offer. A tendency has emerged in the various continental countries for friction to develop between the socialist MPs and the working class. Even the British trade unions, which make frantic efforts to get MPs elected, have witnessed a gradual decline in the number of their members and in their funds. Shouldn't we socialists in Japan pay the greatest attention to this point?

What the working class needs is not the conquest of political power—it is the "conquest of bread."[9] It is not laws—it is food and clothing. Hence it follows

---

9. Reference to Pytor Kropotkin's famous book of the same name.

that parliament is almost of no use to the working class. . . . To repeat: the last thing the workers should do is to put their trust in votes and MPs.

VI

Although I have been talking in this way, I certainly do not think it would be a bad thing to gain the right to vote. Nor am I by any means vehemently opposed to the movement for reforming the election laws. Should universal suffrage be achieved, then the workers' views would at least to some extent have to be borne in mind as parliament went about its business of law making. . . . We can mention the benefits that workers might get from laws dealing with labor insurance, factory inspection, tenant farmers' problems, labor protection, and poor relief. Or the benefits to them of amending or repealing the public peace police law and press law. Because there are advantages to be had here, launching movements to achieve these aims is by no means a bad thing. . . .

The point is that as a socialist and as a member of the Socialist Party, there are certain things I believe are important to attaining our end. What we are aiming at is a fundamental revolution in economic organization: the abolition of the wages system, in other words. Now, I believe that in order to attain this end, it is more important to arouse the consciousness of ten workers than it is to get a thousand signatures on a petition for universal suffrage. . . .

Comrades! The conclusion I draw from the foregoing is as follows: I hope that from now on our socialist movement in Japan will abandon its commitment to a parliamentary policy and will adopt as its method and policy the direct action of the workers united as one. . . .

[Kōtoku, "Waga shisō no henka," p. 1; trans. adapted from Crump, *The Origins of Socialist Thought in Japan*, pp. 341–50]

KAGAWA TOYOHIKO

In the prime of his career as a Christian evangelist, pacifist, and social activist, Kagawa Toyohiko (1888–1960) was one of the most famous men in the world. When he was in his early twenties, Kagawa moved into the Shinkawa slums, east of Kobe, compiling surveys and writing extensively on the need for "human construction" among the flawed and wounded personalities of those afflicted by poverty. His studies of the lumpen proletariat, including large numbers of outcasts, tried to embrace the experience of modern mass poverty, beginning with its social etiology and extending to (un)employment patterns, family forms, spending habits, diet, vices, and criminality. A few years before the rice riots of 1918 and the Great Kantō Earthquake of 1923 (which was followed by a massacre of Koreans in Tokyo), Kagawa predicted that such degradation would predispose individuals with a weakened capacity for self-regulation to mass violence, and this sooner rather than later. A powerful supporter of labor, tenant farmer, and outcast movements, Kagawa tended toward a moralistic evolutionism (he also speculated that Japan's outcasts had a different, and inferior, racial origin from that of the majority of Japanese). Kagawa's concrete hopes for "human construction" were disappointed, not least because of Japan's lurch toward continental aggression and domestic militarism following the Great Depression. In the midst of the Pacific War, even Kagawa felt compelled to renounce his pacifism in favor of Japan's just struggle as a "have-not" against a racist United States. He denounced the incendiary bombing of Japanese cities with particular force and remained conflicted in his views of the war after Japan's capitulation. *Before the Dawn* (*Shisen o koete*) was Kagawa's autobiographical first novel, and its success allowed him to pursue his evangelical and social work. The chapter translated here portrays the atmosphere immediately following the execution of Kōtoku Shūsui and eleven of his codefendants and its effects on Niimi Eiichi, Kagawa's alter ego.

BEFORE THE DAWN
(SHISEN O KOETE)

In the New Year of 1911, before nine o'clock in the morning, there were nineteen fights in the tenement houses in Kitahon-machi.

Then, as happened the year before, Eiichi was asked to assist in funeral expenses. On New Year's Day there was one funeral; on the second of January there were two; and on the fifth there was one more—at all of which he was asked to assist. Each time there was a funeral at the New Year it made Eiichi think of Ikkyū Oshō's saying, "Each New Year is a milestone to the grave, bringing both pleasure and sorrow." Eiichi experienced an indescribable pang each time there was a death among those poor suffering people. He felt that death must be endured and that he must press onward, but he could not help thinking of the wonder of life. . . .

On the twentieth of January the newspapers issued an extra edition announcing the sentences passed on K. and O. and the others, all together twenty-four persons. Twelve of them were sentenced to capital punishment. When he read the announcement, Eiichi thought that it was a sign of the times and paid no further heed to it. That evening Takami came and talked until a late hour.

On the next day a higher police official from the Sannomiya Police Station paid Eiichi a very polite visit. Eiichi had not been visited by the police lately. The police official asked him his opinion on the K. affair and other similar questions.

Trade being dull, the harbor was very quiet. Eiichi, however, went every Friday to Bentenhama to preach the Gospel. The slackness of trade had thrown three [hundred] or four hundred people out of work, and some of them had sought fresh means of livelihood by stowing themselves away on ships for Yokohama, Moji, Korea, Formosa, and even Hong Kong.

Soon after the New Year the emigrants' inns began to fill up with emigrants for Brazil. On the sixth of January a party of nearly six hundred emigrants started, and at the end of January it appeared that there was to be another party of six [hundred] or seven hundred emigrants. At the emigrants' disinfection station near the slums of Shinkawa there were from one [hundred] to two hundred emigrants going in and out every day.

On the morning of the twenty-seventh of January, Eiichi was suddenly visited by Soeda, a young man of nineteen who had been converted at the Friday morning services at Bentenhama. Soeda had decided that he did not want to live in Japan any longer and had arranged to sail on the *Kamo-maru* on the thirtieth of January as one of the emigrants. As unmarried men were not taken, however, he had decided to go under another name as the adopted son of another emigrant. Eiichi thought it was strange to change his name, because he was a Christian, but Soeda was determined not to stay in Japan where trade was so bad and was so determined in his desire to breathe a wider air that Eiichi gave him his blessing and wished him well in his future career.

All the people in the slums had to go out every day to look for work, and it became common to see the men helping their wives making match-boxes as job work. As the number of people making match-boxes increased, the pay for a thousand dropped by five *rin*, from eight *sen* and five *rin* to eight *sen*. Without this pay, however, they would not have had enough to provide themselves even with rice-gruel, and so the work continued to spread.

Because of the depression in trade, wages fell steadily, and every day the papers announced deaths by suicide owing to the difficulty of making a liveli-hood. Every time that Eiichi read of these cases in the paper, he felt strongly that the time had come when Japan could no longer be allowed to sacrifice people like that.

But everybody was silent. "Socialism" was a word prohibited. The workers were dumb and the scholars also. Only the cold north wind from Siberia wailed across the wintry sky.

[Adapted from Kagawa, *Before the Dawn*, trans. Fukumoto and Satchell, pp. 376–78]

SOCIALISM AND THE LEFT

ŌSUGI SAKAE

After Kōtoku Shūsui (and in a far different mode), the most important figure in Japan's anarchist movement was Ōsugi Sakae (1885–1923), whose life was a psy-chobiographer's dream. His autobiography, excerpted here, talks about a distant father (a military officer) and a mother inclined to administer severe physical punishments. Ōsugi stuttered, masturbated, was sexually precocious, and was fond of violence; he bitterly resented all arbitrary restrictions on his freedom, particularly those he encountered as a cadet. At the same time, he had a superb literary talent and became an important participant in the early socialist movement. His *Autobiography* concludes with an account of his several imprisonments between 1906 and 1910. After that, he was jailed four more times. A cofounder in 1914 of the famous journal *Kindai shisō* (*Modern Ideas*), Ōsugi wrote extensively on the philosophy of "life" and on the workers' élan; he also translated many works on anarchism, evolution, and the labor movement. He was a sharp critic of Bolshevism and was active internationally when the socialist labor movement revived following World War I. After he was arrested in Paris during the May Day demonstrations in 1923, Ōsugi was deported to Japan. In September of that year, following the Great Kantō Earthquake and amid the massacre of thousands of Koreans, Ōsugi was one of a number of radicals seized by the military police and murdered. He was strangled, his body thrown down a well.

AUTOBIOGRAPHY

The following selections begin with Ōsugi Sakae's recollections of middle school.

A Young Hooligan, 1895–1899

The headmaster at the middle school was the Professor Miyoshi Aikichi, who was made chief tutor to the imperial princess before his death a few years ago. We nicknamed him Confucius, not only because he had a beard like Confucius, but because he could never say anything without quoting Confucius. With a very solemn and serious expression he would lecture on morals from the *Analects*. One day in the beginning of my second year, he asked each of us in the ethics class to name someone we admired as our idol. Such men as Hideyoshi, Ieyasu, Masashige, and Kiyomaro[10] were named as my turn gradually came around.

Actually there was no one whom I idolized. I liked none of the men who occurred to me as possible choices. I tried to think of someone new, but no one came to mind. When my turn finally came I was at a complete loss. Nevertheless, I stood up, and as I did so suddenly recalled a book I had bought and read recently, somebody's essay on Saigō Nanshū.[11] Trying to make a good

---

10. Wake no Kiyomaro (733–799) and Kusunoki Masashige (d. 1336) were ministers renowned for their loyalty to the imperial throne in times of trouble. Toyotomi Hideyoshi (1536–1598) and Tokugawa Ieyasu (1542–1616) led the unification of the country in the sixteenth century. See de Bary et al., eds., *Sources of Japanese Tradition*, 2nd ed., vol. 1, chap. 19; vol. 2, chap. 20.

11. Saigō Takamori (1827–1877), the hero of the wars of the Meiji Restoration who broke with the government in 1873 and led the last great samurai uprising in 1877, the so-called Satsuma Rebellion. He was pardoned posthumously in 1891.

impression, I answered: "Saigō Nanshū." After everyone had his turn, the teacher commented on each answer. In remarking on mine, he said, "Yes, of course, Saigō was one of the great men of modern times—possibly the greatest Japanese of modern times. But he was a rebel. He was a rebel who drew his bowstring against the emperor. And no matter what the circumstances were or however meritorious his other deeds, he cannot be forgiven for that. So, it goes without saying, it is inexcusable to admire him as an idol."

That's more or less the meaning of the teacher's criticism of my answer. Then the teacher extolled the virtues of Confucius, holding him up as the model of someone whom we all should admire as our idol.

I was very upset with the teacher's criticism. No mention that Saigō's rebellion had been against the emperor was in the book I had read. It had said that his rebellion was to flush out and drive away the corrupt officials from behind the scenes. I had believed this; yet since the teacher had spoken, it was no longer any good. There could no longer be any question of whether Saigō was justified or not. His greatness was flawed. Returning home, I reread his biography and came to admire him even more.

The biography of Saigō Nanshū led me to read biographies of Yoshida Shōin and Hirano Kuniomi.[12] I don't remember clearly which parts interested me most, but after reading how Hirano traveled about raising troops, I liked him immensely. . . .

Cadet School, 1899–1901

The Central Military Preparatory School was in Tokyo, but at that time there was a district cadet school at each of the six army division headquarters. The central school taught the main curriculum, while the district schools taught preliminary courses. Each student attended in his family's home district. For example, those whose families were registered in the district of the First Division attended the district school of the division headquartered in Tokyo. After having the military spirit instilled in them at a district school for three years, all students went on to the central school in Tokyo. Since my family was registered originally in Nagoya, I went to the Nagoya district school.

II.

The third-year students were extremely hard on the students in the class immediately below theirs—that is, the second-year students—but were kind to the

---

12. Both Yoshida Shōin (1830–1859) and Hirano Kuniomi (1828–1864) were activists in the movement against the Tokugawa and inspired some of the heroes of the Meiji Restoration.

first-year students. After I became a member of their group, these veterans made me one of their favorite "companions"—perhaps even more favored than the others. If you were a "companion" of these veterans, you could get away with anything, no matter how wrong. Smoking, for instance, was a guardhouse offense if you were caught. But they had a special place where it was safe. The veterans from Aichi at first hesitated to take me there, but some of those from other provinces—especially Tokyo—took me along with them from the beginning.

It was also these third-year students from Tokyo who taught me something else—something punishable at least by detention or, even more seriously, by expulsion from school. At night after everyone else was asleep, they took me along when they went to amuse themselves in the sleeping quarters of those on the left flank.[13] This was the most serious business in which "companions" took part.

Among the veterans who came from Tokyo was one who wasn't a "companion." This was the son of General Nogi.[14] He was the largest boy in the senior class and the worst at his studies. He had a large mouth that always seemed to be grinning.

I wasn't always engaged in the "vices of *bushidō*." I also made real progress in true *bushidō*. The head teacher, who had a bachelor's degree in letters,[15] lectured on *bushidō* in the ethics course. He said that the soul of *bushidō* was the choice of the right way to die. I was deeply impressed. I thus made a resolution that in order to fulfill *bushidō*, I would not fail to choose in advance how I would die. I began to do research on the ways in which the samurai of old had died. Whenever I found something in a book, I would copy it down verbatim. My notes eventually filled a volume of their own.

Of all those examples of death, the one that most moved me was the story of the crucifixion of Torii Suneemon in the period of the Warring States.[16] In fact, more inspiring than the story was the inscription someone had written on

---

13. The entering class of students was evidently grouped into thirds, starting with the tallest on the right flank. Those on the "left flank" were the smaller students. Ōsugi's place was in the right flank.

14. The father, Nogi Maresuke (1849–1912), was already a national hero for his command of the victorious infantry brigade in the Liaodong Peninsula during the Sino-Japanese War and gained further fame during the Russo-Japanese War (1904/1905) and as president of the Peers' School. By the time of this work, Nogi had become a legend for his ritual suicide at the death of his sovereign, the Meiji emperor. Presumably, this son was one of Nogi's two sons killed in the war against Russia.

15. His degree was in *bungaku*. Often translated as "literature," *bungaku* encompassed a much broader array of subjects in Japanese colleges, including philosophy and history. A bachelor's degree carried considerable prestige in the 1890s.

16. In Japan, war was endemic in the Sengoku period (mid-fifteenth to late sixteenth century).

the picture of his crucifixion: "To die with patriotic fervor is easy—to meet death with tranquillity is difficult." I folded my arms and swore to myself, I will show them that I too can die with tranquillity.

I remember something else about the teacher I just mentioned. It concerned his explanation of the word "redress" in the Imperial Rescript on the Retrocession of the Liaodong Peninsula. I don't remember now what came before or after, but the phrase probably went something like "Nursing our grievances, we seek redress."[17] Whatever the ostensible meaning of "redress," he said that it actually meant "revenge." Even today I cannot remember what the ostensible meaning was supposed to be, so welcome did I find this real meaning.

I've forgotten what month—probably toward the beginning of the summer—there was a holiday to commemorate the capture of Pyongyang.[18] Breakfast that day was the first time I had been served what they called millet gruel. It was slightly sweet and, I thought, rather good. The side dishes were small amounts of green soybeans and tinned beef. This breakfast repast was served throughout the entire Third Division.

The officer of the day, Captain Kitagawa, whom I've also mentioned earlier,[19] spoke to us in the dining room about the story behind this repast: it was the same meal the troops had eaten in celebration on either the morning or the evening of the day Pyongyang was captured.

After we finished eating, we assembled in the lecture hall. On the front wall was hung a large map of Asia. The Liaodong Peninsula in China was colored red, the same color as Japan. All the officers and staff from the school were in attendance, and the head teacher, whom I was discussing above, gave his lecture about "redress." When the head teacher's lecture was over, we were led off to a town east of Nagoya, this time to a military cemetery. Here were the many tombstones of the teacher's comrades-in-arms and we stopped by every stone, one by one, to listen to Captain Kitagawa and the other school officers reminisce. Each concluded with the necessity of waging war on Russia, the ringleader of the Triple Intervention, to take revenge: "For the sake of the departed souls of these brave soldiers, we must take up arms and obtain revenge." We all felt our blood boil within us. . . .

Ōsugi was later expelled from military school after he and another student had fought and knifed each other.

---

17. Stanley's somewhat more literal and perhaps more accurate translation is "We shall endure hardship and privation and will devise our retaliation" (*Ōsugi Sakae*, 3).

18. On September 16, 1894, Japanese troops took this heavily fortified city from its Chinese defenders and achieved control of the Korean peninsula only weeks after the Sino-Japanese War began.

19. This is the first mention of this captain's name; he apparently had divided the new students into language groups.

III.

This joyful infatuation with freedom was not simply a vague instinctive goal for me alone; soon the opportunity came for me to link it with theory and extend it to society. The opportunity came quite unexpectedly.

I have already written about one episode from my memories of the period in "From Amidst the Cremated Ashes" in the volume of *The Honor of Beggars*:

It was around May of my eighteenth year (or perhaps two or three months later). I had only recently arrived from the country and was absorbed in preparing for the school entrance examinations. I knew absolutely nothing about world affairs and at that time never gave any thought to such matters. My lodgings were in the Yarai-chō section of Ushigome. There were five or six students from W (Waseda)[20] University and one cold evening they went rushing pell-mell out of the house. I could hear the noise of what seemed a great crowd waiting outside. I opened the sliding window to look out. At least twenty students were there, all wearing the distinctive four-cornered cap with its tassel, milling about boisterously, holding aloft paper lanterns on poles and waving them like huge banners.

"It's getting late! If we don't run all the way, we'll be late!"

"But that's better! It's too cold to walk. Besides, we'll get a lot of attention if so many of us trot through the streets."

"You're right! Let's run! Let's run!"

And they all flew off, shouting loudly to one another in high spirits.

Even now the scene floats clearly in my memory: the flickering lights in the big paper lanterns illuminating the bold letters "Y (Yanaka) VILLAGE COPPER POLLUTION PROBLEM MASS MEETING." And I can still hear their voices chanting "left right; left right" long after they were out of sight.

This incident was what first impressed on my mind the name of Y village.[21] From then I began to read with considerable care the Y (Yanaka) village articles that appeared frequently in the one newspaper I was taking at the time—the Y (*Yorozu chōhō*) *News*.

The Y village problem soon waned. As I think back on it, that was about the end of the great public commotion over it. Accordingly, my own interest in the Y village also died out for a time. But thanks to this incident I first learned the names of D (Kōtoku) and S (Sakai) of the Y

---

20. Ōsugi provided the identifications in parentheses; all the men were major figures in the left-wing movement as well as successful journalists.

21. Yanaka was among the villages along the tributaries of the Tonegawa River where the mining operations of the Ashio Copper Company caused flooding and pollution and generated national concern in the 1890s. See Notehelfer, "Japan's First Pollution Incident."

(*Yorozu chōhō*) *News*, and K (Kinoshita Naoe) of the M (*Mainichi shin-bun*) *News* and A (Abe Isoo) of W (Waseda) University. Thus I developed an interest in the numerous social issues appearing at the time in these papers; in particular the writings of S and of D were hugely appealing to me. Later at school in the spring of the following year I wrote essays with titles such as "A Discussion of the Gap Between the Rich and the Poor" and began to feel as if I too were a kind of social revolutionary. . . .

I first took the *Yorozu chōhō News* merely because it was the cheapest news-paper. Having just come from the provinces, a world preoccupied with military life, and having for years been forbidden to read newspapers, I did not know its name much less what kind of paper it was. About the only two national events in those years that I recall anything about were the marriage of the crown prince (the present emperor) and the assassination of Hoshi Tōru [1850–1901]. The marriage of the crown prince occurred shortly after I entered cadet school. We were taken to greet the couple at the station precincts as the two passed through on their pilgrimage to Ise Shrine. I recall that we were deeply grateful when they kindly returned our salutes. It is a sidelight, but Yamakawa Hitoshi, who was to become one of my shining mentors, was at that time already publishing a small magazine about Christianity. He made some criticism of the marriage and was sent up for something like three years and nine months on a charge of lèse-majesté.[22]

Hoshi Tōru's assassination took place the year I left cadet school. I heard about it in the schoolyard from a friend who had lived at Hoshi's as a student houseboy. . . . So by sheer chance it fell to the *Yorozu chōhō News* to take me by the hand and lead me out of blindness. Through the *Yorozu chōhō News*, for the first time I was exposed to life as it was lived in the world outside the military. It especially made me see society's unjust and immoral aspects.

To my eyes, however, this injustice and immorality reflected the simple realities of the world. They were purely abstract matters, not subjects that I could say stirred the innermost regions of my heart. Rather, what amazed me was the free and untrammeled tone of the whole newspaper. I was especially astonished by the articles signed with the name Shūsui.[23] Nothing frightened him or blocked his way. Brandishing the pen in his hand exactly as if it were the naked blade his pseudonym implied, he cut his way wherever his beliefs led him. I was absolutely awed by his merciless attacks on militarism and the

---

22. Yamakawa Hitoshi (1880–1958) was a young socialist who in 1897 dropped out of the preparatory school for Dōshisha, a Christian school in Kyoto; moved to Tokyo; and for three years lived a student life not unlike Ōsugi's a few years later. In 1900 Yamakawa was charged with lèse-majesté for writing an article for an obscure monthly that criticized Christians who revered the imperial family.

23. The nom de plume of Kōtoku Denjirō.

military. I, born to a military family, raised among military men, given a military education, and then coming to curse the blind obedience and binding fetters of that military life, was enchanted by these qualities of Shūsui's antimilitarism. . . .

Someone else with whom I had closer contacts also helped open my eyes — a man named Sasaki who had the room next to mine at the lodging house. He was an older student, about thirty, who had graduated from Waseda two or three years earlier. . . . Sasaki had a friend named Onodera whom I knew from the French Language School. In the same advanced class as I, Onodera had also graduated from Waseda two or three years before and was now a researcher in sociology under Dr. Tatebe. He was small and, despite protruding front teeth, handsome with the air of a young court noble. One evening we were returning from class with another student named Takahashi, a captain in the transport corps. Takahashi asked Onodera what sort of thing one studied in sociology.

Onodera answered proudly. His accent was as thick as Sasaki's, but he spoke as if delivering a lecture. "Well, let's consider the state, for example. And below you have the various institutions, you see. In sociology we investigate such thinking as how these came to be and in what manner they have developed."

"That sounds interesting," Captain Takahashi said, sounding really envious, although he was an equestrian instructor at the Army Officer School and was said to be such an accomplished rider that he could control a galloping mount with a single thread for reins.

This was the first I had ever heard of sociology or what it was about. And I joined Captain Takahashi in envying Onodera for doing such scholarship. So I asked Takahashi and Onodera to lend me some books on sociology and on psychology as a fundamental science. . . .

In addition, Onodera urged me to read a French edition of Le Bon's *Psychologie des foules*, saying it was a very interesting book. By checking the dictionary over and over again, I finally managed to finish it, though I didn't understand anything.[24]

There were no vacancies that April at the Gakushūin nor was it possible to get into the Gyōsei Middle School. Therefore I went to take the entrance examination at the only school left, the Seijō Middle School. On the application I put down French as my foreign language and the school accepted it. When the day of the examination finally came, however, they told me, "No more French students are being taken into the fifth-year class at this time." Applying there had been a waste of time.

[Since] I had no choice except to wait until September and take the English examination at some other middle school, I quickly began to study English. I

---

24. A decade later, in 1914, Ōsugi published his translations of Gustave Le Bon's works *La Naissance et l'évanouissement de la matière* and *Les Idées nouvelles sur la matière*.

had heard that you could pass the test at any school if you could read English at the level of the fourth book of the *Union Reader* series. Therefore, stopping my other studies, I started going to an English teacher in the neighborhood for lessons on the fourth book of that series. . . . After a month or two, the fourth book of the *Union Reader* ceased to cause me great problems. . . .

In addition to the rental library in Ikizaka-ue, there was another one in the vicinity of Jinbō-chō that was a favorite of mine. When I was living in a place in Yarai-chō, I started going there, browsing through the books and borrowing ones on philosophy, religion, and social problems. There were two books that I read over and over: *The New Society* by Yano Ryūkei, which I read while living in Yarai-chō, and Dr. Oka's *Lectures on the Theory of Evolution*, which I read while at Ikizaka-shita.[25]

I have no memory of what impression *The New Society* made on me — possibly because I read it too early. But I can still feel the great excitement I felt while reading Professor Oka's *Lectures on the Theory of Evolution*. I seemed to be growing taller as the horizon steadily receded. The world, which until then was entirely unknown to me, was opening up before my eyes with each new page. I was too excited to enjoy Oka's book alone, and I urged, almost forced, all my friends to read it. The work awakened in me for the first time an interest in natural science. At the same time, this theory of the change and evolution of all things, calling as it did for reforms in the social system that still had great authority in my mind, made it exceptionally easy for me to join the ranks of those advocating socialism. . . .

Not long before I graduated from Junten Middle School, I began to visit Christian churches here and there. . . . I ended up attending the Hongō church of Ebina Danjō.[26] It was not only the one closest to my lodgings, but I liked his sermons best. I do not know whether I was unaware of Ebina's nationalism or whether perhaps it suited the military spirit lingering still in the back of my mind. In any case, I was completely entranced by the preacher's eloquence. His wonderful voice enthralled me whenever, pushing back his gray hair and stroking his long beard, he would thrust up his hands and raise the pitch of his voice, invoking God. And when his voice choked with tears, I joined the other believers in weeping.

The reverend often urged that we receive baptism, saying, "No, it does not matter if you do not yet understand Christianity well — no sooner will you receive baptism than you will immediately understand it well." For a rather long

---

25. *Shinshakai* by Yano Fumio (also known as Ryūkei [1850–1931]) was a widely read account of a socialist utopia published in 1902.

26. Ebina Danjō (1856–1937), pastor of this Japanese Congregational church in the Hongō district of Tokyo between 1897 and 1920, was one of the most influential Christian intellectuals of his day.

time I hesitated, but finally I was baptized. Thinking that I would be soaked, I had my hair cropped close before receiving the cup of water.

Christianity had considerable influence on me insofar as it encouraged the "serious and steady-going" side of my personality. But the influence did not last long. . . .

War clouds were steadily gathering between Russia and Japan about this period. A craze of patriotism swept the nation. Even the *Yorozu chōhō News*, which alone had previously maintained an attitude of calm, suddenly changed its tone. Kōtoku, Sakai, and Uchimura Kanzō [1861–1930] together published a bitter farewell message and left the paper. Then Kōtoku and Sakai founded the weekly paper *Commoners News* [*Heimin shinbun*] and began to champion the causes of socialism and pacifism.

Until then my contact with these men had been through their newspaper articles and the eloquent speeches that they made at the occasional meetings in the main hall of the Hongō church. I had never met them personally. Now, however, I decided I wanted to join the ranks of the army they were raising. Kōtoku's book *The Essence of Socialism* had set my brain on fire.[27] . . .

In the Commoners Society [*Heimin sha*] were Kōtoku, Sakai, Nishikawa Kōjirō, and Ishikawa Sanshirō.[28] Of the four, only Ishikawa did not despise religion. But there were outsiders who supported the society who were enthusiastic Christians like Ishikawa: that is, Abe Isoo and Kinoshita Naoe.[29] Moreover, the majority of the youths who came were Christians. After all, Christian ideas were the most progressive in the intellectual world of the day. Or at least, Christianity contained the most numerous elements in rebellion against the ideas of loyalty and patriotism then dominant.

Kōtoku and Sakai sneered at and made scathing attacks on religion. They often brought up religious issues at the study group meetings. Nonetheless, both Kōtoku and Sakai accepted the resolution of the German Social Democratic Party, which held that religion was an individual's private concern, and they did not actually interfere with their comrades' religion.

Ishikawa was my senior at the Hongō church. About that time, however, he seemed to lose all interest in church and stopped going entirely. After I began going to the Commoners Society, under its influence I too became increasingly skeptical—first about religious people and then about religion itself. The war between Russia and Japan cleanly severed my ties with religion.

---

27. This work, *Shakaishugi shinzui*, was originally published in 1903 and reissued by Iwanami bunko in 1953.

28. Both Nishikawa Kōjirō (1876–1940) and Ishikawa Sanshirō (also known as Kyokuzan [1876–1956]) were important left-wing militants.

29. Abe Isoo (1865–1949) and Kinoshita Naoe (1869–1937) were prominent Christian socialists who opposed the war and influenced Ōsugi.

I had believed, as Ebina Danjō taught, that religion had a *cosmopolitanism* that transcended national boundaries and a *libertarianism* that recognized no temporal authority.[30] Tolstoy's views on religion, which had come into vogue in intellectual circles at the time, strengthened my beliefs on this. Moreover, after reading about the origins of Christianity in Ebina Danjō's *Life of Christ* and in *The Life of Buddha* written by a doctor of Buddhism, I had thought it was as Tolstoy had said: primitive religion—in other words, real religion—was a variety of communist movement attempting to escape the insecurity in society that stems from the gulf between the rich and the poor.

But the attitude that religious individuals took toward the war—especially the attitude of Ebina in whom I believed—thoroughly betrayed my faith. The fact that Ebina's Christianity was one of nationalism and the Japanese spirit, was now clearly exposed to my sight. He held prayer meetings for victory. He sang hymns that seemed like military songs. He gave sermons on loyalty and patriotism. And he quoted Christ completely out of context, as in "I came not to bring peace."[31]

I grew thoroughly disgusted. After several arguments with Ebina and with Katō Yokushi [Naoshi], who had translated a great many of Tolstoy's works, I turned my back on churches once and for all. Simultaneously I came to doubt the principle of nonresistance, the "turn the other cheek" that is an essential quality of religion and that I had begun unconsciously to embrace. Thus I could now embrace pure socialism and the class struggle.

When the war broke out, my father was immediately made a battalion commander in one of the mixed brigades of a reserve division and was dispatched to the Liaodong Peninsula. I went to meet him when his brigade passed through Ueno Station and stayed overnight with him at his inn.

When I saw Father on horseback directing his troops, the first time that he had cut such a heroic figure, the sight almost moved even me to tears. But there was almost something ridiculous to me about it when I thought to myself, What is the purpose [of going courageously to war]?[32] Rather than feel sorry for Father, I felt that the scene was ludicrous.

Once we entered the inn my father and the old-timers among the officers in his command went about in high spirits cheerfully telling everyone they met, "This is our last Campaign."

Father had very little to say to me that night except "Study hard." It seemed to be enough for him to have me sitting by his side and to see my face.

---

30. The words in italics are foreign in the original.

31. Matthew 10:34: "Think not that I am come to send peace on earth; I came not to send peace, but a sword."

32. The words in brackets were censored in the 1930 Kaizō edition.

v.

At military school I had thought about the free environment of the Shibata school I knew as a child, when I used to escape the eyes of my parents and the teachers at school to pass the entire day playing at the parade grounds. Now I had gained that freedom completely. My teachers at the Tokyo Gakuin acted as if they were there simply to teach what has to be taught, unconcerned with whether the students learned or did not learn. It did not seem to matter to them whether you came in or left during the class hour, whether you napped or chatted during the class hour, or even whether you attended. At the French Language School, except for me, the students were all adults, and the teachers and pupils all interacted as if friends. In contrast to the military school, where we sat for the whole hour without moving our bodies, hands placed just so on our knees, staring unblinking at the teacher's face, this was a completely different world. My responsibility was to myself and myself only. And I became absorbed solely in the studies for which I was answerable to no one else.

[Ōsugi, *Autobiography*, trans. Marshall, pp. 50–51, 60–67, 94–100, 116–18, 121–22, 124–26]

KANEKO FUMIKO

Kaneko Fumiko (1903–1926) lived a short life exposed to personal and social violence. Born in Yokohama to unmarried parents, Kaneko lived mainly with her mother, who, at best, was barely able to provide for her and finally abandoned her more or less permanently to the grudging care of family members. Unwanted, Kaneko saw the worst of urban, and then rural, life. "Unlike the rice in prison," she was later to recall, at least "the village rice bowls did not have pebbles and worms in them." A major turn came when at age nine, Kaneko was taken by her grandmother to southern Korea, where she lived for seven years. "Carpetbagger" society both replicated and intensified the social hierarchy of the Japanese metropole, and even though her grandmother's was one of the "better" households, Kaneko was thought to lack the refinement needed for an advantageous adoption. Treated sadistically at home, she contemplated suicide but was "rescued" by the discovery (occasioned by the voices of nearby cicadas) of the great beauty of the natural world. Also in Korea, Kaneko felt herself repelled by the arrogance with which Japanese treated their Korean servants and others. The March First movement, including its violent suppression, occurred just before her return to Japan, where at age seventeen, she struck out on her own. Drawn to anarchism and nihilism, Kaneko was also on familiar terms with Korean radicals, including Pak Yeol (1902–1949), with whom the last years of her life were tightly bound. Together, Kaneko and Pak founded a group they called "The Malcontents" (consisting solely of themselves) and were arrested in the aftermath of the Great Kantō Earthquake. After years in "protective custody," they were tried and convicted on charges of having plotted to assassinate the emperor. Offered amnesty, Pak accepted, while Kaneko refused. A few months later, she hanged herself in her cell with a hemp rope that she had woven herself. The following excerpt comes from Kaneko's interrogation record and offers details about and insights into her background and the formation of her political views.

"WHAT MADE ME DO WHAT I DID?"
(NANI GA WATAKUSHI O KŌ SASETA KA?)

The following excerpts are from Kaneko's interrogation on November 22, 1923.

QUESTION: Why did you embrace nihilism?

ANSWER: Because of the circumstances of my family and the ensuing social oppressions.

QUESTION: What about your family?

ANSWER: I have no family in the true sense. . . . I was abandoned by my parents and separated from my brothers and sisters. I had no family life. My birth was not recorded, so I was oppressed by the society. It is the fault of the social system. . . . [After coming to Tokyo] I read the writings of Sakai Toshihiko and socialist magazines. Observing this, my parents seemed to be concerned that I was inclining toward socialism. In about 1922 I became acquainted with a Korean, Pak Yeol, who was unknown and propertyless. I decided to live with him and informed my parents about this. . . . After I started living with him my father wrote me a letter, in May of that year, contending that I was a descendant of a chancellor of the realm, Fujiwara-no-Fusamae [681–737], who lived over a hundred generations ago. I was besmirching this illustrious Saeki family line by living with a lowly Korean. He was disowning me, and henceforth I was not to think of him as my father, he wrote. So I was disowned by my father, who had already abandoned me. Mother too had abandoned me. . . . She even considered selling me to a whorehouse. . . . My parents bestowed no love on me, and yet sought to get whatever benefit they could out of me. Theirs is a truly selfish love, a form of greed. So I, an object of greed, fail to understand the meaning of filial piety. The so-called morality is based on the relationship between the strong and the weak. That morality is always manipulated to serve the convenience of the strong. That is, the strong insists on preserving his freedom of action while demanding the submission of the weak. From the standpoint of the weak, morality means an agreement that calls for one's submission to the strong. This moral principle is common through all ages and all societies. The primary aim of those in power is to preserve this moral principle as long as possible. The relationship between parents and children is also based on this principle. It is only coated over with the attractive-sounding term "filial piety."

QUESTION: How did you come to associate with socialists and eventually arrive at nihilism?

ANSWER: Three intellectual groups influenced me while I was peddling newspapers. . . . One was a Buddhist salvation group, the second was the Christian Salvation Army group who beat their tambourines, and the third, the long-haired socialists who cried out in desperate voices. . . . I first approached the Salvation Army group.

She then relates her experience with Saitō—earlier identified in her memoirs as Itō. She explains that she grew disillusioned with Christianity when he said he had to end his friendship with her.

What an extraordinary contradiction for a Christian to preach love on the street corner then fail to follow through on a pure, unblemished love. Christians have become fettered to the concept of God which they created. Theirs is a cowardly faith of slaves. The virtue and beauty of human beings is to live naturally, ungoverned by external forces. I decided that I could not embrace Christianity, which preaches the doctrine of life that conflicts with the ideals of beauty and virtue. So I abandoned Christianity. . . .

Kaneko was then befriended by a socialist, Hori Kiyotoshi, but she became disillusioned with him also because Hori, she claimed, was a hypocrite. He concealed his relationship with his geisha wife, fearing that it would hinder his chances of getting ahead in the world. He also made all of those under him do all the work in his printing business while he idled his time away.

I was also introduced to another socialist, Kutsumi Fusako. Her family life and principles were no different from Hori's. Kutsumi took care of her own personal needs but paid no heed to her children's needs. She would find some excuse to go out with a young man and stay out all day long. I heard her remark that all she had to do was to get on the platform and make a speech about socialism and say "The present society must be destroyed" to get the police to intervene. The next day the papers would report that Kutsumi Fusako made an extremist speech, and so the police prevented her from speaking. I got disgusted with the widespread desire among the socialists to get their names in the papers. At this time, Kutsumi had no money even to buy food, so she pawned my clothes. She then let the redemption period expire and allowed the pawnshop to sell them without my permission. I am not complaining about losing my clothes, though she knew that I needed them because winter had come. She showed no sense of responsibility. I detested her attitude, a socialist who gives no thought to other people's needs and thinks only of feeding herself.

I had imagined that socialists were people who rose above the meaningless customs and morality of the society. I envisioned them to be courageous fighters with no interests in so-called fame and honor and social reputation. I thought they were warriors fighting to destroy the perverted society of today and striving to create an ideal society. However, even though they denounce the irrational and hypocritical aspects of the society and pretend that they are indifferent to social criticisms and to fame and reputation, they in fact are governed by and are concerned about the standards of the mundane society. They seek to adorn themselves with conventional ornaments and take upon themselves conventional values. Just as generals take pride in the medals on their chests, socialists covet records of arrests in order to earn their bread. They take pride in this. When I realized this fact I gave up on them.

I also came to be appalled at the somnolence of the peasants, who are mired in pain but feel no pain, and the ignorance of the workers, who work diligently while they are being devoured to their bones. If the chains that bind them are removed, they are likely to go to the wielders of political and economic power with their chains and beg them to chain them up again. Perhaps they will be happier if they are allowed just to sleep in ignorance. So I got disgusted at all currents of thought and from the spring of 1922 tightly embraced the nihilistic beliefs I hold today.

As for the significance of my nihilism . . . in a word, it is the foundation of my thoughts. The goal of my activities is the destruction of all living things. I feel boundless anger against parental authority, which crushed me under the high-sounding name of parental love, and against state and social authority, which abused me in the name of universal love.

Having observed the social reality that all living things on earth are incessantly engaged in a struggle for survival, that they kill each other to survive, I concluded that if there is an absolute, universal law on earth, it is the reality that the strong eat the weak. . . . As long as all living things do not disappear from the earth, the power relations based on this principle [of the strong crushing the weak] will persist. Because the wielders of power continue to defend their authority in the usual manner and oppress the weak—and because my past existence has been a story of oppression by all sources of authority—I decided to deny the rights of all authority, rebel against them, and stake not only my own life but that of all humanity in this endeavor.

For this reason I planned eventually to throw a bomb and accept the termination of my life. I did not care whether this act would touch off a revolution or not. I am perfectly content to satisfy my own desires. I do not wish to help create a new society based on a new authority in a different form.

During the course of the interrogation, Kaneko candidly revealed her opinion about the emperor system.

We have been taught that the emperor is a descendant of the gods. . . . But I am convinced that the story of the three sacred treasures[33] is simply a myth plucked out of thin air. If the emperor were a god, then his soldiers would not die. Why were tens of thousands of royal subjects killed by the Great Earthquake in his immediate presence? We have in our midst someone who is supposed to be a living god, one who is omnipotent and omniscient, an emperor who is supposed to realize the will of the gods. Yet his children are crying because of hunger, suffocating to death in the coal mines, and being crushed to death by factory machines. Why is this so? Because, in truth, the emperor is a mere human being. We wanted to show the people that the emperor is an ordinary human being just like us. So we thought of throwing a bomb at him to show that he too will die like any other human being.

We have been taught that the Japanese national polity consists of an unbroken lineage of the imperial family throughout the ages. But the imperial genealogy is really fuzzy. And even if the genealogy is unbroken through the ages, it signifies nothing. It is nothing to be proud of. Rather, it is shameful that the Japanese people have been so ignorant as to acquiesce in having babies foisted upon them as emperors.

[Hane, ed. and trans., *Reflections on the Way to the Gallows*, pp. 111, 119–20, 124]

MARXISM

Marxism was introduced to Japan in the late 1890s, but it took the Russian Revolution, the rice riots of 1918, and related labor strikes to confirm the validity of conflict-centered notions of social progress, providing the impetus for a prolonged struggle between the anarchosyndicalist and Marxist elements of the Japanese socialist movement. While the reasons for the ultimate dominance of Marxism over the Japanese social movement are complex and in no small measure contingent, as a mode of thought anarchism lacked both the capacity to analyze historical structures and an "authorized" canon for the dissemination and popularization of its ideas. Precisely this was to be found in Marxism, which was able to establish itself as a synonym for social science, transcending its role as the ideology of a harried revolutionary movement. Numerous young academics also headed for Weimar Germany, to study directly the original texts and interact with German (and German-speaking) Marxists who represented the entire spectrum of positions within the tradition, from positivist to revisionist to Hegelian. Regardless of the variant, Marxism was "the very first *Weltanschauung* in modern Japan which compelled one intellectually to explicate the transformation of social systems in a total and coherent fashion."[34] Each strength

---

33. The three sacred treasures are the sword, the mirror, and the jewel, which came down from the age of the gods as emblems of imperial authority.

34. Maruyama, "Kindai Nihon no chishikijin," pp. 107–8.

in Marxism, however, brought with it a corresponding flaw. Its systematic character could degenerate into dogmatism; its putative universality recalled its foreign origin (and confirmed Japan's position as a historically backward "object" of knowledge); and its critical modus operandi often provoked infighting and organizational fragmentation.

THE DEBATE ABOUT JAPANESE CAPITALISM

As a social science, Marxism's chief contribution took the form of the "debate about Japanese capitalism" that ran from the late 1920s to the mid-1930s. Occasioned by political disagreements over revolutionary goals and strategy, its task was the historical characterization of the developmental process of Japanese capitalism and the modern state. The so-called Lectures Faction (Kōza-ha), following the position of the Comintern's 1927 and 1932 Theses on Japan, focused its analyses on the entrenched and powerful "feudal" forces controlling the absolutist imperial regime. Japanese capitalism was "special," a kind of hybrid. Bourgeois political institutions were immature or malformed, and the entire state apparatus was supported by a vast base of semifeudal production relations among the peasantry that had been little affected by the political events of 1868. The task of social science, therefore, was to clarify the obstacles to completing the democratic revolution as the necessary first step in a two-stage drive toward socialism. The dissident Labor-Farmer Faction (Rōnō-ha), while cognizant of time lags vis-à-vis the West, took a more conjunctural view, regarding Japan as one of a number of imperialist finance capitalisms. This meant, as a corollary, that before the Restoration, Japan's agrarian economy had already developed production relations characteristic of incipient bourgeois domination. The Meiji Restoration was Japan's bourgeois revolution; "vestiges" of feudalism, while still powerful, were incidental and would be swept away in a socialist revolution.

KAWAKAMI HAJIME

Kawakami Hajime (1879–1946), a gifted journalist, poet, and university professor, was one of the most effective intellectual Marxist spokesmen between the two world wars. His eventful life was marked by three major climaxes, each summed up in a poem. The first was written at the age of twenty-seven when Kawakami, deeply influenced by his reading of the New Testament and Leo Tolstoy's *My Religion*, joined the Unselfish Love movement, a communalist, social service organization founded by a former priest of the True Pure Land sect of Buddhism. In so doing, Kawakami gave up his teaching position at Tokyo Imperial University, stopped writing for newspapers, left his wife and child, and sold everything he owned except a copy of the Bible and the poems of

Shimazaki Tōson. The "thoroughgoingness" that he later identified as perhaps his most characteristic trait led him in this case to renounce everything that did not benefit others, including sleep. Death, the natural consequence of this, he was determined to prepare himself for. It was in the midst of this spiritual crisis that he wrote the following poem:

> To Unselfish Love I have resolved to give my life
> And yet each day bestows new life on me.

Within a few months Kawakami, abandoned both this experiment and the Unselfish Love movement, but briefly took up the study and practice of Zen Buddhism. Eventually he returned to journalism and teaching, advancing rapidly in his academic career at Kyoto Imperial University and becoming a leading writer on economic questions. In his study of Western economic theories, he encountered Marxism, of which he quickly made himself one of the earliest and most authoritative interpreters. After the Russian Revolution, however, younger men newly returned from the headquarters of world Communism subjected him to severe censure for his views. Even though one of these critics was one of his former students, Kawakami humbly accepted correction and resolved to start anew in his study of Marxism. At this point, he wrote:

> Without shaking off
> The dust of the last journey,
> I must set out again on a new road.

This further study led Kawakami to fully embrace Communism. At that time, however, the government was taking stronger measures against the Communists, and his position as professor at an imperial university became untenable. After his resignation in 1928, he found himself drawn more and more into what was called the "actual movement" (i.e., mass political action). This would have been difficult enough for an intellectual quite unused to the hurly-burly of mass movements, but to make it worse, the hazards of open political activity were increasing. Nonetheless, Kawakami felt keenly the need to prove that he was no mere "academician." Like Yoshida Shōin, who had come from the same province of Yamaguchi and had been Kawakami's hero and guiding star in his youth, he set out on the road to possible martyrdom, leaving his protesting wife in tears. After a period of open activity within the Communist-backed New Labor-Farmer Party, for which he ran as a candidate in one election, he was eventually forced underground. Shortly thereafter, he finally gained formal admission to the Communist Party, an event that moved him deeply:

> Here standing at my destination and looking backward—
> How far I have traveled across the rivers and mountains.

After his imprisonment in 1933, Kawakami's estimation of his capacities for the political struggle changed. When he finally was released in 1937, he was a broken man and died in 1946 after years of deprivation and malnutrition. Yet during World War II, he voiced his faith in the future of Communism in characteristically religious terms: "Now, as I spend my remaining years in the midst of World War II and watch things develop, I firmly believe in and eagerly await the advent of the communist society, in which everyone's daily conduct will accord with [the teaching]: 'Give to him that asketh thee, and from him that would borrow of thee turn thou not away.'"[35]

A LETTER FROM PRISON

I went to Tokyo to study at the age of twenty, after graduating from Yamaguchi High School. I had read the *Analects* of Confucius and Mencius but had never laid hands on either the Buddhist scriptures or the Bible. The latter I read for the first time after going to Tokyo. But the moment I came across the passage "Whoever shall smite thee on thy right cheek, turn to him the other also. And whosoever shall compel thee to go a mile, go with him twain. Give to him that asketh thee, and from him that would borrow of thee turn not thou away" [Matthew 5:39–42], it had a most decisive effect on my life. This was something beyond all reasoning. My soul cried out from within itself, "That's right. It must be so." Of course, I was unable truly to put this teaching into practice, but every time something came up, these words stimulated me, encouraged me, and drove me on to "extraordinary" actions. Thus the direction of my life was set toward a concern for others as well as for myself.

Two incidents took place before I moved from Tokyo to Kyoto. One was that I went and heard some speeches appealing for aid for the victims of copper poisoning at the Ashio Mine[36] and donated the scarf and overcoat I was wearing. Furthermore, after going home, I packed up everything except what I had on and turned it over to them. Hearing that many people were on the verge of death from cold and disease in the affected area and being urged to give anything I could spare, even old stockings, I was deeply moved and felt as if I were going to the rescue of somebody on the point of drowning. I thought I had done something good. But later I was scolded severely by my mother and suffered from a tremendous mental dilemma. It was quite natural that she should become angry, because she was supporting me without even having enough for herself to wear. And I freely gave away to others the things she had sent me at such great sacrifice to herself. This happened a little before I graduated from college.

---

35. Kawakami, *Jijoden*, October 28, 1942, p. 157.

36. Pollution from the Ashio copper mine affected farms nearby and became a big social and political issue at the time (1907).

The second incident was my joining the Unselfish Love movement. This was two years after my graduation and while Kishiko[37] was still in her mother's womb. Unselfish Love was a movement propagated at that time by Mr. Itō Shōshin. (He is still engaged in a movement bearing the same name, but over the years it seems to have undergone a change in its content.) I joined the movement, giving up my teaching position and everything. After joining, I found out that the movement was a little different from what I had imagined it to be from the words "unselfish love," but I followed his theory and engaged in a sort of religious movement for a while. It was about this time that I made up my mind not to sleep at all and consequently prepared for imminent death. It was an occasion when "death had to be faced squarely." Ever since, I believe, thanks to that ordeal I attained a great flexibility in life. . . .

[Kawakami, *Jijoden*, vol. 5, pp. 36–38; AB]

CONCERNING MARXISM

The following excerpts are from Kawakami Hajime's *Prison Ramblings* (*Gokuchū zeigo*), written shortly before and revised just after his release from prison in 1937. More of a personal testament than a theoretical discourse, it describes his basic faith in Marxism as the scientific solution to the problems of world depression and world war. Although Kawakami deprecated the value of anything written under the conditions of his confinement, prison memoirs like these were very popular reading after World War II and moved many people who would have been untouched by theoretical works to sympathize with Kawakami's cause.

The ruling classes in the various capitalist countries of today feel that Communism, which is trying to take the place of capitalism, is their greatest menace, and they fear and hate it more than anything else. As a consequence, in capitalistic countries at the present time such a thing as the free study of Communism is unthinkable. Night and day, the spurs are applied to conscious and unconscious counter propaganda designed to slander Communism and Marxism, while all refutations, arguments, and propaganda from the Marxist side that might oppose this are prohibited. Even now, therefore, it is extremely difficult for ordinary people in society—those who are said to enjoy "liberty"—to obtain the books and materials with which to understand Marxism adequately, and they can hardly hope to do so without resorting to illegal methods (such as secretly obtaining books whose importation or publication is prohibited). [pp. 26–28]

In our country, thought-criminals—and not only a small number of leaders but those of all degrees—have come to express a change in their thinking while

---

37. Reference to his first daughter.

imprisoned. It seems to me this may have become a sort of trend. In my view, this phenomenon has two meanings.

In one sense, it is proof that—as I have pointed out before—present-day Japanese prisons provide as many instruments as possible to make people think Marxism is mistaken.

In another sense, it is powerful evidence as to how many among the elements that have devoted themselves to the Communist movement go no deeper than the superficial aspects of it and only echo the views of others. [The reasons for this are] (1) the development of capitalism in Japan has been slower than in western European countries; (2) on the occasion of the Meiji Restoration the bourgeois democratic revolution was not thoroughgoing and left feudal remnants in varying degrees; police restrictions on freedom of discussion and the like persisted throughout and were very cruel; (3) even though the movement for Communist organization in Japan is young (capitalism entered a period of general crisis only after World War I), its growth has been ceaselessly trampled on from the beginning. Hampered by these circumstances, Communist education in Japan has been woefully incomplete. . . . The fact that thought-criminals—who are sometimes called "criminals by conviction"—necessarily lack firm convictions in Japan is certainly rooted in peculiarly Japanese conditions, but these peculiarities are not of the sort spoken of as the "Japanese spirit," or as a "national polity without parallel in the world," but are peculiarities because of the development of Japanese capitalism and hence of the Japanese Communist movement. [pp. 30–32]

Again and again Communists are arrested and accused of being "disloyal to the nation." That this is a simple misconception, however, is made perfectly clear if we take just one glance at actual conditions in the Soviet Union. . . . Detailed figures for economic conditions in the Soviet Union are published annually. If studied carefully, they indicate the following: (1) there is no longer a single unemployed person in the Soviet Union; (2) national income and the wage fund are increasing by a certain percentage each year; (3) some of this revenue comes from the annual increase of treasury expenditures for educational, health, and recreational facilities for the masses; (4) consequently, the standard of living of the masses is rapidly improving; (5) in order to make all this possible the productivity of labor (amount of production per worker), which is the "basic motive force of history," is truly developing rapidly; and (6) in this respect Japan, whose stagnation ranks with that of Hungary, Poland, and Romania, is in a diametrically opposite condition. All this proves beyond doubt that my conjectures while in prison were in no way mistaken.

Reconsidering the question, then, we may well ask: Do such great advances in the fortunes of the Soviet Union and the unusual rise in the standard of living of its people indicate that the Russian Communists have been disloyal to their nation or betrayers of their country? . . .

Since leaving prison, every time I have heard of political conditions in Japan—particularly when I heard of the outbreak of the February 26 [1936] incident—I have realized that the contradictions inherent in Japanese capital-ism are becoming progressively more and more violent. Everything has hap-pened just as we scientifically predicted it would; nothing domestic or foreign has gone contrary to our expectations. How can one say that our thinking is mistaken. [pp. 47, 53–55]

One thing I must say is that the danger of a world war is increasing day by day. The prelude to a world war has already begun; the smell of gunpowder permeates both East and West, and the fire is waiting for some opportunity to break out suddenly and spread over the whole world. Even the most ignorant person must be aware of all this. (This spring—the sixth since the outbreak of the Manchurian incident—there was a special ceremony at the Yasukuni Shrine. I heard on that occasion that from January to December last year [1936] the number of dead commemorated in the Yasukuni Shrine increased by one thousand several hundred. We must realize that it is not only in Spain that war is going on.)

Yet who is it that has proved scientifically that a world war is inevitable? Who has a scientific grasp of the basic causes of it? Who has a scientific faith that they can be eradicated?

It is none other than the Marxists—the Communists. . . . If we reflect on the extraordinary advancement in weapons since the last world war—especially of air forces—the coming second world war, with the misery it will bring to humanity, is truly a cause for alarm. In point of war dead alone, it will probably exceed by thousands upon thousands the dead of the first world war. Every time I think of it, while it engraves on my heart the chaos of the world, I also feel painfully that the responsibility Marxism has taught us to bear is indeed heavy.

Why is this?

Because only the Marxists know the real reasons why world war is inevitable; only the Marxists have the real method that the world offers us for eradicating it and, seeing their duty in regard to this method, fight for it. . . .

Our faith is such that even though we should be imprisoned for a number of years, it would be possible to direct anew the attention of some dedicated men—themselves ready to undergo the same hardships—to the truth of Marx-ism. If we think of this, we can discover the full meaning of daily life, and there will be no real hardship. Since it is to save the hundreds of thousands and millions of lives that would be sacrificed in world wars breaking out among the nations every twenty or thirty years, the jeopardizing of one's own life need hardly be considered. [pp. 56–60]

[Kawakami, *Gokuchū zeigo*, pp. 26–60; AB]

YAMADA MORITARŌ

Yamada Moritarō's *Analysis of Japanese Capitalism* (*Nihon shihon-shugi bun-seki*, 1934) is generally regarded as the highest theoretical achievement of

Kōza-ha Marxism, which, supporting the Communist Party line, saw Japan as being in a semifeudal phase, still in need of bourgeois democratic revolution and thus not yet ready for a proletarian revolution. Yamada (1897–1980) was an economist trained at Tokyo Imperial University, where he also taught. Arrested twice—in 1930 and 1936—Yamada was a contributor to the seven-volume *Nihon shihon-shugi hattatsushi kōza* (*Lectures on the Development of Japanese Capitalism*), the monumental compendium of lectures (sometimes heavily censored) about Japan's capitalist development that had been edited by Noro Eitarō. Yamada's notoriously difficult style and strategic use of neologisms was a challenge to his many readers, but his influence may also have been a source of anxiety for his theoretical opponents in the Rōnō-ha, such as Sakisaka Itsurō, who argued that Japan had already entered a bourgeois stage and that the forthcoming revolution would be a proletarian one to establish socialism. Sakisaka made frequent and sarcastic references to the scriptural status attained by Yamada's work. The famous preface outlines the framework of comparative absolutism within which Yamada's analysis is set. Whatever its flaws, Yamada's *Analysis* was a key text in the "invention" of the tradition of Japanese backwardness, among the longest-standing and (whether or not factually adequate) productive ideas in the history of modern Japanese social thought.

ANALYSIS OF JAPANESE CAPITALISM
(*NIHON SHIHON-SHUGI BUNSEKI*)

This work attempts to analyze the foundations of Japanese capitalism. Its chief task, using this analysis of fundamentals, is to make clear the basic structure—that is, contradictions (*taikō*)—and prospect of Japanese capitalism. I view this task as understanding the reproduction process in Japanese capitalism; I hope, that is, to have concretized the reproduction schema in Japanese capitalism. In this sense, the current study is linked to my earlier work, *Saiseisan katei: Hyōshiki bunseki joron* [*The Reproduction Process: A Schematic and Analytical Preface*, 1931].

Significant attention is given in this work to specifying the process by which industrial capitalism was established. This was a process of roughly the years between the mid-1890s and mid-1900s, that is, a process carried out during just that period marked by the Sino-Japanese and Russo-Japanese Wars; as a result of which the militaristic, semi-serf-like character of Japanese-style capitalism was finally determined. In the particular context of Japanese capitalism, this process was simultaneously one of imperialist transformation and the assumption [by capital] of the configuration of finance capital as well: these are the features specifically defining the process. The process by which industrial capitalism was established in Japan, its elaboration on the basis of the Meiji Restoration reforms, decisively marks the appearance of "Japanese-type" capitalism.

Let us try to compare it with capitalism in other nations. To English capitalism, with its modern large-scale system of landholding. From its basis in the Great Revolution of 1648 [Glorious Revolution of 1688] against the absolutism that had developed since the late fifteenth century, [English capitalism] ultimately took its classic form following the period of manufacture proper (late sixteenth through the last third of the eighteenth century), especially in the Industrial Revolution. To French capitalism, which preserved relations of a petty landholding peasantry: from its basis in the Revolution of 1789 against the *absolutisme* that emerged beginning in the early seventeenth century, it took on its final configuration, following the July Revolution (1830) and February Revolution of 1848, particularly under the form of Bonapartism during the years between 1851 and 1870. To German capitalism, with its domination by the Junker economy and petty landholding peasantry: on the basis of the beginnings of a bourgeois revolution-from-above (1808–1813) carried out under conditions of *Absolutismus* and under the compulsion of Napoleonic control, it assumed its configuration under the sham constitutionalism (1848–1866) and pseudo-Bonapartism (1870–) that followed on the old-line "provincial and Prussian" March Revolution of 1848. To "militaristic and feudal" Imperial Russian capitalism, with its Junker-style economy and *otrabotki* system[38]—that is, debt serfdom. Russia had been forced by defeat in the Crimean War (1845–1856)—in which Russian *absolyutizm*, dominant since the late seventeenth century, fought against advanced capitalist powers of England and France—to emancipate its serfs. After having been elaborated on this basis, [Russian capitalism] took form under the peculiar post-1905 revolutionary condition of "Agrarian Bonapartism" (with Stolypin's 1906 reforms as a keynote), to be abandoned in the second and third revolutions of 1917. Or separately, to American capitalism, with its "purely Russian" system of labor servitude and large-scale capitalist agriculture: this system took shape following the declaration of independence in 1776, in resistance to the British policy of primitive accumulation—that is, colonial control—and the proclamation in 1863 of an end to the system of slave trading and breeding (slaves numbered 697,000 in 1790; approximately 4 million in 1861). Against these various configurations, the characteristics of Japan's special, inverted capitalism stemming from its world-historically low position—those characteristics being a semi-serf system of petty agriculture founded on labor servitude-labor rent, semi-serf-like rule of an in-kind payment of land tax and a general tendency toward debt serfdom—have their basis in the Restoration reforms of 1868. These were undertaken because of the pressure exerted by the advanced capitalist countries on the despotic Tokugawa system that had been in place since the early seventeenth century and assumed condensed

---

38. Yamada's term for the *otrabotki* system is *koeki seido*; for debt serfdom (Russ. *kabalá*), it is *saimu nōdotai*.

structural (categorical, organizational) form in the process of defining industrial capitalism. That Japanese capitalism represents a departure, or deviation, from a [generalized] structural grasp should be clear in view of the points just enumerated. Hence the strong emphasis placed on the fact here.

Nor is this all. It is only through a structural (categorical, organizational) grasp of the configuration set on its way to establishing industrial capitalism that the structural (categorical, organizational) changes during the postwar [World War I] general crisis can be grasped rationally. Thus, by understanding the formative process of industrial capitalism, it becomes possible to understand not only the imperialist transformation and the formation of finance capital that were determined simultaneously with it; it allows us to grasp the primitive accumulation and industrial revolution that were its forerunners, as well as the general crisis (structural transformation) that has succeeded it. In this way, an understanding of the entire life of Japanese capitalism is put on a rational basis. Through this understanding, which takes the establishment of industrial capitalism as its keynote and extends from primitive accumulation to the formation of industrial capitalism itself—that is, imperialist transformation and formation of finance capital—through to the general crisis, we gain for the first time a foundation for criticizing the various errors and delusions concerning the developmental forms of Japanese capitalism and their respective epochs.

Indeed, this work finds, in specifying the formation of industrial capitalism, the key [to the whole problem]. Just as for the theory of reproduction, "simple reproduction" forms the basis of analysis, and just as in agricultural problems, examination of the category of the "peasant" (*shōnō*) provides the key to resolving the entire problem. The "pattern of economic relations" (*die Gliederung der ökonomischen Verhältnisse*) in Japan's militaristic, semifeudal capitalism is revealed through the structural (categorical, organizational) grasp of the configuration set in operation by the formation of industrial capitalism. Here we are provided with the basis for grasping the distinct process of reproduction in Japan's special capitalism. This viewpoint contains a criticism of distortions of the reproduction theory itself, as well as of its mistaken applications to Japanese capitalism. This is the standpoint taken in the present work.

[Yamada, *Nihon shihon-shugi bunseki*, pp. 7–10; AB]

UNO KŌZŌ

Uno Kōzō (1897–1977) is perhaps the only Marxist economist in Japan to have achieved international recognition. Working in considerable isolation, Uno developed a three-level system for analyzing capitalist political economy, made up of "basic principles" of pure capitalism, "stage theory" (mercantilist, liberal, and imperialist), and "analysis of current conditions." Uno's notion of pure capitalism stresses its implacable character as a self-activating, self-perpetuating force; it is a virtual demiurge. Criticized as quietist and even reactionary, Uno countered that only the unfettered scientific exposition of capitalism's basic principles at work would enable the abolition of the "commodification of labor power" that formed its essence. His portrayal of pure capitalism and his anti-Stalinist political stance brought Uno considerable academic influence as well as popularity in the student left of the 1960s. The selection translated here offers a crisp summation of Uno's understanding of capitalism and shows something of his wit and supple intellect.

THE ESSENCE OF CAPITAL
(SHIHONRON NO KAKUSHIN)

By the essence of *Capital*, I mean of course what, having learned it from [Marx's] *Capital*, I consider that essence to be. Not everyone will agree. And actually, rather than being the essence of *Capital*, it's no more than the essence of capitalism itself as I have learned from *Capital*.

Quite some time ago (and circumstances being what they were I can't speak to its accuracy), a colleague of mine in my days at Sendai,[39] a specialist in Japanese religious history, once told me this story: how the venerable Hōnen, having read the entire Tripitaka for the fourth or fifth time, hit upon the invocation of Amida Buddha — "Namu Amida Butsu," or "Hail to thee, Amitabha Buddha." Although I personally have no sense of the preciousness of invoking the name, the fact that out of this enormous text, Hōnen found its heart in these six characters struck me as interesting, and I've never forgotten it. Not that I regard *Capital* as a sutra, to be chanted as my morning devotion. The first time I read *Capital* was also the only time I read it from beginning to end, slogging through and with little understanding of what I read. But since then, from time to time as occasion arose, I've reread it, eventually going through it entirely a number of times and discovering its essence in the notion of the "commodification of labor power." And this has been the central consideration of everything — books, essays — that I've published since the war ended.

Those who have read *Capital* hardly need to be told that capitalism first arose on the basis of the "commodification of labor power" and was then established through a process of constant repetition. But treating commodification as pivotal to the theory not only of accumulation (this goes without saying) but [also] of value and crisis has at times led to a logical development at odds with that of *Capital*. . . . For example, if we account for all the phenomena of imperialism according to the theory of *Capital*, we may be able to know that imperialism is also [a form of] capitalism, but this doesn't necessarily mean

---

39. Sendai is the location of Tōhoku Imperial University, where Uno taught economics from 1924 to 1938.

that we will have clarified what imperialism is in itself. This is what I call a formalistic approach; it is just the same as trying to get by with imperialism in analyzing the contemporary world economy. . . .

It was with this purpose in mind that I set about systematizing *Capital* for myself with the "commodification of labor power" as its crux. . . . There are those, however, who consider "commodification of labor power" too simple a category, while others see it as overly specific. It seems to have been a common feeling among critics of my work "On Crises" that a complex phenomenon cannot be explained in such simple terms. As far as my work "On Value" is concerned, it appears to have been thought that labor power is a peculiar commodity and that to derive from it the substance of value of commodities in general is to take an overly narrow approach. These objections, it seems to me, forget that as a commodity, labor power is not a specific commodity such as wheat or iron nor one that, as with money, is capable merely of purchasing all such commodities; but as one capable of producing these is, rather, a completely special commodity. The contradiction within the commodity between value and use-value does not stop with its actual solution through commodity circulation by means of money; rather, because through the production of commodities by commodities, use value produces value, this contradiction may be termed the foundation for the movement of commodity economy in toto. As a corollary, while for all commodities other than labor power, demand and supply can be adjusted by means of capital, only with labor power as a commodity must demand and supply be adjusted within certain fixed limits for capital. For capitalism, this is simultaneously its indispensable, fundamental condition and its basic weakness. I consider it quite natural to regard this as the essence of capitalism, and therefore also the essence of *Capital* itself.

[Shihonron *no kakushin*, vol. 4 of *Uno Kōzō chosakushū*, pp. 32–34; AB]

MARXIST CULTURAL CRITICISM

Beyond the analysis of capitalist development, Japanese Marxists engaged in a range of cultural phenomena, from writing poetry and literary criticism to engaging in philosophical and scientific debate; this was in keeping with the "totality" of the Marxist Weltanschauung. For committed Communists, partisanship (as an expression of proletarian consciousness) was of course expected, but even in these circles, debates raged over the extent to which autonomous artistic values should be recognized. Bad art, some contended, was ineffective art; the same was said about science. These arguments, perhaps by nature, could not be resolved a priori but had to be left to the judgment of actual practice. In any event, from the 1920s until the beginning of total war with China in 1937 — and as the political atmosphere grew steadily more repressive — "cultural" work continued. And as openly political practice became unsustainable, interventions in the realm of art, culture, and philosophy came to be defined as practice, subject to all the polemics and debates that inevitably accompanied party activity. The following selection illustrates these developments in the area of philosophical critique.

TOSAKA JUN

Tosaka Jun (1900–1945) was born in Tokyo but entered Kyoto Imperial University, intent on a career as a physicist. He was attracted, however, to the philosophy of Nishida Kitarō (1870–1945) and Tanabe Hajime (1885–1962)—the so-called Kyoto school—and graduated from that faculty in 1924. After a year of military service, Tosaka began a teaching career and by the late 1920s was drawn from neo-Kantianism to Marxism, his concerns shifting from scientific methodology to issues of "worldviews" and ideology. A cofounder of the Society for the Study of Materialism, Tosaka tried to make it a vehicle for resistance to militarism and irrationalism. Dismissed from his teaching position in 1934 for "seditious thought," Tosaka threw himself into his movement work but was arrested under the Peace Preservation Law in 1938. He died in Nagano Prison on the day the United States dropped an atomic bomb on Nagasaki. The excerpt translated here is taken from one of his most famous works, *The Japanese Ideology* (*Nihon ideorogī ron*, 1935), a wide-ranging critique and polemic directed at the major intellectual tendencies then being mobilized in support of fascism; here the target is "Japanism."

THE JAPANESE IDEOLOGY
(NIHON IDEOROGĪ RON)

Japanese Spirituality, Japanese Physiocracy, and Japanese Asianism

It seems as if some kind of incoherent emotion, variously termed Japanism, Orientalism, and Asianism, is dominating the present-day life of Japan. Moreover, the social activity backed by this emotion is plainly visible everywhere. That kind of social activity is also reported in the world in detail as if it had some especially significant meaning. . . .

For us to be good critics, Japanism, Orientalism, Asianism—even though they have no inherent capacity for intellectual development—must become objects of our criticism. We shall see that these concepts strike poses as if they were full of meaning; in actuality, however, when we try to probe their content, they turn out to be mere cant. Not limited to Japan but in present-day international society as well, it is an extremely unpleasant but important duty for us to expose the posturing of this rampant and ugly tragicomedy of concepts.

However, as to the power of the kind of ultranationalism (or, to explain it more graphically, this kind of expansionistic ultranationalism) that goes by these names, this is not the first time it is flourishing in Japan. This ideology, which traces back to the Native Studies [National Learning] movement of the later Tokugawa period, first prominently resurfaced during the first three decades of the Meiji period in the form of a countermovement to "Europeanization-ism." In its next phase, it took the form of a startling new growth as reactionary ideology against the early proletarian movement that had arisen as a prominent movement of the Sino-Japanese and Russo-Japanese Wars. In a third stage, it developed very strongly but in a more subtle fashion as a reaction against the Taishō democratic movement that arose at the time of the Great War [World War I]. This entire reactionary legacy has now merged with the crisis of Japanese capitalism as one aspect of a worldwide crisis of capitalism; and, together with the shrill trumpet blasts of the Manchurian incident and the Shanghai incident, is now nothing other than a movement the effects of which are reverberating in every village and hamlet of the nation. If we trace the history of this movement in this way, the dominance of ultranationalism is something that necessarily betrays its own inner essence. Universally, this is the destiny of reactionary ideology.

However, it is certainly a phenomenon of the last two or three years that Japanism, Orientalism, and Asianism, as well as other "Nippon" ideologies (when one reads it *Nihon*, it is classified as dangerous thought) have been produced in great quantities and have begun to penetrate even into the world of free expression, literature, and science. These ideologies have developed in tandem with the establishment of Hitler's dictatorship in Germany, the ultra-nationalistic movement in Austria and Mussolini's actions against Austria, the unprecedented control of national production under Roosevelt in America, and then the establishment of Manchukuo [Manchuria] by Japan and the imposi-tion of its puppet emperor (in 1931), as well as with various other strongly na-tionalistic movements that never cease to sprout in our own beloved great Jap-anese empire. Only by taking its place under the umbrella of this interna-tional situation has Japan been able to emerge as a fanatically ultranationalistic state of its own. Of course, to place our august ultranationalistic movement alongside of this international array may not be approved by some Japanese ultranationalists—who want to maintain that Japanism, in contradistinction to the ultranationalism of the West, is not fascistic—but the facts are the facts, and they do not occur only to please a few people.

In society at large one hears it said that present-day Japan is at a total impasse. . . . For the Japanists of Japan, it matters little what they say theoretically to explain the objective causes of events. If only the explanation enters easily into the common man's ears, it is enough for their purposes. For example, they emphasize that this impasse arises from the fact the "people do not grasp the essence of the Japanese spirit" (according to Takasu Yoshijirō, "Constitutive Elements of the Japanese Spirit," *Keizai ōrai* [*Economic Affairs*], March 1934). . . . This is analogous, they say, to why in China, because there was nobody who clearly grasped the essence of the Chinese spirit the problems of Chinese Communism and the Shanghai riots arose there.

What, then, is the essence of this Japanese spirit? According to Takasu, the constitutive elements of the Japanese spirit consist of such things as that it is "life-creationistic," "centered and unwavering," "excels in cohesion and harmony," "takes as its principle positively to progress and expand," "has the character of clarity," "places emphasis on practice and actualization of the Way"— all the best of things that can possibly be imagined! But while these are all good in themselves, are they not a bit weird in this context? To say that the Japanese spirit is life-creationistic gives us no clue as to what is being stipulated. If we take the example of a philosophy, Bergson's metaphysics is unquestionably worthy of this term. As for its being "centered and unwavering," this is the political sense of the English spirit. As for its spirit of "cohesion and harmony," such things as German scholarly works are even more exemplary. As for "positively to progress and expand" and for "clarity," these are best exemplified by American shipbuilding design and by the "Yankee Girl" [reference to unknown translators]. And needless to say, is not the emphasis on practice and actualization of the Way more appropriately referring to the Soviet Union? If the Japanese spirit is composed merely of these foreign spiritual elements, the situation is unbearably regrettable indeed.

Takasu, in order to put a final touch to his pretty picture, promotes a "self-consciousness of the Japanese national polity." It is indeed regrettable that he did not bring forward this reference to the Japanese polity first. However, whether it is national polity or whatever other card he intends to play, let us not be coerced to adopt this self-consciousness or be manipulated by such underhanded tricks. For a true self-consciousness of Japan's national polity can only be achieved by a scientific cognition of the true history of Japan. And as for the likes of Takasu and other Japanists, what special historical "Japanistic" methodology do they employ? It is their duty to clarify this point to the public and to the world without further subterfuge.

Moreover, I do not understand from what motive Itō Shōshin, the devout believer in "selfless love," wrote his essay "The Essence of the Japanese Spirit" (in the journal *Rhetoric*). When we look at the problem of how the Japanese spirit belongs to a particular "self" known as Japan and then try to connect Itō's selfless love and this love of Japan itself, then the answer that Itō gives is that it is of the nature of the Japanese spirit "truly to love the nation of Japan, and by way of fusing nationalism and internationalism, it is the living spirit, both individually and nationally, that wholeheartedly strives to develop Japan into a truly fine country of the world." Just as he himself says, it is not a way to be trodden only by us Japanese, but for Americans as Americans, for Russians as Russians, it is a universal way to be practiced. Of course, if one speaks from the standpoint of "selfless love," one must naturally speak in this manner. However, what need was there, from the standpoint of selfless love, deliberately to take up the theme of the Japanese spirit? This is precisely the point we do not understand. Is perhaps the hidden reason that, upon the dawn of Japan having subdued the world, the Japanese spirit will turn out to be equivalent to that selfless love? . . .

The words of Yasuoka Masahiro of the Kinkei gakuin seems to give us another kind of hint about the cognition of Japanese history. He writes: "The true realm of the spirit of the Japanese race is expressed sublimely in the three imperial regalia: it shines with the light of wisdom that radiates from the heart of the pure and bright mirror; it courageously brandishes the sword of righteousness; and possesses virtue like the carved jewel; in sum, it consists in the effort to unite the gods and men and to take the world of the ten directions into one's entire being." (A *Study of the Japanese Spirit*). I appreciate how this psychological description is extremely eloquent (and, consequently, abstract) and therefore why this form of Japanism is so readily congenial to the ultranationalistic new bureaucrats. To reduce the reality of history in this old-fashioned ideological rhetoric can be thought actually to reflect the mythic spirit of the ancient Japanese race. But because this is not history and is nothing more than moral didacticism in elegant writing, it is regrettable that even as moral didacticism and beautiful prose it is extremely primitive.

Actually, because this childish literature is not different from a moral law, it is indeed mythology. According to Yasuoka, the three imperial regalia symbolize wisdom, virtue, and courage; the land of Japan is not merely a natural geographical site, but because it is viewed as the "Great Eight Islands" that are born "from the eyes of the gods who give birth to lands," it evokes an explanation of a kind wherein "the emperor and the Japanese race" stand in a relation "of elder and younger brother." In this way Yasuoka's method of historical cognition of the Japanese spirit is nothing other than a mythic method, and it is to be received as something in which the Japanese spirit must eternally remain at a mythic stage. Thus, the Japanese spirit does not advance or develop; it stands firm as something that is the enemy of progress and development.

In the above articulation I have tried to approximate the opinions of people who are devotees of the Japanese spirit. But at least in what I have understood up to now, I venture to conclude that there is no Japanese spirit but, rather, a "Japanese spirituality" that in its theoretical substance is extremely jejune and confused. Thus as to the problem of the Japanese, no answer appears to be forthcoming from the various forms of "Japanese spirituality." Despite the facts that a Research Institute for National Spirit and Culture has been established under the auspices of the Ministry of Education, that there is a magazine called *The Japanese Spirit and Culture*, and that there is a Society for the Japanese Spirit which publishes an organ called *The Japanese Spirit*, the understanding of the Japanese spirit on the basis of Japanese spirituality, at least for the present, must be viewed as a bankrupt enterprise. This Japanese spirituality seems to come down to what the Germans call *Bauchredner* [ventriloquism] — "all fluff and no stuff." . . .

Speaking therefore both from the side of the philosophy of Japanese spirituality and from the philosophy of Japanese agricultural populism, the special
character of Japan appears to reside in the claim that Japan is spiritually superior
to other nations and people. Perhaps all forms of Japanism may be reduced to
this fundamental tenet of Japanese spirituality. Still, what sort of thing the Japanese spirit is and how it is supposed to be the superior essence of Japan have
not, in my mind, been given a rational and scientific explanation. This, too, is
understandable, for in essence even the Japanese spirit—or what Japan is in
itself—is not, according to Japanism's own insistence, an explainable object;
indeed, when closely scrutinized, it is nothing other than a method and a
principle employed in explaining everything rather arbitrarily.

However, arbitrarily bringing forth the single concrete geographical, historical, and social existence in the universe called Japan and letting it become a
kind of philosophical principle is, in essence, something very weird when considered from the standpoint of common sense. Indeed, if this were a philosophy
termed "Venus-ism" or "Daffodil-ism," no one would ever take it seriously from
the beginning.

But the problem is that at the same time that it can be thought that Japanism
has no rational or scientific content whatsoever, one is able arbitrarily to read
into it any content whatsoever.

[Dilworth and Viglielmo, eds., *Sourcebook for Modern Japanese Philosophy*,
pp. 348–57]

THE *TENKŌ* PHENOMENON

Although they were criticized from numerous points of view, Marxist ideas
conditioned the entire history of social thought in Japan. But as a political
movement, Japanese Marxism "failed" doubly: in the attempt both to discover
empirically and to actualize politically a social logic of revolution—that is, a
theory of inevitable revolution stemming from the internal processes of Japanese
society. Part of this failure stems from the fact that until 1945 Marxists were
among the primary victims of political persecution. Indeed, the legitimacy of
the Communist Party after 1945 stemmed from its claim to have resisted longer
than any other organization had. At the same time, it is a fact that the majority
of party members, to say nothing of their many sympathizers and others of varied
leftist inclinations, performed what is termed *tenkō*: an ideological reversal,
renouncing the left and (in many but not all cases) embracing the "national
community." *Tenkō* was performed especially under duress, most often in police
custody, and was a condition for release (although surveillance and harassment
would continue in any case). But it was also a broader phenomenon, a kind of
cultural reorientation in the face of national crisis, that did not always involve

direct repression. For decades, the term served both narrowly as a moral litmus test in evaluating the careers of intellectuals active before and after the war and more broadly as a metaphor for the collective experience of an entire generation of Japanese. One of the most spectacular and consequential instances of *tenkō* came in June 1933, when Sano Manabu (1892–1953) and Nabeyama Sadachika (1901–1979), top figures in the Communist Party leadership, renounced their allegiance to the Comintern and the policy of violent revolution, embracing instead a Japan-specific mode of revolutionary change under imperial auspices, in reaction to the Soviet Union's use of the Comintern for its own power purposes against Germany and Japan. Their proclamation was followed by a wave of defections by the party rank and file and essentially signaled the demise of the party organization, except in exile.

LETTER TO OUR FELLOW DEFENDANTS
(KYŌDŌ HIKOKU DŌSHI NI TSUGURU SHO)

For four years now, we have been shut away in prison, and under the conditions that have been imposed on us, we have both continued to struggle with all our might and, at the risk of many discomforts and dangers, directed our attention to the general situation in the world outside. But recently we have found that there is much to ponder deeply concerning the destiny of the Japanese people and its relationship to that of the working class, as also to the relationship between the vanguard of the Japanese proletariat and the Comintern. At the end of our long meditations, we find ourselves at a point that we have resolved to make important changes in our previous opinions and with respect to our previous actions.

Japan at present faces unheard of difficulties abroad, and unprecedented major changes are bearing down on it. In the face of a domestic and international situation filled with both war and reforms at home, all classes and factions are busy with preparations and countermeasures aimed at resolving the issues at hand. At this time, the Communist Party of Japan, which bears responsibility as the vanguard of the working class, is revealing numerous deficiencies. The foundations of the party have expanded dramatically in both fact and potential, but the social composition of the party's membership, the party's structure, and its activities are turning into the political instruments of the radical petite bourgeoisie. The party has been unable to guide the outrage of the masses in response to the economic panic of recent years and the decay of the capitalistic structure that this has exposed. The party's formalistic policies in response to the Manchurian incident and the succession of war conditions that have followed have failed completely, and its antiwar struggle is limited to a display of demagogic articles in the *China News* (*Shina shinbun*) and the Comintern's agitational literature. The party has been unable either to exercise leadership in important strikes or to provide guidance in the ever more serious struggle of the farmers. At one point in time, the Communist Party of Japan issued calls for armed demonstrations and in fact even organized them, though on a small scale. This was a decisive error; even so, it was grounded in the conviction of mass support and was an expression of the notion of plunging directly into the masses. By comparison, the facts of last year-end appear as nothing but a collection of the bad elements of Blanquism, even seeming to indicate a decaying trend that bears no connection with the proletariat. Viewed objectively, one cannot say that the party itself is a party of the working class. We believe that from our prison cell we should be silent on most matters. Also, we know full well that individual party members are serious and working gallantly, that the struggle is extremely agonizing and serious, and that growing tension in general conditions is working in our favor.

. . . Nevertheless, the fundamental problem is that the party is unable to unite as the vanguard of the proletariat. As a result of our careful deliberations, we have realized that one of the fundamental causes that made the present situation inevitable is to be found in the politics and organizational principles of the Comintern, in which we had placed our unlimited trust. . . .

We acknowledged the need to turn criticism on the Comintern itself, an organization that has until now been accorded the highest authority. We believe that in recent years the Comintern has become conspicuously sectarian and bureaucratized. To an unacceptable extreme it has become the organ of one country, the Soviet Union. . . .

Without conducting fundamental research into what makes Japan unique, the Comintern adapted the experience of the class struggle in Europe and especially of the Russian Revolution and transposed it to the Japanese reality. This tendency is something we have long noted, but in the new theses on the Japan problem that were announced in May of last year it has reached its apex.

Recent world facts (including Soviet Union socialism) are instructive for us. Rather than depending on formalistic internationalism, the realization of world socialism will come by following the path to the construction of socialism in one country that conforms with the special conditions of each country and to which the working class, representing the vitality of that nation, is devoted. The Comintern's political principle, which pits nation (*minzoku*) against class, is an abstraction particularly ill suited to Japan, where the firmness of national unity is a prime characteristic of the society. The process by which the most advanced class represents the development of a people holds especially true for Japan. Not to fear even the sacrifice of one's own country to the goal of achieving world revolution is the culmination of Comintern-style internationalism; we ourselves served this goal. However, now that we have awakened to Japan's superlative conditions, we are determined that we will not offer the Japanese revolution as a sacrifice to anyone, no matter whom. It is not that we are rejecting internationalism among the world proletariat. However, the even higher internationalism of the future is likely to be built out of the efforts to construct single-country socialism in crucial sites across the world.

However, there is nothing so natural or necessary as that Japan's workers should think chiefly of Japan. From ancient times to the modern day, the fact that the Japanese people have progressed through the developmental stages of human society properly, completely, and without interruption from foreign enemies, is evidence of the extraordinarily strong internal developmental capacities of our people. Also, it is exceedingly significant that the Japanese people have not even once had the experience of being the slaves of another; instead they experienced always a free and independent mode of life. The extraordinarily sturdy sense of national fellowship and unity fostered by this experience is internally linked with the experience of a way of life ordered by the state. . . .

The Communist Party of Japan has adopted a slogan calling for the abolition of the monarchy in accordance with the directions of the Comintern. One of the main ideas of the aforementioned theses, taking matters another step forward, is to make the absurd provision that the antimonarchical struggle is the prime mission of the class struggle in present conditions. The Comintern sees monarchism in Japan as identical with czarism in Russia, and it imposes the struggle that took place as is on the Japanese branch. . . . As a political slogan, the party repeats "overthrow the emperor system" as if it were chanting the name of the Amida Buddha. . . .

The social sentiments that place the imperial household at the core of national unity lie deep in the hearts of the working masses. . . . While the working classes instinctively desire the transformation of the capitalistic structure out of their class-based living circumstances, they will have no part of a simplistic program of overthrowing the monarchy that merely replicates that of liberalism or Russian anticzarism. . . .

Along with the antimonarchy struggle, another major problem that the Comintern has imposed on the Communist Party of Japan is opposition to war, and defeatism in particular. Here too, we see an extremely pronounced petite bourgeois quality. . . . The petite bourgeois antiwar arguments that oppose war in general as well as pacifism are not attitudes that we should take up. Whether we participate in or oppose a war is a decision to be made on the basis of whether or not that war is progressive. The war against China's Nationalist clique, objectively, has a progressive significance. Under the current international situation, should there be a war with the United States it could rapidly change from being a mutual war among imperialists to a war of national liberation for the Japanese side. Furthermore, a world war in the Pacific could be turned into a progressive war in world historical terms that would liberate working masses of undeveloped Asia from the clutches of Western capital. . . .

We wish to point out that the official policy of separation of colonial peoples into nation-states that the Comintern demands of our party is not inappropriate for Japan. . . . We reject the capitalistic exploitation and oppression of the peoples of Korea and Taiwan as, above all, the greatest insult to the Japanese people themselves. We fight for completely equal rights for the Korean and Taiwanese peoples. However, the concrete expression of such equal rights will not take the form of a perfunctory separation into nation-states. It is far more realistic and in accord with world history that the working masses of each people, who have drawn closer to one another economically, culturally, and historically, should as a single great nation; and fusing together as a people (*jinmin*) and as a class, make the effort to build socialism. . . .

We believe it is only a matter of time before our comrades in the government of the Chinese soviet and China's Communist Party arrive at the same opinion as ours concerning the Comintern's sectarianism, bureaucratization, and trend toward becoming the instrument of the Soviet Union only. The Comintern probably will collapse totally with the outbreak of a world war. . . .

We have denounced the Comintern, the party, and the radical petite bourgeoisie. While bearing the pain manfully, we acknowledge this as a form of painful self-criticism. . . . We bear a strong joint responsibility for the deficiencies and inconsistencies that are clearly displayed by the Comintern today. There are many things that we have said here that go beyond mere words and have not exhausted our intent. However, it is a huge effort for us to get just these few words out of prison. If we could, we would offer even more detailed opinions. However, while incomplete, we believe that even just what we have said here has allowed us to present the core of the problem. . . .

June 8, 1933 Ichigaya Prison

[Sano and Nabeyama, "Kyōdō hikoku dōshi ni tsuguru sho," pp. 191–99;
AB, Carl Freire]

Chapter 42

THE RISE OF REVOLUTIONARY NATIONALISM

The Meiji period was marked by the rapid growth of Japanese nationalism. In the 1870s, except for the literate samurai, most Japanese were still not aware of and largely indifferent to national affairs. But by the end of the nineteenth century, the Japanese demonstrated striking national unity and determination on matters of national and international concern.

This consciousness of belonging and participating on the part of the Japanese people was the product of many things. Mass education, which made Japan the first literate nation in Asia, made it possible to activate the populace by means of the press. Conscription broadened the horizons of peasant youths who served in various parts of the country that they otherwise would not have seen. Industrial developments that unified the country through better communications brought foreign goods and ideas to all the coastal population centers. The centralization policies of the Meiji government standardized administration throughout the country and weakened the force of particularist customs and dialects. The growing scope of constitutional government increased the responsibilities and interests of community leaders. And Japan's successful wars were both the products and the causes of bursts of national self-confidence. The victory over China in 1895, followed quickly by the refusal of Germany, France, and Russia to allow Japan to occupy the Kwantung Peninsula in Manchuria, and the victory over Russia in 1905, followed by the annexation of Korea in 1910, provided proof of Japanese accomplishment together with evidence of further problems and responsibilities that would require still greater national determination and effort.

Together with the growth of Japanese nationalism—a growth not unlike the development of nationalism in the nineteenth-century West—came the growth of extremist ultranationalism. The ultranationalists feared that Japan was becoming too "Western," and they appealed to ancient and feudal traditions in fighting for their cause. The ultranationalists maintained consistent pressure on their government and countrymen for expansion abroad and orthodoxy at home.

The ultranationalists were indignant because of injustices, real and fancied, that the West had inflicted on Japan. In later years, Western criticism of Japanese imperial aspirations and Western restrictions on Japanese immigration and trade served to convince them of continued oppression and interference. The ultranationalists also were resentful of what they considered an excessive influx of Western ideas and institutions into modern Japan. At all times, they were sharply critical of those Japanese who were infatuated with Western ways of doing things, and they insisted on a priority for Japanese ideas and institutions that culminated in the person and symbol of the emperor. And since the ideas and institutions of Japan were superior to those of the West and since the West was constantly threatening to envelop Japan and the rest of Asia into its economic and ideological embrace, the ultranationalists were convinced that it was Japan's mission to lead and protect Asia. They were critical of their government when it seemed to neglect opportunities for such leadership, and they cooperated with it when it proved alive to its mission. Thus the mainstream of the ultranationalists' movement was vigorously xenophobic, emperor centered, and Asia conscious.

It would be an oversimplification, however, to imagine this mainstream as a consistent and distinct group at all times. There was a large area of agreement between the ultranationalists and others who were less willing to resort to extremist measures. Internally, the ultranationalist movement represented a complicated picture of personal and regional cliques whose standards and objectives shifted frequently in response to the dictates of opportunism.

In terms of social thought and political influence at home, the Japanese ultranationalists attained their true significance only in the twentieth century. Until World War I, their chief efforts were expended on behalf of a vigorous foreign policy. Although the themes and emphases of agitation shifted, for a long time the leaders of twentieth-century extremist organizations were related to those of the patriotic societies formed early in the Meiji period.

JAPAN AND ASIA

In 1881 a group of disgruntled former samurai of Fukuoka formed the Genyōsha. They took this name from the Genkainada, the body of water lying between Fukuoka and the Asian mainland, and in so doing they signified their determination to work for a vigorous policy of expansion in Asia. Tōyama Mitsuru (1855–1944) and the other leaders of his organization were alarmed by the extent of social and ideological change that had followed the overthrow of the feudal regime, and they were indignant because of the treatment given the warrior class. They considered themselves high-minded idealists like the samurai of Restoration days, and they were able to attract youthful activists prepared to show, by deeds of individual heroism and violence, their sincerity in opposing the "Western" policies of the Meiji government. One of their members, who very nearly succeeded in assassinating Foreign Minister Ōkuma Shigenobu in 1889, was thereafter honored by an annual ceremony of rededication. New deeds of valor, as when a Foreign Ministry official was murdered in 1913, drew new recruits for the cause of "Japanism."

At first, the Genyōsha members cooperated with the liberal parliamentarians, but they soon saw that the interests of expansionist groups in the military and business worlds lay closer to their own. They harbored and helped revolutionaries and reformers from Korea and China who sought asylum in Japan, and they encouraged their friends' trips to the mainland for commerce and espionage. They did their best to speed the war with China, which came in 1894, and thereafter they turned to the problem of Russia.

In 1901 the Genyōsha leaders formed the Amur Society (Kokuryūkai, literally, Black Dragon Society). Tōyama and his friends threatened government leaders who sought agreement with Russia; they sponsored trips into Siberia and Korea and the study of Russian; and they helped establish liaisons with Manchurian bandit groups for the coming war.

Yet despite their idealism, their denunciation of the government, and their opposition to the corrupting influence of money and big business on the national morality, the patriotic society leaders did not hesitate to accept financial help from interested individuals in the Westernized industrial world whose influence they professedly sought to curb. They received support from some sectors of the business world, from secret army funds, and at times from other government agencies. In addition, they were involved in many questionable transactions on the borderline between legitimate business and labor racketeering. The ultranationalist groups were not secret societies, for they made every attempt to gain full publicity to exaggerate their influence. Neither were they mass societies; they preferred to remain small elite groups clustered around charismatic leaders.

After the defeat of Russia, most of Japan's overseas aspirations seemed satisfied. But this did not mean that the ultranationalists lacked material for indignation and agitation; domestic issues now came to the fore. After World War I, a larger and more restless proletariat worried some of them, and in the countryside, resentful tenant farmers, unable to maintain the standard of living they had achieved during the war, grew mutinous. Patterns of familial obligation and imperial loyalty seemed endangered by social reformism, internationalism, democracy, and Communism. Moreover, Japan's post-Meiji governments, dominated by big business, showed a willingness to enter into international agreements for naval limitation, and they also tried to ward off Chinese nationalist agitation through a milder policy on the mainland. In the meantime, restrictions on Japanese trade and immigration increased. By the end of the 1920s, the world depression and the resulting distress in Japan provided ultranationalists with persuasive arguments against the business leaders and their moderation in foreign policy.

The patriotic societies thus turned to fight subversion at home. At the same time, they kept alive—and elaborated on—their exploits of the past in order to re-create the sense of urgency and of destiny that had been theirs in the Meiji period.

AN ANNIVERSARY STATEMENT BY THE AMUR SOCIETY

In 1930, for its thirtieth anniversary, the Amur Society (Kokuryūkai) prepared the two-volume *Secret History of the Annexation of Korea*, which stressed the society's prominent part in that achievement. To this history was added a history of the society's past activities and an explanation of its future intentions. Note especially in the following excerpt its proud claims to have assisted nationalist and independence groups in the Philippines, China, and Korea, with no sense of incongruity in subsequent references to the annexation of Korea and Formosa (Taiwan).

Today our empire has entered a critical period in which great zeal is required on the part of the entire nation. From the first, we members of the Amur Society have worked in accordance with the imperial mission for overseas expansion to solve our overpopulation; at the same time, we have sought to give support and encouragement to the peoples of East Asia. Thus we have tried to spread humanity and righteousness throughout the world by having the imperial purpose extended to neighboring nations.

Earlier, in order to achieve these principles, we organized the Heavenly Blessing Heroes in Korea in 1894 and helped the Tong Hak rebellion there in order to speed the settlement of the dispute between Japan and China. In 1899 we helped [Emilio] Aguinaldo in his struggle for independence for the Philippines. In 1900 we worked with other comrades in helping Sun Yat-sen start the fires of revolution in South China. In 1901 we organized this society and became exponents of the punishment of Russia, and thereafter we devoted ourselves to the annexation of Korea while continuing to support the revolutionary movement in China. At all times we have consistently centered our efforts on solving problems of foreign relations, and we have not spared ourselves in this cause.

During this period we have seen the fulfillment of our national power in the decisive victories in the two major wars against China and Russia, the annexation of Korea, the acquisition of Formosa and Sakhalin, and the expulsion of

Germany from the Shantung Peninsula. Japan's status among the empires of the world has risen until today it ranks as one of the three great powers, and from this eminence it can support other Asiatic nations. While these achievements were, of course, attributable to the august virtue of the great Meiji emperor, we cannot help but believe that our own efforts, however slight, also bore good fruit.

However, in viewing recent international affairs, it would seem that the foundation established by the great Meiji emperor is rapidly deteriorating. The disposition of the gains of the war with Germany was left to foreign powers, and the government, disregarding the needs of national defense, submitted to unfair demands to limit our naval power. Moreover, the failure of our China policy made the Chinese more and more contemptuous of us, so much so that they have been brought to demand the surrender of our essential defense lines in Manchuria and Mongolia. Furthermore, in countries like the United States and Australia, our immigrants have been deprived of rights that were acquired only after long years of struggle, and we now face a high-handed anti-Japanese expulsion movement that knows no bounds. Men of purpose and of humanity who are at all concerned for their country cannot fail to be upset by the situation.

When we turn our attention to domestic affairs, we feel more than deep concern. There is a great slackening of discipline and order. Men's hearts are become corrupt. Look around you! Are not the various government measures and establishments a conglomeration of all sorts of evils and abuses? The laws are confusing, and evil grows apace. The people are overwhelmed by heavy taxes; the confusion in the business world has complicated the livelihood of the people; the growth of dangerous thought threatens social order; and our national polity, which has endured for three thousand years, is in danger. This is a critical time for our national destiny; was there ever a more crucial day? What else can we call this time if it is not to be termed decisive?

And yet, in spite of this, our government, instead of pursuing a farsighted policy, casts about for temporary measures. The opposition party simply struggles for political power without any notion of saving our country from this crisis. And even the press, which should devote itself to its duty of guiding and leading society, is the same. For the most part it swims with the current, bows to vulgar opinions, and is chiefly engrossed in moneymaking. Alas! Our empire moves ever closer to the rocks that lie before us. Yet the captains and navigators are men of this sort! Truly, is this not the moment for us to become aroused?

Our determination to rise to save the day is the inescapable consequence of this state of affairs. Previously our duty lay in the field of foreign affairs, but when we see internal affairs in disorder, how can we succeed abroad? Therefore we of the Amur Society have determined to widen the scope of our activity. Hereafter, besides our interest in foreign affairs, we will give unselfish criticism of internal politics and of social problems, and we will seek to guide public opinion into proper channels. Thereby we will, through positive action, continue in the tradition of our past. We will establish a firm basis for our organization's policy, and through cooperation with other groups devoted to similar political, social, and ideological ideals, we are resolved to reform the moral corruption of the people, restore social discipline, and ease the insecurity of the people's livelihood by relieving the crises in the financial world, restoring national confidence, and increasing the nation's strength, in order to carry out the imperial mission to awaken the countries of Asia. In order to clarify these principles, we here set forth our platform to all our fellow patriots:

Principles

We stand for imperial rulership (*tennō shugi*). Basing ourselves on the fundamental teachings of the foundation of the empire, we seek the extension of the imperial influence to all peoples and places and the fulfillment of the glory of our national polity.

Platform

1. Developing the great plan of the founders of the country, we will widen the great Way (*tao*) of Eastern culture, work out a harmony of Eastern and Western cultures, and take the lead among Asian peoples.

2. We will bring to an end many evils, such as formalistic legalism, which restricts the freedom of the people, hampers commonsense solutions, prevents efficiency in public and private affairs, and destroys the true meaning of constitutional government. Thereby we will show forth again the essence of the imperial principles.

3. We shall rebuild the present administrative system. We will develop overseas expansion through the activation of our diplomacy, further the prosperity of the people by reforms in internal government, and solve problems of labor and management by the establishment of new social policies. Thereby we will strengthen the foundations of the empire.

4. We shall carry out the spirit of the Imperial Rescript to Soldiers and Sailors and stimulate a martial spirit by working toward the goal of a nation in arms. Thereby we look toward the perfection of national defense.

5. We plan a fundamental reform of the present educational system, which is copied from those of Europe and America; we shall set up a basic study of a national education originating in our national polity. Thereby we anticipate the further development and heightening of the wisdom and virtue of the Yamato race.

[*Nikkan gappō hishi*, vol. 1, appendix, pp. 1–4; MJ]

AGITATION BY ASSASSINATION

The Amur Society's displeasure with the business world shown in the preceding document was shared by most groups of the Japanese ultranationalist movement. Leaders of the business world were early targets for extremists. Their tremendous wealth contrasted strikingly with the poverty of the masses, and it reflected their success in personal ("selfish") aims, which contrasted with the declared selflessness of the disinterested "idealists" who pursued them. The business leaders were chief agents of the cosmopolitan-ism that the ultranationalists feared. With the decline in number of the genrō (elders) and the decline in prestige of the army after World War I, the businessmen advanced to the center of the political stage. Their control of and contributions to the political parties that formed cabinets during the Taishō period (1912–1926) resulted in periodic disclosures of scandals and corruption. Because the extremists felt that existing laws had been framed to protect the wrongdoers, they had to resort to extralegal violence to achieve their end.

The manner of this violence provided some features that separated the Jap-anese ultranationalist movement from the fascist movements in Germany and Italy. While Hitler and Mussolini strove for large-scale organizations and a mass following, the Japanese fanatics concentrated on individual heroics. They felt that a few spectacular acts of protest by idealists willing to sacrifice their lives would suffice to force major changes in the political and social order. In this belief, they followed honored Japanese traditions, for the loyalist patriots of Restoration days also exploited the possibilities of self-sacrifice and political and ideological assassination. But most of the Japanese fanatics had no blueprint for action to be taken once they succeeded in breaking down the old order. As one of the assassins in a plot that took Prime Minister Inukai Tsuyoshi's life in 1932 explained, "We thought about destruction first. We never considered taking on the duty of construction. We foresaw, however, that once the destruction was accomplished, somebody would take charge of the construction." Thus the first step was to consist of individual, uncoordinated acts of violence against representative figures in society.

ASAHI HEIGO

The first important murder in the campaign against the capitalist leaders came a full decade before the ultranationalist terrorism of the 1930s. On September 3, 1921, Asahi Heigo, a leader of the Shinshū gidan (Righteousness Corps of the Divine Land), assassinated Yasuda Zenjirō, head of the Yasuda *zaibatsu* (finan-cial conglomerate) house, at Yasuda's home. Asahi left a statement explaining his reasons, which illustrates his thorough contempt for the established political and social leaders. Like the young army officers of the 1930s who worked for a "Shōwa restoration," Asahi called for a "Taishō restoration" (Taishō being the reign-name of the emperor ruling from 1912 to 1926, and Shōwa, that of his successor, known to the West as Hirohito).

CALL FOR A NEW "RESTORATION"

The *genrō* set up the model, and today our political affairs are run by scoundrels. Fujita Densaburō became a baron by making counterfeit bills by order of Itō Hirobumi. Ōkura [head of another *zaibatsu* house] became a baron by contributing a part of the money he dishonestly made through selling canned goods containing pebbles. Yamamoto Gonbei[1] built an enormous fortune by his performance in the Siemens warship scandal. Ōkuma, Yamagata, and other old notables are wealthy now because of their corruption while in office. The Kenseikai [political party] raises its campaign funds from the South Manchurian Railroad and from opium. All the other statesmen and dignitaries too are skilled in evildoing, and they work with only their own self-interest in mind. And while the great individual fortunes have been built up by Mitsui, Iwasaki, Ōkura, Asano, Kondō, Yasuda, Furukawa, and Suzuki, the other plutocrats are no better. . . .

Alas, this is a time of danger. Foreign thought contrary to our national polity has moved in like a rushing torrent. The discontent of the needy masses who have been mistreated for long years by this privileged class but who have hitherto kept their bitter feelings deeply hidden is now being stirred up. The cold smiles and reproachful eyes of the poor show that they are close to brutality. There is a growing likelihood that the desperation of the people will take account of neither the nation nor the emperor.

Some of our countrymen are suffering from tuberculosis because of overwork, filth, and undernourishment. Others, bereaved, become streetwalkers in order to feed their beloved children. And those who were once hailed as defenders of the country are now reduced to beggary simply because they were disabled in the wars. . . . Moreover, some of our countrymen suffer hardships in prison because they committed minor crimes under the pressure of starvation, while high officials who commit major crimes escape punishment because they can manipulate the laws.

The former feudal lords, who were responsible for the death of our ancestors by putting them in the line of fire, are now nobility and enjoy a life of indolence and debauchery. Men who became generals by sacrificing our brothers' lives in battle are arrogantly preaching loyalty and patriotism as though they had achieved the victory all by themselves.

Consider this seriously! These new nobles are our enemies because they drew a pool of our blood, and the former lords and nobles are also our foes, for they took our ancestors' lives.

---

1. Yamamoto Gonbei was a premier whose cabinet was overthrown in 1914 after the discovery of corruption in warship contracts.

My fellow young idealists! Your mission is to bring about a Taishō restoration. These are the steps you must take:

1. Bury the traitorous millionaires.
2. Crush the present political parties.
3. Bury the high officials and nobility.
4. Bring about universal suffrage.
5. Abolish provisions for inheritance of rank and wealth.
6. Nationalize the land and bring relief to tenant farmers.
7. Confiscate all fortunes above 100,000 yen.
8. Nationalize big business.
9. Reduce military service to one year.

These are initial steps. But the punishment of the traitorous millionaires is the most urgent of all these, and there is no way of doing this except to assassinate them resolutely.

Finally, I want to say a word to my colleagues. I hope that you will live up to my principles. Do not speak, do not get excited, and do not be conspicuous. You must be quiet and simply stab, stick, cut, and shoot. There is no need to meet or to organize. Just sacrifice your life. And work out your own way of doing this. In this way you will prepare the way for the revolution. The flames will start here and there, and our fellow idealists will band together instantly. So forget about self-interest, and do not think about your own name or fame. Just die, just sleep. Never seek wisdom, but take the road of ignorance and come to know the height of great folly.[2]

[Shinobu, *Taishō seiji shi*, vol. 3, pp. 749–51; MJ]

THE PLIGHT OF THE COUNTRYSIDE

In contrast to the cult of the all-powerful state that distinguished the ultranationalist movements in Europe, much of Japanese ultranationalism was marked by a nostalgic longing for the values of primitive agrarian society. Several theorists turned from the evils of their society to envision a society with less government, more local autonomy, and more closely knit ties of familial solidarity. These ties would, of course, culminate in the person of the emperor as father of the nation, but the overall structure they envisioned would necessarily be very different from the highly centralized and industrialized society that Japan was developing.

---

2. A notion adapted from the Chinese Daoist classics, *Laozi* and *Zhuangzi*.

The most influential exponents of this position were Tachibana Kōzaburō (1893–1974) and Gondō Seikyō (1866–1937), both of whom owed much to traditional Daoist-utopian ideals of social organization. Tachibana wrote that a state could exist forever only under agrarian communalism, and he warned that "Japan cannot be itself if separated from the earth." Gondō, for his part, felt that Japan had been founded on the principle of autonomous living, in which "the sovereign does not go far beyond setting examples, thereby giving his people a good standard." Gondō felt that the small-scale groupings of society in primitive times were the only natural and desirable ones, and his writings show a profound distrust of big government and big army.

Together with this praise of primitive society came laments for the distress of the villagers in modern Japan. Victimized by big government, big business, and the burden of the wasteful military, the villagers were being deprived of their autonomy and their livelihood. Instead of the equality of primitive communalism, Japanese society was showing a very unhealthy class differentiation. For Tachibana, this was an evil of urbanization. "According to a common expression," he wrote, "Tokyo is the hub of the world. But I regret to say that Tokyo appears to me nothing but a branch shop of London." Gondō, too, lamented the decline of agrarian life, "the foundation of the country and the source of habits and customs," while "Tokyo and other cities have expanded out of all proportion to agrarian villages and are built up with great tall buildings." Inequalities of this sort presaged the doom of what he called the "bureaucratic administration patterned after the Prussian style of nationalism."

Thus the agrarian-conscious rightists found traditional grounds for a strong attack against their society. They did not entirely renounce industrialization and machinery, for it had its necessary role in livelihood and national defense. But the unjust social structure on which Japan's modern society rested was, they thought, likely to make all plans for defense and reform go wrong.

Writings of this sort had a considerable appeal to the young officers in the army. By the Shōwa period (1926–1989), Japan's officer corps was no longer dominated by members of the samurai class but was increasingly drawn from the countryside and the peasantry. Discontented with what they saw in the urban sector of Japanese life, unable to understand why their senior commanders worked with the politicians and businessmen, the young officers were prepared to accept Gondō's explanation that the military clique was just another wing of the bureaucratic ruling class.

GONDŌ SEIKYŌ

Gondō Seikyō's works, *Principles of Autonomous People* (*Jichi minpan*) and "Essay on the Self-Salvation of Farm Villages" (*Nōson jikyū ron*), were written during the years of the Great Depression, when distress in the villages was most acute. His writings contributed to the ideology of the young officers who struck down Prime Minister Inukai Tsuyoshi in May 1932. Gondō himself, however, had little or no connection with the extremists who were moved to action by his writings.

THE GAP BETWEEN THE PRIVILEGED CLASSES AND
THE COMMONERS

It was during this period [the late nineteenth century] that the criminal law was codified; civil law was codified; the system of cities, towns, and villages was put into effect; and the protection of private fortunes was really established on the principle of property rights. This made those who profit without working and the members of the privileged classes the pampered favorites of the state. The bureaucracy, the *zaibatsu*, and the military became the three supports of the state; the political parties attached themselves to them; and the scholars fawned on them. These groups allied with one another through marriage, and they all combined to form a single group. In a country so ordered, it is quite obvious that no matter how it may be kept up in the future, the nation's military affairs cannot be supported by means of the privileged class of military alone. I am not an advocate of disarmament, nor am I a pacifist. I have a sincere desire for adequate national defense. For that very reason I have strong misgivings about the present system of military preparation. Leaving aside a detailed discussion for another time, I will say here only that even if we train millions of soldiers, unless we are able to produce the weapons and necessary supplies in quantity, the soldiers in the line will be no more than puppets. . . .

The change in popular sentiment in all nations after World War I, largely a result of economic theories, also was reflected in great changes in this country. Moreover, with the Russian Revolution, the disorders on the China mainland, the ebb and flow of Eastern and Western, old and new thought, took place partly in response to economic pressures and partly to scientific advances. The idea of a militaristic, Prussian, nationalism declined into such a foul state of decay that not even the dogs would eat it. . . .

In militaristic states, whether of early or recent times, the plutocracy never fails to come out on top. When the plutocrats conspire with those who hold political power, the resources of the people fall under their control almost before they are aware of what is happening. When this happens, the common people fall on evil days; they are pursued by cold and hunger, and unless they work in the midst of their tears as tools of the plutocrats and those holding political power, they cannot stay alive. When people are pursued by hunger and have to work tearfully in the face of death, what sort of human rights do you suppose remain? . . .

Since the conditions under which the people live are, in fact, as I have indicated, the foundations of the military regime cannot be secure. To be sure, the military officers—men who hold office for life—are guaranteed an adequate living, and so they are usually conspicuously loyal, brave, and noble. And indeed they have to be. But all the soldiers who dutifully have to shed their blood are sons and brothers of the common people. The great majority of these soldiers were born in poverty and hardship; they entered the barracks and then had to submit to the orders of their superior officers. As the sons and brothers of the common people, they will not under any circumstances forget that they are themselves common people. If, then, we infer what goes on in their minds and take this problem of the commoners' plight and the privileged classes as proportionate, think of the changes that will take place in men's hearts; look back on the labor and tenant problems—from disturbance to struggle, and from struggle, what will come? Granted, it is the army's duty to maintain peace and order, but the good and obedient soldiers in the ranks whom you are leading are for the most part the sons and brothers of the impoverished common people. They are certainly not people who are serving to kill the common people. No, they are persons who offer their lives and bodies for the sake of the wider public morality.

[Gondō, *Jichi minpan*, pp. 185–88; MJ]

KITA IKKI AND THE REFORM WING
OF ULTRANATIONALISM

A group of revolutionaries headed by Kita Ikki stood out in sharp contrast to the primitive utopians like Gondō Seikyō. These were men well read in the radical literature of the West, and they owed more to Marx than they did to Laozi. Their praise of imperial divinity and perfection was combined with some very sharp criticism of the imperial household and its works. They called for radical changes in Japanese society and institutions and held out the promise that a revolutionary Japan would be able to take the lead in a union of resurgent Asian peoples.

Kita Ikki (1884–1937) was the most important spokesman for this group. Born the son of a struggling saké brewer on the island of Sado, he became interested in socialism at an early age. His desire to promote a revolutionary Asia led him to join the circle of adventurers and Amur Society members who cooperated with the nationalist revolution of Sun Yat-sen in China.

Kita was in China during the revolution of 1911, and his chagrin at the failure of that revolution to bring about a democratic China had a profound effect on his later thought. His book *An Unofficial History of the Chinese Revolution*

(*Shina kakumei gaishi*) criticized the Japanese activists in China for relying on Sun Yat-sen, whom Kita now regarded as a superficial user of Western slogans, instead of working for a better balance of Western and Oriental ideologies. Kita's early socialism was now becoming more "Oriental"; henceforth, he called for a blend of Western revolutionary thought and Oriental wisdom, which he called Japanism. Kita also criticized the policy of the Japanese authorities in China. In particular, he resented the maneuverings of the *zaibatsu* houses, whose offers of loans had, it seemed to him, helped drive the Chinese revolutionaries into their compromise with the conservative Yuan Shikai in order to avoid Japanese exploitation. Thus Kita, remaining convinced of the inevitability of a revolutionary Asia, now saw the need for profound changes in Japanese society to enable Japan to assume the leadership in the new Asia. Selfish *zaibatsu* would have to be curbed; corrupt politicians would be done away with; and the imperial household itself would have to undergo changes to free it from the crippling influence of the timid bureaucrats who were at the beck and call of their *zaibatsu*–political party colleagues.

The radicalism of Kita's views was genuine. He advocated sweeping changes in all sectors of Japanese society—the seizure and nationalization of major industries and fortunes, an eight-hour workday, and a land reform program. Nor is there much doubt about his proclivity to extremism. His 1926 preface hailed the murderer of Yasuda Zenjirō, Asahi Heigo, as a man whose ideology had been based on the spirit of his own writings. Kita himself had strong ties with the young officers whose concern about Japan's China policy played such an important role in the military putsches of the 1930s. He was involved with the Imperial Way Faction (Kōdō-ha), the radical group responsible for the mutiny that began with a wave of assassination attempts and ended with the seizure of central Tokyo on February 26, 1936. Arrested then, Kita was executed in 1937. His book, banned until the end of World War II, was reprinted thereafter by men who held that Kita's gloomy forebodings about the need for a thorough reformation of Japanese society as a prerequisite to leadership of a revolutionary Asia had been amply borne out by the events following his death.

AN OUTLINE PLAN FOR THE REORGANIZATION OF JAPAN
(*NIHON KAIZŌ HŌAN TAIKŌ*)

An Outline Plan for the Reorganization of Japan contains Kita Ikki's suggestions for the changes necessary in Japanese society. Written in 1919, while Kita was still in Shanghai, the book was printed secretly and passed from hand to hand by Kita's associates. In 1920 its distribution was forbidden by the police. In 1923, after major excisions, the book was published, only to be banned again shortly afterward. A third edition came out in 1926, but it, too, was later banned.

The outline plan, of which the opening section is translated here, consists of cryptic announcements of steps to be taken, followed by notes justifying the steps and anticipating probable objections.

At present the Japanese empire is faced with a national crisis unparalleled in its history; it faces dilemmas at home and abroad. The vast majority of the people feel insecure in their livelihood and are on the point of taking a lesson from the collapse of European societies, while those who monopolize political, military, and economic power simply hide themselves and, quaking with fear, try to maintain their unjust position. Abroad, not England, America, Germany, or Russia has kept its word, and even our neighbor China, which long benefited from the protection we provided through the Russo-Japanese War, not only has failed to repay us but instead despises us. Truly, we are a small island, completely isolated in the Eastern Sea. One false step and our nation will again fall into the desperate state of crisis—dilemmas at home and abroad—that marked the period before and after the Meiji Restoration.

The only thing that brightens the picture is the 60 million fellow countrymen with whom we are blessed. The Japanese people must develop a profound awareness of the great cause of national existence and of the people's equal rights, and they need an unerring, discriminating grasp of the complexities of domestic and foreign thought. The Great War in Europe was, like Noah's Flood, Heaven's punishment on them for arrogant and rebellious ways. . . .

Truly, our 700 million brothers in China and India have no path to independence other than that offered by our guidance and protection. . . . At a time when the authorities in the European and American revolutionary creeds have found it completely impossible to arrive at an understanding of the "gospel of the sword" because of their superficial philosophy, the noble Greece of Asian culture must complete its national reorganization on the basis of its own national polity. At the same time, let it lift the virtuous banner of an Asian league and take the leadership in the world federation that must come. In so doing let it proclaim to the world the Way of Heaven in which all are children of Buddha, and let it set an example that the world must follow.

Section 1: The People's Emperor

Suspension of the Constitution. In order for the emperor and the entire Japanese people to establish a secure base for the national reorganization, the emperor will, by a show of his imperial prerogative, suspend the constitution for a period of three years, dissolve both houses of the Diet, and place the entire nation under martial law.

(Note: In extraordinary times the authorities should, of course, ignore harmful opinions and votes. To regard any sort of constitution or parliament as an absolute authority is to act in direct imitation of the English and American semisacred "democracy." . . . It cannot be held that in the discussion of plans for naval expansion Admiral Tōgō [Heihachirō]'s vote was not worth more than the three cast by miserable members of the Diet. . . .)

(Note: A coup d'état should be regarded as a direct manifestation of the authority of the nation, that is, of the will of society. All the progressive leaders have arisen from popular groups. They arise because of political leaders like Napoleon and Lenin. In the reorganization of Japan there must be a manifestation of the power inherent in a coalition of the people and sovereign.) . . .

The True Significance of the Emperor. The fundamental doctrine of the emperor as representative of the people and as the pillar of the nation must be made clear.

In order to clarify this, a sweeping reform of the imperial court in the spirit of the Emperor Jinmu in founding the state and in the spirit of the great Meiji emperor will be carried out. The present privy councillors and other officials will be dismissed from their posts and, in their place, will come talent, sought throughout the realm, capable of assisting the emperor. . . .

(Note: Japan's national polity has evolved through three stages, and the meaning of "emperor" has also evolved through three stages. The first stage, from the Fujiwara to the Taira, was one of absolute monarchy. During this stage the emperor possessed all land and people as his private property in theory, and he had the power of life and death over the people. The second stage, from the Minamoto to the Tokugawa, was one of aristocracy. During this period military leaders and nobility in each area brought land and people of their locality under their personal control. . . . The third stage, one of a democratic state, began with the Meiji Revolution, which emancipated the samurai and commoners, newly awakened, from their status as the private property of their shogun and feudal lords. Since then, the emperor has a new significance as the true center of government and politics. Ever since, as the commanding figure in the national movement and as the overall representative of the modern democratic country, he has become representative of the nation. In other words, since the Meiji Revolution, Japan has become a modern democratic state with the emperor as its political nucleus. Is there any need whatsoever for us to import a direct translation of the "democracy" of others as though we lacked something?) . . .

(Note: There is no scientific basis whatsoever for the belief of the democracies that a state governed by representatives voted in by the electorate is superior to a state with a system of government by a particular person. Every nation has its own national spirit and history. . . . The "democracy" of Americans derives from the very unsophisticated theory of the time, which held that society can come into being through a voluntary contract based on the free will of individuals; these people, emigrating from each European country as individuals, established communities and built a country. But their theory of the divine right of voters is a half-witted philosophy that arose in opposition to the theory of the divine right of kings at that time. Now Japan certainly was not founded in this way, and there has never been a period in which Japan was dominated by a half-witted philosophy. Suffice it to say that the system whereby the head of state has to struggle for election by a long-winded self-advertisement and by exposing himself to ridicule like a low-class actor seems a very strange custom to the Japanese people, who have been brought up in the belief that silence is golden and modesty is a virtue.) . . .

The Abolition of the Peerage System. The peerage system will be abolished, and the spirit of the Meiji Restoration will be clarified by removing the barrier that has come between the emperor and the people.

The House of Peers will be abolished and replaced by a Council of Deliberation (Shingiin), which shall consider action taken by the House of Representatives.

The Council of Deliberation will be empowered to reject decisions taken by the House of Representatives a single time. The membership of the House of Representatives will consist of distinguished men in many fields of activity, elected by one another and appointed by the emperor. . . .

(Note: The reason a bicameral system is subject to fewer errors than a uni-cameral system is that in very many cases, public opinion is emotional, uncrit-ical, and changeable. For this reason the upper house will be made up of distinguished persons in many fields of activity instead of medieval relics.)

Universal Suffrage. All men twenty-five years of age, by their rights as people of Great Japan, will have the right, freely and equally, to stand for election to and to vote for the House of Representatives. The same will hold for local self-government assemblies.

Women will not have the right to participate in politics.

(Note: Although a tax qualification has determined suffrage in other coun-tries and this system was first initiated in England, whose Parliament was orig-inally established to supervise the use of tax money collected by the Crown, in Japan we must establish it as a fundamental principle that suffrage is the innate right of the people. . . . Suffrage is a "duty of the people" in the same sense that military service is a "duty of the people.") . . .

(Note: The reason for the clear statement that "women will not have the right to participate in politics" is not that Japanese women today have not yet awakened. Whereas the code of chivalry for the knights in medieval Europe called for honoring women and gaining their favor, in medieval Japan the samurai esteemed and valued the person of a woman on approximately the same level as they did themselves, while it became the accepted code for women to honor the men and gain their favor. This complete contrast in de-velopments has penetrated into all society and livelihood and continues into modern history—there has been agitation by women for suffrage abroad while here women have continued to be devoted to being good wives and wise moth-ers. Politics is a small part of human activity. The question of the place of women in Japan will be satisfactorily solved if we bring about an institutional reorganization guaranteeing the protection of a woman's right to be "mother of the nation and wife of the nation." To make women accustomed to verbal warfare is to do violence to their natural aptitude; it is more terrible than using them in the line of battle. Anyone who has observed the stupid talkativeness of Western women or the piercing quarrels among Chinese women will be thankful that Japanese women have continued on the right path. . . .)

The Restoration of the People's Freedom. The various laws that in the past have restricted the freedom of the people and impaired the spirit of the constitution—the Civil Service Appointment Ordinance, the Peace Preservation police law, the Press Act, the Publication Law, and similar measures—will be abolished. . . .

(Note: . . . Japan today is like a man in his prime and in good health. Countries like Russia and China are like old patients whose bodies are in total decay. Therefore, if there is a technician who takes a farsighted view of the past and the present and who draws judiciously on East and West, Japan can be reorganized through no more than a pleasant talk.)

The National Reorganization Diet. The National Reorganization Diet, elected in a general election and convened during the period of martial law, will deliberate on measures for reorganization.

The National Reorganization Diet will not have the right to deliberate on the basic policy of national reorganization proclaimed by the emperor.

(Note: In this way, since the people will become the main force and the emperor the commander, this coup d'état will not be an abuse of power but the expression of the national determination by the emperor and the people.) . . .

The Renunciation of the Imperial Estate.[3] The emperor will personally show the way by granting the lands, forests, shares, and similar property owned by the imperial house to the nation.

The expenses of the imperial house will be limited to approximately 30 million yen per year, to be supplied by the national treasury.

[Kita, "Nihon kaizō hōan," in *Nihon kaizō hōan taikō*, pp. 6–14; MJ]

THE CONSERVATIVE REAFFIRMATION

During the years in which one branch of the ultranationalist movement turned to suggestions for radical social reforms and produced sweeping denunciations of existing Japanese society, many people were not prepared to follow such a

---

3. This entire section was censored in prewar editions.

headlong course. By the 1930s, a sharp cleavage between social radicals and ideological conservatives was apparent.

The conservatives met the problems of social change and unrest by reaffirming the unique values of "Japanism." Since they furnished a safe alternative to the radicalism of the extremists, the conservative ultranationalists were able to get the financial backing of respected segments of the business and political world. The National Purity Society (Kokusuikai) was founded in 1919 to ward off foreign ideologies, reaffirm traditional values of manliness and chivalry, and reawaken loyalty to the imperial house. It had close contacts with the leading political party, the Seiyūkai. In social issues like labor disputes, it urged mediation or marshaled force as seemed preferable, usually to the advantage of management. The League to Prevent Bolshevization (Sekka bōshidan) was formed in 1921 to fight socialism and Communism, and it was unreservedly opposed to labor and radical movements of all kinds. The National Foundation Society (Kokuhonsha) was founded in 1924 to guide the people's ideology, strengthen the foundations of the nation, advance wisdom and virtue, and clarify the national polity. It was sponsored by Baron Hiranuma Kiichirō and enjoyed the favor of many who were highly placed in the bureaucracy, military, and financial worlds.

The conservative societies appealed more to the established and respectable than to the young and discontented. Their backers were just as convinced of the international inequality from which Japan suffered as Kita Ikki was, but they were more likely to seek solutions through diplomatic and military measures than through social reforms.

The violence of the early 1930s, most of it carried out by young followers of the radical ideologies, culminated in the spectacular mutiny of February 1936. Thereafter, it was perfectly clear to all conservatives that strong measures were necessary to preserve social order and military discipline. It seemed a wise compromise to give the military leaders a freer hand on the continent in return for promises to keep their young extremists under control. Kita and the leaders of the February incident were executed after brief and secret trials. In China, the army prepared for further measures, while at home its control over production, education, and politics was strengthened.

FUNDAMENTALS OF OUR NATIONAL POLITY (*KOKUTAI NO HONGI*)

The movement for the enunciation of "national polity," Japan's unique structure of state and society based on a divine emperor, reached its apogee with the publication by the Ministry of Education of *Fundamentals of Our National Polity* (*Kokutai no hongi*) in 1937. This short work, with an initial printing of 300,000 copies and an eventual sale of 2 million or more, was designed to set the ideological course for the

Japanese people. Study groups were formed to discuss its content; schoolteachers were given special commentaries; and a determined effort was made to reach ideological uniformity by guarding against deviation.

The introduction sets forth the underlying problems of contemporary Japanese thought that require a solution: How are Western influences to be absorbed without permitting them to destroy Japanese national traditions, and how can Japan resolve the dilemma created in the West itself by the inherent contradictions of individualism?

A recurrent theme throughout this work is the transcendent importance of the nation and state as manifested in history. In part, this may reflect the sympathetic reception of German philosophy, particularly that of Hegel, by professional philosophers of Meiji Japan.

Introduction

The various ideological and social evils of present-day Japan are the result of ignoring the fundamental and running after the trivial, of the lack of judgment and the failure to digest things thoroughly. This is because since the days of Meiji, so many aspects of European and American culture, systems, and learning have been imported and too rapidly. As a matter of fact, the foreign ideologies imported into our country are mainly ideologies of the Enlightenment that have come down from the eighteenth century, or extensions of them. The views of the world and of life that form the basis of these ideologies are rationalism and positivism, lacking in historical views, which, on the one hand, place the highest value on, and assert the liberty and equality of, individuals and, on the other hand, place value on a world by nature abstract, transcending nations and races. Consequently, importance is given to human beings and their groupings, who have become isolated from historical entireties, abstract and independent of one another. These political, social, moral, and pedagogical theories based on such views of the world and of life have, on the one hand, contributed to the various reforms seen in our country and, on the other hand, have had a deep and wide influence on our nation's primary ideology and culture. . . .

Paradoxical and extreme conceptions, such as socialism, anarchism, and communism, all are based, in the final analysis, on individualism, which is the root of modern Occidental ideologies and of which they are no more than varied manifestations. Yet even in the Occident, where individualism has formed the basis of their ideas, when it has come to Communism, they have found it unacceptable; so that now they are about to do away with their traditional individualism, and this has led to the rise of totalitarianism and nationalism and to the appearance of Fascism and Nazism. That is, it can be said that in both the Occident and our country, the deadlock of individualism has led alike to a season of ideological and social confusion and crisis. . . . This means that the present conflict in our people's ideas, the unrest of their modes of life, the confused state of their civilization, can be put right only by a thorough investigation by us of the intrinsic nature of Occidental ideologies and by an understanding of the true meaning of our national polity. Then, too, this should be done for the sake not only of our nation but also of the entire human race, which is struggling to find a way out of the deadlock with which individualism is faced. [pp. 52, 54–55]

The body of this work is a résumé of Japanese traditions concerning the founding of the country and the imperial house, the virtues of imperial rule and loyal subjects, manifestations of the Japanese spirit in history, natural features of Japan, and the inherent character of the people, as well as manifestations of these in the nation's social and cultural life. The following selections focus on those attitudes thought to represent the best in Japanese tradition and their superiority to prevailing Western views.

Loyalty and Patriotism

Our country is established with the emperor, who is a descendant of Amaterasu Ōmikami, as its center, as our ancestors as well as we ourselves constantly have beheld in the emperor the fountainhead of her life and activities. For this reason, to serve the emperor and to receive the emperor's great august will as our own is the rationale of making our historical "life" live in the present; and on this is based the morality of the people.

Loyalty means to revere the emperor as [our] pivot and to follow him implicitly. By implicit obedience is meant casting ourselves aside and serving the emperor intently. To walk this Way of loyalty is the sole Way in which we subjects may "live" and the fountainhead of all energy. Hence, offering our lives for the sake of the emperor does not mean so-called self-sacrifice but the casting aside of our little selves to live under his august grace and the enhancing of the genuine life of the people of a state. The relationship between the emperor and the subjects is not an artificial relationship [that means] bowing down to authority or a relationship such as [exists] between master and servant as is seen in feudal morals. . . . The ideology interpreting the relationship between the emperor and his subjects as being a reciprocal relationship and as merely [involving] obedience to authority or rights and duties rests on individualistic ideologies; it is a rationalistic way of thinking that looks on everything as being in equal personal relationships. An individual is an existence belonging to a state and its history that forms the basis of his origin and is fundamentally one body with it. . . .

From the point of individualistic personal relationships, the relationship between sovereign and subject in our country may [perhaps] be looked on as that between nonpersonalities. However, this is nothing but an error arising from treating the individual as supreme, from the notion that has individual thoughts for its nucleus and from personal abstract consciousness. Our relationship between sovereign and subject is by no means a shallow, horizontal relationship, such as [one] implying a correlation between ruler and citizen, but is a relationship springing from a basis transcending this correlation and is that of "dying to self and returning to [the] One," in which the basis is not lost. This is something that can never be understood from an individualistic way of thinking. In our country, this great Way has seen a natural development since the founding of the nation, and the most basic thing that has manifested itself in regard to the subjects is, in short, this Way of loyalty. [pp. 80–82]

Filial Piety

In our country, filial piety is a Way of the highest importance. Filial piety originates with one's family as its basis and, in its larger sense, has the nation as its foundation. The direct object of filial piety is one's parents, but in its relationship with the emperor finds a place within loyalty. . . .

The life of a family in our country is not confined to the present life of a household of parents and children but, beginning with the distant ancestors, is continued eternally by the descendants. The present life of a family is a link between the past and the future, and while it carries over and develops the objectives of the ancestors, it hands them over to its descendants. [pp. 87–89]

Loyalty and Filial Piety as One

The true characteristics of filial piety in our country are its perfect conformity with our national polity by heightening still further the relationship between morality and nature. Our country is a great family nation, and the imperial household is the head family of the subjects and the nucleus of national life. . . .

In China, too, filial duty is important, and they say that it is the source of a hundred deeds. In India, too, gratitude to parents is taught. But their filial piety is not of a kind related to or based on the nation. Filial piety is a characteristic of Oriental morals; but it is in its convergence with loyalty that we find a characteristic of our national morals, and this is a factor without parallel in the world. [pp. 89–91]

Harmony

When we trace the marks of the facts of the founding of our country and the progress of our history, what we always find there is the spirit of harmony. Harmony is a product of the great achievements of the founding of the nation and is the power behind our historical growth. It also is a humanitarian Way inseparable from our daily lives. The spirit of harmony is built on the concord of all things. When people determinedly count themselves as masters and assert their egos, there is nothing but contradiction and the setting of one against the other; and harmony is not created. . . . [A] society of individualism is one of clashes between [masses of] people . . . and all history may be regarded as one of class wars. Social structure and political systems in such a society, and the theories of sociology, political science, statecraft, and so on, which are their logical manifestations, are essentially different from those of our country, which makes harmony its fundamental Way. . . . [pp. 93–94]

The Martial Spirit

And then this harmony is clearly seen also in our nation's martial spirit. Our nation is one that holds *bushidō* in high regard, and there are shrines deifying warlike spirits. . . . But this martial spirit is not [a thing that exists] for the sake of itself but for the sake of peace and is what may be called a sacred martial spirit. Our martial spirit does not have for its objective the killing of men but the giving of life to men. This martial spirit tries to give life to all things and not to destroy. That is, it is strife that has peace at its basis with a promise to raise and to develop, and it gives life to things through its strife. Here lies the martial spirit of our nation. War, in this sense, is not by any means intended for the destruction, overpowering, or subjugation of others; and it should be for bringing about great harmony, that is, peace, doing the work of creation by following the Way. [pp. 94–95]

Self-Effacement and Assimilation

A pure, cloudless heart is a heart that, dying to one's ego and one's own ends, finds life in fundamentals and the true Way. This means it is a heart that lives in the Way of unity between the sovereign and his subjects, a Way that has come down to us ever since the founding of the empire. . . .

In our people's inherent character is strongly manifested alongside this spirit of self-effacement and disinterestedness a spirit of broad-mindedness and assimilation. In the importation of culture from the Asian continent, too, in the process of "dying to self" and adopting the ideographs used in Chinese classics, this spirit of ours has coordinated and assimilated these same ideographs. To have created a culture uniquely our own, even though a culture essentially different was imported, is due entirely to a mighty influence peculiar to our nation. This is a matter that must be seriously considered in the adaptation of modern Occidental culture.

This spirit of self-effacement is not a mere denial of oneself but means living to the great, true self by denying one's small self. [pp. 132–34]

Bushidō

Bushidō may be cited as showing an outstanding characteristic of our national morality. In the world of warriors one sees inherited the totalitarian structure and spirit of the ancient clans peculiar to our nation. Hence, although the teachings of Confucianism and Buddhism have been followed, they have been transcended. That is, although a sense of obligation binds master and servant, it has developed into a spirit of self-effacement and of meeting death with perfect calmness. In this, it was not that death was made light of so much as that man tempered himself for death and in a true sense regarded it with esteem. In effect, man tried to fulfill true life by way of death. . . .

. . . Yamaga Sokō (1622–1685), Matsumiya Kanzan (1686–1780), and Yoshida Shōin (1830–1859) all were men of the most devout character, who exercised much influence in bringing *bushidō* to perfection. It is this same *bushidō* that shed an outdated feudalism at the time of the Meiji Restoration, increased in splendor, became the Way of loyalty and patriotism, and evolved before us as the spirit of the imperial forces. [pp. 144–46]

Conclusion

The conclusion to this work is a general critique of current Western social philosophies and an argument for Japanese tradition as the basis for a new synthesis of Eastern and Western thought. The emphasis on Japan's historical mission as a creative force in unifying and transcending antithetical tendencies suggests the expansive, rather than the purely defensive, character of Japanese traditionalism in the twentieth century.

Every type of foreign ideology that has been imported into our country may have been quite natural in China, India, Europe, or America, in that it sprang from their racial or historical characteristics; but in our country, which has a unique national polity, it is necessary as a preliminary step to expose these types to rigid judgment and scrutiny so as to see whether they are suitable to our national traits. . . .

To put it in a nutshell, while the strong points of Occidental learning and concepts are their analytical and intellectual qualities, the characteristics of Oriental learning and concepts are their intuitive and aesthetic qualities. . . .

Now, when we consider how modern Occidental ideologies have given birth to democracy, socialism, Communism, anarchism, and the like, we note, as already stated, the existence of historical backgrounds that form the bases of all these concepts and, in addition, the existence of individualistic views of life that lie at their very roots. The basic characteristics of modern Occidental cultures lie in the fact that an individual is regarded as an existence of an absolutely independent being, all cultures comprising the perfection of this individual being who in turn is the creator and determiner of all values. . . . As a result, some types of mistaken liberalism and democracy have arisen that have solely sought untrammeled freedom and forgotten moral freedom, which is service. Hence, wherever this individualism and its accompanying abstract concepts developed, concrete historical and national life became lost in the shadow of abstract theories; all states and peoples were looked on alike as nations in general and as individuals in general. Such things as an international community comprising the entire world and universal theories common to the entire world were given more importance than concrete nations and their characteristic qualities; so that in the end even the mistaken idea arose that international law constituted a higher norm than national law, that it stood higher in value, and that national laws were, if anything, subordinate to it.

The beginnings of modern Western free economy are seen in the expectation of bringing about national prosperity as a result of free, individual, lucrative activities. In introducing into our country modern industrial organizations that had developed in the West, as long as the spirit of striving for national profit and the people's welfare governed the people's minds, the lively and free individual activities went very far toward contributing to the nation's wealth. But later, with the dissemination of individualistic and liberal ideas, there gradually arose a tendency openly to justify egoism in economic management and operations. This tendency created a chasm between rich and poor and finally gave rise to ideas of class warfare. Later, the introduction of Communism brought about the erroneous idea that economics was being the basis of politics, morality, and all other cultures and considered that by means of class warfare alone an ideal society could be realized. . . .

The same thing holds true in the case of education. Since the Meiji Restoration our nation has adapted the good elements of the advanced education seen among European and American nations and has exerted efforts to set up an educational system and materials for teaching. The nation has also assimilated on a wide scale the scholarship of the West, not only in the fields of natural science, but also in the mental sciences, and has thus striven to see progress in our scholastic pursuits and to make education more popular. . . . However, at the same time, through the infiltration of individualistic concepts, both scholastic pursuits and education have tended to be taken up with a world in which the intellect alone mattered and was isolated from historical and actual life. . . .

In the Occident, too, many movements are now engaged in revising individualism. Socialism and Communism, which are types of class individualism and the opposites of so-called bourgeois individualism, belong to these movements. Recent ideological movements, such as that called Fascism, which are types of nationalism and racial consciousness, also belong to this category. If, however, we tried to correct the evils brought about by individualism in our country and to find a way out of the stalemate that it has created, it would not help to adopt ideas like Occidental socialism and their abstract totalitarianism wholesale or to copy their concepts and plans, or [conversely] to mechanically exclude Occidental cultures.

Our Mission

Our present mission as a people is to construct a new Japanese culture by adopting and sublimating Western cultures with our national polity as the basis and to contribute spontaneously to the advancement of world culture. Our nation early saw the introduction of Chinese and Indian cultures and even succeeded in evolving original creations and developments. This was made possible, indeed, by the profound and boundless nature of our national polity, so that the mission of the people to whom it is bequeathed is truly great in its historical significance. [pp. 175, 178, 180–83]

[Adapted from Hall and Gauntlett, *Kokutai no hongi*, pp. 52–183]

WATSUJI TETSURŌ

Watsuji Tetsurō (1889–1960) was a major figure in Japanese philosophy during the Shōwa period. He held prestigious posts as professor at Kyoto Imperial University (1925–1934) and Tokyo Imperial University (1934–1949). He is best known for his writings on the effect of climate on Japanese culture and on the distinctive ethics, aesthetics, and spirit (*seishin*) of the Japanese people.

The principal factor in Watsuji's analysis of the benign climatological influence on Japanese life and culture was the alternation of the monsoons (including the typhoon phenomenon):

[The] distinctive Japanese way of life reflected its adjustment—acceptance or resignation—to this alternation of the monsoon seasons, in the form of a copious outflow of emotion constantly changing yet concealing perseverance beneath this change; at every moment in this alternation of mutability and endurance, there is abruptness. This activity of emotions sinks to resigned acquiescence in resistance, and underneath the exaltation of activity there lies a quiet and suddenly apparent abandonment. This is a quiet savagery of emotion, a fighting disinterest. Here we discover the national spirit of Japan.[4]

Most of the major philosophers of the prewar period reacted in some way to Japan's growing nationalism and militarism. Nishida Kitarō (1870–1945 [see chap. 47]) and Tanabe Hajime (1885–1962) are leading examples of this response in the so-called Kyoto school. Tanabe, although much influenced by Nishida, criticized him for his lack of a political philosophy and went on to formulate an alternative to Nishida's philosophy of "place" (*topos*) with one that tended to absolutize the state. At the same time (before World War II), Watsuji was focusing on the distinctive Japanese ethics or spirit.

Watsuji, Nishida, and Tanabe, however, had little to say about the actual political process, organization, or structure of the state, and their philosophies

---

4. Watsuji, *Climate*, pp. 127–28.

left considerable political room for adjustments in the very different atmosphere after World War II.

THE WAY OF THE JAPANESE SUBJECT
(*NIHON NO SHINDŌ*)

The following are Watsuji Tetsurō's views on several of the issues that are dealt with in *Fundamentals of Our National Polity* (*Kokutai no hongi*). They are significant as a reflection on the stages in the development of Japanese thought already presented in earlier chapters of this volume. Watsuji was particularly known for his emphasis on the "stadial," or multilayered, development of Japanese culture and thought, the idea that they grew by incorporating incrementally the main features of the successive phases through which the Japanese had passed.

In the Japanese title of this work, *Nihon no shindō*, the term *shin* (read here as "subject"), had undergone considerable evolution. In Confucianism from early times, it meant "minister" and was most prominently defined in terms of the responsibility of the minister to help the ruler govern in the interests of the people (*min*). The "people," as subjects of the state, were not thought of as participating themselves; rather, it was to be government *for* the people, not government *by* the people. In medieval Japan, *shin* became identified with the retainers of a feudal lord, the samurai who served him with absolute and undying loyalty.

The practice of the samurai was expressed in the moral sentiment that he "should not regret giving his life for his lord." As described repeatedly in such things as the medieval war tales, the warriors of eastern Japan truly abandoned their lives in a dauntless spirit. This was indeed a magnificent ethic that can still be appreciated. But on those occasions the "lord" referred to was the lord of one's own domain or, in the highest case, the shogun, one of his direct retainers, or a lower shogunal official. In this way the samurai were sacrificing their lives within a system of vertical feudal relations. Consequently, even if they said they were attacking an enemy, it was in the context of the necessities of medieval civil warfare. In such a situation, if their sense of love and gratitude toward their lord was extremely powerful, no one would give a second thought to what they were giving their lives for. If those samurai began to reflect on the significance of the death-defying duty they undertook, they would perhaps have become confused. And in point of historical fact, this gave rise to two tendencies in the late Muromachi period. On the one hand, in the samurai class a tendency arose that was referred to as "the lower overcoming the higher" (*gekokujō* [upsetting the vertical hierarchical relations]) and superseding one's lord. On the other hand, some of them sought a deeper point than the feudal vertical system of loyalties for the significance of casting away one's life. This latter tendency gave rise to the Way of venerating the emperor (*sonnō*), which was an ancient cultural legacy from the beginning of the Japanese nation. This latter code of honor came to blend with a deepening understanding of Buddhism or Confucianism as the samurai's code of belief. All these motivations caused the samurai to embody a consciousness that transcended death and life. . . .

For the convenience of discussion, let me first take up the connection of these ideas with Buddhism. The fundamental force that created what is known as Kamakura-period Buddhism was this standpoint of the warrior who willingly sacrificed his life for his lord. Kamakura-period Buddhism undoubtedly represents a Japanization of Buddhism. . . . However, the initial feudal standpoint of willingly sacrificing one's life for one's lord that accompanied this important cultural development in Kamakura Buddhism ripened, through a process of further historical mediation, into the deeper standpoint of transcending death and life. The samurai consciousness matured into an absolute consciousness incomparably greater than their sense of their own individual lives and loyalties.

It was Zen that was deeply linked to the life of the warriors at this stage, permeating every corner of it. For example, it was Zen that permeated their art of swordsmanship. Because the art of swordsmanship is a discipline of killing an enemy, a Westerner might think that it was totally unconnected with religion. But as a matter of fact, the Japanese samurai experienced the consummation of their art of the sword precisely in the teachings of Zen. Hence the literature is replete with such phrases as "the unity of Zen and the sword." . . .

Next, I would like to consider the connection between the idea of dying and Confucianism. This was not an original strain of Chinese Confucianism. It was the Japanese samurai who gave shape to the concept from their own experience. The connection with Confucianism came later. As mentioned earlier, the code of the samurai (*bushidō*) could not attain an ideal resolution in the system of vertical relationships with their feudal lords. In due course, as the samurai class acquired a more profound sense than this vertical form of loyalty to their lords, their own raw struggles for power among themselves gave rise to the sense of another Way—a Way independent of the system of feudal hierarchies. They came to respect the sheer act of courage in itself entailed in sacrificing their lives without personal regrets. They would freely cast aside even their own lives in order to preserve their courage, purity of intention, and nobility of spirit. It was here that they discovered a more precious value than their own lives—the direct opposite of the attitude of preserving one's own life at all costs. In this historical evolution, the standpoint that transcends death and life resurfaced. The senses of dignity and of honor that emerged from this standpoint in the samurai of the late Muromachi period were then clearly linked to Confucianism as it began to gain prominence at the beginning of the Tokugawa period. . . .

Confucianism basically expounds a morality of the Confucian noble man motivated by benevolence, or humanity (*ren*). The literal meaning of the Confucian noble man (*junzi*) concept referred to a person in the position of governing the common people. But the Japanese expounded a philosophy of the superior man's embodying the Way of Confucius, and they further equated this with the Way of the warrior. The samurai class was acquiring a civil status and functions. . . . In this way, *bushidō* came to be recognized as a living embodiment of the Confucian Way—a Way that was grasped as more valuable than life itself.

[This] was at first mediated as a purely formal Confucian concept; consequently, it gained currency not as the theory of venerating the Japanese emperor (*sonnō*) but merely that of venerating a lord (*son'ō*). . . .

This Way of venerating the emperor had in fact been an unbroken thread of thought from the very beginning of Japanese history, taking root deeply in the lives of the Japanese people. Even in the periods in which the samurai were preoccupied with their own system of direct feudal relations, the spirit of venerating the emperor existed in the depths of its heart. . . .

One of the reasons the samurai class subordinated Buddhism to Confucianism three hundred years ago can be found here. However much Zen taught the samurai about an absolute state of existence, they could not allow Zen's accompanying disparagement of the moral domain. This perception was a correct one. Their entering into a state of absolute existence and their serving the emperor had to be directly one process. . . .

The true destruction of the self is certainly not realized in a standpoint in which one thinks of the private interests of one's class, party, or group. A task ordered by the emperor is a public task, a national task, concerning which there should be no admixture or adulteration of selfish or partisan interest. In carrying out such a public task, destruction of the egotistic self involves thoroughly realizing a condition that transcends death and life. The most important matter is that the duty of the subject is a public duty that stands above the people and governs them. This is the basic meaning of subject (*omi/shin*), as distinguished from people (*tami/min*). . . .

This, then, is the Way of the Japanese subject, a Way already understood by our ancestors more than one thousand years ago. Thereafter, as the Way of the warrior based on their system of vertical relationships in the separate feudal domains, it passed through various fires until it has now finally crystallized into an unparalleled beautiful jewel on the world-historical stage of today. . . .

[Adapted from Dilworth and Viglielmo, eds., *Sourcebook for Modern Japanese Philosophy*, pp. 279–87]

Chapter 43

EMPIRE AND WAR

The occupation of Manchuria, planned by Kwantung Army officers in 1931/ 1932, set in motion nearly a decade and a half of Japanese territorial expansion and military aggression on the Asian mainland and in the western Pacific. To be sure, Japan had already become an imperialist power in the late Meiji period. After winning wars with China in 1894/1895 and with Russia in 1904/1905, its colonial possessions stretched from Taiwan in the south through Korea to southern Sakhalin in the north, and under the provisions of the "unequal treaty" system Japan enjoyed the same rights and privileges in China as did the other imperialist countries. None of the Western powers, except perhaps for Russia, had contested these acquisitions, nor did they try to check Japan's expansion. On the contrary, with varying degrees of enthusiasm, they welcomed Japanese power as a "civilizing force" in East Asia.

By the early 1930s, the world had changed. The rise of anticolonial and anti-imperialist movements in European colonial territories like India and French Indochina had found sympathetic support in the newly established Soviet Union, whose leaders proclaimed their own anti-imperialist ideology. The world revolution, declared the Soviet leader Lenin, would begin not in the capitalist home countries but in the colonies or semicolonial areas where their power was weakest. This idea also appealed to Chinese nationalist intellectuals and activists, who embraced a radical anti-imperialist nationalism as they struggled to reunite and strengthen their country after the republican revolution of

1911/1912. In 1924 Soviet advisers helped the Guomindang, the leading nationalist organization, to reorganize, and members of the fledgling Chinese Communist Party joined it in a "united front" against the forces of imperialism and reaction in China.

Imperialism, colonialism, and territorial expansion were no longer unquestioned or unchallenged by Western leaders, either. A critical turning point in Western attitudes came with the peace settlement at the end of World War I. President Woodrow Wilson, who had declared the conflict a "war to end all wars," insisted that the victorious powers respect the right of all nationalities to "national self-determination" and proposed a new system of collective security based on the League of Nations. His idealistic vision was attractive to many Japanese political leaders, who welcomed a respite from the international competition that had driven the country for nearly two generations. During the 1920s, civilian-dominated political party cabinets cooperated with the American and British governments in constructing a diplomatic framework to reduce international tensions in East Asia and to phase out imperialist rights and privileges in China.

Other Japanese leaders, however, found the Wilsonian vision hypocritical and self-serving. Despite its call for "national self-determination," it was clear that Western colonial powers were willing neither to abandon their own colonies nor to include a "racial equality" clause in the League of Nations charter. And when the United States Congress passed legislation in 1924 restricting immigration from both Japan and the rest of Asia, an incensed Japanese press called it a "day of national humiliation." Many politicians called for a "positive" foreign policy more assertive of Japan's strategic interests and more independent of the Anglo-American powers. As Guomindang military forces moved northward in the mid-1920s in an effort to reunite China and unilaterally put an end to imperialist privilege, the Japanese public had become deeply divided over foreign policy issues. It was in this context that the Kwantung Army seized the initiative in Manchuria.

Japan's rapid and successful occupation of Manchuria enjoyed enormous political support and popular enthusiasm at home. But as the country embarked on its new imperialist expansion in the 1930s, Japanese political leaders, intellectuals, and journalists had to explain their policies to themselves, to the Japanese domestic public, and to the world in terms that suited the anti-imperialist temper of the times. Since the late Meiji period, advocates of expansion had been drawn to a Pan-Asian vision of an East Asia united under the Japanese leadership to counter the political, economic, and cultural intrusions of the Western countries, which some Japanese journalists sarcastically referred to as "the white peril." The ideology of Japanese imperialism in the 1930s and 1940s drew heavily on a similar rhetoric, stressing bonds of culture, language, values, and interests linking Japan to the countries it dominated. But imperialistic rhetoric increasingly insisted that Japan's mission was not simply to resist

Western incursions but to liberate colonial and semicolonial regions of Asia from their Western oppressors.

The collapse of the world economy in the late 1920s and early 1930s provided another kind of rhetoric to justify Japan's expansion. The advance into Manchuria, for example, was touted as the opening of a new economic "frontier" or "lifeline" for a Japan struggling to overcome the impact of the world depression. During the 1930s, when Western countries adopted protectionist policies in their domestic and colonial markets to shore up their ailing economies, many Japanese political and intellectual leaders were convinced that the world would soon be dominated by a number of large regional economic and political blocs and that to survive in such a world, Japan would have to build a bloc of its own. The more optimistic saw building such a bloc as a major turning point in human history, with a triumphant Asia under Japanese leadership rising as the morally corrupt and economically defunct West went into decline. Indeed, many intellectuals spoke of the "world historical significance" of Japan's expansion in Asia, and political leaders quickly turned the phrase to their own uses.

In contrast to the late Meiji period, when the Western powers regarded Japanese imperialism with admiration tempered by apprehension, Japanese expansion in the 1930s turned the country into a diplomatic pariah. When the League of Nations issued a report in 1933 censuring Japan for its seizure of Manchuria, the Japanese government responded by withdrawing from the organization. Instead, it forged cordial relations with Nazi Germany and Fascist Italy, which were engaged in their own campaigns of territorial expansion in Europe and the Mediterranean region. Japan signed an anti-Communist pact with both countries in 1936 and then established a more formal diplomatic alliance in 1940. These actions put it on a collision course with Great Britain, France, and, ultimately, the United States.

After an undeclared war between China and Japan broke out in 1937, the government began to gear up the country for a long-term mobilization. Unlike Japan's earlier imperialistic wars, which were fought quickly and decisively, the war in China became a dreary and brutal war of attrition. To organize the population economically and politically, the cabinet of Konoe Fumimaro forced a national mobilization law through the Diet in 1938 and began a "spiritual mobilization" campaign to rally popular morale. When Konoe returned to power again in 1940, he proclaimed the need for a "new political order" to unite the country behind the emperor, and the political parties in the Diet dissolved themselves. While Japan never became a one-party totalitarian state like its allies, Germany and Italy, the country was transformed into a garrison state mobilized for "total war."

When the Japanese leadership decided to move into French Indochina in the fall of 1940 to end the military stalemate in China, Japan found itself face-to-face with the United States. After a series of unsuccessful negotiations intended to deflect American hostility, Japanese naval forces attacked the

American naval base at Pearl Harbor, Hawaii, on December 7, 1941, and then launched a series of strikes that put Japan in control of much of Southeast Asia and the western Pacific. Significantly, the government designated the hostilities as the "Greater East Asia War," indicating that the deepest meaning of the war was the struggle to create an "Asia for Asians" by liberating the region from the thrall of "white imperialism" or "Anglo-American imperialism." In 1943 leaders from Japan together with those from Manchukuo (Manchuria) and several other territories under Japanese occupation issued a "Greater East Asia Declaration" outlining the goals of the war. Almost Wilsonian in tone, it committed the nations of the Greater East Asia Co-Prosperity Sphere to such principles as "coexistence and co-prosperity," "mutual respect for sovereign independence," "mutual cooperation and assistance," and the "elimination of racial prejudice."

THE IMPACT OF WORLD WAR I: A CONFLICT BETWEEN DEFENDERS AND OPPONENTS OF THE STATUS QUO

KONOE FUMIMARO

Konoe Fumimaro (1891–1945), the scion of an aristocratic family that traced its ancestry to the Heian period, served as prime minister during the outbreak of war with China in 1937 and later during the negotiations with the United States in 1941. He inherited a seat in the House of Peers from his father, Konoe Atsumaro, an ardent nationalist who argued for a strong stance toward Russia on the eve of the Russo-Japanese War. In 1918 Konoe, by then a protégé of Saionji Kinmochi, was appointed as a member of the Japanese delegation to the Paris Peace Conference. The following essay, written in November 1918, on the eve of his departure, summarizes a view of the world shared by many Japanese political and military leaders of his generation, who had grown up in a Japan that had emerged as a major world power but whose people still faced racial discrimination abroad.

"AGAINST A PACIFISM CENTERED ON ENGLAND AND AMERICA" (EI-BEI HON'I NO HEIWASHUGI O HAISU)

In my view, the European war has been a conflict between established powers and powers not yet established, a conflict between countries that found upholding the status quo convenient and countries that found overthrowing the status quo convenient. The countries that found upholding the status quo convenient clamored for peace, while the countries that found overthrowing the status quo convenient cried out for war. Pacifism does not always serve justice and humanism, and militarism does not always violate justice and humanism. All depends on the nature of the status quo. If the prewar status quo was the best possible and was consonant with justice and humanism, he who would destroy it is the enemy of justice and humanism; but if the status quo did not meet the criteria of justice and humanism, its destroyer is not necessarily the enemy of justice and humanism. By the same token, the pacifist countries that would uphold this status quo are not necessarily qualified to pride themselves on being the champions of justice and humanity.

Although England and America may have regarded Europe's prewar status as ideal, an impartial third party cannot acknowledge it to have been ideal in terms of justice and humanism. As the colonial history of England and France attests, they long ago occupied the less civilized regions of the world, made them into colonies, and had no scruples about monopolizing them for their own profit. Therefore not only Germany but all late-developing countries were in the position of having no land to seize and being unable to find any room for expansion. This state of affairs contravenes the principle of equal opportunity for all humanity, jeopardizes all nations' equal right to survival, and is a gross violation of justice and humanity. Germany's wish to overthrow this order was quite justified; the means it chose, however, were unfair and immoderate, and because they were based on militarism, with its emphasis on armed might, Germany received the world's opprobrium. Nevertheless, as a Japanese, I cannot help feeling deep sympathy for what Germany has to do.

The Need to Repudiate Economic Imperialism

At the coming peace conference, in joining the League of Nations Japan must insist at the very least, that repudiation of economic imperialism and nondiscriminatory treatment of Orientals and Caucasians be agreed upon from the start. Militarism is not the only thing injurious to justice and humanism. Although the world has been saved from the smoke of gunpowder and the hail of bullets by Germany's defeat, military might is not all that threatens nations' equal right to survival. We must realize that there is invasion through money, conquest through wealth. Just as we repudiate military imperialism, so in the same spirit we should naturally repudiate economic imperialism, which seeks to profit by monopolizing enormous capital and abundant natural resources and suppressing other nations' free growth without recourse to arms. I cannot avoid grave misgivings as to how far economic imperialism can be repudiated at the coming peace conference, led as it is by England and America, which I fear will unsheathe the sword of their economic imperialism after the war.

If we cannot subdue this rampant economic imperialism at the peace conference, England and America, which have profited most from the war, will promptly unify the world under their economic dominance and will rule the world, using the League of Nations and arms limitations to fix the status quo that serves their purpose. How will other countries endure this? Deprived of arms to express their revulsion and indignation, they will have no choice but to follow England and America, bleating in their wake like a flock of meek sheep. England has lost no time in trumpeting a policy of self-sufficiency, and many are advocating that other countries be denied access to its colonies. Such are the contradictions between what England and America say and what they do. This, indeed, is why I am wary of those who glorify England and America. If such a policy is carried out, needless to say it would be a great economic blow to Japan. Japan is limited in territory, [is] poor in natural resources, and has a small population and thus a meager market for manufactured products. If England closed off its colonies, how would we be able to assure the nation's secure survival? In such a case, the need to ensure its survival would compel Japan to attempt to overthrow the status quo as Germany did before the war. If this is the fate awaiting all late-developing countries with little territory and no colonies, not only for the sake of Japan but for the sake of establishing the equal right to life of all nations of the world on the basis of justice and humanism, we must do away with economic imperialism and see that countries do not monopolize their colonies but accord other countries equal use of them both as markets for manufactured products and as suppliers of natural resources.

The next thing that the Japanese, especially, should insist upon is the elimination of discrimination between Caucasians and Orientals. There is no need to dwell on the fact that the United States, along with the English colonies of Australia and Canada, opens its doors to Caucasians but looks down on the Japanese and on Orientals in general and rejects them. This is something at which the Japanese have long chafed. Not only are Orientals barred from employment and forbidden to lease houses and farmland, but still worse, it is reported that in some places an Oriental wishing to spend the night at a hotel is required to have a Caucasian guarantor. This is a grave humanitarian problem that no defender of justice, Oriental or otherwise, should overlook.

At the coming peace conference, we must see that the English and Americans show deep remorse for their past sins and change their arrogant and insulting attitude, and we must insist, from the standpoint of justice and humanism, that they revise all laws that call for discriminatory treatment of Orientals, including of course rescinding immigration restrictions against Orientals. I believe that the coming peace conference will be the great test of whether the human race can bring itself to reconstruct a world based on justice and humanism. If Japan does not rashly endorse a pacifism centered on England and America but steadfastly asserts its position from the standpoint of justice and humanism in the true sense, it will long be celebrated in history as the champion of justice.

[Konoe, "Against a Pacifism," pp. 12–14; "Ei-Bei hon'i no heiwashugi o haisu,"
pp. 23–26]

A PLAN TO OCCUPY MANCHURIA

ISHIHARA KANJI

In 1931 Ishihara Kanji (1886–1949), a staff officer of the Kwantung Army, the Japanese garrison force stationed in southern Manchuria, plotted with fellow officers to seize control of the three northeastern provinces of China (commonly known as Manchuria) by military force. Research into military history had convinced Ishihara that the world faced an apocalyptic "final war" between a West unified by the United States and an Asia under the leadership of Japan. As a first step in preparation for this conflict, Ishihara wished to consolidate Japan's position on the Asian continent. The following position paper, written in May 1931, on the eve of the takeover of Manchuria, outlines his fundamental views on continental policy.

PERSONAL OPINION ON THE MANCHURIA–MONGOLIA PROBLEM (MANMŌ MONDAI SHIKEN)

The Value of Manchuria and Mongolia

A world dominated by the five superpowers that emerged from the Great War in Europe will eventually be united into one system. A struggle for supremacy between the United States, as the representative of the West, and Japan, as the champion of the East, will decide who will control it.

The basic principle of our national policy must be to acquire rapidly what we need to qualify as the champion of the East.

To overcome the current economic depression and to secure what we need to become the champion of the East requires rapidly expanding the borders necessary to maintain our sphere of influence. Although the Manchuria–Mongolia region is not suited to the solution of our population problem or endowed with sufficient natural resources for Greater Japan, at the present moment the solution of the so-called Manchuria–Mongolia problem should be our first priority, for the following reasons.

POLITICAL VALUE

1. For a nation-state to play an active role in the world, its most essential requirement is a favorable national defense position. The reason why Germany's defensive position is so unstable today is that the British hegemons established an advantageous defensive position in the nineteenth century. As the American navy grows, the British Empire in turn will find its defensive position seriously

threatened; and as American economic power advances, the United States will become the champion of the Western peoples.

Our country must resist the encroachments of Russia to the north as it simultaneously confronts British and American naval power to the south. The Hulunbeier region in the Greater Xiangan Range [in northern Manchuria] is of especially important strategic value to Japan. If our country brings northern Manchuria under its influence, Russia will find it extremely difficult to advance to the east. It will not be difficult to [block Russia] simply by building up our strength in Manchuria and Mongolia. If our country is relieved of its burden to the north, depending on the dictates of national policy, it can then make bold plans for development toward China proper or toward the South Sea region.

The Manchuria–Mongolia region is of enormous strategic importance with respect to the destiny and development of our country.

2. If the Manchuria–Mongolia region is brought under our influence, then our control over Korea will be stabilized.

3. If our country shows firm determination by resolving the Manchuria–Mongolia problem through force, it can assume a position of leadership toward China; it can promote China's unity and stability; and it can guarantee peace in the East.

ECONOMIC VALUE

1. Agriculture in the Manchuria–Mongolia region is sufficient to solve the problem of food supplies for our people.

2. Iron from Anshan, coal from Fushun, and other resources [in Manchuria] are sufficient to build up our present heavy-industrial base.

3. Various business enterprises in the Manchuria–Mongolia region will enable us to break out of economic depression by helping those currently unemployed in our country. Even though the natural resources of the Manchuria–Mongolia region will not be enough to make us the champion of the East, they are sufficient to relieve our present plight and to build a foundation for a great leap forward.

The Solution of the Manchuria–Mongolia Problem

It is clear from the history of the past twenty-five years that it will be difficult to expect even limited development under the aegis of today's crafty Chinese politicos. To stabilize our national defenses as the guardian of the East against Russia, we must be aware that there is no solution to the Manchuria–Mongolia problem but to make the region our own territory.

The solution to the Manchuria–Mongolia problem rests on two assumptions: first, that making Manchuria–Mongolia into our territory is a just action; and, second, that our country has the power to carry this policy out resolutely.

Of course, we should heed those who argue that since Chinese society is finally making advances toward becoming a capitalist economy, our country should withdraw its political and military facilities from the Manchuria–Mongolia region and pursue our economic development in harmony with the revolution of the Han people. But on the basis of direct observation, I think that it is extremely doubtful that the Chinese will be able to build a modern nation-state by themselves. On the contrary, I firmly believe that if our country establishes peace and order, it will contribute to the natural development and well-being of the Han people [in Manchuria].

The mission of our Japan is to overthrow the warlords and bureaucrats who are the common enemy of the 30 million people living in Manchuria. Our country's control over the Manchuria–Mongolia region, moreover, will bring about the unification of China proper. . . .

Some [people] may be pessimistic about war from an economic point of view, but the costs will be slight. Since war expenses can be recovered in the war zone, we have little to fear financially, and if need be, we will resolutely establish a planned economy embracing both the homeland and the occupied territory. Naturally we may not be able to avoid a temporary major turmoil in the economic world, but eventually we will be able to overcome the economic crisis and progress to the same level as the advanced industrial countries. . . .

The Timing of the Solution

The present situation in our country raises concerns about how easy it will be to achieve national unity in the event of war. For that reason, at first it might seem logical to give priority to the domestic reconstruction of the country. But we fear that it will be difficult to achieve a so-called internal reconstruction and national unity and that it will take much time to achieve political stability. . . .

If we can first draw up war plans and convince our capitalists that victory is possible, it will not be at all impossible to move the present political regime toward a positive foreign policy. History has shown that military success, especially at the early stage of a war, arouses and unites popular sentiment.

[*Ishihara Kanji shiryō*, vol. 2, *Kokubō ronsaku*, in *Meiji Hyakunenshi shiryō*, vol. 18, pp. 76–79; PD]

THE ECONOMIC NEED FOR EXPANSION

HASHIMOTO KINGORŌ

Hashimoto Kingorō (1890–1957), an army officer who organized plots against the civilian government in 1931, advocated military insurrection at home and aggressive expansion abroad. After he was forced to resign his commission because of his involvement in the unsuccessful military putsch of February 26, 1936, he organized the Greater Japan Youth Party, a radical right-wing organization, and eventually was elected to the Diet. Tried and convicted as a class-A war criminal after World War II, he was sentenced to life imprisonment in Sugamo Prison. This 1939 speech, justifying the takeover of Manchuria on economic grounds, was used as evidence against him.

ADDRESSES TO YOUNG MEN

We have already said that there are only three ways left to Japan to escape from the pressure of surplus population. We are like a great crowd of people packed into a small and narrow room, and there are only three doors through which we might escape, namely, emigration, advance into world markets, and expansion of territory. The first door, emigration, has been barred to us by the anti-Japanese immigration policies of other countries. The second door, advance into world markets, is being pushed shut by tariff barriers and the abrogation of commercial treaties. What should Japan do when two of the three doors have been closed against her? It is quite natural that Japan should rush upon the last remaining door.

It may sound dangerous when we speak of territorial expansion, but the territorial expansion of which we speak does not in any sense of the word involve the occupation of the possessions of other countries, the planting of the Japanese flag thereon, and the declaration of their annexation to Japan. It is just that since the Powers have suppressed the circulation of Japanese materials and merchandise abroad, we are looking for some place overseas where Japanese capital, Japanese skills, and Japanese labor can have free play, free from the oppression of the white race.

We would be satisfied with just this much. What moral right do the world powers who have themselves closed to us the two doors of emigration and advance into world markets have to criticize Japan's attempt to rush out of the third and last door? If they do not approve of this, they should open the doors which they have closed against us and permit the free movement overseas of Japanese emigrants and merchandise.

At the time of the Manchurian incident, the entire world joined in criticism of Japan. They said that Japan was an untrustworthy nation. They said that she had recklessly brought cannon and machine guns into Manchuria, which was the territory of another country, flown airplanes over it, and finally occupied it. But the military action taken by Japan was not in the least a selfish one. Moreover, we do not recall ever having taken so much as an inch of territory belonging to another nation. The result of this incident was the establishment of the splendid new nation of [Manchukuo]. The Powers are still discussing whether or not to recognize this new nation, but regardless of whether or not other nations recognize her, the Manchurian empire has already been

established, and now, seven years after its creation, the empire is further consolidating its foundations with the aid of its friend, Japan. . . .

This is quite a convenient argument for them. Let us take it at face value.
Then there is another question we must ask them. Suppose that there is still
on this earth land endowed with abundant natural resources that have not been
developed at all by the white race. Would it not then be God's will and the will
of Providence that Japan go there and develop those resources for the benefit
of mankind?

And there still remain many such lands on this earth.

[IMTFE, document 487B, exhibit 1290]

KONOE FUMIMARO

On November 3, 1938, nearly a year and a half after the outbreak of war with
the Guomindang government under Chiang Kai-shek, Prime Minister Konoe
Fumimaro proclaimed in a radio address the establishment of a "new order in
East Asia" as the objective of Japan's policy toward China. Although prompted
by the hope of winning the cooperation and collaboration of anti-Chiang leaders like Wang Jingwei, the new slogan became a rallying cry at home as well.

RADIO ADDRESS

It is a historical necessity that the three great neighbor nations—China, Manchukuo, and Japan—while fully retaining their respective individuality, should
stand closely united in their common duty of safeguarding East Asia. It is deeply
to be deplored not only for the sake of Japan but for that of all Asia that the
attainment of this goal has been thwarted through the mistaken policy of the
Guomindang government. The policy of the Guomindang government was
based on a transient fashion of the period that followed the Great War. It did
not originate in the native intelligence and good sense of the Chinese people.
In particular, the conduct of that government, which in its efforts to stay in
power cared not whether the nation was left prey to Communism or relegated
to a minor colonial status, cannot but be regarded as treason toward those many
patriotic Chinese who had risked their lives in order to erect a new China. It
was in those circumstances that Japan, reluctant as she was to be involved in
the tragedy of two great kindred nations fighting against each other, was compelled to take up arms against the Chiang Kai-shek regime. . . .

The nations of the world must surely be able to comprehend these new
developments in East Asia. It is undisputed history that China heretofore has
been a victim of the rivalry between the powers whose imperialistic ambitions
have constantly imperiled her tranquillity and independence. Japan realizes the

need of fundamentally rectifying such a state of affairs, and she is eager to see a new order established in East Asia, a new structure of peace based on true justice.

Japan is in no way opposed to collaboration with foreign powers, nor does she desire to impair their legitimate rights and interests. If the Powers, understanding her true motives, will formulate policies adapted to the new conditions, Japan will be glad to cooperate with them. Japan's zeal for stamping out Communism is certainly well known. The aim of the Comintern is to sovietize the Orient and to overturn the world. Japan is firmly determined to eradicate the Communistic influence, which is behind the so-called long-term resistance of the Chiang regime. Germany and Italy, our allies against Communism, have manifested their sympathies with Japan's aims in East Asia, and we are profoundly grateful for the great encouragement that their moral support has given our nation during this crisis. In the present emergency, it is necessary for Japan not only to strengthen still further her ties with those countries but also to collaborate with them on the basis of a common world outlook toward the reconstruction of world order.

[*Tokyo Gazette* 2 (December 1938): 17–20]

NATIONAL MOBILIZATION

ARMY MINISTRY

Beginning in 1934, the army published a series of pamphlets explaining its policies in Manchuria and calling for plans to mobilize the country for a prolonged war. After declaring that "war is the father of creation and the mother of culture," the pamphlet *On the Basic Meaning of National Defense and Its Intensification (Kokubō no hongi to sono kyōka no teishō)* outlined why future wars could no longer be fought as they had been in the past. It called for the establishment of a "national defense state" geared for war preparation. Many left-wing politicians supported the views expressed, but centrist-conservative parties in the Diet protested against this and other army pamphlets as unconstitutional military interference in politics.

ON THE BASIC MEANING OF NATIONAL DEFENSE AND ITS INTENSIFICATION (KOKUBŌ NO HONGI TO SONO KYŌKA NO TEISHŌ)

The essence of national defense policy must be the organization and administration of the nation-state to manifest the highest level of its total energy. . . .

The extraordinary development of science and technology and the growing complexity of international relations have invariably widened the scale of war. Armed warfare does not occur in isolation but develops simultaneously with diplomatic warfare, economic warfare, ideological warfare, and other kinds of warfare. Coordinating these elements into war goals and preparing a wartime leadership structure during peacetime have become inextricably linked to the achievement of victory in war.

From these circumstances sprang the idea of total mobilization as the basis for armed conflict, an idea much talked about since the Great War. Total mobilization is the means by which the army and the people unite in a single body to carry on armed warfare. . . .

National defense is not aimed just at armed warfare arising from international competition; it is the energy and force behind the life of the nation. The idea that national defense is the actualization of the fundamental energy sustaining the creation and development of the nation-state is absolutely central to the life of the nation. As international rivalry intensifies and international struggle for supremacy spreads, national defense is of the utmost necessity to clarify the ideals of our imperial land and to emerge victorious in the violent competition. . . .

To secure the future of our imperial land, we must adopt various necessary emergency measures to overcome the current emergency. It will be difficult, but we must succor the masses who have grown poor under the present system and improve the living standards of the nation's people. We must exert ourselves to achieve the highest level of our national strength by reexamining all our national state organizations in light of our relations with the outside world; by resolutely carrying out a fundamental reconstruction of our national finances, our national economy, our diplomacy, and our education of the people; by organizing and harnessing the enormous latent spiritual strength of our imperial land for the sake of national defense; and by managing all this in a consistent and unified way. These measures will at the same time serve as policies to deal with the crisis now confronting our imperial land.

Some take the optimistic view that international conflict is not inevitable in the present situation and that we can turn things to our advantage solely through diplomatic means. But such are the views of people who do not understand international conditions. . . .

We have described the goal and essence of national defense. To summarize, it is the fundamental energy behind the creation and development of the nation-state. Naturally, it is wrong to argue that the scale and content of a country's absolute national defense should be tied to how large or small a country is or how wealthy or poor it is. In this world it is an undeniable axiom that every country has an autonomous and independent right of national defense. It is clear that efforts in the past to limit or prohibit military preparedness by means of international treaties have been little more than subterfuges of the Powers to maintain the superiority of their own national defense under the name of pacifism. No internationalist can deny this fact.

[Rikugunshō, *Kokubō no hongi to sono kyōka no teishō*, pp. 2–4, 10–13; PD]

KONOE FUMIMARO

Using the mounting sense of crisis created by the military stalemate in China, the Konoe cabinet decided in the summer of 1940 to establish a "new political order," entailing wide-ranging domestic political reforms to strengthen Japan in its confrontations with the outside world. In its original conception, as outlined in the following statement by Prime Minister Konoe Fumimaro, the "new political order" was envisioned as a way to end the political infighting and opposition that had persisted even after the outbreak of the China War. Shortly before this statement was issued, on August 28, 1940, the political parties in the Diet dissolved themselves, paving the way for the creation of a new domestic political order. Critics accused the Konoe cabinet of setting up a "*bakufu*-like structure" between the people and the emperor, but Konoe insisted that the system would exist only to serve the emperor.

CONCERNING THE NEW NATIONAL STRUCTURE
(SHIN TAISEI)

In the midst of a world upheaval of unprecedented magnitude, Japan is today going forward with the unparalleled task of creating a new order in East Asia. If she is to bring the China affair to a successful conclusion while adjusting herself to the international situation and taking a leading part in the establishment of a new world order, she must concentrate upon the accomplishment of this task the moral and material resources of the nation to the utmost degree so as to be in a position to take independently, swiftly, and resolutely appropriate measures to meet whatever situation may arise. To this end Japan must perfect a highly organized national defense structure, the basis of which is a powerful internal structure. Consequently, there has arisen the pressing demand for the setting up of a new structure in politics, economy, education, culture, and in all phases of the life of the state and of the people.

This demand is indeed the expression of the will of the nation, transcending cabinet, faction, or individual; nor is it of an ephemeral character for the carrying out of a specific policy but, rather, of a lasting nature for rendering possible the energetic pursuance of any policy when the necessity arises. Whether or not Japan can firmly set up such a strong national structure will decide the rise or fall of the nation. . . .

The aim of the new national structure is to unite all the forces of the state and people, welding into one living whole our hundred million fellow countrymen and enabling them to fulfill in the highest degree their duty as subjects of the throne. The realization of this purpose can only reside in the due performance by each of his appointed task. It is but natural when, as has been the case in the past, the majority of the people have no other opportunity of taking part in government than by casting a vote as the occasion arises once every three or four years, that the nation as a whole should find itself unable to take to heart the destiny of the country.

The organization of the nation is to be that in which the people serve the state in their everyday life, and must therefore embrace the economic and cultural spheres. There must be a solid nationwide structure in which each component part is organized vertically and yet works in coordinated unity on a horizontal plane. It is because there does not exist such a structure, in which the people can effectively assist the throne, that we see today a tendency toward conflict between those who govern and those who are governed; an absence on the part of the authorities who formulate the nation's policies of a true understanding of the people's real activities; and an indifference on the part of the people toward the formulation of state policies. . . .

The new national structure movement aims at superseding the old party politics predicated upon liberalism. It is essentially national, all-embracing, and public spirited in character. It aims at the concentration and unification of all the forces and resources of the nation. Its activities extend to the whole life of the nation. Even were this movement to rise as a popular movement, its character would not be that of a political party in the old sense. It would, on the contrary, be a national movement standing above any political party, embracing all parties and factions, economic and cultural bodies, and uniting all in the spirit of public service. When such a movement is led by the government, those who hold the reins of government and are entrusted with the task of assisting the throne are always placed in a position where they must seek the welfare of the whole but never be permitted to indulge in party politics which, in their very nature, contain elements of sectional antagonism and conflict.

As I have just stated, the national structure cannot take the form of a political party, especially when it is led by the government. Nor can it be allowed to take the form of a single party system. Such a political system takes a "part" and makes of it a "whole"; it considers the state and the party as one and the same thing and views any opposition to the party as a revolt against the state; it renders permanent the ruling position of one party, with the head of that party as a permanent wielder of the power to govern. No matter what brilliant results such a system may have reaped in other lands, it is not acceptable in Japan, as it is contrary to the basic principle of our national polity of "one sovereign over all." In Japan, it is the privilege of every one of His Imperial Majesty's subjects to assist the throne, and that privilege cannot be monopolized by the power of either a single person or a single party.

If there should arise a difference of opinion concerning the assistance to be offered, the final decision would rest with the throne. And once an imperial decision has been given, all the subjects of the throne should unite in obeying His Majesty's command. That is the very essence of Japanese polity.

[*Tokyo Gazette* 4 (October 1940): 133–36]

THE IMPERIAL RULE ASSISTANCE ASSOCIATION

In October 1940, the Konoe government organized the Imperial Rule Assistance Association (Taisei yokusankai), a national political organization intended to act as the core of the "new political order." The following radio address by Prime Minister Konoe, delivered on September 28, 1940, explained the reasons for establishing it.

CONFRONTING THE CRISIS

In a period of peace and tranquillity, a nation is liable to live a life of laxity and irresponsibility in all its phases. Nevertheless, once the country is threatened with a national crisis, the entire nation will band together to surmount it. No room is left then for sectionalism, dissensions, or untrammeled discussions. Personal comforts and living must be sacrificed willingly to the common welfare; personal renown and profits must likewise be jettisoned for the sake of the throne and the country. The true character of the Japanese nation finds expression in the unfaltering, courageous service for the cause of the state on the part of all its members in time of emergency. It devolves, on the one hand, on the emergency cabinet to see to it that every member of the nation each finds his or her proper place while serving the state, with heart and soul to the best of his or her ability. What the new structure aims at is the perfection of a political system founded on the principle of the unity of sovereign and subject, under which the will and ideas of those who govern will be made known to those who are governed for the guidance of the latter; and the will and ideas of those who are governed will be communicated to those who govern. In other words, the function of government is to see that the people are enabled to find each his proper place; the duty of each subject is to devotedly serve the throne. This constitutes the essence of our national polity, which predicates loyalty as a supreme virtue existing between sovereign and subjects, a loyalty that is con-terminous with the mutual affection of father and son. Herein lies the key to the ideals of the new national structure.

[*Tokyo Gazette* 4 (November 1940): 176]

SPIRITUAL MOBILIZATION

MINISTRY OF EDUCATION

After nearly a decade of fighting in China, the national leadership feared a decline in popular morale. To boost support for the war and to affirm the country's moral and political superiority over its adversaries, the Ministry of Education produced several textbooks aimed at counteracting foreign intellectual influences and clarifying the nature of the "Japanese spirit." *The Way of Subjects* (*Shinmin no michi*), published in early 1941, was used as a textbook in ethics (*shūshin*) and history courses in schools all over the country. Its call for a return to what many regarded as Japan's traditional values had enormous influence on public discourse during the wartime period.

THE WAY OF SUBJECTS
(*SHINMIN NO MICHI*)

The way of the subjects of the Emperor issues from the polity of the Emperor, and is to guard and maintain the Imperial Throne coexistent with Heaven-and-Earth. This is not in the sphere of the abstract, but a way of daily practice based on history. The life and activities of the nation are all attuned to the task of giving great firmness to the foundation of the Empire.

In retrospect, this country has been widely seeking knowledge in the world since the Meiji Restoration, thereby fostering and maintaining the prosperity of the state. With the influx of European and American culture into this country, however, individualism, liberalism, utilitarianism, and materialism began to assert themselves, with the result that the traditional character of the country was much impaired, and the virtuous habits and customs bequeathed by our ancestors were affected unfavorably. . . .

If this situation is left unremedied, it will be difficult to eradicate the evils of European and American thought that are deeply penetrating various strata of the national life of Japan, and to achieve the unprecedentedly great tasks by establishing a structure of national solidarity guarding and maintaining the prosperity of the Imperial Throne. . . .

The Construction of a New World Order

An old order that has been placing world humanity under individualism, liberalism, and materialism for several hundred years since the early period of the modern epoch of history is now crumbling. A new order is now in the making amid unprecedented world changes. . . .

. . . Thus, the orientation of world history has made the collapse of the world of the old order an assured conclusion. Japan has hereby opened the start for the construction of a new world order based on moral principles. . . .

Japan's Ethical Code

The Imperial Family is the fountain source of the Japanese nation, and national and private lives issue from this. In the past, foreign nationals came to this country only to enjoy the benevolent rule of the Imperial Family and become Japanese subjects spiritually and by blood. The Imperial virtues are so great and boundless that all are assimilated into one. Here is the reason for the present glorious state, in which the Emperor and his subjects are harmonized into one great unit. . . .

In Japan, filial piety cannot exist singly without its absolute counterpart. It is loyalty. Loyalty is the principle. Filial piety at home must be loyalty. Both are one and inseparable. This is the Japanese characteristic unexcelled by other countries. In Japan, husband and wife do not form the standard of home, as in the Occident, but the relations of parents and sons are its center. It is natural that filial piety is given great prominence. The first requisite of filial piety is to fulfill the duty of subjects of guarding and maintaining the Imperial Throne in observance of the bequeathed will of their ancestors. This is the essence of filial piety. . . .

The China affair is a holy task for Japan to propagate the ideals of the Empire-founding throughout East Asia and also the world over. . . .

[Tolischus, *Tokyo Record*, pp. 409–10, 408, 416, 424–27]

ECONOMIC MOBILIZATION

RYŪ SHINTARŌ

In March 1938, the Diet passed the National Mobilization Law, which gave the government extensive new powers over the county's manpower, resources, trade, and other economic activities. Big business leaders and their political allies in the Diet objected to many of these changes. In 1940, Ryū Shintarō, a journalist close to Prime Minister Konoe Fumimaro, wrote a best-selling book explaining the economic reorganization. The following excerpt deals with government controls over the profits of business firms.

JAPAN'S ECONOMIC REORGANIZATION
(*NIHON KEIZAI SAIHENSEI*)

Investment and Controls on the Profit Rate

Investors of capital argue that if profits are placed under government control, productive activities will stagnate. . . . Others object [to government controls on company profits] on the fundamental economic ground that according to the tenets of liberalism the source of all productive activity lies in the human impulse toward "gain." This view dominates the conventional wisdom of today's businessmen (*jitsugyōka*).

With respect to the first point . . . [the fear that production will stagnate] is an illusion that results from the concentration of capital in the high-profit sector. The high-profit sector invigorates and stimulates productive activity, but it does so only relatively compared with other sectors. If the present dividend rate were to continue fluctuating at around 30 percent, would investment slow down if dividends were held under 30 percent? . . .

The Pursuit of Gain

Let us turn to the second point. This is the problem of *Homo economicus* (economic man) familiar to every first-year economics student wrestling with Adam Smith. In these final days of liberalism, it is probably inevitable that we must mention Smith, the founding father of liberalism.

The essence of liberalism lies in the proposition that when individuals pursue their own gain as they compete with one other to express their distinctive characteristics, they are acting in complete accord with the public good (*kōeki*). Basically, this proposition rests on the assumptions that an individual's "creativity" or "originality" derives from his "pursuit of gain" and that without pursuing one's gains, it is not possible to display one's creativity or originality.

This way of thinking lies at the core of economic liberalism. Transcending this way of thinking must be the point of departure for building a new economic system. . . .

. . . In a liberal economy "pursuit of gain" must be tolerated, but in itself it is nothing more than the economic psychology of those who find themselves in an economy organized on liberal principles. . . .

The Motive for Action in Modern Business Firms

Since the modern business firm is organized for the continual pursuit of profit, what is at issue here is clearly not a question of human nature but a question of economic organization. It is safe to say that even systems based on liberal [economic] principles are, for the most part, moving in the direction of "functionality."

Looked at in this way, the idea that controls on profits will slow down productive activity or bring the economy to a halt is behind the times. It reflects the mentality of a small shopkeeper who thinks the commercial spirit of the greengrocer or the fishmonger is what drives the modern business firm. The problem clearly is to free the development of productive power by stripping the old shell from modern business firms that have developed on the basis of functional specialization, by emphasizing their "functional" position and by transforming them from "organizations based on profit" to "organizations based on function."

The Control of Profits and the Freedom of Creativity

However, since an organization based on function constitutes a unified whole, we must decisively regulate profits, which are at the core of a liberal economic system.

The control of profits involves both a reduction and a fixing of the dividend rate. What the system must determine is not how high the dividend rate should be but, rather, how upper limits on the dividend rate can be fixed at a level appropriate to current conditions. Since we can imagine that at some point there will be an economic turndown, it ought to be set at a low level . . . the point of departure for the new system lies in whether or not dividends should be considered equivalent to interest payments. More specifically, since profits over and above the fixed dividend are either retained as company reserves or used directly in the expansion of the business firm, not only must profits be considered as interest payments but the meaning of invested capital also must change to some degree. Since the owners of capital simply collect fixed dividends similar to a kind of interest payment, the function of the businessman (*kigyōka*) and the position of the capitalist differ. There is no reason why a capitalist cannot also be a businessman at the same time, of course, but his function [in each role] is quite distinct. The businessman assumes the role of a purely managerial technician charged with running the business firm. He sees to it that the company pays fixed dividends on capital, but beyond that he has no responsibility toward the capitalist. On the other hand, as a business manager, he has an enormous responsibility toward the state and society. His function is to manage the enterprise in its state and social roles with the highest degree of efficiency, and it is for that that he is rewarded.

Just as the engineer carries out his state and social functions through his technical contributions, . . . so too the businessman [in his role as manager] acts like an "engineer" for a particular business firm. In that sense he stands as a true leader of production. Since he is completely liberated from the supervision of the capitalist, he acquires freedom of "creativity" in running the business firm. His "creativity" is not driven by moneymaking, as it once was. As he becomes conscious of his role in society, he achieves a new and purer freedom. Today both the businessman and the capitalist must put aside the notion that profit is everything, or to put it another way, a framework based on individualistic economic activity. By carrying out their own particular "function" in state or society, they finally will be able to express an influential "public voice" in state and society. If they act individualistically by putting profit ahead of everything else, businessmen will gradually lose their "public voice." . . . Only by putting aside their individualism and their profit seeking will their public views acquire political weight. In the view of the current political situation facing Japan, it is extraordinarily important that they do so.

[Ryū, *Nihon keizai no saihensei*, pp. 147–48, 149–54; PD]

THE GREATER EAST ASIA WAR

ARITA HACHIRŌ

When war broke out in Europe in September 1939, the Japanese leadership found itself with opportunities to break out of the military stalemate in China by expanding into the European colonial territories left vulnerable by the German occupation of France and Holland and its aerial assaults on England in 1940. On June 29, 1940, in a radio address entitled "The International Situation and Japan's Position," Foreign Minister Arita Hachirō proposed a new vision of a Greater East Asia Co-Prosperity Sphere under the leadership of Japan. This vision assumed that the future world would be divided among large regional blocs dominated by major powers like Nazi Germany, the Soviet Union, and the United States.

THE GREATER EAST ASIA CO-PROSPERITY SPHERE

Japan's ideal since the foundation of the empire has been that all nations should be enabled to find their proper places in the world. Our foreign policy has also been based upon this ideal, for which we have not hesitated at times even to fight by staking our national existence.

What all mankind longs for is the firm establishment of world peace. But it goes without saying that peace can never endure unless it is a peace in which all nations enjoy their proper places. Unfortunately, however, the establishment of world peace in this sense is difficult of speedy realization at the present stage of human progress. In order to realize such a high ideal, therefore, it seems to be a most natural step that peoples who are closely related with one another geographically, racially, culturally, and economically should first form a sphere of their own for coexistence and co-prosperity and establish peace and order within that sphere and, at the same time, secure a relationship of common existence and prosperity with other spheres.

The causes of strife mankind has hitherto experienced lie generally in the failure to give due consideration to the necessity of some such natural and constructive world order and to remedy the irrationalities and injustices of old. The war in Europe brings home the truth of this with special emphasis. Accordingly, in order to establish international peace on a permanent foundation, every effort must be exerted for the rectification of the errors that have been committed in this regard.

It is in this spirit that Japan is now engaged in the task of establishing a new order in East Asia. . . .

The countries of East Asia and the regions of the South Seas are geographically, historically, racially, and economically very closely related to each other. They are destined to cooperate and minister to one another's needs for their common well-being and prosperity and to promote peace and progress in their regions. The uniting of all these regions under a single sphere on the basis of common existence and insuring thereby the stability of that sphere is, I think, a natural conclusion.

The idea to establish first a righteous peace in each of the various regions and then establish collectively a just peace for the whole world has long existed also in Europe and America. This system presupposes the existence of a stabilizing force in each region, with which as a center the peoples within that region are to secure their coexistence and co-prosperity as well as the stability of their sphere. It also presupposes that these groups will respect one another's individual characteristics, political, cultural, and economic, and they will cooperate and fulfill one another's needs for their common good.

When the present European war broke out, the Japanese government at once declared their policy of noninvolvement and made it clear that this country did not intend to intervene in Europe and at the same time did not want to see the war spread into East Asia. Quite naturally Japan expects that the Western Powers will do nothing that will exert any undesirable influence upon the stability of East Asia.

> [Arita, "The International Situation and Japan's Position," June 29, 1940;
> reprinted in *Tokyo Gazette* 4 (August 1940): 78–79]

THE DECISION FOR WAR WITH
THE UNITED STATES

After the cabinet of Konoe Fumimaro signed the so-called Axis Pact with Nazi Germany and Fascist Italy and sent troops to occupy the northern part of French

Indochina in the fall of 1940, Japan's relations with the United States, already strained by the Japanese invasion of China, steadily deteriorated. The two countries opened bilateral talks in the spring of 1941, but the United States insisted that Japan accept four "basic principles" that would have compelled it to give up all its territorial gains since 1931. In early September 1941, the Konoe cabinet decided to prepare for war while continuing to negotiate with the Americans. In October, Tōjō Hideki, the war minister, replaced Konoe as prime minister, and the final decision for war was made at an imperial conference on December 1, 1941. The following excerpts from the discussion make clear the frustration of the Japanese leaders in dealing with the Americans.

STATEMENT BY PRIME MINISTER TŌJŌ HIDEKI

On the basis of the Imperial Conference decision of November 5, the Army and Navy, on the one hand, devoted themselves to the task of getting everything ready for military operations; while the Government, on the other hand, used every means at its disposal and made every effort to improve diplomatic relations with the United States. The United States not only refused to make even one concession with respect to the position she had maintained in the past but also stipulated new conditions, after having formed an alliance with Great Britain, the Netherlands, and China. The United States demanded complete and unconditional withdrawal of troops from China, withdrawal of our recognition of the Nanking Government, and the reduction of the Tripartite Pact to a dead letter. This not only belittled the dignity of our Empire and made it impossible for us to harvest the fruits of the China Incident, but also threatened the very existence of our Empire. It became evident that we could not achieve our goals by means of diplomacy.

At the same time, the United States, Great Britain, the Netherlands, and China increased their economic and military pressure against us; and we have now reached the point where we can no longer allow the situation to continue, from the point of view of both our national power and our projected military operations. Moreover, the requirements with respect to military operations will not permit an extension of time. Under the circumstances, our Empire has no alternative but to begin war against the United States, Great Britain, and the Netherlands in order to resolve the present crisis and assure survival. . . .

STATEMENT BY FOREIGN MINISTER TŌGŌ SHIGENORI ON JAPANESE–AMERICAN NEGOTIATIONS

The United States Government has persistently adhered to its traditional doctrines and principles, ignored realities in East Asia, and tried to force on our

Empire principles that she herself could not easily carry out. Despite the fact that we made a number of concessions, she maintained her original position throughout the negotiations, lasting for seven months, and refused to budge even one step. I believe that America's policy toward Japan has consistently been to thwart the establishment of a New Order in East Asia, which is our immutable policy. We must recognize that if we were to accept their present proposal, the international position of our Empire would be reduced to a status lower than it was prior to the Manchurian incident, and our very survival would inevitably be threatened. . . .

STATEMENT BY PRIVY COUNCIL PRESIDENT HARA YOSHIMICHI

In negotiating with the United States, our Empire hoped to maintain peace by making one concession after another. But to our surprise, the American position from beginning to end was to say what Chiang Kai-shek wanted her to say and to emphasize those ideals that she had stated in the past. The United States is being utterly conceited, obstinate, and disrespectful. It is regrettable indeed. We simply cannot tolerate such an attitude.

If we were to give in, we would give up in one stroke not only our gains in the Sino-Japanese and Russo-Japanese Wars, but also the benefits of the Manchurian incident. This we cannot do. We are loath to compel our people to suffer even greater hardships, on top of what they have endured during the four years since the China incident. But it is clear that the existence of our country is being threatened, that the great achievements of the Emperor Meiji would all come to naught, and that there is nothing else we can do. Therefore, I believe that if negotiations with the United States are hopeless, then the commencement of war, in accordance with the decision of the previous Imperial Conference, is inevitable.

I would like to make a final comment: there is no doubt that initial operations will result in victory for us. In a long-term war, however, it is necessary to win victories, on the one hand, while, on the other hand, we keep the people in a tranquil state of mind. This is indeed the greatest undertaking since the opening of our country in the nineteenth century. We cannot avoid a long-term war this time, but I believe that we must somehow get around this and bring about an early settlement. In order to do this, we will need to start thinking now about how to end the war. Our nation, governed by our magnificent national structure [*kokutai*], is, from a spiritual point of view, certainly unsurpassed in all the world. But in the course of a long-term war, there will be some people who will fall into erroneous ways. Moreover, foreign countries will be actively engaged in trying to undermine the morale of the people. It is conceivable that even patriotic individuals will on occasion attempt to do the same. It will be very difficult to deal with these people. I believe that it is particularly important to pay attention to our psychological solidarity. We must be very concerned about this. Be sure you make no mistakes in handling the inner turmoil of the people.

I believe that the proposal before us cannot be avoided in the light of present circumstances, and I put my trust in officers and men whose loyalty is supreme. I urge you to make every effort to keep the people in a tranquil state of mind, in order to carry on a long-term war.

CONCLUDING REMARKS BY PRIME MINISTER TŌJŌ HIDEKI

I would now like to make one final comment. At this moment our Empire stands at the threshold of glory or oblivion. We tremble with fear in the presence of His Majesty. We subjects are keenly aware of the great responsibility we must assume from this point on. Once His Majesty reaches a decision to commence hostilities, we will all strive to repay our obligations to him, bring the government and the military ever closer together, resolve that the nation united will go on to victory, make an all-out effort to achieve our war aims, and set His Majesty's mind at ease.

I now adjourn the meeting.

[During today's Conference, His Majesty nodded in agreement with the statements being made, and displayed no signs of uneasiness. He seemed to be in an excellent mood, and we were filled with awe.]

[Ike, *Japan's Decision for War*, pp. 263, 270, 281–83]

THE WAR'S GOALS

Japan's war planners envisioned a long struggle, in several stages, to achieve their new Asia. The new Asia was to be known as the Greater East Asia Co-Prosperity Sphere. The southern region would supply raw materials and surplus food, while Manchuria and northern China would provide the materials and basis for a heavy-industry complex. The rest of Asia would become a vast market, defended and integrated by Japanese planning, tools, skills, and arms.

DRAFT OF BASIC PLAN FOR ESTABLISHMENT OF GREATER EAST ASIA CO-PROSPERITY SPHERE

This document, produced in January 1942 as a secret planning paper by the Total War Research Institute, a body responsible to the army and cabinet, reveals the nature of long-range planning during the early war years before defeats began to take their toll on optimism and confidence.

Part I: Outline of Construction

The Plan. The Japanese empire is a manifestation of morality, and its special characteristic is the propagation of the imperial way. It strives but for the achievement of *hakkō ichiu*, the spirit of its founding. . . . It is necessary to foster the increased power of the empire, to cause East Asia to return to its original form of independence and co-prosperity by shaking off the yoke of Europe and America, and to let its countries and peoples develop their respective abilities in peaceful cooperation and secure livelihood.

The Form of East Asiatic Independence and Co-Prosperity. The states, their citizens, and resources, comprised of those areas pertaining to the Pacific, Central Asia, and the Indian Oceans formed into one general union, are to be established as an autonomous zone of peaceful living and common prosperity on behalf of the peoples of the nations of East Asia. The area including Japan, Manchuria, north China, lower Yangtze River, and the Russian Maritime Province forms the nucleus of the East Asiatic Union.

The above purpose presupposes the inevitable emancipation or independence of eastern Siberia, China, Indochina, the South Seas, Australia, and India.

Regional Division in the East Asiatic Union and the National Defense Sphere for the Japanese Empire. In the Union of East Asia, the Japanese empire is at once the stabilizing power and the leading influence. To enable the empire actually to become the central influence in East Asia, the first necessity is the consolidation of the inner belt of East Asia, and the East Asiatic Sphere shall be divided as follows for this purpose:

The Inner sphere—the vital sphere for the empire—includes Japan, Manchuria, north China, the lower Yangtze area, and the Russian Maritime area.

The Smaller Co-Prosperity Sphere—the smaller self-supplying sphere of East Asia—includes the inner sphere plus eastern Siberia, China, Indochina, and the South Seas.

The Greater Co-Prosperity Sphere—the larger self-supplying sphere of East Asia—includes the smaller co-prosperity sphere, plus Australia, India, and island groups in the Pacific. . . .

For the present, the smaller co-prosperity sphere shall be the zone in which the construction of East Asia and the stabilization of national defense are to be aimed at. After their completion there shall be a gradual expansion toward the construction of the Greater Co-Prosperity Sphere.

Outline of East Asiatic Administration. It is intended that the unification of Japan, Manchoukuo, and China in neighborly friendship be realized by the settlement of the Sino-Japanese problems through the crushing of hostile influences in the Chinese interior and through the construction of a new China in tune with the rapid construction of the Inner Sphere. Aggressive American and British influences in East Asia shall be driven out of the area of Indochina and the South Seas, and this area shall be brought into our defense sphere. The war with Britain and America shall be prosecuted for that purpose.

The Russian aggressive influence in East Asia will be driven out. Eastern Siberia shall be cut off from the Soviet regime and included in our defense sphere. For this purpose, a war with the Soviets is expected. It is considered possible that this northern problem may break out before the general settlement of the present Sino-Japanese and the southern problems if the situation renders this unavoidable. Next the independence of Australia, India, etc. shall gradually be brought about. For this purpose, a recurrence of war with Britain and her allies is expected. The construction of a Greater Mongolian State is expected during the above phase. The construction of the Smaller Co-Prosperity Sphere is expected to require at least twenty years from the present time.

The Building of the National Strength. Since the Japanese empire is the center and pioneer of Oriental moral and cultural reconstruction, the officials and people of this country must return to the spirit of the Orient and acquire a thorough understanding of the spirit of the national moral character.

In the economic construction of the country, Japanese and Manchurian national power shall first be consolidated, then the unification of Japan, Manchoukuo, and China shall be effected. . . . Thus a central industry will be constructed in East Asia, and the necessary relations established with the Southern Seas.

The standard for the construction of the national power and its military force, so as to meet the various situations that might affect the stages of East Asiatic administration and the national defense sphere, shall be so set as to be capable of driving off any British, American, Soviet or Chinese counterinfluence in the future. . . .

Chapter 3: Political Construction

Basic Plan. The realization of the great ideal of constructing Greater East Asia Co-Prosperity requires not only the complete prosecution of the current Greater East Asia War but also presupposes another great war in the future. Therefore, the following two points must be made the primary starting points for the political construction of East Asia during the course of the next twenty years: (1) preparation for war with the other spheres of the world and (2) unification and construction of the East Asia Smaller Co-Prosperity Sphere.

The following are the basic principles for the political construction of East Asia, when the above two points are taken into consideration:

a. The politically dominant influence of European and American countries in the Smaller Co-Prosperity Sphere shall be gradually driven out, and the area shall enjoy its liberation from the shackles hitherto forced upon it.

b. The desires of the peoples in the sphere for their independence shall be respected, and endeavors shall be made for their fulfillment, but proper and suitable forms of government shall be decided for them in consideration of military and economic requirements and of the historical, political, and cultural elements peculiar to each area.

It must also be noted that the independence of various peoples of East Asia should be based upon the idea of constructing East Asia as "independent countries existing within the New Order of East Asia" and that this conception differs from an independence based on the idea of liberalism and national self-determination.

c. During the course of construction, military unification is deemed particularly important, and the military zones and key points necessary for defense shall be directly or indirectly under the control of our country.

d. The peoples of the sphere shall obtain their proper positions; the unity of the people's minds shall be effected; and the unification of the sphere shall be realized with the empire as its center. . . .

Chapter 4: Thought and Cultural Construction

General Aim in Thought. The ultimate aim in thought construction in East Asia is to make East Asiatic peoples revere the imperial influence by propagating the imperial way based on the spirit of construction and to establish the belief that uniting solely under this influence is the one and only way to the eternal growth and development of East Asia.

And during the next twenty years (the period during which the above ideal is to be reached) it is necessary to make the nations and peoples of East Asia realize the historical significance of the establishment of the New Order in East Asia and, in the common consciousness of East Asiatic unity, to liberate East Asia from the shackles of Europe and America and to establish the common conviction of constructing a New Order based on East Asiatic morality.

Occidental individualism and materialism shall be rejected, and a moral worldview, the basic principle of whose morality shall be the imperial way, shall be established. The ultimate object to be achieved is not exploitation but co-prosperity and mutual help, not competitive conflict but mutual assistance and mild peace, not a formal view of equality but a view of order based on righteous classification, not an idea of rights but an idea of service, and not several worldviews but one unified worldview.

General Aim in Culture. The essence of the traditional culture of the Orient shall be developed and manifested. And casting off the negative and conservative cultural characteristics of the continent (India and China), on the one hand, and taking in the good points of Western culture, on the other, an Oriental culture and morality, on a grand scale and subtly refined, shall be created.

[IMTFE, International Prosecution Section, document 2402B, exhibit 1336 (Draft of Basic Plan for Establishment of Greater East Asia Co-Prosperity Sphere)]

316 JAPAN, ASIA, AND THE WEST

THE GREATER EAST ASIA CONFERENCE

In November 1943, two years after the outbreak of the Greater East Asia War, the cabinet of Tōjō Hideki convened the Greater East Asia Conference at the Diet Building in Tokyo to strengthen ties with leaders in occupied territories like the Philippines or allied countries like Thailand. Five such leaders, including the prime minister of Manchukuo, attended, and the conference issued a final declaration intended to challenge the principles enunciated in the Atlantic Charter, promulgated by President Franklin Roosevelt and Prime Minister Winston Churchill in the summer of 1941. The following excerpt from Prime Minister Tōjō's inaugural speech encapsulates the basic rationale for the Greater East Asia War.

INAUGURAL ADDRESS TO THE GREATER EAST ASIA CONFERENCE

During the past centuries, the British Empire, through fraud and aggression, acquired vast territories throughout the world and maintained her domination over other nations and peoples in the various regions by keeping them pitted and engaged in conflict one against another. On the other hand, the United States who, by taking advantage of the disorder and confusion in Europe, had established her supremacy over the American continent, spread her tentacles to the Pacific and to East Asia following her war with Spain. Then, with the opportunities afforded by the first World War, the United States began to pursue her ambition for world hegemony. More recently, with the outbreak of the present war, the United States has further intensified her imperialistic activities and has made fresh inroads into North Africa, West Africa, the Atlantic Ocean, Australia, the Near East, and even into India, apparently in an attempt to usurp the place of the British Empire. . . .

Movements for emancipation have occurred from time to time among the nations and people of East Asia, but due to the ruthless and tyrannical armed oppression by America and Britain or due to their malicious old trick of division and alienation for ruling other races, these patriotic efforts ended largely in failure. Meanwhile, Japan's rise in power and prestige was looked upon by America and Britain with increasing dislike. . . .

It is my belief that for all the peoples of greater East Asia, the present war is a decisive struggle upon whose outcome depends their rise or fall. It is only by winning through this war that they may ensure forever their existence in their greater East Asian home and enjoy common prosperity and happiness. Indeed, a successful conclusion of this war means the completion of the very task of constructing the new order of greater East Asia. . . .

It is my belief that to enable all nations each to have its proper place and to enjoy the blessings of common prosperity by mutual efforts and mutual help is the fundamental condition for the establishment of world peace. And I must furthermore say that to practice mutual help among closely related nations in one region, fostering one another's national growth and establishing a relationship of common prosperity and well-being, and, at the same time, to cultivate relations of harmony and concord with nations of other regions is the most effective and the most practical method of securing world peace. . . .

Japan is grateful to the nations of greater East Asia for the wholehearted cooperation which they are rendering in this war. Japan is firmly determined, by cooperating with them and by strengthening her collaboration with her allies in Europe, to carry on with indefatigable spirit and with conviction insure victory [in] this war, the intensity of which is expected to mount from day to day. Japan, by overcoming all difficulties, will do her full share to complete the construction of a greater East Asia and contribute to the establishment of world peace which is the common mission of us all.

[Tōjō, "Address to Greater East Asia Conference," pp. 1343–47]

DEFEAT

After initial spectacular successes at Pearl Harbor and in Southeast Asia, Japan suffered defeats in the central Pacific that led to the fall of the government of Tōjō Hideki and, after the United States's attack on Okinawa, to diplomatic initiatives to obtain peace terms from the Allies, resulting in the Potsdam Declaration in July 1945 demanding unconditional surrender. Although it was divided on the issue, the Japanese government was finally compelled by the atomic bombing of Hiroshima and Nagasaki to resolve the matter at a meeting of the Supreme War Council on August 14, at which the emperor insisted on making peace. The next day, he took the unprecedented step of broadcasting to the nation at large the following rescript.

IMPERIAL RESCRIPT ON SURRENDER

To our good and loyal subjects:

After pondering deeply the general trends of the world and the actual conditions obtaining in our Empire today, we have decided to effect a settlement of the present situation by resorting to an extraordinary measure.

We have ordered our Government to communicate to the Governments of the United States, Great Britain, China, and the Soviet Union that our Empire accepts the provisions of their joint declaration.

To strive for the common prosperity and happiness of all nations as well as the security and well-being of our subjects is the solemn obligation that has been handed down by Our Imperial Ancestors, and we lay it close to the heart.

Indeed, we declared war on America and Britain out of our sincere desire to ensure Japan's self-preservation and the stabilization of East Asia, it being far from our thought either to infringe upon the sovereignty of other nations or to embark upon territorial aggrandizement.

But now the war has lasted for nearly four years. Despite the best that has been done by everyone—the gallant fighting of the military and naval forces, the diligence and assiduity of our servants of the state, and the devoted service of our one hundred million people—the war situation has developed not necessarily to Japan's advantage, while the general trends of the world have all turned against her interest.

Moreover, the enemy has begun to employ a new and most cruel bomb, the power of which to do damage is, indeed, incalculable, taking the toll of many innocent lives. Should we continue to fight, it would not only result in an ultimate collapse and obliteration of the Japanese nation, but also it would lead to the total extinction of human civilization.

Such being the case, how are we to save the millions of our subjects, or to atone ourselves before the hallowed spirits of our Imperial Ancestors? This is the reason why we have ordered the acceptance of the provisions of the joint declaration of the powers.

We cannot but express the deepest sense of regret to our allied nations of East Asia, who have consistently cooperated with the Empire toward the emancipation of East Asia.

The thought of those officers and men as well as others who have fallen in the fields of battle, those who died at their posts of duty, and those who met with death and all their bereaved families, pains our heart night and day.

The welfare of the wounded and the war sufferers, and of those who have lost their homes and livelihood is the object of our profound solicitude. The hardships and sufferings to which our nation is to be subjected hereafter will be certainly great.

We are keenly aware of the inmost feelings of all you, our subjects. However, it is according to the dictates of time and fate that we have resolved to pave the way for a grand peace for all the generations to come by enduring the unendurable and suffering what is insufferable. Having been able to save and maintain the structure of the Imperial State, we are always with you, our good and loyal subjects, relying upon your sincerity and integrity.

Beware most strictly of any outbursts of emotion that may engender needless complications, and of any fraternal contention and strife that may create confusion, lead you astray and cause you to lose the confidence of the world.

Let the entire nation continue as one family from generation to generation, ever firm in its faith in the imperishableness of its divine land, and mindful of its heavy burden of responsibilities, and the long road before it. Unite your total strength to be devoted to the construction for the future. Cultivate the ways of rectitude, nobility of spirit, and work with resolution so that you may enhance the innate glory of the Imperial State and keep pace with the progress of the world.

All you, our subjects, we command you to act in accordance with our wishes.

Hirohito
(The Seal of the Emperor)
The fourteenth day of the eighth month of the twentieth year of Shōwa
(Countersignatures of the Ministers of State)

[Adapted from Jones, *Japan's New Order in East Asia,* pp. 474–75]

PART VI

Postwar Japan

At noon on August 15, 1945, the emperor of Japan announced the end of the war. With this unprecedented radio broadcast, Imperial Japan (1868–1945), too, came to an end, its military defeated, its empire in ruins, and its homeland in ashes. And yet within a few months, the moment of unconditional surrender had come to mean not only the end of a long and catastrophic war but also the bright beginning of a "new Japan," whose people had turned resolutely away from aggression and empire toward peace and democracy. This is what John Dower calls "embracing defeat" in his study of Japanese attitudes toward the galvanic changes that took place during the Allied Occupation following the war. Japanese frequently referred to the immediate postwar period as the "second opening" of the country and compared the postwar reforms with those that followed the Meiji Restoration. The reforms undertaken between 1945 and 1947 were indeed wide ranging, including everything from land reform and a new constitution to educational reform and the rights of women. Whereas the Meiji reforms had looked to the future to establish a modern society and state, the postwar reforms first had to sort out the past, identifying the factors that had led Japan to war so they could be altered to pave the way for democracy and peace.

Although the postwar reforms were carried out under the often strenuous leadership of the American Occupation, many of them drew on previous Japanese blueprints, and nearly all were implemented by Japanese officials. The most successful measures, like the land reform, also had the deepest Japanese base, whereas the American-style policies, like a decentralized police force and daylight saving time, disappeared when the Occupation did, sometimes sooner. In short, General Douglas MacArthur and his General Headquarters supplied the authority and the Japanese provided the energy for reconstruction and reform. The Occupation also used coercion, as it did in forcing the government to approve the constitution almost exactly as the Americans had written it, although it was the subsequent half-century of constitutionalism that established the constitution in Japanese belief and practice. Some aspects of Japan's reconstruction owed little to either Americans or Japanese. This was particularly true of the economic effects of the Korean War, which finally launched the disabled economy on its way to recovery after a series of Occupation policies had failed to do so.

Although Japanese (and Americans) habitually spoke of the postwar (*sengo*) period as if history had begun anew in 1945, in fact the rise of Japan was based on prewar antecedents as well as on the structural effects of mobilization for total war. These "transwar" factors helped account for the nature of Japan's postwar democracy and prosperity and were also linked to its longer modern history. This fact did not, however, alter the general sense of postwar Japan as a phoenix risen from the ashes. After a decade of recovery, Japan entered a period of "high growth" that lasted until the oil and dollar "shocks" of the early 1970s sent the economy into recession. At the same time, environmental pollution and other problems made the Japanese conscious of the costs of high growth, although this consciousness ebbed as the economy reached new heights in the 1980s. Japan became an economic superpower and creditor to the world, and millions of middle-class Japanese enjoyed the benefits of a "lifestyle revolution."

The boom ended in the 1990s. The conclusion of the Cold War made the world more complicated than it had seemed when the U.S.–Japanese alliance had occupied the central place on Japan's international agenda. Reestablishing relations with Asia now became a new focus, made more complicated by Japan's long silence concerning its colonial past in Korea and its wartime actions in China and other parts of Asia. In economic affairs, the "lost decade" began with the recession at the beginning of the 1990s, and by the decade's end, the media overflowed with gloomy talk of the "disappearance of Japan" and the "second defeat." The pessimism at the turn of the new century contrasted sharply with the optimism that had attended the beginning of the postwar period in 1945. Japan's postwar era, which had lasted for decades, appeared finally to be over.

Chapter 44

THE OCCUPATION YEARS, 1945–1952

In July 1945, the land, air, and sea forces of the United States were massed in the western Pacific, poised to invade a Japan already devastated by intensive aerial bombardments. On July 26, the Allied Powers issued the Potsdam Declaration, an ultimatum calling on the Japanese to surrender or face "utter destruction." Then, in rapid succession, on August 6 the United States dropped an atomic bomb on Hiroshima; on the eighth, the Soviet Union entered the war; on the ninth, the United States dropped another atomic bomb, this time on Nagasaki; on the tenth, the Japanese government opened communications with the Allied Powers; on the fourteenth, the Japanese government communicated to the Allied Powers its decision to surrender; and on the fifteenth, in an unprecedented radio address to the nation, the emperor announced the end of the war.

By August 28, American troops had begun to take up positions in Japan, and two days later General Douglas MacArthur arrived in Japan as the Supreme Commander for the Allied Powers. The American Occupation of Japan had begun.

POTSDAM DECLARATION

Proclamation by Heads of Governments, United States, United Kingdom, and China, July 26, 1945

1. We—the President of the United States, the President of the National Government of the Republic of China, and the Prime Minister of Great Britain, representing the hundreds of millions of our countrymen, have conferred and agreed that Japan shall be given an opportunity to end this war.

2. The prodigious land, sea, and air forces of the United States, the British Empire and of China, many times reinforced by their armies and air fleets from the west, are poised to strike the final blows upon Japan. This military power is sustained and inspired by the determination of all the Allied Nations to prosecute the war against Japan until she ceases to resist.

4. The time has come for Japan to decide whether she will continue to be controlled by those self-willed militaristic advisers whose unintelligent calculations have brought the Empire of Japan to the threshold of annihilation, or whether she will follow the path of reason.

5. Following are our terms. We will not deviate from them. There are no alternatives. We shall brook no delay.

6. There must be eliminated for all time the authority and influence of those who have deceived and misled the people of Japan into embarking on world conquest, for we insist that a new order of peace, security, and justice will be impossible until irresponsible militarism is driven from the world.

8. The terms of the Cairo Declaration shall be carried out, and Japanese sovereignty shall be limited to the islands of Honshu, Hokkaido, Kyushu, Shikoku, and such minor islands as we determine.

9. The Japanese military forces, after being completely disarmed, shall be permitted to return to their homes with the opportunity to lead peaceful and productive lives.

10. We do not intend that the Japanese shall be enslaved as a race or destroyed as a nation, but stern justice shall be meted out to all war criminals, including those who have visited cruelties upon our prisoners. The Japanese Government shall remove all obstacles to the revival and strengthening of democratic tendencies among the Japanese people. Freedom of speech, of religion, and of thought, as well as respect for the fundamental human rights, shall be established.

11. Japan shall be permitted to maintain such industries as will sustain her economy and permit the exaction of just reparations in kind, but not those which would enable her to rearm for war. To this end, access to, as distinguished from control of, raw materials shall be permitted. Eventual Japanese participation in world trade relations shall be permitted.

12. The occupying forces of the Allies shall be withdrawn from Japan as soon as these objectives have been accomplished and there has been established in

accordance with the freely expressed will of the Japanese people a peacefully inclined and responsible government.

13. We call upon the government of Japan to proclaim now the unconditional surrender of all Japanese armed forces and to provide proper and adequate assurance of their good faith in such action. The alternative for Japan is prompt and utter destruction.

[SCAP, Government Section, *Political Reorientation of Japan*, vol. 2, p. 413]

INITIAL OFFICIAL POLICIES, AMERICAN AND JAPANESE

INITIAL U.S. POLICY FOR POSTSURRENDER JAPAN: REQUIRED REFORMS

Although the Pacific War had ended much more abruptly in mid-August than U.S. foreign policy planners anticipated, they were already in the final stages of drafting a comprehensive postsurrender policy for defeated Japan. After being endorsed by President Harry S. Truman on September 22, this draft was well publicized in the foreign and Japanese press. Along with the Potsdam Declaration, the postsurrender policy served as basic guidance for General Douglas MacArthur, amplified by a more detailed and secret directive from the Joint Chiefs of Staff on November 4. In addition, Washington sent MacArthur numerous detailed position papers on a wide variety of political, economic, educational, and social reforms. This initial policy, exclusively American in formulation, was to be implemented by working through the organs of the existing Japanese government, although without necessarily endorsing them. By March 1946, seven months into the Occupation, when the Allies succeeded in joining policy discussions through the creation of the nine-member Far Eastern Commission in Washington, D.C., and the four-power Allied Council for Japan in Tokyo, the basic reforms were well advanced and firmly under American direction.

In tone, the initial U.S. policy was moderately reformist in its statement of general provisions for the democratization and demilitarization of Japanese institutions, thought, and culture. It reflected the expertise of foreign service officers and academic scholars who had language competence, living experience, and scholarly knowledge of Japan dating from the 1920s and 1930s. As reformers, their prime concern was to revive those democratic tendencies that had developed in pre-1930s Japan and to eliminate totalitarian measures and laws. Although opposed to revolution of any kind, the reformers endorsed punishment for war crimes, reorientation of Japanese values, and control of the mass media.

In contrast, the initial U.S. economic and fiscal policies were harsh and radical, calling for vast agrarian, labor, and corporate reform and for reparations.

The job of economic recovery was left strictly to Japan's devices, with no regard for its loss of empire, external resources, and foreign trade. These policies were the work of economists who had joined the official U.S. planning process in 1945 but had relatively little firsthand knowledge of Japan. They were heavily in favor of grassroots egalitarianism and against big business, believing that it had been a driving force in war and empire. For reasons of security, Okinawa, a prefecture that had been part of Japan proper since the 1870s, was retained as a key U.S. base and placed under direct American military rule until 1972. Most of the Kurile Islands, or Northern Territories, were lost to Soviet rule.

This initial policy was closely followed by General MacArthur and the members of the special staff sections that he set up in his General Headquarters, Tokyo, for liaison with the still-intact Japanese government. Indeed, they used its guidelines to order and, when possible, to persuade Japanese officials to carry out political, social, and economic reforms. This policy was the source for the first orders from the Supreme Command of the Allied Powers (SCAP) in the opening months of the Occupation to transform the Japanese government into a more open and democratic system, legalize labor unions, dissolve giant trusts, engage in agrarian reform, demobilize the armed forces, repatriate Japanese soldiers and civilians from liberated colonies and territories, and end state-sponsored Shinto. In late 1945, 200,000 American troops, arriving in several stages, were stationed at strategic points throughout Japan to ensure sole U.S. control of the military occupation. In early 1946, 37,000 British Commonwealth Forces joined the Americans. Whenever possible, MacArthur's staff sought out sympathetic Japanese to act as spokespersons, collaborators, and perfecters of envisioned reforms.

GENERAL MACARTHUR'S STATEMENT TO THE JAPANESE GOVERNMENT

Even more basic than Washington's policy was General Douglas MacArthur's interpretation of his orders. In one of his earliest and most dramatic moves, on October 4, 1945, he issued the Civil Liberties Directive, which ordered the annulment of all laws restricting political, civil, and religious liberties, as well as the release of political prisoners from prison. At a meeting on October 11, with the new prime minister, Shidehara Kijūrō, a member of the House of Peers and a former foreign minister, MacArthur simplified and reduced his policy guidelines to liberalization of the constitution and five major reforms, adding certain emphases of his own. Technically, he presented this as a public "statement" to the Japanese government and not as an order, but he clearly expected compliance. The only variation from Washington's priorities was MacArthur's emphasis on the emancipation of Japanese women, about which U.S. policy planners had had little to say except for a few lines on the importance of women and the home in nurturing and sustaining pacific values. In common with

Japanese officials, MacArthur expressed grave concern about the economy, warning the government to find ways of meeting basic needs and preventing social upheaval. He did not mention agrarian reform, but quickly corrected the oversight after receiving additional guidance from Washington.

Concerning Required Reforms, October 11, 1945

In the achievement of the Potsdam Declaration, the traditional social order under which the Japanese people for centuries have been subjugated will be corrected. This will unquestionably involve a liberalization of the Constitution.

The people must be freed from all forms of government secret inquisition into their daily lives which holds their minds in virtual slavery and from all forms of control which seek to suppress freedom of thought, freedom of speech, or freedom of religion. Regimentation of the masses under the guise or claim of efficiency, under whatever name of government it may be made, must cease.

In the implementation of these requirements and to accomplish purposes thereby intended, I expect you to institute the following reforms in the social order of Japan as rapidly as they can be assimilated.

1. The emancipation of the women of Japan through their enfranchisement—that being members of the body politic, they may bring to Japan a new concept of government directly subservient to the well-being of the home.

2. The encouragement of the unionization of Labor—that it may be clothed with such dignity as will permit it an influential voice in safeguarding the working man from exploitation and abuse and raising his living standard to a higher level; with the institution of such measures as may be necessary to correct the evils which now exist in child labor practices.

3. The opening of the schools to more liberal education—that the people may shape their future progress from factual knowledge and benefit from an understanding of a system under which government becomes the servant rather than the master of the people.

4. The abolition of systems which through secret inquisition and abuse have held the people in constant fear—substituting therefor [sic] a system of justice designed to afford the people protection against despotic, arbitrary, and unjust methods.

5. The democratization of Japanese economic institutions to the end that monopolistic industrial controls be revised through the development of methods which tend to ensure a wide distribution of income and ownership of the means of production and trade.

In the immediate administration field, I hope for vigorous and prompt action on the part of the government with reference to housing, feeding, and clothing the population in order to prevent pestilence, disease, starvation, or other major social catastrophe. The coming winter will be critical, and the only way to meet its difficulties is by the full employment in useful work of everyone.

[SCAP, Government Section, *Political Reorientation of Japan*, vol. 2, p. 741]

REVISED REPORT TO THE DIET AND PEOPLE BY THE SHIDEHARA CABINET

A month and a half later, on November 28, 1945, in an address to an extraordinary session of the Diet broadcast on national radio, Prime Minister Shidehara Kijūrō, who had taken office on October 9, indicated considerable acceptance of Occupation requirements, as did his subsequent legislative agenda. Although careful to express gratitude for the emperor's generosity and to extol virtue and peace over the sword and the gun, the address displayed overwhelming preoccupation with the economic problems of a devastated country and a demoralized people. And although Shidehara spoke of elections, the popular will, and the resumption of democracy, he spent little time on spiritual rehabilitation and did not call for collective repentance. As before, the Japanese seem to have had more interest in the causes of defeat than in the origins of the war or the victimization of their Asian neighbors.

It fills me with trepidation that unworthy as I am, I should have been commanded to head the government at a time when our nation is confronted with a difficult situation unparalleled in history. I only hope to conform to the august will of our Sovereign by doing everything in my power.

His Majesty the Emperor visited the Grand Shrine and the Imperial Mausoleum of Unebi and Momoyama on the thirteenth and fourteenth and the Imperial Tama Mausoleum on the seventeenth of this month to report personally the termination of the war. On express orders of the Sovereign, the journey was arranged as simply as possible, but it was attended with the most touching manifestations of the genuine feeling of the people who flocked all along the way to give sincere welcome to His Imperial Majesty. . . .

The war has been ended between Japan and the Allied Powers. But the way is still long to the final restoration of peace. In our foreign relations, we are incapacitated; we do not possess the power to uphold and carry out our policies, which we ourselves may believe to be just and equitable. Such is the inevitable lot of a vanquished nation. Of course, there exists in human society a universal sense of justice, also the inviolable right of public opinion to express itself. Only, as you may readily understand, the postwar conditions in all countries of the world are yet too abnormal to permit them to be brought into full play. Nevertheless, the ultimate power that controls the minds of men and regulates internal and external affairs of all countries must be neither the sword nor the gun but virtue.

There must be a rule of the rational spirit. That this is so will, I think, be admitted readily by world public opinion. What is wanted of our people today is not to be downhearted or bewildered but to march forth bravely toward the construction of a new Japan on the basis of justice and fair play. That is the only way, and there we may find hope for the future. . . .

Japan, having accepted the Potsdam Declaration, is obliged to remove all obstacles to the revival and development of democratic tendencies among the people. Such tendencies were gradually growing in this country following the Meiji Restoration, but they have been in recent years suppressed by reactionism. Fortunately, those tendencies have not been killed entirely; their roots remain alive; and it is expected that with the elimination of reactionary forces, they will recover rather easily and grow up again. We will see to it that no obstacle is put in the way of their growth and development.

First of all, it is necessary for us to allow the Diet to function fully as an organ for reflecting the popular will. For that purpose, there must be a full and fair election. When viewed from this standpoint, the existing Election Law does not fit in entirely with demands of the day. Accordingly, we are making haste to draft a plan for its revision which will be submitted to the present session of the Diet. In fact, that is one of the primary reasons for convening this extraordinary session.

Secondly, another prerequisite for the revival and growth of democracy lies in the renovation of the country's educational system. By wiping out all vestiges of militarism and ultranationalism from the schools, the government has set the goal of education in service to state and society by a complete development of the individual. Special emphasis is to be laid upon effecting an epoch-making advance in the training of the younger generation in civics. . . .

We must by all means renovate the system of social education and seek the elevation of the ethical standard; at the same time we must strive to keep alive in the hearts of all people the spirit of liberty and independence and the enthusiasm for resurgence and reconstruction.

Since its formation, the present government has annulled various laws and regulations restricting political, civil, and religious liberties in order to ensure the freedom of speech, thought, and religion. By abolishing the Higher Special Police, it has also paid particular attention to realizing a wholesome police administration such as will deserve the confidence and cooperation of the public. Liberalism calls for a sense of responsibility on the part of every individual; it does not imply lawlessness or absence of discipline. Any act detrimental to public order or morals will, of course, be dealt with according to law without the least leniency.

The most urgent task facing the country is the stabilization of the people's life. With the major portion of its production power destroyed and the national wealth exhausted almost to nothing on account of the war of these past years, it is imperatively necessary that we devise measures for stabilizing the people's life and put those measures in operation without delay. . . .

Deleted here are sections devoted to resolving food shortages; helping war victims; pro-
tecting nationals in North Korea, Taiwan, Sakhalin, and Manchuria; finding jobs for
an army of unemployed; explaining the necessity for commodity controls; and improving
land and sea transportation.

The rehabilitation of devastated areas is possible only through the revival of industries, which calls for the importation of necessary materials and which in turn requires the securing of funds for payment. It means we must develop export industry as much as we must increase the production of civilian goods. Since the success of industrial policies along these lines depends largely upon private initiative and enterprise, the government is doing away, as far as it is permitted by circumstances, with the hitherto existing controls.

However, in the face of the present extreme scarcity of materials and the terrible havoc that has been wrought by war, control is necessary on such basic commodities as iron, coal, and textiles in order to ensure the stability of national life and to accelerate economic recovery.

It is the policy of the government to limit control to these categories of goods and to exercise the control in such a manner as to leave as much room as possible for autonomous operation of industry on the basis of individual initiative and ingenuity.

It is believed that in the coming years Japan's economic activities will largely be carried on by medium and small industry and trade enterprises, to which the government should afford positive guidance and assistance.

On the other hand, it is most desirable to bring about a healthy growth of labor unions as a means of solving labor questions in a democratic way. To that end the government is now engaged in drafting the necessary laws. . . .

Finally, the War Inquiry Commission has been set up in the cabinet because it is believed necessary to probe the cause and the actual conditions that brought on defeat in order that egregious errors committed may not be repeated in the future.

I have now stated the views of the government concerning the major aspects of administration. Let us hope that our entire people, united as one man, will exhibit the most vigorous constructive spirit in response to the imperial wishes to consolidate the foundation of peace for all ages to come.

[*Contemporary Japan* 14 (April–December 1945): 289–93;
Nippon Times, November 28, 1945]

A NEW BASIC DOCUMENT:
THE 1947 CONSTITUTION

Liberalization of the constitution, including a change in the image and role of the emperor, became uppermost in the Occupation's early agenda for Japan.

Political parties, which had been ruled out of existence in October 1940, rebounded and were thriving in a variety of persuasions by the end of 1945. The mass media, although closely monitored by Occupation authorities, provided a wide forum for political debate and commentary. Some defended the Meiji constitution, while others pointed to flaws, such as the continued existence of the House of Peers. A few even proposed a new constitution. While MacArthur and his staff waited expectantly, Prime Minister Shidehara appointed a special cabinet committee to investigate the possible revision of the Meiji constitution.

On January 1, 1946, the issue of the emperor's being "sacred and inviolable" was partly settled by Emperor Hirohito's imperial rescript, which paid homage to the Five-Article Charter Oath of 1868 and renounced his divinity. "The ties that bind us together," he proclaimed, "rest in our shared history." When MacArthur and his staff learned in late January that the cabinet committee was on the whole satisfied with the existing constitution, including the position of the emperor, and envisioned only a few changes, they decided to prepare a model draft constitution for the government. This was done in secret, taking only six days, by a team of Americans working under the authority of General Courtney Whitney, the head of MacArthur's Government Section. MacArthur's personal participation was limited to a brief outline of four recommendations: (1) the emperor as head of state only, (2) total disarmament, (3) adequate budget powers for the Diet, and (4) an end to feudalism (by which he seems to have meant reform of the outmoded social order). The Americans, a diverse group headed by three lawyers, had guidelines from Washington, reference books, and their own political ideals. The urgency was only in part explained by the superficial nature of the cabinet proposals. Also relevant, MacArthur had just learned that the emperor, whom he had come to believe was crucial to social stability and to the success of the Occupation, had been named by Australia as the number-one war criminal. Moreover, the Far Eastern Commission, which was scheduled to begin meeting in March, had ultimate authority over revision of the constitution. The general, with visions of running for the U.S. presidency, wished to be perceived as the great man who remade Japan. Basic revision of the constitution was necessary to enhance his reputation, ensure democratization, and secure Japan's return to international society. In other areas, too, such as labor and land reform, SCAP resorted to pressure to extract more drastic reforms than Japanese officials were able or willing to produce.

The model draft—in effect a new constitution—was handed to Yoshida Shigeru, Shidehara's foreign minister, by a delegation from the Government Section on February 13, 1946, giving the Japanese only a short time to review the contents. General MacArthur was prepared, as General Whitney, the head of the Government Section delegation, told them, "to leave the sponsorship of the document to your government with his firm approval, but failing in that, if necessary, he is prepared to lay it before the people himself." Yoshida asked for secrecy, and Whitney agreed, reportedly "for your convenience and protection, not for that of the Supreme Commander."

Carefully translated into Japanese under watchful American eyes, the draft was thoroughly discussed over the next six months by Japan's cabinet, the Privy Council, the House of Peers, and the newly elected Lower House of the Diet, which included thirty-nine women representatives. Yoshida, who emerged as the new prime minister following the April elections and was the dominant political figure on the Japanese side for the duration of the Occupation, appeared frequently on the Diet floor to answer questions from all points of view, conservative to Communist. In the process, the text was rewritten into more idiomatic language, and the contents were somewhat amended by the Diet and the Far Eastern Commission. The constitution was promulgated by the emperor on November 3, 1946, and became effective on May 3, 1947. During the interval, an intensive six-month campaign of political education, designed by Americans and Japanese and utilizing all the media, explained and promoted the virtues of the new constitution. The story of how it actually came into existence, although suspected by the Japanese and the foreign press, was kept an official secret until the end of censorship controls in late 1949.

A close reading of the final text indicates that to a considerable extent, the makers had respected Japan's parliamentary tradition and history and its multiparty system but had replaced imperial sovereignty with popular sovereignty, by transforming the monarch into a "symbol emperor" who was not even the head of state. As Japanese liberals had long advocated, the drafters also expanded the authority of the Lower House, replaced the appointed House of Peers with the elected House of Councillors, stipulated that the prime minister be the head of the majority party and that all cabinet members be civilians, and required the election of prefectural governors. In the most American of the changes, they incorporated the concept of judicial review. The guarantee of inalienable rights was expanded from freedom of speech, conscience, and religion to include academic freedom, freedom of choice in marriage, and gender equality. Article 9 abolished the right to wage aggressive war or to maintain war matériel. Amending the new constitution was a difficult process, requiring a two-thirds vote of the Diet and a popular referendum. Before its promulgation, small changes in the wording, mutually acceptable to Diet members and Occupation authorities, gave Japan's courts in future years an opening to declare the right of self-defense. Neither the Americans nor the Japanese, however, dealt with another basic feature of Japanese political life: the central bureaucracy.

Even though its origins, manner of imposition, and content were controversial, Japan's 1947 constitution quickly became popular with a large segment of the population. Socialists, at first suspicious, became devoted supporters of article 9, which renounced war. For women, it was a gift in undercutting Japanese patriarchy and stemming militarism. Conservatives lamented the loss of the imperial mystique, social controls, and a standing army—to them the basic requisites of a normal state—but they could perhaps find some small comfort in the document's promulgation by means of imperial rescript.

Preamble

We, the Japanese people, acting through our duly elected representatives in the National Diet, determined that we shall secure for ourselves and our posterity the fruits of peaceful cooperation with all nations and the blessings of liberty throughout this land, and resolved that never again shall we be visited with the horrors of war through the action of government, do proclaim that sovereign power resides with the people and do firmly establish this Constitution. Government is a sacred trust of the people, the authority for which is derived from the people, the powers of which are exercised by the representatives of the people, and the benefits of which are enjoyed by the people. This is a universal principle of mankind upon which this Constitution is founded. We reject and revoke all constitutions, laws, ordinances and rescripts in conflict herewith.

We, the Japanese people, desire peace for all time and are deeply conscious of the high ideals controlling human relationship, and we have determined to preserve our security and existence, trusting in the justice and faith of the peace-loving peoples of the world. We desire to occupy an honored place in an international society striving for the preservation of peace, and the banishment of tyranny and slavery, oppression and intolerance for all time from the earth. We recognize that all peoples of the world have the right to live in peace, free from fear and want.

We believe that no nation is responsible to itself alone, but that laws of political morality are universal; and that obedience to such laws is incumbent upon all nations who would sustain their own sovereignty and justify their sovereign relationship with other nations.

We, the Japanese people, pledge our national honor to accomplish these high ideals and purposes with all our resources.

Chapter I: The Emperor

Article 1. The Emperor shall be the symbol of the State and of the unity of the people, deriving his position from the will of the people with whom resides sovereign power.

Article 2. The Imperial Throne shall be dynastic and succeeded to in accordance with the Imperial House Law passed by the Diet.

Article 3. The advice and approval of the Cabinet shall be required for all acts of the Emperor in matters of state, and the Cabinet shall be responsible therefor [*sic*].

Article 4. The Emperor shall perform only such acts in matters of state as are provided for in the Constitution and he shall not have powers related to government. . . .

Chapter II: Renunciation of War

Article 9. Aspiring sincerely to an international peace based on justice and order, the Japanese people forever renounce war as a sovereign right of the nation and the threat or use of force as means of settling international disputes.

In order to accomplish the aim of the preceding paragraph, land, sea, and air forces, as well as other war potential, will never be maintained. The right of belligerency of the state will not be recognized.

Chapter III: Rights and Duties of the People

Article 11. The people shall not be prevented from enjoying any of the fundamental human rights. These fundamental human rights guaranteed to the people by this Constitution shall be conferred upon the people of this and future generations as eternal and inviolate rights.

Article 13. All of the people shall be respected as individuals. Their right to life, liberty, and the pursuit of happiness shall, to the extent that it does not interfere with the public welfare, be the supreme consideration in legislation and in other governmental affairs.

Article 14. All of the people are equal under the law and there shall be no discrimination in political, economic or social relations because of race, creed, sex, social status, or family origin.

Peers and peerage shall not be recognized. . . .

Article 15. The people have the inalienable right to choose their public officials and to dismiss them.

All public officials are servants of the whole community and not of any group thereof.

Universal adult suffrage is guaranteed with regard to the election of public officials.

In all elections secrecy of the ballot shall not be violated. A voter shall not be answerable, publicly or privately, for the choice he has made.

Articles 16 to 18 guarantee the right of peaceful petition for redress of damages or removal of public officials and protection against bondage or involuntary servitude except as punishment for crimes.

Article 19. Freedom of thought and conscience shall not be violated.

Article 20. Freedom of religion is guaranteed to all. No religious organization shall receive any privileges from the State, nor exercise any political authority.

No person shall be compelled to take part in any religious act, celebration, rite or practice.

The state and its organs shall refrain from religious education or any other religious activity.

Article 21. Freedom of assembly and association as well as speech, press, and all other forms of expression are guaranteed.

No censorship shall be maintained, nor shall the secrecy of any means of communication be violated.

Article 22. Every person shall have freedom to choose and change his residence and to choose his occupation to the extent it does not interfere with the public welfare.

Freedom of all persons to move to a foreign country and to divest themselves of their nationality shall be inviolate.

Article 23. Academic freedom is guaranteed.

Article 24. Marriage shall be based only on the mutual consent of both sexes and it shall be maintained through mutual cooperation with the equal rights of husband and wife as a basis.

With regard to choice of spouse, property rights, inheritance, choice of domicile, divorce, and other matters pertaining to marriage and the family, laws shall be enacted from the standpoint of individual dignity and the essential equality of the sexes.

Article 25. All people shall have the right to maintain the minimum standards of wholesome and cultured living.

In all spheres of life, the State shall use its endeavors for the promotion and extension of social welfare and security, and of public health.

Article 26. All people shall have the right to receive an equal education correspondent to their ability, as provided by law.

All people shall be obligated to have all boys and girls under their protection receive ordinary educations as provided for by law. Such compulsory education shall be free.

Article 27. All people shall have the right and the obligation to work.

Standards for wages, hours, rest, and other working conditions shall be fixed by law.

Children shall not be exploited.

Article 28. The right of workers to organize and to bargain and act collectively is guaranteed.

Article 29. The right to own or hold property is inviolable.

Property rights shall be defined by law, in conformity with the public welfare.

Private property may be taken for public use upon just compensation therefor [sic].

Article 31. No person shall be deprived of life or liberty, nor shall any other criminal punishment be imposed, except according to procedure established by law.

Chapter IV: The Diet

Article 41. The Diet shall be the highest organ of state power, and shall be the sole law-making organ of the state.

Article 42. The Diet shall consist of two Houses, namely the House of Representatives and the House of Councillors.

Article 43. Both Houses shall consist of elected members, representatives of all the people.

Article 44. The qualifications of members of both Houses and their electors shall be fixed by law. However, there shall be no discrimination because of race, creed, sex, social status, family origin, education, property, or income.

Articles 45 to 64 provide for four-year terms of office for representatives, except for termination by dissolution of the Diet, and six-year terms for councillors, with half to be elected every three years. Provisions are also made for salaries, ordinary and extraordinary sessions of the Diet, general elections after dissolutions, quorums, rules for members, procedures for passing laws and budgets, records of proceedings, the selection by each house of a president and officers, official investigations, approval for the conclusion of treaties, the Diet's interpellation of the prime minister and ministers of state, and the impeachment of judges.

Chapter V: The Cabinet

Article 65. Executive power shall be vested in the Cabinet.

Article 66. The Cabinet shall consist of the Prime Minister, who shall be its head, and other Ministers of State, as provided for by law.

The Prime Minister and other Ministers of State must be civilians.

The Cabinet, in the exercise of executive power, shall be collectively responsible to the Diet.

The remaining articles, 67 to 75, deal with procedures and provisions in the case of a vacancy in the post of prime minister and with additional functions of the cabinet, such as the management of foreign affairs, the conclusion of treaties with the Diet's approval, the administration of the civil service, preparation of the budget, legal immunities while in office, and decisions on amnesty, commutation of punishment, and restoration of rights.

Chapter VI: The Judiciary

Article 76. The whole judicial power is vested in a Supreme Court and in such inferior courts as are established by law.

No extraordinary tribunal shall be established, nor shall any organ or agency of the Executive be given final judicial power.

All judges shall be independent in the exercise of their conscience and shall be bound only by this Constitution and the laws.

Articles 77 to 82 deal with the organization of the Supreme Court and the appointment, review, and tenure of its judges, as well as the high court's nomination of judges of the inferior courts. Trials and judgments are to be public except in cases in which the court "unanimously determines publicity to be dangerous to public order or morals."

Chapter VII, Finance (articles 83–91), provides for the Diet's administration of national finances, including new tax laws, expenditure of moneys, reserve funds, state ownership of the property of the Imperial Household, and the Diet's appropriation of all expenses of the Imperial Household. Article 89 bans the appropriation of public money or property for "the use, benefits or maintenance of any religious institution or association, or for any charitable, educational or benevolent enterprises not under the control of public authority."

Chapter VIII, Local Self-Government (articles 92–95), stipulates local autonomy for local public entities, the establishment of assemblies as "deliberate organs," and direct popular vote for chief executive officers of local entities and members of assemblies.

Chapter IX: Amendments

Article 96. Amendments to this Constitution shall be initiated by the Diet, through a concurring vote of two-thirds or more of all the members of each House and shall thereupon be submitted to the people for ratification, which shall require the affirmative vote of a majority of all votes cast thereon, at a special referendum or at such election as the Diet shall specify.

Amendments when so ratified shall immediately be promulgated by the Emperor in the name of the people, as an integral part of this Constitution.

Chapter X: Supreme Law

Article 97. The fundamental human rights by this Constitution guaranteed to the people of Japan are fruits of the age-old struggle of man to be free; they have survived the many exacting tests for durability and are conferred upon this and future generations in trust, to be held for all time inviolate.

Article 98. This constitution shall be the supreme law of the nation. . . .

Chapter XI, Supplementary Provisions (articles 100–103), deal with the enactment of such laws and procedures as were necessary for enforcement of the constitution on May 3, 1947. They also address the mechanics of transition periods for representatives, ministers of state, and judges.

[*Kodansha Encyclopedia of Japan*, vol. 2, pp. 9–13]

INTRODUCING A NEW CIVIL CODE

Basic among the changes required for enforcement of the constitution was a thorough revision of the civil, criminal, and other codes, which dated from the

1890s and were widely perceived by the reformers as barriers to further democratization. Revisions would affect every man, woman, and child in the exercise of individual freedom. What to conservative elites was a radical break with the social order and an affront to Japanese morals was to others a welcome and overdue liberation.

The Revised Civil Code and the Revised Family Registration Law, both of which went into effect on January 1, 1948, were the result of considerable interaction between like-minded radical reformers on the Japanese and American sides, particularly Japanese women's groups and American women officers in SCAP. They had to deal with the prejudices of not only Japanese men but also skeptical American men. For both women and younger sons, the new Civil Code was important to mandating changes in family law and inheritance rights. The main target was the *ie*, or household, as codified in the Civil Code of 1898. Critics saw it as a wrong turn in the Meiji enlightenment and charged that it enshrined a family system that in fact was based on idealized elite samurai households of late Tokugawa Japan. The old code recognized a single male patriarch, usually the eldest son, who possessed extensive rights and responsibilities. Under it, for example, the head of the household controlled all property or income. Women under twenty-five and men under thirty could marry only with parental consent. Because the patriarch could refuse to enter the bride's name on the family register, marriage was held as not the union of a man and a woman, but the admission of a bride to her husband's household. Divorce was difficult, and husbands retained legal custody of the children.

THE REVISED CIVIL CODE

The new Civil Code of Japan, a product of numerous sessions involving Japanese legal experts and Occupation authorities as well as public hearings in the Diet, is lengthy and detailed. Its underlying General Provision is "the individual dignity and the essential equality of the sexes." Book I promises the enjoyment of private rights, which "commence at birth." Book II deals with real rights, such as property and ownership; book III, with obligations, such as contracts, leases, and the hiring of services. Book IV, entitled "Relatives," describes marriage and property, and books V and VI discuss succession and wills. The code also establishes the Court of Domestic Relations, an innovation in Japanese law. The key passages establishing individual rights within the family are in book IV and focus on marriage, matrimonial property, divorce, parental power, adoption, and guardianship.

Book IV: Relatives

Article 731. A man may not marry until the completion of his full eighteen years of age, nor a woman until the completion of her full sixteen years of age.

Article 732. A person who has a spouse may not contract an additional marriage.

Article 733. A woman may not remarry unless six months have elapsed from the day of the dissolution or annulment of her previous marriage.

Article 750. Husband and wife assume the surname of the husband or wife in accordance with the agreement made at the time of the marriage.

Article 752. Husband and wife shall live together, and shall cooperate and aid each other.

Article 760. Husband and wife shall share the expenses of the married life with each other, taking into account their property, income and all other circumstances.

Article 762. Property belonging to either a husband or wife from a time prior to the marriage and property acquired during the subsistence of the marriage in his or her own name constitutes his or her separate property. . . .

Article 763. Husband and wife may effect by agreement divorce.

Article 766. In case a father and mother effect a divorce by agreement, the person who is to take the custody of their children and other matters necessary for the custody shall be determined by their agreement, and if no agreement is reached or possible, such matters shall be determined by the Court of Domestic Relations. . . .

Article 770. Husband or wife can bring an action for divorce only in the following cases:

1. If the other spouse has committed an act of unchastity;
2. If he or she has been deserted maliciously by the other spouse;
3. If it is unknown for three years or more whether the spouse is alive or dead;
4. If the other party is attacked with severe mental disease and recovery therefrom is hopeless;
5. If there exists any other grave reason for which it is difficult for him or her to continue the marriage. . . .

[SCAP, Government Section, *Political Reorientation of Japan*, vol. 2, p. 1261]

THE REVISED FAMILY REGISTRATION LAW

Together with the Revised Civil Code, the Revised Family Registration Law effectively abolished the *ie* system. It ended the old *koseki* (family register) system, further removing the power, influence, and obligations of the single male head of household (*koshu*). In previous practice, all household members were registered together; no changes were possible without the consent of the head. In the new system, registers were to be made up for each single individual or married couple. The family was to consist of a husband and wife and their minor children, both natural and adopted, as well as any children born out of wedlock but recognized by the father. Registers were required for marriage, birth, divorce, remarriage, parental power and guardianship, entry into or separation from the parental register, death and disappearance, and acquisition or loss of nationality. Any person could apply to the domestic relations courts to rectify statements, mistakes, or omissions. In short, every married couple was a separate family. Members were no longer under legal obligation to the head of the household. Any married man, not just an elder son, could head a family. An unmarried woman of adult age could create her own family and household. Bans on changing first and second names were lifted.

Article 6

Any Family Register shall be made up for each husband and wife who have their registered locality within the district of a City, Town or Village and their children whose surnames are the same as that of such husband and wife, but in cases where a family register is newly made up for any person having no spouse, it shall be made up for such person and his children whose surnames are the same as that of such person.

[SCAP, Government Section, *Political Reorientation of Japan*, vol. 2, p. 1076]

THE NEW EDUCATIONAL SYSTEM

Crucial to the Occupation's goal of reorientation and to the Japanese goal of reconstruction was educational reform. On its own initiative, the Ministry of Education took steps toward classroom and textbook reform while awaiting the formulation of the Occupation's policy. The initial moves of SCAP's education experts, starting in the first months of the Occupation, were to eliminate military drill and martial arts from the schools, ban militaristic and ultranationalist content from textbooks and inaugurate work on new textbooks, revise curricula to include social sciences, and extend educational opportunities in higher education. They were especially anxious to eliminate *shūshin* ethics, which emphasized loyalty and filial piety. The overall goal was to redefine the entire education system, extending from its organization and administration to its underlying ideology and classroom pedagogy.

Before the passage of the final reform legislation, as in labor laws, General MacArthur invited an education commission from the United States, which toured Japan in the spring of 1946. After much discussion with their counterparts on the Japan Education Reform Council, which had its own ideas, the commission offered extensive recommendations to MacArthur. They were heavily tinged with American models and much debated in the Diet, mass media, and academic journals. To accord with the new constitution, two basic laws were passed in March 1947: the School Education Act and the Fundamental Law of Education.

The new patterns became permanent, although they were challenged in following decades by critics who questioned the quality of standards and lamented the absence of moral education. As for language reform, a few Americans wanted to abolish the use of Chinese characters (*kanji*), but the Occupation left the final decision to the Japanese. The result was simplification of the existing system by reducing the number and strokes of characters for mass communication. Americans also pressed hard—though in the end unsuccessfully—for decentralizing the administration of education along the American pattern of local controls. They wanted more power for parent–teacher associations and less for the Ministry of Education in Tokyo. As a safeguard, the Occupation also insisted on a recision in 1948 of the 1890 Imperial Rescript on Education.

THE SCHOOL EDUCATION ACT

The School Education Act, passed on March 29, 1947, revamped the existing educational structure of multiple tracks into a single track system of six years at the primary level, three in junior high, three in senior high, and four-year universities—the 6/3/3/4 American pattern. It also required the provision of universities, higher professional schools, kindergarten, and special schools for the blind, deaf, and handicapped.

Article 17. The primary school shall aim at giving children elementary general education according to the development of their minds and bodies.

Article 18. In primary school education efforts shall be made to attain the principles mentioned in each of the following items. . . .

1. To cultivate a right understanding and the spirit of cooperation and independence in connection with relationships between human beings on the basis of the children's experience in social life both in and outside the schools.
2. To develop a proper understanding of the actual conditions and traditions both of children's native communities and of the country and, further, to cultivate the spirit of international cooperation.

Article 21. At elementary school, the textbooks to be used shall be those authorized by the Minister of Education, Science and Culture, or textbooks, copyrighted by the said Ministry.

Article 77. The kindergarten's aim shall be bringing up young children and developing their minds and bodies, and providing a suitable environment for them.

Article 78. In order to realize the aim in the foregoing Article, the kindergarten shall endeavor to attain the objective in each of the following items:

1. To cultivate everyday habits necessary for a sound, safe and happy life and to effect a harmonious development of bodily functions.
2. To make children experience group life and to cultivate a willingness to take part in it, as well as to foster the spirit of cooperation and independence.

3. To foster an understanding of the correct attitude toward social life and events.
4. To guide the correct usage of language and foster an interest in fairy-tales and picture books.
5. To cultivate an interest in expressing themselves through music, dance, pictures and other means.

[SCAP, Civil Information and Education Section,
Education in the New Japan, vol. 2, pp. 112–30]

THE FUNDAMENTAL LAW OF EDUCATION

The Fundamental Law of Education, part of which is quoted here, states the basic premises of a democratic education, using rhetoric similar to that of the preamble to the constitution and that of the new Labor Standards Law. Passed on March 31, 1947, it envisions the building of a peaceful and cultural state, and on a more practical level, it requires the extension of compulsory education from six to nine years and mandates coeducation.

Preamble

Having established the Constitution of Japan, we have shown our resolution to contribute to the peace of the world and welfare of humanity by building a democratic and cultural state. The realization of this idea shall depend fundamentally on the power of education.

We shall esteem individual dignity and endeavor to bring up the people who love truth and peace, while education aimed at the creation of culture, general and rich in individuality, shall be spread far and wide. . . .

Article 1: Aim of Education

Education shall aim at the full development of personality, striving for the rearing of the people, sound in mind and body, who shall love truth and justice, esteem individual value, respect labor and have a deep sense of responsibility, and be imbued with the independent spirit, as builders of a peaceful state and society.

Article 3: Equal Opportunity in Education

The people shall all be given equal opportunities for receiving education according to their ability, and they shall not be subject to educational discrimination on account of race, creed, sex, social status, economic position, or family origin. . . .

Article 4: Compulsory Education

The people shall be obligated to have boys and girls under their protection receive nine years' general education. . . .

Article 5: Coeducation

Men and women shall esteem and cooperate with each other. Coeducation, therefore, shall be recognized in education.

[SCAP, Civil Information and Education Section,
Education in the New Japan, vol. 2, pp. 109–11]

LABOR UNIONS

As in educational reform, the Occupation pressed on with more drastic labor and land laws than had been contemplated by prewar Japanese labor leaders, agrarian reformers, government bureaucrats, or, as it turned out, policy makers in Washington. When the Japanese government was slow to act on its own to carry out social reconstruction, the Occupation stepped in. This pattern of pressure, resistance, compliance—or active seizure of opportunity—was repeated many times.

In accordance with the Occupation's initial goals, labor unions and collective bargaining were legalized by the end of 1945 when the Trade Union Law was approved by the Diet on December 21. It guaranteed the right to organize, bargain collectively, and strike. By September 1946, the Occupation not only was sponsoring innovative welfare legislation and a more effective means of worker–manager mediation, but also was promoting stronger labor legislation.

THE LABOR STANDARDS LAW

The Labor Standards Law (enacted, as were so many other laws at this time, to accord with the new constitution) was passed by the first postwar Diet on April 1, 1947. The Japanese drafters, who were closely monitored by SCAP experts, were familiar with the conventions of the International Labor Organization and U.S. labor practice, as well as the history of labor repression in Japan. The final law was a comprehensive labor protection code setting minimum standards for contracts, wages, working hours and conditions, paid holidays and annual vacations, safety and sanitation, and accident compensation—and singling out women and minor workers for special attention. Its aims were to offer workers a better life under a capitalist democracy and to help counter elitist attitudes toward the working class. Police authority was eliminated from labor affairs.

Article 1 (Principle of Working Conditions). Working conditions should meet the need of the worker who lives a life worthy of a human being.

The standard of working conditions affixed by this law is minimum. Therefore parties of labor relations must not reduce working conditions with the excuse of this standard and, instead, should endeavor to raise the working conditions.

Article 2 (Decision of Working Conditions). Working conditions should be decided by the worker and employer on an equal basis.

The worker and employer must abide by the collective agreement, rule of employment, and labor contract and must discharge their respective duties faithfully.

Article 3 (Equal Treatment). No person shall discriminate against or for any worker by reason of nationality, creed, or social status in wages, working hours, and other working conditions.

Article 4 (Equal Wages for Men and Women). The employer shall not discriminate women against men concerning wages by reason of the worker being women.

Article 5 (Prohibition of Forced Labor). The employer shall not force workers to work against their will by means of violence, intimidation, imprisonment, or any other unfair restraint on the mental or physical freedom of the workers.

Article 7 (Guarantee for the Exercise of Civil Rights). The employer shall not refuse when the worker requires necessary time to exercise franchise and other civil rights or to execute public duty during the working hours. However, the employer may change the required time as far as the change does not hinder the exercise of the right or the execution of public duty.

Further detailed provisions for working hours, rest days, recesses, women and minor workers, minimum age, restrictions on dangerous work, and the like follow.

[SCAP, Government Section, *Political Reorientation of Japan*, vol. 2, pp. 872–84]

RURAL LAND REFORM

Even more than labor legislation, agricultural reform went beyond the initial policy of the United States. The basic law in 1947 was heavily influenced by the views of the non-American members of the Allied Council and was considered key to the democratization of Japan. There was wide agreement in Japan, even among conservatives, that something more fundamental was needed. Ironically, although the rural land reform was attacked in the United States Congress as socialistic, it helped create a strong core of conservative support for the subsequent Liberal Democratic Party, which formed in 1955.

RURAL LAND REFORM DIRECTIVE

Douglas MacArthur's first order on agricultural reform was issued on December 9, 1945, to the Japanese government.

1. In order that the Imperial Japanese Government shall remove economic obstacles to the revival and strengthening of democratic tendencies, establish respect for the dignity of man, and destroy the economic bondage which has enslaved the Japanese farmer to centuries of feudal oppression, the Japanese Imperial Government is directed to take measures to ensure that those who till the soil of Japan shall have a more equal opportunity to enjoy the fruits of their labor.

2. The purpose of this order is to exterminate those pernicious ills which have long blighted the agrarian structure of a land where almost half the total population is engaged in husbandry. The more malevolent of these ills include:

   a. Intense overcrowding of land. Almost half the farm households in Japan till less than one and one-half acres each.
   b. Widespread tenancy under conditions highly unfavorable to tenants. More than three-fourths of the farmers in Japan are either partially or totally tenants, paying rentals amounting to half or more of their annual crops.
   c. A heavy burden of farm indebtedness combined with high rates of interest on farm loans. Farm indebtedness persists so that less than half the total farm households are able to support themselves on their agriculture income.
   d. Government fiscal policies which discriminate against agriculture in favor of industry and trade. Interest rates and direct taxes on agriculture are more oppressive than those in commerce and industry.
   e. Authoritative government control over farmers and farm organizations without regard for farmer interests. Arbitrary crop quotas established by disinterested control associations often restrict the farmer in the cultivation of crops for his own needs or economic advancement. Emancipation of the Japanese farmer cannot begin until such basic farm evils are uprooted and destroyed.

3. The Japanese Imperial Government is therefore ordered to submit to this Headquarters on or before 15 March 1946, a program of rural land reform. This program shall contain plans for:

   a. Transfer of land ownership from absentee land owners to land operators.
   b. Provisions for purchase of farm lands from nonoperating owners at equitable rates.

   c. Provisions for tenant purchase of land at annual installments commensurate with tenant income.

   d. Provisions for reasonable protection of former tenants against reversion to tenancy status. Such necessary safeguards should include:

      (1) Access to long- and short-term farm credit at reasonable interest rates.

      (2) Measures to protect the farmer against exploitation by processors and distributors.

      (3) Measures to stabilize prices of agricultural produce.

      (4) Plans for the diffusion of technical and other information of assistance to the agrarian population.

      (5) A program to foster and encourage an agricultural cooperative movement free of domination by non-agrarian interests and dedicated to the economic and cultural advancement of the Japanese farmer.

   e. The Japanese Imperial Government is requested to submit in addition to the above, such other proposals as it deems necessary to guarantee to agriculture a share of the national income commensurate with its contribution.

[SCAP, Government Section, *Political Reorientation of Japan*, vol. 2, p. 575]

VIEWS OF YOSHIDA SHIGERU

In his memoirs, Yoshida Shigeru offered an interesting account of land reform from a conservative's viewpoint. Over the years, he was involved with the question as a cabinet minister (September 1945–May 1946) and the prime minister (May 1946–May 1947, October 1948–December 1954).

The reform of agriculture was . . . [a] major objective of Occupation policy. Viewed from the standpoint of the Allied Powers, the Japanese land system was not only feudalistic, but it weakened the national economy while providing the militarists with one of their firmest bases of support. The agrarian half of the nation represented a reservoir of soldiers and cheap labor. Rural landlords impeded the democratization of Japan equally with the militarists, the financiers, and the bureaucracy. To end this state of affairs by liberating the agricultural classes and raising their living standards was, therefore, regarded by the Occupation authorities as a vital step in bringing about the demilitarization and democratization of Japan.

We had, indeed, anticipated that this would be the case. The agricultural problem had been a major issue confronting successive Japanese Cabinets since the early years of the century. Furthermore, agricultural controls enforced during the Pacific war had the effect of placing small farmers in a specially favored position in the country, so that by 1945 the existing state of affairs, whatever the outward form might suggest, differed to a marked degree from what was widely imagined abroad from available textbooks on the subject. It was true that the change had been occasioned by the need to maintain the food supply during the period of hostilities. But that objective became even more pressing with the end of the war, so that Japan's agricultural system would in any event have had to be reconsidered in order to bring it closer in line with the actual situation.

That circumstance led to the passing of the first agricultural reforms at the time of the Shidehara Cabinet, when Mr. Kenzō Matsumura was Minister of Agriculture, and before any SCAP directive had been issued on the subject. . . . Two main points [of the reform] were the substitution of payment of farm-rent in money, instead of in kind as previously, and the restriction of individual ownership of agricultural land to three *chō* (one *chō* being approximately 2.45 acres), beyond which amount the plan made it compulsory for landowners to turn over the land to the tenants, a revolutionary step at the time.

This Japanese plan was doubtless evolved with knowledge of GHQ's [General Headquarters] intentions to seize the opportunity of solving the agricultural problem that had been troubling the nation for so long. But even so it met with a chorus of objections when it was originally outlined at one of our Cabinet meetings. In particular, the compulsory acquisition of agricultural land by tenants was a revolutionary idea never before proposed in Japan. . . . In the event, the plan was endorsed by the Cabinet after the limit of individual holdings had been raised from three to five *chō*. . . .

Although, as I have mentioned, agricultural land reform was one of the more important Occupation objectives, both the Allied Council for Japan and General MacArthur's headquarters adopted a somewhat more leisurely attitude to this question than toward other problems and appeared disposed to give the question serious consideration before proceeding to take any definite steps. This was, no doubt, because reforms and changes connected with farm land had invariably been accompanied by a good deal of trouble and rural unrest, and sometimes even by bloodshed, in other countries. Thus it happened that the first plan for agricultural reform proposed by Mr. Matsumura must not only have furnished GHQ with a practical blueprint for carrying out the reform, but also have been instructive in indicating to the Occupation authorities, at the time of its publication, that, while some objected to it as being too radical, the number of those in Japan who expressed a contrary opinion—that the plan did not go far enough—was by no means small. . . .

The law based upon the Matsumura plan was promulgated before the end of 1945 and became effective from February 1946. That part of the measure dealing with the compulsory transfer of land was not enforced because General MacArthur's headquarters thought the provisions of the law on that point could be improved upon; wherefore land ownership remained unchanged until the implementation of the second agricultural land reform.

Officially, GHQ was waiting for the Japanese Government's reply to be submitted by 15 March 1946, but, unofficially, the Occupation authorities had early indicated to the Ministry of Agriculture flaws which they had detected in the details of the first agricultural reform. These were made public for the first time at a press conference held by William J. Gilmartin and Wolf I. Ladejinsky, the experts within the GHQ in charge of the reform, on 12 March 1946, just before the deadline fixed for the Government's reply to SCAP, and consisted of two points: that the maximum holding of five *chō* was too large and would leave too many tenant farmers in the same position as before, and that, in order to ensure that land transfers were carried out and to shorten the period for this to be accomplished, the Government itself should act as agent instead of transfers being direct between landlords and tenants. . . .

The final details of the reform measure were decided upon in the course of our negotiations with GHQ, and then brought together and communicated to the Japanese Government, not officially as a directive, but more privately in the form of advising us of their opinion. Apparently General MacArthur took that step because he thought that such an undertaking as agricultural land reform—affecting as it did the fundamental economic structure of our society—could only bear fruit if it was planned by the Japanese themselves and of a nature genuinely acceptable to the Japanese people. I think that the methods employed in this matter of land reform, at least, enabled GHQ and the Japanese Government to work well together which was not always the case.

The general election was held on 10 April 1946, as a result of which the Shidehara Cabinet resigned on 22 April. By that time the food shortage had become acute and social unrest had grown. What was called "Food May Day" was held on 19 May, following the usual May Day observance on 1 May, and the political scene at the time appeared mainly composed of masses of red flags and demonstrators. In such an atmosphere . . . the first Yoshida Cabinet came into being on 22 May, with agricultural land reform now a matter of pressing importance. . . .

The major points of the reform as finally agreed upon were that all agricultural land belonging to landowners who did not reside in the districts where the land was located, and which was being tilled solely by tenants, was to be transferred to the tenants; and that individual ownership of tenant land was to be limited to the average of one *chō* (four *chō* in Hokkaido); that the total amount of agricultural land to be owned individually, including tenant land was to be limited to three *chō* (twelve *chō* in Hokkaido); that it was to be made compulsory for land beyond that limit to be sold to the Government for resale to tenant farmers; and that payment to landowners for their requisitioned land was to be made in Government bonds. A bill embodying these provisions was introduced into the Lower House of the Diet on 7 September 1946 and passed both Houses without amendment on 11 October 1946. . . .

The final result [when implemented in 1950] was that two million *chō* of agricultural land were requisitioned from some 1,500,000 landowners and turned over to those who had previously been tenant farmers, numbering around four million persons. In addition to which operation 450,000 *chō* of pasturage and 1,320,000 *chō* of uncultivated land were also disposed of in the same manner. Tenant-tilled land, which until that time had accounted for 46 percent of Japan's agricultural land, diminished to 10 percent. The tenant farmer practically ceased to exist, while the great landowners of the old days and absentee landlords passed into history.

The effects of such sweeping changes on Japan's agriculture as a whole are, of course, incalculable. The agricultural land reform was, in fact, a revolutionary measure, and to have carried it out without any major friction, and certainly without anything in the nature of serious disturbance or bloodshed, was an achievement that cannot be dismissed lightly, particularly when one remembers the unsettled state of the country at that time. The possible outbreak of such troubles had been feared by some during the deliberations on the reform bill in the Diet, but the event showed our apprehension to have been groundless.

There occurred, of course, a certain amount of confusion in some districts; there were bound to be details in the reform plans that were open to criticism. But no one can deny that the reform contributed immeasurably toward raising the standards of living of the agricultural classes, or that the effects this stabilization and improvement of life in the rural areas had on the social unrest in Japan as a whole were profound. This was one of the immediate benefits of the land reform. And when we think of what that fact saved us from, we should also remember at the same time the sacrifice paid by the landowners and their uncomplaining attitude throughout. Had they been so minded, they could have expressed their discontent in political and social activities of no uncertain kind, that would not only have hindered the implementation of the reform, but would have endangered still further the precarious state of our country. It is not too much to say that it is to the admirable behavior of the landowners that the success of the reform is largely due. . . .

Following the signing of the San Francisco Peace Treaty, there were those who demanded, and others who vaguely expected, that as the agricultural land reform had been enacted with the strong support and encouragement of the Occupation authorities, some of its measures should be repealed. We decided, on the contrary, to incorporate the principles of the reform into the body of our national laws by combining them in one law, for which purpose a bill was introduced during the thirteenth session of the Diet held in 1952, while my third Cabinet was in office, under the title of the Agricultural Land Bill. This was passed by both Houses by an overwhelming majority, including the Socialists, and became law on 15 July 1952.

The agricultural land reform thus enacted and enforced does not by any means solve all the problems which confront Japanese agriculture, if only for the simple reason that there is not enough farm land in Japan to provide our large rural population with a sufficiently high standard of living. But the aim of the reform lies in helping to increase total agricultural production in order to permit the raising of the standard of living of those engaged in agriculture. The reform is not an end in itself, but a means.

[Yoshida, *The Yoshida Memoirs*, pp. 196–203]

ECONOMIC STABILIZATION AND RECONSTRUCTION

Economic reconstruction along capitalist lines was a prime goal of the first postwar cabinets. While Japan floundered in economic malaise, the Occupation, as ordered, at first gave little positive help beyond shipments of food. Instead, SCAP, in the name of economic democratization, demanded the dissolution of family-controlled holding companies (*zaibatsu*), the enactment of an antimonopoly law, and the payment of harsh reparations. As Japanese bureaucrats, politicians, and businessmen struggled to overcome high rates of inflation and revive domestic production, they drew selectively from prewar experiences in mobilizing the economy to fight the Great Depression and the more recent military-led mobilization for total war. The state's economic guidance of the private sector was already a fixed pattern, although the degree and extent of it were contested, as was the shift toward heavy industry and mass production. Still to be sorted out, however, were postwar interrelationships among state, capital, and labor in the Japanese model of modified capitalism and the creation of an industrial policy geared exclusively to peacetime industries and the revival of foreign trade.

POSTWAR RECONSTRUCTION OF THE JAPANESE ECONOMY

In September 1946, the Special Survey Committee, a study group formed in the Ministry of Foreign Affairs as the war was ending in mid-August 1945, issued an extensive report, *Postwar Reconstruction of the Japanese Economy*, with copies to SCAP and Japanese government agencies. This was shortly after the cabinet of Yoshida Shigeru had set up the Economic Stabilization Board (ESB; forerunner of the Economic Planning Agency, 1955) to deal with Japan's shattered economy. The various members included bureaucrats and economists of varying opinions and expertise, as well as businessmen and a journalist. The group took note of Japan's wartime state central controls and the necessity of postwar economic democratization but retained the concept of economic planning. Contrary to the emphases in the initial policy of the

United States, their report stressed the promotion of heavy industries and a return to export-driven trade as the best way to create a viable, self-sustaining economy and genuine worker livelihood. Years later, in 1991, when preparing the report for an English-language edition, Ōkita Saburō—by then a veteran economic planner of world renown and a former foreign minister—characterized Japanese "postwar economic development" as "catch-up capitalism" or "latecomer capitalism" and justified planning as a necessary complement to the operation of free-market mechanisms. Others might reasonably argue that Japan, until 1943 the world's fastest-growing economy, was far more advanced than Ōkita cared to admit and that state involvement in economic planning had preceded mobilization for total war.

The report, which gives great insight into the thinking of many of Japan's most influential economists, was more concerned with Japan's near or mid-future than with solving immediate problems of food supplies and inflation. The purpose was to help generate economic rehabilitation while refashioning the economy along modified capitalist and socialist lines and ridding it of any militaristic and feudalistic vestiges. Divided into two parts, "Prerequisites for Reconstruction" and "Measures for Reconstruction," and backed up with statistics, the report analyzes Japan's economy under the new conditions of defeat and occupation, including the loss of empire. It also addresses the postwar international environment and lists special Japanese characteristics. Throughout the report are constant reminders that Japan has a large population, is poor in natural resources, and, in some ways, is still backward in economic development. Since foreign trade was deemed vital, the report offers recommendations to make Japan more competitive once it returns to world markets. One of the major problems it does not address, although Japan had had ample experience with it, is the impact of industrialization on the environment.

Difficulties in the Resumption of Production

The resumption of production is a most basic task for the present-day Japanese economy. Without an increase in production, no improvement in the national life can be expected. There can be no real democratization where there is no substantive guarantee of the people's standard of living. The production of essential goods has decreased of late to a fraction of the figures registered during the war. If production in general remains stagnant at such low levels for a long time, then even the production of the export commodities required to pay for minimally required food imports cannot be realized.

The fundamental reasons why things have come to this pass are the abstraction of people's behavior due to the defeat in the war and their psychological uncertainty owing to the sharply changed environment. Further, the various new conditions stated above—the loss of territory, the effect of war damages, the progress of inflation, the burden of reparations, and food shortages—are all powerful factors obstructing the resumption of productive activities.

Meanwhile the government, which has lost the capability of comprehensive planning and leadership, has remained an idle onlooker to the collapse of the wartime control system and the resultant confusion in the economic community. . . . Thus the whole productive structure of the Japanese economy has come to a standstill, as if a big wheel has stopped turning, and cannot be reactivated unless some well-coordinated, planned, and systematic measures are taken.

The report proceeds to list the many problems of resuming production, among them the loss of independence, the sluggish production of basic materials, the interruption of commodity imports, the progress of inflation, labor unrest, an arrested entrepreneurial system, and the conversion from wartime heavy industry to peacetime civilian production. The agricultural sector was confronted by many difficulties, although less so than urban areas: consumption of productive capital, mass return of labor to rural areas, indifference to improving farm management, and delays in shipments of rationed foods. Nonetheless, there were favorable conditions in rural Japan, such as advances in mechanical engineering, experience and training in a planned economy, relief from military burdens, mechanization of agriculture, progress toward cooperative farming, and the rise of democracy.

The Rise of Democracy

Even though touched off by outside forces, the rise of democracy is a step forward that will ultimately bring about a fundamental gain in the nation's productive capacity through an increase in the number of people who will have self-consciousness and who will take responsibility for themselves, although the change may give rise to confusion in various forms during the transitional period.

The authors next offer several recommendations for the direction that Japan must follow to achieve reconstruction (some of the named reforms were already under way). For example, economic democratization and the upgrading of technological standards, as in the rationalization of agricultural production, are necessary—"that is, the abolition of oppressive tenant relations and the enlargement of managerial scale"—as is the promotion of manufacturing industries and foreign trade. The various measures of democratic reconstruction, which were governed by external "American coloration" of disarmament and destruction of Japanese militarism as well as by internal demands, required the prohibition of industrial monopoly, limitations on government intervention in the economy "in order to encourage free competition in the private sector," the encouragement of the growth of trade unions, the modernization of agriculture, assurance of an equality of national life, bans on international cartels and restrictive international contracts, and equal opportunity for foreign capital. Basic to the thinking of this committee were the promotion of manufacturing, overall planning, and resumption of foreign trade.

Promotion of Manufacturing Industries and Foreign Trade

The starting point for the democratization of the Japanese economy is the modernization of agriculture and the improvement of farmers' living standards. In order to realize these objectives, the excess of farmers relative to arable land has to be eliminated, and farmers have to be provided with arable land of optimal size. In other words, it is necessary to extract surplus population from farm villages. But as most of the population thus extracted will have no place to go other than the manufacturing industries, the promotion of manufacturing industries is regarded as indispensable for furnishing a specific basis for economic democratization.

Meanwhile, in order to import food, clothing, and other necessary goods in large quantities every year, it is necessary to promote exports to pay for these imports. Japan is, however, endowed very poorly with natural resources within the country. The nation has only manpower in abundance. In case direct exports of labor are not permitted, emphasis has to be placed on the export of industrial goods by changing labor into commodities. The promotion of manufacturing industries is needed from this standpoint, too. As to which industries should be developed in Japan hereafter, it will be appropriate from the viewpoint of international division of labor to choose those that require as much labor as possible in manufacture and do not allow easy automation of the production process, based on the condition that labor is abundant but natural resources are in short supply.

The report attempts to sort out what Japan should and could do on its own initiative and from internal demand while governed by conditions of external control and mandated reform. Sooner or later, Japan would return to the "world international community" and participate in the 1944 Bretton Woods Agreement for trade and investment and the recently established International Monetary Fund. Because Japan's industries were in an intermediate stage of development, Japan would "be required for the time being to take part in international labor division by combining cheap labor with relatively high-level technology and to increase wages gradually, backing up such measures with mechanization of production processes and upgrading technological standards based on future capital accumulation." Here the report stresses the importance of a planned economy.

Planning required careful preparation, beginning with a scientific study of the causes for the failure of the wartime controlled economy. Data should also be gathered about other planned economies, particularly the Soviet Union's five-year plans, the United States's New Deal, and Britain's postwar policies. Properly trained planning experts and a "large-scale, powerful, and comprehensive research organ, either private or governmental," are needed. Whether Japan's economy became capitalist or socialist in the

future, it would require "well-prepared statistical data" and statistical publications. A
planned economy was inevitable.

Toward a Planned Economy

A comprehensive and specific year-to-year reconstruction program will have to
be formulated in order to revive the Japanese economy from the extreme destitution in which it finds itself now. The waste of economic power that would
result from allowing laissez-faire play to market forces will not be permitted in
order that all the meager economic power remaining may be concentrated in
a direction toward reproduction on an enlarged scale and that the process of
reconstruction may be expedited. . . .

Contents of a Planned Economy

The specific process of devising a plan for economic reconstruction would be,
first, to fix a target living standard to be attained and the time period during
which this target should be reached; then, taking as a starting point a demand
and supply plan for essential materials and also a national land reconstruction
plan formulated on the basis of the target and time period, to work out in a coordinated manner programs regarding production, exports and imports, funds,
public finance, employment, and so on. . . . Such a plan should not be drawn
in the bureaucratic and coercive way, as was done in the past, but would need
to be formulated in a democratic manner that would fully reflect views in
private business or at the labor site. Striving for the creation of the objective
conditions would allow the achievement of a planned economy by placing a
clear-cut responsibility on the parties concerned for the materialization of the
plan formulated by such a democratic process and also by constantly reviewing
actual performance in order to prevent the plan from being too distant from
reality. The scale and speed of Japanese economic construction would be affected greatly by the form of government taken by the nation and also by the
political party in power. Therefore an economic program ought to be drawn
up on the basis of the outlook of political situations and also in accordance with
the need to contrive for its realization at the political level by taking into consideration the form of government that would promote the accomplishment of
the program. Only after a comprehensive grasp of such interactive relations
between politics and the economy could a truly realistic economic program be
drawn up.

A truly democratized economy, the report continues, should guarantee freedom of eco-
nomic activity and a minimum standard of living and should provide social security and
welfare. To avoid social unrest and bankruptcy of the economy, labor leaders were cau-
tioned to keep workers well disciplined and to look constructively at the "aggressive

economy" in expanding their activities. Recommendations for restructuring the economy covered the fiscal and monetary systems, capital accumulation, currency reform, and the budget. Not to be overlooked was an increase in spending "for cultural objectives" so that Japan might in fact be reconstructed as a "cultural nation." The manufacturing sector was seen as playing "the principle role in Japan's economic reconstruction."

The Future of Heavy Industries

Although a large part of Japanese heavy industry will be lost as a result of implementing reparation payments, that does not imply that Japan will be wholly denied heavy industries. Japanese heavy industries had a strong militaristic character in the past, but in the future, heavy industries of a peaceful nature will have to be developed through opening up a new market for them within the country. . . . Various favorable conditions, such as the proximity of marine transport, a diligent and large labor force, and the ready supply of electric power and industrial water, provide a foundation favorable to the growth of the manufacturing industry in Japan. Therefore when the Japanese political and economic systems have been democraticized and their aggressive character wiped out, the nation's heavy industries should be allowed to grow to a considerable extent. . . . As Japanese heavy industries are certain to be subjected to international competition in the future, on the one hand, and because the benefit of adequate governmental protection as experienced in the past will become difficult to obtain, on the other hand, they will have to cultivate — through the rationalization of management and the elevation of technological levels — the ability to withstand the competition from foreign goods in terms of production costs as well.

In its key message, the report once again stresses proper organization of the industrial setup: the rationalization of business management, importance of large-scale operations in certain industries, elevation of technological levels, place of smaller enterprises, reform of corporate organization, and modernization of the civil service system by removing its feudalistic character. Inevitably, "state assistance" by a democratic government "will be much relied on in economic operations in the future, too, due to the nation's economic backwardness, narrowness of markets, and insufficiency of raw material resources." The bureaucracy should not intervene, but "provide private enterprise with information and guidance on the basis of careful investigation and research." To this end, an agency for comprehensive planning and investigation should be established, and national research institutions expanded.

Establishment of an Agency for Comprehensive Planning

The function of the Economic Stabilization Board should be strengthened so that it may assume the task of collecting basic data and drafting overall plans for economic reconstruction. . . . The staff of the Stabilization Board should not be a mere group of ordinary administrative officials, as was the case in the past; instead, it must be a systematic collection of excellent experts in various fields selected from both government and private circles. By making such an agency a brain trust for the prime minister and giving the premier the power to give orders to various ministers if necessary, a systematic and unified administrative operation should be made possible. Such a system would correspond to the general staff in the armed forces. . . .

Industrial Structure in the Future

A consideration of Japan's prospective industrial structure must proceed on the premise that the nation is poorly endowed with natural resources but has an abundant labor supply and must aim at establishing an equilibrium in the international payments balance while realizing the maximum employment of domestic labor. Japan in the future has to sustain and develop industries as varied as possible, partly in order to export industrial manufactures in quantities necessary to cover its imports of large quantities of food, clothing, and other essential commodities and partly in order to provide job opportunities for its huge population. . . . Furthermore, the nation's industries must shift gradually to the manufacture of sophisticated and high-grade commodities that will not only be competitive with their counterparts in the rest of the world but also require as much human labor as possible. The production of industrial goods for domestic consumption, too, must be contrived so that job opportunities can be provided for the domestic labor force and that the nation's burden of payments to the rest of the world can be reduced by importing, as much as practicable, necessary raw materials in the form of crude materials for processing into finished goods within the national boundaries.

In other words, it will be essential for Japan to have highly developed industries in order to maintain a peaceful economy and guarantee the people's livelihood. It is also necessary that because of the geographical location of the country, Japan's industrial ability should be utilized fully for the industrialization of the Asian regions.

As the report draws toward a conclusion, the focus shifts to trends in overseas markets as well as Japan's special conditions as basic to determining precisely what it should export. To reduce burdens on foreign exchange and provide employment, Japan should aim for domestic self-sufficiency in the production of iron and steel, ships, rolling stock, machinery, chemical goods, paper, fertilizers, and cement. As in the past, exports of industrial manufactures for daily use (the report did not specify to where), such as textiles, toys, bicycles, rubber goods, electric bulbs, together with machinery and chemical goods, would enable Japan to import food, fertilizers, clothing, and other products for its growing population. In order to modernize and rationalize the economy, electric power development and utilization were crucial. For a peaceful economy, Japan should revive its fishing and shipping industries and promote tourism. It should formulate plans for the development of national land, the full utilization of river water and hilly districts, improved transportation and communications, and the spread of technology.

Tasks for Japanese Technology

The development of advanced technology and constant research are needed not only for the conservation of such resources, products, and imported goods but also for the purpose of using them effectively without waste. In other words, the nation's technology must support such technical tasks as the creation of new resources, making unutilized resources useful, sophisticated product processing, economization in the per unit consumption of raw materials in factories, reduction in product wastage, increasing product durability, and so forth.

The second task of Japanese technology is the maintenance and development of export trade through technological advancement. Japan must maintain a superiority in know-how over other Asian countries by constant advancement of its own technology so that it may be able to export industrial manufactures to such countries. The nation must also improve the quality of its exports so as to contribute to reductions in unit prices or to the cultivation of reliable markets abroad. . . .

Third is the contribution of technology to the elimination of cheap labor. . . .

Through advances in technology, Japan would be able to contribute to Asian industrialization and provide technical assistance: "It is considered inevitable that the economy will move in a direction toward a planned economy," requiring "a new type of technician." However, Japan's future technology would not be utilized to strengthen military power but to serve the people and better living standards: "Japanese technology must also get rid of its traditional, imitation-centered colonialistic character and strive for the development of a technology that conforms to the nation's environment." It must strive for economy in the use of raw materials. Engineers should awaken to their responsibilities in economic revival and concentrate on "the lowering of production costs, qualitative improvement, economization of materials."

At the end, the report briefly discusses rationalization in daily life and consumption, including the economic emancipation of Japanese housewives.

Real Emancipation of Housewives

Japanese housewives are too busy. A way must be opened for them to have leisure hours in which to acquire the culture worthy of humans by emancipating them, in terms of both time and physical conditions, through ample introduction into households of such modern facilities as electricity and gas. Only after such real improvement has been realized in their daily lives can women effectively exercise the franchise that has been extended to them.

It is also a requisite for an expansion of the domestic-market manufacturing industry that electrical appliances and other modern equipment be used widely in Japanese households. If the living standards of Japanese people are so low that they cannot afford to purchase appliances, the joint use of such equipment may be promoted through the groups of residential housing. . . .

Economic Reconstruction and Education

In a rapidly changing period, such as the present age in particular, the educational system must be rebuilt on a clear recognition of the direction that Japan will follow in the future. Of course, because education is endowed with the primary objective of the training of character, we should refrain from treating education as a means to pursue actual profits. At the same time we must reconsider whether an ideal character training that is apart from real life is advisable. Education in the future should aim at the training not of careerist-type utilitarians but, among others, of those many nationals who are diligent, reliable and regard their jobs as duties entrusted by Heaven, and of a great number of producers. . . .

[Adapted from Special Survey Committee, Ministry of Foreign Affairs, Japan, *Postwar Reconstruction of the Japanese Economy*, pp. 65–66, 74, 78, 98, 130, 139, 175, 184–86]

JAPAN'S FIRST WHITE PAPER ON THE ECONOMY

Economic conditions remained chaotic in 1947 and 1948, during the two coalition cabinets headed first by Katayama Tetsu (1887–1978), the Christian Socialist leader of Japan's first leftist government, and then by Ashida Hitoshi, a former career diplomat and conservative Speaker of the House (1947/1948). Commerce was at a standstill; workers were antagonistic; and households were desperate. SCAP continued to press its reformist programs, but sympathy was building for more positive assistance. In July 1947, the new head of the Economic Stabilization Board, Wada Hiroo (reformist minister of agriculture in the first Yoshida cabinet until January 1947), attempted to check inflation and stabilize the economy by instituting increased price controls as part of an emergency program. Once again, planning was stressed. As he explained in a speech delivered on July 1 to both houses of the Diet, in lieu of foreign trade, Japan had to do the best it could with materials at home. To effect rehabilitation, "it is absolutely essential to operate our economy by an overall planning."

A few days later, on July 4, 1947, in a historic move, the cabinet issued Japan's first White Paper on the Economy. The sixty-thousand-word report, highly factual and written in plain and readable language, was a frank depiction of Japan's broken economy. Although little colored by ideology, it promoted a mixed economy and statistical planning. The chief drafter was Wada's colleague on the ESB, Tsuru Shigeto (b. 1912), a Marxist economist with a doctorate from Harvard. The paper was divided into three parts: government (national finance), private enterprise (production), and household economy (consumption). If the people were well informed about the actual condition of the economy as a whole, the assumption was, they would take their share of responsibility and face up to continued hardship. Under manufacturing, the White Paper reiterated the vital importance of coal production. It took a stand on war guilt, placing blame on the military and officials for starting the war against the will of the people. It introduced a wide variety of statistics: on prices, wages, and cost of living; people's livelihood; production; transportation; public finance and banking; labor and employment; and foreign trade. Equally important was its introductory tone:

As prerequisites, let us lay stress on two important facts. The first is the necessity to grasp the movement of our national economy in a dynamic manner. The other is the necessity of an overall analysis of our national economy. . . . It cannot be said that we have yet fully realized the profound misery our military leaders have brought upon us by starting a reckless war against the will of the people at large. Furthermore, we cannot say that in the two years that have elapsed since the end of the war we have done all that we might have done. There are some things we should have done sooner and will try to do now. We have to work with a more or less inaccurate forecast—growth in production and an improved international account.

Part 2 of the White Paper, offering statistics on food, clothing, daily commodities, house-hold fuel, and housing, attacks the black market. It concludes:

We were apt to lack in courage in the past to face the reality straight. During the war, which was like a bad dream, our leaders' cowardice helped to bring tragedy to our nation; they tried to lead our nation to close their eyes to the facts which they did not like and to distort the facts in such a way as to suit the direction in which they wanted to lead the nation. . . . The facts that honest men are quite often fooled and that those who work sincerely suffer from losses, testify to the "physiological" malady of the economic organism of this country. The Government desires to share the facts of these difficulties frankly with the people, and to make such realization a basis for the reconstruction and reha-bilitation of our country. . . .

The stages in which the people, after going through conditions in which the base of reproduction gets more and more restricted, emerge, with hope for the future, into the road to rehabilitation and reconstruction, shall be the stages in which those who work honestly in close relation with each other, will make their livelihood easier through their own effort. . . . The starting point of a democratic government must mean that we are faced with the question of forming a government of the people, by the people and for the people. . . .

[*Nippon Times*, July 6, 1947]

REVISED U.S. POLICY FOR OCCUPIED JAPAN

Midway through the Occupation, on October 18, 1948, President Truman endorsed a considerably revised policy for Japan in National Security Council (NSC) Document 13/2. Based on a year-long study, the recommendations reflected a calculated shift from punitive measures to positive support of Japan's economic recovery to a level of self-sufficiency but did not necessarily require a reverse course in all other reforms. Instead, emphasis was placed on Japan's "assimilation of the reforms in place." The eventual peace settlement with Japan, moreover, should be as "nonpunitive" as possible. The altered direction came on the urging of SCAP experts, Japanese and American businessmen, high-level officials on both sides, and a fiscally conservative American Congress. Of prime importance was a visit to Japan in early 1948 by George Kennan, head of the State Department's Policy Planning Staff and a major author of the United States's Cold War policy to contain Communism. The underlying conviction in Washington was that a vibrant democracy and a healthy economy were interdependent. Japan was reenvisioned as a workshop for Asia, similar to the role already projected for West Germany in postwar Europe, although the Japanese version was not expected to be as advanced in heavy industry and quality products. The key recommendation stated the following.

Economic Recovery. Second only to U.S. security interests, economic recovery should be made the primary objective of United States policy in Japan for the coming period. It should be sought through a combination of United States aid programs envisaging shipments and/or credits on a declining scale over a number of years, and by a vigorous and concerted effort by all interested agencies and departments of the United States Government to cut away obstacles to the revival of Japanese foreign trade, with provision for Japanese merchant shipping, and to facilitate restoration and development of Japan's exports. In developing Japan's internal and external trade and industry, private enterprise should be encouraged. . . . We should make it clear to the Japanese Government that the success of the recovery program will in large part depend on Japanese efforts to raise production and to maintain high export levels through hard work, a minimum of work-stoppages, internal austerity measures and the stern combating of inflationary trends including efforts to achieve a balanced internal budget as rapidly as possible. . . .

[Department of State, *Foreign Relations of the United States*, 1948, vol. 6, p. 861]

RECONSTRUCTING JAPAN AS A NATION
OF PEACE AND CULTURE

Throughout the Occupation, there was much rhetoric about reconstructing Japan as a nation of both peace and culture. It crept into the speeches of prime ministers and Diet members and into the writings of journalists and critics. At times vague, this inseparable equation envisioned the re-creation of a non-militarist Japan, a new Japan that would regain the respect of the world through its promotion of philosophy, science, and the arts. It also entailed deep thinking about the real meaning of pacifism, especially after the adoption of the peace constitution. Was a peace state in fact not a normal state, or somehow a lesser state, or was it something to cherish as Japan's singular contribution to a new world of international politics? The discourse embraced new issues as the Cold War progressed in Asia and as Japan came closer to a peace and security settlement.

MORITO TATSUO

In January 1946, an important essay, "The Construction of a Peaceful Nation," appeared in the first postwar issue of *Kaizō* (*Reconstruction*), an influential magazine that Japanese officials had suspended during the war. Its author, the economist Morito Tatsuo, had been the central figure in a famous case in 1920 involving academic freedom. For publishing an article about the Russian anarchist Pyotr Kropotkin, he was dismissed from Tokyo Imperial University and briefly jailed. To earn a living, Morito spent the next two decades at the Ōhara Institute for Social Research. In postwar Japan, he was elected as a Social Democrat to the House of Representatives and in 1947 became minister of education in the short-lived cabinet of Katayama Tetsu. This was followed by a long tenure as president of Hiroshima University.

In his lead essay for *Kaizō* in January 1946, which predated by one month the incorporation of a peace clause in the model draft constitution, Morito raised several hypothetical questions about the meaning and requirements of a peaceful nation and discussed their application to a defeated Japan. Two of his passages in the Japanese version were deleted by American censors. Ironically, when the essay appeared in English translation a few months later, it was again censored, but different passages were selected and for different reasons. This is a reminder that freedom of debate was sometimes seriously circumscribed in Occupied Japan. At the same time, censored remarks often served to betray the bias of both the writer and the censor. In the excerpt, the italicized words are those that were deleted because they criticized the Allies.

Throughout history, Morito began, peace, not war, had been a high ideal in international relations. But on second thought, a peaceful state "can mean either 'a state that cannot wage a war' or 'a state that does not desire war.'" In which of the two categories did Japan belong? In Japan's present condition, it was obviously the first, but the Allies would also try to make Japan incapable of war in the future by disarming the military and prohibiting a war industry.

"THE CONSTRUCTION OF A PEACEFUL NATION"

The democratization of politics with the revision of the constitution as the initial, basic step, the democratization of national economy with the dissolution of *zaibatsu* as an important beginning, and the emphasizing of antimilitarist education as the most effective means of psychological disarmament will be indirect steps yet to be completed.

This nation, devoid of war potential, might be regarded as an absolutely peaceful state. But is this the peaceful state that humanity has so long sought as an ideal? *Had we the Japanese sought such a state when we desired peace?*

To speak frankly, Japan is now forced to be such a peaceful state as her punishment for the aggressive war, and she has in no way chosen it of her free will. Under the circumstances, her being a peaceful state is merely superficial, not affecting her inner life to the core. It is true that an antimilitarist education is carried out vigorously to influence the coming generations as the militarist education had done in the former days. Since, however, it is an education forced upon them from outside, its effect does not go deep enough to change their inner life.

Should the complete pacification of the mind of its people not be effected, what road will the outwardly peaceful state follow? There may be two possibilities. The first case is that of a morally weak people where they will inevitably fall in decadence, losing the spirit of independence, liberty, and self-reliance under the pressure of the enforced peace while at the same time falteringly observing the wish of the victor nation. If that is the destiny to be followed by a peaceful state, it has to be called a slave state, or a collective existence unworthy of the name of a state, far from the peaceful state in its highest sense.

The second case is that of a morally strong people, where the spirit of independence will not only remain unsmashed by war defeat, but all the more be strengthened in its certain respects. When peace is forced upon this type of people, in the sense of inability to fight, it certainly will revolt against the fate of a slave state brought upon it under the beautiful name of a peaceful nation. Yet, being unable to resist with force, it will acquiesce in being such a nominally peaceful state, while cherishing resentment against the forces compelling it to be so.

Consequently, the possibility of its joining in the anti-peace camp rather than consistently standing for peace cannot be precluded.

When viewed in this light, to keep a people long in a state of a forced peaceful nation will result either in reducing it to a slave state or in driving it to be a psychologically bellicose country, which is the type of state radically different from what is originally intended. Such a policy, therefore, can never be commended. The question is, what is a peaceful state in the true sense of the term? It is no other than one which does not desire war, or a state that seeks peace of its own free will and from its own inner conviction, striving with all its moral powers for the realization of that ideal. In this case the possession or nonpossession of armed forces is totally out of the question.

The essential prerequisite to the peaceful state, therefore, is that it is independent and free; in other words, it must have free will to seek peace instead of war. . . . It must be a state which has economically attained a certain level in productive capacity and culturally in morality and arts. . . .

A truly peaceful state, Morito continued, "must stand for pacifism in a particular sense"—a pacifism of the present and not as a future social idea. To do so was not easy. It would require sacrifice and "spiritual effort." Real peace, like liberty, "must be gained by our own efforts, not being a gift from outsiders." To prepare for peace required the removal of social evils and the establishment of three foundations: a socialist economy, democracy, and a cultural revolution. A socialist state, he thought, would weaken the motive for exploitation. Democracy would eliminate despotism and liberate "the working masses and women." A cultural revolution would help wipe out notions of Japan as a chosen people. However, the perfection of a peaceful state was a matter for all nations, not one in isolation: "Just as militarist nations have always prepared for aggressive wars, so the nations should not neglect to prepare for peace." This might be accomplished through a single democratic world federation of all states, a worldwide planned economy, and a world culture "that does not belittle the original culture of any people." A peace offensive should seek to harmonize conflicting ideologies and "accelerate the tendency of independent states limiting the exercise of their sovereign right as a step toward forming a single world federal state."

Morito discussed the roles of major and minor powers in this peace offensive: "Under present conditions, without doubt, the United States, the Soviet Union, and Great Britain, and particularly the former two will be the propellant powers." (In the Japanese version, he clarified that America represented democracy; the Soviet Union, socialism; and Britain, a combination.) To construct a peaceful international society, the major powers would have to give up selfish interests and refrain from victimizing minor states. The road would not be easy. Advocates of democracy did not understand socialism, and socialists did not fully appreciate democracy. At this point, Morito lost in the Japanese version (which was therefore deleted in English translation) the added thought: "Also, who is there who can definitely say that there is no mixture of racial and national egoism and obstinacy within the natural pride and self-esteem of these victor nations? And in *such cases, would it not be that the construction of a peaceful international society will, again, in some shape or other be deformed?"*

Lesser powers, like the defeated Japan, could play important roles "simply because they are small and weak. Japan, who has suddenly fallen from the rank of a major power to that of a lesser nation as a result of the defeat, is apparently destined to become a sort of leader of minor powers ideologically, for good or ill." Since Japan was no longer an imperialistic threat, it could revive relations on an equal basis with its neighbors. Since it was a poor and starving country, it could sympathize with "other suffering peoples" and advocate "the rational distribution of world wealth and resources." Since Japan was disarmed, it could denounce militarism and aggression "and severely criticize without any reserve the armed peace, which is only a mask for militarism." Here, apparently in this paragraph, censored in the Japanese text (and therefore also omitted later in English), Morito was not permitted to say the following.

We belong to the colored races which are apt to receive discriminatory treatment. Of course, this fact was not too strongly felt while our nation remained a first-rate power, but now that we have fallen into the class of a sixth-rate or eighth-rate nation, there is no doubt that we shall strongly feel this as an irrational drawback. But at the same time, we must not overlook the fact that this will serve as a tie between us and the other numerous colored races. That is, this strong awareness, together with the history and capability of our race, will not only make them (other colored races) our real friends, but will also make us the main leading power in effecting a common battle line for their liberation and elevation. . . .

Lastly, our culture now faces a serious crisis caused by the war and the defeat. Our cultural life and institutions were destroyed by the vandalism of war, the political confusion after the defeat, and the economic destitution. Consequently the moral and cultural level of the people is appreciably lowered. This state of things is brought about by our fostering militarism, which was the direct outcome of the promotion of feudalistic culture before and during the war, as well as by our blind acceptance of the cultures of the victor nations after the surrender. Thus even the higher phases of our original culture are being threatened with being discarded. By denying the mistaken notion of cultural aspects of war, and by backing up the cultural revolution of backward nations, as taught by our own bitter experience, we will be able to devote ourselves to the creation of a harmonious world culture based on the peculiarities of different cultures, eliminating every vestige of cultural imperialism.

In the light of the foregoing considerations we fully realize that the historic mission of Japan as a lesser state in the construction of a peaceful international society is as vital as that of major powers. Are we prepared to shoulder this high responsibility?

[Morito, "Heiwa kokka no kensetsu," pp. 3–16;
"The Construction of a Peaceful Nation," pp. 109–17]

YOKOTA KISABURŌ

Article 9 in Japan's constitution converted Morito Tatsuo's speculation into reality, and for the remainder of the Occupation, it provoked considerable controversy about the renunciation of war, disarmament, and security. Yokota Kisaburō, a professor of international law at Tokyo Imperial University and a future chief justice of Japan's Supreme Court, argued in the April 1947 issue of *Shakai shichō* (*Social Thought*), an organ of the Social Democratic Party, that the keynote of Japan's future diplomacy under the new constitution should be to uphold pacifism. Moreover, he believed that the Social Democrats were the best equipped to do so.

ON PEACE

Under the new constitution, Japan has definitely renounced war and has decided on the complete abolition of armaments. This is, indeed, a very important decision for a state to take. The decision is of great import domestically, but of still greater import internationally.

How Japan, shorn of all its armaments, can safeguard its security or can maintain its territorial integrity and independence is a big problem confronting its people. Whether or not a country is armed or how heavily it is armed has hitherto been the criterion of first importance by which to judge its international position. From this point of view, Japan's total disarmament means its fall to a very low and weak position. How, then, should its position be improved and elevated? To rearm itself is, of course, out of the question. Is it, then, possible to elevate its international position by some other means, and, if it is possible, how can it be done? This is a big problem awaiting solution.

In order that the new constitution may be acted on faithfully so that Japan may be transformed into a perfectly peaceful state, it is of prime importance for the Japanese people generally to become convinced of the imperative need and the absolute justice of the renunciation of war and the total abolition of armaments. . . .

Now that Japan has adopted pacifism, pure and simple, the like of which has never been adopted by any other country, it is up to all political parties in this country to understand it thoroughly, study it in all its bearings, and work out a detailed and concrete diplomatic policy in strict accordance therewith.

Pacifism of the highest order will necessarily be the keynote of Japan's future diplomacy.

Yokota castigated the Social Democratic Party for not living up to this mission and challenged it to do better.

[Yokota, "Shakaitō to gaikō," pp. 305–13; MM]

REGAINING SOVEREIGNTY IN A BIPOLAR WORLD

For Japan, the restoration of its sovereignty and political independence was a constant, if often elusive, goal from the time of its surrender in August 1945 to the signing of the San Francisco Peace Treaty and the U.S.–Japan Security Treaty in September 1951 (effective in April 1952). As Japan conformed to the Potsdam Declaration and to the requirements of the United States and the Far Eastern Commission, Japanese officials and diplomats wondered and worried about the terms of the ultimate treaty—how harsh or how generous and how acceptable to the public they would be. At first it seemed that a reborn Japan, peaceful and democratic and operating under a new constitution that renounced war, was the best way to regain the respect of the international community and earn entry into the United Nations. But as the Cold War intensified in Asia, another crucial issue was Japan's future security as an unarmed state. Could Japan honor article 9 and exercise the right of self-defense? Was it possible or even wise for Japan to be neutral in a bipolar world, or should Japan rely for security on the continued military presence of the United States in Japan?

The possibility of a formal peace treaty was first raised by American and Japanese officials in 1946. Douglas MacArthur, too, made an early but abortive move in 1947, motivated in part by his presidential aspirations. Various methods were advocated, including bilateral negotiations and joint conferences, and ideas were exchanged, often behind the scenes. After his return to power, Prime Minister (and Foreign Minister) Yoshida Shigeru told the Diet in November 1949 that Japan was ready to accept a peace treaty. The question, however, was precisely what the Allies and the Japanese government had in mind. The Peace Problems Discussion Association was already pressing for an overall peace and unarmed neutrality, trusting for Japan's security in the United Nations. It was also building strong connections with the media and labor movement. In the Diet, the opposition Social Democrats were in complete support of article 9 and disarmament. As the negotiations became more concrete, the official U.S. position in early 1950—a few months after the takeover of mainland China by Mao Zedong's Communist forces—was that Japan should sign a separate peace with the Allies and take its place with the free world in the global struggle against Communism. Japan should also guard against Communist subversion at home—a warning that Yoshida did not need—and, less welcome to him, it should also consider gradual rearmament.

In an address to the Diet on January 24, 1950, as Japan began to show mixed signs of economic recovery within the framework of the Dodge Plan, an economic stabilization program sponsored by the Occupation to develop Japan's export capacity, Yoshida declared that article 9 did not forbid the right to self-defense. By May, it had become clear that his cabinet was ready to accept a separate peace with the West and to rely on the United States for post-Occupation security. Privately, Yoshida hoped somehow to revive economic ties with mainland China. The international situation changed abruptly in late June with the arrival in Tokyo of the State Department's foreign policy adviser, John Foster Dulles, and the invasion a few days later of South Korea by North Korea. Dulles had just told the U.S. Chamber of Commerce in Tokyo, on June 22, that Japan had the responsibility of choosing between the Free World or the Captive World. The Japanese "have seen what the Free World can produce in terms of military might. They have seen the moral authority for righteousness of free people who, having conquered, stoop to lift up the conquered, offering them economic aid and fellowship. Our material might was exemplified by the atomic bomb; our moral might is exemplified by General MacArthur."[1] Within a month of the outbreak .of the Korean War, Yoshida laid the foundations of the future Self-Defense Forces when he authorized in July, at MacArthur's directive, an armed police reserve. Tokyo and Washington were even more firmly opposed to an overall peace settlement. That autumn, with the massive military intervention in Korea of Communist Chinese forces and rumors of the possible use of nuclear weapons, Japan's media, peace groups, and opposition parties increasingly voiced their concerns, in a prelude to the contentious decade ahead.

NEGOTIATING A FORMAL PEACE SETTLEMENT

In defending his position on the forthcoming peace settlement and rearmament to the House of Representatives of the Diet in January 1951, Yoshida Shigeru was subjected to sharp questioning from Social Democrat Mrs. Tokano Satoko (from Tochigi Prefecture).

The foreign policy of Yoshida, Ashida, and Shidehara is a remnant of prewar royal court diplomacy. Diplomacy today should represent the peace-loving desires of the people and strive to secure national independence and obtain a proper international position for Japan . . . Statesmen should not betray the wish of Japanese women, baptized by atomic bombs, never again to send their sons and husbands to the battlefield . . . Even if we call for security from the U.S., we should abide by the New Constitution. Japan should call upon the U.N. to guarantee its security as an unarmed nation. Britain, U.S., China, and Russia should be held responsible for our security.

Even more outraged was Communist representative Mrs. Tajima Hide (Aichi Prefecture).

---

1. Dulles, "Free or Captive World?"

All of Japan has been made a military base for aggressive war and is being placed in a state of war. Entertainment of American soldiers, blood donations, and compulsory contributions of money are being conducted, while war-wounded Japanese soldiers are begging on the streets. Which of these, American soldiers or Japanese, requires more protection? The remains of Japanese workers and seamen who died in Korea have been sent back to Japan, but what kind of disposal do you think was made of those victims? Are you not resolved to discontinue once and for all the war collaboration with the U.N.? . . . What is the Prime Minister's opinion on rearmament? The question of rearmament is not limited only to the size of a regular army or to an increase in police reserve forces. Wages for women are deplorably low; widows are unable to keep body and soul together; streets are overrun with homeless and disreputable girls; hungry peasants in Yamagata Prefecture are even selling their children for about four kilograms of dried gourd. This is the economic basis of the proposed rearmament. The general tendency at present is to regard prostitution as a desirable thing; education tries to give the impression that the U.S. is a paradise on earth; militaristic education urges willing participation in the police reserve force. This is the moral foundation of the proposed rearmament. Mr. Yoshida's assertion that he will move cautiously with regard to rearmament is only a gesture to sell us a separate peace. Is not the Yoshida government practically going ahead with rearmament? Japanese women, who want peace, will arise boldly to oppose rearmament.

Yoshida's reply was simply: "The interpellation amounts to nothing more than a bit of communist propaganda based on misrepresentation. Hence, I don't think it deserves a serious answer."

[SCAP, Government Section, January 30, 1951,"Opposition Representatives Interpellate PM on Treaty" (January 29, 1951)]

TREATY OF PEACE BETWEEN THE ALLIED POWERS AND JAPAN

The San Francisco Peace Conference commenced in the first week of September 1951, with Prime Minister Yoshida and a delegation from Japan present. The Allies, India abstaining, signed a multilateral peace treaty with Japan on September 8. Technically, the pact ended the Occupation by recognizing the full sovereignty of the Japanese people over Japan and its territorial waters and by restoring independence. In fact, however, it was a partial peace treaty that excluded the Soviet Union and the newly established People's Republic of China. It made a point of recognizing Japan's right of individual or collective self-defense but did not take specific note of or require Japan to maintain the Occupation's reforms. Indeed, chapter II, article 3, was a source of turmoil for decades to come. Okinawa was to be placed under United Nations trusteeship, with the United States as the sole administrative authority, although Japan was to retain residual sovereignty. Okinawans had little to say in the matter. The prefecture remained under U.S. military occupation until 1972 and was used as a staging base during the Korean and Vietnam Wars.

Whereas the Allied Powers and Japan are resolved that henceforth their relations shall be those of nations which, as sovereign equals, cooperate in friendly association to promote their common welfare and to maintain international peace and security, and are therefore desirous of concluding a Treaty of Peace which will settle questions still outstanding as a result of the existence of a state of war between them;

Whereas Japan for its part declares its intention to apply for membership in the United Nations and in all circumstances to conform to the principles of the Charter of the United Nations; to strive to realize the objectives of the Universal Declaration of Human Rights; to seek to create within Japan conditions of stability and well-being as defined in Articles 55 and 56 of the Charter of the United Nations and already initiated by postsurrender Japanese legislation; and in public and private trade and commerce to conform to internationally accepted fair practices;

Whereas the Allied Powers welcome the intentions of Japan set out in the foregoing paragraph;

The Allied Powers and Japan have therefore determined to conclude the present Treaty of Peace, and have accordingly appointed the undersigned Plenipotentiaries, who, after presentation of their full powers, found in good and due form, have agreed on the following provisions:

Chapter I· Peace

Article 1.

a. The state of war between Japan and each of the Allied Powers is terminated as from the date on which the present Treaty comes into force between Japan and the Allied Powers concerned as provided for in article 23.

b. The Allied Powers recognize the full sovereignty of the Japanese people over Japan and its territorial waters.

Chapter II: Territory

Article 2.

a. Japan, recognizing the independence of Korea, renounces all right, title and claim to Korea, including the islands of Quelpart, Port Hamilton and Dagelet.

b. Japan renounces all right, title and claim to Formosa and the Pescadores.

c. Japan renounces all right, title and claim to the Kurile Islands, and to that portion of Sakhalin and islands adjacent to it over which Japan acquired sovereignty as a consequence of the Treaty of Portsmouth of September 5, 1905.

Japan also renounced claims to the Pacific islands formerly under the mandate of Japan, to any part of the Antarctic area, and to the Spratly Islands and Paracel Islands.

Article 3. Japan will concur in any proposal of the United States to the United Nations to place under its trusteeship system, with the United States as the sole administering authority, Nansei Shoto south of 29 degrees north latitude (including the Ryukyu Islands, and the Daito Islands), Nanpo Shoto south of Sofu Gan (including the Bonin Islands, Rosario Island and the Volcano Islands) and Parece Vela and Marcus Island. Pending the making of such a proposal and affirmative action thereon, the United States will have the right to exercise all and any powers of administration, legislation and jurisdiction over the territory and inhabitants of these islands, including their territorial waters.

Chapter III: Security

Article 5.

c. The Allied Powers for their part recognize that Japan as a sovereign nation possesses the inherent rights of individual or collective self-defense referred to in article 51 of the Charter of the United Nations and that Japan may voluntarily enter into collective security arrangements.

Article 6.

a. All Occupation forces of the Allied Powers shall be withdrawn from Japan as soon as possible after the coming into force of the present Treaty, and in any case not later than ninety days thereafter. Nothing in this provision shall, however, prevent the stationing or retention of foreign armed forces in Japanese territory under or in consequence of any bilateral or multilateral agreements which have been or may be made between one or more of the Allied Powers, on the one hand, and Japan on the other. . . .

Chapter IV: Political and Economic Clauses

Article 10. Japan renounces all special rights and interest in China. . . .

Article 11. Japan accepts the judgments of the International Military Tribunal for the Far East and of other Allied War Crimes Courts both within and outside Japan, and will carry out the sentences imposed thereby upon the Japanese nationals imprisoned in Japan. . . .

[Dennett and Durance, eds., *Documents on American Foreign Relations*, vol. 9, 1951, pp. 470–79]

BILATERAL SECURITY TREATY BETWEEN THE UNITED STATES
OF AMERICA AND JAPAN

Since a constitutionally unarmed Japan could not effectively engage in self-defense, Yoshida was required, at the insistence of the U.S. Joint Chiefs of Staff, to sign a separate security treaty with the United States, also on September 8, 1951, as a condition for the peace treaty. In requesting American military aid and continuance of American military bases in Japan, Japan sided officially with the United States in the Cold War. It, too, became effective on April 28, 1952. Many Japanese, including those who accepted the peace treaty, regarded the security treaty as an infringement on Japanese sovereignty and contrary to article 9. The preamble states that the United States expected Japan to "increasingly assume responsibility for its own defense against direct and indirect aggression." The United States gained the right to dispose of its Japan-based troops or supplies to meet trouble anywhere in the Far East but made no specific commitment to defend Japan. It promised assistance to the Japanese government in putting down large-scale internal riots and disturbances. The expiration date was indefinite. The allusions to Japan's right to "inherent self-defense," however, provided a loophole in later court rulings concerning the constitutionality of the U.S. military presence in Japan and the emerging Japanese self-defense forces.

In addition, a lengthy administrative agreement, signed on February 18, 1952, laid down detailed conditions for areas and facilities pertaining to the presence of U.S. troops in Japan. Its provision of extraterritoriality for American troops accused of committing crimes while on official duty in Japan would be yet another source of future controversy and protest throughout the 1950s reminiscent of nineteenth-century battles over unequal treaties. In another pressure tactic, Yoshida Shigeru was required to state that he would deal with nationalist China (Taiwan) in trade and diplomacy and not the Communists in control of mainland China. Otherwise, he resisted, even during the Korean War, anything more than a light and gradual buildup of Japanese defense forces. As the war progressed, Japan's factories and sex industry gained a considerable and questionable profit from the vast expenditures by the United Nations and the United States. Misbehavior by GIs, once censored in the media, became open season in Japanese film, fiction, and newsprint.

Japan has this day signed a treaty of peace with the Allied Powers. On the coming into force of that treaty, Japan will not have the effective means to exercise its inherent right of self-defense because it has been disarmed.

There is danger to Japan in this situation because irresponsible militarism has not yet been driven from the world. Therefore, Japan desires a security treaty with the United States of America to come into force simultaneously with the treaty of peace between the United States of America and Japan.

The treaty of peace recognizes that Japan as a sovereign nation has the right to enter into collective security arrangements, and further, the Charter of the United Nations recognizes that all nations possess an inherent right of individual and collective self-defense.

In exercise of these rights, Japan desires, as a provisional arrangement for its defense, that the United States of America should maintain armed forces of its own in and about Japan so as to deter armed attack upon Japan.

The United States of America, in the interest of peace and security, is at present willing to maintain certain of its armed forces in and about Japan, in the expectation, however, that Japan will itself increasingly assume responsibility for its own defense against direct and indirect aggression, always avoiding any armament which could be an offensive threat or serve other than to promote peace and security in accordance with the purposes and principles of the United Nations Charter.

Accordingly, the two countries have agreed as follows:

Article 1. Japan grants, and the United States of America accepts, the right, upon the coming into force of the Treaty of Peace and of this Treaty, to dispose United States land, air, and sea forces in and about Japan. Such forces may be utilized to contribute to the maintenance of international peace and security in the Far East and to the security of Japan against armed attack from without, including assistance given at the express request of the Japanese Government to put down large-scale internal riots and disturbances in Japan, caused through instigation or intervention by an outside power or powers.

Article 2. During the exercise of the right referred to in Article 1, Japan will not grant, without the prior consent of the United States of America, any bases or any rights, powers or authority whatsoever, in or relating to bases or the right of garrison or of maneuver, or transit of ground, air, or naval forces to any third power.

Article 3. The conditions which shall govern the disposition of armed forces of the United States of America in and about Japan shall be determined by administrative agreements between the two Governments.

Article 4. This treaty shall expire whenever in the opinion of the governments of the United States of America and Japan there shall have come into force such United Nations arrangements or such alternative individual or collective security dispositions as will satisfactorily provide for the maintenance by the United Nations or otherwise of international peace and security in the Japan area.

[Dennett and Durance, eds., *Documents on American Foreign Relations*, vol. 9, 1951, pp. 266–67]

SOME JAPANESE VIEWS OF THE WAR

KURIHARA SADAKO

Kurihara Sadako was born in Hiroshima in 1913 and was a longtime resident of that city and its vicinity. She therefore witnessed the atomic bombing of the city and, along with her husband, Kurihara Tadaichi, became an important leader of the antinuclear movement, which had a long record of antiestablishment activities. Kurihara fought vigorously on behalf of peace, social justice, and human rights, but at the same time, she and her husband did not hesitate to denounce Japanese wartime atrocities.

A DISSIDENT POET'S CRITIQUE OF WAR

WHAT IS WAR?

I do not accept war's cruelty.
In every war, no matter how beautifully dressed up,
I detect ugly, demonic intent.
And I abhor those blackhearted people
who, not involved directly themselves,
constantly glorify war and fan its flames.
What is it that takes place
when people say "holy war," "just war"?
Murder. Arson. Rape. Theft.
The women who can't flee take off their skirts
before the enemy troops
and beg for mercy—do they not?
In fields where the grain rustles in the breeze,
sex-starved soldiers chase the women,
like demons on the loose.
At home they are good fathers, good brothers, good sons,
but in the hell of battle,
they lose all humanity
and rampage like wild beasts.

LET US BE MIDWIVES

An Untold Story of the Atomic Bombing

Night in the basement of a concrete structure now in ruins.
Victims of the atomic bomb
jammed the room;
it was dark—not even a single candle.
The smell of fresh blood, the stench of death,
the closeness of sweaty people, the moans.
From out of all that, lo and behold, a voice:
"The baby's coming!"
In that hellish basement, at that very moment,
a young woman had gone into labor.

In the dark, without a single match, what to do?
People forgot their own pains, worried about her.
And then: "I'm a midwife. I'll help with the birth."
The speaker, seriously injured herself,
had been moaning only moments before.
And so new life was born in the dark of that pit of hell.
And so the midwife died before dawn, still bathed in the blood.
Let us be midwives!
Let us be midwives!
Even if we lay down our own lives to do so.

Kurihara, along with the teachers' unions, was opposed to SCAP's relaxation in 1950 of the rule prohibiting the flying of the rising-sun flag (Hinomaru), not only on holidays, but on any occasion. She wrote the following poem in June 1952.

THE FLAG, I

As if nothing at all had gone wrong,
the flag fluttered once more
high over the roofs
and began to dream again of carnage in broad daylight.
But no one looked up to it,
and people resented its insatiable greed
and gnashed their teeth at its monstrous amnesia. . . .
Ah! Red-on-white flag of Japan!
The many nightmarish atrocities carried out at your feet.
Manila and Nanjing, where they splashed gasoline
over women and children
and burned them alive—
consummate crimes of the twentieth century.
Yet today the flag flutters again, shameless,
all those bloody memories
gone;
fluttering, fluttering in the breeze,
in dreams once more of redrawing the map.

[Kurihara, *Black Eggs*, trans. Minear, pp. 53, 67, 246–47]

ŌE KENZABURŌ

In 1965, a newly famous novelist and future Nobel laureate, Ōe Kenzaburō (b. 1935), looked back on his generation, which was born during the war and raised during the Occupation.

GROWING UP DURING THE OCCUPATION

When the war ended I was only ten years old, a grade-school boy in a mountain village, and I couldn't understand what the Emperor was saying over the radio when he announced that we had surrendered. The grownups sat in front of the radio and cried. I watched them from the garden, which was bathed in strong summer sunlight. The room where the grownups sat, crying, was dark.

Soon I got bored and went out to play. As all the adults were inside, listening to the radio, there were only children on the village road. We gathered here and there in small groups, and talked.

Not one of us knew exactly what had happened. We were most intrigued by the strange and somewhat disappointing fact that the Emperor had spoken in a *human voice* no different from any ordinary adult's. None of us understood what he had been saying, but we had certainly heard his voice. One of my friends was even able to imitate it very cleverly. We surrounded him, a boy in grimy shorts who spoke in the *Emperor's voice*, and we howled with laughter. . . .

My present image of the Emperor bears no resemblance to the awe-inspiring figure I imagined when I was an indiscriminating schoolboy. I feel no particular affection for the Emperor himself or for the Imperial Household. My mother, on the other hand, if she were given the opportunity, would hurry to the great square in front of the palace to do reverence to the Emperor as though he were a god, and seems keenly interested in all the doings of the Imperial Household.

But this attitude is not unique with my mother: at least half of the Japanese people demonstrate a keen interest in the Imperial Court. The feeling of deep esteem for the Emperor himself also seems to be general all over Japan. . . .

I remember seeing a picture of some grade-school children parading and flag-waving in celebration of the Crown Prince's betrothal. This crowd of young, cheering faces was rather a shock for me.

What made those children parade the streets with banners in their hands? Was it the influence of their parents and teachers? Was it the Emperor worship that remains embedded in some recess of the Japanese consciousness? Or was it merely an innocent love of fun and parades?

As long as every Japanese is able to formulate for himself whatever image of the Emperor he pleases, the word *symbol* will denote something wholesome. But what if the power of journalism created that parade and set those voices cheering by forcing on the children some specific image of the Emperor?

Those grade-school boys and girls were wreathed in smiles, but when we were children, we passed before the Imperial portrait with frightened faces and bowed heads.

Hallo-Hallo!

The children had gathered on the stone-paved wharf and now they were shouting. They faced the men on the decks of the foreign ships, and they shouted *Gibu mee monee—Gibu mee monee*. The foreigners threw some coins; the children fought for them. Shouting and screaming, these unmistakably Japanese children scrambled for a few cents worth of coins.

When I read the newspaper articles about this incident and the criticism that it provoked, I couldn't help thinking about myself, for I too am unmistakably Japanese. Yet I am not qualified to criticize these children, for I have shouted as they did; I too, in my youth, used to scream without knowing shame. And now I am a young man who cannot forget it. The only difference between these children and me is that their shouting is greeted by indignant glares from the adults, the same adults who taught me how and what to shout. . . .

Foreigners enter a country, a place where other people live, and they are clad in military uniform. Surely such an invasion cannot always proceed naturally and smoothly. It would seem unavoidable, proper even, that various frictions arise.

And yet the Japanese people, who had surrendered unconditionally, welcomed the victors into their country with smiles and waves and shouted *hallos*. There were no resistance movements of any significance. And looking back today, we can be thankful that the futile spilling of blood was thus avoided. Nevertheless, it is significant that resistance movements just naturally did not occur, and that the defeated Japanese were willing and able to grin and shout *hallo*. I discovered some years later when I first read French history that the people of a defeated nation are capable of behaving very differently than we Japanese did. It was the first time that such a possibility had ever occurred to me. I had often heard people say that World War II was Japan's first defeat since the beginning of recorded history. Considering it was something that we had never done before, it seemed to me that we had accepted defeat with remarkable poise and skill.

At any rate, when the occupation troops first arrived in our village, we children shouted to them at the top of our lungs. We put everything we had into those shouted *hallos*, but the foreign soldiers looked very grim as they rode past us in their jeeps. I suppose it was a weird experience for them, entering a small village at the bottom of a hushed valley deep in the mountains to be greeted by beaming Japanese children who were shouting *hallo*. That is probably why they wore such sullen expressions as they rode past in the jeeps, hands tightly gripping their automatic rifles.

But the soldiers very quickly grew accustomed to our way of welcoming them. They began to wave back, and sometimes they would throw us gum and chocolate. At that point we began to grow decadent. Some of the cleverest in our group managed somehow to equip themselves with more elaborate phrases.

Gibu mee chocorayto, they would shout, or *Gibu mee cigarayto*, requests that seemed to have been inspired by their parents.

The foreign soldiers threw candy and cigarettes to the children; the children fought each other for these spoils. I have no intention of hiding the fact that my own fingers have fastened on chocolate bars which were hurled out of a jeep. It is an embarrassing recollection, but there is no denying that it happened. I have no right to criticize the children who turned to the sailors on a foreign ship and shouted *Gibu mee monee!*

But the average Japanese undoubtedly sees in these children a reflection of his own shame. There is no essential difference between occupied Japan and Japan today, yet the child who shouts *Gibu mee monee* today is certain to be severely reproved.

But how, we might ask, do the Japanese react when positions are reversed? Some time ago a member of the Diet—he was a conservative—traveled around Asia, and I remember reading his account of the trip. Apparently, whenever he went into the streets of a certain Asian seaport, a group of children would surround him and scream *Gibu mee monee*. A familiar phrase. At first he threw them coins, but after a while he began to get very annoyed and would flee to his hotel. But even in the hotel, he said, he encountered people who began right away by asking for money.

It was clear from the tone of the Diet Member's story that he, as a Japanese, had been arrogant and patronizing with the people of another Asian country. In other words, his attitude toward the people of Asia was precisely the same as the Occupation Army's attitude toward us. Of course he is not the only one: the average Japanese feels superior in some way to the other people of Asia. When they see photographs of celebrations in the People's Republic of China, for example, pictures of young women parading in the streets, many Japanese must clench their teeth against a giggle, as though they were being tickled. This sort of defiant pride in Japan's isolation from the rest of Asia goes a long way toward explaining the difficulties, many of them incredibly trivial frictions to begin with, which constantly beset Japanese–Asian relations. The Japanese tendency to submit to mastery by the Westerner with smiles and shouts of *hallo* while he maliciously snubs his Oriental brothers, this somewhat effeminate tendency, is poisoning not only the Japanese economy but all of Japanese culture as well.

[Ōe, "Portrait of the Postwar Generation," pp. 347–51]

TANAKA KŌTARŌ

A graduate of Tokyo Imperial University, the training ground of statesmen and jurists, Tanaka Kōtarō (1890–1974) was a follower of Uchimura Kanzō (see chap. 47) before being converted to Catholicism in 1926. While chief justice of the Supreme Court in postwar Japan, Tanaka gained prominence as an interpreter of the new constitution and as an outspoken critic of Marxism at a time when few writers dared oppose it on intellectual grounds. In the following selections, Tanaka discusses the main trends of thought in modern Japan as they affect the success of democratic institutions. The "search for truth" in his title relates to questions of natural law, individualism, and morality, and to issues underlying both the Meiji and postwar constitutions.

Tanaka responds to many of the same trends as does Ōe Kenzaburō in his reminiscence of the Occupation period, but Tanaka's reactions are more sanguine with respect to the possible convergence of Japanese and Western values.

IN SEARCH OF TRUTH AND PEACE

Ethics and Politics

Surveying the general trend of political thought in the modern world and particularly in Japan, we may observe that its most striking characteristic is its ethical indifference. This reflects the domination of humanistic studies in the nineteenth century by the dogmas of natural science. After the Meiji Restoration, with the introduction into Japan of European and American culture, we ignored the ethical and religious bases of that culture and sought only to adopt its natural science, its material technology, and its external institutions. The subsequent trend of Japanese political thought has further intensified that tendency. The only thing that has lent any ethical character at all to our political life has been the consciousness of our "national polity" and a sense of reverence for the emperor. In recent times, however, not only did these attitudes lead to superstition and a loss of sanity, but also they developed into a form of ultranationalism that recognized no ethical restraints on the nation's conduct and justified immoral policies of imperialistic aggression.

The Japanese people cannot be considered traditionally unethical. The enlightened leaders of the early Meiji period themselves had faith in Buddhism and were trained in Confucianism, but the generation that followed them was exposed neither to the discipline of Oriental moral codes nor to the influence of the Christian faith that underlies Western culture. As a result they lapsed into ethical indifference or lack of conviction. . . .

A serious weakness in our political thinking that has not yet been corrected is the attitude of relativism. In the postwar period, with the adoption of the new constitution, democracy and pacifism have been loudly acclaimed; but do our people today really have faith in these fundamental principles? Do they, in the bottom of their hearts, realize how greatly they have erred in the past, or do they take the attitude that, having been beaten, there is nothing else they can do? . . .

Politics has as its end the realization of the common good (*bonum commune*), which is inconceivable apart from the mission or destiny of man. What, then, is man's mission? Is man's mission to be found apart from his individuality, as, for instance, in an organization embracing the individual or in the service of culture existing apart from man? . . .

From the standpoint of collectivism, the supreme value lies in organization. The individuals who represent its parts are absorbed into the organization that stands for the whole and, serving it, are considered mere means for the enhancement of its power and prosperity. The extreme example of this point of view is Nazism, the errors of which need not be elaborated upon here. From the standpoint of "culturism," which places a supreme value on culture, the meaning of human life is to be found in service to culture, in the creation of cultural value. Nevertheless, just as organization should exist for the sake of man, culture should exist for the sake of man and not man for the sake of culture. In the last analysis, man's value as an individual comes first, and the value of organization or culture has no more than a subordinate significance. . . .

So to the common good that is the aim of government, although the material and economic life is by no means negligible, the most essential thing is morality, and all else is, at best, secondary in significance. . . . Our new constitution is permeated with the "lofty ideals which govern human relationships," based on the universal principle of humanity, the laws of universal political morality, equity, good faith, justice, peace, freedom, and order. Thus the primacy of morality is recognized in the conduct of both our domestic and foreign affairs. Moreover, those who discuss politics today, almost without exception, acknowledge the necessity for a moral transformation of our political life. But to achieve this will require of our political analysis that their whole worldview be reintegrated in this direction. That is, they can no longer insist on the importance of morality while permitting themselves the contradictory view that in fact, economics and military power take precedence over morality. . . . [pp. 30–43]

On Authority

An utter denial of the idea of authority could well be called the characteristic of our present era of transition. It had been thought that authority was the most essential property of militarism and extreme nationalism. Now that they have been driven to the wall and face extinction, it is thought that authority too must be banished with them.

Authority, however, is not the special property of militarism or extreme nationalism. Like "rights" or "freedom," it is not intrinsically either good or bad but ethically neutral. It works for good or ill depending on the end it is made to serve. . . .

Let us consider first the government. In the old constitution the supreme authority in government was the emperor, but in the new constitution it is what is called "the people as a whole." . . . The Meiji constitution was adopted unilaterally by the will of the emperor; it was a so-called constitution by imperial grant. The new constitution, however, was adopted by the Diet, that is, by representatives of the people. The people's right to adopt the supreme law of the land, or constitution, derives from their possession of sovereignty.

Even assuming that the people possess absolute authority in the matter of government, can the Diet in fact decide anything and everything by majority vote? There are some things that not even the English Parliament, which is recognized as having absolute authority, can do, such as change males into females. The majority vote of the people is likewise limited by the laws of nature and the principles of things, which may take the form of natural laws or the ethical laws of human society. The constitution adopted by majority vote may not be in conflict with such fundamental principles. . . .

If this interpretation is correct, then while the constitution is the supreme law in relation to other actual laws, still . . . as an actual law itself, there stands above it, behind it and under it as a base, the natural law that represents truth and order in the universe. This natural law is what defines the limits of actual laws. It demonstrates that even the will of the people, though having the supreme authority in the adoption of a constitution, nevertheless is not absolute but is relative to and governed by a higher principle. Whether sovereignty rests with the majority of the people or with the emperor makes no difference. The question was never raised under the Meiji constitution, but it should be understood that even the supreme will of the emperor cannot be in conflict with the natural law.

The third article of the preamble [to the new constitution] states that "the laws of political morality are universal," and the eleventh article asserts that "the basic rights of man are enduring and inviolable." Such laws—such natural laws—are not confined to one nation or one period of time. They endure, and they do so because they are founded on the true nature of man.

Therefore, to say that the people possess sovereignty and supreme authority is true in a formal sense, but intrinsically the people are limited to what in a true sense is the supreme norm: the natural law. To put it another way, it is truth itself which governs social life. In truth itself rests true authority. . . .

Japan in the World

Situated at the extreme eastern end of the known world, an isolated island with its back to the Pacific, Japan has never achieved a position, culturally speaking, as a cooperating member of the international community. It is true that Buddhist and Confucian culture were introduced by way of Korea and imported directly from China and that four hundred years ago Catholicism was introduced and showed signs of spreading with striking rapidity before being suppressed for political reasons. But in return for what Japan received from other cultures, what does it have to offer other peoples?

Since 1868 European and American culture and institutions have been introduced to Japan, but whereas the assimilation of Buddhism and Confucianism extended even to their underlying ways of thought, the transplanting of Western culture and institutions was done in such a way that they could send down no deep roots here. Our society has been culturally no more than a colony of Europe. . . . Faced by the urgent need to fashion a centralized state, to develop the material prosperity of the nation, to revise the unequal treaties that had humiliated us internationally, Japan could not help but take a superficial and imitative approach to the adoption of Western culture. What we imported was, in a word, the individualism of the Enlightenment and the material technology—the natural science—of the West. Such tendencies were quite characteristic of the exponents of Europeanization in the Meiji era [1868–1912], who believed that this type of culture actually represented Western civilization. Therefore it was not at all surprising that in reaction to this there should have appeared the exponents of Japan's "national polity." They mistook individualism and materialism for Western culture and opposed to it a Japanese culture stressing collectivism and the national spirit. . . .

At the beginning of its history, Japan kept its doors completely open to the world. Today Japan finds itself thrown completely into the maelstrom of world politics and world culture. Because of this, we should remember, we have acquired new responsibilities to the peoples of the world and to our times. To fulfill these responsibilities is the highest destiny of the Japanese people. . . . Japan must not only fulfill its own peculiarly creative mission among the peoples of the world but also realize its universal mission. Japan possesses its own characteristic moral convictions and fine social traditions which are a legacy from Buddhism and Confucianism. Of these it must preserve all that is good. The Oriental peoples, including the Japanese, have always recognized the natural [moral] law. This [recognition of] natural law is the common spiritual basis uniting the cultures of East and West. . . . Faith in its own national moral virtues, as perfected in Christianity, could be for a reborn Japan its qualification as a member of the world community of peoples, giving us for the first time in our history a sense of Japan's place and mission in the world, and providing a spiritual bond between East and West, as well as a firm basis for world peace. [pp. 191–95]

[Tanaka, *Shinri to heiwa o motomete*, pp. 30–195; WTdB]

Chapter 45

DEMOCRACY AND HIGH GROWTH

Japan's postwar era was a long one. For decades, people grappled with the consequences of war, defeat, and the radical changes of the Occupation era. They struggled to define the proper relationship among citizens, state, and monarch and, at the same time, argued about the proper place of Japan in the global order of the Cold War era. Many of the documents in this section present the varied and evolving visions offered in the debate over these fundamental issues.

Peace was embraced by many as the essence of Japan's postwar reformation. This pacifism sprang primarily from a determination to never again be horribly victimized by war. It mobilized a powerful constituency against the U.S.–Japan security alliance [Anpo], established in 1952, and made this the most contentious foreign policy issue in Japan for at least twenty years. By the early 1950s, the concepts of "peace" and "democracy" had acquired a clear political meaning. Allegiance to these concepts defined a person as a member of the "opposition" or the "progressive" forces. In the 1950s, progressive labor unions also mobilized both their members and local communities in important campaigns for higher wages and greater control of the workplace. Such causes as a ban on nuclear weapons testing gained broad support well beyond the political left, which was centered on the Socialist and Communist Parties. Women joined these movements in large numbers. An active student movement emerged, led by the Zengakuren (All-Japan Federation of Student

Self-Governing Associations). In the divided political culture of early postwar Japan, these voices sought to give meaning to the postwar reforms through grassroots activism.

Not everyone shared this enthusiasm. Members of the prewar and war-time ruling elite, especially those in the bureaucracy and those in the Liberal and Democratic Parties, managed to preserve their positions of power. Many of these leaders tried to roll back institutional reforms at home, revive Japan's military power, open the way to an independent foreign policy, and restore the imperial symbol to something closer to its prewar perch at the apex of the social and political hierarchy. Although they were unable to realize these ambitious goals, they did gain significant popular support and enjoy some success. They reconcentrated economic power under the banks of the old *zaibatsu* (business conglomerates) and restored centralized control over education policy and the police force. They even built a new military, called the Self-Defense Forces, albeit one with no prospect of projecting power beyond Japanese borders. In the 1950s, business and co-operatively inclined labor unions consistently confronted and defeated militant unions.

The conflict in the divided politics of the early postwar era came to a peak in 1960 when the government overrode a huge protest movement to renew the U.S.–Japan Security Treaty. But the reactionary drive of the 1950s fell short of its most cherished goal of amending the constitution by eliminating article 9 and banishing its democratic "excesses." Over the next two decades, the ruling elites shifted to a strategy of accommodating the new order rather than dismantling it. They moved to capture a growing political center by co-opting programs of citizens' movements or left-wing parties with initiatives such as the "income-doubling plan." As they did so, some of the local bases and national leaders of the progressive forces moved to the center as well. A new breed of union leaders consolidated control, first in private-sector workplaces in the 1960s and gradually in the public sector in the 1970s and 1980s, arguing that cooperation with management and short term moderation in wage and other demands would guarantee the long-range prosperity of the corporation and its employees. But in the 1960s and 1970s, other forms of political activism emerged with new force to challenge the established powers. In addition to a substantial movement opposing Japanese support for the American war in Vietnam and a new wave of activism among women demanding legal and economic equality with men, the environmental movement gained great force by defending the victims of industrial pollution in several famous cases.

As people in postwar Japan dealt with these political issues (and as the exchange in 1960 between Maruyama Masao and Yoshimoto Takaaki makes clear), they also worked hard to rebuild shattered homes and enjoy private lives, returning to more normal routines of school, work, family, and play.

The economy recovered in the 1950s, surged in the 1960s, and continued to grow through the 1970s and 1980s when other global economic leaders suffered bouts of stagflation and recession. Consumers were exhorted in print, on radio, and on television to partake of the "bright new life" of the modern era by purchasing products flooding from Japanese factories, especially electrical appliances. By the 1970s, the consumerist commercial culture that had emerged in the early twentieth century, especially among middle-class city dwellers, included the vast majority of people. Japanese society was no longer a place where most worked just to fulfill their basic needs for food, clothing, and shelter. To wit, the proportion of household budgets spent on food fell from about one-half in the early 1950s to just under one-quarter by the late 1970s.

As people were "liberated" to pursue their wants and desires as shaped and manipulated by mass advertising, a succession of consumer durables moved from undreamed luxury to possibility. In the mid-1950s, in a play on the three sacred regalia of the emperor (jewel, mirror, and sword), irreverent pundits began to speak of the "three sacred regalia" of modern life: television (black and white), washing machine, and refrigerator. By the mid-1960s, more than 90 percent of the population owned these consumer goods, and observers began to talk of the "three new regalia," also referred to as the "three C's": car, cooler (air conditioner), and color television.

More and more people became able to afford the "typical" modern life emblematized by these possessions, or at least reasonably hope to obtain this life for themselves or their children. As this happened, a large majority of people in Japan came to identify themselves as members of mainstream or middle-class society. This change in social consciousness is neatly reflected in social surveys beginning in the 1950s, which indicated that nearly 75 percent of the population felt they belonged to the upper, middle, or lower level of "the middle class." By the late 1970s, this proportion topped 90 percent. Perhaps most notable was a significant decline over these years in the number of members of the self-identified "lower-middle class," matched by a sharp rise, from about 35 to 60 percent, of those who placed themselves squarely in the middle of the middle class. This and other surveys producing similar results led observers to marvel at the advent of a nearly universal middle-class society in what had recently been a society marked by sharp divisions of social status, wealth, and power. The 1980s were a high point of Japan's celebratory rhetoric as a model to the world of economic affluence and social stability. Methods of Japanese business management, in particular, were promoted for exporting to flagging economies in the West. But as the final document of this chapter makes clear, by the end of the 1990s a decade of economic stagnation had generated a profound sense of stasis or crisis for many and a belief that the glory days of middle-class prosperity and security had come to an end.

THE MOVEMENT AGAINST THE SEPARATE TREATY AND THE U.S.–JAPAN MILITARY ALLIANCE

In the late 1940s, when the prospect of a peace treaty loomed on the horizon, an impassioned debate began over Japan's proper international role, particularly the nature of its relationship to the United States. After more than fifty years, this debate continues. Among the most important early statements of principle was the following declaration issued by a group of Japan's prominent intellectuals. In early 1949, they began to organize the Peace Problems Discussion Group. Then, when the Cold War intensified, it became clear that the Soviet Union and its allies were unlikely to sign a peace treaty allowing the United States to maintain a military presence in Japan. The debate thus centered on whether Japan should insist on a "comprehensive" treaty with all the nations of the world or sign a "separate" treaty with the United States and its allies, which would implicitly or explicitly commit Japan to a military alliance with the American side in the Cold War. In later years, the advocates of a comprehensive peace took the lead in opposing as unconstitutional the U.S.–Japan Security Treaty and the buildup of a Japanese military in the form of the Self-Defense Forces.

DECLARATION OF THE PEACE PROBLEMS DISCUSSION GROUP ON QUESTIONS SURROUNDING AN AGREEMENT ON PEACE (KŌWA MONDAI NI TSUITE NO HEIWA MONDAI KONDANKAI SEIMEI)

In late October 1949, questions surrounding the conclusion of peace with Japan occupied for a time the center stage of a lively debate, both inside Japan and abroad. When it appeared likely that peace plans could soon materialize, the two Peace Problems Discussion Groups of Eastern and Western Japan agreed to meet again for joint discussions of this question, as they had in the preceding year.

The declaration that is reproduced here . . . originated in our shared concern for the fate of Japan and our yearning for peace in the world. . . . Its conclusions were reached only after being subjected to scholarly scrutiny from every imaginable side. [Thirty-five signers' names are omitted.]

Declaration

We, who one year ago announced to all our shared opinion regarding the causes of war and the foundation of peace, issue here again a declaration regarding the latest problems related to the conclusion of peace and its subsequent guarantees. The gravity of this matter is unparalleled for us. We are convinced that its resolution will ultimately determine the fate of Japan. As we reflect deeply on the fact that at the opening of the war, we ourselves let pass the opportunity to determine our own fate, we wish at precisely this juncture to determine our own fate by our own hands. That is, guided by a desire for peace and by love for our ancestral country, we have investigated with great care the various problems surrounding the conclusion of peace and finally come to state in public a common view that transcends our individual political positions. All will probably agree that the Occupation by the Allied Forces has afforded important stimuli and left a solid foundation for the democratization of Japan. At the same time, none can doubt that further progress toward democratization depends on the responsibility and creativity of the Japanese people themselves. In other words, it is imperative that the Japanese people firmly establish relations built on free interchange and sincere cooperation with all the peoples of the world, by securing a formal peace agreement with them. The conclusion of peace and an end to the Occupation are the urgent need and demand of the Japanese people as a whole.

Yet for a peace agreement to be truly meaningful in both content and form, it cannot be an agreement in name only; such an agreement will only heighten the danger of another war. An agreement must be all-encompassing. The present situation certainly is marked by worldwide confrontation, which obstructs the conclusion of an all-encompassing peace. We are greatly encouraged that the principles of international justice and morality, recently affirmed by the International Military Tribunal, persist even as they seem to be submerged by this confrontation. And if we reflect on the reasons that led Japan to accept the Potsdam Declaration and capitulate to the Allied nations, our desire to restore peaceful relations with the Allied Powers is surely reasonable.

Such is our general conclusion. Before summarizing the conclusions to our earnest debate, we must point out two fundamental maxims that undergird our debate. They are (1) our sacred duty to contribute to preserving world peace in accord with the peaceful spirit indicated by our constitution and (2) our fervent wish that Japan attains economic independence as soon as possible and no longer imposes a burden on other countries.

1. As its most important condition, Japan's economic autonomy requires that it engage in comprehensive, close, and free trade relations with all Asian nations, especially China. Needless to say, this condition can be met only through a comprehensive peace. Separate peace treaties will sever the relations between Japan and China as well as other nations; they will by necessity place the Japanese economy in a position of dependence on, and subordination to, particular nations. Undeniably, if it were allowed to persist, the loss of economic autonomy would lead to the loss of political autonomy. And although Japan does not wish for this result, a deteriorating livelihood for the people poses a latent threat to peace. More than the short-term gains promised by a separate peace, we seek to emphasize the economic and political autonomy of Japan.

2. Without question, the controversy over concluding a peace treaty stems from the fact that the world is divided into two opposed camps. Our own fervent hope for a comprehensive peace and peaceful coexistence of these two worlds

is strongly encouraged by continuing determined efforts of those on both sides to adjust their differences and reach a comprehensive peace with Japan. While we adhere to the peaceful spirit of our constitution, we must not approach this problem with a passive attitude in the face of a volatile international situation; rather, we must approach it with a positive determination to work toward a reconciliation of the two worlds. In addition, our obligation here to encourage a rapprochement between these two sides derives in part from the debt of our war responsibility. If we conclude a so-called separate peace, it will catapult us into one of two opposing camps. This would strengthen our ties with that side, but it would result in a continued state of war with the other side. It would further intensify the unfortunate enmity with the latter and more generally exacerbate the polarization of the world. We find this simply unacceptable.

3. With regard to post-treaty security arrangements, we call by all means for a position of neutrality and nonaggression and for membership in the United Nations. The United Nations, as is apparent from its charter, crystallizes in the present mankind's ancient, time-honored quest for peace. Together with all the people in the world who pray for peace, we invest great trust and hope in this body. The Declaration on Human Rights adopted by the third General Assembly of the United Nations enables us to demand these rights not only within our own country but in the international arena as well. This fact gives us new courage. Without doubt, both the principles of neutrality and nonaggression as well as our membership in the United Nations are premised on reaching a comprehensive peace. A separate peace treaty or a de facto separate peace will involve military cooperation with specific countries or the granting of military bases to specific countries. However one describes such arrangements, they will contradict the preamble and article 9 of our constitution. They will further contribute to the destruction of Japan and the world. Under no circumstances can we accept this. The fate of Japan will turn to the better only when Japan devotes itself fully to the spirit of peace and proceeds resolutely on the road to self-determination and independence.

Conclusions

1. We Japanese must insist on a comprehensive peace.
2. Japan's economic autonomy cannot be achieved through a separate peace.
3. In regard to post-treaty security, we desire neutrality, nonaggression, and membership in the United Nations.
4. We absolutely oppose granting military bases to any country for any reason.

January 15, 1950, The Peace Problems Discussion Group

Supplement: As has become evident already, our declaration rests on the demand for a comprehensive peace. At the same time, some of us see considerable meaning in the conclusion of a separate peace but are no less moved by a desire for peace and a loving attachment to Japan. Respecting these desires and attachments, we devoted due deliberation to these various arguments.

[Peace Problems Discussion Group, in *Sekai*, no. 51 (March 1950): 60–64; AG]

NAKASONE YASUHIRO: A CRITICAL VIEW OF THE POSTWAR CONSTITUTION

On July 30, 1953, a young parliamentarian named Nakasone Yasuhiro gave the following speech (in English) to an international forum at Harvard University. Part of why the speech is important is that Nakasone later became a leading politician in the Liberal Democratic Party, serving as prime minister from 1982 to 1987. The speech also is noteworthy for articulating the dissatisfaction felt by many other politicians and citizens at the time, who viewed Japan's postwar political system, particularly the constitution, as imposed on the nation by the United States. Nakasone objected especially to the presence of American forces in Japan under the security treaty—as did his political opponents on the left, the authors of the declaration of the Peace Problems Discussion Group.

It is noteworthy, too, that Nakasone later modified his views of the need to revise the constitution. In the late 1950s, politicians in the Liberal Democratic Party pushed the government to convene a constitutional commission as a first step toward revision, against fierce opposition from the political left. Over several years, the commission heard testimony from many individuals, including Nakasone. But in 1963, he argued that the position of the emperor in the new constitution, as "the symbol of the state and of the unity of the people," more appropriately reflected his traditional, pre-Meiji role. According to this reasoning, which many Japanese people came to accept, it was the powerful imperial institution of the Meiji constitution that was the exception. Such an interpretation led Nakasone and other conservatives to accept the postwar constitution's treatment of the emperor.

THE "MACARTHUR" CONSTITUTION

The present Japanese constitution given by General MacArthur (sometimes called the MacArthur Constitution) has many commendable points, and I believe that especially those points related to pacifism, democracy, harmony between internationalism and nationalism, and respect for the basic human rights are worthy of preservation. However, the question is not entirely one of content. The important factors of democracy lie in methods of establishment. This constitution was drawn up in English by the Occupation Forces and swallowed whole by the Japanese in their anxiety to gain independence from foreign military powers as soon as possible. Such a document could hardly be called a constitution in the true sense of the term.

If Lincoln's words "Government . . . by the people" have any truth, a constitution for the Japanese should be made by the Japanese. I have no doubt that when such a constitution is made, Americans will be satisfied and pleased with the result—the birth of real democracy in Japan.

A constitution should be of such a sacred nature that a majority of the people would risk their lives to defend it. But how many Japanese are there today who would risk their lives to preserve the MacArthur Constitution? The present Japanese constitution is a product of the honeymoon period between the United States and Russia soon after the war. In making the constitution, Russia exerted its influence to weaken Japan. Today, it has even become a strong weapon for the Communists in their so-called peace approach. In 1947, the United States changed its policy to take a strong stand against Russia, but Japan is still floundering about due to its political disability.

There are many technical points which should be revised, but two important points in the MacArthur Constitution require immediate revision. I refer to the prohibition of armaments and the article relating to the Diet cabinet system. . . .

With a view to accelerating permanent friendship between Japan and the United States, I am anxious to see the following points taken up as soon as possible:

1. To revise the MacArthur Constitution in order to establish Japan's own defense force.
2. At the same time, to convert the present security treaty into a Japanese-American alliance to be formed with both countries on an equal footing.
3. To withdraw American forces gradually in proportion to the increase of Japanese forces.
4. At the end of the Pacific War, the Allies ordered the total dissolution of Japan's armed forces. Today, in view of the menacing situation in Korea and Manchuria, that dissolution has proved to be an unexpected mistake. We hope, therefore, that the United States will now furnish us with aid sufficient for us to rebuild our defenses.

[Nakasone, "The Problems of Japanese Democracy," pp. 331–42]

THE GOVERNMENT'S VIEW OF THE ECONOMY IN 1956: "THE 'POSTWAR' IS OVER"

Published in the wake of a year of remarkable economic growth—considered by many the start of Japan's "high-growth era"—the government's 1956 White Paper on the Economy was simultaneously positive in its view of past achievements and cautionary for the future. It suggested that the economy was shifting from an era of easy gain through simple "recovery" to a time when investment in costly new technologies would be the engine of growth. The White Paper accurately described the critical importance of technological innovation in the economic takeoff of high-growth Japan. In addition, buried midway through a concluding paragraph in the introductory chapter of this long publication was a famous statement: "already, the 'postwar' is over" (*mohaya sengo de wa nai*). The phrase had appeared as the title of a magazine article several months earlier, written by a professor of literature at Tokyo University.[1] It resonated in popular imagination, and in short order it became a widely circulated buzzword that defined the upbeat spirit of the era. Perhaps nothing conveys the cultural, political, and economic centrality of the bureaucracy in modern Japanese history as well as the fact that the use of this expression in a dry government document helped it become a long-remembered slogan.

DECLARATION OF THE DIRECTOR OF THE ECONOMIC PLANNING AGENCY ON THE OCCASION OF THE PUBLICATION OF THE WHITE PAPER ON THE ECONOMY

Concluding Remarks

The swiftness of the recovery of the postwar Japanese economy has defied all expectations. It was nourished by the diligence and hard work of the Japanese people and favorable global circumstances.

However, it must not be forgotten that the very depth of the valley into which we were thrown by defeat heightened the speed of our climb out of this valley. The economy has been buoyant. During the process of recovery, it was enough for our policies to steer clear of the pitfalls of inflation, on one hand, and a deterioration in the balance of international payments, on the other. Consumers bought more goods, and businessmen eagerly made investments. Now the buoyancy of the era of recovery has run its course. To be sure, because Japan is poor, latent consumer demand and a latent need to invest remain high in comparison to other countries of the world. But compared to the time just after the war, the intensity of desire has clearly declined. Already, the postwar is over. We now face a different situation. The growth spurt of recovery has ended. Growth from now on must be buttressed by modernization. And progress in modernization is possible only through swift and, at the same time, stable economic growth.

Introducing new things always brings resistance. It is possible that for a time contradictions in backward sectors of economy and society will be intensified by modernization. But in the long run, the manifold contradictions inherent in all sectors, such as small- to medium-size businesses, labor, agriculture, etc., can be resolved through economic development. Since modernization is the

---

1. Nakano Yoshio, "Mohaya sengo de wa nai," *Bungei shunjū*, February 1956.

only direction the national economy can take, the burdens that accompany its pursuit have to be shared among the people in accord with their abilities. . . .

We have to adapt ourselves as quickly as possible to the constant progress of global technology and the resulting changes in the world environment. If we fail to do so, not only will a bigger and bigger gap open between ourselves and the advanced industrialized nations in qualitative levels of technology, but our quantitative lead in industrial production over the developing nations that pursue the industrialization of their countries according to long-term plans will probably narrow as well.

Reflecting on such world trends, we must not become drunk with the successes of a quantitative economic boom brought about by strokes of good fortune. Our urgent need at this point is to embark on building a new nation by riding the wave of the world technological revolution.

[Economic Planning Agency, *Economic White Paper*, 1956, pp. 42–44]

THE TRANSFORMATION OF THE POSTWAR MONARCHY

One of the most important changes in twentieth-century Japan was the postwar transformation of the monarchy. Under the Meiji constitution, the emperor was a ruler with theoretically absolute powers. He used these powers to influence decisions of state, and others wielded them in his name. Under the postwar constitution, that same emperor was limited to a role as "the symbol of the state and of the unity of the people." The significance of this change, and its pros and cons, has been a subject of impassioned debate. The following insightful commentary on the character of the postwar imperial institution was written in 1959 at the height of the "prince and princess craze" sparked by the announcement that Crown Prince Akihito (the son of the Shōwa emperor, Hirohito) would marry Shōda Michiko, a commoner (albeit an extremely wealthy one, the daughter of a leading industrialist). The author, Matsushita Keiichi, was a professor of European political thought. Although he was a sharp critic of the prewar monarchy and had a detached view of the enthusiasm for the upcoming wedding, Matsushita took issue with those who lamented the "Michiko boom" as a revival of the old emperor system. Instead, he astutely interpreted it as a sign of the throne's ironic transformation into something far less menacing.

THE EMPEROR SYSTEM OF THE MASSES

On November 27 of last year, a "Chrysanthemum Curtain" covered all of Japan. At the very moment when the Chrysanthemum Curtain that shrouds the imperial house itself was said to have been lifted with the "love match" of a "commoner" princess, it rode a wave of media attention to envelop the whole of Japan.

Certainly, people will differ in their response to this Chrysanthemum Curtain. Yet no matter how they react, they cannot remain wholly indifferent. In this way, the crown prince has become "our crown prince."

In the December 8 edition of the *Yomiuri* [newspaper], Murakami Hyōe spoke of this situation as an "unconditional surrender" to the crown princess boom. He went on to state: "Times when the whole world goes crazy, so that a sane person seems mad, are not limited to far-off antiquity after all." Yet I believe Murakami is mistaken when he argues that "[the fuss over the wedding] has simply brought old things to the fore, covered in new cosmetics, for all to see." . . .

What has come to be called the princess boom is not, in Murakami's sense, a revival of "various old things" using "new cosmetics." Rather, haven't the "new cosmetics" dealt a decisive blow to these "various old things"? Surely, the boom of the commoner princess's love match could have taken place only under this new constitution. Isn't it more appropriate to call this a new constitution boom?

The objective conclusion that can be drawn from the recent designation of a crown princess is that the emperor system under the new constitution—the emperor system of the masses, so to speak—has matured. The *grief* and *resentment* felt toward the absolutist emperor system of old must be linked to the *recognition* that a new emperor system of the masses has matured. After all, what Murakami has called an "unusual response" to the crown princess is a normal reaction in the sort of mass society that is developing in Japan today. It is therefore an urgent task to delineate the contours of the emperor system of the masses, that is, the emperor system under the new constitution, or the "democratized" emperor system. The emperor system that is being revived today is, of course, not absolutist, nor is it a limited monarchy along the lines that developed in Europe in the nineteenth century and was sought in Japan during the period of Taishō democracy [1920s]. While it is changing into a monarchy of the masses, the imperial house is absorbing new energy from the cheers of the "masses." Today we must transcend the *feelings* of the wartime faction and must clearly *understand* this transformation.

The political romanticism that sees "the entire Japanese people offering their congratulations together" may be rather silly, but we ought to reject the vulgar political cynicism that maintains a clever stance of "indifference to the private affairs of the imperial house." The princess boom cannot be simply dismissed as a state of rapture over saccharine phrases. Nor is it simply a private affair of the imperial house. Hidden in this boom is the core problem of Japan's postwar political transformation.

From Living God to Star

"Love! That's so cool!" A female university student is transported with joy. "The two of them in a love marriage, at their age! This will really influence the rest of us [not to give up]." People sigh with relief, and cliques of girls burst into giggles: "If only we'd gone to Sacred Heart [as did Princess Michiko]!" Others console their peers: "You know, there's still hope for us. The crown prince's younger brother is still around!" . . .

Not all Japanese have gone crazy, to be sure. Yet the trend in the media's treatment of this event has been set, and the younger generation has no remembrance of the idea that the emperor is a god in human shape or a living god. This does not mean that the emperor or the imperial house emerged from among the masses. Rather, it is the reverse [he has come down to the masses]. Since the imperial house is no longer the object of awe or fear, it has come to be viewed with affection.

When a personality plays a political role, it can do so in two fundamentally different ways. One would be the style of rule through intimidation. Here private matters are shrouded in secrecy. A ruler looks out over the masses as a superhuman being. A second is the style of rule through intimacy, in which private matters are laid out in the open and authority rests on a personalized affection. Under the old absolutist emperor system thus far, the emperor, while occasionally acting with benevolence, remained "above the ninefold clouds" as a living god always to be feared. Imagine the emperor's portrait of prewar days, in its enclosed sacred altar. This conveys a sense of the former situation. But since the surrender the emperor has worn a suit and tie. His picture is even taken with his family. And the crown prince even falls in love. This change in the atmosphere surrounding the imperial house is more important than the change in the emperor's constitutional position. . . .

Looking at the matter in this fashion, existing theories of the emperor system such as Inoue Kiyoshi's cannot account for the emperor system of the masses. The so-called progressive critique was paralyzed in the face of that boom of last November because it had prepared no theoretical perspective on this emperor system of the masses. From now on into the future, stories such as "The [New] Couple's First Voyage Together" or "A Baby Is Born" will surely be broadcast one after another. The degree of interest in these may vary, but this princess boom is by no means going to be a one-time abnormal reaction.

[Matsushita, "Taishū tennōsei ron," pp. 30–32, 46; AG]

TWO VIEWS OF THE SECURITY TREATY CRISIS OF 1960

In 1960, while a year-long coal miners' strike dragged on in southern Japan, unprecedented demonstrations and protest greeted the government's effort to renew the U.S.–Japan Security Treaty. For several weeks, tens of thousands of demonstrators filled the streets of Tokyo in the vicinity of the Diet building.

The government literally rammed the renewal through the Diet on May 19, 1960 (as security guards shoved the Speaker of the House sideways like a ramrod through a crowd of opposition-party Diet representatives to call a snap vote). Although the ruling Liberal Democratic Party prevailed, the protests were sufficiently volatile to cause the United States to cancel a planned visit by President Dwight Eisenhower to mark the renewal.

In the wake of these events, some of the nation's leading intellectuals debated the meaning of the popular uprising against the treaty. In these excerpts from two famous essays, Maruyama Masao first offered his critical view of this popular consciousness and action. He lamented the self-interested stance of a new breed of postwar individualists and the lack of connection between the activists on the streets and the everyday lives of working people. In reply, the poet and philosopher Yoshimoto Takaaki presented a different reading. Using the idiosyncratic label of "a fictitious system," he criticized the consciousness and behavior of the mainstream left-wing forces as rooted in a concept of the "public," with overtones of the wartime ethos of self-sacrifice for the "public" state. He then found cause to celebrate the phenomenon of private political and social consciousness that Maruyama deplored, as a possible harbinger of a "true" system.

MARUYAMA MASAO

"8/15 AND 5/19"

Maruyama Masao's essay "8/15 and 5/19" is presented in interview format. Although most of the questions have been deleted, in one case the "Q" refers to the questioner.

In prewar Japan, there was the curious notion of the *kokutai* [national polity]. In one aspect, the *kokutai* was a state system that placed the emperor as its apex. On the other hand, it was sustained by emotional factors that cannot be dissolved into the political structure or the legal system. Rather, the system of the state built on this kind of irrational emotion by its subjects. But while the *kokutai* as a total structure has vanished like mist, the governing elite has made no efforts to replace it with a democratic ethos from below, which has a comparable emotional effect. In essence I think it has instead set up a legalistic democratic system in the expectation that an acquiescent consciousness of the imperial subject still endures. Therefore, it is still likely that ideas of democracy will lean toward a formal legalism. When the new constitution was adopted, the governing elite expected that *kokutai* emotions were still deeply rooted among the people. This also led to the famous "theory of longing" [for the monarch] in [postwar] popular sovereignty. But if the consciousness of the imperial subject retreats into the background and a democratic consciousness of some sort takes hold, the ruling class will be in a bind. Even now, it cannot rely on anything like the emotionalism expressed in the concept of the *kokutai* in the past.

The definition of democracy that Minister of Labor Matsuno [Raizō] advanced at the roundtable discussion on the June 4 strike . . . is a classic case in point. He said: "There are rules in democracy. No one can deny that the demonstrators' collective action broke the rules. What I am referring to here as rules is law, and for someone who has broken the law to shout for democracy is quite presumptuous." He further stated the following: "It is the rule of democracy to engage in consultation within the limits of the law." Here, first of all, a formalistic legalism has replaced the rule of law. The *spirit* of law has dissolved into existing legal rules. This is how the great majority of government officials think. Second, democracy has been replaced by "consultation," the peace-and-harmony myth of the village community. Under Japan's wartime system this consultation-ism was practiced in countless deliberative bodies. This was, so to speak, a totalitarianism built on consultation. There was no consciousness of definitive decisions, so that responsibility for decisions vanished like morning mist. The ruling class's image of democracy has been formed through a combination of such legalism and consultation-ism. For this reason, it is not aware that one side is in a position to resort to lawful force and turn its decisions immediately into law. In other words, it lacks an awareness of power and a consciousness of responsibility. In its place, there is always the illusion or self-deception that an unimpeded consultative relationship exists between the government and the people. . . .

Shinmin, the Japanese word for "imperial subject," is a synthetic combination of "ruling official" and "common people." Under the extreme circumstances of total war during the Pacific War, the *min*, or "people," were completely transformed into *shin*, or "vassals." "One hundred million assisting imperial rule" and "sacrificing the private, serving the public" were ideological expressions of this. The postwar began as an enormous reverse flow from *shin* to *min*. Democracy started out in such a form. Roughly speaking, in my opinion, the revived *min*, or "people," have then branched out into two directions. One is the direction of "privatizing" the "people." The slogan of "sacrificing the private, serving the public" was reversed. In the rural villages we see this mainly in individual farmers' increased interest in economic gain and the collapse of the prestige of local notables. In the big cities we see this in the overwhelming drive to enjoy private life in the sphere of consumption. This is well known. The second direction the "people" are taking is toward active reform movements. Here, a measure of "sacrificing the private, serving the public" remains as an underlying ethos. From the perspective of the privatized citizen, the activist's movements and behavioral style seem aggressive and noisy, and his enthusiasm is rather boring.

But in my view, in the absence of the people's former subject consciousness, these divergent tendencies among the people have favored the governing elite to no small degree. The political indifference of the privatized group, although it differs in form from the imperial subject consciousness, is very convenient for the governing elites who wish to "contain" the activist group. In addition, in positive terms, the rulers can tap the farming households' interest in profits by offering so-called subsidies. It seems to me that these policies toward the "people" of "divide and rule," however painstaking they may be for the ruling elites who must now control society without the charisma of the emperor, have continued to this day. To put the matter in more positive terms, if these two groups among "the people" were to happen to come together in human relations and patterns of action, this would mark an important turning point in the history of postwar Japan. The struggle to oppose the Police Duties Law [of 1958] was a good start, and I believe that the surge of mass demonstrations this May and June signifies another huge step in this direction. To be sure, the farming villages and small regional towns certainly remain a problem for the future. In the big cities, the frequent comparison of the demonstrators to sports spectators, made by Prime Minister Kishi [Nobusuke] and his supporters, exaggerates the situation. But there is a kernel of truth in what they say. In the face of this, I thought Yoneyama Mamako's remark quoted in the June 8 issue of *Josei jishin* was marvelous:

> I had always thought that politics was something that specialists handle for us, but when I saw the vote forced through parliament on May 19, I had the feeling that this was really odd. So far I have never had an interest in politics, but I thought this was something one could not simply leave to others. This is something one has to keep an eye on. . . .

This expresses wonderfully an attitude of keeping watch on authorities even as one maintains one's own "place."

Q: Since public intellectuals or celebrities can act independently, it is easy enough for them to recognize that "There's something wrong here!" and it is easy enough for them to take action to resist. But won't the ordinary organization man, such as the downtown business district "salaryman," find it impossible to act in this way?

That's right. I think the article entitled "Seen from the Inside of the Building," which appeared in the July feature edition of *Shisō no kagaku* (*The Science of Ideas*), depicts this aspect of the situation extraordinarily well. It states that the clamor is only in the streets, only among a small segment of the people. Within the office buildings an orderly discipline is maintained, as always, and regular work [is] performed. As soon as one steps inside, the heaviness of modern architecture, in which one is isolated by walls, merges with the naturalism of the Japanese building. In addition, the feeling of being torn away from the "street" is enhanced by the minute division of labor necessary for modern production. The reality of daily work presents task after task. Therefore, even for a person who conscientiously completes his daily job and goes to present a political petition only after [his] work is done, the fact remains that work is work. On the other hand, people who skip work to join protests will be ostracized from their place within the system and lose all respect. In this sense, unless one finds a way in one's own consciousness to connect one's work to the world beyond the wall, this thick wall will not be broken down easily.

[Maruyama, "8/15 and 5/19," pp. 51–54; AG]

YOSHIMOTO TAKAAKI

"THE END OF A FICTITIOUS SYSTEM"

Maruyama Masao has assigned the movement for citizen democracy its place in postwar history, from his position on the sidelines. In his "8/15 and 5/19," Maruyama Masao argues that the rise of the movement for citizen democracy since [the demonstrations of] May 19 [1960] constitutes the principled foundation for spontaneous and voluntary action. He believes that such a social consciousness among the citizens has been generated by the same process that imposed democratization policies *from outside*, which then produced Japan's constitution *from above*, a constitution that in the fifteen postwar years the ruling elite has come to view as a nuisance.

According to Maruyama Masao, the masses who were uniformly organized in the form of "imperial subjects" under the emperor system of the war years have, in the postwar era, reverted back to the status of masses in the form of "the people." In this process they have branched out in two directions. One has been a turn toward the private self, a move toward an assertion of individual rights and private interest as the highest priority. The other has been a flow into an activist reform movement. This current, he believes, preserves in its ethos the consciousness expressed in such [wartime] slogans as "sacrifice the private, serve the public" or "give priority to the public good." According to Maruyama Masao, the "people" exhibiting the first tendency have drifted toward political indifference and indirectly assisted the efforts of the rulers to "contain" the second sort of activism. In this view, the security treaty struggle is assessed in positive terms as a first step—in terms of both personal relations and patterns of action—toward a broadening of desirable interaction between these two streams of the "people."

Stated in this way, Maruyama's view expresses the typical logic of progressive enlightenment thought or false democracy. It well represents the general views of the present leadership of the Japanese Communist Party.

To be sure, the fifteen postwar years have witnessed a process by which bourgeois democracy has matured among the masses. From the confusion of defeat—the world of the black market and rubble in which a state of nature obtained—a consciousness inevitably took root that valued sectoral interests over the interests of society as a whole and that further valued private self-interest over the interests of social sectors. In tandem with the maturation of postwar capitalism, this sort of democratic consciousness was able to develop, particularly in the postwar generation that was spared the intellectual experience of the prewar and war eras. Maruyama takes a negative view of this consciousness that gives priority to private interests. He criticizes it as the consciousness of the politically indifferent. Yet the truth is precisely the reverse. This private sense of interest forms the basis of postwar "democracy" (bourgeois democracy). If we do not recognize something positive at the root of this development, we can recognize no progressive developments whatsoever in Japanese society since World War II. Such a privatized consciousness neither idolizes the organization nor exalts state authority. . . .

When this autonomous consciousness that grants "private" interests priority over the interests of society emerged in combination with revolutionary political theory, it relativized the myth of the established vanguard [political party]. It gave rise to the independent actions of Zengakuren, which simply ignored organizational bureaucratism. It demonstrated a dynamism unimaginable in the case of the prewar faction that was terror stricken by a self-imposed illusion of suppression. When the prewar faction called the Zengakuren faction reckless youth, it felt the pain of the wounds inflicted on it by the authority of the prewar emperor system. The Zengakuren faction was as free as it could be, at least from an imagined fear of suppression. Here the cleavage between the understanding held by the prewar faction and the postwar generation of the level of development of postwar society, the transformation in the structure of power, and the transformation in the consciousness of the masses, has become apparent.

I regard as true "democracy" (bourgeois democracy) the spread of a situation in which "private" interests are the highest priority. In contrast, I cannot but think that what Maruyama refers to as "democracy" is a fictional "democracy." It is nothing but a mutation of the fictional progressivism that came into being as it flowed down from the pyramid of fictional vanguard thought. . . .

These thinkers [Maruyama and Takeuchi Yoshimi] have probably misunderstood the meaning of "democracy," just as they completely misunderstood the meaning of "dictatorship." The report "Seen from the Inside of the Building"[2] by the association for "Ideas in the World of Practical Business" made this clear. One "salaryman" is noted to have written as follows:

On the morning of May 20, I took a look at the newspaper and was thunderstruck. In a state of undiminished agitation, I swayed in the jammed commuter train, then rushed to my company longing for someone to speak

2. *Shisō no kagaku*, July 19, 1960.

with. Yet, certainly not on the morning of the twentieth and not to this day, was even a single word spoken at work on the topic of the government violence on this occasion. For my part, I started no conversations but immersed myself in my daily business as always. It would appear that the most natural thing to do, from the moment one faces one's desk at the company, is indeed to keep silent on such matters as this violence and slowly drop one's pen. In short, one is overwhelmed by the peculiar atmosphere of the corporate body.

The author of this report touches on this note and confesses that since the inside and outside of the building are divided into two different orders and atmospheres, we inevitably feel confused as to our own proper position as we run back and forth from the inside to the outside. This report goes beyond the fictions of the citizen-democrat intellectuals and the like, as it points out the error of praising those who participated in the Anpo [U.S.–Japan security alliance] activities as progressive and condemning the inactive elements on the inside as backward and as mere bystanders. . . .

The activism of the citizens and common people during the Anpo period is not only different from the enlightenment thought of the citizen-democracy intellectuals. Rather, it is completely unconnected to it. These people bear the continually increasing burden of a sensibility gripped with an amorphous boredom, enjoying a bloated material life and a relatively improved standard of living but an overall feeling of impoverishment. In this situation, having lived through the growth and stabilization of society since 1955, these people grasped in the Anpo protests for the first time an opportunity to freely vent their own feelings of alienation. At least, this was the first opportunity for citizens as well as common folks to grasp the opportunities of large-scale mass action that those in the labor movement experienced several times soon after the war. As they rallied under the banners of the principles of citizenship and the People's Joint Struggle Committees, they may have brought to mind memories of the war or perhaps memories of the anarchic state at the time of defeat when they were cast adrift, bombed out of their homes. At the very least, only ideological blindness could fail to see that these citizens and common people possessed a different sort of destructive force from that of the ideologues of the people's joint struggle committees and of citizenship.

The security treaty struggle was a strange battle. In the fifteenth year of the postwar era, the fictitious system has ended. Despite this, a true system is still being forged, in an immature form, within the vanguard movement, among the citizens' thought, and within the worker's movement. We are now entering a period of stormy transition, a period of severe confusion, a period of intense confrontation. Thus the situation appears strange. The fictitious system that has come to an end has nonetheless grown large as if it were completely unscathed, and it talks about the future in rosy terms. That is, it is able to talk about it only in rosy terms. By passing through the security treaty period unscathed, it has in truth perished already. And because it has perished, it cannot but talk in rosy terms. Whether we will be able to respond to this quiet but certain reversal of the situation will depend solely on the maturity reached by the elements among the intelligentsia and the workers' and citizen movements, who may consti- tute the vanguard of a true system.

[Yoshimoto, "Gisei no shūen," pp. 70–76; AG]

THE CONSUMER REVOLUTION IN POSTWAR JAPAN, 1960

In addition to its annual White Paper on the Economy, the government's Eco- nomic Planning Agency published an annual White Paper on the People's Livelihood. The 1960 edition is noteworthy for its upbeat description of a rev- olution in lifestyles that had been under way for several years. This White Paper describes the changing habits of daily life that accompanied postwar economic growth and presents an image of the salaryman household of the new middle class that would soon become a social cliché. In the final section, it also alludes to the worried spirit that moved state bureaucrats to try to guide and regulate social change.

THE ECONOMIC PLANNING AGENCY'S WHITE PAPER ON THE PEOPLE'S LIVELIHOOD

The Lifestyle Revolution and Its Background

Looking at the transformed consumption patterns among the people of the past few years, one sees numerous radical changes. No one at the recovery stage of the postwar years, not to mention the prewar era, could have imagined this. Lifestyles have changed with special speed. In a word, this can be called Westernization. One can see this in eating habits . . . clothing habits . . . and housing habits. Let us now try to analyze this lifestyle revolution from various angles.

First, in daily household life, purchases of labor-saving goods are on the rise. At mealtime we see an increase in the use of canned and processed foods like ham or sausage and, most recently, the appearance of instant curry rice, soups, noodles, and other instant foods and also more eating out or buying prepared food from caterers. In dress, we note more purchases of ready-to-wear clothes for women and children and a shift toward Western-style clothing at home [as well as in public]. All this reduces the amount of sewing done at home. A reduction in household labor due to the introduction of washing machines and vacuum cleaners, electric rice cookers, and refrigerators is marked as well.

A second noteworthy trend is the rapid proliferation of consumer durable goods. In the prewar era, even a wealthy household might at best own a radio, a sewing machine, and an electric fan. Yet now households in large cities own TV sets, cameras, washing machines, and the like at a rate of one per two households, and electric refrigerators and vacuum cleaners are also spreading gradually.

A third trend is the increase in leisure consumption. The proliferation of TV sets is one example, but recently everything, from the sale of indoor leisure goods to recreational travel and sports outside the home, has been flourishing. . . .

What has brought about these transformations in our consumption habits, which one might fairly call a lifestyle revolution? If we sort through the various reasons involved, we come up with roughly five factors.

The first is more income. . . . Consumer outlays in 1960 exceeded prewar levels by 35 percent. Needless to say, this is enabled only by larger incomes owing to the expansion of the national economy.

The second is the influence of the technological revolution in the postwar period. The appearance of TV sets, washing machines, refrigerators, and plastics as well as synthetic fibers is due to the postwar technological revolution. . . .

Third is the advent of a new mass of consumers brought into being by the changes in social structure from the prewar era . . . when the spread in incomes was extremely large. This has shrunk significantly in the postwar era.

In addition, the social base for mass consumption is nurtured by postwar changes in the family system, such as the fragmentation of extended families into nuclear ones, the move of women into the workplace, and the rise in the number of two-income couples.

A fourth factor is value change. From the Tokugawa era to World War II, our people's basic attitude toward life focused on diligent saving and restrained consumption. Frugality was among the great virtues of everyday life. After the war, opportunities to encounter the living patterns of Europeans and Americans increased, and our people's attitudes changed significantly. Values of frugality gave way to the idea of enjoying life. . . .

Fifth is the influence of aggressive marketing by producers and retailers of consumer goods. Some even argue that all demand for goods beyond the basic necessities of clothing, food, and housing is in a sense created by the producers through advertising. . . .

The social stratum in which the lifestyle revolution has made the greatest inroads is that of employee households in the big cities. Above all, we can call the households of big-company employees the emblem of this stratum. Their incomes are higher than average; their livelihoods are secure; their working hours are shorter; and they have more spare time. In addition, they have access to company-run support facilities and all kinds of amenities for leisure activities. . . .

Future Problems in National Life and Tasks for Its Administration

[Finally there] is the problem of consumer protection, which has assumed greater importance as the lifestyle revolution progresses. The government has supported consumer protection all along and has imposed regulations and control based on the Foods Hygiene Law, the Law for Quality Standards for Agricultural Products, the Textile Goods Quality Labeling Law, the Regulations for Control of Electrical Appliances, and the Industrial Standards Law. However, in the present situation, when new consumer goods appear one after another as the technological revolution continues, consumer protection through such controls is insufficient. Our task from now on in protecting consumers will be to help them obtain the necessary information and knowledge that will allow them to make autonomous choices and integrate these new goods rationally into their lives, without being at the mercy of the advertising jingles of producers and retailers. In America, nongovernmental consumer organizations have a long history. They provide consumer-oriented information about the purchase and choice of goods and conduct information campaigns. Consumers in our country must develop a greater consumer consciousness; consumers must become more active in a healthy fashion; and we must develop the new field of consumer education.

[Economic Planning Agency, *Kokumin seikatsu hakusho*, pp. 11–22]

THE ECONOMIC PLANNING AGENCY'S NEW LONG-RANGE ECONOMIC PLAN OF JAPAN, 1961–1970

The "income-doubling plan" of 1961 was among the most important government statements in the postwar era. It was noteworthy, first, as a sign that the Liberal Democratic Party's political leadership, under Prime Minister Ikeda Hayato, had shifted its strategy for achieving political control and stability from revising the constitution and suppressing the political left to promoting economic development and popular welfare. In addition, the plan was an important example of the ambitious reach of Japan's economic bureaucrats in bodies such as the Economic Planning Agency and the Ministry of International Trade and Industry. Here, the government not only set targets for growth rates, but also indicated which industries should be the focus of investment and growth, determined specific amounts for investment, recommended mergers, called for interfirm cooperation, and specified an active government role to guide the private sector toward these goals.

THE INCOME-DOUBLING PLAN

Purpose of the Plan

[The] Doubling National Income Plan[3] should have an objective of achieving full employment and radically raising people's living standard by rapidly doubling the gross national product. Special effort must be made to rectify the existing disparity of living standards and income between farming and nonfarming population, between major enterprises and smaller business, between urban and rural residents, and between high- and low-income strata, to promote balanced development of national economy and people's living.

Targets of the Plan

The plan is aimed at raising the gross national product to ¥26,000,000 million (in fiscal 1958 prices) within 10 years to come . . . from the ¥13,600,000 million (¥13,000,000 million in fiscal 1958 prices) in 1960. . . .

Advancement of Manufacturing Industries and Strengthening of International Competitive Power

It is necessary to seek expansion of scale and diversification of production, based on the healthy growth of industries, as well as to further the reorganization of the industrial structure with emphasis on the heavy and chemical industries, which has been in progress since the end of World War II.

In this case, emphasis must be placed upon advanced processing industries, which look toward solidification of export structure suitable to the international market. The entire process of development, moreover, must be so arranged as to pivot on the machine and chemical industries. In particular, the machinery industry is most counted upon not only as an export industry but also for its ability to absorb surplus labor. In other words, the industry will occupy an important "strategic" position for a rapid growth of economy and advancement of the industrial structure. . . .

Many obstacles are foreseen in working toward the increase in industrial output and diversification of industries as outlined above, and efforts to overcome these obstacles will be required. The following policies will have to be

---

3. This document was published in English by the government, in addition to the Japanese version.

carried out not only to expand industrial output quantitatively but also to meet demands for the advancement of the industrial structure with trade liberalization as the stimulus.

First of all, it is necessary to modernize equipment, establish and specialize the mass production system, standardize products, and strengthen competitive power in the international market through combination of industries. Secondly, as for the mining and manufacturing industries, it is essential to secure an estimated ¥16,000,000 million required for equipment investments and accumulate owned capital for that purpose in the next 10 years. The sum includes ¥5,500,000 million for the machine industry, ¥3,000,000 million for the iron and steel industry and ¥2,500,000 million for the chemical industry. Third, there is a need for a stable import of low-priced fuels and raw materials, such as energy sources, mineral products, and timber. Fourth, the environment of the industrial areas must be improved, and industries properly distributed to eliminate regional differences, while it is necessary to build new industrial areas. Fifth, national research institutes must be reinforced and assistance extended to private research work. At the same time, measures should be taken to train scientists and technicians; promote science and technology, especially for industrialization; and foster new industries. Sixth, small- and medium-size enterprises must be modernized, and the social division of work be established between large industries and smaller industries and also among smaller industries themselves. Lastly, in order to carry out the above-mentioned policies, the government must take adequate measures to supplement and guide private enterprises. . . .

[T]he following problems should be considered in studying a new industrial order in a long-range perspective.

The first is the expansion of enterprises to put up with international competition. For this purpose, consideration must be given to concentration, merger, and grouping of enterprises and establishment of the system of specialized production. Secondly, strong measures must be taken against economic recession. Efforts must be made to narrow gaps in business cycles through flexible customs policy and promotion of cooperation among enterprises. Third, close cooperative relations must be established between large and small- and medium-size enterprises. Fourth, an orderly import of raw materials from abroad must be secured through expansion of joint purchase and joint development of overseas resources. In this connection it is necessary to give due consideration to the prevention of excessive competition in overseas markets.

Measures for the maintenance of proper order have special significance in the transitional period of trade liberalization. They must be designed mainly for (1) prevention of confusion in the transitional period, (2) protection and encouragement of new industries and "growth" industries, and (3) smooth transformation of waning industries.

Only through these measures can trade liberalization and high growth rate be smoothly and securely realized.

[Economic Planning Agency, *New Long-Range Economic Plan of Japan*, pp. 8–10, 85–89]

ENVIRONMENTAL ACTIVISM IN POSTWAR JAPAN: MINAMATA DISEASE

In the 1950s, the devastating symptoms of what later was identified as mercury poisoning began to destroy the health, lives, and livelihoods of fishermen, their families, and the residents of Minamata City in Kyushu. The mercury was discharged into the bay by the Chisso Corporation as a waste by-product in the production of chemical fertilizer. Local residents and then a network of supporters nationwide organized a movement to provide compensation and redress and to prevent future pollution. A settlement reached in the 1950s offered meager payments to a small number of recognized victims and half-measures of prevention. The company denied responsibility and covered up evidence of the link between its production process and mercury poisoning. Then, from the late 1960s into the 1970s, a far more effective protest movement developed in a changed context. Economic growth had made compensation easier to afford, and it also made it easier for activists to communicate to a broader audience. The settlement was a landmark in the history of political activism by pollution victims and ordinary citizens, a case of effective mobilization outside the framework of both parliamentary politics and the mainstream political parties. The following statement conveys something of the emotional appeal to a broader constituency and the sense of betrayal and anger felt by citizens toward the corporation and the state. (The title of the book of Minamata-related documents that contains this statement is a grim pun. The word *shimin* in the title normally means "citizens" but here is written with the characters that mean "dead people." "We citizens" thus becomes "We dead people.")

WE CITIZENS: SIT-IN STRIKE DECLARATION
(WAGA SHIMIN)

As we who suffer from Minamata disease and our families continue our sit-in strike in front of the company president's office at Chisso headquarters [in Tokyo], how can we possibly thank the many people throughout the nation who have provided us with their warm support?

Although we began our negotiations with Chisso this past December 6, we have met nothing but a scheme to avoid us, in the form of a note mentioning the company president's (feigned ?) sickness. From Minamata to Tokyo, even if we families and victims did not expect to reach a final solution thereby, we did hope that our path would lead us to some tangible hint of a solution. These hopes were brutally shattered. What became clear, what was proved to us in Tokyo, was the immorality, the inhumanity, uncivility, the utter depravity of Chisso's leadership. These robotlike men raised a storm and tried to intimidate those of us who suffer from Minamata disease, our families, and all those who fervently love humankind. The cacophony of their pleas to "Let us do our job," uttered in unison by these robotlike men, has ignited the wrath of the many who suffer or who have died from Minamata disease. Our five or six encounters with Chisso's executive board have only strengthened our resolve and made us even more adamant in our determination. A string that is stretched to the limit is about to break. Even though we are in such an overextended state, we strive to retain our flexible and rich humanity and the abundant fighting spirit that lies hidden deep within us.

Our conversation with Mr. Satō continued far into the night as we talked about soothing our pain, gaining foresight, and repaying all the people throughout the nation for their cherished support. . . . As we enter the fifteenth day [of our sit-in], we continue to shout our "gratitude and appreciation for the privilege of life, health, and livelihood." Even if our voices may sound faint, from the site of our sit-in in front of the company president's office, we rejoice day by day in our fortitude. In Tokyo, the center of a Japan fast becoming an archipelago of pollution, an archipelago of wrath, we are able to meet our daily needs in the "Chisso Central Headquarters" building due to your kind support. . . .

A new year is about to arrive. We hereby solemnly declare that we will continue our sit-in strike into the new year, just as we continue it this day today with the support of people throughout the whole nation. We rely on the mighty tree of material and spiritual help of the people from the "Committee to Publicize the Minamata Disease."

(December 24, 1971. Issued by Kawamoto Teruo and other sufferers from Minamata disease taking part in the sit-in demonstrations)

[Ishimure, ed., *Waga shimin*, pp. 333–34; AG]

BULLDOZING THE ARCHIPELAGO: THE POLITICS OF ECONOMIC GROWTH

A little more than a decade after the income-doubling plan was announced, the newly installed prime minister, Tanaka Kakuei, issued his plan to "remodel" the Japanese islands. His *Building a New Japan* quickly became a best-selling book. Tanaka was adroitly responding to the growing popular unease at the price of affluence, in the form of environmental destruction in the industrial centers of Japan and the decline of rural areas. With this project to invest huge sums in roads and high-speed railways to reverse the flow from country to city that he lamented, Tanaka was also aiming to serve the construction industry, which had so richly supported his political machine. Scandal tarnished Tanaka's own career a few years after this declaration, but over the following decades the government indeed poured billions of dollars into public-works projects throughout the archipelago. These investments did not in fact stop the exodus of people into urban and industrial centers, but they did lead rural communities to undertake numerous projects to bring tourists "home" to the countryside.

EPILOGUE OF *BUILDING A NEW JAPAN*

Those born in the Meiji (1868–1912) and the Taishō (1912–1926) eras have a deep sense of love and pride in their native locales. While life in these rural villages may not have been rich, it was home. Home was the place where your stern father and gentle mother lived, where you could always find your child-hood friends, and whose green fields, rolling hills, and fresh streams remained with you forever. Seeking their fortunes, village youths left their ancestral homes for faraway cities where they studied, worked, married, and followed the course of their lives. Saisei Muroo, a poet of those days, sang in praise of his homeplace, "It is where my mind travels from afar." Whatever their fate, whether in success or failure, they always remembered the people and scenes of their unchanging homeplace.

I believe that the endless fountain of energy which has built today's Japan derives from the cherished and respected rural homes from which all of us have originally come.

In this great enterprise of remodeling the Japanese archipelago, I am moti-vated by a strong desire to rebuild the home of the Japanese people, which has been lost and destroyed and is declining today but which, once restored, will again give to our society a sense of tranquillity and spiritual enrichment.

It is true that the urban concentration of both people and production has been the driving force in building today's prosperity. The process of this massive flow has given rise to many whose only home is a two-room apartment in a big city, sapped the villages of their youth, and left behind only the aged and house-wives to sweat and toil in back-breaking labor. How can such a society generate the energy necessary to build a new Japan in the next hundred years?

It is such considerations as these that have impelled me to work on the policy of "dispersion" to reverse the tide of people, money, and goods and to create a flow from urban concentrations back to outlying areas, using industrial relo-cation and the nationwide communication and transportation networks as the main tools.

This plan for building a new Japan is a set of policy programs to solve simultaneously both overcrowding and underpopulation through the relocation of people and industry into less populated areas. It is, more importantly, an action program to implement these prescribed solutions.

I wish to activate the dynamo of our nation's powers to revitalize the declining rural areas of Japan. By moving pollution-free industries from large cities to outlying areas, local cities can be made strategic cores of development with improved income opportunities. Educational, medical, cultural, and leisure facilities will be adequately provided to enrich the local life environment. Those leaving the farm will find new jobs in local factories and stores while still being able to cultivate enough land to produce some rice and vegetables for their own consumption. Land they do not need can be leased for salaried cultivation. No longer will they have to leave their villages to seek seasonal employment in the large cities.

Japanese farms of fifty to seventy-five acres will be mechanically cultivated by a small number of highly efficient farmers raising stock in spacious pastures, growing fruit and rice in well-tended fields and paddies. Life in the large cities will also be improved. By relocating those industries and universities no longer needed in big cities, urban areas will be freed of pollution and high costs and made comfortable places to live in. City dwellers will work five days a week at worthwhile jobs. While they will live in apartments near their work in their twenties and thirties when they are in the prime of life, in their forties they will have homes in suburbia where they can take care of their aged parents. On weekends, they may enjoy family outings by car to nearby mountains, rivers, or beaches, or they may choose to engage in do-it-yourself carpentry or agriculture in their spare time.

Only when life in both metropolitan and rural Japan is reshaped into one humane, livable environment will the people take pride in their own communities and develop a strong sense of solidarity and mutual cooperation. So long as the people can enjoy the same conveniences and opportunities for self-development wherever they may live, their love for their homeplaces will be firmly restored and will develop into an abiding love of their homeland Japan.

[Tanaka, *Building a New Japan*, pp. 217–19]

THE PHILOSOPHY OF JAPANESE LABOR MANAGEMENT IN THE HIGH-GROWTH ERA

In this excerpt from his memoir, *Twenty Years of Labor Management* (*Rōmu kanri 20 nen*), recounting more than two decades as a labor manager at the Nippon Kōkan steelworks in Kawasaki, Orii Hyūga neatly summarizes the reigning ideology of Japanese corporate management toward the end of the high-growth era. By this time, corporate management had made its peace with labor unions, which for their part had generally adopted a stance of cooperation (critics would call it co-optation) toward the enterprise. Managers like Orii, as much as their counterparts in the union movement, denied that the interests of employees and employers necessarily conflicted. Instead, they presented an idealistic vision of the corporation as a cooperative body, the emblem of both productivity and human values in modern society. At the same time, Orii makes clear that harmonious industrial relations did not emerge naturally. He graphically describes the confrontations of workers with managers during the early postwar years. He also notes that such struggle seemed "unimaginable" in the early 1970s, when he wrote his book. In his view, the harmonious industrial relations of later years were nurtured by managers through scientific social analysis and careful policies to produce appropriate attitudes and behavior among employees.

TWENTY YEARS OF LABOR MANAGEMENT
(*RŌMU KANRI 20 NEN*)

I believe that a corporation is a cooperative body whose purpose is to produce social value and that the highest aim of personnel management is to produce a cooperative orientation among employees. To this end, my strong desire has been to promote policies that allow all employees to expand their abilities and improve their own lives while simultaneously developing the enterprise. I also came to believe that labor unions were indispensable as a check to ensure that management maintains this correct posture. . . .

Steps Toward a "Scientific Approach" to Personnel Management . . . Inaugurating "Job Surveys" in Search of a Basis for Labor–Management Dialogue

In May 1949 I was appointed head of the [NKK Kawasaki mill's] labor section [which oversaw negotiations with the union]. Labor–management relations consisted of one continuous string of confrontations. To be honest, I was more than a little worried about taking on this position. . . . Negotiations back then were menacing to an extent impossible to imagine today. Large crowds of union members were present, in addition to the union and management committee representatives who sat at the bargaining table. It was a sort of mass bargaining, probably a strategy to intimidate management with the force of the crowd. . . .

When I was appointed head of the labor section, I thought that this kind of [confrontational] labor–management relations could not bear any real fruits. I felt, above all, the need to somehow provide for the possibility of a more productive dialogue. I was interested in objective data that could provide a foothold for labor–management dialogue and become a basis for objective and calm judgments on both sides. For this purpose I thought that a point of departure might be careful analysis of the actual situation in the workplace. This was the strongest motive for us to conduct "job surveys" on a grand scale.

An additional trend in our company as a whole led us to push forward with these "job surveys." In the confusion after the war's end, all of us were groping in the dark to figure out what labor management was supposed to be. Before and during the war, labor management was authoritarian in character. It relied on coercive power from above to force obedience regardless of circumstances. In reaction to this, workers after the war tended to go too far in their refusal to accept any kind of authority. Thus, we were groping in the dark to come up with a basis for restoring order to the workplace. In this circumstance we began to talk of "approaching labor management as a science." In other words, we collected "scientific data" to provide a third-person perspective independent from the interests of either labor or management. The idea took root that if we took such data as a standard of judgment for settling problems in labor management relations, we could resolve impasses and reach agreements.

If one thinks about it, Frederick W. Taylor, the man who turned labor management into a systematic science, was a technician just like us who had accumulated on-the-job experience in the steel industry. His conclusions, also reached after racking his brain for some way to restore health to the extremely turbulent labor–management relations of his time, was nothing other than the realization that labor management had to be approached in a scientific way, its administration improved by collecting objective data concerning the actual situation in the workplace. In this sense, one might say that the "job surveys" we undertook aimed at a "scientific labor management" as envisioned by Taylor.

[Orii, *Rōmu kanri 20 nen*, pp. ii, 3–7; AG]

THE JAPANESE MIDDLE CLASS AT THE END OF THE TWENTIETH CENTURY

As the Japanese economy surged in the 1960s, proved resilient through the oil crises of the 1970s, and took off once more in the booming 1980s, a tone of celebration began to dominate journalistic and even academic views of society. Commentators praised the egalitarianism of Japan's new "mass middle-class" society. But by the end of the 1990s, after nearly a decade of economic stagnation, social commentary had decidedly turned gloomy. The stability of the middle-class mainstream seemed to be crumbling. The jobs of male breadwinners, even in large corporations, appeared insecure. The prospects for working women seemed especially poor. Access to higher education and home ownership, for decades the symbols of middle-class success, seemed endangered. This feature story, by Yada Giichi, in one of Japan's two most widely read national newspapers wrote of the demise of "mainstream" (*chūryū*) consciousness and typified the new pessimism.

"FAREWELL, MAINSTREAM CONSCIOUSNESS!"

For all of us who have been firmly confident about our mainstream life, the ground beneath our feet is shaking. With the economic future uncertain, enterprises have intensified their efforts at "restructuring." The stability of the work environment is crumbling. Real-estate prices, counted on as a source of collateral and capital, are plunging. Stock values, already hard hit, seem headed for a further decline. Interest rates are extraordinarily low, eroding the value of savings. Yet medical and other basic costs are steadily rising. In addition, the only growth sector in the working world takes the form of part-time or "temp" jobs. It is impossible for a regular full-time employee to continue at a job with any sense of security. There are no grounds for optimism. How does one live in an era when the once buoyant consciousness of the middle-class mainstream is surrounded by fog?

The Temp Business Is Thriving, but Employee Protection Is Lagging

Until now, temp work has been women's work, but lately businesses that dispatch men on a contract basis to work at construction sites or in warehouse jobs have rapidly expanded. According to placement companies such as Recruit, in recent years many businesses have reassessed those jobs they assign to regular employees and have tended more and more to reassign these tasks to temporary contract employees. The only sectors showing a strong continued demand for regular employees are fields such as computer networking, which need specialized technicians. In January of this year [1997] Nikkeiren [Japan Federation of Management Organizations] published "The New Japanese Model—In Search of a Third Way." In a survey conducted for this report, 64 percent of businesses replied that the category of employees engaged in "activities requiring long-term accumulated skills" had shrunk. Conversely, more than 70 percent responded that the employee categories described as "highly specialized skills" and "flexible hires"—in other words, both the categories of contract and temp employees—had expanded.

"What Japan needs to do to change its industrial structure is nothing less than making its employees more flexible. As things now stand, opportunities for employment will decline steadily," worries Arakawa Hajime, Nikkeiren's section chief for labor law.

Needless to say, businesses will have some need in the future for long-term or lifetime employees who form an enterprise's nucleus. Yet it appears that their percentage will fall in the next few years, from 80 percent at present to about 70 percent [of the workforce]. This means that [the number of] secure jobs will decrease. Even as the deregulation of labor markets gains force and the opportunities for temp agencies and similar businesses expand, a system of rules to protect working people is lagging behind. No one can feel secure.

[Yada, "Sayonara chūryū ishiki," p. 13; AG]

PART VII

Aspects of the Modern Experience

The chronological order followed in this book makes it possible to show the relationship between thought and its historical context. No reader would miss the connection between the early Tokugawa efforts to secure the realm and the efflorescence of Neo-Confucianism or, similarly, the link between early Meiji discourse and the establishment of the modern nation-state. In each case, the language, concerns, and arguments are characteristic of the times, immersing us in the life-worlds of the past. These historical episodes are connected to one another across time, not only by temporal accumulation or influence, but also by conscious retrievals of earlier traditions by later figures. Thus the reader can trace the changes in Neo-Confucianism during the Tokugawa period and afterward and the changes in the debates engendered by modernization from the Meiji era until the end of the twentieth century.

In this concluding part of the book, the chapters are organized by themes rather than chronology, precisely in order to trace such changes and continuities over time. The reader will notice many obvious links with earlier chapters, which treat similar themes chronologically. Here the thematic approach is intended to highlight what one might call the "sources of Japanese modernity." The four aspects of modern experience—new religions, cultural debates about Japan in the world, gender politics and feminism, and history writing and historical consciousness—are meant to be neither representative nor exhaustive but merely exemplary of the kinds of connections across time that existed in countless other domains of modern life. Following the lineages of the "old" new religions that emerged in the early nineteenth century through the new religions of the mid-twentieth century to the "new" new religions of the late twentieth century provides a sense of their commonalities and differences, in effect, a definition of what was "new" about the new religions in modern Japan. Similarly, it helps to see the development and vicissitudes experienced by one sect in different contexts. The history of Ōmoto, for example, reveals much about late Meiji modernity, ideological suppression in the 1930s, and postwar pacifism. Comparing one new religion with another provides a different angle of vision, not least the social insight afforded by the mettle of the two rural women whose revelations became the founding bases of Tenrikyō and Ōmo-tokyō. Indeed, their spiritual charisma and organizational effect suggest that their stories would not be out of place in the chapter on gender politics.

Chapter 48, "Gender Politics and Feminism," focuses on the relationship between gender and modernization, making clear the effects of industrialization, the nation-state, mass communications, and multiple shifts in power relations on the real women (and men) who lived through them. The image of the "traditional" Japanese woman, expressed in the phrase "good wife, wise mother," was a modern invention produced by a combination of late Meiji government ideology, the new civil code, and collective social opinion. Modern women were allotted this "traditional" role because, in the words of Harriet Taylor Mill, "men like it." That some women did not like it was the reason for the emergence of late Meiji feminism and the "new women," whose counterparts in Europe and North America held similar political and social attitudes. Just as in other societies, even though Japanese women did not agree among themselves about motherhood, suffrage, family, or work, their active engagement in these issues produced waves of feminism from the late Meiji "Blue-stockings" to Ueno Chizuko's "reflexive feminism" of the 1990s. And just as there was no single "traditional" woman or man, there was no singular "modern" feminine or masculine either but, rather, a complex landscape of gender and sexuality that has continued to change over time.

The same might be said of the ceaseless debates about the relation of Japanese culture and tradition to Asia, the West, and the world. Although the filings of ideas tended to arrange themselves, as if by magnetic force, around the polar imaginaries of East and West, in fact the cultural debates treated in chapter 47 usually revolved around the nature of the modern. The question was always what kind of modernity Japanese ought to have or what was wrong with the one they had and how it might be fixed. Some Meiji figures spoke optimistically about being both Japanese and modern at the same time, defining modern in Western terms, whereas others, like Natsume Sōseki, focused on the darker sides of modernization, both foreign and homegrown. In the 1920s and 1930s, intellectuals turned to culture in general and Japanese traditions in particular as a critique of the mass society and culture they associated with European and

American-style modernity. In the 1930s, what began as an antimodern nostalgia for the folk past and traditional ways turned into a strident anti-Western nationalism, culminating in the famous debates of 1942 about "overcoming the modern." In the postwar period, when Mishima Yukio celebrated the Japanese martial spirit and the cultural emperor, and Ōe Kenzaburō criticized Japanese ways and its emperor-system politics, they both were arguing less about the past than the present, less about tradition than modernity.

It was no different in the realm of modern history writing. From the beginning of the new "national history" in the Meiji period to the calls for transcending the nation at the turn of the twenty-first century, historians addressed the past according to their notions of what the future should look like. Their changing interpretations were grounded in changing and competing ideas and ideals of modernity. Chapter 49, "Thinking with the Past," follows history writing and popular historical consciousness across a century or more to show how historians' politics and methods changed and how differently epochal events like the Meiji Restoration and World War II were viewed by different people at different times. As has often been remarked, the modern mentality is everywhere obsessed with newness, which has only made it more attentive to the past from which it wanted to distance itself. History, it turns out, was a way of positing the condition of being modern.

Chapter 46

THE NEW RELIGIONS

Japanese religions of the modern period are commonly divided into the "established religions" and the "new religions." The term "established religions" refers to temple Buddhism, shrine Shinto, and older varieties of Christianity, while "new religions" refers to lay movements founded from around the beginning of the nineteenth century to the present. Because "new religions" can refer to religions that are two hundred years old, it is widely acknowledged that the term is problematic, but it has become firmly established in both scholarly usage and popular discourse. The doctrines of the new religions may derive from Buddhism, Shinto, or Christianity, or they may be independent creeds originating in revelations experienced by their founder. With an estimated one-quarter of the Japanese population as their members, the new religions represent an important part of modern Japanese life. Whereas temple Buddhism and shrine Shinto have declined since 1945, the new religions have experienced phenomenal growth in the postwar decades, making them the most vital sector of the postwar religious world. An authoritative work published in 1990 lists more than six hundred significant new religions in Japan today, and these are only the ones with sizable national or regional followings.[1] More are founded each year, although not all survive.

---

1. Inoue et al., eds., *Shinshūkyō jiten*.

New religions have appeared since the end of the Tokugawa period. The first cluster emerged near the beginning of the nineteenth century, when the system of social control was weakening and the legal prohibitions against the formation of novel religious societies under the shogunate were loosening. Continuing roughly until the Meiji Restoration of 1868, this first stage saw the founding of Nyoraikyō (f. 1802), Kurozumikyō (f. 1814), Tenrikyō (f. 1838), Butsuryūkyō (f. 1845), and Konkōkyō (f. 1855). The founder of Kurozumikyō, Kurozumi Munetada (1780–1850), was originally a Shinto priest; the founder of Butsuryūkō, Nagamatsu Nissen (1817–1890), was originally a Buddhist priest of the Nichiren sect. These two groups illustrate the importance of established religions as a source of doctrine and ritual adapted by founders for use in lay organizations. In Kurozumikyō and Butsuryūkyō, such practices as the recitation of Shinto prayers and the reading and study of Buddhist scripture, usually monopolized by clergy up to that time, were extended to the laity under the influence of distinctive founders who broke down the distinction between clergy and laity. But the founders of Tenrikyō and Konkōkyō were lay people before their revelations, and their prior religious affiliations played comparatively minor roles in the formation of their doctrines. Like many founders of new religions, Tenrikyō's founder, Nakayama Miki (1798–1887), was a woman.

Ōmoto was one of the most significant new religions. It was founded in 1892 by Deguchi Nao (1837–1918), whose son-in-law Deguchi Onisaburō (1871–1948) also had a part in its beginnings. Ōmoto doctrine had a prominent millenarian component, and Nao believed that a "renovation of the world" was imminent. Ōmoto was among the first of the new religions to utilize modern media, including a national newspaper. The newspaper was an invaluable aid in spreading Ōmoto beyond its original base in rural Kyoto Prefecture, and its novel doctrines attracted a broad spectrum of people. Its rapid expansion, however, led in 1921 to its suppression and, in 1935, to the most severe instances of state suppression of religion in modern Japanese history.

In the early twentieth century there appeared many new religions, including the Buddhist movements Reiyūkai kyōdan and Sōka gakkai, both founded in 1930 and both deriving from Nichiren Buddhism. In addition to them, religions formed by schism from earlier new religions, such as Honmichi (f. 1913, originating with Tenrikyō), Sekai kyūseikyō (f. 1926, originally an offshoot of Ōmoto), and numerous groups emerged from Reiyūkai, such as Risshō kōseikai (f. 1938). Gedatsukai (f. 1929) and Shinnyo'en (f. 1936) were the first new religions derived from Shingon Buddhism. Many new religions, as well as Christianity, were suppressed by the state before 1945, often on charges of lèse-majesté if their doctrines appeared to conflict with state Shinto.

After 1945, the state restrictions on religious life were lifted, and it was as if the floodgates had been opened. Religions suppressed before 1945, such as Tenrikyō and Sōka gakkai, regrouped their members and grew rapidly to become mass organizations. Many novel groups, large and small, were founded in the aftermath of war, not all of which have survived until the present. Tenshō kōtai jingukyō (f. 1944), Perfect Liberty kyōdan (f. 1946), Myōchikai (f. 1950), and many others flourished. The Ark of Jesus (f. 1960) was one of the most distinctive Christian new religions.

The new religions have flourished in the cities, where they offer small-group counseling in various forms with a powerful appeal, especially to women. In urban society, the new religions provide a surrogate family or community compensating for the cities' emotional aridness. When members face a problem of any kind, they can count on the sympathetic assistance of their fellow members. New religions provide accessible structures of rank in which women, the young, retired persons, and others can rise in authority through doctrinal study, proselytization, and volunteer work. New religions have contributed to society by constructing schools and hospitals, by engaging in volunteer activities of all kinds, and, in some cases, by creating nongovernmental organizations (NGOs) actively involved in the work of the United Nations. Political activity is an extension of this work. The most notable example is the 1964 formation by Sōka gakkai of the Clean Government Party (Kōmeitō).

How are the new and old in religion related? We first should note that between established Buddhism and Shinto, there is a "division of labor" in the performance of ritual, so that the shrines generally perform the rites of birth and marriage, and Buddhism maintains graveyards and performs funerals and ancestral memorials. Established Buddhism (temple Buddhism) is organized by complex ecclesiastical institutions and ordains its priests after a period of training and study, according to textually prescribed ritual. The priesthoods of both Buddhism and Shinto are mostly "hereditary" occupations in modern Japan, and both temples and shrines are frequently passed from father to son. Lay persons' affiliations also are passed from one generation to the next, more as a matter of family tradition than personal conviction. A definite distinction between priest and laity is maintained, and lay people are unable to perform the central rites of funerals and merit transfer to ancestors. In shrine Shinto as well, there are clear distinctions between priest and lay person, so that a priest's observance of purifications and abstinence entitles him (nearly all priests of both established Buddhism and shrine Shinto are men) to draw nearer to the gods than lay people can. Both traditions have ideas about the pollution of women and have historically barred women from priestly roles and leadership positions.

Since new religions frequently originate with a founder's revelations, their doctrines vary widely. Founders, both male and female, tend to be highly charismatic individuals who attract their first followers through healing and other "this-worldly benefits." Founders are sometimes seen as living gods, and their writings or sayings are regarded as sacred or as authoritative guides for members. At least in the first generation, followers are recruited through distinctive religious experiences, followed by conversions. The ethics resemble those of the established religions, being generally conservative and stressing sincerity, frugality, harmony, family solidarity, diligence, and filial piety. Whether they are Buddhist, Shinto, or independent, they usually place a premium on worship of the ancestors, although these practices occupy an ambiguous position in Christian groups. Shamanistic or spiritualistic practices to contact the ancestors are common. For the most part, anyone, including women, may acquire leadership qualifications, and leaders and ordinary members are separated by only a thin line. While some new religions provide for "ordination" and a monastic life for some members, this is rare.

Despite the variety of doctrine in the new religions, they tend to have a broadly shared perspective or worldview. The universe is seen as a vital, living thing sustained by divinities who usually are benevolent. Humanity shares the life of the universe and its divine beings through the heart-mind (*kokoro*). A major task of the religious life is maintaining harmony with the universe by nurturing one's own heart-mind, family relations, and ties with other people generally. Beyond that, harmonious relations with one's ancestors and the divinities are preserved through correct ritual and correct conduct. These lay societies frequently regard marriage as the most important occasion for religious training, requiring individual aspiration to be sacrificed for the larger interests of parents, children, and the family as a whole. Buddhist new religions deriving from the Nichiren line typically speak of their believers as bodhisattvas whose work in society improves the conditions of religious practice for all.

In the mid-1970s, around the time of the oil shocks, a cluster of new religions appeared that seem to be oriented differently from earlier religions. Whereas those that had been founded up to that time have a pervasively optimistic outlook on the possibility of salvation, stressing that all people can perfect themselves by their own efforts, the new religions that were established or experienced significant growth after that time tend to have a more pessimistic or fatalistic outlook. Groups such as Sekai mahikari bunmei kyōdan (f. 1962), Glad Light Association (f. 1969), and the offshoots of these two—Kōfuku no kagaku (Science of Happiness, f. 1896) and Agon-shū (f. 1954, but growing significantly after the oil shocks)—tend to stress the influence over human life of essentially unknowable, and not necessarily benevolent, forces. Another tendency of recently founded groups is the attenuation of the intensive small-group interaction characteristic of earlier new religions. In rare cases it has been reported that new religions' founders have such absolute influence over their followers that believers give over their own will in blind obedience. Aum shinrikyō (f. 1986), the religion linked to the 1995 poison gas attack on the Tokyo subway, fits this description. The group's writings record extreme predictions of apocalypse. At this early stage in the histories of these so-called new-new religions, it is impossible to know whether the current tendencies will endure or whether (as seems more likely), they will "mellow" as they gain age and stability and come to resemble their predecessors more closely.

The new religions also have developed distinctive religious thought. Kurozumikyō, one of the religions whose sacred texts are presented here, has nearly two centuries of history, and it regards the writings of its founder, Kurozumi Munetada, as sacred texts, along with Shinto prayers. Many of these are in the form of *waka* poetry. Tenrikyō's scriptures also are largely poetic writings, and some of them are accompanied by music, dance, and ritual. Some of the sacred writings of Tenrikyō and Ōmoto are delivered as the words of the deity, incarnated as the founder, as his commandments to humanity and predictions of millennium. Other groups' writings set out divinity's requirements of humanity both as general principles and in the context of specific cases. Buddhist groups identify special Buddhist scriptures, notably the Lotus Sutra, and they study them according to their distinctive interpretations and sometimes create abridged versions for daily recitation. The texts excerpted here illustrate the variety of sacred texts in the new religions. They were selected in consultation with adherents of each of the religions concerned, in order to present the most representative sample possible of each organization's central doctrines.

Nonetheless, any small sampling of the new religions is somewhat arbitrary, and it is inevitable that highly significant religions would be omitted. Five new religions were selected for this book on the basis of their historical and social significance: Kurozumikyō, Tenrikyō, Ōmoto, Reiyūkai kyodan, and Sōka gakkai. Collectively, they represent a cross section of the whole. Kurozumikyō is one of the earliest new religions and a sectarian form of Shinto, founded by a Shinto priest. Tenrikyō was founded by a woman on the basis of novel revelations not directly derived from either Buddhism or Shinto. Its headquarters has expanded into the religious city of Tenri. Ōmoto, founded by a male–female pair, emphasized a millenarian doctrine and spiritualistic practices; it gave rise to highly influential offshoots. Reiyūkai kyōdan was founded in the aftermath of the Great Kantō Earthquake of 1923 as a new type of Buddhism entirely for lay people. Its founders, a male–female pair, created an abridged version of the Lotus Sutra for use in ancestor veneration and attracted a large urban following, giving rise to many schisms that perpetuate its main beliefs and practices. Like Reiyūkai, Sōka gakkai was founded in 1930, but it was suppressed and its founders were imprisoned, so that it did not achieve significant growth until after 1945. Now it is the largest of the new religions and has sponsored the creation of a political party.

TENRIKYŌ

Founded in 1838 by Nakayama Miki (1798–1887), Tenrikyō was based on religious revelations that she received from the God of Origin, God in Truth (Tenri Ō no Mikoto). Born in Yamato Province (present-day Nara Prefecture), Miki grew up as a devout Jōdo-sect Buddhist in a prosperous landholding family, with a love of visiting temples and chanting *jōdo wasan* hymns. She received a level of doctrinal training exceptional for women and hoped to become a nun.

When Miki was thirteen, however, her parents arranged her marriage into a village headman's family named Nakayama. Miki was entrusted with many duties, which included caring for her husband's parents, managing the agricultural workers on the family's land, as well as working in the rice and cotton fields herself. Above all, she was expected to produce heirs to the family name and its position in the village as headman. She bore six children in all, always continuing her Buddhist devotions.

Miki lost two of her daughters to illness, and she feared the worst when in 1837 her only son, Shūji, came limping home from the fields complaining of excruciating pain in his foot. Miki was forty years old and in the latter stages of pregnancy when this happened. Desperately she sought out a doctor, but when he brought no relief, she went to a *yamabushi* (mountain monk) known as a skilled exorcist. Several times over a period of years, she brought the exorcist to her home to conduct healing rites. The *yamabushi*'s healing method was to summon the spirit responsible for the son's foot ailment into his female assistant, who would go into a trance. Then the *yamabushi* would interrogate the spirit incarnated in his assistant, exhorting it to leave Shūji so that his foot would heal. On the last of these exorcisms, however, the female assistant was not available, and Miki was suddenly called on to serve in her place. Quite unexpectedly, when Miki went into a trance under the *yamabushi*'s direction, the oracle she delivered bore no relation to the problem at hand: "I wish to take Miki as a shrine within which to dwell!" This demand was directed to Miki's husband. The *yamabushi* was unable to rid Miki of this spirit, and she remained in a state of trance for three days, sometimes sitting quietly, and at other times delivering oracles in an awesome voice, with her hands and body shaking violently. The possession was so violent that at times she seemed to be dragged about the floor, leaving her skin raw and bleeding, by the god who announced himself as the Heavenly Shogun, and then as Tenri Ō no Mikoto, the God of Origin, God in Truth.

Miki remained in this state until her husband relented. This was no small concession, as the prospect of Miki's becoming the "shrine" for this unknown deity implied that she would be released from her primary roles in the headman's family as wife, mother, and manager. When her husband yielded, Miki's trance came to an end, and Tenrikyō dates its founding from this time in 1838. She continued to receive oracles from the deity, who ordered her to "sink to the lowest depths of poverty." Eventually, Miki not only tore down the dwelling but also gave away the Nakayama family's wealth to the poor. Villagers regarded her as insane. Her husband died in 1853.

The scriptures of Tenrikyō refer to deity as God of Origin, God in Truth (Tenri Ō no Mikoto), as God the parent (Tsukihi, literally Moon-Sun), and as Parent (Oya). These different names refer to distinct aspects of deity. "God of Origin" refers to deity's creation of the universe and all humanity, and "God in Truth" refers to deity's constant sustenance of the universe and humanity. The name Tsukihi refers to deity's free and unlimited workings, day and night. In these ways, Tenrikyō developed a complex theology of a benevolent, universal creator who sustains humanity. This theology was neither Shinto nor Buddhist but the independent thought of Nakayama Miki.

Little is known about Miki's life during the sixteen years between the time of her first revelations in 1838 and 1854, the year she became known as a living god of safe childbirth. Miki gained fame as a midwife who rejected the local food taboos for pregnant women, instead telling them to have faith in god. As she later wrote, "The conception of a baby is by Tsukihi; giving birth to it, also, is by the work of Tsukihi."[2] Women flocked to receive her grant of safe childbirth, which consisted of blowing lightly on the abdomen and stroking it. She said that pregnant women did not need to wear a special sash (*obi*) or observe food taboos, and she rejected contemporary ideas that childbirth was ritually polluting.

When Miki extended her works to faith healing, she encountered opposition from Buddhist priests and *yamabushi*, but she also gained many stalwart followers. She received followers without regard to wealth, social status, or their other religious affiliations: "The souls of all people are equal, whether they live on the high mountains or at the bottom of the valleys."[3] Originally she had only a simple altar in her residence before which she received believers, but when she was joined by the carpenter Iburi Izō in 1864, he took the lead in constructing Tenrikyō's first sanctuary. Miki wanted a place where she could proclaim her doctrine and receive followers for counseling and where followers could gather and worship together. At that time, temples and shrines were mainly places for the clergy's performance of ritual, and Tenrikyō's emerging custom of assembling large numbers of people was viewed with suspicion. Shinto priests, Buddhist priests, and *yamabushi* invaded the sanctuary on numerous occasions, sometimes causing serious damage and bodily harm. Miki was detained, interrogated, and imprisoned by the police nearly twenty times.

The creation of a sanctuary in 1865 established Miki's birthplace as the *jiba*, the place where humanity was created, and to mark this sacred center, a pillar called the "stand for heavenly dew" (*kanrodai*) was erected there in 1875. The *jiba* is also the religion's headquarters. The stand consists of thirteen hexagonal blocks, its size and shape having been specified in all details by Miki, to symbolize human creation and spiritual maturity. Returning to the *jiba* on pilgrimage is a central practice in Tenrikyō, understood as a return to the original place of creation.

Miki saw creation as expressed in mythic form and directly linked to her understanding of salvation. "In the beginning, the world was a muddy ocean," begins the story. God drew forth myriad "seed" of human beings, whom he thereafter nurtured through many rebirths over an immense period of time.

---

2. Miki, *Ofudesaki*, vol. 6, p. 131.
3. Miki, *Ofudesaki*, vol. 13, p. 45.

The formation of the earth, the heavens, and the whole universe progressed in parallel with human development. Humanity's salvation comes through enacting the truths taught in the story of creation, which explains why God the parent took Miki as his shrine; why the *jiba* is the spiritual home of all humanity; why all humanity are the children of God and hence are siblings of one another; why humanity receives life only through God's providence; why humanity is to lead the "joyous life" (*yōkigurashi*) and manifest it to God; and, finally, why humanity should not conquer nature but coexist peacefully with it.

From 1866 to 1882, Miki developed a worship service consisting of two sacred dances, both accompanied by musical instruments and singing. The songs sung during both dances are compiled in the sacred text *Songs for the Service* (*Mikagura-uta*). The first sacred dance is called Kagura[4] and is a reenactment of Tenrikyō's myth of creation. It is performed only at the *jiba*, around the sacred pillar *kanrodai*, by five men and five women taking the parts of ten deities. The dancers wear carved wooden masks that symbolize ten aspects of divinity. The second sacred dance is called Teodori, or "Dance with Hand Movements," and it represents the "joyous life." Teodori is performed at both the *jiba* and local churches' monthly services, by three men and three women standing in a line. The hand movements express the meaning of the *Mikagura-uta* songs that accompany the dance.

Because the interference and persecution from other religionists continued, Miki's son, Shūji—who had, indeed, recovered from his ailment—sought and obtained affiliation with the Yoshida house of Shinto in 1867. Miki opposed this alliance with Shinto, saying, "True, the Yoshida clan is apparently great. But in fact it is no more than one of the branches of a tree. The time will come when it will wither."[5] Similarly, she was unimpressed by rumors that talismans of the Ise Shrines were falling from the sky, saying, "To compare it to the human body, it is like vomit and diarrhea. When vomit and diarrhea are excessive, the flesh itself will be drained. God is concerned."[6]

Tenrikyō grew through the Meiji period, continuing its expansion and suffering suppression under the influence of state Shinto until 1945. Tenrikyō's formal affiliation with Shinto ended, and its headquarters grew into a major religious city. At the end of the twentieth century, Tenrikyō remained an important presence in the Japanese religious world, with roughly 2 million members throughout Japan and in thirty foreign countries.

Tenrikyō has three sacred scriptures. The most important is called *The Tip of the Writing Brush* (*Ofudesaki*) and contains the religion's central doctrines.

---

4. The Kagura service is also known as the "Service of the Kanrodai," "Joyous Service," "Main Service," and "Salvation Dance," since its ultimate purpose is to bring about universal salvation.

5. Tenrikyō Church Headquarters, *The Life of Oyasama*, p. 76.

6. Tenrikyō Church Headquarters, *The Life of Oyasama*, p. 76.

It was composed by Nakayama Miki between 1869 and 1882 and is written in 1,711 *waka* verses. The remaining two scriptures are considered interpretive aids to the *Ofudesaki. Songs for the Service (Mikagura-uta)*, also composed by Miki, was compiled between 1866 and 1882. It consists of five parts and twelve counting songs to be sung while performing Kagura and Teodori dances. The third text, *The Divine Directions (Osashizu)*, is a collection in spoken vernacular form of transcriptions of God's directions and instructions from 1887 to 1907, given by Miki, and, after her death, continued by Iburi Izō (who held the title *honseki* [mediator of revelations]). Some of these directions were given in response to followers' requests for counsel, and others were delivered as "timely directions" not directly responding to an inquiry.

THE TIP OF THE WRITING BRUSH
(OFUDESAKI)

Part 8 of *The Tip of the Writing Brush* is the most complete portrayal of the founder and her mediation of the god Tsukihi. It explains that the founder is Tsukihi on earth and defines the meaning of the *jiba* and the *kanrodai*. It was composed by Nakayama Miki in May 1875, when the *jiba* had been determined and in the midst of her persecution. It consists of eighty-eight verses.

The mountainous regret of Tsukihi piled up day by day:
To clear it away is My desire.

This talk, given step by step, is about the intention of Tsukihi:
to bring forth universal salvation.

If the mind is sincere,
the performance of any kind of Service will all bring salvation.

To Tsukihi, all of you throughout the world are My children.
My only desire is to save you.

Despite this, to My regret,
they attempted to stop Me and, after that, even to forbid.

Because of this, the Salvation Service cannot be performed.
Oh, the regret in the mind of Tsukihi!

As for the Service, it is Tsukihi who teaches you the
hand movements step by step. It is not a human mind (*kokoro*).

Whatever I may do,
never think that it is from the human mind.

At this place, every talk is by Tsukihi
and every preparation is by Tsukihi.

Whatever disorder may come to you,
never think that it is from the human mind.

Since it is Tsukihi who began this world,
there is nothing unknown to Me.

The innermost heart of everyone in the world
is all reflected to Tsukihi.

Unaware of this, in the human mind,
everyone has only self-centered thoughts.

Hereafter, I shall teach you everything
about the true path step by step.

The beginning of this world was by Tsukihi.
I began to teach everything fully in detail.

Until then, there was no one who knew.
There were only the thoughts of Tsukihi.

Even until today, I have been telling you that everything
is by Tsukihi, but still you do not understand. . . .

I shall teach you only of things that have not existed before
and bring true salvation.

What do you think this salvation is about?
I am preparing the amulet to protect you from smallpox.

Another salvation: My free and unlimited workings
for the time of childbirth, either to delay or to quicken.

About these free and unlimited workings of which I speak:
do not think of them as being trivial. . . .

If only your mind is truly accepted by Tsukihi,
you will be assured of any salvation whatever.

Tsukihi assures you any and every salvation
because your true Parent lives.

Because the Jiba or Origin and the causality of origin exist,
Tsukihi works freely and unlimitedly.

You may wonder why I repeat this teaching so persistently.
It is the basis of My assurance of single-hearted salvation.

Wherever you may seek to find the origin,
there will be no one who knows.

So should it be, for this is the first time
that Tsukihi has entered a body and speaks.

To Tsukihi, who can see everything in this world,
nothing is unknown.

Watching each and every one of you,
Tsukihi will discern the good and evil.

If you wonder why Tsukihi is so persistent,
it is because I pity you when evil appears.

If you let your debts pile up,
a path of oxen and horses will finally appear.

But Tsukihi will save all of you, whoever you may be,
if only your sincerity is accepted. . . .

Even until now, all things have already appeared,
but you have not known their true origin.

Thunder, earthquakes, great winds, and floods:
these are from the regret and anger of Tsukihi.

Because no one has ever understood this matter,
this time Tsukihi will tell you about them beforehand.

To Tsukihi, each of you, one and all, is a child of Mine.
I am filled with love for you.

But the innermost heart of every one of you
is covered with piles of dust.

Unless this dust is cleanly swept away,
the deep concern of Tsukihi will come to naught. . . .

Hereafter, when I begin My work of single-hearted salvation,
every one of you will only be spirited.

Whatever Tsukihi has once said
will never become false through all time. . . .

You have heard of the Gift of Heaven to be given
to the Parent of this world's human beginnings.

You may not know what this talk is about. . . .
Tsukihi wishes to bestow the Food of Heaven.

Further about this talk:
place a flat vessel on the Kanrodai.

Hereafter, bodily disorders will appear here and there.
Know that it is the care being given by Tsukihi.

When you come, compare your disorder with this place.
If the condition is the same, quickly begin the sweeping.

Walk over where you have swept,
and you will come to a standstill. There, the Kanrodai . . .

When it is done, assemble the performers
and quickly begin the Service. Your minds will be spirited.

Indeed, wherever else you may seek it, it will never be found.
It is the central pillar of Nihon.

If only this comes surely into being,
there will be no one whomever to fear.

In any case, unless you are able to see the proof of the truth,
I cannot set out on My next preparations.

On however high a place you may be,
I shall talk to you freely.

[Nakayama, *Ofudesaki*, part 8, pp. 18–24]

SONGS FOR THE SERVICE
(*MIKAGURA-UTA*)

SONGS FOR THE KAGURA

Sweeping away evils, please save us,
Tenri Ō no Mikoto.[7]

Just a word: Listen to what God says.
I will never tell you anything wrong.
Representing heaven and earth
I have created husband and wife.
This is the beginning of the world.

Sweeping away evils, hasten to save us
All mankind equally purified.
The Kanrodai. [p. 3]

TEODORI, SONG 5

First, As this world is so wide,
There may be various places to save people.
Second, Miraculous salvation at this place
I grant you safe childbirth and freedom from smallpox.
Third, God, the same as water
Washes away the dirt from your minds.
Fourth, Though there is no one who is free from greed,
Before God there is no greed.
Fifth, However long you may continue to believe,

---

7. This verse is repeated twenty-one times during the service.

Your life shall ever be filled with joy.
Sixth, Forgetting away a cruel heart,
Come to me with a gentle heart!
Seventh, Assuredly I shall never leave you in suffering.
Because this is the place of single-hearted salvation.
Eighth, Not only in Yamato,
I will go also to other countries to save you all.
Ninth, This is the *jiba*, the origin of this world.
Indeed, a remarkable place has been revealed.
Since firmly we are determined to believe,
Let us form a brotherhood.[8] [pp. 13–15]

[Nakayama, *Mikagura-uta*, pp. 3, 13–15; HH]

THE DIVINE DIRECTIONS
(*OSASHIZU*)

The Home Ministry notified local authorities to suppress Tenrikyō, and believers requested instructions. Iburi Izō, speaking as the *honseki* (mediator of revelations), gave these directions in the name of the founder. During the 1880s, Tenrikyō leaders repeatedly sought the government's permission to establish the religion independently of Buddhism and Shinto, but without success. The organization's continued expansion after the Sino-Japanese War (1894/1895) without such approval made it vulnerable to suppression, especially in the wake of a press campaign against it in 1895.

April 21, 1896

Sah, sah, they will come to tell you, come to tell you all kinds of things. I have already told you about this in full. They will not achieve whatever plans they may have. The matter about which you ask contains many problems, many problems. On this occasion, I shall have them investigate you thoroughly. You may think it strange that I allow this investigation. You applied and reapplied for a church permit from the district authority; rejected, rejected. All was in vain. Of the many problems you have had time after time, you think that this one is insurmountable. I intend to unify sincere minds once and for all, once and for all. You must ask me about this. This problem may frighten you at first glance, but there is good in frightening events. The waters will rise; mountains will crumble; it will rain heavily and rain heavily; there will be no escape. But pure will be the aftermath. You are wondering what will happen. If you just set your minds, I shall do my work. Those who oppose me also are children dear

---

8. *Kō*, a religious confraternity of lay people.

to my heart. Yet dearer are those who pray to me. But even with those who pray to me, if they do not follow my will, they are the same as those who oppose me. I have already directed you by my words, my words. Even some leading members say that these divine directions are not divine. That the world should oppose me is natural. Opposition from within the path. Opposition from within the path washes away the fertilizer I have spread. You will clearly see, you will clearly see the wrongs that have been done. Never, never be regretful. Unite instead. Unite your minds in accord with my will. From now on I shall gather, I shall gather all of you by all means. Mountains will crumble; the waters will rise; great wind and rain. There will be no escape. I shall wash away the muddy water thoroughly. While the water remains muddy, your thoughts will be of no avail. Unite your minds in accord with my will, unite. If they tell you, "Don't," then answer, "Very well." If they tell you, "No," then answer, "Very well." I shall be watching, I shall be watching.

[Tenrikyō Overseas Mission Department, *Selections from the Osashizu*, pp. 56–57]

ŌMOTO

Ōmoto was founded in 1892 by Deguchi Nao (1837–1918), after she received revelations from the god Ushitora Konjin. She attracted a small group of followers in the rural town of Ayabe, north of Kyoto, but it was not until she was joined by the man who became her son-in-law, Deguchi Onisaburō (1871–1948), that their proselytization was extended to the cities. Thereafter, the religion attracted an educated, urban stratum in addition to rural people and quickly grew to become one of the fastest-expanding religions of the early twentieth century. Nao and Onisaburō are regarded as its cofounders.

Nao lived at a time of rapid social change, when rural Japan was becoming industrialized through the establishment of textile mills in the countryside. Nao's husband was a carpenter who was unable to provide for his large family, forcing Nao to take on menial work of all kinds. He died when she was fifty. Of their eight children, two daughters went mad. Nao then began to experience revelations and was imprisoned by the police, who feared that she also might be insane. Although she had no formal education, she began to write down her revelations in her cell, and these formed the basis of her work *Divine Revelations* (*Ōmoto shin'yu*).

Nao had been drawn to religion since childhood, and she had had contact with both Tenrikyō and Konkōkyō. She identified the god of her revelations as Ushitora Konjin, also revered in Konkōkyō, as a universal parent god mistakenly believed to be a mere directional deity guarding the northeast in a popular religion of the region. But unlike any other popular understandings of this deity, Nao's Ushitora Konjin revealed that he intended to "reform and renovate" (*tatekae-tatenaoshi*) the entire world in a millenarian upheaval that would overthrow the current materialist society and establish an agrarian utopia based on a reverence for God. In *The Tip of the Writing Brush* (*Ofudesaki*), later included in the work translated here, *Divine Revelations*, Nao explains that a divine kingdom would be established on earth and urges people to prepare themselves.

In 1899 Nao was joined by Ueda Kisaburō, who took the name Deguchi Onisaburō when he married Nao's fifth daughter, Sumi (1883–1952). Onisaburō had wide experience in the religious world of his day. He had undergone mountain austerities, belonged to a confraternity dedicated to Inari, and served as a Shinto priest. He helped systematize Nao's ongoing revelations and convey her message of world renovation to a wider segment of the population, especially during and after World War I. Following the loss of life in the Sino-Japanese and Russo-Japanese Wars, the interest in spiritualism grew, which dovetailed with Onisaburō's expansion of Nao's teachings to a wider understanding of the spiritual world. After Nao's death in 1918, he spoke of her revelations as a second opening of the heavenly rock cave, thus connecting her thought to the ancient mythic collection, the *Record of Ancient Matters* (*Kojiki*). Onisaburō identified Ushitora Konjin as the Shinto deity Kunitokotachi and prophesied that this deity would displace the evil deities ruling the material and spiritual worlds and restore them to divine rule. The Ōmoto religion bought a national newspaper to promulgate these prophecies, which provoked the state to suppress it in 1921 on charges of lèse-majesté and violation of the Newspaper Law. Onisaburō and other group leaders were imprisoned.

After this first suppression, Onisaburō began to record his experiences in the spiritual world in *Stories from the Spiritual World* (*Reikai monogatari*), a massive work of more than eighty volumes. This doctrinal compendium laid out Ōmoto's conceptual foundation, which was expressed in artful language and parables.

Ōmoto was suppressed again in 1935, but this time more than three thousand members were arrested; sixty-one leaders were prosecuted; its facilities were confiscated and destroyed; and Onisaburō was imprisoned until the end of World War II. In the background of charges of lèse-majesté and violation of the Peace Preservation Law was the state's fear of Ōmoto's rapid expansion and its millenarian prophecies. Its buildings were reduced to rubble; all signs bearing the religion's name were obliterated; and Ōmoto was forced to pay for the demolition. This second suppression of Ōmoto was the most extreme case of state persecution of religion in modern Japanese history.

After 1945, Ōmoto pursued the theme of world peace, from 1945 to 1952 under the name Garden of Brotherly Love (Aizen-en) and after 1952, under its original name, Ōmoto. During its history, Ōmoto underwent many schisms, giving rise to new religious movements that preserved aspects of Ōmoto's thought, in turn attesting to Ōmoto's enduring influence in modern Japanese religious life.

Ōmoto has two main sacred texts: Deguchi Nao's *Divine Revelations* and Deguchi Onisaburō's *Stories from the Spiritual World*. Onisaburo's *Divine Signposts (Michi no shiori)* and *The Path of Ōmoto (Ōmoto no michi)* are also considered to be sacred texts.

DEGUCHI NAO

DIVINE REVELATIONS
(ŌMOTO SHIN'YU)

[Section from 1892]

When the reign of Ushitora Konjin begins, the plum blossoms of all the three thousand worlds will bloom in unison. The world as it is now is a bestial place full of demons, a world where the strong prey on the weak. Japan, too, has become bestial. If the world continues on its present course, it will soon come to an end. For this reason I have come forth to bring about the demolition and reconstruction of the Greater World. Make ready! I will establish an everlasting divine kingdom, pacifying the entire world in perfect peace through a great cleansing and purging. Know ye that the word of Kami will be fulfilled unerringly, without even a hair's width of difference. If not, Kami does not exist in this world.

Like the hosta plant, from which leaves appear on the root [as well as from the stems above], if flowers fail to bloom both above and below, this world will know no peace. I will bring about a Heavenly Kingdom on Earth that will endure through all the ages to come. In various lands and places in the world, many messengers of Kami will come forth to announce the demolition and reconstruction of the world. All this is arranged by me, Kami Ushitora, otherwise known as Kami Kunitokotachi, to inform the world about Kami's plan. As the mountain streams eventually flow together to form huge rivers, in the end all of them will become one. That is Kami's plan. I will bring the world together and rule it under one king. Although it is a monumental undertaking, this plan has been set in motion by Kami from ancient times and hence is infallible.

When I, Kami, come forth into the world, I will hold a contest of strength against human science. The time of science is over. No one can defeat Kami. I will sort out souls so that only crystalline souls are left, and [all others will face] absolute death.

People of the world, change your hearts! The world will change, and you will be astounded. You may be able to change [your] outward appearance today, but the soul cannot change so easily. Cultivate your soul and reform yourself! Do not imagine that leaves will survive when the trunk is cut down. Leaves will survive only if the branches and the trunk remain. The leaves of a felled trunk will wither away.

[1893]

I, Kami Ushitora, use Deguchi Nao's hand to inform [humanity] about the happenings in the world. I, Kami Ushitora, will come forth to watch over this world and will no longer allow the egotistical manner that has dominated the world until now. The thinking of many people will be in error. Because, through ignorance, the *kami*—guardian spirits and people who ruled the world for millennia—wreaked havoc, this world has degenerated into a bestial wilderness. With no means of repairing the damage, this world cannot long endure.

The world will never be at peace as long as so much value is placed on gold and silver. In the epoch when I, Kami Ushitora, am completely guarding the world, all people will be able to live on natural products produced in their own land. As I fulfill this plan, I will show it to Heaven-and-earth. I will make people change even their clothes, food, houses, and storehouses. I will not allow them to live in luxury.

I will bring happiness equally to all people in the world. If not, it would not merit the name of the kingdom of Heaven. In ancient times I fell into adversity, went through infinite suffering and tribulations, and explored every corner of the world. In that way I arranged my plan so that it will be fulfilled without even the tiniest error. Thus, everyone must return to his or her original pure soul and take part in the sacred work of building the heavenly kingdom on earth. Thus is the great undertaking to demolish and reconstruct the spiritual and material worlds, once and for always.

There is only one sun for this world. With seven or eight kings, the world will always be in turmoil. Therefore, I have set in motion my plan to rule the world with one divine king. Mark my words, people of the world, and change your hearts! I will restore the world to its original heavenly state. . . .

. . . When I am completely manifested on Earth, I will make the world totally pure and give favor first to those who change their heart.

When the crystalline Kingdom of Heaven on Earth has come into being, everything will happen according to one's wishes. I will search out crystal clear souls and use them for the sacred work. Starting now, I will make the whole earth a heavenly kingdom, and I will make *kami* and people live happily and heartily. I will purify Shintoism and other religions and peoples in the world and will restore the world to the sacred epoch. When the sacred epoch has come, I, Kami Ushitora, will do everything.

Extraordinary things will come to pass!

[Deguchi Nao, *Ōmoto shin'yu*, in *Ōmoto shiryō shūsei*, ed. Ikeda, vol. 1, pp. 13–17; HH]

DEGUCHI ONISABURŌ

Chapter 12: Unity of the Spiritual and Material Worlds

In all the universe there is no absolute good or evil. The material and spiritual worlds, good and evil, are one. Accordingly, if there is no absolute happiness, neither is there absolute misery. In pleasure there is suffering, and in suffering can be found pleasure. After death, if a person falls into the infernal realm in the spiritual world and receives unlimited suffering, that is only the recompense that he himself has produced with his own body and spirit while he lived in the material world. The souls living in the material world are always communicating with those parts of the spiritual world that are appropriate to them, and spirits in the spiritual world are constantly communicating with human souls in the material world that are in accord with them. This will never change. . . .

If ordinary humans didn't exist, there could be no *kami*. In other words, good and bad are not separate elements, and justice and injustice are identical. This [understanding] is supported by a sutra: earthly passion and enlightenment, delusion and nirvana, this world and paradise, Buddha and an ordinary human, all these are essentially the same. Fundamentally, there is little difference among the great compassion of Buddha, the blessing of the Divine Way, and the desires of an ordinary person. It can be said that human nature is in fact God. Every quality of God, without exception, can be found in the ordinary human.

In essence, there is no difference between paradise and this world. So why are such essentially identical natures separated into two different qualities: sacred and vulgar, pure and filthy, right and wrong, good and evil? Those qualities are nothing more than a provisional code given to the levels of activity, that is, whether or not one acted properly and fully in accordance with one's innate character. Good and bad are not unchangeable: depending on the time, place, and situation, good may become bad, and bad may become good. . . . No matter how good something is, it cannot be qualified as good if one acts to make it his private possession. Even if it contains some bad, a deed must be qualified as good if it is done for the public good. When King Wen [of the Chinese Zhou dynasty] became angry, peace and order began to be restored in the world. It must be said that even anger is good. . . .

. . . This society, this world (the real world) is an environment of small pleasure and small suffering; the spiritual world is a place of great pleasure and great suffering. In the sutra Rishu-kyō can be found the following teaching: "Great avarice and cynicism are ecstasy and pure enlightenment; sexual desire is the way to nirvana." This in fact means that an honest candid form is the road to enlightenment.

It is a common mortal who believes that asceticism is of no use and that romantic love is sacred and tries to put it into practice naturalistically and instinctively, that is, at his own level. It is a *kami* who expands love and implements it on a universal scale. God makes all people in the Greater World his beloved children and has a great desire to save all living beings. An ordinary person loves only his own family and relatives and those who serve him, and [he] remains indifferent to others. Furthermore, he indulges in such petty selfishness that he knows no joy other than self-contentment. The human soul is itself essentially God. Therefore it has the innate ability to act on a universal scale. And it is a life duty of every human to develop the true nature of his naturally given spirit, which is wisdom, love, courage, and harmony. If we look at this from a standard of good and bad, we could tentatively call it self-fulfillment. Our two-sided conduct, good and bad, directly spreads to display great activity for society and for the salvation of the human race through the administration of justice, rewarding and punishing. This great power and activity is in fact God, the expansion of oneself on a universal scale.

After all, our great purpose, and our way of realizing a Heavenly Kingdom on Earth, is not by separating ourselves from this suffering, defiled, unclean, evil, and unfair society but instead to beautify and make it pleasant. This is our concept of evolving into *kami* and the main point of our teaching.

[Deguchi Onisaburō, *Reikai monogatari*, vol. 1, chap. 12; HH]

DIVINE SIGNPOSTS
(*MICHI NO SHIORI*)

February 8, tenth year of Taishō (1921)

There is only one god (or *kami*) that created the universe. We adore him using the name Ame-no-minaka-nushi. Ame-no-minaka-nushi is called, for short, "God," or, the True God. There is only one True God, so sacred that he has no beginning and no end. God split his spirit, force, and body and created all beings such that he created first the body and then gave to it force and spirit. In order to rule the heavens and the earth, including all beings, God created many *kami* and gave to each its own task; this is how God guards and evolves the vast world. God has various functions, which together make up the activity of the one and only God. Those many functions are called *amatsu-kami yaoyorozu* (eight million heavenly *kami*) and *kunitsu-kami yaoyorozu* (eight million local *kami*).

Some teachings obstinately insist that there are no spiritual entities (*kami*) other than God himself. But that is the opinion of those who look at only one side of God. The sun, the moon, all beings in the world, everything lies in the bosom of God. God (Ame-no-minaka-nushi) is omnipotent. His activity is unlimited, with immense variety and never-ending changes. So there cannot exist any place in the universe where God is not present.

Among the Shintoists are some unapologetic bigots who say that Japan is a divine land where the *kami* dwell, while foreign countries are bestial places without *kami*. There are *kami* wherever the light of the sun shines. While the Japanese differ from foreigners in the color of their hair and the color of their skin, we all are the divided spirits of the ruler of heaven. We all are children of *kami* and are ruled by Heaven. But the Shintoists who say that despite this the Japanese are the direct descendants of *kami* and that foreigners have souls no better than beasts are barbarians in darkness about the truth. Inasmuch as the ruler of heaven, as an expression of his love, created the races of the world—yellow, white, black, and brown—we are not fundamentally different. . . .

The earthly world will be ruled in peace, not by strong armies, but because the people will believe in God and will follow the real path. Because there are armies in the world, people become greedy and make war. War in the world spites the heart of God, who is displeased when someone is fortunate while others are unfortunate. There is a calm after a storm: the war is an inevitable stage until the world finally becomes peaceful. But nothing in the world is more cruel than war.

A nation's strength or weakness depends on whether its citizens' conduct is good or bad. If the people's conduct is just, their mores are beautiful; if the mores are beautiful, the nation will be in accord. The strongest nation in this world is the one whose people are united. . . .

Military buildup and war cause unlimited suffering to the poor. People should not be burdened with heavy taxes and conscription for military buildup and war. . . . Tens of millions of youths in the world are forced to serve as soldiers and be trained only in the art of killing. People are suffering much hardship from being trained in the art of killing, which is heinous. For any nation, there is nothing more useless than military buildup.

There are five kinds of love. One of them is the love between parents and their children. The love of parents for their children, and of children for their parents, is not unique to humans; even birds and beasts have it. It is the natural love of all animals. There is no one in the world who does not have this kind of love. But because the world now is coming near its end, few children respect and love their parents, although almost all parents love their children. Even a dove knows how to love its parents, and a crow will certainly repay its debt of gratitude to its parents. That was said already from ancient times. So it can be said that he who, as a son, does not esteem his parents and love his parents is inferior to a bird or beast. . . .

The second is the love of preference. Because one fancies horses, one loves a horse; because of an inclination toward women, one loves a woman; because of a fondness for miniature plants (*bonsai*), one loves a miniature plant. Preferential love is the love of oneself to please one's fancy. One does not love the horse itself. The same also with a woman or a miniature plant. Therefore, any love not bestowed on the object itself is nothing but the love of one's own fancy.

The third is love for honor's sake. Love for honor's sake does not come from the depths of the heart. It is possible that a stepmother loves her stepchild with a pure love from the heart, but in most cases, a stepmother loves her stepchild for her husband, for the family, or for public opinion. All this is love for honor's sake.

The fourth is false love. This is the love of one who does not have it in his heart, although he says it with his mouth. Love proclaimed by a hypocrite is false. . . . The love of narrow-minded Shintoists and obstinate missionaries often turns out to be false.

The fifth is divine love. It is love that is genuine and beautiful. He who has this kind of love loves even his enemy. To love a perverse person, and lead him to the path of virtue, is divine love. It is love directed toward everyone, even foreigners. To love an evildoer the same as a good person is divine love; God grants sunshine not only to good people's rice paddies but also to those of evildoers. Divine love is love that especially favors scoundrels.

God is supreme love itself. Therefore no matter how heavy and deep a human soul's sin is, God is not offended, nor does he create hell specially to punish it. The human soul or spirit itself builds hell and, of its own accord, falls into its unceasing fire because of its own selfishness, which it had in its life on earth. God has absolutely no idea of hate, blame, punishment. . . . God is always eager to form the Kingdom of Heaven on Earth: He gives part of his divine qualities to prophets in order that all peoples may be convinced of his love and benevolence. If God had even a tiny bit of hate, it would mean that he himself had come to ruin. Therefore, in the sacred teachings can be found the words "God is universal love."

[Deguchi Onisaburō, *Michi no shiori*, p. 174; HH]

SŌKA GAKKAI

Sōka gakkai was originally founded in 1930 by Makiguchi Tsunesaburō (1871–1944) for the purpose of implementing his distinctive Buddhist theory of value in the educational system of the day, hence the original name Sōka kyōiku gakkai (Society for Value-Creating Education). Makiguchi affiliated his organization with Nichiren shōshū, a branch of Nichiren Buddhism, and this connection was continued by Makiguchi's successor, Toda Jōsei (1900–1958). In 1943 Makiguchi was imprisoned along with Toda and other leaders for refusing to enshrine a talisman of the Ise Shrines. Makiguchi died in prison in 1944, leaving Toda to revive the movement after 1945.

Sōka gakkai regards the Lotus Sutra as the most profound scriptural expression of Buddhist teaching, and doctrinal study is a central activity. Nichiren's writings also are studied as sacred, and the saint's life is regarded as the paradigm of the bodhisattva in the latter days of the Dharma. The *daimoku* (Hail to the Lotus Sutra) is chanted before Nichiren's calligraphic mandala (called the *gohonzon*) as an expression of the entire truth of the Lotus Sutra, as a form of self-cultivation, and as a means to obtain practical benefits. The largest of Japan's new religious movements, Sōka gakkai has developed a lay person's Buddhism in which followers regarded as bodhisattvas active in the present world pursue value in the life of the individual, linked to the improvement of society, as the core of bodhisattva practice.

The religion originated when Makiguchi spread his beliefs among schoolteachers in the Tokyo and Yokohama area. This group then widened to include small-scale businessmen, housewives, and students. From a membership of about sixty in 1937, it expanded to fifteen hundred by 1942. The imprisonment of Makiguchi and Toda from 1943 to 1945 temporarily halted the group's expansion, and it was not until the 1950s that it began to grow conspicuously. At that time, the religion produced a manual on proselytization, and the membership responded vigorously, proclaiming that the *gohonzon* could bring so many practical benefits to the faithful that it could be regarded as a "happiness-making machine." By the mid-1960s, Sōka gakkai claimed about 2 million members, and by the end of the twentieth century it had 16 million adherents.

Sōka gakkai was headed by three generations of distinctive leaders. Makiguchi established the pursuit of value as a central idea, in conjunction with Nichiren shōshū, although his leadership was cut short by imprisonment and death before the end of World War II. Toda Jōsei revived the religion after the war and presided over its explosive expansion in the 1950s, boldly setting the goal of converting the entire nation by forceful proselytization (*shaku-buku*). Under him, significant rifts with Nichiren shōshū appeared as Sōka gakkai began to overshadow the older sect and to assert its autonomy. Sōka gakkai's rapid expansion was inevitably controversial and brought criticism of the religion. Ikeda Daisaku, the third leader, persuaded the religion to soften its forceful proselytization, to widen its appeal beyond the blue-collar class, and to initiate significant international activities for world peace. In 1964 Sōka gakkai launched the Clean Government Party (Kōmeitō), which emphasized the expansion of social welfare, becoming Japan's third largest political party and wielding the decisive vote in issues dividing the conservative and opposition parties. While some aspects of Ikeda's leadership remained controversial, he gave the religion greater influence in society and led it to become the most powerful religion in Japan at the turn of the twenty-first century.

The texts translated here represent central elements of Sōka gakkai thought as developed by its three leaders: Makiguchi's theory of value, Toda's theory of "life force," and Ikeda's theory of "health and welfare."

MAKIGUCHI TSUNESABURŌ

As an educator, Makiguchi Tsunesaburō tried to reform Japan's educational system by infusing it with humanistic values, so that benefits to the individual, such as achievement and happiness, would be understood as rightful goals of education. He stressed the cultivation of religious values and harmony between religion and science. His system of values emphasized benefits to the individual and society as essential to the happiness of the individual and to social good. His views were grounded in the doctrines of the Lotus Sutra and substituted "benefit" for the traditional element "truth" in the triad "truth, goodness, and beauty." The educational system of his day, however, was less humanistic than authoritarian, oriented much more toward making the people obedient subjects, in line with such government proclamations as the Imperial Rescript on Education (see chap. 38). Makiguchi foresaw a reconciliation of religion and science and frequently referred to the power of the Lotus Sutra and the power of the *daimoku*. He believed also that Christianity and Buddhism could be reconciled.

WHAT IS RELIGIOUS VALUE?

On what basis should we establish religious value? Konishi Shigenao[9] holds that saving a life from extreme suffering and establishing the "settled mind"[10] is a sacred value. If that is correct, would this match the value of virtue, in terms of society? And again, if we consider the matter from the standpoint of the individual, can we call the "settled mind" a beneficial value? Is it not a beneficial value to save people? Is it not a virtuous value to save the world?

The sixteenth chapter of the Lotus Sutra, "The Life Span of the Tathagata," is the highest-ranking sermon of Shakyamuni's fifty years. Its central tenet is the promise that all suffering humanity, without exception, will attain Buddhahood and that they will abide in eternal, undying life. When we hail the Lotus Sutra as the absolute object of worship by saying *namu*,[11] we attain the

---

9. Konishi Shigenao (1875–1948) was an early-twentieth-century educator.

10. Also called "settled heart," this is a Buddhist concept meaning faith, firm belief, assurance of salvation.

11. *Namu* (hail or praises to) appears in the phrase (called the *daimoku*) chanted to hail or praise the Lotus Sutra, "Namu myōhō renge kyō."

only absolute joy of true life, liberated from suffering. Is this absolute not a benefit to us, and should we not attribute value to this condition? Is this not the good?

It may be objected that we are attributing sacrality to individual benefit or to social good. But I think that simply praising the good, purely rejoicing in benefit, also is sacred. . . . I will say it again: Value can be found only in benefit, good, and beauty.

["Shūkyō to kagaku," in *Makiguchi Tsunesaburō zenshū*, vol. 1, pp. 340–43; HH]

THE RELATIONS AMONG RELIGION AND SCIENCE, MORALITY, AND EDUCATION

Society seeks a standard by which to judge good and evil, but there is a difference between the relative good and an absolute, highest good. The science of morals, which takes the laws of human life in this world as its object, lacks the power to transcend the relative level. One can go no higher by the power of science, but human aspiration does not end with this. This is the point at which the sphere of religion develops. The reason that religion arises is the desire running through the depths of all human hearts to discover a law of cause and effect governing the life of the eternal soul, valid for all time: past, present, and future. Such a law establishes the absolute, highest standard to discriminate truth from falsity, good from evil, and enables us to judge how to achieve—for the first time—a life of the greatest happiness. . . .

The objects of faith of those stagnant Buddhist sects that adhere to the teachings promulgated in the forty-odd years (of Shakyamuni's preaching) before the Lotus Sutra are anthropomorphic incarnations called *kami*, or Buddhas. Because these objects structure the interior consciousness of those individuals who worship them, these sects are utterly different from science's ideals of truth and law. This means that science and religion are irreconcilable in such cases, and thus their ideas of morality also are at odds. However, the vital point of the Lotus Sutra, as expressed in its title is "Law" (Dharma), and the sutra is praised as "Wonderful Law." The Law is likened to a lotus, which appears out of the mud, incarnated as a Buddha who lived in accord with an utterly pure law. This [truth] was expounded as a sutra. When admiration is expressed by the word *namu* and by "Namu myōhō renge kyō," there is an exact correspondence with the ideals of the scientists of the entire world. . . .

If we take Shakyamuni's teaching of the identity of the Buddha Dharma and worldly law to its final conclusion, not only do we find an agreement of religion and science. We also actually find that science is entirely enfolded in the Buddha-Dharma. If there is a point of difference [between religion and science], it is in the treatment of the social laws of cause and effect of ethical morality, which in science is limited to the present world, limited by the laws of cause and effect in the phenomena addressed by the separate branches of science. Even the comprehensive science of philosophy is limited by a concept of human life and a worldview unable to transcend the present. By contrast, Buddhism teaches that the Five Eyes of Wisdom not only comprehend the present world but also illuminate the laws of cause and effect of the three worlds of past, present, and future. . . .

When humanity develops the intellect, rids itself of the sensual life from which it is so hard to separate because we are so caught up in egotistical advantage and loss, becomes empty, and enters the broad way of Heaven-and-earth, then we will certainly achieve the condition set out in Shakyamuni's last admonition: Adhering to Dharma, Not Adhering to Persons. Without this, there can be no unification of religions, it is needless to say, nor can there be any reconciliation of religion and science, or religion and virtue. Accordingly, there can be no reconciliation of religion and education, nor will true education be possible. But we must not fall into despair like the pessimists of the world. Through education that aims to develop the intellect, by following the path of science that seeks to rely on laws rather than persons, I believe that [such a reconciliation] will be possible. In Christianity also, through the development of human wisdom, just as the Buddha taught, the sensual element gradually declines, and the intellectual element of adhering to law deepens. Gradually, we come closer to science's goal of truth, and the history of change shows the possibility that science and religion will ultimately become one. I believe that soon it will be possible to speak of Christianity in the same terms as Buddhism. If we give up our historical attachment to the notion that Buddhism and Christianity have nothing whatever to do with each other because of the separation of East and West, and if we humbly conform to the teaching of Adhering to the Dharma, Not Adhering to Persons, and if a candid comparison is undertaken for the sake of achieving a broad way of humanity, we will be able to return to the period of ninety-five philosophical schools, as in India three thousand years ago. I think we would, in a flash, be able to realize an awakened unification, worthy of both the so-called Hinayana and all subsequent sutras.

If religionists forsook their prejudices, abandoned their egos, open their hearts, and recognized the truth, and if scholars stopped vacillating and admitted the limits of their knowledge, then if meekly, humbly, we [could] admit the narrow extent of our experiential wisdom, then we could slough off the limited wisdom of the phenomenal world and cultivate the magnanimity with which to abide in the great, eternal truth of the past, present, and future worlds. If we all obeyed the teaching of Adhering to the Dharma, Not Adhering to Persons, then we could look forward to the time when science and religion, and religion and education would surely be reconciled.

["Shūkyō to kagaku," in *Makiguchi Tsunesaburō zenshū*, vol. 1, pp. 343–44; HH]

TODA JŌSEI

"ON THE NATURE OF LIFE"
(SEIMEIRON)

Shinto was exploited by ultranationalism and absolutism and when this abuse escalated into the misguided Pacific War, my revered mentor Makiguchi Tsunesaburō, my beloved comrades, and I spoke out vehemently against this. We explained that forcing the Japanese people to worship at shrines went against reason and morality. For this reason we were persecuted in the summer of 1943 and thereafter spent two years in jail. While I was spending miserable days in that dank cell, innocent but imprisoned, I pondered that most difficult problem: the essence of life. What is life? Is this world the only one? Or does life continue eternally? These problems were eternal mysteries to which the ancient saints and sages each gave their own answers.

Lice flourished in that filthy jail, coming out to take pleasure in the light of the springtime. I put two of them on a plank. They waved their limbs about. I crushed one of them, but the other one kept moving about unconcernedly. Where had the life of the crushed one gone? Had it disappeared from the world forever?

Long before [this], a daughter of mine died just after her birth, and I remembered how bitterly I grieved for her. I thought to myself at the time, "If I grieve so at the death of my daughter, how could I endure it if my wife should die?" My wife did die, and I grieved for her, thinking, "What if my parents should die?" They died also, and I cried as if my heart would break. Then, quivering with fear, I thought, "Now what would I do if I had to face my own death?" After that, I tirelessly searched for the way, trying Christianity, then drawn to the Amida Sutra. But nothing convinced me to the bottom of my heart about the problem of life.

I looked back on this suffering in my cell. For me, having grown up with an interest in science and mathematics, I could not believe in something that did not convince me logically. Then I began to study fervently the Lotus Sutra and the writings of Saint Nichiren. When I encountered the mysterious verses of the Lotus Sutra, I prayed to be able to read with full understanding, and I began to recite the *daimoku* with all my might, following Saint Nichiren's teachings. About the time I reached two million recitations, I came up against something extremely mysterious, and an unfathomable state of mind unfolded before my eyes. Trembling with joy, I stood in my cell and shouted to all the Buddhas, bodhisattvas, and all beings of the three worlds and the ten directions. After five years of searching, I finally realized my sacred mission. Based on that experience and on the Lotus Sutra's understanding of life force, I will speak of the essence of life force. . . .

[The Lotus Sutra teaches that] the life of Shakyamuni extends to the three worlds of past, present, and future. Buddhist philosophy without this concept of life force extending for all time would have no basis. Nevertheless, in each sutra we can see degrees of profundity of life force, revealing to us the scripture's relative standing. In addition, it goes without saying that Saint Nichiren also based himself on a limitless concept of life force. Of the two (Shakyamuni and Nichiren), Nichiren's thinking on the existence of life force was more profound. . . . The Buddha-Dharma is unthinkable without a limitless life force. This was precisely the first step, the real face of Nichiren's enlightenment. However, many intellectuals call this a superstition, laughingly rejecting it. But from our standpoint, those who deny the life force are not thinking of their own lives scientifically, and their stupidity is risible. Could science be sustained if it ignored causation? For every phenomenon of the universe, there is certainly a cause and result. . . . If we suppose that life simply arose by accident and that when we die life disappeared like so much froth on water, then we are being unpardonably indifferent to our own lives.

No matter how much natural science may develop, proclaiming equality and the destruction of social class, it cannot explain or understand the actual facts of the life force. All around us we see people, animals, the natural world— are their lives all the same? How are they related to one another? People have different degrees of intelligence, beauty, and health. Some are poor no matter how hard they work, while others suffer from desire and jealousy, and science can do nothing about it. There must be causes for such differences, and they cannot be understood without thoroughly searching for the causes. But in speaking of a limitless life force, I am not saying that we have a soul existing apart from the body and mind or that we are controlled by such a thing, nor am I recognizing that such a thing is eternal.

In saying that the life force of human beings extends from past, to present, to future, just how long is it? Again I turned to the Lotus Sutra as the root and branch of the Buddha-Dharma. . . . This is the most important of Shakyamuni's many sutras, and it is the basis of enlightenment. . . . [Shakyamuni says to his disciples,] "You all believe that I became a Buddha in this life, but it was actually an immeasurable eternity ago that I attained Buddhahood. I have always been working in the world." In other words, his life is not limited to the present world, nor is his enlightenment but has existed from an eternity in the past.

Life force coexists with the universe, neither preceding it nor produced either accidentally or by human design. The universe is itself life force, and it is mistaken to see it as uniquely belonging to the earth. We are bathed in the broad unbounded, limitless compassion of the great saint [Nichiren]. By clinging to the Gohonzon, . . . we are able to grasp the wondrous actual existence of life force.

[Toda, "Seimeiron," pp. 1–68; HII]

IKEDA DAISAKU

HEALTH AND WELFARE

Capitalism has sacrificed the happiness and welfare of individual human beings to the pursuit of profit. Socialism has suppressed human liberty for the sake of standardized equality. Failure to take into consideration the dignity of human life is behind the faults of both systems. . . . The current trend is to regard production and economy as the total of human society and not merely as a subsystem, which is in fact all that they are. This great modern illusion has wrongly put all other aspects of human activity—culture, religion, technology, and politics—in a position where they are subject to and must serve the needs of the economy. . . . The time has come for us to revise our way of thinking about the precedence currently being given to economic matters. We must put the economy in a place subordinate to culture and education, and we must devote all our energy to the creation of a richly humane society in which the economy will promote human spiritual development and will serve as a means of enabling human beings to manifest their creative abilities. . . . Let us turn . . . to contemporary efforts to establish welfare states. . . . As the distribution of wealth becomes more equal and as the lives of the people become more stable, economic growth tends to slow down or even to stagnate. In other words, the very achievement of the ideal of the welfare state inevitably acts as a brake on the economic growth of the country. A second problem has to do with the attitudes of the people themselves. As social security becomes a reality, the citizens lose independence and grow to rely more and more on services provided by the state. . . . The third, and in my opinion the most important, problem in the welfare state is a weakened understanding of the meaning of life, a loss of the competitive spirit, and the growing difficulty people find in manifesting their creative talents. . . . I am by no means categorically rejecting the welfare system. On the contrary, I am one of the people who earnestly hope for the establishment of such a system in Japan. . . . I see a possibility for solving these problems only on the spiritual plane. . . . It is necessary now to effect a fundamental turnabout in the popular way of thinking about the relations between the spiritual and the material. Elevation of the level of spiritual welfare must become our first concern, and raising of the physical level of welfare must be given second priority. . . . Emphatically a spiritual revolution is indispensable to human welfare.

[Toynbee and Ikeda, *Choose Life*, pp. 100–105]

Chapter 47

JAPAN AND THE WORLD IN CULTURAL DEBATE

The relationship between Japan and the rest of the world expressed as a cultural divide between East and West is a subject as old as modern Japan itself, dating back at least to late Tokugawa times. Sakuma Shōzan's famous formulation of "Eastern ethics, Western science" sought to combine the best of both worlds in an ultimately futile attempt to benefit from the material and technological superiority of Western ways without affecting the thought and values of Asian civilization. As it turned out—not only in Japan but around the world—such a separation was impossible. Foreign ideas and alien traditions arrived together with the railroads and the cannons, by the force of Western power as well as by the power of new ideas to realize visions that the Japanese already had.

The ubiquity of the East–West imaginary can be found in nearly every chapter in this book that deals with modern Japan, whether about institutions like constitutions and political parties, foreign relations of empire and war, or ideologies like nationalism and socialism. This chapter addresses the same question in cultural and personal terms. Although it includes only a few such considerations, they are texts of some controversy, sometimes even notoriety, that are often quoted or evoked as representing the cultural dilemma of relating Japan and Asia to the West and the world. Frequently, the dilemma was also a personal one, a tension between the individual's faith or art and the nation.

For Uchimura Kanzō and Endō Shūsaku, Christianity posed the problem of reconciling a foreign religion and its singular God with their own national identity and tradition. For Natsume Sōseki, the problem was less that of Western ideas than of the Meiji incarnation of modernity that dissolved earlier links of self and society while denying the individual any meaningful independence from the nation-state. Nishida Kitarō, modern Japan's premier philosopher, was as deeply anchored in Zen Buddhism as in the thought of Kant, Hegel, and William James, and his philosophy reflected and transformed the influences of both Asian and Western traditions. In the 1930s, as nationalism surged and Japanese intellectuals redrew the cultural line between Japan and the West— now rejecting Western modernity in favor of Japanese tradition—Nishida attempted to link Japanese and world culture. This led him, on the one hand, to argue the possibility of a universal culture, with each culture, including Japan's, retaining its distinctiveness, and, on the other hand, to assert the superiority of Japan's *kokutai* and emperor system as a justification for Japan's imperial dominance in Asia.

Two preeminent novelists of postwar Japan, Mishima Yukio and Ōe Kenzaburō, represented nearly opposite views in their literary and political stance on questions of Japanese tradition and an appropriate modernity for contemporary Japan. Their very different critiques of postwar society and their different literary styles and subjects were not divided along an East–West binary, but along the lines of the equally old debate about the nature of modernity. This was a debate already familiar to Natsume Sōseki and Uchimura Kanzō in the Meiji period. Indeed, at the end of the twentieth century, as at the time of Sakuma Shōzan, it seemed that the East–West divide was as irresistible in rhetoric as it was misleading in reality.

UCHIMURA KANZŌ

Uchimura Kanzō (1861–1930) exemplified the challenge experienced by Meiji Japanese who sought to integrate their strong sense of national identity into their new Christian faith. Like other young samurai Christians of the time, Uchimura was first drawn to Christianity when he was a student of the American William Clark at the government agricultural school in Hokkaido in the late 1870s. His faith was later confirmed at Amherst, a college with close ties to Japanese Christians. Niijima Jō, the founder of Dōshisha University, had graduated from Amherst in 1870, just two years after the Meiji Restoration. For both Niijima and Uchimura, their encounter with the moral rigor of New England Protestantism both resonated with and strengthened their samurai values and patriotic spirit. After Uchimura returned to Japan, he became notorious for refusing to bow before the Imperial Rescript on Education when it was presented to the First Higher School in Tokyo, where he was a teacher. As a result of this "disrespect incident," Uchimura was forced to resign, and the loyalty of Japanese Christians became a political and ideological issue. For Uchimura, however, it was a matter of faith and loyalty to God. He took a similarly independent position when he opposed war with Russia in the early twentieth century, and his pacifism forced him to resign his position at a national newspaper.

After withdrawing into a life of writing and study, Uchimura founded what he called the "Nonchurch" movement. Without a professional clergy or an ecclesiastical organization, the movement was as independent as Uchimura himself, eschewing ties to Western mission groups in favor of a wholly Japanese Christianity. He was revered by later generations for both his integrity and his willingness, as a patriot, to resist the state.

HOW I BECAME A CHRISTIAN

Uchimura Kanzō's most famous work is *How I Became a Christian*, his spiritual autobiography written in 1895. Like Okakura Tenshin's *The Book of Tea*, another well-known Meiji essay that addressed the question of Japan and the world in cultural terms, Uchimura's autobiography was written in English and later published in Japanese.

One Sunday morning a schoolmate of mine asked me whether I would not go with him to "a certain place in foreigners [*sic*] quarter, where we can hear pretty women sing, and a tall man with a long beard shout and howl upon an elevated place, flinging his arms and twisting his body in all fantastic manners, to all which admittance is entirely free." Such was his description of a Christian house of worship conducted in the language which was new to me then. I followed my friend and was not displeased with the place. Sunday after Sunday I resorted to this place, not knowing the awful consequence that was to follow such a practice. An old English lady from whom I learned my first lessons in English took a great delight in my church-going, unaware of the fact the sight-seeing, and not truth-seeking, was the only view I had. . . .

Christianity was an enjoyable thing to me so long as I was not asked to accept it. Its music, its stories, the kindness shown to me by its followers, pleased me immensely. But five years after, when it was formally presented to me to accept it, with certain stringent laws to keep and much sacrifice to make, my whole nature revolted against submitting myself to such a course. That I must set aside one day out of seven specially for religious purposes, wherein I must keep myself from all my other studies and enjoyments, was a sacrifice which I thought next to impossible to make. And it was not flesh alone which revolted against accepting the new faith. I early learned to honor my nation above all others, and to worship my nation's gods and no others. I thought I could not be forced even if by death itself to vow my allegiance to any other gods than my own country's. I should be a traitor to my country, and an apostate from my national faith by accepting a faith which is exotic in its origin. All my noble ambitions which had been built upon my former conceptions of duty and patriotism were to be demolished by such an overture. I was then a Freshman in a new Government College, where by an effort of a New England Christian scientist, the whole of the upper class (there were but two classes then in the whole college) had already been converted to Christianity. The imperious attitude of the Sophomores toward the "baby Freshmen" is the same the world over, and when to it was added a new religious enthusiasm and spirit of propagandism, their impressions upon the poor "Freshies" can easily be imagined. They tried to convert the Freshies by storm; but there was one among the latter who thought himself capable of not only withstanding the combined assault of the "Sophomoric rushes" (in this case the religious-rush, not cane-rush), but even of reconverting them to their old faith. But alas! mighty men around me were falling and surrendering to the enemy. I alone was left a "heathen," the much detested idolater, the incorrigible worshiper of wood and stones. I well remember the extremity and loneliness to which I was reduced then. One afternoon I resorted to a heathen temple in the vicinity, said to have been authorized by the Government to be the guardian-god of the district. At some distance from the sacred mirror which represented the invisible presence of the deity, I prostrated myself upon coarse dried grass, and there burst into a prayer as sincere and genuine as any I have ever offered to my Christian god since then. I beseeched that guardian-god to speedily extinguish the new enthusiasm in my college, to punish such as those who obstinately refused to disown the strange god, and to help me in my endeavor in the patriotic cause I was upholding then. After the devotion, I returned to my dormitory, again to be tormented with the most unwelcome persuasion to accept the new faith.

A few years later, Uchimura went to the United States and there deepened his faith and devotion to Christ.

With all of the ups and downs that followed the final grasping of the Crucified Son of God, I will not trouble my reader. Downs there were; but they were less than ups. The One Thing riveted my attention, and my whole soul was possessed by It. I thought of it day and night. Even while bringing up scuttles of coal from the basement floor to the topmost story where my lodging was, I meditated upon Christ, the Bible, the Trinity, the Resurrection, and other kindred subjects. . . . Whenever Satan left me free to myself, I pictured to myself the dear and blessed homeland away beyond the seas, and spotted it with churches and Christian colleges, which of course had their existence in my imagination only. No inspiring thought ever came to my mind but I reserved it as a message to my countrymen. Indeed, an empire and its people swallowed up all my leizure [sic] hours. [pp. 117–18]

Much impressed by the thought that God's providence must be in my nation. If all good gifts are from Him, then some of the laudable characters of my countrymen must be also from on high. We must try to serve our God and the world with gifts and boons peculiar to ourselves. God does not want our national characters attained by the discipline of twenty centuries to be wholly supplanted by American and European ideas. The beauty of Christianity is that it can sanctify all the peculiar traits which God gave to each nation. A blessed and encouraging thought that J– too is God's nation. [p. 124]

[*Uchimura Kanzō zenshū*, vol. 3, pp. 117–18, 124]

THE DISRESPECT INCIDENT
(FUKEI JIKEN)

This letter, written by Uchimura to an American friend two months after he had refused to bow before the Imperial Rescript on Education in 1891, describes the personal consequences of his decision to become a Christian. The "disrespect incident" (*fukei jiken*) is sometimes translated as the "case of lèse-majesté."

March 6, 1891

Dear Mr. Bell,

Since I wrote you last, my life has been a very eventful one. On the 9th of Jan. there was in the High Middle School where I taught, a ceremony to acknowledge the Imperial Precept on Education. After the address of the President and reading of the said Precept, the professors and students were asked to go up to the platform one by one, and *bow* to the Imperial signature affixed to the Precept, *in the manner as we used to bow before our ancestral relics as prescribed in Buddhist and Shinto ceremonies.* I was not at all prepared to meet such a strange ceremony, for the thing was the new invention of the president of the school. As I was the third in turn to go up and bow, I scarcely had time to think upon the matter. So, hesitating in doubt, I took a safer course for my Christian conscience, in the August presence of sixty professors (all non-Christians, the two other Xtian prof.'s beside me having absented themselves) and over one thousand students, I took my stand and did not take a bow! It was an awful moment for me, for I instantly apprehended the result of my conduct. The anti-Christian sentiment which was and still is strong in the school, and which was a very delicate affair to soothe down by meekness and kindliness on our part, found a just cause (as they suppose) for bringing forth against me accusations of insult against the nation and its Head, and through me against the Christians in general. . . .

For a week after the ceremony, I received several students and prof.'s who came to me, and with all the meekness I can master I asked them if they found anything in me which was contrary to the Imperial Precept, in my daily conduct in the school, in my conversations among the students, and in my past history as a loyal subject of Mikado [emperor]. I told them also that a good Emperor must have given the precepts to his subject *not* to be bowed unto, but to be obeyed in our daily walks in life. My logic and demonstrations were enough to silence them individually, but as a body, their anger and prejudice were unquenchable. . . . They called up the principal of the school out of his sickbed to have satisfaction for my case. He, the principal, had been my good friend ever since my first connection with the school; so he tried his best to retain me in the school without compelling me to go through the humiliation of *bowing* before the precept. But the cry of my enemies was that of the Jews to Pilate, "If thou let this man go, thou are not Caesar's friend." He wrote me a very kind letter, approving and applauding my conscientious act, and almost imploring me *to conform to the custom* of the nation, assuring me that the *bow* does *not* mean *worship*, but merely respect to the Emperor. Then he described the real state of the school, that to appease the students who could not understand me, the only course will be to bear the humiliation on my part. The latter touched me, especially as I was in great physical weakness. That the *bow* does *not* mean *worship*, I myself have granted for many years. Here in Japan, it often means no more than taking off of the hat in America. It was not *refusal* but *hesitation* and *conscientious scruples* which caused me to deny the bow at that moment; and now that the Principal *assured* me that it was *not worship*, my scruples were removed, and though I believed the ceremony to be a rather foolish one, for the sake of the school, the principal, and *my* students, I consented to bow.

[*Uchimura Kanzō zenshū*, vol. 20, pp. 206–9]

"TWO J'S"

"Two J's" was composed in parallel English and Japanese five years before Uchimura's death. He wrote his tombstone inscription (in English) while he was working in a home for mentally retarded children.

I love two J's and no third; one is Jesus, and the other Japan.

I do not know which I love more, Jesus or Japan.

I am hated by my countrymen for Jesus' sake as a *yaso* [Jesus, hence Christian] and I am disliked by foreign missionaries for Japan's sake as national and narrow. . . .

Jesus and Japan; my faith is not a circle with one center; it is an ellipse with two centers. My heart and mind revolve around the two dear names. And I know that one strengthens the other; Jesus strengthens and purifies my love for Japan; and Japan clarifies and objectivises [*sic*] my love for Jesus. Were it not for the two, I would become a mere dreamer, a fanatic, an amorphous universal man.

Jesus makes me a world-man, a friend of humanity; Japan makes me a lover of my country, and through it binds me firmly to the terrestrial globe. I am neither too narrow nor too broad by loving the two at the same time.

O Jesus, thou art the Sun of my soul, the saviour dear; I have given my all
to thee!

To Be Inscribed Upon My Tomb
I for Japan;
Japan for the World;
The World for Christ;
And all for God.

> [*Uchimura Kanzō zenshū*, vol. 15, pp. 599–600; vol. 20, frontispiece; Tsunoda et al.,
> eds., *Sources of Japanese Tradition*, 1st ed., vol. 2, pp. 349–50]

NATSUME SŌSEKI

Natsume Sōseki (1867–1916), together with Mori Ōgai (1862–1922), exemplified
literary expression in the late Meiji period. Both men developed new fictional
forms and engaged in the cultural debates of the day. Sōseki remained the most
popular writer throughout the twentieth century. His early novels, especially
Botchan and *I Am a Cat* (*Wagahai wa neko de aru*), were widely read for generations, while his later, and darker, novels, including *Kokoro* and *The Gate*
(*Mon*), soon entered the modern literary canon. In the later works, Sōseki frequently evoked the spiritual costs of Meiji modernization: "Loneliness," he wrote
in *Kokoro*, was "the price we have to pay for being born in this modern age."

Sōseki's life coincided with the Meiji era, a fact he noted more than once.
After graduating from Tokyo Imperial University in 1893 and teaching in provincial secondary schools, the government sent him to study in England, where
he was lonely and unhappy. He resigned from Tokyo University in 1907 and
joined the *Tōkyō Asahi shinbun*, one of Japan's largest national newspapers,
which published his fiction in serial form. Between 1905 and 1916, Sōseki wrote
fourteen novels. At the same time, he took public positions critical of the government's ideological attempts to control literature, even refusing to accept a
doctoral degree from the Ministry of Education in 1911.

"MY INDIVIDUALISM"
(WATAKUSHI NO KOJINSHUGI)

"My Individualism" is an often-quoted speech delivered by Natsume Sōseki in 1914 to
the students of the Gakushūin, an elite academy for the sons of peers and the upper
classes. In the years following the Russo-Japanese War of 1904/1905, educated youth
were increasingly attracted to the notion of individualism, while the government and
conservatives treated their attraction as subversive to the social order. Sōseki used his
own experience to fashion an argument for an individualism grounded in the self that
depended on neither Western referents nor the Japanese nation.

In my day, it was even worse. Attribute something—anything—to a Westerner and people would follow it blindly, acting meanwhile as though it made them very important. Everywhere, there were men who thought themselves extremely clever because they could fill their speech with foreign names. Practically everybody was doing it. I say this not in condemnation of others, however: I myself was one of those men. I might read one European's critique of another European's book, for example. Then, never considering the merits of the critique, without in fact understanding it, I would spout it as my own. This piece of mechanically acquired information, this alien thing that I had swallowed whole, that was neither possession nor blood nor flesh of mine, I would regurgitate in the guise of personal opinion. And, the times being what they were, everyone would applaud.

No amount of applause, however, could quiet my anxiety, for I myself knew that I was boasting of borrowed clothes, preening with glued-on peacock feathers. I began to see that I must abandon this empty display and move toward something more genuine, for until I did so, that anxiety in the pit of my stomach would never go away. . . .

My next step was to strengthen—perhaps I should say to build anew—the foundations on which I stood in my study of literature. For this, I began to read books that had nothing whatever to do with literature. If, before, I had been other-centered, it occurred to me now that I must become self-centered (*jiko hon'i*). I became absorbed in scientific studies, philosophical speculation, anything that would support this position. Now the times are different and the need for self-centeredness should be clear to anyone who has done some thinking, but I was immature then, and the world around me was still not very advanced. There was really no other way for me to proceed.

Once I had grasped this idea of self-centeredness, it became for me an enormous fund of strength, even defiance. Who did these Westerners think they were anyway? I had been feeling lost, in a daze, when the idea of ego-centeredness (*jiga hon'i*) told me where to stand, showed me the road I must take.

Self-centeredness became for me a new beginning, I confess, and it helped me to find what I thought would be my life's work. I resolved to write books, to tell people that they need not imitate Westerners, that running blindly after others as they were doing would only cause them great anxiety. If I could spell this out for them with unshakable proof, it would give me pleasure and make them happy as well. This was what I hoped to accomplish.

My anxiety disappeared without a trace. I looked out on London's gloom with a happy heart. I felt that after years of agony my pick had at last struck a vein of ore. A ray of light had broken through the fog and illuminated the way I must take. . . .

So let me explain individualism as simply as I can. Individual liberty is indispensable for the development of individuality that I spoke of earlier. And the development of your individuality will have a great bearing on your happiness. Thus it would seem to me that we must keep for ourselves and grant to others a degree of liberty such [that] I can turn left while you turn right, each of us equally unhindered so long as what we do has no effect on others. This is what I mean by individualism. . . .

Evils arise because people . . . are incapable of understanding ethical individualism. They try, instead to aggrandize themselves at the expense of the general public, to use their power—be it financial or otherwise—to further their own selfish ends. Thus it is that individualism—the individualism that I am describing here—in no way resembles the danger to the nation that ordinary people imagine it to be. As I see it, individualism advocates respecting the existence of others at the same time that one respects one's own existence. I find that a most worthy philosophy. . . .

Many people seem to think of individualism as something opposed to—even destructive of—nationalism. But individualism in no way justifies such a misguided, illogical interpretation. (Actually, I don't like these labels I've been using. People are not to be neatly defined by any single "ism." For clarity's sake, however, I am forced to discuss a variety of subjects under one heading.) Some people nowadays are spreading the idea—and they believe it—that Japan cannot survive unless it is entirely nationalistic. Many go so far as to assert that our nation will perish unless this terrible "individualism" is stamped out. What utter nonsense! All of us, in fact, are nationalists *and* internationalists *and* individualists as well. . . .

The nation may well be important, but we cannot possibly concern ourselves with the nation from morning to night as though possessed by it. There may be those who insist that we think of nothing but the nation twenty-four hours a day, but, in fact, no one can go on thinking only of one single thing so incessantly. The bean curd seller does not go around selling bean curd for the nation's sake. He does it to earn a living. Whatever his immediate motives may be, he does contribute something necessary to society and, in that sense, perhaps, the nation benefits indirectly. The same may be said of the fact that I had three bowls of rice today for lunch and four for supper. I took a larger serving, not for the nation's sake but, frankly, to suit my stomach. These things might be said to have some very indirect influence on the country, and, indeed, from certain points of view, they might bear some relation to the entire drift of world affairs. But what a horror if we had to take that into account and eat for the nation, wash our faces for the nation, go to the toilet for the nation! There is nothing wrong with encouraging nationalism, but to pretend that you are doing all of these impossible things for the nation is simply a lie. . . .

We are all aware that Japan today is not entirely secure. Japan is a poor country, and small. Who knows what could happen—or when? In that sense all of us must maintain our concern for the nation. But this country of ours is in no danger of suddenly collapsing; we are not about to suffer annihilation; and as long as that is true, there should be no need for all the commotion on behalf of the country. It is like running through the streets dressed in firefighting clothes and full of self-sacrifice before any fire has broken out. . . .

There is just one other point that I would like to bring to your attention — namely, that a nationalistic morality comes out a very poor second when compared with an individualistic morality. Nations have always been most punctilious over the niceties of diplomatic language, but not so with the morality of their actions. They swindle and cheat and trick each other every chaotic step of the way. That is why you will have to content yourself with a pretty cheap grade of morality when you take the nation as your standard, when you conceive of the nation as an indivisible monolith. Approach things from a foundation of individualism, however, and you arrive at a far loftier morality; the difference between the two deserves a good deal of thought.

> [Sōseki, "Watakushi no kojinshugi," trans. Rubin,
> "Sōseki on Individualism," pp. 21–48]

NISHIDA KITARŌ

Nishida Kitarō (1870–1945), the leading philosopher of the Kyoto school, was the founding figure of modern philosophy in Japan. As a devoted practitioner of Zen Buddhism and a lifelong student of Western philosophy — from the ancient Greeks through Hegel and Johann Fichte to Heinrich Rickert and Edmund Husserl — Nishida's philosophical universe had encompassed Japan and the world from his student days. His best-selling early work, *Studies of the Good* (*Zen no kenkyū*, 1911), established his reputation and, with it, the field of academic philosophy as the inquiry into human experience rather than the history of (Western) philosophy. His mature *Fundamental Problems of Philosophy* (*Tetsugaku no konpon mondai*, 1933/1934) further developed his core concept of the "place of absolute nothingness" (*mu no basho*), drawing on both Mahayana Buddhism and European metaphysics to define the dialectical relationship between the conscious self and the world of action.

The emphasis on culture and "culturalism" among intellectuals during the 1930s joined with the imperialism and rising nationalism of the time to revive the debate about the relation of Japanese culture to Asian and world culture in a new and increasingly aggressive register. Nishida first delivered his *Problem of Japanese Culture* (*Nihon bunka no mondai*) as a series of lectures at Kyoto University in 1938, and then revised it for publication in 1940. This is a text that could be, and was, read in different ways. Some emphasized Nishida's consistent concern with world culture, quoting statements like that from *Fundamental Problems of Philosophy*: "A true world culture will be formed only by various cultures preserving their own respective viewpoints but simultaneously developing themselves through global mediation." These defenders also cited the fact that during the war, nationalists had denounced Nishida as a seditious "globalist." Others, and they were far more numerous, pointed out Nishida's insistence not only on the specialness of Japanese culture but also on its superiority and the proper historical role of its imperial and national polity to lead East Asia. The postwar critique of Nishida and the Kyoto school for their intellectual support of empire and war was both sharp and contested, a mark of the ways in which prewar philosophical debates had indeed been swept up in the political tide of the times.[1]

THE PROBLEM OF JAPANESE CULTURE
(NIHON BUNKA NO MONDAI)

I believe that underlying the Oriental view of the world and of humanity there has been something equal, if not superior, to Occidental conceptions. Underlying both Chinese and Indian cultures there was something truly great, but they lacked a spirit of resolutely seeking out the facts and therefore became rigid and fossilized. That the Japanese alone in the Orient, though sharing in these cultural influences, have gone forward to absorb Occidental culture and have also been considered the creators of a new Oriental culture is due, is it not, mainly to that same Japanese spirit, free and unfettered, that "goes straight to things"? . . . [p. 1]

In order to explain what Japanese culture is like, we must look back on its history [and] study its institutions and civilization. I stated at the outset of this lecture that I appreciate such studies very highly. At the same time, I believe that we must examine in what sense Japanese culture may today be considered [to be becoming] a world culture and how it may develop as such. The question also arises: Now that the Orient and Occident form one world, in what sense can Oriental culture contribute as a world culture to future world history? They say those who are ignorant of foreign languages know nothing about their own language, and indeed, only through comparison with other things can we achieve a true understanding of a given thing. We can know ourselves by projecting ourselves into the mirror of objectivity, and by knowing ourselves objectively we can act objectively; otherwise we cannot escape the charge of being boastful and conceited. It is not enough just to explain the distinctive features of Japanese culture. In the Japan of today, which is attempting to establish itself as Japan, a nation of the world, this point requires special attention. . . .

What in Japan has thus far passed for comparisons of Eastern and Western culture has tended to be done by lining up two cultures and comparing their external characteristics. For example, people say that in the West there is such-and-such a theory; in the East there is a similar one. Or alternatively, in the East there is such-and-such a thing, but in the West it is lacking. Needless to say, men

---

1. Heisig and Maraldo, *Rude Awakenings*.

as members of the same species, *Homo sapiens*, have thought the same things often enough. However, even doctrines of a purely theoretical character are not independent of their historical backgrounds; any discussion of them must therefore start with their historical bases and treat them as living things. To compare these ideas in such abstract terms as "isms" is bound to be superficial. For example, Fazang's "free interaction of event with event" and Hegel's dialectics seem much alike at first glance, but one is Buddhistic while the other is Christian, which means that they are essentially different in spirit. Again, although we may speak of possessing something in Oriental thought that is lacking in Occidental thought, the difference may be merely extrinsic, like the long-necked giraffe and the short-necked whale [both of which are nonetheless mammals]. Such characterizations may be acceptable if it is merely a matter of description, but in discussing the relative merits of both cultures, we must reexamine things in terms of the intrinsic character of our historical life. . . . [pp. 280–83]

Let us ask whether there is not any sort of logic underlying Oriental culture — the culture that has nurtured us for several thousand years. Doesn't our conception of human life and the world possess its own original way of looking at and thinking things or, in short, its own logic? Is it, as many people think, simply emotional? I do not deny that Japanese culture is a culture of emotion; I made a remark myself elsewhere to the effect that Japanese culture is *rhythmical*. Nevertheless, it is only through the attainment of reality that we can be creative, can live in truth. We must, therefore, obtain a logical grasp of our way of life at its very foundations. . . .

Leaving aside those who are studying the special character of Oriental culture from a historical point of view, don't the majority of those who treat Oriental culture from a philosophical point of view deal with it in Occidental terms? And on the other hand, don't the remainder take something particular [i.e., specifically Oriental] for the universal, in other words, regard subjective hope or desire as the basic principle? Is "logic" in general nothing more than the mode of thought and way of looking at things that underlies Western culture today? Must we assume Occidental logic to be the only logic, and must the Oriental way of thinking be considered simply a less-developed form [of the same thinking]? In order to decide these problems, we first have to go back and reexamine the underlying sources from which logic emerged into the historical world and the part logic played in history.

In the last analysis, thinking is nothing but a historical event, which acts as the self-formative function of our historical life. Willing as I am to recognize Occidental logic as a magnificent systematic development and intent as I am on studying it first as one type of world logic, I wonder whether even Western logic is anything more than a special feature of the historical life, an aspect of self-formation of the historical life. Such a thing as formal, abstract logic will remain the same anywhere, but concrete logic as a form of concrete knowledge cannot be independent of the specific features of historical life. . . . [pp. 286–87]

I am not saying that logic is of two kinds, Occidental logic and Oriental logic. Logic must be one; it is only as the form of self-formative function of the historical world that it has taken different directions in the course of its development. Roughly speaking, we might say that Occidental logic is the logic that takes things as its object and that Oriental logic is the logic that takes mind as its object. Some may say that a logic with mind as its objective is an impossibility, for logic must always be the logic of the objective object. [On the one hand,] what we call this self of ours is also a fact or event in the historical world. Only as such is it something thinkable, something we can discuss. [On the other hand,] what we call a "thing" really exists only as a fact in the historical world, and nothing exists in the historical world as mere object entirely apart from what we call "self." All [i.e., things and selves], therefore, should come under the logic of historical fact. Now in the logic of Buddhism, I think, there are the germs of a logic that takes the self as its object—a logic of the mind— even though it has remained a sort of personal experience and developed no further. It has not developed into what could be called a logic of fact. We first need to study Occidental logic thoroughly, but at the same time we must have a critical attitude toward it. What we call the study of the Orient today only means taking the Orient as an *object* of study. As yet, a profound reflection about the Oriental way of thinking, in order to evolve a new *method* of thinking, has not been undertaken. [pp. 289–90]

At this point, Nishida presents a brief statement of the theoretical position on which he bases the evaluation of Oriental and Occidental culture given in the concluding selection.[2]

To distinguish among the intellectual trends of different peoples, we must note their respective characteristics. I believe that the principle of self-formation of the historical world formed the foundation of Japanese thought. For the Japanese people who attained their distinctive development as a society almost entirely secluded on isolated Oriental islands for thousands of years, what they called Japan was the same as the world. Japan was a vertical world. The Japanese spirit emerged in the construction of Japanese history. But today Japan is no longer the isolated Oriental islands or secluded society it once was. It is Japan of the world, Japan turned toward the world and rising. Japan's formative principle must therefore become the formative principle of the world as well. Herein lies what I consider a great problem in the present time. To my mind, what must be most cautioned against is making Japan into a subject (*shutai*). That reduces the imperial Way (*kōdō*) to nothing other than imperialism (*teikokushugika*). . . . [Instead,] we must contribute to the world by discovering

---

2. See Tsunoda et al., eds., *Sources of Japanese Tradition*, 1st ed., vol. 2, pp. 356–62.

in the depths of our historical development that principle of self-formation of the world of self-identity and contradictions. This is the realization of the imperial Way and the true meaning of "all the world under one roof" (*hakkō ichiu*). [p. 341]

> [*Nihon bunka no mondai*, vol. 12 of *Nishida Kitarō zenshū*, pp. 1, 280–83, 286–87, 289–90, 341; CG; see also Tsunoda et al., eds., *Sources of Japanese Tradition*, 1st ed., vol. 2, pp. 350–64]

ENDŌ SHŪSAKU

Endō Shūsaku (1923–1996) was one of the most popular writers in the postwar years. His historical fiction, including the famous *Silence* (*Chinmoku*, 1966), depicted the dilemmas of faith caused by the Tokugawa persecution of Christianity in the seventeenth century. In his novels about Japan's Christian martyrs, whose refusal to tread on a metal image of the crucifix or the Madonna (*fumie*) cost them their lives, Endō portrayed Japanese Christianity as a maternal religion that looked less to God the Father than to the Mother, the Virgin Mary, and often in the form of the images of Maria Kannon that sustained the faith of the "hidden Christians" during the centuries of persecution.

"MY COMING INTO FAITH" (WATASHI NO NYŪSHIN)

Endō Shūsaku's confessional account of his coming into faith explains his spiritual and cultural journey from a perfunctory baptism in childhood through his study abroad in France to his confrontation with his own alienation in novels about those who had faced dilemmas of belief in earlier times.

My Relationship with Christianity

Why did I become a Christian? I did not choose this religion of my own volition. Among the various Christian sects, I am a follower of Catholicism, but I did not choose Catholicism after conducting a comparison of Catholicism and Protestantism. Neither did I choose Christianity after comparing it with Buddhism or with Communism.

My parents divorced when I was in elementary school, and it seems my mother tried to find solace from her pain after the divorce through religion. Her older sister was a Catholic, and so my mother ended up attending church and was baptized. It was natural for my older brother and me, though reluctantly, also to go to church.

To be perfectly honest, the talks at church were totally uninteresting to me, and I dozed through most of them. It turned out that all the children in my group were to be baptized, and I joined in with them and said I would be baptized, too. I received baptism without giving a thought to its significance. I was in the fourth grade at the time, so I must have been ten or eleven years old.

That was the manner in which I received baptism, so there was no philosophical motivation whatsoever behind it. Like an infant getting baptized, I was converted without any idea of what I was doing. . . .

When I was eighteen or nineteen years old, around the time I was taking preparatory classes to enter Keiō University, I began reading books and decided that perhaps I would cast off this "Western religion." It was like being coerced into a marriage with a woman chosen by my parents, since I hadn't made the choice of my own volition, and I felt like saying to her "Get out!" But she wouldn't leave. Just like a wife. It felt like she was there to stay. . . .

A Religion Retailored to My Body

I think, because I was very strongly attached to my mother, that somehow inside I felt I couldn't look her in the face if I were to flatly reject something she had believed in so fervently. It seemed as if it would be shirking my duty to my mother to discard something she had given me. It seemed inexcusable of me to throw off something without really studying it or thinking about it when my mother had lived it with her whole soul and bequeathed it to me, and somewhere I felt that I, too, had to put my soul into it.

I finally came to the conclusion that I would have to retailor the suit of Western-style clothes that my mother had given me into Japanese attire that would fit my body. . . .

I went to France as a student shortly after the end of World War II, and while I was there I became very ill. I'm sometimes asked whether I began to think seriously about Christianity at that time, since it is very lonely to become ill in a foreign land and one suffers spiritually in many ways. But I didn't give it that much thought at the time. Not that I gave it no consideration at all, but it was actually more during the time of a later illness that I began to take the issue seriously. . . .

It was after I became a novelist, when I had to spend two and a half to three years lying in bed, that I thought about Christianity. . . . I became ill just after I had finished writing *The Sea and Poison* (*Umi to dokuyaku*), and every time I opened up a literary journal, there was something a friend of mine had written. Knowing that I would be writing, too, if I were healthy, I felt bitter disappointment. . . .

When I fell ill as a student, I still retained the image in my mind that Christianity was a force that was oppressing me, strangling me. Just as Europe was oppressing me. No matter how much I studied about Europe, I could never understand it. Even though I studied very hard. Among those elements oppressing me was Christianity. European-style Christianity, that is. I was stifled by it and wanted to go back to Japan as quickly as possible.

When I got sick the second time, after I became a novelist, I gradually came to realize that Christianity did not belong exclusively to Europe—in other words, that Christianity wasn't just a suit of Western clothes but had elements of Japanese dress as well. And so I began to think about how I could bring it into my own life. I think that feeling emerges in the novel I wrote after I was released from the hospital, *Silence (Chinmoku)*. . . .

I wrote a novel entitled *The Samurai,* but the image of the samurai there was of one who serves, who surrenders himself and his life to another. I'm sure that people who believe they can handle everything in their lives through their own strength feel they don't need religion, but I'm the kind of man who can't take care of everything in my life on my own; just like the protagonist in my novel *The Samurai*, I have to give myself over to something greater. It's just as Luke records in his Gospel: "Into thy hands I commend my spirit." . . .

I think that Japanese writers in particular are seeking after something religious in nature. We speak of a literature in search of truth, but I think you could replace that concept of truth with the idea of religion. Yoshiyuki Junnosuke is a man deeply sensitive to the sincerity and gentleness and compassion one finds in prostitutes. He responds to the sympathy that such women show him. To turn the whole idea on its head, just as I have sought a maternal religious spirit in God, he has sought something humanly sublime in the redlight district. I suppose this is a bothersome thought for a man like Yoshiyuki who believes in no religion, but I think he'll make it to heaven sooner than I do.

I don't think there are irreligious people and religious people. I think there are two types of people: those who claim to be religious individuals and those who would not make such a claim but for whom the experiences they seek are in fact religious. . . .

Some say that the Jesus in my novels is very gentle, very easy for the Japanese to relate to. Some are critical that he is too Japanese, but that is Jesus as I see him. To say that Jesus is a mirror that reflects each individual's heart is to say that there is one image of Jesus for me and another image of Jesus for others.

And yet . . . I am most drawn to the gentle Jesus. That is the Jesus I love. That is why I have written throughout my career about such a Jesus and why the image of him raging in the temple does not quite come into focus for me. And so the Jesus about whom I write is not the absolute Jesus, not all there is to Jesus. There are other ways of looking at him. Each Christian has a separate image of Jesus, but the true image of Jesus emerges when we put all those views together.

[Endō, "Watashi no nyūshin," pp. 5–25; VG]

MISHIMA YUKIO

Mishima Yukio (1925–1970) was another of the brilliant writers—including Kawabata Yasunari, Abe Kōbō, and Ōe Kenzaburō—who made postwar Japanese literature an indispensable part of world culture. A prolific novelist, dramatist, and flamboyant figure, Mishima was distinguished from these other literary giants by his powerful commitment to a Japanese imperial tradition that led eventually to his dramatic suicide in the name of a martial spirit he considered lost in the peace and democracy of postwar Japan. Mishima was learned in traditional culture and widely read in Western literature. He insisted on using traditional orthography even after writing had been simplified by the postwar government, displaying contempt for writers who, when they wrote about the former nobility, could not reproduce its distinctive language. Although he criticized the upper classes for their pretension and their materialism, he believed that their language and social behavior preserved Japanese traditions. Mishima's daily life, however, was not marked by any obvious adherence to these traditions. His house was built in a Spanish style and featured a marble statue of Apollo in the garden. He wore the latest fashions and the most stylish sunglasses and, to the end of his life, disdained Japanese cuisine as insufficiently filling.

Mishima did not think of these aspects in his life as inconsistent with Japanese tradition—a tradition he spoke of as a refined eroticism—a *joi de vivre* that manifested itself in an elegant sensuality, which he contrasted to the moralistic puritanism of the West. In choosing the emperor as its focal point, he did not refer to Hirohito, whom he was perfectly willing to openly mimic or criticize. Rather, for him, the emperor was not a particular person but the incarnation of an unbroken tradition extending to the beginnings of Japanese history—Japanese tradition given visible form. Feeling intense disgust at the bourgeois culture and commercialism that had infected Japan, he believed that the imperial institution could provide an axis around which Japanese culture might be reinvigorated. His *On the Defense of Culture (Bunka bōei ron)* dates from 1969.

Mishima's sensational suicide in 1970 had little apparent effect on the youth of Japan, the audience to whom he directed his final appeal. But his novels and plays continued to draw audiences in Japan and the West, not because of their political philosophy, but because of the beauty of their language and Mishima's mastery of Japanese literary tradition.

"THE NATIONAL CHARACTERISTICS OF JAPANESE CULTURE"
(NIHON BUNKA NO KOKUMINTEKI TOKUSHOKU)

There is something dubious about such abstract concepts as "world culture" and "the culture of humanity." Especially in the case of a country like Japan, which has a distinct national character, history, geographical situation, and climate, a grasp of the national characteristics revealed in the culture is essential.

First of all, even if the end product of a culture is material, while in a living state it is not material nor is it immaterial like the national spirit before it has manifested itself; it is a form, a kind of transparent crystallization through which the national spirit can be seen, and no matter how turbid the form may become, it is likely that the degree of transparency already achieved will be sufficient for the soul to be glimpsed in the form. For this reason, culture includes not only what may be termed works of art but also actions and modes of action. Culture includes not only the prescribed movements of a nō play but also the actions of the naval officer who was killed after he jumped from a human torpedo as it surfaced in the moonlit sea off New Guinea and brandished his Japanese sword over his head, and it includes all the many last letters written by members of the Special Attack Force (*kamikaze*). Everything points to the form through which the Japaneseness of things can be glimpsed in the two aspects of the "chrysanthemum and the sword," from *The Tale of Genji* to a modern novel, from the *Man'yōshū* to avant-garde poetry, from the Buddhist statues in Chūson-ji to contemporary sculpture, from flower arrangement and the tea ceremony to kendō and jūdō, and even from kabuki to gangster movies or from Zen to military etiquette. Literature in its use of the Japanese language is an important element in the creation of Japanese culture as form.

It is not adequate to extract from Japanese culture only its static side and to ignore the dynamic side. Japanese culture has a special tradition of transforming modes of action themselves into works of art. It is a special feature of Japan that the martial arts belong to the same genre of artistic forms as the tea ceremony and flower arrangement; all come into being, are continued, and disappear within a short space of time. *Bushidō* is a system of making ethics beautiful or perhaps of giving ethical content to beauty; it is a union between life and art. The importance accorded to the traditions of performance that have arisen in nō and kabuki prepares from the outset clues to how the art is to be transmitted, and these clues themselves are forms that constantly give rise to free expression. Even in the modern novel, which might seem at first glance to be the genre with the greatest freedom, the efforts expended at times ever since the rise of naturalism, albeit unconscious, on the creation of novelistic forms, have been many times the efforts expended on intellectual formation.

Second, Japanese culture has never distinguished between originals and copies. In the West, where culture consists mainly of things, they built with stone, but wood was used in Japan. In the West the destruction of an original building was final; it could not return to life a second time. For a culture based on material things, this was tantamount to extinction; that was why Paris was surrendered to the enemy, as we have seen.

However, it is true equally of the West and Japan that material culture, before plans for organic preservation were drawn up in accordance with the emphasis on culture of modern times, was subjected to frightening license. When one thinks back on the wartime destruction and the conflagrations of the past, it is evident that the survival of material culture has been simply a matter of accident. One cannot say that only objects of good quality, carefully selected by the hands of history, have been preserved. The supreme work of the Greek sculptor Praxiteles may still be sleeping today at the bottom of the Mediterranean. The fate imposed in the past on the Japanese plastic arts, based on a culture of wood and paper, was far more thorough. An incalculable number of cultural properties were lost during the Ōnin War. It was a miracle that the temples and shrines of Kyoto escaped the flames.

One reason that adherence to material culture has been comparatively rare in Japan and that there has been the special feature of transference of cultural forms to forms of action that take disappearance as intrinsic is related to the nature of the materials employed. The extinction of the original is not absolute. Far from it. No definitive difference in value between the original and the copy has been established.

The most extreme example of this tendency can be found in the buildings of the Ise Shrine. The ceremonial renewal of the buildings every twenty years has recurred fifty-nine times since the time of Empress Jitō. The newly erected Ise Shrine is always the original, and the [former] original at this point disappears, passing on to the copy the life of the original; the copy itself becomes the original. The uniqueness of the cultural concept of rebuilding the Ise Shrine becomes apparent if it is compared with the handicap shouldered by Roman copies for preserving the ancient Greek sculptures, most of which survive only in these copies. The rules of *honkadori* (allusive variation) in *waka* poetry and other similar examples show that this kind of cultural concept still today occupies a deep place in our hearts.

The special features of this cultural concept correspond to the special feature of the emperor system in that each successive emperor is indisputably the emperor and the relationship between him and Tenshō Daijin [Amaterasu, the Sun Goddess] is not one of original and copy. . . . [pp. 227–29]

The Emperor as a Cultural Concept

The imperial institution, as a cultural concept of this nature, satisfies the two requisites of cultural totality: temporal continuity has been preserved by religious rites, but at the same time, spatial continuity at times has gone so far as to tolerate even political disorder; it is as if the most profound eroticism corresponds on the one hand to ancient theocracy while being bonded with anarchism.

Miyabi (elegance) was at once the fine flower of the court culture and the yearning it inspired, but in times of emergency, *miyabi* might even take the form of terrorism. That is to say, the emperor, being a cultural concept, was not always on the side of state authority and order; he sometimes held out his hand to disorder. When state authority and order had separated the country from the people, the emperor, in his role as a cultural concept, functioned as a revolutionary principle attempting to restore "the indivisibility of country and people." The patriots who, in response to the wishes of Emperor Kōmei, carried out the incident at the Sakurada Gate,[3] were putting into practice "single-hearted *miyabi*." An uprising for the sake of the emperor, as long as it did not violate cultural tradition, was to be accepted, but the "emperor system" under Shōwa,[4] adhering to the European system of constitutional monarchy, had lost the ability to understand the *miyabi* of the February 26 [1936] incident.[5]

While it proclaimed "the unity of religion and government," the emperor system under the Meiji constitution provided only a temporal continuity and did not concern itself with spatial continuity, thus giving way to the danger of political instability. In other words, it did not concern itself with the problem of freedom of speech. The political concept of the emperor could not help but abet the sacrifice of the cultural concept of the emperor, which should have been freer and more embracing. Hence in postwar Japan, a "cultural nation" with an emperor system that barely managed to survive under the American Occupation, both these aspects of the system lost their real force. As a result of the "educationalism" in the style of the Taishō period [1912–1926], promoted by low-class bureaucrats and low-class "men of culture," it was made subservient to a mass socialization, and its true dignity was lowered to the realm of "the emperor system" as it appeared in the weeklies. It ended without any attempt having been made to revive and reestablish "the emperor as cultural concept" or "the emperor as unifying agent of a cultural totality." On the one hand, the nobility of the culture died, and on the other, it came about that those looking for a revival of the ancient order could hope for no more than a revival of the emperor as a political concept.

At the same time, the figure of the emperor as priest and poet still lived in the rites of the palace sanctuary and the ceremonies of the Imperial Office of Poetry Composition. The tradition of imperial poetry composition signifies that it is the emperor who presides over poetry. However, this has almost nothing to do with the emperor's individual talent or cultivation as a poet. [Instead,] it invests the people's poetizing work with a certain elegance (*miyabi*); it attests to the continuance of the cultural holism that has come down from the *Man'yōshū*. Originality is pushed to the periphery, and the commonplace

---

3. Reference to the assassination of Ii Naosuke on March 24, 1860, by samurai of the Mito domain. Ii, the chief adviser (*tairō*) of the shogun, had relentlessly attempted to stamp out opposition to his policy of peacefully concluding treaties with foreigners. Emperor Kōmei bitterly opposed this policy.

4. Shōwa was the reign-name of Hirohito as emperor (1926–1989).

5. The emperor, not approving of the revolt of young army officers against the alleged corruption of the government, ordered the soldiers back to their barracks.

radiates at the core. Poems by the people participating in this courtly elegance and linking up with the imperial composition form an unbroken chain from the summit of the imperial composition all the way down to the skirts of the mountain. By the people's not merely "looking" at the cultural tradition but participating in it with their compositions, glory is thrown back on them by the cultural continuity. The reigning emperor is, like the renewal of the Ise Shrine, at once the present emperor and the first emperor. The secret rituals of Great Thanksgiving (Daijōsai) and "Offering of the First Fruits" (Niinamesai) preserve this tradition well.

The imperial institution, representing the cultural holism that provides the formal link between the cultural present and its origins in the past, between its creation and its preservation, appears to have become almost completely effaced from the consciousness of the bearers of culture today. At the same time, apart from the sense of courtly excellence, we no longer possess a truly typical model of classical beauty. The holism of culture is not to be found in the flatness of the contrast between freedom and responsibility but in the three-dimensional structure of freedom and excellence. Even now, we have no poetic form that completely combines the chrysanthemum and the sword except for the *waka*. Just as the Japanese novel developed from the prefaces to poems, the *waka* is the generic form of Japanese culture, and other genres are extensions of this. The fluid structure based on the operation of images in accordance with the continuing effects of resonant language continues even in contemporary literature almost unconsciously to infuse and diffuse throughout all our literary practice. Caught between the elegance of court poetry and the imitative elegance of popular poetry, there persists only this slender rootless grass in all contemporary culture. The break in tradition is none other than the break in the tradition of what at first glance might seem to be conventional poetry. There is no sign that contemporary Japanese culture has provided anything of the generic beauty we associate with the concepts of *yūgen* (mysterious depth), *hana* (flower), *wabi* (simple beauty), and *sabi* (faded beauty). Without the essential intermediary agency of the emperor, poetry and politics have fallen into diametrical opposition, and politics have swallowed up the domain of poetry. . . . [pp. 244–46]

[*Mishima Yukio hyōron zenshū*, vol. 3, pp. 227–29, 244–46; DK]

ŌE KENZABURŌ

Ōe Kenzaburō (b. 1935), the winner of the Nobel Prize for Literature in 1994, viewed Japanese tradition very differently from the way Mishima Yukio did. Marked by his childhood experience of the war, Ōe became an ardent supporter of postwar democracy as an ideal and a steadfast critic of its violations in practice.[6] Ōe wrote in many genres, including novels, short stories, and essays. His preoccupation with personal authenticity and integrity evolved together with a profound engagement with Western literature and philosophy, from William Butler Yeats to Gershom Scholem. He was a persistent public opponent of the myths of the imperial institution, of rearmament and Cold War geopolitics, and of Japan's inadequate relations with Asia, both political and cultural.

"JAPAN, THE AMBIGUOUS, AND MYSELF"

Ōe Kenzaburō's Nobel Prize acceptance speech, an excerpt of which follows, represents his mature views, but the title suggests his continuing anxieties and doubt with regard to unresolved personal and cultural tensions. Ōe's sense of ambiguity, expressed in images he refers to as "grotesque realism," affected him both as a Japanese and as an individual, who, according to the Nobel citation, "with poetic force creates an imagined world, where life and myth condense to form a disconcerting picture of the human predicament."

Ōe introduced his remarks by referring to the Nobel speech of his predecessor, Kawabata Yasunari (1899–1972), the first Japanese writer to receive this literary distinction, in 1968. Kawabata had identified with Japanese tradition as represented by Zen poetry, but Ōe found this too vague and struggled to make his own ambiguities less so.

During the last catastrophic World War, I was a little boy and lived in a remote, wooded valley on Shikoku Island in the Japanese archipelago, thousands of miles away from here. At that time there were two books by which I was really fascinated: *The Adventures of Huckleberry Finn* and *The Wonderful Adventures of Nils*. . . .

Kawabata Yasunari, the first Japanese writer who stood on this platform as a winner of the Nobel Prize for Literature, delivered a lecture entitled "Japan, the Beautiful, and Myself." It was at once very beautiful and *vague*. I have used the English word *vague* as an equivalent of that word in Japanese *aimai na*. This Japanese adjective could have several alternatives for its English translation. . . .

Under that title Kawabata talked about a unique kind of mysticism which is found not only in Japanese thought but also more widely Oriental thought. By "unique" I mean here a tendency towards Zen Buddhism. Even as a twentieth-century writer, Kawabata depicts his state of mind in terms of the poems written by medieval Zen monks. Most of these poems are concerned with the linguistic

---

6. For his immediate postwar views, see chap. 44; for his views of the atomic bomb, chap. 49.

impossibility of telling truth. According to such poems, words are confined within their closed shells. The readers cannot expect that words will ever come out of these poems and then get through to us. . . . After those years of his pilgrimage, only by making a confession as to how he was fascinated by such inaccessible Japanese poems that baffle any attempt fully to understand them was he able to talk about "Japan the Beautiful, and Myself," that is, about the world in which he lived and the literature which he created.

It is noteworthy, furthermore, that Kawabata concluded his lecture as follows:

> My works have been described as works of emptiness, but it is not to be taken for the nihilism of the West. The spiritual foundation would seem to be quite different. Dōgen entitled his poem about the seasons "Innate Reality," and even as he sang of the beauty of the seasons he was deeply immersed in Zen.[7]

To tell you the truth, rather than with Kawabata, my compatriot who stood here twenty-six years ago, I feel more spiritual affinity with the Irish poet William Butler Yeats, who was awarded a Nobel Prize for Literature seventy-one years ago when he was at about the same age as me. Of course, I would not presume to rank myself with the poetic genius Yeats. I am merely a humble follower living in a country far removed from his. As William Blake, whose work Yeats revalued and restored to the high place it holds in this century, once wrote: "Across Europe and Asia to China and Japan like lightning." . . .

As someone living in the present world such as this one and sharing bitter memories of the past imprinted on my mind, I cannot utter in unison with Kawabata the phrase "Japan, the Beautiful, and Myself." A moment ago I touched upon the "vagueness" of the title and content of Kawabata's lecture. In the rest of my lecture I would like to use the word *ambiguous* in accordance with the distinction made by the eminent British poet Kathleen Raine; she once said of William Blake that he was not so much vague as ambiguous. I cannot talk about myself otherwise than by saying, "Japan, the Ambiguous, and Myself."

My observation is that after one hundred and twenty years of modernization since the opening of the country, present-day Japan is split between two opposite poles of ambiguity. I, too, am living as a writer with this polarization imprinted on me like a deep scar.

This ambiguity, which is so powerful and penetrating that it splits both the state and its people, is evident in various ways. The modernization of Japan has been oriented toward learning from and imitating the West. Yet Japan is situated in Asia and has firmly maintained its traditional culture. The ambiguous orientation of Japan drove the country into the position of an invader in Asia. On

---

7. Translation by Edward Seidensticker.

the other hand, the culture of modern Japan, which implied being thoroughly open to the West, long remained something obscure that was forever inscrutable to the West (or at least that impeded understanding by the West). What was more, Japan was driven into isolation from other Asian countries, not only politically but also socially and culturally.

In the history of modern Japanese literature, the writers most sincere and aware of their mission were those "postwar writers" who came onto the literary scene immediately after the last war, deeply wounded by the catastrophe yet full of hope for a rebirth. They tried with great pains to make up for the inhuman atrocities committed by Japanese military forces in Asian countries, as well as to bridge the profound gaps that existed not only between the developed countries of the West and Japan but also between African and Latin American countries and Japan. Only by doing so did they think that they could seek with some humility reconciliation with the rest of the world. It has always been my aspiration to cling to the very end of the line of that literary tradition inherited from those writers.

The contemporary state of Japan and its people in their postmodern phase cannot but be ambivalent. Right in the middle of the history of Japan's modernization came the Second World War, a war which was brought about by the very aberration of the modernization itself. The defeat in this war fifty years ago occasioned an opportunity for Japan and the Japanese as the very agent of the war to attempt a rebirth out of the great misery and sufferings that were depicted by the "postwar school" of Japanese writers. The moral props for Japanese aspiring to such a rebirth were the idea of democracy and their determination never to wage a war again. . . .

After the end of the Second World War it was a categorical imperative for us to declare that we renounced war forever in a central article of the new constitution. The Japanese chose the principle of eternal peace as the basis of morality for our rebirth after the war.

I trust that the principle can best be understood in the West, with its long tradition of tolerance for conscientious rejection of military service. In Japan itself there have, all along, been attempts by some to obliterate the article about renunciation of war from the constitution, and for this purpose they have taken every opportunity to make use of pressures from abroad. But to obliterate from the constitution the principle of eternal peace will be nothing but an act of betrayal against the peoples of Asia and the victims of the atom bombs in Hiroshima and Nagasaki. . . .

The prewar Japanese constitution that posited an absolute power transcending the principle of democracy had sustained some support from the populace. Even though we now have the half-century-old new constitution, there is a popular sentiment of support for the old one that lives on in reality in some quarters. If Japan were to institutionalize a principle other than the one to which we have adhered for the last fifty years, the determination we made in the postwar ruins of our collapsed effort at modernization—that determination of ours to establish the concept of universal humanity would come to nothing. . . .

What I call Japan's "ambiguity" in my lecture is a kind of chronic disease that has been prevalent throughout the modern age. Japan's economic prosperity is not free from it either, accompanied as it is by all kinds of potential dangers in the light of the structure of world economy and environmental conservation. The "ambiguity" in this respect seems to be accelerating. It may be more obvious to the critical eyes of the world at large than to us within the country. At the nadir of the postwar economic poverty we found a resilience to endure it, never losing our hope for recovery. It may sound curious to say so, but we seem to have no less resilience to endure our anxiety about the ominous consequences emerging out of the present prosperity. From another point of view, a new situation now seems to be arising in which Japan's prosperity is going to be incorporated into the expanding potential power of both production and consumption in Asia at large.

I am one of the writers who wish to create serious works of literature which dissociate themselves from those novels which are mere reflections of the vast consumer cultures of Tokyo and the subcultures of the world at large. What kind of identity as a Japanese should I seek? W. H. Auden once defined the novelist as follows:

> . . . , among the dust
> Be just, among the Filthy filthy too,
> And in his own weak person, if he can,
> Must suffer dully all the wrongs of Man.[8]

This is what has become my "habit of life" (in Flannery O'Connor's words) through being a writer as my profession.

To define a desirable Japanese identity, I would like to pick out the word *decent*, which is among the adjectives that George Orwell often used, along with words like *humane*, *sane*, and *comely*, or the character types that he favored. This deceptively simple epithet may starkly set off and contrast with the word *ambiguous* used for my identification in "Japan, the Ambiguous, and Myself." There is a wide and ironical discrepancy between what the Japanese seem like when viewed from outside and what they wish to look like.

I hope Orwell would not raise an objection if I used the word *decent* as a synonym of *humanist* or *humaniste* in French, because both words share in common qualities such as tolerance and humanity. Among our ancestors were

---

8. W. H. Auden, "The Novelist," lines 11–14.

some pioneers who made painstaking efforts to build up the Japanese identity as "decent" or "humanist." . . .

I learnt concretely from [Watanabe Kazuo's] translation of Rabelais what Mikhail Bakhtin formulated as "the image system of grotesque realism or the culture of popular laughter"; the importance of material and physical principles; the correspondence between the cosmic, social, and physical elements; the overlapping of death and passions for rebirth; and the laughter that subverts hierarchical relationships.

The image system made it possible to seek literary methods of attaining the universal for someone like me, born and brought up in a peripheral, marginal, off-center region of the peripheral, marginal, off-center country, Japan. Starting from such a background, I do not represent Asia as a new economic power but an Asia impregnated with ever-lasting poverty and a mixed-up fertility. By sharing old, familiar yet living metaphors, I align myself with writers like Kim Ji-ha of Korea[9] and Chon I and Mu Jen, both of China. For me the brotherhood of world literature consists in such relationships in concrete terms. I once took part in a hunger strike for the political freedom of a gifted Korean poet. I am now deeply worried about the destiny of those gifted Chinese novelists who have been deprived of their freedom since the Tiananmen Square incident.

Another way in which Professor Watanabe has influenced me is in his idea of humanism. I take it to be the quintessence of Europe as a living totality. It is an idea which is also perceptible in Milan Kundera's definition of the spirit of the novel. . . . As someone influenced by Watanabe's humanism, I wish my task as a novelist to enable both those who express themselves with words and their readers to recover from their own sufferings and the sufferings of their time and to cure their souls of the wounds. I have said I am split between the opposite poles of ambiguity characteristic of the Japanese. I have been making efforts to be cured of and restored from those pains and wounds by means of literature. I have made my efforts also to pray for the cure and recovery of my fellow Japanese. . . .

"Weak person" though I am, with the aid of this unverifiable belief I would like to "suffer dully all the wrongs" accumulated throughout the twentieth century as a result of the monstrous development of technology and transport. As one with a peripheral, marginal, and off-center existence in the world, I would like to seek how—with what I hope is a modest decent and humanist contribution—I can be of some use in a cure and reconciliation of mankind.

[Nobel Museum, Nobel Lecture, December 7, 1994; English text in Allén, *Nobel Lectures in Literature*, pp. 66–75]

---

9. See Ch'oe et al., eds., *Sources of Korean Tradition*, vol. 2, p. 400.

Chapter 48

GENDER POLITICS AND FEMINISM

In Japan, as elsewhere, the upheavals and transformations accompanying the advent of modernity produced new identities and social formations while dismantling, excluding, and marginalizing others. Out of this conflictual and uneven process emerged possibilities for new social alliances and movements, as well as for the writing of new histories representing new perspectives. Indeed, the telling of these histories often meant creating new frameworks for understanding the temporal process of modernity itself.[1]

This was certainly the case for those who have tried to account for how gender, as a fundamental social division, has evolved with the formation of a modern social structure in Japan. Denied the status of legal subjects of the Japanese state until 1945, women (as well as other sexual and ethnic minorities) since the Meiji Restoration have been largely refused active participation in the crucial ideological work of providing the modern nation-state with its historical narratives and cultural canons. With a few exceptions, representations of women's experiences in these bodies of work have been either absent or, equally likely, produced by others. As long-neglected texts and other expressive artifacts

---

1. For background on the status and role of women, see de Bary et al., eds., *Sources of Japanese Tradition*, 2nd ed., vol. 1, chap. 17; vol. 2, abr., chaps. 25, 36, 37, 38, 42, 45.

created by women continue to be reclaimed, however, our stories of modern Japanese history will continue to be revised.

That the selections included in this chapter represent an unusually broad time span—from the late nineteenth to the late twentieth century—is indicative of the far-reaching implications of the question of gender for the writing of modern Japanese history. Each piece may be linked, directly or indirectly, to the existence of a social movement calling for women's equality or, as we move closer to the present, for an end to forms of social discrimination based on gender and/or sexual preference. Gender roles have varied greatly throughout history, however, so to assume a single definition of "woman" linking these writings is not entirely satisfactory. That the term *feminizumu* was not used in Japan until the 1970s also complicates our chronology. For example, should the transcription by a feminist anthropologist in the 1970s of interviews with Japanese women sent as contracted sex workers to Southeast Asia in the 1920s be viewed as an aspect of postwar women's studies or as a long-occluded chapter of Taishō history? What are the implications for our current understanding of the emergence of modern Japanese literature of the publication of an anthology of Shimizu Shikin's little-known writings, a hundred years after her birth? Narrowly speaking, such events may be linked to the social movements known as *ūman ribu* (women's liberation) and *feminizumu*, which emerged in Japan in the 1970s and without which, no doubt, these events would not have occurred. Yet insofar as they entail a revision of the story of modern Japan itself, they also require us to rethink the foundations of Japanese modernity.

GENDER AND MODERNIZATION

The nature of modernization and its impact on gender remained a crucial area of debate among late-twentieth-century Japanese feminists. Today, the advent of modernization in Japan is seen not so much as an unqualified advance for women as a historical process in which gender itself was radically redefined, producing both new forms of freedom and new restrictions for women. Many feminists now argue that gender inequality in modern Japan has much in common with that of other societies in which industrial capitalism emerged on a preindustrial patriarchal base. The onset of industrialization in such societies was experienced differently in the countryside and in the cities and affected differently those in varying socioeconomic circumstances. Thus while preindustrial societies were undoubtedly organized around principles of patriarchal authority, depending on the context, forms of gender segregation may have been quite different from what they are in industrialized societies. Marriage, work, child-rearing practices, and codes of sexual conduct in Tokugawa Japan, for example, differed among the four major social classes. While the lives of women in samurai households were highly restricted and codified, women in the other three classes were more likely to work alongside men, with whom they often shared, to a greater or lesser degree, responsibility for both productive and child-rearing labor. As Japan's efforts to build mines and factories in order to compete in a global economy progressed and as life in the countryside was slowly transformed, young women from farming families were drawn in unprecedented numbers out of the small household units in which they had worked. Although this move took them beyond the confines of the family, they often were segregated more decisively from men because of their low-paying jobs. Within thirty years of the Restoration, however, the Meiji government's new Civil Code took as the national standard a modified version of the samurai household (ie), which had secluded women in the family. For middle- and upper-class women, the government's ideal of the "good wife, wise mother" (ryōsai kenbo) reflected a new emphasis on education for women, but it also defined their roles exclusively in terms of mothering and caring for the household, from which men were now absent. As Tokugawa literary and theatrical practices associated with cross-dressing and homoerotic relations also were eclipsed, less fluid notions of biologically based feminine and masculine social roles became the norm.

MAGAZINES FOR WOMEN'S EDUCATION

Under the Meiji Civil Code, only men were legally recognized persons. Patriarchal authority in the household was explicitly linked with the emperor. In a departure from the more diverse practices of the Tokugawa period, the oldest son inherited all the household property, in accordance with strict principles of primogeniture. Adultery was punishable and was grounds for divorce only when committed by the wife. Although women were, for the first time, given the right to sue for divorce in court, divorced women faced overwhelming public censure. In the Meiji period, because political (and cultural) institutions were controlled exclusively by men, the number of texts written by women was comparatively small. And an even smaller number of texts written by late-nineteenth-century women continued to be known and read in the twentieth century.

The groundwork for producing and publishing writings by women was established by the Meiji state's early emphasis on universal education and by the emergence of newspapers, journals, and other mass media printed with movable type. Initially, the vast majority of Meiji women lacked both reading and writing skills. But in the immediate aftermath of the Restoration, the abolition of hereditary class distinctions and an 1873 decree that required four years of schooling for all children (stating that "there is no difference between men and women as human beings") sparked efforts to transform education for women. As early as 1872, the mother of Fukuda Hideko (see chap. 37) became a teacher in a girl's middle school established by Okayama Prefecture; soon after, she started her own private school for girls. As the Freedom and People's Rights movement elicited the participation of women like Kishida Tokiko, Shimizu Toyoko (later known by her pen name, Shikin), Fukuda, and others, the movement for women's education gained strength, so much so that the "girl student," or *jo-gakusei*, became an emblematic figure in such pathbreaking early Meiji fiction as Futabatei Shimei's *Ukigumo* (*The Drifting Cloud*, 1886). Tsuda Umeko, sent at the age of seven by Education Minister Mori Arinori in 1871 to the United States to learn English and "Western manners," returned after ten years and became a pioneer in women's education. A decree in 1879, however, required that after the first four years of elementary school, girls were to be segregated from boys, attending only girls' middle schools. The first public normal school for women was opened in Tokyo in 1874, but national universities did not admit women until 1913. Families with means, therefore, sent their daughters to private secondary schools, most of which were run by Christian missionaries, for training in English and exposure to new ideas. It was in one such school, Tokyo's famous Meiji jogakkō (Meiji Women's Higher School), in 1885, that educator Iwamoto Yoshiharu started the first magazine devoted to political and cultural commentary surrounding the "woman question," including articles written by women. In this magazine, *Jogaku zasshi* (*Journal of Women's Issues*); its successor, *Bungakkai* (*Literary World*); and other new print media, a few talented young Meiji women published their fiction and social commentary. Much of their writing, however, was received dismissively by critics. Unable to make a living as writers and facing strenuous demands from their families, many of these writers either died or stopped writing when they were in their early twenties or early thirties.

SHIMIZU TOYOKO: "THE BROKEN RING" (KOWARE YUBIWA)

Shimizu Toyoko (pen name Shikin) was the daughter of a Kyoto bureaucrat who joined the Freedom and People's Rights movement, traveling and lecturing with Ueki Emori and Fukuda Hideko in the late 1880s. She became an editor of *Jogaku zasshi* and an instructor at Meiji Women's Higher School in 1891. "The Broken Ring," her semifictional account of events leading to her divorce from her first husband, was published in the journal in 1891. Shimizu published her final short story, dealing with the Meiji *burakumin* or former "outcasts," in 1899, and then lapsed into silence. Her writings were buried in obscurity until her son collected them in an anthology in celebration of the hundredth anniversary of her birth.

I know you are bothered by this ring of mine with the stone missing. Wearing a broken ring like this does not, as you say, look very good. You are probably thinking that I should put in a new stone, that anything would do. But this broken ring is a kind of remembrance for me, and so you see, there is no way I could possibly repair it. How quickly the days and months have passed since the day I broke it two years ago. During that time, you have asked me again and again, "Why are you wearing that ring? It doesn't really become you." Still, there are things that force me to keep on wearing it, and to you I feel I can try to explain what it means to me.

Every time I look at this ring, I feel a stab of pain and am reminded of how I suffered. But I cannot take it off, even for a single moment, because it has been a great benefactor to me. And if you were to ask why I am so deeply indebted to it, I would tell you that it is thanks to the suffering and grief it has caused me that I have somehow been able to discover in myself the strength and willpower to really mature. It has been both a kind of medium, inspiring me to make great efforts, and an unsurpassable source of encouragement. To others, it no doubt appears unsightly, but to me it is a jewel, a treasure that I would not be able to exchange for enormous amounts of money. It is, on the contrary, something that does suit me very well.

So let me tell you the details of my story. My life has been very much like this broken ring. Like it, I have been criticized by many people, but knowing from the start that I should expect this sort of thing, I wasn't really bothered. Yet sometimes when I look at it [the ring] and think, "Ah, dear ring, how pitiful we are," I cannot help but shed tears of regret. I don't know whether or not others do, but when I regain my composure, I take comfort in the notion that God is merciful and knows what is in my heart. I'm afraid that not until a hundred years have passed will there be a few who understand the precious value of this ring.

As I start to tell this story again, I suddenly feel as though my heart is about to burst. It was on that unforgettable day five years ago, in the spring of my eighteenth year, that I came to wear this ring. That was the day of my marriage. Although it was given to me by my husband, he hadn't really intended it to be what they now call an engagement ring. But looking back on it, I suppose one could call it that. At about that time, the seeds of women's education were at last beginning to be sown in our country, but I myself didn't have even halfway modern views. Also, even though it was a mere five years ago, things were quite different in the region where I was living than they were in Tokyo. The kind of relationship Western women have with their husbands was something I could not possibly have imagined. I knew only of traditional Japanese marital customs and had never heard about the new marriage laws that had been established by then. At the girls' school where I was first educated, we were taught only morals in the Chinese manner and read only books like *Ryūkyō retsujoden* (Liu Xiang's *Lives of Notable Women*). I was, of course, influenced by these things without being aware of it. We were taught that if a young girl's hand were promised to a boy whom she had not even met and that boy were to die young, the girl was bound by custom to cut off her nose or an ear to prove that she would never be of two hearts. We also learned that even if a young bride's mother-in-law tried to strangle her out of cruelty, that would not be reason enough for her to leave her husband's home. Enduring such things was considered to be an unsurpassable virtue in women. And according to custom in those days, a woman could never be sure of what sort of husband she might end up with. All she could do was decide to uphold her own principles and live purely and leave the choice of her husband up to fate. Like shaking the box of fortune sticks, there was no telling whether she would get a good one or a bad one.

My mother was a woman who took it as a matter of pride to model herself after the ideal of womanhood in "The Great Learning for Women" (Onna daigaku), and so when she spoke to my father, she would almost always respectfully kneel in the doorway to his room. Because she always treated him as though he were an honored guest, I was amazed when I saw other fathers and their children who seemed to get along so easily. I was greatly influenced by my mother's subservient and reserved behavior toward my father and, for no apparent reason, had come to think of the fate of woman as a pitifully unhappy one. But at the same time, I was already beginning to be aware of my own misgivings about this notion. Having realized women's regrettable fate, I even began to wonder whether there might not be some way for me to spend my life in peace, without marrying at all.

But just at about that time—it was probably when I was fifteen or sixteen— my parents began to urge me to marry. This happened more than once or twice, and oddly enough, even though I objected each time, they went on recommending various men, saying, "Now, how do you like this one," or "What about that one?" Each time I thought to myself, "Oh no, not again," and somehow managed to tell them, "No, I don't like him."

At first my mother would speak up on my behalf saying, "Because she's still young, perhaps we should think it over." But when I turned eighteen, my mother was no longer able to fend off the demands of a father who would anger quickly and sometimes even scold my mother, saying things like, "The girl is just being selfish! And it's all because you've brought her up badly."

One day, my father called me into his room; I knew immediately from the look on his face that he was too impatient to wait for me to sit down. Before I knew it, he had commanded me to accept a new marriage offer. How shocked I was at that moment! Recalling it now, I almost break into a cold sweat. Although I had guessed that this might happen and had planned responses to the arguments I predicted he would make, it had never occurred to me that he would confront me with such utter, uncompromising authority. Feeling so completely overwhelmed by this, I could do no more than look meekly at his stern face, which seemed to say, "If you dare to say no, say it now!" I waited for a moment, believing that my mother, who was sitting beside him, would say something to help me, but she was silent. Whether this was because she also feared my father's authority or because she had in fact discussed the matter with him beforehand, I could not tell. She only looked at me with a worried expression that seemed to say, "Tell him yes, and do it quickly!"

With one parent glaring at me sternly and the other looking at me plaintively, I was at a loss for words. Despite my intense embarrassment in front of my father, with whom I had never learned to feel at ease, I finally managed to bite my trembling lips and, with great effort, to say in no more than a whisper, "Please allow me a little more time to finish my studies." Before I was through, he flashed a sharp glance at me and said, "What unfinished studies! Don't be a fool. I've seen to it that you've been given a good education. What do you mean? What are you complaining about, you selfish girl?" My mother looked at me as if to say, "It's too bad you've made your father so angry." I wanted to explain myself further but, for a moment, could find no words. Finally, I somehow managed to say, "But please, I would like to go on to the Teachers' Training School in Tokyo."

Again, I was cut off by my father's sharp words. "What! Teachers' school! Absurd! Just how do you think you'd manage as a schoolteacher? It's no easy thing for a girl to go through life alone. I'll hear no more of this nonsense. You must do as I say. It's too late to change the arrangement now, anyway. I've told your mother all the details, so listen carefully." With that, he stood up quickly and stormed out of the room.

My mother then tried to console me, pleading in a soft, tearful voice. "Your father's character is such that whenever he speaks like that he isn't likely to change his mind, especially since this time he seems to like the young man in question. The go-between is Mr. Matsumura, who is surely acting on your behalf. You know it's not easy to find someone who is so accomplished and learned. And it's better for a young woman to marry at the right age because otherwise she will lose all her chances."

If this happened today, I would never agree to these things, but then, I was truly innocent of the world. Because I had resigned myself to the fact that I would have to marry someone, sometime, I weakheartedly acquiesced, even though I had only been half convinced by my mother's words. But when I look back on it now, I find myself thinking it odd that I didn't refuse more forcefully. My mother then began to tell me about the *miai* (prospective marriage meeting, literally "see-meet"). A message had arrived suggesting that it be held two days later. She said that I should start arranging my hair and should quickly select a suitable kimono with matching accessories. I could not think of how I should reply and so ended up agreeing. But later, when I went back to my room and thought it over, I realized that because my father had already made a more or less final decision about the matter, even if I were to protest at the formal *miai*, there would be no reason to expect them to listen, and I would only suffer great embarrassment. Having the young man see me would be truly unpleasant, and so with singular resolve I told my mother that I did not want to attend the *miai*. But again, it was no use.

Looking back, I wonder whether this was also a foolish failure of strategy on my part. But now I have come to realize that there was nothing I could do. As a child, I rarely had the chance to meet anyone other than relatives and school friends. When my father had visitors, I was rushed into the back room by my mother, who always told me to stay out of sight. Because of this, I was not a good judge of people. At the *miai*, I was unable to understand a thing, and so before the rash decision was finalized, even though I still thought marriage would be unpleasant, rather than feeling worried, I enjoyed a few minutes of pleasant anticipation wondering what sort of person he might be. Now I have resigned myself to thinking that at least this is a remembrance to look back on.

The ceremony was held in March of that year, just when the cherry blossoms were beginning to bloom. But after two or three months, I still couldn't get used to living with my husband and began to doubt more and more that I could stay in that house for the rest of my life. I really didn't know whether or not my husband cared for me. Sometimes he would take me to a museum or some other place and would offer to buy me things. But I never felt comfortable accepting gifts from him. Again, this was because of the uneasy feeling I had of not really being a member of his household. If we did go somewhere and do something, I didn't enjoy it in the least. On such outings I would be thinking constantly of my village at home and wishing that my mother and sister could be there too.

Then one day, a girl of fifteen or sixteen came to the house with a letter. Our house girl took it and started to bring it to me, but my husband thrust out his hand and glared at her as if to say, "Bring that over here!" I did not have the slightest notion of what the letter might contain and only remember thinking what a short-tempered person my husband was for getting angry over such a trifling thing. He read the letter and awkwardly rolled it up and put it in his sleeve. After telling the girl to convey the message that he would send a reply soon, he sent her away. That very night, he went out saying he was taking a short walk in the neighborhood. He wasn't back by ten or even twelve o'clock. Thinking I should naturally wait up for him, I did not ask to have the bedding laid out. As I sat writing letters to school friends, the night grew later and later, so I told the house girls to go to bed before me. One of them came and sat beside me, saying she thought I must be lonely. As she watched me writing letters, she carelessly commented, "How nice your brushwork is. . . . The former mistress didn't have such a . . . I had just caught the words "former mistress" and, without really intending to, asked, "Oh, was there someone here before me?" The girl had been working in that house for some time and felt obliged to answer my question. I watched her face closely as she half murmured to herself, "How could I have been so careless." Then she turned to me and said, "Although it will make the master angry, I must tell you. Until five or six days before you arrived, there was someone else here. Most certainly she is the daughter of the family where he boarded during his student days." . . .

After that evening, my husband's outings became more frequent, more in April than in March, more in May than in April, and finally he would go out and not return home at all for three or four days at a time. In the beginning, I stayed awake for two or three nights in a row waiting for him, but then, unable to keep my eyes open any longer, I finally dozed off. It was just my misfortune that he came home late that very night. I was suddenly awakened by the sound of knocking at the gateway, and when I rushed to open it, my husband, the smell of saké heavy on his breath, glared at me sharply and said, "What's this? I was pounding hard enough to break down the door, wasn't I? Why didn't you open it? If the neighbors heard me, that would have caused a stir, now wouldn't it! What a fine wife I have, who makes her husband stand outside while she sleeps like a log."

How I suffered at hearing his harsh words. I somehow managed to endure this but would have been deeply embarrassed if one of the house girls had been awakened by that loud, angry voice in the middle of the night and had mistakenly thought that I was arguing with my husband because he had returned so late. I knew that if I were to try and talk with him about it, he would only start grumbling even louder, so even though I knew he was being unreasonable, I handled him as gently as one would a piece of damp paper, placating him with apologies. I somehow managed to get him to bed without further mishap. . . .

Things like this accumulated until my mother, who had always been weak, suddenly took to her bed in a constant state of worry about me. Then in the autumn of my nineteenth year, she passed away like the morning dew. (And was I not the real cause of her death?) Although it may be useless for me to tell you what was deep in my heart, I then realized that the very marriage that my mother had thought would put her at ease and to which I had agreed unwillingly, thinking it would relieve her, had itself resulted in the premature end of her precious life. I felt as though my heart would break under the weight of this discovery. Knowing that my own lack of foresight and limited understanding had brought this about, I resigned myself to a state of unhappiness and, for two more years, spent every day deep in sorrow.

As you may imagine, I had come to feel deeply disturbed by these events. During the two or three years after my marriage, a strong sense of indignation on behalf of young women had begun to grow in me. Just at that time, new ideas about women's rights were being discussed and, along with them, the notion that sorrow and tragedy are not necessarily a woman's fate had gradually spread. As a matter of habit I always kept new publications near at hand to glance at between tasks around the house, and what I read about Western views of women's rights impressed me deeply. Thus, I began to see that Japanese women too had a right to seek the fulfillment and happiness that were their due.

Out of both a need to console myself and a desire to help relieve the unhappiness of women, I began to write occasionally on these difficult subjects, and in doing so, my own way of thinking also changed. Up until then I had believed in the Chinese code of morals, which teaches that it is virtuous for a woman to endure all kinds of suffering and to sacrifice her own happiness for the sake of her husband. In this sense, I had held a passive view of things. But from about this time on, I ceased to be satisfied with this view and came to hold more progressive ones. I decided to put aside the question of my own unhappiness and try to guide my husband to change his ways so that he might become a fine person of whom one need not feel ashamed. But even though I made the most sincere effort to influence him, because he was my senior by several years and was much more experienced in worldly affairs than I, he would not readily listen to what I said. . . .

But just as the torn cloth cannot easily be mended and the broken stone cannot easily be restored to its original form, here too it had become impossible to make amends. Knowing that it would be more harmful to him for me to remain there, for his sake, too—although I was loath to do so—I left him.

Since then, I have decided to work solely for the betterment of society. As a reminder of that vow, I myself removed the stone from the ring I am wearing. Although I cannot say I have learned from Kōsen's scowl, I gaze at the ring every morning and evening and recall the heavy responsibility it represents.[2] And although my humble gestures cannot compare with lying on burning coals or tasting bitter meats,[3] I most certainly have vowed to work to ensure a better future for the many beautiful young women of today in the hope that they will not follow the same mistaken path as I have.

With reforms of the marriage laws, there are many fine couples nowadays. When I observe their way of living, I can't help but wonder, as I gaze at my broken ring, why I failed to earn the love of my husband and was myself unable to love him.

It is by good fortune that my father still is in good health and now has come to have great sympathy for me in my long years of suffering. He often writes consoling letters expressing regret that the foolish interference of an old man resulted in the breaking of a fresh, young branch. Now he praises my aspirations and offers encouragement, which has given me the greatest pleasure in the midst of these days and months of sorrow. My only remaining hope is that this broken ring may somehow be restored to its perfect form by the hand that gave it to me. But of course I know such a thing is not yet to be. . . .

[Shimizu, *Shikin zenshū*, pp. 14–23; Jennison, "Narrative Strategies in Shikin's 'The Broken Ring,'" pp. 28–35]

---

2. Goujian was a prince of the state of Yue, enthroned in 486 B.C.E., who suffered defeat in an ill-considered attack on the state of Wu and thereafter drank a potion of gall every day to remind himself of the bitterness of defeat.

3. Lying on burning coals and tasting bitter meats refers to the phrase *gashin shōtan*, originally used to describe the king of Go as he was preparing himself physically and mentally before taking revenge on Kōsen for the death of his father. Colloquially, the phrase *gashin shōtan* means to endure severe hardship for the sake of future success.

WOMEN AND LABOR

By the early twentieth century, socialist groups had begun to appear in Japan, claiming a small number of women among their members. These women were the first to call attention to the problems of working women, who had played a significant role in the first three decades of Japan's intense industrialization. Women made up the majority of workers in the textile industry, the site of Japan's first industrialization. In 1880s, these female textile workers were the first workers to strike in modern Japan. By the 1920s, half of all Japanese factory workers were women. Because the land tax imposed by the government to provide capital for modernization was a particularly heavy burden for rural families, they often sent their daughters to work in the pleasure quarters in the cities (or overseas, where they became an important source of foreign currency). As was the case in Europe, the number of prostitutes increased markedly with the advance of industrialization and urbanization. Whether as factory workers or sex workers, young women were exposed to severe health hazards, received little pay, and were subjected to strict surveillance.

Those women in the various wings of the socialist movement at the turn of the twentieth century were often family members or lovers of male leaders, as was the case with Nobuoka Tameko (wife of early leader Sakai Toshihiko), Itō Noe (lover of Ōsugi Sakae), and Yamakawa Kikue (wife of Yamakawa Hitoshi, who founded the Japanese Communist Party in 1922). After the demise of the Freedom and People's Rights movement, Fukuda Hideko also joined the socialist movement. Because article 5 of the Meiji constitution banned them from attending political meetings, these women found themselves, and women's issues, marginalized in the socialist political agenda. In 1907, therefore, Fukuda founded the women's magazine *Sekai fujin* (*Women of the World*), advocating that the struggle against gender hierarchy be made an immediate priority for socialist politics. The journal and Fukuda's socialist women colleagues then launched a movement for the repeal of article 5, a movement that was the forerunner of the women's suffrage movement of the 1920s.

YAMAKAWA KIKUE: *RECORD OF THE GENERATIONS OF WOMEN* (*ONNA NIDAI NIKKI*)

Yamakawa Kikue was active in the prewar socialist and Communist movements and published important articles on women's issues. After the Pacific War, she became the first head of the Women and Minors Bureau in the Ministry of Labor. In her memoirs, she expresses her frustration with the failure of the Meiji women's education movement to address adequately the situation of poor and working women. She also describes her first encounters with textile workers and the early efforts to draft labor laws.

Mistress Tsuda could not abide the politics of the Gakushūin [school for children in the royal family and aristocrats], which focused on educating "little princesses." Moreover, she did not get along with the director of the school, Shimoda Utako, so she left the Gakushūin in 1900 and started her own academy at her home with a few students. Her goal was to establish an institution that would enable her to implement her own educational philosophy. Unlike other educators of this pe-riod, she ignored the Ministry of Education's policy that girls should become "good wives and wise mothers." She was a pioneer in educating women to be-come professionals. She rejected the slave morality and spineless submissiveness that characterized schools like Tokyo Women's College. She herself was independent-minded and forceful and was a natural-born teacher. . . .

Professor Yasui Tetsuko taught ethics and psychology briefly at our school. We read in Higuchi Ichiyō's diary that Professor Yasui had studied under her as a young student. So a couple of my friends and I visited her at her home to talk about Higuchi Ichiyō. The professor poured some tea for us and talked about her experiences. Among her comments were these: "Ichiyō was beautiful and strong and talented. But I feel that she wasted her talents writing mostly about lower-class people. She had dealings with upper-class people. If she wanted to, she could have written about more refined matters. It's a shame, since she was such a talented writer." We didn't know what to say and just looked at each other. Just prior to this, we had heard an older person who studied under Higuchi Ichiyō say that Ichiyō often spoke highly of Professor Yasui's character. We had been impressed by this.

Professors Tsuda, Yasui, and Kawai were all pure idealists. They were like angels and saints frolicking about in heaven. They were naive and innocent, totally cut off from the real world. They were completely unaware of what the students were thinking about and what they were searching for. After all, Professor Tsuda once told our class that Tolstoy was an apostate and a harborer of dangerous thoughts, so she did not want students in her school to read his writings. The institution was as strict as a convent. Even letters from family members were opened and inspected, and the school authorities intervened in a host of other personal affairs. . . . Since it was a language school, it was only natural that they concentrated primarily on language instruction, but I was not satisfied with this and felt frustrated. . . . So I looked into the requirements of Tokyo University. They stipulated that qualified students would be admitted. Nowhere did it say that admission was restricted to male students only. So I asked our teacher of psychology, Sugawa Kyōzō, to help me get permission to audit some courses at the university. The university authorities responded that the term *student* signifies male students. Females do not fall into this category. . . .

At the end of 1908 I went to the headquarters of the Salvation Army in Kanda to do volunteer work. I helped them distribute Christmas presents and Salvation Army pamphlets among the slum dwellers. I was not a Christian, but I admired the dedicated missionary work the Salvation Army performed and their efforts to help inmates of brothels gain their freedom. I had read and been enlightened by Mr. Yamamuro's writings on public brothels. So I went to them more or less as an outside observer.

Early on Christmas morning, I joined Mr. Yamamuro, Kawai Michiko, and others to visit a textile factory. . . . At that time the factory was running twenty-four hours a day. A few of the girls who had worked for twelve hours through the night began to show up in the lecture hall after breakfast. . . . They looked to be twelve to fifteen years of age, but they lacked the vitality of the young. They looked pale and tired as if they were sick. Eventually, fifty to sixty girls came to the lecture hall and sat on the straw mats that were placed on the cold wooden floor. The only heat in the room came from the charcoal brazier that had been provided for the speaker on the platform. The sky was gray, and it seemed as if it would start snowing at any moment. The cold penetrated deeply into our bones. Directed by the lecturer and accompanied by an organ, the girls sang a Christmas carol that was written out on the blackboard. Then Mr. Yamamuro got up to speak.

He told the girls that Our Lord, Jesus Christ, was a laborer just like them. Labor is sacred. "You too must become good workers, just like Our Lord Jesus. You must be grateful that you are able to work every day in good health. God will answer your prayers."

Mr. Yamamuro was followed by Kawai Michiko, and she also spoke of the sacred nature of work and in a highly emotional voice intoned a lengthy prayer. The meeting closed with a psalm. All during the ceremony I was seated on the platform but hated being there. I was filled with shame and anger. The girls had worked all night beside roaring machines. They were pale and bloodless. How could they be told that the life they led was due to God's blessings and that they should view this kind of slave labor as sacred and holy?

I had hoped that we would be permitted to see the work area, dormitory, and dining hall and be given a chance to question the girls about their work, but we were not allowed to do so. It seemed that the company authorities did not look favorably on this kind of Christian missionary work. None of the company officials came to the meeting. Only those girls who wanted to come were there. After the meeting Mr. Yamamuro and his group left. I felt that I could never join them in their activities again. . . .

In 1916 a labor act was finally passed, but only after it had been tampered with in a hundred different ways and had been emasculated. At that time Yamakawa Hitoshi criticized the law as a public endorsement of the fourteen-hour workday. Fujii got his dander up at this. "Socialists can't see that this law makes a big difference for the women factory workers. If they had any criticism, why didn't they speak up sooner? If they had spoken up and stirred up public support, our draft legislation would not have been cut to bits this way. The labor legislation was not such a tepid proposal when it was being drafted."

The *Shokkō jijō* would have been the best instrument to arouse public opinion in favor of labor legislation, but it did not see the light of day for about a half-century. Only in 1947, after imperial Japan had been destroyed, did it appear in print publicly. . . .

In 1912 the Bluestocking Society (Seitōsha) sponsored a lecture on women's rights.

Concerning the discussion on birth control and abortion, Miyajima Reiko wrote, "Harada [Kōgetsu] sponsored abortions, Itō Noe supported birth control but opposed abortions, Hiratsuka Raichō approved of both measures, while Yamada Waka opposed both." Yamada also opposed the marriage of young people who were not yet ready to have and rear children. Everyone, except Raichō, held poverty and difficulties in maintaining a living as grounds for abortion and birth control. Raichō argued that aside from poverty, intellectual and psychological grounds existed to justify these practices. She argued that "traditional-minded Japanese women who have no awareness of their individuality and have not had the opportunity to live their own lives [may oppose these practices.] Likewise for lower-class, working women who have no education and who have no leeway in thinking about anything but staying alive. But it puzzles me to find people like you not fighting for these causes."

Needless to say, under current social conditions, it is impossible for women to devote all their energies to becoming totally free, autonomous personalities. Does Raichō believe that those who are frustrated by this dilemma are only those women who are self-aware and cultured, engaged in mental and spiritual work, that they are distinct from lower-class, working women who are ignorant and have to devote their efforts to eating and staying alive? Does she believe that lower-class, working women deliberately give their lives over to the single task of finding enough food to stay alive? That they live like animals out of choice? Such questions about Raichō's contention were harbored by us too.

Ōsugi Sakae praised Baba Kochō's speech at the same meeting. In the audience was Baba's younger sister. She stopped by at Baba's house that evening, waited for him to come home, and castigated him for speaking "such fine words publicly" and behaving like a tyrant at home. Ikuta Chōkō [a literary critic, 1882–1936] also was a supporter of the Bluestocking Society (Seitōsha) and was sympathetic to socialism, but a decade later he made a 180-degree turn and wrote, "Compared with men, women are closer to savages and animals. If it is permissible to maintain a hierarchy of superior and inferior between adults and children, then it must also be permissible to maintain a hierarchy of superior-inferior between men and women."

Iwano Hōmei, who also spoke at the meeting, soon abandoned his wife, Kiyoko, and his child and moved on to his third wife.

At just about this time my older sister wrote me: "There are many men who appear to be allies of women and speak on women's issues and argue for equal rights and equal status for women. But you must not be taken in facilely. Many of them, when they leave their homes, become allies and friends of women, but take a look at their households to see how they behave at home. They turn into tyrannical princes and treat their wives and daughters as slaves. Their credo regarding women is 'Let them be dependent; keep them ignorant' [the feudal ruling class's policy toward the masses]. They are like tombstones painted in white."

Again, "Before we criticize others or blame society, we mothers must change our ways and stop rearing our sons differently from our daughters. If we carelessly continue to allow our precious daughters to be reared by an educational policy and system that are designed to produce future mothers who believe in treating boys and girls differently, it would be akin to exposing ourselves to a deadly sword."

[Yamakawa, *Record of the Generations of Women*, in *Reflections on the Way to the Gallows*, trans. and ed. Hane, pp. 165–69]

HIRATSUKA RAICHŌ AND THE BLUESTOCKING SOCIETY

Although Hiratsuka Raichō and her colleagues have often been called Japan's "first feminists," she was in fact close in age, but not in socioeconomic background, to the women socialists of Yamakawa Kikue's generation. Entering the upper-class Japan Women's University in 1903, Hiratsuka chafed at the emphasis on domestic sciences and, after graduating, chose to undertake training in Zen Buddhism, study Nietzsche, and seek out the company of female literary scholars and writers. With their encouragement, she founded *Bluestocking* (*Seitō*), a literary journal exclusively for women. Boldly committed to women's right to self-expression, including sexual expression, *Bluestocking* was initially devoted largely to creative writing and commentary on new cultural trends. The journal's founding, moreover, took place in tandem with an expansion of commercial publishing, which eventually resulted in the establishment of commercial magazines for women and the emergence of larger numbers of publicly recognized women writers. Hiratsuka and her group of "New Women," as they came to be known, became the objects of sensational press coverage, and at one point a rock-throwing crowd converged on Hiratsuka's home. In response to this public reaction, the journal increasingly explored explicitly feminist issues and published translations of writings by European and American feminists. In the early 1920s, feminism was the locus of intense and influential discussions among women writers. The major topics were motherhood and the desirability of state support and protection for mothers and children (the *bosei hogo* debate). Hiratsuka, Yamakawa, and the poet Yosano Akiko argued this issue from three different viewpoints, and it was later examined from the perspective of "maternalism" by Takamure Itsue, a feminist anarchist and great scholar of women's history. The questions of chastity, birth control, abortion, and prostitution were heatedly debated by Yamakawa, Itō Noe, and Yasuda Satsuki.

In 1920, Hiratsuka, no longer the editor of *Bluestocking*, banded together with the socialist Ichikawa Fusae and women of different political persuasions to form the broadly based New Women's Society, which launched the long but ultimately unsuccessful struggle for women's suffrage. Although a bill for limited female suffrage was passed by the Lower House in 1930, it failed to win the approval of the Upper House. The last Woman's Suffrage Conference was held in 1937. The movement had reached an impasse, and its members were gradually co-opted into joining women's associations supporting Japanese imperialism and the war in Asia.

"IN THE BEGINNING WOMAN WAS THE SUN"
(GENSHI, JOSEI WA TAIYŌ DE ATTA)

In September 1911, Hiratsuka Raichō wrote the now famous lines carried in the first issue of the *Bluestocking* (*Seitō*) magazine.

> In the beginning, woman was the sun,
> An authentic person.
> Today she is the moon,
> Living through others.
> Reflecting the brilliance of others. . .

And now, *Bluestocking*, a journal created for the first time with the brains and hands of today's Japanese women, raises its voice.

[Sievers, *Flowers in Salt*, p. 163]

"NEW WOMAN"
(ATARASHII ONNA)

In 1913 Hiratsuka was asked to define the "New Woman" in a special issue of *Chūō kōron*. Although her earlier writings had advocated women's autonomy and creative self-expression, her definition of the "New Woman" includes a critique of male privilege.

The new woman; I am a new woman.
I seek, I strive each day to be that truly new woman I want to be.
In truth, that eternally new being is the sun.
I am the sun.
I seek; I strive each day to be the sun I want to be.

. . .

The new woman curses yesterday.

The new woman is not satisfied with the life of the kind of woman who is made ignorant, made a slave, made a piece of meat by male selfishness.

The new woman seeks to destroy the old morality and laws created for male advantage. . . .

The new woman does not merely destroy the old morality and laws constructed out of male selfishness, but day by day attempts to create a new kingdom, where a new religion, a new morality, and new laws are carried out, based on the spiritual values and surpassing brilliance of the sun.

Truly, the creation of this new kingdom is the mission of women. . . .

The new woman is not simply covetous of power for its own sake. She seeks power to complete her mission, to be able to endure the exertion and agony of learning about and cultivating issues now unknown to her. . . .

The new woman today seeks neither beauty nor virtue. She is simply crying out for strength, the strength to fulfill her own hallowed mission.

[Sievers, *Flowers in Salt*, p. 176]

POSTWAR JAPANESE FEMINISM

The process by which most prominent Japanese women leaders, including Yoshi-oka Yayoi, the founder of the first medical school for women, and Takamure Itsue, a scholar and historian, were drawn in the 1930s into supporting Japanese imperialism is a chapter of Japanese feminist history that is just beginning to be studied. A few women resisted such pressures: Yamakawa Kikue sequestered herself in the countryside, whereas the feminist Communist Miyamoto Yuriko was subjected to police surveillance and repeated jailings during the war years. Under the American-authored postwar constitution, women experienced dramatic gains in status, attaining goals for which they had fought for half a century or more. Women gained the vote, and several women were elected to the Diet in 1946. (Their numbers, however, have never risen beyond 2 to 3 percent of the Diet's membership in the postwar period.) Women were allowed to own and inherit property. The postwar Occupation, moreover, transformed the legal status of women in other ways, which were seen as excessively liberal by those who tried to overturn them in the ensuing decades. A few legal grounds for access to abortion, which had been defined as a crime since 1907, were established, although access to birth-control medication remained illegal, reinforcing the state's long-standing emphasis on women's reproductive roles. The new constitution's pioneering article 14 forbade discrimination based on sex (and the Meiji Civil Code was revised accordingly to permit marriage based on mutual consent). Lacking sanctions for noncompliance, however, article 14 was largely unenforced until demands from Japanese and international feminist groups in the 1980s pressured the government into signing and eventually acting on the United Nations Treaty of Women's Rights.

As the instability of the early postwar years receded, a gendered division of labor not entirely dissimilar from the one that had supported earlier modernization efforts was reestablished. The content of public education continued to differentiate between boy and girl students. While access to higher education for men and especially for women dramatically increased in the postwar years, even in 1988 the majority of women students were still concentrated in two-year junior colleges emphasizing preparation for their role as homemakers and mothers. The faculty of Japanese four-year universities was almost overwhelmingly male. As mothers and as low-paid, part-time workers before and after their child-rearing years, women supported first the postwar recovery and then the high-speed economic growth.

Despite their lack of representation in formal national politics, women and women's organizations played leading roles in grassroots political movements throughout the early postwar years and were especially influential in the peace movement, the consumers' movement, and the antipollution movement. Four major women's organizations were active during this period: the National Coordinating Council of Regional Women's Associations, the Housewives' Council of the Japan Coal Miners' Union, and two women's organizations linked with the Socialist and Communist Parties. In their many and varied struggles—for improved health care, education, and protection from layoffs for women working part time, to name just a few—they advocated political reform based on women's domestic labor and responsibilities, as well as on a generalized concept of "rights." In their discussion of women's reproductive roles and responsibilities for mothering and child rearing, these groups echoed the concerns for "protection of motherhood" articulated by some Japanese feminists of the 1920s.

Out of the movements protesting both the renewal of the U.S.–Japan Security Treaty and the Vietnam War, however, emerged what is often called the postwar's "second-wave feminism," which insists on the right of women to choose not to become mothers and wives. In the mid-1960s, Saitō Chiyo organized the Bank of Creativity to help those mothers who had left the workforce to raise their children to retrain themselves for new jobs. In 1972 she founded the journal *Agora* as a forum for feminist debate. Also in 1972 Tanaka Mitsu founded the Fighting Women's Group (Tatakau onna). In her well-known book *To Living Women* (*Inochi no onnatachi e*), Tanaka asked, "What is it to live as a woman, and what in the world is a woman?" She urged women to radically explore self-definitions outside existing forms of marriage, including same-sex relationships, while maintaining their concern for the emotional needs of mothers and children. From its origins in flourishing networks of mimeographed pamphlets (*mini komi*) in the early 1970s, feminist writing in the late twentieth century achieved broad visibility in journalistic and academic publishing.

Feminist historians have retrieved or reconstructed heretofore hidden stories of women's daily lives in modern Japan and redefined modern social relationships and the political and ethical responsibilities they entail. This revisionist historical work has extended to a newly critical consideration of modern nationalism and imperialism (especially as they affected Japanese relations with Asia), as well as an intense discussion of war responsibility. Feminist activists continue to confront the legal complexities surrounding reproduction, reproductive technologies, and the conditions of women's work, including sex work. As these processes move forward, Japanese feminism has continued to redefine itself as its goals and areas of activism have become more diverse.

AOKI YAYOI AND ECOFEMINISM

Aoki Yayoi is a well-known feminist and critic who has published articles on the relationship of gender politics to technological and environmental issues and on the rights of indigenous peoples. Her essay "Feminism and Imperialism" (Feminizumu to teikokushugi), from the book *Feminism and Ecology* (*Feminizumu to ekorojii*), reexamines modern ethics in light of the historical impact on women's daily lives of the *ie* system and its relation to the imperial institution.

IMPERIALIST SENTIMENTS AND THE PRIVILEGE OF AGGRESSION

Within the Japanese system of "nation-as-family," the imperial household holds the position of the main house, and the people become the branch families. An adoptive relationship is formed between nation and family, and within this framework "loyalty" and "filial piety" are inextricably bound to each other at a structural level. Consequently, it became even more difficult to distinguish between the controller and the controlled in the modern period than during the feudal period. In the modern period, in matters related to government (the emperor and the nation), the concepts of loyalty and "voluntary" self-sacrifice were internalized by the people as the ultimate virtues. This process provided a uniquely favorable environment for the internal systems of a late-developing country, keen to achieve the goals of national unity and industrialization. The union of nation and self-sacrifice around the common goal of "Japan as number one" has formed the foundation of a Japanese work ethic that proposes low wages and overwork as the raisons d'être of the individual worker. At the same time, this approach has fostered the continued existence of selfless patriotism as a key component of the Japanese national character. It was a primary force behind the social predisposition toward giving priority to the "public good" while placing social welfare on the shelf, a predisposition still apparent in Japan today.

Fundamentally, what the household head and the emperor had in common was the fact that neither of them had the rights of a dictator in the modern sense of the word. The authority they could claim was only whatever came to them as the representatives of their ancestors. It was not an autonomous authority, which they could claim in their own right. And their responsibilities and duties were held not in relation to the individual members of their particular family group but in relation to the ancestors they shared with that group. Within a group organized on this basis, even if an individual member is sacrificed for the sake of "family name," "company," or "country," the leader does not need to suffer from any sense of conscience or responsibility. Not only are vertical relations of political influence and power structure clearly in place but it is also difficult for any oppositional relationship to develop between victim and aggressor.

The social action taken by the Japanese people in August 1945 is best understood in the context of this psychological makeup. Hungry, burned out of their homes, and bereaved of loved ones—all for a war fought in the name of the emperor—there was almost no one who blamed the emperor himself. Some suffered the defeat as the direct result of the incompetence of the people and took their own lives to atone for what they considered a disloyalty that had endangered the continuity of the imperial line. The majority of the people, rather than identify themselves as victims and pursue those responsible for the war, chose to try to close the door on the whole situation, referring to it simply as "a crime of the people." While those who fought in the war considered it a "senseless" war, they did not consider the young war-dead "senseless victims." The people fashioned the dead into tragic "war heroes," enshrined them, erased their victim status, and exempted themselves from all responsibility.

The same general structures are found between men and women. If anything, the structural mechanisms are even more complex in the case of gender. For example, in the premodern warrior class, a woman's virginity was considered more important than life itself. The wives and daughters of the samurai class were educated to choose death rather than risk rape. If we consider that men of the same period who kept mistresses and frequented the brothels of the pleasure quarters were regarded as men of the world, we can discern a gross inequity. In the modern period there are practices related to the status of the female that are even more difficult to comprehend. It has to be seen as a modern irony that the burgeoning trade in young female bodies from the Meiji period onward was a consequence of the poverty caused by the downfall of the old samurai families and the impoverishment of the farmers. There were many young women who lost their freedom through a system of prepaid labor that sold them into the spinning mills—the location of so many "sad histories of working women"—but still worse off were the girls sold into brothels. Why was the traffic in female bodies possible in an environment where the prevalent sexual morality continued to claim that it valued virginity over life? A filial ethic has come into play here—"for the sake of the family"; "to save the household from ruin." Though the daughters could probably predict the ultimate fate of their bodies once they were sold, if they refused to go, they would be branded as unfilial; and, as the Imperial Rescript on Education stated, filial piety and loyalty were inseparable components of the national ethic. For young girls, whose position was already weak, there was no hope of defeating this ethic. They threw themselves into the world of prostitution, taking their only solace in the fact that they would be the future heroines of tales of filial piety. In exercising their "parental rights," the parents themselves ended up in exactly the same position of victim as their daughters. They were no more able to question their role of aggressor than the daughters could question their role as victim. There are even records of praise for this unification of parent and child in the act of self-sacrifice: "What is needed today is beauty of the human heart. It was evident in the many brothels in the days of the Yoshiwara. In this time of emergency we must sustain our national ethic, built as it is upon the memory of the beauty of such human devotion."

These words were spoken by Funada Chū [Funada Naka], a Diet member, in an address to the Special Congress of the National Federation of Brothels in the year Shōwa 10 (1935), when Japan was mobilizing for war.

From a modern perspective, it is nothing short of grotesque that a Diet member should have praised the prosperity of brothels as an aspect of the national ethic and then gone on to aestheticize the sale of young girls' bodies as representing "beauty of the human heart" as Funada did. But this structure, where the compassion of the powerful is prerequisite to the self-sacrifice of the powerless, is a special characteristic of a Japanese style of discrimination nurtured within the emotional climate of imperialism. This structure is still in place today. Incidentally, the same Diet member, Funada, continued to be active in the political arena after the end of the war and, if my memory serves me correctly, served as speaker of the Lower House.

[Buckley, ed., *Broken Silence*, pp. 23–26]

MATSUI YAYORI AND ASIAN MIGRANT WOMEN IN JAPAN

At the time of her death in 2002, Matsui Yayori was a senior staff editor with the *Asahi shinbun*, one of the few women to hold a senior editorial position. The author of numerous books and articles on women's issues, Matsui also helped create activist networks in the Asian region. In 1977 she founded the Asian Women's Association, devoted to maintaining stronger links between Japanese women and women in the rest of Asia. The following is an excerpt from her address to the Conference on International Trafficking in Women, held in New York in 1988. In her talk, Matsui briefly connects the postwar exploitation of Asian sex workers to the forcible recruitment of "comfort women" from Japanese-controlled territories by the Japanese Imperial Army during the Pacific War. The emergence and the testimony of former "comfort women" who demanded reparation from the Japanese government in the early 1990s had a profound impact on Japanese feminism in that decade. Matsui was the organizer of the Women's International War Crimes Tribunal held in Tokyo in December 2000, at which many former "comfort women" gave testimony.

THE VICTIMIZATION OF ASIAN MIGRANT WOMEN IN JAPAN

I am here to make heard the painful cries of victimized Asian women.

I come from Japan, the country that grew rapidly into an economic giant only four decades after the devastation of World War II. On the surface, such rapid economic growth really does look like a miracle. It is little known, however, that this "miracle" was achieved at the expense of countless women both inside and outside Japan. One of Japan's most serious social problems is an expanding sex industry—this is the other, less publicized side of economic prosperity.

In the 1970s, Japan was known as the country that sent men on sex tours to neighboring Asian countries; today it has become the country that receives the largest number of Asian migrant women working as entertainers in the booming sex industry. Some estimate that nearly 100,000 such women come to Japan every year, including both legal female workers with entertainer visas and those who work illegally on tourist visas.

More than 90 percent of these female migrant workers come from only three countries: the Philippines, Thailand, and Taiwan. The number of Filipinas now accounts for 80 percent of that total, although the number of Thai women coming to Japan is also increasing at an alarming rate. Their jobs are concentrated in the sex industry, with most of them working as prostitutes, hostesses, striptease dancers, and other sex-service-related entertainers. . . .

The growing number of migrant women who find their way to shelters all over the country also indicates the scope of human rights violations, inhuman humiliating treatment, and sexual abuse. Over the last three years, 1,200 women have sought refuge and assistance after being subjected to physical violence, psychological threats, nonpayment of wages, or forced prostitution. While migrant women suffer from this gross exploitation, traders—including recruiters, promoters, club owners, and pimps—make enormous profits at their expense; the returns from forced prostitution are particularly high.

Exactly why is it, then, that such huge numbers of Asian women are flooding into Japan? Essentially, this phenomenon results from the unjust economic imbalance between the north and the south. In other words, it is a symptom of deep-rooted economic problems on a global scale. . . .

But why does the sex industry flourish in Japan, creating such a high demand for female workers? The answer to this question is an inseparable part of Japan's economic system and reflects the situation of women and men in Japan. Japanese men are forced to work very hard and are virtually enslaved by the companies that employ them. Under the "Japanese-style management system," which is supported by the three pillars of life-long employment, seniority, and cooperative management–labor relations, employees are treated as members of the company family. In return, they are expected to be loyal and to devote their life to the company.

Employees average more than 2,000 working hours per year, compared to 1,600–1,700 hours in Western European countries; they take only nine days of paid holidays. They will even work on Sundays. Seeking relief from these extremely tense work patterns, Japanese business "warriors" frequent entertainment facilities with their colleagues or business customers. The companies themselves often provide their employees and customers opportunities to drink and enjoy entertainment with women. Sometimes the companies organize sex tours abroad for their employees as a reward for hard work or successful business deals.

In the context of such business practices, the role of Japanese women is either, as hostesses, to extend sexual services to men or, as wives and mothers, to take care of their husbands and teach children to be future business warriors. Temporary work is another option, yet this is low-paid and unstable.

It cannot be overemphasized that the sharp increase in Asian female migrant workers coming to Japan is fundamentally linked to the very economic system that has brought about Japan's unprecedented rapid economic development. Based on the dehumanization of both Japanese men and women and on imported cheap labor, that development supports a growing sex industry in Japan, estimated at ¥10 trillion. . . .

Trafficking in women is part of a consumer culture created by transnational corporations, which strongly influences third-world countries. Everything is utilized as a commodity to be sold. Even women are commodified and traded to satisfy men's desires, which are stimulated by all forms of mass media. In this context, Asian women are favorite goods because of the "Oriental charm" and exoticism that Western and Japanese men see in them. Thus, countless women in the third world are victimized by racism, colonialism, commercialism, and sexism.

The tidal wave of such sexual exploitation should be stemmed by all available means. What kind of actions should we take? Here I would like to present a brief history of our campaign against sex tours since the mid-1970s. Japanese women were shocked when Korean women protested against Japanese male sex tours in 1973. First, Korean Christian women's groups published a very strong statement condemning the wealthy Japanese men who were dehumanizing their country's women. Then a handful of Korean women students went to Kimpo airport carrying placards stating: "We are against prostitution tourism!" "Don't make our motherland a brothel for Japanese men!" Some of these women were arrested because the dictatorship didn't like such protests.

Responding to the courageous action of these Korean women, we Japanese feminists organized demonstrations at Haneda Airport, distributing leaflets to tourists bound for Seoul. We used strong language, such as "Shame on you!" "Stop your shameful behavior!" and "We will never allow you to repeat your sexual aggression!" During the war, the Japanese Imperial Army forced young Korean women to serve as prostitutes. Hundreds of thousands of them were sent to the battlefields of China and Southeast Asia, and they were abandoned in the jungle when Japanese troops had to withdraw in defeat.

It was during this demonstration against "*Kisaeng* tourism" that I coined a new word for prostitution. In Japanese, prostitution is called *baishun*, written with two Chinese characters meaning "sell spring." I changed the characters so that it meant "buy spring." I wanted to change attitudes toward and concepts of prostitution. Traditionally, women who sold their bodies were blamed, while men who bought their sex were not condemned. Therefore, the word had to be changed. It may seem a rather small thing, but it is revolutionary to shift the responsibility from women to men. Those who buy sex are to be condemned more than those who sell.

We should not look at prostitution from a perspective of moral judgement but rather analyze the problem within the context of the global economic structure.

[Buckley, ed., *Broken Silence*, pp. 143–53]

UENO CHIZUKO AND THE CULTURAL CONTEXT OF JAPANESE FEMINISM

In the mid-1990s, sociologist Ueno Chizuko was appointed professor at Tokyo University. In the following short essay, she considers Japanese feminism in a broad historical perspective. Ueno answers the frequently heard argument that feminism is a "foreign" or an "imported" movement in Japan, suggesting that in the context of an overwhelmingly culturally hybrid modernity, such accusations are merely ways of dismissing political activism by women. She also calls attention to the dangers of the contention that once the modern is rejected as foreign, Japanese women may be linked to the essence of the native and the premodern. Reflecting on the work of Takamure Itsue, she warns that such reasoning may lead to nationalistic feminism.

ARE THE JAPANESE FEMININE? SOME PROBLEMS OF JAPANESE FEMINISM IN ITS CULTURAL CONTEXT

A remarkable intellectual event in Japanese feminist theory has taken place. It is the publication of a book about Takamure Itsue, a critical biography of one

of the greatest Japanese feminist philosophers and historians of the prewar period. The book, written by a young feminist scholar, Yamashita Etsuko, is an
attempt to reevaluate Takamure's achievements in the light of developments in
recent French postmodernist philosophy.

This attempt is itself rooted in two wider intellectual contexts: first, the rediscovery and reevaluation of premodern thought as postmodernist; second, the
reconstruction of a critical history of feminist thought that also problematizes
the active participation of Japanese feminists in World War II. The former
reflects the current revisionist tendency to reevaluate what was once considered
to be backward. The latter demonstrates a feminist "reflectiveness" in relation
to women's history. The latent messages are, in the first case, that the Japanese
are not always wrong and, in the second case, that women are not always victims. As a cultural product, contemporary Japanese feminism is located within
the same cultural context. Feminism is under considerable pressure to respond
to these two trends. The purpose of this paper is to see Japanese feminism as a
constructed cultural ideology and place it within a wider political context. To
this end I will use a "sociology of knowledge" approach. In a sense, this is an
attempt at a meta-anthropology of gender.

In the concept of Orientalism proposed by Edward Said, the East is to the
West as woman is to man. Taking an Orientalist approach to national identity,
Japanese intellectuals have described Japan as an oppressed woman. Some have
gone even farther, to equate Japan with a poor woman raped by the West,
particularly when describing the period after World War II. After the Western
concept of Orientalism was imposed on the East, the intellectuals of this region
took up the same framework as a basis for their own expression of self-identity.
The use of gender metaphors to refer to the East and the West has become
common. However, on reflection, this is somewhat tautological, given that gender difference is shaped by a romantic worldview that sees men and women as
existing only within such binary relations as positive/negative, active/passive,
rational/irrational, dominant/subordinate, and ultimately, superior/inferior.
However, the "East-as-woman" is inhabited by both men and women. By implication, within this framework Oriental men can, to some extent, be assigned
such feminine "traits" as passivity and irrational thinking. Some research has
shown that if an individualist orientation is used as the criterion of gender
difference, then Japanese men are more feminine than French women. However, this finding does not mean that a Japanese man adopts a woman's role
more than a French woman does. He is, after all, a man. There will always be
gender politics regardless of the ethnic context.

With the rise of new nationalism since the 1970s, in the wake of the so-called
Japanese economic miracle, there has been a tendency for Japanese indigenous
thought of the prewar years to be reevaluated as postmodernist, as ideas that
had the potential to overcome the constraints of Western-influenced models of

modernization. The reevaluation itself has only taken place in the light of the most recent wave of European philosophy. Japanese intellectuals repeatedly take advantage of the cycles of self-criticism within European thought. This could be described as the product of reverse Orientalism—a process of devaluation followed by a process of reevaluation, in which an Orientalist perspective is taken up to define a positive national identity. This approach both fits the existing dominant paradigm for the East and is appealing for its ability to express a fundamental weakness of Orientalism, namely, Western ambiguity toward the non-Western world.

It is in this context that the reevaluation of an indigenous feminist thinker, Takamure, can be understood as an example of reverse Orientalism. Takamure shaped her thought in the face of the modern world, more specifically in reaction to the disintegration of the traditional community structures that had been based on such oppositions as rural/urban, nature/culture, and human/technological.

Takamure's own countermodernism is obviously a modern product, something that would not have existed without modernism. It is a reactionary response to modernism. Takamure stood for the past, for tradition, for things that were rapidly disappearing. She was particularly worried about what she considered the loss of traditional gender roles or identity. The recovery of national identity and gender identity were the same thing for her. She attempted to achieve both goals by tracing women's history all the way back to ancient times. With no professional training as a historian, she strove to prove the existence of matrilineality in ancient Japan by tracing the genealogical documents of the ancient clans. Though she mistook matrilineality for matriarchy, she did offer a challenge to a dominant historical view that had never admitted to the possibility of women's power.

In her search for women's power, Takamure also turned to the Japanese creation myths. According to those cosmological myths, Japan's first great ancestral goddess was Amaterasu, from whom all creations derived. Takamure proposed the idea of "maternal self" as a Japanese cultural ideal, identifying herself and all Japanese women with the first, great goddess. For her, this solution went beyond the Western individualism to which she attributed the destruction of Japan's traditional community structures. Within her concept of a "maternal self," woman is at the center of everything. There is no conflict between community and individual in this ideal culture, and it is only women who can lead.

Her argument was an exercise in countermodernism and problematized the questions related to the debate surrounding the overcoming of modernity. The countermodernists generally sought a process of modernization that was not bound to Westernization or Western models. Among these countermodernists, Nishida Kitarō was an outstanding philosopher who wrote extensively on these issues. He questioned the Western modernism that appealed so much to young Japanese intellectuals of the prewar period. The same young men later had to fight the United States in World War II. When the time came, Nishida encouraged them to participate in the war. The anti-Westernization of countermodernism lent itself to nationalist goals.

Takamure offered a feminist counterpart of countermodernism. Her countermodernism also led her to participate actively in the war. In the late 1930s, she wrote: "The maternal self sees humankind as one family. As our sacred war is a challenge to what interferes with this familyhood, the war is ours, for women." She also described what she saw as the close relationship of women and fascism: "Fascism, which encourages women to have more children, values womanhood and therefore is liberating for women."

Takamure was committed to forming a maternalistic feminism, as opposed to an individualist feminism. From her point of view, individualist feminists, with their focus on such issues as the woman's vote, were effectively destroying feminine virtues and cultural tradition in their attempts to overcome male standards. This was not the first debate between individualist and maternalist feminists in Japan. The most famous precedent occurred as early as the 1910s.

The two main figures in that debate were Hiratsuka Raichō and Yosano Akiko. Raichō was the founder of the first feminist journal in Japan and a strong maternalist. She argued for the specificity of womanhood and demanded maternal welfare from the state and the community. From the beginning, Japan's indigenous feminism defined itself as distinct from Western individualism. Takamure considered herself a legitimate heir to this first maternalist feminist and received her enthusiastic approval. Takamure's emphasis on motherhood and femininity functioned as an attempt to overcome Western individualism. She was by no means a right-wing woman or a conservative but a strong feminist from the start. However, once locked into a framework of reverse Orientalism (the rejection of the Western model in the search for a Japan-specific one), she became increasingly implicated in fascism.

Not only Takamure, but also leading feminists in the struggle for the women's vote, participated actively in the war effort. In order to earn their share of political rights, women felt obliged to demonstrate a positive contribution to the state in the time of national crisis. A problem shared by most Asian feminists is that of locating a female identity and a feminist movement in relation to questions of national and cultural identity. Since feminism is frequently criticized at the local level as a Western import, feminists are under continuous pressure to distinguish themselves from Western feminists and must always define themselves negatively or oppositionally in order to establish a distinctly indigenous feminist identity.

This is confusing in a country such as Japan, where the national identity is already, at least to some extent, constructed as a somewhat feminine identity.

If the Japanese as a cultural group are considered to have "feminine" traits and to have internalized the understanding of their own culture as "feminine" (in contrast to other cultures, such as that of North America, which might be characterized as "masculine" within this framework), then feminists are faced with a dilemma: on the one hand, if feminists ask for equal rights, they are accused of being anti-Japanese; on the other hand, if they stress feminine virtues, men think it over and say, "Look, in contrast to Western men, we are already feminine enough. Why do we have to become more feminine?"

This dilemma was reproduced in the 1980s, a half-century after the first feminine/feminist controversy. The feminist debate in the 1980s was between "maximalist" and "minimalist" feminists. Maximalist feminism was a new wave of feminism that followed radical feminism. It was also referred to as "ecological feminism" and drew support from a countercultural movement for alternative technologies. Its critique of Japanese industrial society paralleled the logic of the earlier countermodernist movement. It began to resemble a new nationalism when it proclaimed the virtues of such concepts as nature, motherhood, and "vernacular" values (after Ivan Illich).

An oppositional or reactive cycle of Orientalism and reverse Orientalism has been reproduced again and again throughout Japanese history. During the Edo [Tokugawa] period Motoori Norinaga, a philosopher, proposed a counter-Orientalism of the Japanese mind, in opposition to Chinese universalism (*karagokoro*, or Chinese mind). The Chinese model of the Orient and its relation to the rest of the world was the dominant model of identity in the East. Japan was as much the "other" to China as it was later to the West. Before contact with the West, everything—writing, law, technology, philosophy, and art—derived from China. Norinaga was a student of the classical literature of the Heian period. He was particularly known for his study of *The Tale of Genji*, a work written by a woman of the court and renowned as the world's oldest novel. In the Heian period Japanese official documents were always written in Chinese, but women were not allowed to use the Chinese language. It was during the same period that the Japanese writing system, *kana*, was developed. This invention took place among the court women. Gradually a system emerged within which women and men had clearly distinguishable written and spoken languages. Paradoxically, women could express themselves more easily than men in the vernacular of women's speech and the indigenous *kana* syllabary. The Heian period is considered to have seen the birth of Japanese culture, as opposed to Chinese universalism.

Norinaga developed his own theories of *The Tale of Genji* and of a Japanese aesthetic, theories which were based on the premise that the Japanese mind could be characterized as feminine while, by contrast, Chinese universalism could be characterized as masculine. Ironically, the creation of a "Japanese" culture led to the ghettoization of Japanese traits. The particularism of this conscious production of cultural identity is still evident in many contemporary theories of Japanese culture and society. In its attempts to define the feminine positively, maximalist feminism shares much with Japanese cultural particularism. We could point out the following similarities: first, this particularism falls within the same frame of binary oppositions as that imposed by Orientalism—nature/technology, soft/hard, positive/negative, masculine/feminine. It is actually a reversed expression of universalism, Western or Chinese, in that it strives to redefine or reallocate the positive and negative qualities of the existing, traditional oppositions. Second, this particularism is achieved only by ghettoizing the same qualities it claims to valorize. The dominant paradigm is ultimately left intact.

The nature of the relation of feminism to nationalism starts to become ambiguous when feminism and cultural particularism approach one another. In more recent times, a right-wing woman, Hasegawa Michiko, has criticized feminism as being responsible for the destruction of cultural traditions. As a philosopher and, not coincidentally, a student of the works of Norinaga, she has referred to feminism as *karagokoro*, or "Chinese mind." Hasegawa is the Japanese equivalent of Jean Bethke Elshtain, the American political scientist who, rather confusingly, claims to be a feminist. Fortunately, our "Japanese Elshtain" distinguishes herself clearly from feminism, so we can comfortably and fairly position her as antagonistic.

Hasegawa made a speech at the sixtieth anniversary of the Shōwa emperor's reign, in which she referred to the emperor as the "mother of the nation." Strangely enough, her statement did not cause any anger on the right. Though the Japanese imperial system is patrilineal, the emperor is no longer a powerful patriarch but an embracing mother; conservatives also agree with this view of the Japanese empire. There has been a transmogrification of the image of the emperor from a fatherlike to a motherlike figure. The current imperial system has gone through changes parallel to the transformation of capitalism—from hard to soft, visible to invisible, industrial to information- and service-oriented, centered to decentered. Accordingly, the entire discourse surrounding imperialism has changed. The new discourse of a soft, invisible empire was first posited by the French philosopher Roland Barthes in 1970 in his book *L'Empire des signes*, or *Empire of Signs*. In this book, he describes the emperor as an empty center: the center is there, but it is an empty, passive one. Japanese postmodernists were quick to take up his vocabulary. It is now common to refer to the emperor as the zero sign of Japanese culture: everything derives from this empty center, and everything collapses into one at this center. It functions like a black hole. This model has served as a strategy for enabling the imperial system to survive the transformation of Japanese capitalism. The transformation of the emperor into an empty center can be seen as equivalent to the emergence of the "soft capitalism" of the 1980s, a process often described as a feminization.

To sum up, we find ourselves trapped in a vicious circle that oscillates between Orientalism and a reverse Orientalism. Feminism as a cultural product cannot escape from this closed framework. It is especially difficult when gender is fundamental to many of the oppositional metaphors mobilized in the production of cultural identity. When a feminist chooses to stress the feminine, as in the case of maternalist and maximalist feminists, any alignment with either position will be achieved only by the effective ghettoization of "Japaneseness" and "womanhood." How can we avoid getting trapped by these frustrating alternatives?

In conclusion, it should be said that although I have limited this discussion to the Japanese case, these problems are in no way unique to Japan but are common to all nations. These issues are particularly evident in developing societies where mechanisms of reverse Orientalism have prevailed in the attempt to define local identities. Developed societies in which the formation of a national identity is at issue will also be faced with the same potential problems. Any feminist backlash that effectively ghettoizes the feminine—for example, the emergence of women's religions—also raises these same questions. In considering the issues I have raised here in relation to Orientalism and reverse Orientalism, feminist and cultural particularism, and nationalism—all of which are specific (not mutually exclusive) strategies for the construction of identity— it would be naive to forget the political specificity of difference.

[Buckley, ed., *Broken Silence*, pp. 293–301]

SAITŌ CHIYO AND JAPANESE FEMINISM

Saitō Chiyo, founder of the feminist journal *Agora*, attempted to redefine the concept of a "Japanese feminism" in the context of the movement's diversification in the late twentieth century. In her remarks, Saitō also alludes to the positions of Aoki Yayoi and Ueno Chizuko, other feminists who are her contemporaries.

WHAT IS JAPANESE FEMINISM?

I usually don't like definitions, but if I was asked for my own definition of feminism today, I might say the following, emphasizing that it refers only to the current situation:

An international cultural and human rights movement to "cleanse" experience and knowledge, a movement that adopts a female perspective rather than the traditional male value system. Opposition to the privileging of production and efficiency models. The privileging of human life and sexuality. The elimination of all discrimination based on gender, economic status, race, culture, education, etc.

This would be my definition for the present, but it might well change in the future. It is a definition that is informed by all my own priorities, and so I would invite others to disagree. I believe that the first wave of feminism developed philosophically out of a humanist tradition. If we begin to consider the relationship between humanism and feminism, there is material for a book and still some. I don't feel I am familiar enough with this problem to touch on it here in detail, but as a passing observation I would say that the origins of this relationship go back a long way.

There are various theories as to when the word *feminism* first came into use. The widely told official version is that the term was coined by Alexandre Dumas, the French dramatist, in his work *L'Homme-femme* in 1872, where he used it to name the contemporary movement for women's rights. Other explanations trace the first use back to the eighteenth century, but in all cases the country of origin remains France. In that respect it is interesting to note that despite the fact that there is ample record of the numbers of women at Versailles in 1789, the expression "Freedom, Equality, and Brotherhood" (*fraternité*) excludes sisterhood (*sororité*). The expression *sororité* is still rarely used officially in France today outside limited feminist circles.

The Renaissance is known as the period of the discovery of mankind, the restoration of mankind, and yet, be it the Renaissance or the French Revolution, women are excluded from the category of mankind. Perhaps some will consider it an exaggeration to say that feminism has played a major role in the movement to restore the excluded group—women—but that is my impression. In its earliest forms feminism called for sexual equality in political, economic, educational, and social rights, and these focuses led to the popularization of such terms as "Women's Liberation" and "Women's Rights Movement." However, the radical feminism and second wave of the feminist movement that grew out of the anti-Vietnam and civil rights movements of the 1960s brought major qualitative changes. As early as the nineteenth century some people had questioned whether the Women's Rights Movement went far enough, wanting also to assert the value of woman as reproductive subject. This movement focused on the maternal female. Radical feminism went another step further, calling not only for the glorification of female life and sexuality but also for the feminization of all fixed value systems and future social principles. Perhaps it is because the women of this movement repeatedly brought such massive numbers of demonstrators onto the streets in support of their demands that today American feminists credit their country with the birth of the movement. The Women's Liberation Movement spread quickly across the world under the abbreviated title of "Lib." In contrast to the emphasis on certain aspects of female identity and the fight for equal rights that characterized the classic feminism, the new radical feminism was remarkable in its resolute demand for a realization of the total identity of all women as living subjects. Ueno-*san* has said that we have seen such diversification because feminism has matured and reached its outer limits. From the perspective of feminism's long history, one could say that it has reached a period of maturity, but it is on this solid foundation that radical feminism has come into being. . . .

While one dimension of any movement is an emphasis on basic principles, a movement will also usually confront the reality of its time. Those associated with feminism have consistently called for reforms in the context. Of all the realities whose paths they have tread, each of these calls for reform has developed a theoretical base of its own. In response to Ueno-*san*'s claim that the abundance of theoretical positions represents the demise of feminism, I would argue that the richer the movement, the richer the range of theories. I predict that the more women who join the ranks of feminism, the more vigorous feminist discourse will become. I should add, however, that at one level I do agree with Ueno-*san* when she says that in some sense the proliferation of theory is an attempt to change the way we see the world in the face of the apparent impossibility of changing the reality of the world. When I hear people labeling one another—"Oh, she's a radical feminist," "She's an ecological feminist"—I get the feeling that if theory is ever reduced to just this, a collection of intellectual labels to wear, then the movement will be dead.

If feminist theory and the movement are two sides of the same coin, surely what links them is the fact that both originate from the same basic emotions. This, too, could be seen as another source of the recent proliferation of feminisms. Some people came to feminism from their experience of discrimination in the workplace, others due to hardship caused by the restrictions of the family system or the difficulty for women with young children to return to the workforce. The range of experiences is not unlike that suffered in a state of war. Some suffered psychological injuries, and some the pain of discrimination due to race, culture, class, or other "identifications." For others the starting point was their concern over nuclear weapons or the contamination of food supplies. Still others came to feminism out of a religious love. There are so many paths that bring people to feminism. When I was in New York in 1982 for a peace rally, I tried to meet with as many of the feminist groups there as possible. There were mothers who had become involved over the contamination of milk by radioactive rain, black activists, supporters of cooperation with the third world, minority groups, lesbians, and many others from different interest groups. It is not surprising then that so many different tactical approaches have emerged ranging from antipatriarchy, the elimination of class, sexual liberation, new ecology, rethinking the body, a rejection of the male principle, and cooperation with the third world to talking from the heart and relaxation.

At yet another level, this diversification is fundamental to understanding the movement itself. The most basic foundation of feminism is each woman's own emotions and perceptions. Feminism is opposed to standardization and regulation. The entrenchment of the standardized concept of "women in the home, men in the workplace" should be questioned. Another example of such questioning is the criticism from lesbians of heterosexual dominance and their call for equal rights for homosexuals. The other unavoidable question is whether the fight for the expansion of rights can be limited to women. The territory has been shifting to include race, culture, birthrights, the handicapped, and others. Even the very category of humanity is coming under question. Ecological feminism, with its call for alternative ways of life that reject high-production society and its questioning of the conditions of human life, will have a major impact.

With this level of diversification it is inevitable that at different times different approaches will generate a barrage of sparks as they come in contact with one another, but as long as no one group attempts to adopt a dominant position, the stimulation of these fiery encounters can become the ground for new ideas and actions. It is here that we can identify the boundless potential of feminism. I believe that this diversity will continue to breed still further differentiation.

Let's return to the idea of a Japanese feminism. If we accept the concept of diversity as a characteristic of feminism, then there is no reason why there should not be a multitude of feminisms in direct relation to geographic, historical, and contextual variables. Within this system the possibility that we would nurture a Japanese feminism in Japan is perfectly acceptable, and indeed, I believe it to be the reality. I may not have met even a hundred foreign feminists in my time, but even so they have come from as far afield as Asia, Africa, the Middle East, Central America, North America, Australia, northern Europe, southern Europe, and the Eastern Bloc. I have felt very subtle variations among the feminisms of each of these countries. It is only natural that, given the differences in social conditions in each place, the tone and hue of the feminisms should also differ. . . .

[Buckley, ed., *Broken Silence*, pp. 262–68]

Chapter 49

THINKING WITH THE PAST:

HISTORY WRITING IN MODERN JAPAN

Like all modern nations, Japan takes its history seriously, mobilizing the past in the service of national identity, cultural value, and political critique. Such uses of history are by no means new to modern Japan, which inherited the historical mindedness associated with East Asian Confucianism as well as a centuries-old habit of defining Japan against China by evoking a distinctive national past. This combination of new and old reasons for attending to history may help explain the prominence of historical concerns in contemporary Japan. From public politics to popular culture, from early Meiji to the beginning of the twenty-first century, Japanese have used the past as something to think with.

History is thus no academic matter but part of the national consciousness, in which the story of "Japan" is collectively told. The modern version emerged in the Meiji period under the sign of the nation-state that was then under reconstruction. This newly designated "national history" (*kokushi*) employed the methods of a newly "scientific" history writing. Both the national story and the academic discipline of history belonged to what Narita Ryūichi called a "grammar of modernity" common to nation-states in the late nineteenth century. Its legacy, in Japan as elsewhere, was to make the nation the main subject of most historical sentences, whether stated or implicit, and to give precedence to historical knowledge based on written sources and expressed in written form.

The logic of modernity further challenged historians in Japan and other places to situate their nation in world history, understood as a universal progress toward modern forms of politics, society, and culture. This meant comparing Japan with the West, regarded as the source of models of modernity and theories of history, and with China, which became an antimodel and icon of an antiquated past. On the one hand, such historical comparisons justified Japan's wars and imperialism in Asia. On the other, the allegedly universal models, which were in fact Western, injured national pride. The result was nationalistic histories asserting the uniqueness of Japan. This tension between a common modernity and a distinctive national history was itself nearly universal, a dilemma that Japan shared with most twentieth-century societies, outside a very few Western countries.

Even the categories of history writing made comparison inevitable. Japanese history was fitted, for example, into Western chronologies of ancient, medieval, and modern, or into Marxist stages of development from feudalism to capitalism. European conceptions of revolution and democracy provided the interpretive framework for understanding the Meiji Restoration, the parliamentary system, and so on. For a long time, Western modernity was set against Japanese "tradition" in an absolute dichotomy that led historians and social critics to idealize and demonize either one term or the other. Centuries of Japan's long history were viewed from the vantage point of the present, as if the entire past had been prologue to the modern nation-state. These strong concepts, typical of modern historical consciousness as it developed in the nineteenth-century West, produced great debate among historians as well as in the wider domains of politics and culture. At stake were both the understanding and the production of a Japanese modernity.

This challenge generated a creative and contentious historiography, which wrestled with the common questions of modern history writing everywhere while producing powerful interpretations of Japan's particular experience. The master narrative of history since 1600 amounted to the story of becoming modern, with the contention arising from different notions of what modernity ought to look like. For Meiji historians, it looked like Western-style "civilization," toward which Japan was rapidly "advancing." For Marxist historians, who dominated Japanese history writing for much of the twentieth century, true modernity required a revolution to make the transition from capitalism to socialism, which, in their view, "backward" Japan continually failed to achieve. For liberal progressives like Maruyama Masao, being modern meant a democratic parliamentary politics based on the will of autonomous individuals, whose absence these historians linked to the rise of fascism and aggressive war. For scholars of modernization, in contrast, modernity comprised economic growth, social change, and political democracy, which they judged Japan to have "succeeded" in acquiring in the decades after World War II. For "people's historians," a proper modernity ought to concern society, not the state, the daily lives of ordinary people, not the protected provinces of a self-selected elite, and so they rewrote the story to make the people the protagonists of history. Social and cultural historians then sought to include in the national narrative those previously excluded because of gender, status, location, ethnicity, or colonial rule and, in the process, deconstructed the very notion of a singular homogeneous "Japan."

Different definitions of modernity thus produced different approaches to history, and these in turn resulted in changing stories about the past. But modern history writing is also oriented to the future, which is supposed to be better than the present, to make "progress," that most fundamental of modern beliefs. So historians constantly reinterpret the past for what it has to say about why the present is as it is and how to move forward from it. Nowhere is this clearer than in the changing interpretations of the two main epochal events in modern Japanese history: the Meiji Restoration and World War II. Both events were considered absolute ruptures between an old past and a new future. The Restoration, as the founding event of the modern nation, and the war, as the new beginning of postwar democracy, were examined with an eye to their causes and consequences. But they were also understood as charges to the future, and historians interpreted them according to their views of what that future should hold.

Their openly declared present and future mindedness impelled Japanese historians to practice their history in public, their activism ranging from the support of revolution in the 1930s or democracy in the 1960s to continued engagement with the politics of textbooks and history education. As public intellectuals, Japanese historians appeared prominently in the press and the mass media, welcome contributors to the successive "history booms" that swept popular discourse since the first "history fever" was identified in the 1890s. The public appetite for history was manifested in the popularity of historical fiction, drama, and television, where heroes like the spirited samurai Sakamoto Ryōma were reinterpreted as often as the Restoration itself. But not all popular history was about heroes or the safely distant past. Toward the end of the twentieth century, as World War II became more prominent in public memory in many places, Japanese were called on to confront the enormity of their wartime actions in Asia, including the excesses of colonial rule in Korea, the military's exploitation of "comfort women" as sex slaves, and atrocities such as the Nanjing massacre. The received national story of the war, which had focused on the victimization of the Japanese people by their own leaders, now had to recognize the Asian victims of war and empire. The result was a heated national and international controversy about Japan's twentieth-century past. Whether commentators were celebrating Tokugawa tradition or condemning Shōwa imperialism, Japanese public culture remained "saturated with history."

NEW HISTORIES IN MEIJI JAPAN

As with many things in Meiji Japan, the new history writing, repeatedly heralded as a complete break with the past, was in fact a blend of Western approaches and established Tokugawa habits. Because both the Western approaches and the Tokugawa habits encompassed diverse and conflicting views of their own, the mix made for considerable turbulence among those contending for a place in the new historical landscape.

History was accorded importance from the beginning. Already in April 1869—even before the country was fully unified—the new Meiji government established the Office of Historiography. In a slap at the shogunate, the office was charged with resuming the imperial tradition of writing national histories, which had lapsed during the eight centuries of warrior rule. But the times were no longer propitious for state history defined as the compilation of materials in Chinese arranged in chronological order by imperial reign, and in the 1890s, faced with criticism from several quarters, the government abandoned its effort. Not so the compilers, whose successors at the Historiographical Institute at Tokyo Imperial University were still collecting and publishing primary sources as the twenty-first century began. They were not, however, writing history.

Writing history, as opposed to compiling sources, took two main forms in the Meiji period, each declaring itself especially appropriate to the new age. The first, histories of civilization (*bunmeishi*), were lively national narratives dedicated to showing where Japan stood in the universal course of progress and how its past exhibited the same "laws of history" described by nineteenth-century European historians like Henry Buckle and François Guizot and thinkers like Herbert Spencer. These civilizational histories were written not by academic historians but by public intellectuals and journalists such as Fukuzawa Yukichi (see his *Outline of a Theory of Civilization* in chap. 36) and Tokutomi Sohō (see his *Future Japan* later in this chapter), who took it as their mission to impel the nation forward by enlightening the people. They consciously centered their histories on the people, society, and culture, not on the government or the state, in works that were optimistic, hortatory, and enormously popular. Nothing interested them more than the "trends of the times" (*jisei*), the "progress of civilization" (*bunmei no kaika*), and the future of Japan.

What interested the pioneers of the new "national history" (*kokushi*)—the second stream of Meiji history writing—was a scientific understanding of the past based on "facts" recounted without bias or moral purposes. Influenced by German historicism, their respect for verifiable data led them to debunk hallowed heroes and events in Japanese history, earning them public condemnation for their "theories of obliteration." They denounced Confucian praise-and-blame history as moralistic, yet their method of verifying facts was an updated form of textual criticism (*kōshōgaku*) inherited from Tokugawa Chinese studies (and from Qing philology). With the establishment of the Department of National History at Tokyo Imperial University in 1889, these historians—Shigeno Yasutsugu and Kume Kunitake, in particular—became the founding figures of the modern academic discipline of history.

Like the new categories of "national literature" and "national language," the discipline of national history emerged together with the intensified nation-mindedness of the late 1880s and 1890s. While this concern was clearly linked to the Meiji pursuit of modernity, it was also part of the wider nineteenth-century evolution of the nation-state. Indeed, the professionalization of national history occurred in roughly the same period in Japan as it did in France, Britain, and the United States, suggesting that the contemporary global context was as important as any need specific to the recently unified Meiji state. In each country, the new professional historians employed the latest scientific, or "objective," methods to narrate the nation as a continuous unitary entity, thus contributing the weight of the past to the modern catechism of national identity.

This link between history and the nation provoked public controversy. In the early 1890s, both Shigeno and Kume were dismissed from the university for having violated the sanctity of national myth, hounded out by Shintoists and others who resented either Chinese or Western approaches or both. School textbooks repeatedly aroused debate, and in 1911 the "controversy over the Northern and Southern Court" reached the highest political levels. The Meiji constitution, after all, stated that the emperors reigned in a line "unbroken for ages eternal," making it inopportune to suggest the existence of two contending imperial lineages in the fourteenth century.

By the end of the Meiji period, both civilizational and academic history had spawned a new generation of historians. Public intellectuals like Yamaji Aizan carried on the tradition of popular national narrative, and professional historians such as Hara Katsurō and Uchida Ginzo inaugurated the academic fields of medieval and Tokugawa (*kinsei*) history. It became the prevailing fashion for later historians to condemn the Meiji founders as either unrigorously popular in the case of histories of civilization or rigorously pedantic in the case of professional historians, whose method was denigrated as "academism." But the truth—as the academic professionals might have asserted—was that these historians thought of themselves as the vanguard of a new age of history writing. In their combat against old forms of Confucian moralism, imperial annals, and ungrounded mythologies, they were indeed radical, if not quite as free of the Tokugawa past as they were wont to claim.

TAGUCHI UKICHI

Taguchi Ukichi (1855–1905) exemplified the spirit that produced the new histories of civilization (*bunmeishi*), which both recounted Japanese history as progress toward enlightenment and hoped to enlighten Meiji Japanese about the "universal laws" of history. Like Fukuzawa Yukichi, Taguchi criticized feudal rule and Confucian scholarship, arguing that historians should identify "fixed principles" and cause and effect, not merely produce "chronologies" or praise moral individuals. Always both historian and participant, Taguchi— sometimes known as the Adam Smith of Japan—founded the important *Tokyo*

Economic Journal in 1878 on the model of England's *Economist*, took part in the political Freedom and People's Rights movement, tried his hand at private enterprise, and spent the last decade of his life as an elected member of the Diet. His popular history magazine, *Shikai* (*Historical World*), of 1892 ignited the controversy that cost the academic historian Kume Kunitake his job, while Taguchi's indefatigable publishing efforts produced large-scale collections of historical documents that remain invaluable.

A SHORT HISTORY OF JAPANESE CIVILIZATION
(*NIHON KAIKA SHŌSHI*)

Published between 1877 and 1882, Taguchi Ukichi's famous *Short History of Japanese Civilization* made the economic argument that material progress is fundamental to cultural development and the historical claim that the people (*jinmin*), not the state, propelled history forward during the Tokugawa era. This excerpt shows the way in which Taguchi constructed his historical arguments for the progress of Japanese civilization.

The Phenomena of Civilization that Emerged During Tokugawa Rule

ON THE GREAT PROGRESS OF MATERIAL AND IMMATERIAL GOODS AFTER THE CALMING OF SOCIETY [UNDER THE TOKUGAWA]

During the era of war-torn chaos [of the sixteenth century], the people (*jinmin*) suffered from hunger and thirst and could not afford to choose their food and drink. Although they desired better, it was impossible for them to improve their sustenance and shelter. But in the era of Great Peace, when circumstance no longer suppressed these demands, people worked as hard as they could to obtain what they wanted to make their lives comfortable. And just as plants bring forth their shoots in the spring breezes, nothing could keep the elements of civilization from thriving in the nurturing air of the Great Peace.

It is in the nature of man to protect life and avoid death. To protect life and avoid death, man must clothe, feed, and shelter himself, but clothing, food, and shelter that merely stave off hunger and cold are not enough. What is desired is clothing soft to the skin, food sweet to the taste, and comfortable shelter against the elements.

To satisfy these desires, people must use their intellectual abilities. This leads to material progress and, with it, progress in the inner human spirit. Material progress depends on progress of the spirit, and as long as material conditions do not devolve, the spirit will not regress either. This is because material goods develop intellectual abilities, and the human spirit makes material progress possible. . . .

ESTABLISHING THE CRITERION OF PROGRESS ON THE BASIS OF WHAT ARE CALLED LUXURY GOODS

It is not easy to advance standards of living. Some believe that the extravagance of the people would know no bounds unless the government set limits to it, but this is not at all the case. Because standards of living progress as the property and capital of the general populace increase, this striving, far from leading to ruin, is in fact the very criterion of civilization.

THE CHARACTER OF CIVILIZATION THAT EMERGED UNDER FEUDALISM

The feudal system values the family. The eldest son is esteemed, the younger sons slighted, and even if the heir is a fool, the intention to continue the family unbroken into perpetuity prevails. A familial blood line may be entirely severed, and yet by adopting an heir, the family may still appear to the world to continue. Such practices, based as they are on man's nature (to avoid death and protect life), resulted in great progress under the feudal system.

Recognizing this in retrospect, it is easy to see that there is a fixed principle in society, which merely operates differently under different systems. . . .

SOCIETY REMEDIES ITSELF

Reasoning from the facts stated above, we understand that it is in the nature of society for civilization to progress. When the debates over distinctions of rank in the aristocratic lineages became extreme in the Heian court, for example, the localities sought freedom, thus giving rise to feudal power. When feudalism descended into the chaos of the warring states like that of late Ashikaga rule, the lords sought to achieve the Great Peace, eventually uniting the country. And after achieving the Great Peace, the people sought to make their lives comfortable, engendering progress in all things from literature to the practical arts. Society always moves in this way. The actions of heroes and great men merely hasten or delay these forces. Thinking of the future in the light of this principle, we can foresee the prospects for our nation.

[Taguchi, *Nihon kaika shōshi*, pp. 181–83, 232–33; CG]

SHIGENO YASUTSUGU

Caricatured in the press as Dr. Obliterator for his denials of the historical existence of legendary heroes, Shigeno Yasutsugu (1827–1910) was a founding figure of academic history at Tokyo Imperial University. Both roles derived from

Shigeno's sure sense of the historian's vocation, which he defined as a search for the truth, based on facts verified through close textual criticism (*kōshō*) of primary sources. Thus when he found no corroborating textual evidence for the existence of Kojima Takenori, the famous imperial loyalist who appears in the military tale *Taiheiki*, Shigeno said so, arousing the wrath of traditionalists. From the time of his appointment to the government's Office of Historiography in 1875, he practiced the strict textual methods of his early training in Chinese learning, eschewing any sign of unreliable narrative and sticking close to the sources. This earned him the hostility of Shintoists, nationalists, people who thought that official history should be written in Japanese rather than Chinese, historians of civilization who found textual criticism insufficiently inspiring for progress, and younger critics who thought his history antiquated and him an old fogy.

Like many Meiji figures who came of age under the Tokugawa, Shigeno was a transitional figure between the old and the new history, who nonetheless left his mark as the founder of "academism," which dominated the halls of Tokyo Imperial University. When the Department of National History was founded there in 1889, Shigeno and Kume Kunitake were among its first professors. When the Historical Society was established the same year, Shigeno became its president, and when the society began its *Historical Journal* (*Shigaku zasshi*), Shigeno wrote for it. In response to the following speech published in the inaugural issue in 1889, Shigeno was denounced as deficient in loyalty and national feeling, and when the Office of Historiography was closed in 1893, he lost his university post. The journal, still published by Tokyo University, remains the professional home of academic, "positivist" history to this day.

"THOSE WHO ENGAGE IN THE STUDY OF HISTORY MUST BE IMPARTIAL AND FAIR-MINDED IN SPIRIT" (SHIGAKU NI JŪJI SURU MONO WA SONO KOKORO SHIKŌ SHIHEI NARAZARU BEKARAZU)

In light of the current recognition of the need for history, my lecture today concerns the many articles published in various journals which are one-sided and lacking in impartiality. Anyone engaged in the study of history must first faithfully follow his art. If the historian's spirit is partial and unfair, all his views will be biased, creating abuses that make it impossible to achieve the objectives of scholarship and that obstruct the development of the study of history. The historian must therefore strive for an impartial spirit, avoiding bias and self-interest. . . .

Because their discipline involves study and speculation about enormous numbers of people over thousands of years, any partiality of spirit on the part of historians may lead both people and the world astray, causing immeasurable harm. . . .

Unfairness leads to bias and partiality, to the habit of preferring the eccentric and extolling the new, to the malady of favoring victory and harshly criticizing error, and in myriad ways turns out to be either too much or not enough. In the end the historian falls into prejudice, unable to choose the good or select the virtuous, obstructing thereby the progress of the age. This ought to be the greatest concern of scholars of history.

History is the reflection of the conditions of an age, and the point of historical scholarship is to examine those conditions and establish the facts. Yet those who write in the belief that history is primarily a moral teaching tend to distort the facts in the service of morality. As commendable as the concern with social teachings may be, distorting the facts contravenes the essence of history, which is to reflect the conditions of the world. Conveying this reality through "impartial views and impartial writing" also works naturally to praise good and blame evil and serves as the source of moral teaching.

In the writings of the ancients I found two lines which ought to serve as the historian's guide:

Examine by following evidence.
Write directly based on facts.

The first line comes from a "Comprehensive Explanation of the Study of History" (Shitong tongshi), and the second from Zhu Xi. Seek evidence, examine it, establish the facts, and write things just as they are. The first line pertains to investigation; the second, to compilation. History consists of both investigation and compilation, and although the study of history is largely concerned with investigation, compilation is always linked to it. These lines express the substance of history: it is the historian's task to encounter a phenomenon and conjecture as to its character, consulting and employing the methods of Eastern and Western history. . . .

We now convene this society in the hope of benefiting the nation, dedicating ourselves to textual criticism (*kōshō*) of the traces of our national history and to its compilation based on the materials collected by the Bureau of History and utilizing Western methods of historical investigation.

> [Shigeno, "Shigaku ni jūji suru mono wa sono kokoro shikō shihei narazaru bekarazu," *Shigaku zasshi*, December 15, 1889, pp. 2–5; CG]

KUME KUNITAKE

Shigeno Yasutsugu's colleague in founding the new academic history, Kume Kunitake (1839–1931) was the most accomplished historian of his generation. His long and prolific career began with his "true account" of the Iwakura Mission of 1871 to 1873 (see chap. 35), which he accompanied on its travels to the

West. He worked in the Office of Historiography, cowrote the first national history textbook (*Kokushigan*), and was one of the first professors in the new Department of National History at Tokyo Imperial University until he was ousted in the famous Kume incident of 1892. He then moved to Waseda University, where he continued research and publication until he retired in 1922.

Kume experienced firsthand the dangers of writing national history in a charged ideological atmosphere. As one of the "obliterators," he published such articles as "The *Taiheiki* Is of No Value for Historical Scholarship," which inflamed nativist scholars. Like the Shintoists, they opposed the Chinese text criticism and Western methods that were usurping their position as arbiters of national history. So when Taguchi Ukichi reprinted Kume's article "Shinto Is a Primitive Form of Nature Worship" in his popular history journal, the Shintoists and nativists promptly attacked Kume and succeeded in provoking his dismissal from the university. One year earlier, the Christian Uchimura Kanzō had been forced to resign his post for refusing to bow before the portrait of the emperor in the "disrespect incident." Such nationalist feelings ran high in the early 1890s, often without the instigation of the state, and national history, always linked to identity and ideology, met with constant controversy.

"THE ABUSES OF TEXTUAL CRITICISM IN HISTORICAL STUDY" (SHIGAKU KŌSHŌ NO HEI)

In the 1901 lecture excerpted here, Kume Kunitake refers to the institutional characteristics peculiar to national history in the university. By then, the study of history had been divided into national history, Asian history, and Western history. While this separation typified nineteenth-century national history in other countries as well, the result was that the study of the history of Japan was severed from that of Asia and the world. It was also subject to ideological scrutiny and suppression. Kume nonetheless counseled academic historians against retreating to the safe haven of antiquarian source criticism, which is precisely what many of them did. "Academism" in Japanese history in the universities thus owed its longevity not only to a commitment to scholarly objectivity but also to a professional impulse to stay out of political trouble.

Although textual criticism (*kōshō*) is absolutely essential to the study of history, it is equally obvious that textual criticism alone is not sufficient. The first step in historical research is to ascertain the facts. The sole rule—the fundamental law (*kenpō*)—of historical study consists of presenting one's opinion based on scientific research, founded on reliable facts, in a context of free academic inquiry.

And reliable facts are ascertained by textual criticism, which is thus the first essential of historical study, though not in itself adequate to genuine scholarship. Yet ever since the public uproar about [the authenticity of the historical figure] Kojima Takanori, national history (*kokushi*) has been severely attacked in public.

In response to the continual cannonade of "national polity" (*kokutai*), "national essence" (*kokusui*), and even "national traitors" (*kokuzoku*), national history defended itself against the siege with the shield of textual criticism. Thrusting textual criticism to the fore, they disclaimed responsibility for their statements, inasmuch as they could do nothing about the facts revealed in the old documents they examined. This issue has dogged history writing ever since. When I presented some small opinions of my own, I was dismissed from the university. The discipline of history has been beset by difficulties from the start, and even now one cannot be optimistic about a discipline so reviled by the public. . . .

To avoid these public attacks, national history had little choice but to give in and commit itself to conduct research following the steadfast and appropriate course of practicing textual criticism founded on reliable facts. And indeed, practicing textual criticism on the basis of reliable facts is an eminently reasonable course to follow. Yet however much we believe this, it is of no use against the attacks of antiquated thought. . . .

Thus, while textual criticism is essential to the discipline of history, textual criticism alone does not constitute historical study. Making judgments that determine one's opinions is essential to any genuine scholarship. But because history writing faces so many obstacles, we cannot develop our opinions in open display, as is done in other fields. Still, because scholarship is a matter of one's own learning, I intend to devote myself to developing my interpretations and to relishing historical research. And I would like to recommend that you gentlemen do the same.

[Kume, "Shigaku kōshō no hei," pp. 60–61, 70; CG]

MARXIST HISTORY WRITING

The prominence of Marxist approaches to history was one of the most impressive characteristics of twentieth-century Japanese scholarship, impressive in intellectual achievement and in prominence despite a political environment largely hostile to the left. The upsurge of interest in Marxism in the interwar period occurred around the same time as the liberal trends described in chapter 40, but in the field of history and in intellectual life more generally, it was Marxism, not liberalism, that had the greater impact, from the 1920s through the 1970s. Marxism became synonymous with the institutionalization of "social science" in Japanese universities after World War I, and educated youth of the interwar period immersed themselves in the texts and theories of Marxist analysis. Notably, the first full edition of the *Collected Works of Marx and Engels* appeared in Japan, not Europe, edited and translated in thirty volumes between 1928 and 1932. Although Marxist scholars suffered repeated suppression during the late 1920s and 1930s, they emerged from World War II to dominate the academy in a postwar context that initially seemed favorable to their visions of a democratic revolution. In the ensuing decades progressive historians remained steadfast in their opposition to conservative trends, receiving a respectful public hearing in the media even as they lost hope of realizing their social and political goals.

Marxist history writing began as a response to an environment of social and economic crisis in the 1920s and 1930s. In contrast to Meiji historians who had ridden the crest of national progress, Marxist historians confronted the crisis of capitalism and world depression, the contradictions of social unevennesses engendered by modernity, and the possibility, even the necessity, of revolutionary change. These "world historical" phenomena impelled Japanese intellectuals, like their counterparts elsewhere, to seek solutions on the left. In the ferment of political commitment, which ranged from Bolshevism and Communism to socialism and social democracy, historians saw their task as understanding Japan's past in order to bring about a new future. For them, history was no armchair calling but a call to arms. They railed against academic historians as antiquarian and irrelevant; timid positivism (*jisshōshugi*), they judged, could not change the world in the way a properly scientific historical materialism could.

Prewar Marxist historians worked within a difficult double mandate. First, they had to place Japanese history in the universal developmental scheme, which necessarily led from feudalism to capitalism to socialism. In China, this periodization resulted in identifying a feudal era that was some two thousand years long; in Japan it produced what Andrew Barshay called a "logic of backwardness," stressing the "feudal remnants" that prevented modern Japan from developing an authentic form of capitalism. The second mandate came not from Marx but from Moscow, where the Comintern produced its own changing diagnoses of Japanese history in accordance with Communist Party strategies for revolution (see chap. 40).

The main scholarly split between the Lectures Faction (Kōza-ha) and the Labor-Farmer Faction (Rōnō-ha) arose from this double mandate, one historiographical and the other political. Any analysis of the Meiji Restoration, for example, had to explain why it resulted in what the Lectures Faction called an "absolutist emperor-system state" and to identify where it stood in the developmental typology of revolution, with the English, French, and Russian Revolutions as historical models. The reason for this was also political: if the Restoration was a failed bourgeois revolution, as the Lectures Faction argued within the Comintern framework, then Japanese activists had two revolutions to bring about in the twentieth century: first the bourgeois and then the proletarian. But if the Restoration qualified as a genuine, if incomplete, bourgeois-democratic revolution that had produced a Japanese form of capitalism, as the Labor-Farmer Faction contended, then Japan could move directly to a socialist revolution. History and politics were thus closely conjoined.

In history writing, the Lectures Faction prevailed, its two-stage revolution theory emphasizing the ways in which Japan had diverged from the universal scheme of social, economic, and political development. In real life, both factions met with suppression, including imprisonment, and no revolution of any kind occurred in the years of fascism and war. But after 1945, the possibility of a democratic revolution's emerging from the ashes of defeat energized Marxist historians as they continued their debates, the Lectures Faction still prevailing, for several decades to come.

LECTURES ON THE HISTORY OF THE DEVELOPMENT OF JAPANESE CAPITALISM
(NIHON SHIHONSHUGI HATTATSUSHI KŌZA)

Many pioneers of Marxist history writing worked outside the academy, some by choice and others because they were forced out of universities by police repression. Their political commitment, scholarly energy, and amateur status combined to galvanize the intense "debates on Japanese capitalism," which put Marxist scholarship on the intellectual map in the late 1920s and the early 1930s.

The landmark work of this period was the seven-volume *Lectures on the History of the Development of Japanese Capitalism (Nihon shihonshugi hattatsushi kōza)*, which gave the Lectures Faction its name. Its charismatic editor, Noro Eitarō (1900–1934), taught at the Workers School, joined the Communist Party in 1930, and died, ill, in prison in 1934. His collaborators in this series, which reflected the shifting views of the Comintern, included such central figures in the Lectures Faction as Hirano Yoshitarō, Hattori Shisō, Hani Gorō, and Yamada Moritarō, whose famous analysis of Japanese capitalism is excerpted in chapter 41. Noro enlisted the prestigious press Iwanami to publish the work, which met with repeated censorship. The published essays focus on the deviant character of Japanese capitalism, the developmental level of the late Tokugawa economy, and the nature of the Meiji Restoration, employing the analytic methods of social and economic history. Despite the complexity of argument, the often contradictory views it contains, and the sheer danger of such material in the increasingly dark times of the 1930s, the series sold extremely well, laying the cornerstone for decades of historical debate to come.

Features, 1932

1. The series approaches the historical development of capitalism in Japan as part of the total system of world capitalism; it analyzes the fundamental contradictions in this development, constrained as it was by various special factors; and it elucidates the conditions for a fundamental resolution of these contradictions, with particular reference to the present general crisis of postwar capitalism.

2. The series pursues a thoroughly scientific view of history, rejecting the textual source criticism, narrow specialization, idealist methodology, and simple analogies with processes in foreign countries that characterize conventional histories of the *bakumatsu* [late Tokugawa], Meiji Restoration, and Meiji–Taishō periods as well as the history of the development of capitalism, political history, and the rest. It takes into account—scientifically, systematically, and dialectically—the total structure of economy, politics, and culture, based on the concrete interrelatedness of their historical development. . . .

Prospectus, 1931

The prospectus was written by Noro Eitarō, the editor of the multivolume work.

The world economic depression is shaking the foundations of the entire capitalist system, and with it that of the Japanese capitalist system as well. The mounting general crisis of capitalism, the catastrophic deepening of the ongoing depression, the threatening tension of international antagonisms, and the unsustainable intensification of class struggle—the rapid deterioration of all these circumstances, which, though one may try to conceal them can no longer be concealed, has led the ruling class and its agents finally to cry that a national crisis (*kokunan*) is upon us. "A national financial crisis!" says one; "a national crisis of thought!" says another; and yet another proclaims a "national crisis unprecedented since the founding of the nation!"

Imperialists flustered by the increasingly desperate situation are apt to think only of war and fascism. Yet the sole way to find solutions to such problems as the economic dead end, political instability, and social unrest is to delve into the fundamental contradictions that made this chain of changes necessary and inevitable. Reflection on the history of the establishment of Japanese capitalism and examination of the characteristics of its contradiction-filled development are therefore the key to discovering the path to a fundamental resolution of the problems facing Japanese capitalism. This series attempts to provide such a key.

Originating in response to these pressing present demands, the series does not stop with the mere enumeration and explanation of historical facts. Nor, however, do its contributors have any notion whatsoever of fabricating facts to fit some hidden agenda. What we resolve to undertake is not the interpretation but the transformation of history. Transforming history does not mean altering the historical facts of the past but creating the history of the future. We cannot, however, create this history just as we please. Only on the basis of already given conditions is it possible to transform and create history and to expect any true resolution to the problems at hand.

. . . This series includes the great majority of researchers capable of cooperatively contributing to the true resolution of these problems. It is literally the collaborative effort of some thirty authors. And while each contributor's originality is amply displayed within his assigned scope, each article also constitutes a part of the tightly integrated structure of the whole.

The series provides the most comprehensive scientific research on Japanese capitalism and the most fundamental analysis of its contradictions to date. Yet it merely offers the key to the fundamental solution of the problems facing us. We expect the task to be completed only by the active efforts of many readers, themselves searching to find a way out of the crisis of Japanese capitalism. . . .

[Uchida et al., eds., *Marukushizumu* I, pp. 37–39; CG]

THE ASSOCIATION OF HISTORICAL STUDIES

In 1932, amid the political ferment that produced the "debates on Japanese capitalism," a group of young historians at Tokyo Imperial University formed the Association of Historical Studies (Rekishigaku kenkyūkai). Influenced by Marxism and dedicated to scientific history, they saw themselves as scholarly progressives in contrast to their elders and peers, the "academic" historians of the Historical Society, which had been founded in the mid-Meiji period. Compared with outsiders like Noro Eitarō and Hattori Shisō, however, these historians were professional academics, and although they were subjected to police surveillance and some suppression, they published their journal, held academic conferences, and pursued detailed research until finally forced to suspend activities in 1944. They combined progressive politics and Marxist approaches with a deep-seated empiricism that they in fact shared with the "academic" historians whose "positivism" they so often criticized. Just as Meiji scholars had joined Tokugawa text criticism with Western historicist methods, Marxist historians matched their new theoretical frameworks with an old respect for facts and data. This was the reason they prevailed in the academy and the reason the Association of Historical Studies and its journal have endured for so long as a progressive national organization alongside the "academism" of the more methodologically and politically conservative Historical Society.

DRAFT OF THE CHARTER OF THE ASSOCIATION OF HISTORICAL STUDIES

When the Association of Historical Studies formed again in 1946, both its politics and its scholarship seemed suddenly more in tune with the times. Progressive historians, who ranged from Communist Party Marxists to social democratic left-liberals, soon gained prominence in universities, their earlier arguments for scientific history now further strengthened by their critique of wartime "imperial history" (*kōkoku shikan*) for its chauvinistic manipulations of the past. The progressives also came "out of the study," as they put it, in self-critical reflection for not having done more to resist the forces of imperialism and war. Many worked tirelessly for social causes, peace, and accurate history teaching in the schools. The great progressive historians of the 1940s, such as the medievalist Ishimoda Shō and the historian of ancient Japan Tōma Seita, joined with earlier Marxists like Hani Gorō to propel the association into dynamic scholarly and public activity after the war. Their successors—among them Tōyama Shigeki, Nagahara Keiji, Fujiwara Akira, and many others—continued the Marxist and progressive traditions of history writing associated with the association and its journal, *Journal of Historical Studies* (*Rekishigaku kenkyū*).

In 2002 the association commemorated its eightieth anniversary, continuing its scholarly mission with a conference on the theme of "global capitalism and historical knowledge" and its public activism with interventions opposing the nationalistic re-vision of history textbooks and the potential violation of the Peace Constitution by antiterror legislation authorizing the dispatch of the Self-Defense Forces abroad in the wake of the attacks of September 11, 2001.

First, we advocate at all times the freedom of research and total independence of scholarship, without regard for any authority except scientific truth.

Second, we assert that the freedom and development of historical studies exists only within a correct relationship between the study of history and the people (*jinmin*).

Third, we seek to destroy all nationalistic, ethnocentric, and other old biases and advocate a democratic and world-historical position.

Fourth, we intend to establish a tradition of scientific study of history, prop-erly using the fruits of earlier scholarship and developing them further.

Fifth, we intend to enhance the culture of our ancestral land and its people by joining forces with all progressive scholars and organizations, regardless of their national origin.

[*Rekishigaku kenkyū*, no. 122 (June 1946): 47; CG]

WRITING ABOUT THE MEIJI RESTORATION

As the iconic event marking "the emergence of modern Japan," the Meiji Res-toration of 1868 played a role in Japanese historical thinking similar to that of the French Revolution in France. Like the Revolution, the Restoration was understood as the end of an ancien régime, in this case the Tokugawa shogun-ate, and the beginning of a new age that laid the foundations of the modern nation. Like the Revolution, the Restoration was subject to continual reinter-pretation as times and notions of modernity changed. To debate the Meiji Restoration was to question the origins of modern politics and society and the reason—depending on one's point of view—Japan's modernity either had turned out for the best or had gone somehow awry.

The Restoration figured in every precinct of historical representation, both scholarly and popular, its depiction shifting with the concerns of the times.

Three large themes, however, remained constant over the years. First, the debate over change and continuity posed the question of whether the Restoration had in fact created a "new Japan" severed from the Tokugawa age, which preceded it. One result of this juxtaposition of new against old was the reinvention of the Tokugawa (or feudal) past as Japanese "tradition," represented, whether negatively or positively, as the historical Other of modernity. A second result was a counterargument that emphasized continuities across the alleged rupture of 1868. Some proponents stressed the gradual nature of change across a "long Restoration" from the 1820s through the 1880s. Others claimed that deeply fundamental change did not occur during the transition, suggesting to conservatives that Tokugawa "tradition" remained to undergird modernization for the better and to progressives that feudal survivals prevented the development of an authentically modern economy and politics for the worse.

Second, the relation of external to internal factors in the Restoration raised the question of the role played by the West in this most nationally significant of historical moments. In regard to causes, how important was the catalytic appearance of Matthew Perry's black ships and the impending peril of Western imperialism? In regard to consequences, how did Euro-American models of civilization operate in the Meiji reforms that established the institutions of modern Japan? In regard to comparison, how did internal historical factors impel or impede Japan's taking its place in world "trends of the time" or universal "laws of history"? Writing the history of the Restoration demanded an inside–outside perspective that sometimes wounded national pride, which preferred an originary event that owed more to indigenous than to international factors.

Third, the nature of the Restoration itself presented a problem for historians, who combined the restoration (*ōsei fukkō*), narrowly construed as the events of 1868, with the Meiji renovation (*Meiji ishin*), the reforms that followed between 1868 and 1873, and asked: Was it a revolution; if so, what kind, if not, why not? (see chap. 35). Was it merely a change in political rule, from shogun to emperor; a social leveling of the feudal status system to a nation of equal subjects; an economic transition produced by a class alliance of low ranking samurai and well-off merchants; or an intellectual transformation in the way people knew and construed their world? Depending on their answers to such questions, subsequent historians judged the Restoration to have succeeded "smoothly" or to have failed to "complete" its task.

TOKUTOMI SOHŌ

The civilizational historians of the 1870s and 1880s produced the earliest narrative accounts of the Restoration, expressed in their customary register of optimism and progress. Perhaps the most popular and influential was *Future Japan* of 1886, whose author, Tokutomi Sohō (1863–1957), epitomized the new generation of Meiji youth imbued with Western ideas, Japanese potential, and a confidence in their own ability to combine the two for the sake of the nation. Tokutomi was a journalist, prolific writer, and prominent political gadfly who advocated democratic "commonerism" (*heiminshugi*) in his early work, imperialism in his middle years, and ultranationalism in his old age during World War II, all the while holding fast to a Meiji-inspired nationalism.

FUTURE JAPAN
(SHŌRAI NO NIHON)

Future Japan, which inspired many youthful readers, borrowed from Herbert Spencer to argue for Japan's inevitable transition from a militant (samurai) to an industrial (democratic) society. In his account of the causes of the Meiji Restoration, note Tokutomi Sohō's views of what moves history and also the way he treats the themes of new–old, inside–outside, and the nature of the change brought about by the Meiji reforms.

Even though thirty years ago the civilization of Japan was gasping for breath and was headed on an extremely uncertain course toward the future, strangely enough the country changed direction with lightning speed, reversed course, [and,] with a buoyant spirit, set off in pursuit of Western Civilization, and produced a state of affairs in which it appeared as if Japan desired to compete with it. . . .

. . . Behold! The downfall of our feudal society, reminiscent of the similar conditions of the Dark Ages in eleventh-century Europe, took place a mere ten years or so ago. Behold! The establishment of a parliament, which is expected to derive from nineteenth-century European parliamentary institutions, is already about to take place in four or five years. The slavelike commoners have suddenly risen in status, while their samurai masters have suddenly fallen in status. Already they are coming to meet on an equal footing. In the old days, people who did not have long swords at their side were not even regarded as human beings; nowadays you cannot see anyone bearing swords, except for soldiers or police. Now there are even those who bend their knees to the cross, the symbol of the Christian religion, which was trampled under bare feet in the past. Think of it! From the argument for closed ports to that for the total abolition of import tariffs and for free trade; from the advocacy of "repelling barbarians" to that of "mixed residence." How many days and how many generations have elapsed?

The more we think about it, it is like a dream or a fantasy, and it is not improper to say that it is just as if the phrase "this time of ours is like a great, confused dream" had been created to describe this era.

Such rapid changes are not confined to politics, social activities, food, clothing, and shelter, things that we see and hear of in daily life. We must also consider the spiritual plane. For example, everything in standards of morals, religion, human relations, honor, ideas, and so on, has been completely overturned. . . .

For this reason, we should not call this the transformation of Japan but, more appropriately, the restoration and regeneration of Japan. For the old Japan has already died, and what exists in the present day is the new Japan. . . .

Why is it that only the history of our Restoration reforms has progressed vigorously, exceeding people's expectations at every turn, and utterly astonishing them? I can assert that it has been because the great reform of the Meiji Restoration was a result of internal and external stimuli coming at the same time, the outside pushing and the inside shoving, which were eventually exhibited in a grand spectacle. To be more precise, the world trend awakened the spirit of the people, which then had to succumb to this inevitable pressure of the world trend and finally embark on an unforeseen and great undertaking, performing a fresh and extraordinary play that we had never seen and of which we had never heard. Not only we, the onlookers, but even the patriotic and righteous leaders of the Restoration themselves, the actors in the play, must surely have been taken completely by surprise. . . .

. . . The leaders of the Restoration reforms wavered lest they sacrifice both good and bad people indiscriminately. Nevertheless, they were spurred on by unrelenting pressure from this general world trend. Hence, one reform stimulated another. One overthrow invited another. Even the leaders wished to stop; they were not allowed to. Even they wished to pause; they were not allowed to. Finally, this thunderous approach led to reforms that in their magnitude are perhaps without precedent to date. . . .

Extemporaneous measures, designed to meet immediate needs, unintentionally completely changed our militant society into an industrial society and our aristocratic society into a democratic society. . . .

[Adapted from Tokutomi, *The Future Japan*, trans. Sinh et al., pp. 16–17, 158–59]

NORO EITARŌ

The optimism of the mid-Meiji period had long disappeared when the Marxists turned their attention to the Meiji Restoration in the late 1920s. For them, it was society rather than the nation that required urgent historical attention, what with capitalism in crisis, a rural economy in recession, and politics beset by forces of reactionary nationalism and imperialism. Toward that end, they debated the revolutionary nature of the Restoration, comparing it with the bourgeois (English and French) and socialist (Russian) revolutions of the West. With political economy as their frame and historical materialism as their method, they situated Meiji Japan as a stage in the inevitable world-historical development from feudalism to capitalism to socialism.

HISTORY OF THE DEVELOPMENT OF JAPANESE CAPITALISM
(NIHON SHIHONSHUGI HATTATSUSHI)

In this excerpt from the *History of the Development of Japanese Capitalism*, published in 1930, Noro Eitarō introduces a precursor of the Lectures Faction argument about the Restoration as a failed bourgeois revolution that resulted in an absolutist imperial state. In regard to political economy, Japanese capitalism emerged without ridding itself of "feudal remnants" in social and economic relations, among both capitalists in industry and "parasitic landlords" in agriculture. Here Noro criticizes, in turn, academic historians, bourgeois liberals and socialists, and rival Marxists of the Labor-Farmer Faction. At the same time, he suggests how Lectures Faction Marxists viewed the three main themes of Restoration history writing.

The Meiji Restoration was clearly a powerful political revolution, and—precisely because of that—it was a far-reaching social revolution as well.

It was not what it is generally understood to be: merely the restoration of imperial rule (*ōsei fukko*) or a struggle for political power within the feudal ruling class. Nor, however, was it [as some scholars say] a straightforward bourgeois revolution in which the propertied groups grasp political power.

Without doubt it was an epochal social change that constituted the beginning of the shift from feudal relations of production to the developing dominance of capitalist relations of production, and consequently also from the former feudal rulers to the establishment of the dominant authority of capitalists and "capitalistic" landlords. The Restoration thus comprised extremely far-reaching and complex political, economic, and social aspects.

Any detailed analysis and development of the revolutionary nature of the Meiji Restoration must be deferred to a work on "the history of the Meiji Restoration." Here I investigate just the epochal importance of the Meiji changes as the first step in the development of the dominance of capitalistic relations of production in Japan.

[Noro, *Nihon shihonshugi hattatsushi*, pp. 121–23; CG]

NAKAMURA MASANORI

The postwar period changed many things in Japan, including views of the Meiji Restoration. In the immediate postwar years, some invoked the *Meiji ishin* (literally, Meiji renovation) as a direct historical antecedent of the thoroughgoing reforms of the Occupation period, while others stressed the need to complete finally what the Restoration had left unfinished. The peace and prosperity of the 1960s returned the Restoration to its place as the narrative beginning of a successful modernity, at least in official and non-Marxist academic circles. Similarly positive appraisals appeared in translations of American works of what

Japanese scholars call the "modernization theory" school, referring (not always accurately) to most of the studies published by U.S. historians in the 1960s and 1970s. Marxist historians, meanwhile, continued to develop their prewar critiques and debates into the 1980s. By 1989, the year that both the Cold War and the Shōwa era ended, Nakamura Masanori (b. 1935), an economic historian who had once declared himself to be "the last of the Lectures Faction" in Marxist history writing, published an article entitled "The Meaning of the Meiji Restoration Today" in a leading national newspaper.

In it, he criticized the existing scholarship on the Meiji Restoration, including his own earlier views, and called for a reinterpretation in the light of postwar domestic and international developments, with a concomitant shift in vocabulary and emphasis. In addition, his world-historical characterization of the Restoration as a "revolution from above" reflected a different comparative perspective. Rather than the classic cases of England and France, he referred to modernization in what Immanuel Wallerstein called "semiperipheral" countries—in this instance, Scandinavia and central Europe—whose experience Nakamura likened to that of nineteenth-century Japan. Here, then, is a post-postwar progressive rendering that tells a differently weighted story of the Restoration.

"THE MEANING OF THE MEIJI RESTORATION TODAY" (MEIJI ISHIN KENKYŪ NO KONNICHITEKI IMI)

Because the prewar and, for a time, the postwar debates about the *Meiji ishin* were directly linked to revolutionary strategies in the present, they had an extremely politicized character, from whose fetters they are now freed.

Far more important than these debates, I believe, is the effect on Restoration scholarship of the high growth of the Japanese economy. After Japanese capitalism overcame the two oil shocks of the 1970s and the world came to see Japan as an "economic superpower," the view emerged that the origin of contemporary Japan's prosperity lay in the *Meiji ishin*. Added to this are the increasing numbers of foreign researchers from Asia and the Middle East who come to Japan to ask why Japan succeeded in modernizing in the *Meiji ishin* and to learn from its experience. This is a research context unimaginable twenty years ago.

In such circumstances, what issues should we consider in order to move Restoration scholarship forward once again?

The first is not to waste any more energy on the conceptual debate over whether the *Meiji ishin* represented a bourgeois revolution or the establishment of absolutism. The theories of the *kōza-ha* (lectures faction) originally rested on dual explanations of the *Meiji ishin* as either a bourgeois revolution or absolutism. And even the *rōnō-ha* (labor-farmer faction) version of the Restoration as a bourgeois revolution usually qualified it as an "incomplete" or a "backward-country-type" bourgeois revolution. Neither group thought that the

Meiji ishin had resulted in a classical Western-style bourgeois revolution or absolutism. As for myself, I have lately come to understand the *Meiji ishin* as a "bourgeois revolution from above"—neither a revolution nor a restoration but a reform—the "Meiji Reform." . . .

Second, I believe that one must consider the interpretations of the *Meiji ishin* as a "set" with those of the "postwar reforms" after World War II. . . . This is fine to define the meaning of the *Meiji ishin* itself, but to grasp the historical significance of the Restoration in the context of modern Japan, I think the postwar reforms must also be included.

This approach involves making clear which issues broached by the *Meiji ishin* were resolved and which remained unresolved and, further, which of the outstanding issues were resolved by the postwar reforms and which were not. . . .

Third, the most important part of the task is to clarify the relation between economic development and democracy. Previous research has shown that despite the hyperspeed of economic development in the modernization since Meiji—or indeed because of it—political modernization was retarded. And this question, I think, has a broader global scope. . . .

The Meiji Restoration and the postwar reforms offer excellent material for such a study. I predict that future research on the *Meiji ishin* will—and must—develop within this broader global framework.

[Nakamura, "Meiji ishin kenkyū no konnichiteki imi,"
Asahi shinbun, April 4, 1989; CG]

BANNO JUNJI

The postwar period saw a rise of non-Marxist interpretations of the Restoration that granted the revolutionary aspects of the Meiji reforms while stressing the contingencies—rather than the historical necessity—of the political process that resulted in the imperial nation-state. In general, these narratives present a fitful evolution of modern parliamentary politics within the framework of a constitutional monarchy, from the 1870s to the 1930s, and shift the focus from large-scale socioeconomic structure to the thoughts and deeds of political actors. Combining archival empiricism with the precepts of postwar social science, this work resonated with American accounts of the Restoration, such as Albert Craig's *Chōshū and the Meiji Restoration* and Thomas Smith's "Japan's Aristocratic Revolution," both published in the 1960s.

Impelled by concerns about contemporary parliamentary politics in its postwar forms, Banno Junji (b. 1937), a political historian at Tokyo University, concentrated on the Meiji outcomes of the Restoration rather than on the event itself. In the following excerpt from a book published in 1996, he summarizes his views of the historical strands woven, one way and another, into the political fabric of imperial Japan.

"MEIJI JAPAN'S NATION-BUILDING PROCESS"

The familiar expression "nation-building process" implies a complicated mix of revolutionary upheaval and construction. Such "construction" in Japan's case did not mean a time of pragmatic political leadership. Many leaders were driven by their own personal ideals of what the Meiji Restoration's "governmental revolution" implied and advocated practical measures based on these perspectives. As a result, even policies that at first glance seem completely pragmatic were simply attempts to achieve such ideals; on the other hand, quite violent and reactionary policies were proposed as feasible and realistic. A prime model for such reasoning in the former case was Industrialization from Above; in the latter, the demand for war with China in 1874. The first policy was enforced regardless of Japan's economic weakness and was therefore broken by fiscal realities. The second was rejected by the government, but its advocates were fully engaged in plans to mobilize troops and in making internal arrangements for war leadership.

Industrialization and expansionary nationalism were not the Meiji Restoration's only revolutionary aims. Even as early as 1868, after establishing imperial rule, the emperor's Charter Oath publicly promised Democracy from Above; after the Iwakura Mission to Europe and the United States of 1871–1873, leaders who regarded this as the Restoration's fundamental principle insisted on framing a constitution to embody the Charter Oath in detail. In short, productive industry, expansionary nationalism, and guided democracy became the basic ideals for nation building by the Meiji government after the "revolution." . . .

In the nation-building process of all countries, expansionary nationalism and democratization cannot always stand together in an equal balance. The Meiji Restoration was a "samurai revolution," not the result of demands by farmers who had been newly mobilized as conscript soldiers. . . . Nationalism of this kind and democratization were mutually opposed. If democracy was to advance, it had to supplant New Exclusionism; on the other hand, if complications with East Asia grew more constricting, progress toward democracy would be frozen.

. . . After victory in the 1894/1895 war against China, Japan succeeded in achieving a harmonious blend of the three aims of industrialization, expansionary nationalism, and democratization. At the same time, the fierce ideological struggles seen during the nation-building process faded away.

[Banno, "Meiji Japan's Nation-Building Process," in *Democracy in Pre-War Japan*, trans. Fraser, pp. 1–3]

BITŌ MASAHIDE

The surge of cultural nationalism in the 1980s and 1990s brought another wave of celebrational interpretations of the Meiji Restoration. Some took the form of civilizational histories, which found aspects of a distinctively Japanese modernity already present in Tokugawa "tradition." Others praised the Meiji leadership for providing an Asian model of pragmatic reform. In this selection, Bitō Masahide (b. 1923), an academic historian of Tokugawa Confucianism, presents a little of each of these, plus some others, in his treatment of the themes of new–old, inside–outside, and the nature of change—or lack of it—that characterized the Meiji Restoration.

WHAT IS THE EDO PERIOD?
(EDO JIDAI TO WA NANI KA?)

The boundary between the early modern [Tokugawa or Edo] and modern eras seems easily drawn because of the clearly defined changes of the Meiji Restoration. . . .

In the process there was resistance like that of the Satsuma Rebellion, and yet, smoothly, in a little more than twenty years a constitution was written and the Diet [parliament] was convened. Although this was a foreign system, it functioned to an extent because it was modern. In the context of world history, this was clearly a singular phenomenon. If one considers why this was possible, it comes down to the fact that—despite the great changes that occurred when Western civilization entered Japan before and after the Meiji Restoration—the actual organization of society scarcely changed at all. This was especially true of the villages, where the peasants, who comprised 90 percent of the population, lived, so that village organization constituted most of social organization as a whole. Names changed: village headmen became village officials and mayors, and other such changes were made. But these only introduced new names, leaving the actual village collective organization unaltered. In some sense, it persists to this day. . . .

Those in the higher strata of political authority as well—the court, shogunate, and feudal lords—were not entirely stripped of authority. On the contrary, they remained at the center of power, just as in the past, and only the form of the authority structures was changed. Of course, the higher strata were gradually pushed aside, as competent lower-level samurai and low-ranking court nobles assumed actual power. And yet the political authority of the former samurai and court nobles and court officials was not overthrown, but changing its form, it survived intact within the Meiji government. Therefore, to take the critical view, the Meiji Restoration was nothing more than an extremely compromised and incomplete reform, which left feudal authority intact, with the negative effect of preserving the feudal character of Japanese society until the end of World War II. It is perhaps no wonder that this criticism arose and that people still argue this way today.

. . . We must think, therefore, in terms of continuity. And precisely because of this continuity the Meiji Restoration was able to accomplish reform so smoothly. We can also see that since that time, Japan has managed to continue

to the present without any great disturbance. In this way, while the Meiji Restoration may seem clearly to demarcate a line between the period before and
after it, we now acknowledge that in fact the early modern and the modern are
continuous. At least that is what I think.

[Bitō, Edo jidai to wa nani ka, pp. 12–14; CG]

SHIBA RYŌTARŌ

In popular culture, the Meiji Restoration was rarely out of fashion, whether in
print, film, theater, television, or cartoons. Historical fiction and drama always
favored periods of turbulent change—in particular, the age of the Warring
States in the sixteenth century and the closing decades of the Tokugawa era,
which culminated in the Restoration. And whereas professional historians
stressed the role played by socioeconomic structures, political forces, and intellectual trends, popular history preferred exemplary heroes like Sakamoto
Ryōma and the forty-seven masterless samurai, whose individual or collective
actions were portrayed as having made history happen.

Shiba Ryōtarō (1923–1996), the most famous writer of postwar popular history, epitomized the so-called optimism boom of the 1960s. Turning away from
the dark years of imperialism and war, Shiba reveled in stories of "bright Meiji,"
which to him and his readers seemed to presage the prosperous status quo of
high-growth Japan. Youth and salarymen counted prominently among his millions of fans, whose enthusiasm meant that Shiba often had a best-selling novel,
a newspaper serial, ubiquitous magazine articles, and a blockbuster television
drama in the media at the same time. In 1968, the year of the Meiji centennial,
he published the Restoration novel *The Mountain Pass* (*Tōge*), which had been
serialized in the *Mainichi* newspaper for eighteen months. . . .

As in most of Shiba's works, the people in this excerpt from *The Mountain
Pass* are real historical figures engaged in a fictionalized conversation. Some of
his characters were famous, like Fukuzawa Yukichi, who here represents the
advocates of Western-style civilization in the remaking of the nation. Others
attained national fame after Shiba wrote about them, as was the case with Kawai
Tsugunosuke, the loyal samurai retainer whose devotion to his domain remained steadfast even after the cause was lost. No less forward-looking than
Fukuzawa, Kawai wielded Western firearms as he led his domain to defeat and
was killed in 1868 resisting the new imperial forces. Shiba's respect for the two
samurai says a great deal about his own view of the Restoration.

THE MOUNTAIN PASS
(TŌGE)

During the banquet, [Kawai] Tsugunosuke said to himself, "Ah, so that's how
it is," and now he understood everything about Fukuzawa [Yukichi]. . . .

"I've got it—who you are. But you're . . . how shall I say?" Tsugunosuke thought a bit, "a very unusual person."

Tsugunosuke understood that Fukuzawa's ideals and enthusiasm were bringing civilization to the country. To import the civilization that had ripened in Europe to the foreign environment of Japan, the soil had to be prepared for transplanting. The soil must first be fertilized with the thought of freedom and rights, and with this fertilizer, everything would have to change from the ground up.

The list of ideals that Fukuzawa embraced included such freedoms as the abolition of the status system, freedom of speech, freedom of belief, freedom of choice of occupation, and freedom of enterprise. Rights are the obverse side of freedom. And these rights are protected by the state. Creating a state that guarantees and protects rights was the ideal of Fukuzawa Yukichi, translator in the shogunal bureau of foreign affairs.

"That is why he's neither against the shogunate nor for it. For Fukuzawa, it's not a question of choosing the Tokugawa or Satsuma–Chōshū. As long as the people in power create the right kind of state, it's fine with him," thought Tsugunosuke, then confirming his thoughts aloud, "That's so, isn't it?"

Fukuzawa replied, "Yes, exactly. Because the state is supposed to protect civilization. That's all it is, and nothing more." . . .

. . . The saké bottle in front of Fukuzawa was now empty. Fukuchi Genichirō motioned for a waitress with his hand.

"Now, Kawai," said Fukuzawa, passing the cup to Tsugunosuke, "I want to hear about you."

"First I'd like to know whether you are for a monarchy centered on the Tokugawa or on Kyoto," inquired Fukuzawa.

Tsugunosuke shook his head.

"I take care to be as little interested as possible in such debates."

"In such debates?"

"Yes. I'd rather leave the debates over what to do with the realm to other samurai of spirit (*shishi*). For me, being a chief retainer of the Nagaoka domain of Echigo is more important, and that's all there is to Kawai Tsugunosuke."

"I'm surprised. You're purposely keeping your windows shut."

"That I am. I exist in this world solely as a chief retainer of the Nagaoka of Echigo. That's what I believe."

"That's just an argument from position."

"A person lives in his position. And I do not allow myself to step outside mine. That is my unshakable point of view."

"Difficult," said Fukuzawa, summing up his impression of Kawai Tsugunosuke with these words. . . .

Walking home, Tsugunosuke thought about the tragic character of human beings.

"I guess that describes me," he mused.

He understood Fukuzawa's point. More than understood, for he agreed with Fukuzawa Yukichi in advocating the complete opening of the country, and in farsightedness there was no difference at all between Fukuzawa and Tsugunosuke.

He also agreed that "a nation and society that distinguishes people by high and low status will not prosper." But since Fukuzawa was a thinker and Tsugunosuke was a politician, Tsugunosuke's expression of his beliefs had to take shape in reality, not words. Such a goal might well be a national task in the future, but his intention was to implement it, however late, within his own domain.

Not that Tsugunosuke considered this from the standpoint of the people's welfare. His interest in dismantling the status system of high and low lay instead in drawing men of talent from lower strata to serve the prosperity of the domain. While Tsugunosuke's opinion on this point was coming to resemble that of Fukuzawa, it had a slightly different tinge.

Tsugunosuke was a follower of Confucianism. He believed the tenets of Confucian political thought that serving the ruler promotes the welfare of the people and that the people should be ruled as benevolently as possible from above.

This was what Tsugunosuke meant by the "people," whereas Fukuzawa invoked a "people" whose expanding wealth, culture, and power would themselves produce a flourishing nation and society. Although Fukuzawa had doubtless not read Rousseau's original text on the right of liberty, he had grasped its very substance and made it his own. In any case, it was on this point alone that the two men differed; on the rest they felt the same.

And yet Tsugunosuke was not able to reach the same conclusion as Fukuzawa. . . .

. . . Fukuzawa understood progress through pure reason, but Tsugunosuke was strong in feeling. He regarded feeling as the virtue of a samurai and a gentleman and the most important value for him as a person.

[Shiba, *Tōge*, pp. 70–73; CG]

A HIGH-SCHOOL HISTORY TEXTBOOK

MODERN JAPANESE HISTORY
(*GENDAI NO NIHONSHI*)

This general summary is the introduction to modern Japanese history in a high-school textbook for Japanese History A, a course that deals with the modern and contemporary periods. It situates the Meiji Restoration in this longer history in a way that is conventional and also reflects its times, the 1990s, providing a comparison with other versions of this epochal event.

Modern and Contemporary Japanese Society

Around the middle of the nineteenth century, Japan gave up the policy of seclusion that had lasted for more than two centuries and set about modernizing itself on the lines of the countries of the West. Realizing that moves by the West to dominate the world had begun to extend to the vicinity of Japan, the men of the day decided, in order to safeguard Japan's independence, to open up the country and adopt the advanced civilization of the West, radically transforming the Japanese nation and its society. With the series of reforms that are referred to as the Meiji Restoration, Japan shifted from the closed, placid society of the Edo [Tokugawa] period to a society that was ceaselessly changing and developing, all the while deepening its relations with other countries. The Japan in which we live today is founded in the accumulated efforts toward modernization that began at this time.

Not all the things that this involved were desirable in themselves. In order to improve the national life, a long period of endurance was necessary. In the process, Japan committed aggression against neighboring countries, inflicting grave harm on them, then launched a major war, as a result of which it was defeated and occupied by foreign forces—the first such experience in its history. Because of its emphasis on trade, economic development—while creating for the first time a society in which people could live hopefully and enjoy an affluent consumer life—changed not only life within Japan but also the lives of people in other countries, creating in the process new problems such as environmental pollution and the depletion of resources.

In the following chapters, we shall study Japan's process of modernization, taking note of its relationship with trends in the West and Asia, getting to know the aspects that we can be proud of as well as those we have to reflect on in the legacy bequeathed us by our ancestors as we consider the way we should live from now on.

[Toriumi et al., *Gendai no Nihonshi*, p. 65; trans. adapted from International Society for Educational Information, *High School*, vol. 2 of *Japan in Modern History*, p. 65]

ALTERNATIVE HISTORIES

Because national histories are, by definition, ideologically and institutionally entrenched, they are frequently challenged from outside the halls of established scholarship. Modern Japan has a long and vital tradition of such alternative histories.

Alternative histories flourished in the early decades of the twentieth century, according to the historian Kano Masanao, who identified five attributes of this kind of history writing. Written against the state, it stressed the darker sides of modernization, focusing on the oppressed or discriminated against, including Okinawa, women, and the natural environment. Written against official national history, it preferred the private to the public, the daily life of the people to events in the life of the nation. It was also a social movement, which both studied the history of ordinary people and engaged ordinary people in the study of history, particularly in local history. Avoiding the imported rhetoric and missionary tone of academic history writing, it used ordinary language and valued experience and observation. Finally, as a part of the popular movements associated with Taishō democracy, these histories imagined an alternative modernity to the state-led version produced by the Meiji transplant of Western civilization. Where academic history was "external" in nature, these histories were "internal" to the understanding that ordinary Japanese had of their own experience.[1] For all these reasons, these "lay historians" had an impact on Japanese historical consciousness that was often stronger at the end of the century than at the time they wrote.

IFA FUYŪ

By the end of the twentieth century, Okinawa had become a favored site from which to relativize the dominant storylines of national history. Still seeking alternatives to the narratives of modernity focusing on the nation-state, historians looked to the margins and inner borders of an allegedly homogeneous Japan. They paid renewed attention to the Ainu and *burakumin* (former outcast communities) inside their national boundaries and to the Koreans, Taiwanese, and other colonial subjects of the empire outside the "home islands." Modern Okinawa had attributes of both: when the Meiji state annexed the Ryūkyū Islands and established Okinawa Prefecture in 1879, its people became Japanese nationals (*kokumin*), but with a distinction that was in fact discrimination and with legacies of an inner colonialism that outlasted Japan's formal empire.

Okinawans, of course, had long confronted the ambiguities of their place in modern Japanese history. Ifa Fuyū (1876–1947) played a pioneering role in the scholarly articulation of the abiding ambivalence of Okinawans caught between a desire to be fully accepted as Japanese and a wish to retain a distinctive identity derived from their own history and culture. Ifa's famous early work, *Old Ryūkyū* (*Koryūkyū*, 1911), reflected this ambivalence in the mirror of late Meiji times. By claiming "common ancestry," he was asserting a Ryūkyūan historical subject, but in the context of a Japanese national identity. By invoking the ethnic, racial, civilizational, and linguistic markers of a newly introduced anthropology, he aligned Ryūkyūans with the "nations" of Japanese and Chinese and, one step of kinship removed, Koreans as well, while distinguishing Okinawans from the

---

1. Kano, *Kasei suru rekishigaku*, pp. 239–41.

allegedly primitive Ainu and Taiwanese aboriginal "peoples" who were judged to be civilizational inferiors.

This was a hard line to draw, and in later years, Ifa came close to Yanagita Kunio in viewing his fellow "southern islanders" as fully Japanese, although with cultural attributes of earlier ages. Thus was Okinawa inserted into the prehistory of Japan, a place where Japanese might find living signs of their own lost past. Later-twentieth-century historians rejected this ethnographic colonialism but still faced the dilemma confronted by Ifa of how to do justice to the commonalities and the differences between Okinawan history and the national story that remained in the grasp of the main islands.

OLD RYŪKYŪ
(KORYŪKYŪ)

The most important thing to understand about today's Okinawans is that they are the descendants of people from Kyūshū who settled in the southern islands more than two thousand years ago. For a long time these ancient colonists maintained contact with their homeland. But in the fourteenth century all contact was cut off as a result of the hostilities between the Northern and Southern Courts in the homeland and the conflict among the three principalities in Okinawa. At this time, the Okinawans came into contact with the Chinese continent and became tributary subjects of the Ming, actively importing Chinese institutions and culture. The Okinawans of the time were Japanese in Chinese costume. In the fifteenth century, a heroic figure from Okinawa island named Shō Hashi unified the three principalities [in 1429, into the Ryūkyūan kingdom] and reestablished the long-severed contact with the homeland. The thought of Japan and China flowed into Okinawa, and by the beginning of the sixteenth century Okinawans had assimilated Japanese and Chinese civilizations and created an Okinawan culture. During this era of centralization under King Shō Shin [r. 1477–1526], Omoro poetry—which may be called the Man'yōshū of Okinawa—flourished, and stone inscriptions and personal letters were written in the Okinawan language. This spirit eventually issued forth, and trade began in the Southern Seas, with Yanbara ships sailing as far as the eastern shores of Sumatra, to the amazement of the Portuguese adventurer Mendez Pinto. The Okinawans of this period showed a character not unworthy of the valiant Yamato people. But in the misfortune of being wedged between two empires, Okinawans were unable fully to manifest their true character, and over time they came to be treated as the instruments [of others' interests]. And so, even during the era of national seclusion, the Shimazu clan [of Satsuma] took advantage of its location to trade with China by way of Okinawa. . . .

. . . I believe that Okinawans actively exerting their common character will make Okinawans a part of the powerful Japanese empire. Any attempt by force of habit to completely destroy the distinctiveness of Ryūkyūans would amount to severing the spiritual connection between the two peoples and ignoring their history. As I have just said, it is essential to let Okinawans exercise their common character [with Japanese], but it is perhaps necessary for them to display their differences as well. This is particularly true for Okinawans in the arts. To speak of differences may be a bit misleading, so let us speak rather of qualities that others cannot imitate. I believe that everyone possesses characteristics that others cannot possibly imitate. . . .

[Ifa, *Koryūkyū*, pp. 62, 89–90, 100; CG]

YANAGITA KUNIO

After Marx and Marxism, the greatest single influence on postwar history writing was neither a historian nor a theorist, but the founder of Japanese ethnography (*minzokugaku*) and folklore studies, Yanagita Kunio (1875–1962). Similar to the impact of cultural anthropology on Western history writing, Yanagita's works encouraged historians to shift their event-oriented and document-bound gaze to cultural practices and meanings expressed in oral, visual, and material form. In the context of Japanese history writing, Yanagita also offered an alternative to the dry positivism of academic history and the socioeconomic determinism of Marxism. He criticized both for their inattention to the lives of ordinary people, the textures of everyday life, and the rituals of community. Yanagita's romance of custom and the countryside amounted to a "new nativism" (*shin-kokugaku*), which mixed a critique of modernity with folk nationalism in the conservative culturalism characteristic of the 1930s.

ON FOLKLORE STUDIES
(*MINKAN DENSHŌRON*)

In this canonical summary of 1934, Yanagita Kunio outlined the new folklore studies, which, while owing its name to a translation of the French *tradition populaire*, is here described in Japanese terms. Yanagita matched the three objects of study in everyday life—material culture and custom, oral traditions, and beliefs and values—with three degrees of social distance, concluding that only the local people themselves could understand the last and most important of the three. Privileging the people as ethnographic insiders echoed his cultural arguments about the primacy of the folk and the singularity of national history. Later historians who drew on Yanagita for an alternative populist history also ran the risk of romanticizing the nation in the form of the ethnic people (*minzoku*).

1. The study of folk tradition is a discipline of the future. It is a sapling. It is up to us whether we plant it in the mountains or turn it into a bonsai. And so its adherents are able at the same time to be its prophets.

2. All disciplines once experienced a period of infancy, and many disciplines have already aged. Only our study of folk tradition is still malleable. . . .

4. Over the past thirty years, folklore studies has evolved sufficiently to draw attention to its future prospects. In Japan the ground for this discipline is as yet untilled, but the precedents in foreign countries have already shown us the path of its development.

5. We are now able to answer three important questions that must be settled first. The first is that of objectives, or to what degree knowledge can in fact be gained by collecting and analyzing folk traditions. It is clear that this knowledge may extend over nearly the whole history of human culture.

6. It is true that the areas in which we previously achieved results through these methods were limited. Also, since we collected so-called residual sources, they could easily be applied to any issue. In addition, the amount of material depended in the first instance on regional character (*kunigara*).

7. Scholarship begins with doubts arising in real life, and its judgments should be based on a knowledge of facts. This means that no cultural theory can ignore the course of a nation in earlier times. Much of folklore studies is the discovery of things that have previously gone unnoticed. All past explanations must now be reexamined in this light. . . .

9. The second issue concerns scope; that is, our present practices notwithstanding, what ultimately is the extent of folklore research relative to other disciplines? Historical study has certainly expanded its domain in recent times, but its capacity still is limited. What lies outside history's purview should now be taken over by other disciplines, so that no unclaimed spaces remain between them.

10. From the perspective of historical study, our discipline is so-called supplementary learning. Yet the areas in which documentary sources can be used are themselves extremely limited. As life's problems crowd in on us and the demand for explanations of past uncertainties grows, there are many instances that call for the aid of new methods. Although anthropology initially appeared with limited goals, it has now become a suitable name for the sum total of these methods. . . .

19. . . . The third issue arises from the question of "classification," which is essential to our consciousness of the value of our research. . . .

24. The first category includes the outward forms of daily life (*seikatsu*), collected by observation and by travelers. One might also call this a record of techniques of daily life (*seikatsu gijutsu*). What we know as compilations of indigenous customs were largely limited to this type, which folklore research in other countries did not ordinarily include.

25. The second category consists of interpretations of daily life, collected visually and orally by temporary residents. These are traditions that can be learned through the knowledge of language. From the names of things to narrative tales, all verbal arts are included in this category, which stands at the "marketplace on the boundary" between existing compilations of indigenous customs and the study of folk tradition.

26. The third category comprises the core, which is the consciousness of daily life (*seikatsu ishiki*), which involves collecting by inner feeling, that is, by the local people themselves. With rare exceptions, outsiders are not privy to this category, which is why local research is essential.

[Yanagita, *Minkan denshōron*, pp. 1–7; CG]

TAKAMURE ITSUE

The founding female figure in women's history, Takamure Itsue (1894–1964), worked for more than three decades secluded in the Tokyo suburbs writing comprehensive and provocative histories of women in Japan. Her most famous studies dealt with matrilineal and matrilocal marriage in early periods, in which she expressly countered Yanagita Kunio's male-centered views of marriage customs focused on "becoming a bride" with the "female principle" of "taking a groom," which was common practice until well into medieval times.

For Takamure, women's history and women's liberation belonged together, and she dedicated both her activism and her scholarly writings to the struggle against the long dominance of patriarchy in Japanese society. As an anarchist, in 1930 she founded the magazine *Women's Front* (*Fujin sensen*), in which she opposed all forms of state power, including socialism. As a historian, her concern with the family system and her "maternalism" were connected to contemporary social and political debates about the "protection of motherhood." Takamure's "new womanism" (*shinjoseishugi*), as she called it, places her among the early generation of twentieth-century feminists discussed in chapter 48.

The imposing *History of Women*, 1,261 pages in four volumes (1954–1958), presents Takamure's master narrative of Japanese history on the basis of "historical research from the standpoint of women." By this she meant a total women's history, not a female supplement to a narrative dominated by men. Writing from the perspective of Marxist historiography, she saw Japanese history as part of a universal world history, at least in its ultimate outcome, but her vision of that outcome made women, rather than class or the state, the pivot of a better world.

HISTORY OF WOMEN
(*JOSEI NO REKISHI*)

Volume 1: *Women-Centered Society*

PREFACE

This book may serve to encourage the correction of the conventional—in particular, the male-centered—view of history. "How should we live?" is a perennial human question, but never has the answer been as urgently sought as today, when the peace of humankind and the independence of peoples are threatened and the advance of women, too, is liable to be distorted. History must provide the answer to this question. . . .

CHAPTER 1: THE WOMEN-CENTERED ERA

In my view, the difficulty of women's movements and of the women's history that I am writing here is that in the end they are inseparable from "motherhood" (*bosei*). If women's history and women's movements remain solely a question of women's rights, they are easily understood and can be discussed by anyone. But when it comes to motherhood, things are not so simple. Such matters absolutely must be grounded in the genuine awareness and actions of women themselves. . . . I want it to be understood that the rights of mothers and children are in fact the ultimate women's rights and that they are unique to women. . . .

In short, what I attempt to do in this book is consider the history of the development in Japan from a primitive matriarchal society based on maternal identity through a patriarchal society based on the individual male self, to its correction in the present and the future. . . .

In the women-centered primitive era, there was no "home" (*katei, hōmu*). At the time, people were satisfied with group or visitation marriage, and the care of children was secured by the group or clan.[2] . . . [In modern times], the home is a symbol of patrilineality and patriarchy. . . .

The desire of our ancestors to seek the support and protection of the group was great indeed. So they created a "social organization" under the leadership of the clan matriarchs, who were the most spiritually powerful individuals of the time, thus taking the first step in the glorious history of humankind. And of course they began with what was extremely close at hand: the security of mothers and children. . . .

CHAPTER 2: HOW THE POSITION OF WOMEN REGRESSED

THE COLLAPSE OF WOMEN'S CULTURE: WHAT IS WOMEN'S CULTURE? In my view, the culture of the matrilineal era was a kind of naturalistic culture that preceded all forms of discrimination or categorization. Thus, at that time neither women nor men knew the sorts of oppression that appeared in later eras, and they were able to manifest their own naturalness with abandon and without fear. In this sense one might call it natural culture rather than women's

---

2. Visitation marriage refers to the husband's visiting the house where the wife resides and he does not.

culture. But since I wish to emphasize that this natural culture emerged through the female sex, I will call it women's culture. . . .

Until the end of the Kamakura era [in the fourteenth century], Japanese women had the capacity to see with their own eyes, think with their own minds, and act according to their own wills. As far as we can tell from the documents, Nara maidens (*otome*), Heian working women (*shokugyō fujin*), and Kamakura housewives (*shufu*) all possessed this ability.[3] Thus it is only in these periods that we can explore the tradition of women's culture of old. From the Muromachi era on, we women became almost completely incapacitated and, as a result, left no cultural legacy. . . .

Volume 2: *The Prison of Sex*

CHAPTER 3: THE ERA OF WOMEN'S HUMILIATION

JAPANESE WOMEN'S HISTORY SEEN THROUGH THE FUNDAMENTAL PRINCIPLES OF WORLD HISTORY: ANCIENT GREEK WOMEN AND JAPANESE WOMEN AFTER THE MUROMACHI ERA

The Muromachi era [1392–1573] in Japan corresponds to the extended patriarchal system in ancient [Greek] times. In the Edo era [of Tokugawa rule, 1600–1867], a rapidly maturing feudal authority suppressed this system, and a divided patriarchal system (*bunkai kafuchōsei*) emerged under its regime. As a composite of feudal and ancient practices, Edo was a "semiancient" era, which displayed its most backward dimension in the family system in particular. . . . I therefore regard this period as the peak of oppression of women in our country and call Edo the era of women's humiliation. By grasping the conditions of this age of humiliation as accurately as possible, I hope to make clear the origins of the ancient and feudal fetters that still afflict us today. . . .

The enslavement of women is synonymous with the commodification of sex. . . . In one case, women become merchandise as brides; in the other, they become merchandise as prostitutes. In civilized society, every demand is met in the form of commodities. And women are clearly one of those "demand goods." When there is a demand for labor, slaves are sold on the slave market, and when there is a demand for sex, sex slaves (*sei dorei*) are sold on the sex market. These two types of "human commodification" typically emerge together with the development of commercial and urban economies. It is obvious that in this respect, classical ancient Greece corresponds to the Muromachi era [and] onward in our country.

---

3. "Working women" and "housewives" are twentieth-century terms associated with modernity, used here to highlight the subjectivity of women that existed in earlier times but was later eclipsed by patriarchal feudalism.

ASIAN SOCIETY AND JAPANESE WOMEN'S HISTORY

The path of history is singular. Although the manner of concrete expression may vary, there is only one direction to history. Both our Asian society (in which blood relationships are more distorted and exploited) and European society (in which individualistic tendencies are more pronounced), while attaining historical development each in its own way, will in the end follow the single linear path that leads from a blood kin-based communal age to one of land-based individuals and, finally, to an era of social collectivity.

SO-CALLED COMMONER CULTURE: COMMONER CULTURE AND WOMEN

In the Momoyama times of Hideyoshi [late sixteenth century] . . . an invigorating and expansive atmosphere permeated society. The cities continued to flourish, frequent efforts to suppress them notwithstanding. . . . Meanwhile, however, the family system became stricter; trade in household slaves and transactions in brides were conducted ruthlessly and expansively under a strong patriarchal authority. Women had become dependents, losing almost entirely the property rights they had once possessed. We should not therefore be deceived by the word *expansive*. Consider the Greeks—let us remember that in the shadow of that civic freedom, slaves were writhing in iron chains. . . .

I conclude that this civic culture (*shimin bunka*)—townsmen culture (*chōnin bunka*) or so-called commoner culture (*shomin bunka*)—was in the end founded on the victimization of women and slaves, and, in the Edo period, on that of peasants as well. . . .

Volume 3: *The Dawn of Liberation*

PREFACE

Stirrings of the liberation of women in Japan began with the so-called opening of the country and the Meiji Restoration. [In imperial Japan] women endured the oppression of semifeudal Japanese capitalism and the reorganization of the family system. Then, as a result of the new constitution promulgated with the establishment of a bourgeois democracy after World War II, liberation reached the stage of the realization of equal rights for men and women.

CHAPTER 4: WOMEN ARE NOW RISING (1)

THE OPENING OF THE COUNTRY AND GEISHA GIRLS

The opening of the country brought a stream of foreign officials and merchants. Fujiyama and geisha girls (*geisha gaaru*) became the symbols of an international Japan. . . . We cannot overlook the important significance of geisha girls in

Meiji women's history [1868 1912]. Geisha girls caught the eyes of foreigners precisely because they were active on the front lines of social life, in place of ordinary women, who were enslaved in the household.

JAPANESE-STYLE "GOOD WIFE, WISE MOTHER"-ISM

Japanese-style "good wife, wise mother"-ism suited the reorganized patriarchal system [of imperial Japan] because it was an ambiguous composite of Confucian and some Western-style values. . . . The main characteristic that distinguishes the Japanese-style "good wife, wise mother" ideology from that of the West derives from two of its fundamental ideas: "no need for serious learning for women" (denial of women's education) and "boys and girls separate after age seven" (denial of mixed society). Thus, the good wife of Japan, unlike the good wife of the West, who is a helpmeet in all aspects of life, was more on the order of a housekeeper. A wise mother, too, was meant to be more a nanny than someone wholly in charge of her children's education.

THE REORGANIZATION OF THE PATRIARCHAL SYSTEM

In the Meiji Civil Code, which went into effect in 1898, patriarchal authority was reorganized in the authority of the head of household, with some touches of modernism added. . . . The Civil Code was a retrograde law that harked back to the old patriarchal system, bypassing even the limited patriarchal system of Edo samurai (which did not include married younger sons) in favor of the even more backward divided patriarchal system of commoner families (patriarchal extended families). . . . In the patriarchal system, the family in general is enslaved, but the women's position is that much more slavelike, and after daughters grow up and are married into another family, their status remains similarly low.

CHAPTER 5: WOMEN ARE NOW RISING (2)

WOMEN'S SELF-AWARENESS AND WOMEN'S MOVEMENTS

Although Seitō [Bluestocking] was a purely literary movement, there is no doubt that the single sentence "in the beginning, woman was the sun," [which Hiratsuka Raichō wrote in 1911] in the founding issue of its journal, was the initial "declaration of women's rights" in Japan [see chap. 48]. . . . It can be said that her "declaration of women's rights" was quite Japanese in that it was the voice of a tradition that stemmed from women's rituals in primitive Japan (the ideology of primitive communal society). . . . The latent genius of Japanese women lies in transcending the process of equal rights for men and women associated with present-day capitalist society, passing through the stage of socialist revolution by the masses, and envisioning the recreation of the primitive in a new form. . . .

Volume 4: A *Century of Women Workers*

CHAPTER 6: WOMEN ARE NOW RISING (3)

It was assumed that woman's employment was marriage and that her calling lay in housework. For men, in contrast, marriage was understood as employing a female servant called a wife, and beyond that men were expected to follow [the dictates of] national production. These assumptions were undercut in the Meiji period. The main national industries were built on women's labor because as household industry was socialized (*shakaika*), women's labor was socialized with it. A woman who was pulled out of the household in this way came to bear double labor, both of the household and of society, in a single body. This double labor constitutes the greatest inevitable and tragic duty of women in a capitalist society. . . .

CHAPTER 7: WOMEN ARE NOW RISING (4)

CRISIS CULTURE AND WOMEN

Paying no heed to the voices calling for woman's duty in the home, cruel capitalism hauled women out of the house in numbers. Those who disliked having women wrenched from the home would have had to oppose capitalism itself, which they could not do. Women's labor was no exception but was everywhere a necessary component of modern production, including in the main national industries. . . . In this way, the conflict between home and workplace surfaced in the realm of women's labor, and as the old-style family system gradually waned, the reconstruction of a new family system became inevitable. . . .

CHAPTER 8: TOWARD A CENTURY OF LOVE AND PEACE

THE PEACE MOVEMENT: MOTHERS RISING UP

A mother's love is a love of life. For a long time, mothers entrusted their children's lives to their fathers, but that history has been largely tragic. The fathers' century was a century of "power," in which wealth and brute force were praised and the philosophy of the survival of the fittest reigned. And because of this, the fathers' century has seen unceasing war. . . .

THE AWAKENING OF THE WORLD (2)

Mothers demand peace. In the eyes of mothers no time has ever seemed as terrible as the present. . . .

The world is awakening . . . except for a portion of the ruling strata, the conscience of the masses is already widely and irrepressibly awakening to the voices of peace. Capitalism will not immediately perish, but people are gradually comprehending that civilized people trust the progress of society to issue from peaceful coexistence. From the viewpoint of mothers especially, peace itself is everything. And so it is clear that the awakening of the mothers of the world to peace will continue to grow.

Mothers of the world and the masses, unite! Halt the utterly tragic war of human extinction that threatens us, and go forward in a century of peace and love. . . .

A CENTURY OF LOVE

Throughout this book I have emphasized that "when the economic system becomes communal, the kinship system becomes matrilineal." In a matrilineal society, child care is communalized, housework is socialized, and mechanized production is promoted on the principle of the labor of all the people. It is, in short, the society of a "century of women workers."

[Takamure, *Josei no rekishi*, vol. 4, pp. 1, 4–5, 11, 68, 225–27, 240, 248–49, 261, 469–70, 473–74; vol. 5, pp. 1, 497, 553, 583–84, 721, 723, 902, 995, 1031, 1040, 1046, 1053; CG]

JAPANESE HISTORY IN COMPARISON

Historical thinking everywhere favors analogy, and scholars scan the past for instances of similarity to or difference from the subject at hand. Modern history writing, of the sort that originated in Europe and is now practiced in hybrid forms around the world, built Western exemplars into the very categories of history, from the term "modernity" itself and an array of opposites like "pre-modern" and "tradition" to component parts such as revolution and the nation-state. By definition, then, histories of modern Japan are always already comparative. Whether the comparison is with the West, Asia, the world, or some "universal" principle, every text here is implicitly or explicitly set in a comparative frame.

The examples of comparison in this section represent influential attempts since the 1960s to approach the perennial problem of how and why Japan's history differs from other experiences in the universe of historical possibilities. Individual historians, of course, defined this universe in different ways and often left unstated the comparisons that drove their analysis. It is therefore worth examining the following excerpts to identify what the historians had in mind for what was "not Japan" as they argued the case for what was. Recurrent themes again included the dialectic between internal and external factors, the relation between change and continuity, and the undertow of a cultural essentialism that seemed to postulate some enduring Japaneseness that stood outside, or underlay, the course of history. In the background, too, was the general assumption of modern history writing that the early national modernizers, England and France in particular, set the pattern with which all subsequent cases necessarily had to be compared. The history of modern Japan, like that of Germany and other countries, was thus saddled with what Narita Ryūichi called the burdens of "negative particularism," which treated historical difference as a deviation from the proper course of modern development. One reaction to this burden of difference was an insistence on an indigenous path to a distinctively Japanese modernity. This often nationalistic view retained the comparative framework while turning negative difference into positive distinctiveness, even uniqueness.

MARUYAMA MASAO

As a scholar and public intellectual, Maruyama Masao (1914–1996) was one of the emblematic figures of the early postwar period. Influenced by Marxism and Anglo-American liberalism in his youth, Maruyama emerged from the war with a left-liberal commitment to civil democracy and civic responsibility. To realize these goals, Maruyama and others engaged in a sustained diagnostic effort to ascertain what had gone wrong in the past. In his view, the postwar challenge was to rectify the flawed modernity of imperial Japan, which had culminated in imperialism, fascism, and war.

Maruyama described his field as the study of politics (*seijigaku*). Whether his subject was Tokugawa Confucianism, Meiji intellectuals, prewar fascism, or postwar democracy, Maruyama pursued the question of what constituted modern politics and what had prevented it from developing in Japan. His European definitions of both modernity and politics led historians of other persuasions first to label his work "modernism" and later to accuse of him of an elitist nationalism of the sort espoused in the Meiji period by Fukuzawa Yukichi, one of Maruyama's lifelong interests. In both respects, he was a man of his times, poised like the title of one of his books, "between the war and the postwar," examining a bad past for the sake of a better future.

"THE STRUCTURE OF *MATSURIGOTO*: THE BASSO OSTINATO OF JAPANESE POLITICAL LIFE"

In this essay from the 1970s, Maruyama Masao describes principles that he claimed have operated in Japanese history since ancient times. In other works, he uses a geological metaphor of "ancient strata" to evoke the practices of the remote past that continued to affect the present. Here he adds the musical metaphor of a "basso ostinato," which he identifies as the determining mechanism of the relation between change and continuity, internal and external factors. What comparisons did he have in mind that generated this interpretation and with what implied effect for modern history and politics?

In recent years I have been working on the problem of continuity and change in Japanese intellectual history. Often this problem is discussed as general theory, using one of the world's cultures as an illustration. My problematic, however, is not simply to apply this kind of general inquiry to the case of Japan. Japan is characterized by a degree of homogeneity—homogeneity in terms of race, language, mode of agricultural production, etc.—unusual among the highly industrialized nations of the world. This homogeneity has profoundly affected the ways in which continuity is related to change in the course of Japanese history. Often it is emphasized how much Japan has changed despite basic continuities; I, however, prefer to ask whether historical changes occurred not in spite of, but precisely because of, some basic continuous factors that underlie the Japanese experience. It is in this context that I believe Japan's exceptional homogeneity is relevant, since it has allowed those continuities to persist over a long period and through diverse kinds of historical change.

In grappling with this inquiry I hope to elucidate what might be called the basso ostinato of Japanese history. I use this musicological metaphor, for no other adequate expression comes to mind. In music the basso ostinato, as distinct from the basso continuo, is a recurrent pattern of bass notes. It is an underlying motif that is independent from the treble part, and if the main theme appears in the treble part, it is bound to undergo some modifications by this basso ostinato. This metaphor may be applied to the historical development of Japanese thought. Most of the main themes have been imported from abroad since ancient times, beginning with Confucianism, Daoism, [and] Buddhism and including modern ideologies such as liberalism, constitutionalism, anarchism, socialism, and so on. In this context, any attempt to construct a coherent system of political thought deserving to be called the Japanese Way was bound to fail. If, however, we examine the circumstances in which those ideologies underwent modifications after they arrived in Japan from the Asian continent or from the West, certain patterns of thinking similar in each case emerge, each responsible for subtly changing the original. These recurrent patterns of thinking are those which I have termed the basso ostinato of Japanese intellectual history.

In this chapter I intend to examine the basso ostinato of the Japanese political way of thinking. First, I have selected certain pivotal words which ancient Japanese used in their references to government and politics. Second, I have made a paradigm from these words in order to show the structure of political consciousness in ancient Japan. The documents from which I have selected the pivotal words were compiled around the seventh and eight centuries and include such works as the *Kojiki, Nihon shoki, Shoku-Nihongi, Fudoki, Man'yōshu, Engishiki, Kogoshūi*, and others. Needless to say, these texts, the oldest extant examples of Japanese literature, are valuable sources of ancient

Japanese myth and history. In the seventh and eight centuries the Yamato dynasty established a system of government modeled on the centralized bureaucracy of the Tang dynasty, and the paradigm here relates directly to the political institutions that emerged during that period, which later came to be called the *ritsuryō* system. My purpose here, however, is not to describe the political history of ancient Japan as such. My selection of pivotal Japanese words from the documents mentioned above is made because I think the period of intense encounter with continental Chinese civilization is best for isolating those bass notes that give color to the main theme which the ruling class of Japan intentionally adopted from the Chinese empire.

. . . The word *matsurigoto*, which is used here in the sense of "matters governmental," in which sense it is expressed by the Chinese characters, which in turn may also be read *seiji* (politics). . . .

. . . The first point is the way in which the separation of the level of legitimacy from the level of actual political power—this particular bass note—influenced the large-scale adoption, both theoretical and institutional, of the Chinese system of centralized bureaucracy by the Yamato court in the seventh century. The dramatic change of the system of government under the influence of Tang China at that time may well be compared with the adoption of the Western political system after the Meiji Restoration. Nevertheless, what was noteworthy was that a new institution was interposed between the emperor and his ministers. It was called the *dajōkan*. The *dajōkan*, literally translated, was a council of great government and became the highest organ of the Japanese state. In China there was no counterpart to the *dajōkan*, since it was taken for granted that the emperor was both the source of legitimacy and the holder of supreme power. . . . In Japan, however, the emperor did not govern. His subordinates conducted *matsurigoto*. Hence an organ like the *dajōkan* was necessary. Thus, though the Japanese were thorough in their adoption of Tang institutions, setting up even the most minor of offices, they nonetheless found it necessary to invent a new organ, the *dajōkan*, which was an intermediary between the emperor and the bureaucracies.

Another important modification of the Chinese imperial system was the notion of joint rule. This was expressed in ancient documents as *tomo ni osamu* (ruling together). This idea had already been expressed in the half-legendary constitution issued by Prince Shōtoku in 604. There had been various kinds of joint rule in ancient and early medieval Japan; for example, the joint rule of emperor and crown prince, of emperor and a member of a powerful clan (such as the Fujiwara), of emperor and abdicated emperor. . . . In this sense the basso ostinato of Japanese emperorship has been poly- rather than mono-archic. . . .

The above-mentioned points, first on the separation of the level of legitimacy from the level of decision making and, second, on the concept of joint rule, were bound to obscure the locus of ultimate responsibility concerning matters governmental. The other side of the coin was that this same pattern made it difficult for despotism or dictatorship to establish itself in Japan.

These patterns of institutional modification that occurred in the seventh and eighth centuries were repeated again and again in the course of Japanese history. For example, imperial regents, *sesshō* and *kanpaku*, soon became permanent institutions instead of temporary ones as existed in imperial China. Beginning with *sesshō* and *kanpaku*, extralegal officials not mentioned in the *ritsuryō* codes emerged during the Heian period. These have come to play important roles in the governmental process, thus increasing distance not only between the levels of legitimacy and actual power but also between the *dajōkan* and formally inferior bureaucrats. This trend was even more dramatically revealed by the establishment of the Kamakura shogunate at the end of the twelfth century. With the emergence of the Kamakura shogunate, the power of decision making in Japan moved, on a large scale, to the shogun and away from the court. And yet the emperor remained the source of legitimacy; it was from him or, more strictly, from the imperial family that the shogun derived his legitimate power to rule. And what is striking was that this same pattern was revealed within the shogunal government itself, since the internal structure of the Kamakura shogunate soon came to resemble that of the court bureaucracy it had replaced. From as early as the thirteenth century, the Hōjō clan came to exercise power on behalf of the shogun in the name of the shogunal regent (*shikken*). . . .

In all these cases, the relationship between power and legitimacy is the same, always separate and distinct, whether between the *dajōkan* and the emperor, or between the regent (*sesshō* or *kanpaku*) and the emperor, or between the shogun and the emperor, or between the shogunal regent (*shikken*) and the shogun. The same relationship persists throughout. In every case the nominal servant, the one who offers service, is the actual wielder of power.

This state of affairs produced two trends as the official system began to degenerate. First, power tended to devolve downward to subordinates; that is, to lower and lower status levels. . . . Second, public power tended to become more and more informal and private, so that the private employee of a family or a group set up within a private household to manage the household finances ended up by conducting public affairs of government. This informalization had already begun even when the imperial court still retained public authority, and it continued in the successive shogunal governments. . . .

The two trends mentioned above converged: power developed downward at the same time as it became more informal and private. The climax of this convergence was *gekokujō*, or inferiors overpowering their superiors, a phenomenon which characterized the fifteenth and sixteenth centuries when powerful local warriors rose to power and chaos prevailed. The remarkable thing, however, is that no matter how extreme *gekokujō* may have been, it never led to any change in the level of political legitimacy in Japan as a whole. Toyotomi

Hideyoshi, one of the great unifiers of the late sixteenth century, was symbolic of his age. He rose from the peasantry to the highest level of political power; and yet only the title of *kanpaku* (regent to the emperor), conferred on him by a powerless emperor, could legitimate his supreme position.

Where government is conceived primarily in terms of service offered to a superior by a subordinate and where the source of legitimacy is strictly separated from the actual possessor of power, revolution of the system is most unlikely to occur. This paradox is revealed in modern history as well. In what is known as *gekokujō* within the military in the 1930s, power devolved downward from the general staff to low-ranking field officers. The climax of this downward movement was the insurrection of February 26, 1936. Yet this incident failed to bring about a revolution even in the structure of the army, let alone the state. A court noble serving Emperor Hirohito, as the Duc de la Rochefoucauld-Liancourt served Louis XVI, might well have replied to the emperor's question: "Is it a revolution?"

"No, sire, this is nothing but a revolt called *gekokujō*—a recurrent phenomenon in Japanese history."

[Henny and Lehmann, eds., *Themes and Theories in Modern Japanese History*, pp. 27–29, 38–43]

IROKAWA DAIKICHI

The rise of "people's history" (*minshūshi*) in the 1960s entailed a commitment to resituate historical action and agency outside the state and its elites, usually among the common people of the countryside. The people's historians expressed dissatisfaction with Marxist history writing because of its overly exclusive focus on impersonal socioeconomic structures, and they criticized Maruyama Masao's style of modernism for its concern with elites and its European orientation. Most belonged to the generation too young to have played a role in the road to war but old enough to have been affected by the defeat. Their dedication to popular democracy and to people's history also reflected the political mood of the 1960s and the scholarly trends of "history from below" in other places, although the emphasis in Japan fell less on social history than on a cultural history of popular mentalities and values.

The landmark work of Irokawa Daikichi (b. 1925), literally translated as *A Spiritual History of Meiji* (*Meiji seishinshi*), was filled with accounts of colorful local figures, collective popular action, and the contributions of educated peasants to such modern phenomena as parliamentary politics and constitutions. No less concerned with the baneful effects of the "emperor system" of 1868 to 1945 than the postwar Marxists and Maruyama, people's historians identified an alternative tradition in the popular past. In their view, this indigenous dynamic, rooted in Tokugawa villages and Meiji local society, was squelched by modernizing elites in the name of the imperial state. Like historians elsewhere who were increasingly drawing on anthropological approaches, the popular historians evoked the ethnography of Yanagita Kunio, who for Irokawa effectively replaced Karl Marx and Max Weber as a methodological guide for writing a modern history of the common people.

Enshrining the popular tradition in the historical mainstream in no way resolved the problems posed by the dominant narratives of modernity. The relation of Japan's experience to that of Asia, the West, and the world remained a leitmotif even for those who insisted on the importance of internal factors in the historical passage to modern times. The following selection from the introduction to Irokawa's best-selling book, *The Culture of the Meiji Period* (*Meiji no bunka*), written in the wake of the Meiji centennial of 1968, suggests the comparative frame for his understanding of the nature of Japan's modern history.

THE CULTURE OF THE MEIJI PERIOD
(MEIJI NO BUNKA)

Where does what we call "Meiji" fit in with world history and culture, and what significance does it have? To answer those questions we have to decide what qualitative change was involved in the mid-nineteenth-century response to Western influence by a Japan that had maintained the "independent culture of an island country" for over a millennium without being enveloped by a continental world power. In this respect Japan is too unusual for it to be taken as a model for underdeveloped countries. That is, countries like Japan and Russia, which maintained their independence when they came into contact with the modern civilization of the West, provide a contrast to countries that were colonized or dependent. They proved relatively adept at receiving and adapting and managed to develop economic and military strength, but on the other hand their appropriation of the imported culture was partial, and it brought an extended period of facile imitation and confusion. . . .

. . . [T]he cultural level and degree of national consciousness people attained when their countries experienced the impact of the West constitutes an important consideration for their ability to resist subjugation. In the case of Japan there was the maturity of early modern culture and the legacy of Dutch studies; the wide diffusion of education and the spiritual self-discipline the masses had developed were combined with the patriotic spirit that they came to share. . . .

If it was only in the Meiji period that the Japanese were able to bring forth things that had begun to germinate in Tokugawa times, then what are these modern "elements" that we can designate in "Meiji culture"? One is a clear response to human rights. Democratic self-awareness became particularly evident during the 1880s as a popular groundswell during the Movement for People's Rights. Another is probably an awakening individualism, a kind of self-consciousness, as we have seen in the poems of Takamura Kōtarō. This was particularly strong among those who had direct experience of the West or with the concepts of Christianity, and it was notably current among members of the former samurai class and the intelligentsia. But even among ordinary people a modern kind of individual consciousness was developing slowly, in concert with the breakdown of ideas of "village" and "household" that had characterized feudal society; to be sure, it was seldom felt as sharply as it was by Takamura. Third, elements of capitalism—materialistic values, utilitarianism, and practicality—began to replace the old values that had had a more spiritual basis. Striking aspects of this transition were to be found in the decline of Confucian ethics and the ideals of *bushidō*.

A fourth and final aspect of modern culture was the rapid strengthening of an ethnic and national self-consciousness that encompassed virtually all of society. This showed itself through the rediscovery of Japanese aesthetics after an infatuation with those of the West and in the reevaluation of Japanese morality, tradition, and view of life. Okakura Tenshin's new Japanese Art movement, Kōda Rohan's movement for native literature, the folklore movement of men like Yanagita Kunio, and the National Essence movement of Miyake Setsurei and Kuga Katsunan were all examples of this. . . .

I think these four elements (self, democracy, capitalism, and nationalism) are the principal components that make up modernity in all countries and not in Japan alone. General theory can be developed only after definite determination of the relationship of these elements to each other in other countries, in addition to an examination of the way those relationships posed logical inconsistencies.

For instance, when self and democracy were unable to mature because of the suppression of the movement for people's rights, the growth of capitalism and of nationalism became distorted; with that, in the Meiji period, came the emergence of the "emperor system" as the focus and node of this set of contradictions. We have to understand that those special characteristics that are cited as fundamental characteristics of Meiji culture—eclecticism, family (*ie*) consciousness, nativism, localism, naturalism, shortcomings in civic and in public consciousness—are all ultimately elements in the "emperor system as a spiritual and mental structure."

Consequently it is of vital importance to trace the historical process in which that emperor system was hammered out and then to examine the process whereby it penetrated the minds of the Japanese. Furthermore, in order to relativize it, and to overcome it from within, to avoid regarding it as something transcendental and foreordained, we have to examine carefully the subterranean consciousness of Japan's common people from early to recent times. That task in turn requires us to employ, however modestly, the findings of specialists in related disciplines like folklore, religion, sociology, geography, and anthropology.

[Irokawa, *The Culture of the Meiji Period*, pp. 15–18]

YASUMARU YOSHIO

An influential analyst of people's history, Yasumaru Yoshio (b. 1934) made his mark by identifying popular consciousness as a driving force in modernization. Changes in what he called the popular, or conventional, morality (*tsūzoku dōtoku*) of Tokugawa villages transformed Confucian values into practices of collective self-formation that enabled the people to become the active agents of their own, and Japan's, social transformation. At the same time, Yasumaru recognized that local visions of change could also subject the people to the totalizing forces of capitalism and the emperor-system state. He neither romanticized the countryside nor essentialized Japan as unchanging, but instead sought the historical specificities that accounted for the way Japanese modernity evolved. The following passage includes his criticisms of other approaches and suggests his view of the appropriate uses of comparison in writing the history of modern Japan.

"NATIONAL RELIGION, THE IMPERIAL INSTITUTION, AND INVENTED TRADITION: THE WESTERN STIMULUS"

Explanations of Japan's modernization put forward since World War II generally fall into two categories. One approach stresses discontinuity, citing premodern elements and backwardness that had to be overcome by modernization. The other emphasizes continuity, asserting that particularistic aspects of Japanese society and culture furthered modernization.

A break with the past accorded with Japanese thinking in the early postwar years when the national psyche was battered by defeat and hopeful for a fresh start. Discontinuity was the hallmark of the sweeping postwar reforms and democratic movements. From about 1960, as rapid economic growth began to define popular consciousness, continuity came to the fore. Groupism and its underlying values, for example, were lauded as determinants of modernization and the economic "miracle."

Selective affirmation of the past sparked a flurry of books from the 1960s celebrating the uniqueness of Japanese and Japanese culture—*Nihonjin-ron*. This introspective, self-congratulatory genre was a response to and finally supplanted the crusading social science and Marxist historiography dominant through the 1950s. Even Maruyama Masao, the famous scholar of political thought who personified postwar enlightenment, addressed such themes as the "prototypes" and "ancient strata" of Japanese thought, on the assumption that enduring features of Japanese society were sustaining economic growth. Amino Yoshihiko, the most influential Japanese historian from the 1970s, disputed the standard paradigm of Japanese society—rural communities engaged in paddy-field rice agriculture—and demonstrated the importance of nonfarming occupations such as commerce and fishing, showing that trade and transportation via coastal waters and rivers had created a national market. Although both Maruyama and Amino were critical of social oppression as well as of Japan's colonialism and aggression in East Asia, they were interested in the vitality and energy that drove modernization. Maruyama noted that Japan's communal-style society had a semi-open functional rationality, while Amino emphasized its diversity and dynamism. For them to conclude that openness and diversity characterized ancient Japan suggests that even Maruyama and Amino favored a cultural essentialist explanation of rapid economic growth.

It is clearly impossible to show that distinctive aspects of modern and contemporary Japanese society existed in earliest times, or to prove such a thesis historically. But European history provides two valuable insights: (1) new phenomena tend to be created freely from an existing tradition and then take root, and (2) in the formative period of the modern nation-state, legitimacy based on ancient folk or ethnic traditions is a powerful truth of the new nationalism. In the transition to a modern society, Japanese, too, re-created a premodern artifact; "invented tradition," the term used by Eric Hobsbawm and others, is applicable to Japan.

It is my contention that in the case of Japan, new institutions were molded to fit the nation-state and affected social norms and individual attitudes far more than the government system and advanced civilization imported from the West. Western stimuli were incorporated into the invented tradition, but the prototype was unrecognizable, facilitating the transformation.

Critics of the emperor system have considered it the embodiment of feudal elements and backwardness, the antithesis of modern enlightenment. They often affix adjectives like "ancient" and "Asian" to denote its extreme repression of individuality and autonomy.

Defenders asserted that the monarchy was an immutable tradition and spiritual pillar for Japanese; since World War II, they have stressed that the throne is a cultural device unrelated to aggression and militarism. From this standpoint, the merger of religious ritual and government administration (*saisei itchi*) at the start of the Meiji period (1868–1912) and the ultranationalism from 1931 to 1945, when Japan invaded China and went to war against the Allied Powers, were deviations from the original imperial tradition. The emperor's status in the 1947 constitution—a "symbol of the State and of the unity of the people" under popular sovereignty and democracy—is consistent with tradition, say the monarchists.

Both the critics and supporters describe the institution in value-laden terms and offer a suprahistorical explanation of the monarchy, in my view. Of course, one can treat the monarchy as an institution by showing its ancient origins; however, when particular historical moments are examined in detail we find a very different reality in each era. For example, there is an enormous difference between an emperor who was not permitted to leave the Imperial Palace, the case for more than two hundred years from the sixteenth to the eighteenth centuries, and an emperor who toured the country in military uniform surrounded by generals and martial pomp. In the Tokugawa period (1600–1867) emperors were permitted only a ritual role in a restricted space; from the Meiji period emperors were at the pinnacle of absolute authority over political and military affairs. Historians must examine the specific conditions and causative forces behind this amazing transformation. . . .

[Hijiya-Kirschnercit, cd., *Canon and Identity*, pp. 167–69]

THE ASIA-PACIFIC WAR IN HISTORY AND MEMORY

Like the Meiji Restoration, World War II appeared in Japanese historical consciousness as a break in time, suggesting the end of one era sharply sundered from the beginning of another, as if history could start "anew." History, of course, could do no such thing, and the illusion of rupture only made questions of continuity and change that much more pressing. People tended to see everything before the two epochal events as leading toward them, as in the (inevitable) decline of the Tokugawa shogunate culminating in the Restoration and the (inevitable) rise of fascism culminating in war and defeat. It took a long time for historians to reconnect the nineteenth century across the divide of 1868 and the twentieth century across that of 1945, all the while arguing among themselves about what had changed and what had not—and what they thought ought to have changed, according to their particular version of the tale of modernity.

But the war was different from the Restoration, not least in its catastrophic outcome. The so-called reckless war was taken as a judgment not only on the conflict itself but on the whole of Japan's modern history, strengthening the widespread feeling of need for a "new beginning." This was one reason why John Dower described the Japanese as "embracing defeat" under the Allied Occupation, which followed unconditional surrender in 1945. This embrace included reflecting on the prewar past and recounting the war in such a way that its story could serve the postwar future. This meant identifying the actors and factors responsible for the conflict and reforming the conditions that had made war possible. In the original narrative that emerged in 1945, the war was told as a cataclysm brought on the Japanese people by a misguided leadership acting within a flawed political, social, and ideological system. Once the leaders were replaced, the system reformed, and the Peace Constitution established, the existence of a peaceful and prosperous Japan seemed to validate the original story of the war as a bad past now replaced by a good present. As chapters 44 and 45 make clear, postwar Japanese continued to speak as if 1945 marked an epochal moment in their history. Whether conservative politicians were celebrating the economic rise of the "new Japan" or progressive intellectuals were criticizing democracy and Cold War geopolitics for resembling the old Japan too closely, the postwar myth of a new beginning retained its power.

Although the postwar myth nurtured identity, it created problems for history and memory. This was not because people forgot the war or refused to speak of "war responsibility" (*sensō sekinin*). On the contrary, the debates about responsibility began immediately and recurred frequently. The original war story of a people victimized by their leaders was underscored by American Occupation reforms and dramatized in the Tokyo war crimes tribunal, which tried twenty-eight of these leaders for aggressive war and atrocities. The renunciation-of-war clause in the constitution and the atomic bombings of Hiroshima and Nagasaki symbolized the nation's postwar mission for peace. The problem, then, was not collective amnesia but the all-too-simple story enshrined in public memory of the war. It focused on Pearl Harbor and the atomic bomb but not on Manchuria and the Nanjing massacre, assigned responsibility to the leadership but not to the people, and told of the victims of war in Japan but not in Asia.

The historians had their work cut out for them as they sought to disturb the comforts of memory with the complications of history. Progressive historians and intellectuals, who had dominated the scene for so long, led this effort. Politically, they held high hopes for postwar democracy (or the democratic revolution), only to be continually disappointed. They were for peace and against nuclear weapons, and they opposed the Cold War politics of the U.S.–Japanese alliance. They resisted the conservative consensus that upheld the original war story and protested the government's version of the war as it appeared in national textbooks. They never lacked antagonists, or "revisionists" who repeatedly tried to replace the "reckless war" with a "holy war" of national pride. From the mid-1940s to the late 1990s, historians engaged in research and public activism to foster a deeper and more responsible understanding of the war. The success they began to achieve toward the end of the century owed as much to changes in the world—in particular, the end of the Cold War and the rise of the importance of Asia—as to their own intellectual tenacity and political commitment.

MARUYAMA MASAO

In the months immediately after the defeat, Maruyama Masao, together with many others, wrote impassioned diagnoses of the structural flaws that had led the imperial state to fascism, imperialism, and war. His influential formulations included the evocation of a "system of irresponsibility," which referred all agency upward to the emperor; the hypothesis of "fascism from above," brought about by premodern survivals in a "sham constitutional system"; and, from his famous 1946 essay excerpted here, the concepts of "transfer of oppression" and "the interfusion of morality and power," referring to the vertical hierarchy of power and the concentration of supreme value in the emperor. Maruyama's structural critique of Japanese history stressed the primacy of society over the independence of the individual, an independence he regarded as the only possible basis for genuine democracy.

"THE LOGIC AND PSYCHOLOGY OF ULTRANATIONALISM"
(CHŌKOKKASHUGI NO RONRI TO SHINRI)

We are faced, then, with a situation that might be described as the rarefaction of value. The entire national order is constructed like a chain, with the emperor as the absolute value entity, and at each link in the chain the intensity of vertical political control varies in proportion to the distance from the emperor. One might expect this to be ideal soil for the concept of dictatorship, but in fact it was hard for this concept to take root in Japan. For the essential premise of a dictatorship is the existence of a free, decision-making agent, and this is precisely what was lacking in our country. From the apex of the hierarchy to the very bottom it was virtually impossible for a truly free, unregulated individual to exist. Society was so organized that each component group was constantly being regulated by a superior authority while it was imposing its own authority on a group below.

Much has been made of the dictatorial or despotic measures exercised by the Japanese military during the war, but we must avoid confusing despotism as a fact or a social result with despotism as a concept. The latter is invariably related to a sense of responsibility, and neither the military nor the civilian officials in Japan possessed any such sense.

This emerges in the question of responsibility for starting the war. Whatever may have been the causes for the outbreak of war in 1939, the leaders of Nazi Germany were certainly conscious of a decision to embark on hostilities. In Japan, however, the situation was quite different: although it was our country that plunged the world into the terrible conflagration in the Pacific, it has been impossible to find any individuals or groups that are conscious of having started the war. What is the meaning of the remarkable state of affairs in which a country slithered into war, pushed into the vortex by men who were themselves driven by some force that they did not really understand?

The answer lies in the nature of the Japanese oligarchy. It was unfortunate enough for the country to be under oligarchic rule, and the misfortune was aggravated by the fact that the rulers were unconscious of actually being oligarchs or despots. The individuals who composed the various branches of the oligarchy did not regard themselves as active regulators but as men who were, on the contrary, being regulated by rules created elsewhere. None of the oligarchic forces in the country could ever become absolute; instead, they all coexisted, all of them equally dependent on the ultimate entity [the emperor] and all of them stressing their comparative proximity to that entity. This state of affairs led one German observer to describe Japan as *Das Land der Nebeneinander* (the land of coexistence), and there is no doubt that it impeded the development of a sense of subjective responsibility. . . .

In the absence of any free, subjective awareness, an individual's actions are not circumscribed by the dictates of conscience; instead, he is regulated by the existence of people in a higher class—of people, that is, who are closer to ultimate value. What takes the place of despotism in such a situation is a phenomenon that may be described as the maintenance of equilibrium by the transfer of oppression. By exercising arbitrary power on those who are below, people manage to transfer in a downward direction the sense of oppression that comes from above, thus preserving the balance of the whole.

This phenomenon is one of the most important heritages that modern Japan received from feudal society. . . .

With the emergence of our country on the world stage, the principle of "transfer of oppression" was extended to the international plane. . . . Just as Japan was subject to pressure from the Great Powers, so it would apply pressure to still weaker countries, a clear case of transfer psychology.

> [Maruyama, "The Logic and Psychology of Ultranationalism,"
> trans. adapted from Maruyama, *Thought and Behavior in
> Modern Japanese Politics*, pp. 16–18]

IENAGA SABURŌ

His own experience and helplessness in the face of what he called the "evils of war" turned the historian Ienaga Saburō (1913–2002) into a lifelong crusader for a fuller understanding of the "Pacific War." He noted the irony in the title of this 1968 book, which he wrote in part to correct the simple story that began with the attack on Pearl Harbor in 1941 and ended with the atomic bombings and surrender in 1945. The Americans had decreed the change in name to the Pacific War, which was the war they had fought against Japan. Ienaga was urging his countrymen to remember the war in China, beginning with the Manchurian incident in 1931 and escalating into total war in 1937. To make the point of sustained continental aggression, historians used the term "fifteen-year war," but the public knew only the "Pacific War." For this reason, Ienaga decided to stay with the familiar name despite its inaccuracy. Around the fiftieth anniversary of the end of the war in 1995, a new term, "Asia-Pacific War," gained currency. The expanded name had the signal advantage of including Asia, which was the place, after all, where Japan began the war and where Asians fought it. In the following passage, Ienaga's characterizations of the Tokyo war crimes trial and the constitution reflected widely held progressive views.

THE PACIFIC WAR
(*TAIHEIYŌ SENSŌ*)

The terms "Manchurian Incident," "China Incident," and "Greater East Asia War" were both official and popular usage until Japan's defeat in 1945. "Incidents" became war with the start of hostilities against the United States and England on December 7, 1941, and the government designated the expanded conflict the Greater East Asia War. The new name included the fighting in China since 1937 but did not retroactively encompass the Manchurian Incident, the Chang Tso-lin Incident, the Nomonhan Incident, and the other covert operations and military clashes of the 1930s. They were thought of by the public as disparate events separate from the larger conflict.

Japan's leaders, however, regarded all the fighting after the Manchurian Incident in September 1931 as one war. Major General Kawabe Torashirō stated in 1940 that "Many reasons may be cited for the China Incident, but I think it was an extension of the Manchurian Incident, which continues to the present." Colonel Mutaguchi Ren'ya, a regimental commander at the clash which started the China Incident, said in 1944, "I am responsible for the Greater East Asia War. I fired the first shot at the Marco Polo Bridge and started it." To these professional soldiers, from the Manchurian Incident to the Greater East Asia War was one continuous conflict. Civilian premier Konoe Fumimaro, in a February 1945 report to the emperor, echoed this view: "The Manchurian and China Incidents were provoked, the hostilities expanded, and we were finally led into the Greater East Asia War."

Premier Tōjō Hideki's explanation at the Imperial Conference on December 1, 1941, when the decision to go to war against America, England, and the Netherlands was made, contains the following passage about the consequences of accepting American demands: "Japan will be forced to withdraw completely from the Asian continent. Our status in Manchukuo will be jeopardized. All our successes in China will be completely lost." War with the United States and England was inevitable in order to defend Manchukuo, which was established as a result of the Manchurian Incident. The highest national leadership thereby confirms that the Greater East Asia War began with the push into Manchuria. The conflict was acclaimed as a "holy war" and enthusiastically supported in Japan. The great mass of the public sincerely believed in the cause. A small number of people, however, either because they saw it as an "imperialistic war" or for other reasons, were critical or opposed the hostilities. This dissent was completely suppressed; the attitudes and opinions openly expressed or published until August 1945 showed only total support for the war.

Japan's defeat and the Allied Occupation changed the name and interpretations of the war. On December 15, 1945, the term Greater East Asia War was prohibited; it was replaced by Pacific War (Taiheiyō sensō). . . . The term Pacific War reflects the fact that to America the Pacific was the main battlefield. . . .

The [Allied] Occupation's assessment of the conflict as an illegal war planned by Japanese militarists is well known; reforms of Japan were predicated on this assessment of war responsibility. The IMTFE (International Military Tribunal for the Far East) called it a war of aggression in violation of international law and a criminal act involving inhumane conduct contrary to the rules of war. Several Japanese leaders were brought to trial; those thought most responsible were designated class-A war criminals, found guilty, and sentenced to death. The tribunal was criticized on both moral and legal grounds by the defense attorney Kiyose Ichirō, by Justice Radhabinod Pal in his minority opinion, and by others. The main objections were that the victors were ignoring their own responsibility for the war and unilaterally blaming only the losers and that the penalties were based on an ex post facto law, contrary to the legal principle that both crime and punishment should be specified in the law. If the Japanese people of their own volition had determined legal responsibility for the war, these objections would not have been raised, and it should have been possible to reach a clearer judgment. No such attempt was made, however, and the problem of legal responsibility for the war was limited to a moot issue: the legitimacy of the IMTFE. The basic issue—war responsibility—was obscured in legalistic charges of "victor's justice" and never resolved. . . .

The preamble to the postwar constitution states that the Japanese people "resolved that never again shall we be visited with the horrors of war through the action of government." The renunciation of war and war-making capacity in article 9 of the constitution bespeaks a judgment about World War II. . . . When a draft of the constitution was published, although a majority of the public did not fully understand its peace provisions, there was no opposition to the proposed law. Indeed, the reaction was favorable because most Japanese had personally experienced the loss of loved ones, the bombing, or near starvation. Their passionate hatred of war was a cry from the heart by a people who had been misled: it was not the path of glory they found but the "horrors of war." Some of the ruling elite feigned compliance with Occupation policies and the new constitution while sabotaging them, but the public had no reason to dissemble. Their approval was genuine.

[Ienaga, *The Pacific War*, trans. Baldwin, pp. 246–51]

THE IENAGA TEXTBOOK TRIALS
(*IENAGA SABURŌ KYŌKASHO SAIBAN*)

Ienaga Saburō's best-known effort on behalf of undistorted national history was the thirty-year-long series of lawsuits that he brought against the government for its censorship of history textbooks. Ienaga had been writing high-school history texts since 1952 when, in 1963, the Ministry of Education demanded deletions in the sections about the war, removing even previously permitted terms such as the once ubiquitous "reckless war." From 1965 to 1997, Ienaga and the legions of historians supporting him challenged the textbook approvals system as unconstitutional. The verdicts went against Ienaga in upholding the constitutionality of the system, but over the years the courts yielded on important historical points, admitting, for example, that the existence of the biological-warfare Unit 731 had been established as historical fact and could be included in the texts.

When the ministry changed Japan's continental "invasion" to an "advance" in another of Ienaga's submissions, it set off the 1982 "textbook flap" between China and Japan. Even as Ienaga lost his final suit in the late 1990s, textbook issues were again dogging diplomatic relations with China and South Korea. Indeed, inadequate or inaccurate textbook treatments of colonial rule in Korea and wartime atrocities in China figured prominently in what Asian officials now called Japan's "history problem." Meanwhile, however, progressive historians had succeeded in including once forbidden topics like Unit 731, the Nanjing massacre, and the "comfort women" in the middle- and high-school texts of the early 1990s. It was these inclusions that aroused conservatives to another outburst of textbook nationalism beginning in 1996. The rightwing Association to Create New Textbooks promoted the so-called Liberalist View of History; the Ministry of Education responded by softening or removing the new treatments of the Nanjing massacre and other facts of war and empire; and the Chinese and South Korean governments angrily denounced Japan in yet another "textbook controversy" in 2001. When it came to imperialism and war, the domestic politics of national history had international implications.

The Errors of Prewar Japanese History Education

In the education we received in the prewar period, Japanese history was whitewashed in the extreme—with no mention whatsoever of social contradictions or mistakes that Japan committed. We learned only a sanitized and superficial history. Postwar education must be different. Because we received such a blinkered education, we were unable to prevent the tragedy of the disastrous "fifteen-year war."

To keep this from happening again, we will honestly reflect on Japan's errors even as we acknowledge its distinguished traditions and put them in service of the development of a better Japan. At the same time, we believe that as a nation we should not avert our gaze from its contradictions but instead boldly confront and resolve them. Resolving social contradictions and improving the lot of the people were blind spots in prewar history education. In my view, the greatest flaw was the lack of any reflection on the errors made by Japan itself.

The Definition of True Patriotism

For example, the constitution contains a statement resolving that "never again shall we be visited with the horrors of war through the action of government," thus squarely confronting Japan's errors and acting not to repeat them. Far from bringing harm to Japan, this is the path of true patriotism required by the constitution. . . .

The mission of history education lies in the people's becoming clearly aware of political errors and rectifying them. The lesson we must learn is that if we do not do so, tragedy will occur again. This, I believe, is genuine patriotism; trying to foster patriotism by whitewashing Japanese history is a terrible mistake.

My Anguish over the Restrictions on Textbooks and the Grave Abuses of Textbook Approval

For someone like me for whom writing is a vocation, it causes considerable mental anguish to have my work suppressed for reasons that make no sense to me. Of course, I appreciate having my errors pointed out and am not so foolish as to refuse such attention. But I absolutely cannot tolerate being coerced by the authorities to write something I find unacceptable. . . .

The harm caused by an inappropriate action of individual writers or teachers is confined to their sphere of influence, but the officials' authority of national approval extends to the whole system. Moreover, while the errors of individuals can be corrected through mutual criticism, the errors of the authorities can be repaired only through the enormous efforts and costs of trials like this one. As I said earlier, my own experience with the standardized history texts controlled by the prewar state authorities left me with lifelong aftereffects. And it wasn't only me but millions of people in my generation who were victims of the same evil. . . .

Motives for the Lawsuit

I am a member of the prewar generation, and because of that reckless war, millions of my countrymen suffered wretched deaths in the wilds of the continent, the depths of the sea, and the recesses of the jungle. And they died miserable deaths in air raids and atomic bombings. Fortunately, I survived. But I was unable to make any effort for the sake of my ancestral country to stop the reckless war, and I feel heartfelt remorse for the sin of having been a futile bystander to the tragedy of my country. If I were to die today without opposing educational policies that extol war and, under subordination to America, drive Japan toward war, on my deathbed I would ask why I had once again done nothing to prevent it. I never want to repeat the experience of such remorse. Although I am a single citizen with little power, I embarked on this lawsuit with the desire to atone for even a tiny fraction of the sin of not having resisted the war.

[Ienaga, *Ienaga Saburō kyōkasho saiban*, pp. 2–7; CG]

ŌE KENZABURŌ

The atomic bombings of Hiroshima and Nagasaki on August 6 and 9 and the emperor's radio announcement of Japan's surrender on August 15, 1945, constituted two of the most powerful symbols in Japanese public memory of the war. The emperor evoked the bombings as a reason for accepting the terms of surrender, speaking of "a new and most cruel bomb" that could result in the "obliteration of this Japanese nation" and the "total extinction of human civilization." Afterward, the atomic bombs justifiably supported the story of the Japanese as victims, on the one hand, and provided the grounds for postwar Japan's commitment to pacifism, on the other. Over the years, the anniversaries of Hiroshima, Nagasaki, and the surrender became the main dates of national commemoration of the war, establishing the narrative sequence of "atomic bombs, surrender, peace" in official ceremonial.

But the atomic bombings also propelled Japan's strong antinuclear movement and, in the context of the Cold War, the opposition of the left to the Japanese–American alliance and to Japan's rearmament. Ōe Kenzaburō (b. 1935), a novelist and Nobel laureate, had been affected by the violence of war as a young boy.[4] Later, in his role as a prominent public intellectual, he remained steadfast in his commitment to the original progressive vision of postwar peace and democracy. He wrote *Hiroshima Notes* in 1965, the year after he published his most famous novel, *A Personal Matter* (*Kojinteki na taiken*), each dealing in very different ways with the atomic bombs and the antinuclear activities of the time. Like the artists Toshi and Iri Maruki, the cartoonist Nakazawa Keiji (the author of *Barefoot Gen*), the poet Kurihara Sadako (see chap. 44), and many others, Ōe emphasized the real victims of the bomb, the *hibakusha*, and the importance of Hiroshima and Nagasaki for all humankind. These intellectuals literally painted and wrote the experience of the atomic bombs into postwar Japanese memory.

By the 1990s, the national and human story of the bombs had finally come to include other victims, such as the many Koreans and Korean-Japanese *hibakusha* who suffered both the bombings and the subsequent decades of discrimination. Meanwhile, post–Cold War debates about constitutional revision,

---

4. See Ōe's short story "The Catch" (Shiiku) and chap. 44.

nuclear weapons, and regional security once again challenged the way the atomic bombs would be remembered, or forgotten.

HIROSHIMA NOTES
(HIROSHIMA NŌTO)

. . . In this age of nuclear weapons, when their power gets more attention than the misery they cause, and when human events increasingly revolve around their production and proliferation, what must we Japanese try to remember? Or more pointedly, what must I myself remember and keep on remembering? . . .

. . . In such a time as this, I want to remember, and keep on remembering, the thoughts of the people of Hiroshima—the first people and the first place to experience full force the world's worst destructive capability. Hiroshima is like a nakedly exposed wound inflicted on all mankind. Like all wounds, this one also poses two potential outcomes: the hope of human recovery and the danger of fatal corruption. Unless we persevere in remembering the Hiroshima experience, especially the thoughts of those who underwent that unprecedented experience, the faint signs of recovery emerging from this place and people will begin to decay and real degeneration will set in. . . .

In the broadest context of human life and death, those of us who happened to escape the atomic holocaust must see Hiroshima as part of all Japan, and as part of all the world. If we survivors want to atone for the "Hiroshima" within us and give it some positive value, then we should mobilize all efforts against nuclear arms under the maxims "the human misery of Hiroshima" and "the restoration of all humanity." Some people may hold to the fairy-tale view, in this highly politicized age, that the new acquisition of nuclear arms by one country actually advances the cause of nuclear disarmament. Since the world has in fact taken the initial step forward in that direction, there may be some ultimate possibility of completely eradicating nuclear weapons. . . .

. . . To put the matter plainly and bluntly, people everywhere on this earth are trying to forget Hiroshima and the unspeakable tragedy perpetrated there. . . . All who fortunately survived, or at least luckily suffered no radiation injury, seek to forget the ones who, even now, are struggling painfully toward death. Forgetting all these things, we go on living comfortably in the crazy world of the late twentieth century. . . .

It was in the summer of 1960 that I first visited Hiroshima. Although at that time I had not yet begun to understand Hiroshima, I had one clear intimation of it. A short essay that I wrote for the Chūgoku newspaper included this passage: "Today I visited Hiroshima and attended the A-bomb Memorial Ceremony. It was a precious experience for me. I still feel it is. The impact of that experience will grow and deeply influence me. During the fifteen years since the bombing, I passed the springtime of my life. I should have visited Hiroshima earlier; the earlier, the better. But it was not too late for me to visit there this year."

This intimation became reality. Hiroshima has, indeed, become the weightiest and most influential factor in my thinking. I often dream very suffocating, painful dreams. For instance, in a certain place at high noon in midsummer, I see a small, strained, middle-aged man in his pajamas and robe with his head held erect like an Awa doll, and he speaks in a scarcely audible voice. In this dream, I listen to his voice and realize that in a few months he will die, wasted away by an A-bomb disease. . . .

In Hiroshima, I met people who refused to surrender to the worst despair or to incurable madness. I hear the story of a gentle girl, born after the war, who devoted her life to a youth caught in an irredeemably cruel destiny. And in places where no particular hope for living could be found, I heard the voices of people, sane and steady people, who moved ahead slowly but with genuine resolve. I think it was in Hiroshima that I got my first concrete insight in human authenticity, and it was there also that I saw the most unpardonable deception. But what I was able to discern, even faintly, was altogether only a small portion of an incomparably larger abominable reality still hidden in the darkness. . . .

[Ōe, *Hiroshima Notes*, trans. Toshi and Swain, pp. 90, 98–99, 168–69]

FUJIWARA AKIRA

The resurgence of controversy in the 1990s about Japanese war memory sparked a new wave of nationalist revisionism centered on the liberalist view of history, which glorified the "holy war" and criticized the depiction of wartime atrocities in textbooks and public discourse. In response to this latest rash of denials of the Nanjing massacre and justifications of the "comfort women," the progressive historians once again took up the tools of history to dispute the manipulations of memory. This was nothing new for them: already in 1982, the historian Fujiwara Akira (1922–2003) and his colleagues had established the Nanjing Massacre Research Group in reaction to the "textbook flap" with China. The studies they produced over the years made it increasingly difficult for "Nanjing deniers" to assert that the "rape of Nanking" in 1937/1938 had never occurred, prompting them to shift their tactics but not their position. The historians reacted by persisting in pursuit of the facts, their public impact aided now by vocal outrage in Asia and the United States.

Historians played a similar role in regard to the comfort women. It became difficult for the Japanese government to continue to deny its involvement in military sex slavery after the historian Yoshimi Yoshiaki found documents that proved it in 1992.[5] While the combination of historical research and victims' testimony did not silence the revisionists, it did bring the stories of the comfort

---

5. Yoshimi, *Comfort Women*.

women and the Nanjing massacre into the media spotlight for all to see. And judging by opinion polls, many Japanese believed their eyes.

HOW TO VIEW THE NANJING INCIDENT
(NANKIN JIKEN O DŌ MIRU KA)

Sixty years have passed since imperialist Japan began its total war of aggression in China in July 1937 and, in November of that year, committed large-scale atrocities during the occupation of Nanjing, the Chinese capital. . . .

In Japan today, some forces still refuse to acknowledge the war of aggression and persist in affirming and glorifying the war. And these war glorifiers focus particularly on denying the facts of the Nanjing massacre. Just as Nazi glorifiers tried to deny Auschwitz, the symbol of German war crimes, their Japanese counterparts are vehement deniers of the Nanjing massacre, which symbolizes the war crimes committed by Japan. Now, sixty years later, researchers must investigate the Nanjing incident in order to stop these denial arguments and demolish the glorification of war. . . .

When Japan accepted the Potsdam Declaration and surrendered in August 1945, the state officially acknowledged the war of aggression and the Nanjing massacre committed by the Japanese army. The Potsdam Declaration denounced Japanese aggression and specified the punishment of war criminals. After the surrender, the International Military Tribunal for the Far East convened in Tokyo. In November 1948 the court handed down its judgment that the war was a war of aggression for which Japan was responsible, and it also acknowledged that 200,000 people had been massacred in Nanjing. Then, in article 11 of the San Francisco Peace Treaty concluded in San Francisco in 1951, Japan signaled its acceptance of the judgments of the war crimes trial about the war of aggression and the Nanjing massacre. And because most Japanese, having experienced the horrors of war, welcomed the Peace Constitution and were deeply critical of the war, they, too, accepted the treaty.

But this provision was disregarded almost as soon as the treaty came into effect. Because the postwar purge of public officials was lifted around the same time, right-wing politicians, journalists, former military officers, and right-wing activists returned to politics in force. The affirmation and glorification of the war began with a publishing boom in war books and the assault on history textbooks for being critical of the war.

As a result, the pursuit of war responsibility in Japan remained inadequate and insufficient in the extreme. . . . And the exoneration of the emperor for the administrative convenience of the Occupation played a role as well, while most of the politicians, industrialists (*zaibatsu*), and bureaucrats also survived in place. Because those responsible for the war returned to the forefront of politics after the treaty went into effect, it was to be expected that they had no desire either to condemn the war they had made or to speak of atrocities they had committed. . . .

One focus of the present movement of politically motivated historical revisionism is the denial of the facts of the Nanjing massacre. In order to counter the views of these war glorifiers and "liberalists" who distort history for their own purposes, it is up to us to make the facts clear. However abhorrent these events are to Japanese, that they occurred is a fact, and only by confronting these facts can they become "lessons for the future." . . .

Recently the denials of the Nanjing massacre have centered on the question of numbers. At the beginning, the war glorifiers had labeled the massacre as an "illusion" or a fiction, but this view was completely bankrupted by advances in scholarly research. So now they are reduced to arguing about the number of victims, to the effect that because the numbers are small, it was not a massacre. This debate limits the time frame and geographic extent of the events in order to calculate as small a number of victims as possible, [calculations refuted by recent scholarly works in both China and Japan]. . . .

. . . Yet another question that must be addressed is why Japanese became the perpetrators. Believing in emperor-system militarism, poisoned by sexism and ethnocentrism, without offering any resistance whatsoever, they became the perpetrators of a massacre. Understanding the conditions that made this possible is essential to preventing such offenses of history from ever happening again.

[Fujiwara, *Nankin jiken o do miru ka*, pp. 7–13; CG]

KOBAYASHI YOSHINORI

The most influential example of liberalist revisionism was surely the thick comic book *On War* by the popular cartoonist Kobayashi Yoshinori (b. 1953). Published in 1998, it sold 500,000 copies within a few months, arousing great enthusiasm among its readers, many of whom were young people who knew little about the war and found the book exhilarating, and great concern among progressive Japanese and many Asians, who knew quite a lot about the war and found the book repugnant.

Kobayashi introduced the war with a critique of postwar Japanese society gone soft from too much peace and too little devotion to the nation, egged on by progressive intellectuals and the media that supported them. Against this, Kobayashi celebrated the patriotic sacrifice of "our forefathers" willing to die for their country and of the "comfort women," who "consoled the Japanese soldiers." Nostalgic for the spirit of the *kamikaze* pilots, Kobayashi rehearsed the reasons for their brave deaths in defense of Japan's waging a "just war" against Western imperialists. Filled with descriptive detail and personal stories based on soldiers' diaries and other sources, the comic book persuaded many young readers of the "truth" of its history of national "pride" and "the thrill of war." Here was an antistory to the dominant narrative of a "reckless war," designed to rouse nationalism in the present by rewriting the "Tokyo war crimes trial view" of the past.

ON WAR
(SENSŌRON)

[*P. 567, TOP*] . . . Soon after the war began, Japan decided on the name "Greater East Asia War," and the Japanese fought the Greater East Asia War. After the war, General Headquarters (GHQ) [of the Occupation] prohibited the term "Greater East Asia War" and created the name "Pacific War" in order to deny the principles and ideals of the "Greater East Asia Co-Prosperity Sphere." So even now, we use "Pacific War," a term that did not exist at the time but suited the convenience of the United States [after the war].

[*UPPER RIGHT*] Our opponents were the Communist army led by Mao Zedong and the Nationalist army led by Chiang Kai-shek in continental China, and the United States, the Netherlands, Great Britain, France, and others.

[*UPPER LEFT, ABOVE*] The "Pacific War" of the textbooks implies that we fought only the United States.

[*UPPER LEFT, BELOW*] It makes more sense to say "Greater East Asia War," even if the name did come later, because Japan fought for the tremendous idea of creating a Greater East Asia Co-Prosperity Sphere in Asia.

[*LOWER RIGHT*] Some people label others as "right-wing" just for saying "Greater East Asia War," but that doesn't bother me. Since "Greater East Asia" means "greater" "East Asia," it makes the scene of battle clear.

[*LOWER LEFT*] In any case, that this small island country waged a war of such a scale without regard for its own status is more than amazing, it's thrilling. To express it in the feelings of innocent boys, it was "great"! . . .

[*P. 568, UPPER RIGHT*] And still, to the whites of the discriminatory Western powers who regarded the colored races only as lowly monkeys and colonized East Asia. . . .

[*UPPER LEFT*] Applause for the Japanese army that stuck it to them!

[*LOWER*] At the outset of war, the Japanese army appeared extremely powerful. In Malaya and at Singapore, a British and Indian army of 130,000 men could not stop the 40,000-man Japanese army. Although an allied army of 50,000 British, Dutch, and Australia soldiers defended Bandung in Indonesia, a Japanese army of only 750 men charged and forced them to surrender. . . .

[Kobayashi, *Sensōron*, pp. 28, 30; CG]

日本は開戦直後に戦争名称を「大東亜戦争」と決定。日本人は「大東亜戦争」を戦った。戦後GHQは「大東亜共栄圏」の理念、理想を否定するために「太平洋戦争」という名称を作り「大東亜戦争」という呼称の使用を禁止した。そして今でも、当時は存在しなかったアメリカにとって都合のいい呼称「太平洋戦争」が使用されているのである。

教科書に載ってるように太平洋戦争っていったらアメリカとだけ戦ったような気がするが…

相手は支那（中国）大陸の毛沢東率いる中共軍蔣介石率いる国民党軍アメリカ・オランダ・イギリス・フランスなどである

日本はアジアに大東亜共栄圏を作ろうという、とんでもない構想を後づけにせよ掲げて戦ったので大東亜戦争と呼んだほうが わかりやすい

無邪気に男の子の感覚で言えばグレイトなのである

こんな小さな島国が身のほど知らずながらこんなスケールの大きい戦争をやってしまったってことが 驚きというか痛快である

なにしろこんな小さな島国が

中には「大東亜戦争」と聞いただけで右翼とレッテル貼りしてくる人もいるが知ったこっちゃない

「大・東亜」のほうが大・東アジアだから戦場がわかりやすいのだ

ISHIZAKA KEI

Over the years, many comics depicted the progressive views of the war that so angered Kobayashi Yoshinori. A well-known example from 1991, originally serialized in the youth comic *Yangu janpu* in the 1980s, was created by Ishizaka Kei (b. 1956) with the ironic title "A Just War," glossed in English as "Goodwar Is Badwar." In this excerpt, she offers the home-front view, the part of the original war story that focused on the hardships of women and children during the war. When Shōwa Hall, the national museum commemorating the war, finally opened in 1999 after twenty years of contentious debate, the same homefront story occupied nearly the entire exhibit. In contrast, Ishizaka presented a critical view of what the war had meant to women.

A JUST WAR
(*TADASHII SENSŌ*)

The White Legions

[*P. 571, RIGHT*] [Local leader (man)]: I assume you've all heard about the lieutenant's wife who committed suicide the day before he was to leave for the war.

> She wanted her husband to be able to go to battle without leaving worries behind.

> Isn't this the paragon of a warrior's wife!!

[*LEFT*] Why did Germany lose the last war?

> Because the women in charge of the kitchen dragged the men down, complaining of material hardship.

[*P. 570, RIGHT*] And so in Japan, women must be firm about the importance of national defense to their daily lives.

[*LEFT*] [Woman, wearing sash of the Greater Japan Women's National Defense Association]: Our soldiers sacrifice their lives for the nation.

> At least let's care for them so they can leave with their minds at ease.

> Isn't that our duty as the women of the homefront!
> National Defense begins in the kitchen!!

[*P. 572, UPPER RIGHT AND CENTER*] [Song] "I am the pink flower [woman of Japan] blooming on the homefront; Off to war, off to war, be bold and brave."

[*UPPER LEFT*] Well, that's over. Thanks for the good work.

[*CENTER, ABOVE*] For us who believed in the words "holy war" and did not doubt them. . . .

やれ
やれ
ごくろう
さまでした

「聖戦」という
言葉を
信じて疑わなかった
私たちに——

大陸で どんなに
恐ろしい光景が
おこっていたかなど

どうして
想像することが
できたでしょう

母は よく
昔を思い出して
……………

あのころが
一番
充実していた
なんて
言ってました
……………

[CENTER, BELOW] How could we imagine . . . the horrible things that happened on the continent?

[BOTTOM] My mother often recalled the past . . . and said that life then was the most fulfilling for her.

[P. 573, UPPER RIGHT] As a bride from a poor farm family, she felt inferior . . . and must have had a rough time for many years.

[UPPER LEFT] After Father went to war and died an honorable death in battle . . . Mother was finally recognized as a woman in her own right.

[BOTTOM] Oh Mrs. Hattori, what a shame.

[Ishizaka, *Tadashii sensō*, pp. 154–55, 166–67; CG]

TWENTIETH-CENTURY DESIGN STAMPS

The dominant narrative of the war appeared nearly unchanged in this series of special commemorative stamps issued in 2000, at the end of the twentieth

20世紀デザイン切手 第9集

① 「杉原千畝副領事がビザ発給」から

② ③
④ ⑤

① 杉原千畝副領事がビザ発給：
　肖像とユダヤ人に発給したビザ（通過査証・部分）と
　イスラエル政府より贈られたメダル
② 国民学校始まる：教科書「ヨミカタ」の挿絵（部分）
③ 真珠湾攻撃・太平洋戦争勃発：
　真珠湾上空を飛ぶ日本軍の飛行機
④ 高村光太郎が詩集「道程」で第一回帝国芸術院賞：
　肖像と初版本の中扉題字と詩（部分）
⑤ 昭和新山：噴煙を上げる昭和新山

⑥ ⑦

⑧

⑥ 広島被爆：広島の原爆ドーム
⑦ 長崎被爆：長崎の平和祈念像

⑧ 終戦：戦艦ミズーリ号の上で行われた
　降伏文書の調印式

⑨ ⑩

高村智恵子 作 「パンジー」（紙絵）

⑨⑩ 黄金バット：（左）紙芝居「黄金バット」・加太こうじ画
　　　　　　　（右）マンガ「黄金バット」・永松健夫画

平成12年 4月21日　　　大蔵省印刷局製造

century. Note the dates marked in public memory; the cultural icons; and the inclusion of Sugihara Chiune, the so-called Schindler of Japan, honored for saving Jews from the Holocaust. Note, too, the absences, or silences, in the story.

NO. 9: 1940–1945

1. Vice Consul Sugihara Chiune Issues Visas [1940]
   Portrait of Sugihara, with visa issued to European Jews for transit through Japan and the medal presented to Sugihara by the Israeli government
2. [Wartime] "national schools" begin [1941]
   Illustration from the textbook *Yomikata*
3. Attack on Pearl Harbor and outbreak of the Pacific War [December 8, 1941]
   Japanese military aircraft flying over Pearl Harbor
4. Takamura Kōtarō's poetry collection *Dōtei* [*Journey*] awarded the first Imperial Japanese Art Academy Prize [1942]
   Portrait, with title lettering and poem from the first edition
5. The new mountain Shōwa [1943]
   The new mountain Shōwa erupting
6. The atomic bombing of Hiroshima [August 6, 1945]
   The Atomic Bomb Dome at Hiroshima
7. The atomic bombing of Nagasaki [August 9, 1945]
   The Peace Prayer Statue, Nagasaki
8. End of the war [August 14, 1945]
   Ceremony signing articles of surrender aboard the USS *Missouri* [September 2, 1945]
9. *The Golden Bat*
   Illustration by Kata Kōji from the children's picture-card show (*kami-shibai*) of *The Golden Bat*
10. *The Golden Bat*
    Illustration by Nagamatsu Takeo from the comic *The Golden Bat*
    [*right*] Illustration of papercut of "pansies" by Takamura Chieko
    [Ministry of Finance, Printing Bureau, *20-seiki dezain kitte*, 2000, no. 9; CG]

RETHINKING THE NATION

Both history writing and popular historical consciousness shifted during the last two decades of the twentieth century. As is almost always the case, several trends converged to produce these changes. The first was what historians called "the end of postwar historiography," in reference to the Marxist history writing that had occupied so prominent an academic place since the end of the war. Marxist categories of analysis now seemed less useful, and debates about the Meiji Restoration seemed more tedious than in earlier years. At the same time, recent trends in social and cultural history directed scholarly attention away from socioeconomic structures like state monopoly capitalism to the lived experiences of everyday life. In part an outgrowth of people's history, these interests combined with contemporary social concerns to focus history writing on questions of gender, ethnic minorities, and people on the social margins at home and in the colonial empire abroad.

Second, ideas of modernity, which determined the way that historians viewed the past, also had changed as Japanese grappled with the unfamiliar notion of living in postmodern times. Ever since the Meiji period, the modern had been conceived in comparison with Western exemplars as a condition that Japanese were striving to achieve in accordance with the imperatives of some universal scheme. Now they confronted less a failed modernity than a completed one, and like that modernity or not, it forced them to think about history differently. The assumptions of universal progress, whether linear or dialectical, no longer seemed so sturdy a guide to a future for which there were "no more models" to establish a ready-made comparative frame. In conservative circles, this development was taken as proof of Japan's having "overtaken the West" by virtue of a superior civilization. A new wave of popular civilizational histories appeared in the 1990s that echoed their Meiji counterparts of a century earlier, except that the West was now omitted in a story that attributed the achievement of Japanese modernity entirely to indigenous cultural factors. Meanwhile, many historians were critical both of this sort of growing nationalism and of the nature of Japan's "completed" modernity. Criticism of modernity was, of course, nothing new for progressive historians, as they wrote against the main narratives of national history in ways that reflected the changing times.

The changing relations between Japan and Asia particularly affected their views, constituting the third determinant of the shift in historical thinking in the last years of the century. With the end of the Cold War, the long laserlike focus on U.S.–Japanese relations gave way to a wider and more complicated view of the world. After four decades of relative neglect—or, in the case of war memory, repression—Asia finally reappeared on Japan's political and economic agenda. Historians turned to the study of empire, bringing the experience of the peoples of Manchuria, Taiwan, Korea, and the South Seas into the purview of a national history that had been almost entirely "Japanese" since 1945. They explored ancient connections and commonalities between Japan and Asia, writing about "Japanese history as seen from the seas" to show the close economic and cultural links that had existed since earliest times. As a counterpart to this stress on regional over national history, they de-nationalized the past internally as well, emphasizing regional differences within Japan that the modern narrative of the nation-state had all but entirely erased.

Yet even this writing against received views of national history bore the unmistakable marks of history written under the sign of the nation-state. "Japan," however expanded and inclusive, still remained the subject of the historical sentence, and the imperial institution, however historicized and de-mythologized, remained the touchstone of Japanese identity even for its strongest critics. However linked to its regional past, the nation still remained rhetorically separated, a question of Japan *and* Asia rather than of a common transnational history. Thus at the end of the twentieth century, history writing and popular consciousness in Japan, as in nearly every place else, were still national and, in this sense, still modern: a continuation of the Meiji project to rethink the nation's future through rewriting its past.

AMINO YOSHIHIKO

Amino Yoshihiko (1928–2004) was the scholar most closely associated with the new trends in social and cultural history in the 1980s and 1990s. Certainly he was the most famous, with more than 140 books, countless television appearances, and a noticeable influence on popular culture, including the huge animated-film (*anime*) success, *Princess Mononoke.* The 1997 feature incorporated Amino's unorthodox views of the importance of ethnic minorities into the history of a country relentlessly described as homogeneously "Japanese."

A medieval historian, Amino traversed the central terrain of postwar history writing during his long career. He joined the Association of Historical Studies as an activist Marxist historian after the war and worked as an ethnographic researcher for an institute inspired by Yanagita Kunio's interest in the lives of ordinary people. Like the people's historians, he considered such inquiry both a truer account of the past and a means to combat the power of the modern state and its emperor system. Writing against the national grain, Amino contested the ideological link among rice, the emperor, and "Japan" by focusing on "nonagriculturists" who had been extruded to the social margins by the Tokugawa political and taxation system. These included the people who made their living in the mountains and from the sea, as well as itinerant artists, artisans, and outcasts, who, in Amino's view, occupied a spatial and social zone of freedom in the borders between the rice-growing villages—a freedom that was lost with the establishment of the modern state, which wrote them, and women, out of its history.

Amino also sought to disaggregate "Japan," the unitary historical subject, into its distinctive regional histories, especially the division between eastern and western Japan, only part of which, he argued, had belonged to "Japan" proper in early times. At the same time, he linked these regions to areas in Asia both across nearby seas and at farther-flung ports of maritime trade. As the following excerpt shows, Amino contested even the most hallowed myths and institutions, from rice and race to the emperor and the folk.

"DECONSTRUCTING 'JAPAN'"

One Country, One Name

It is self-evident that neither Japan nor the Japanese people existed prior to the use of the name "Japan" (*Nihon*), and needless to say, the name of the country is a central problem in "the discourse on Japaneseness" (*Nihonron*). Yet it is a problem that has not been squarely confronted in previous discussions about "Japan.". . . . There are few states like Japan, whose name is neither a place name, a dynastic title, nor the family or clan name of a royal line. . . .

The generally accepted view among ancient historians today . . . emphasizes the usage of Nihon by the envoy sent to Tang China in the first year of Taihō [701] . . . however, it is important to note the close correlation between the time when the name "Japan" was adopted and when the appellation *tennō* (emperor) came into systematic use. . . . This would suggest that "Japan" and *tennō* have been inseparably linked from earliest times.

There are also all sorts of theories, and no consensus, as to the meaning of "Japan." Most widely held is the view that emerged in the Heian period, which identified the "prince of the place where the sun rises" mentioned in the *Sui-shū* with the Eastern *tennō* (emperor) of the *Nihon-shoki*, holding that Japan was so named because, looking eastward from the Tang Court, it was where the sun rose. If one adopts this view, it means that the name "Japan" has a Tang or at least a Chinese continental perspective. . . . [One scholar] has also noted the working of a deep-rooted tendency on the part of the society of the archipelago to "see its essence in terms of the sun and the direction from which it rises," a tendency also evident in "the creation of the mythology of imperial authority."

Thus the name Nihon signifies a natural phenomenon or orientation and is neither the name of the place of origin of the dynastic founders nor that of a dynasty or tribe. . . . Probably nowhere else, at least in East Asia or Europe, is there to be found a royal or imperial house without a clan or family name, while, as we have noted above, the name of the country itself, Nihon, is inextricably linked to the *tennō* institution. . . .

Nihon itself is a purely historical construct, and for that reason we should firmly reject historical images rooted in the "In the beginning were the Japanese" sort of framework that is still widely adhered to. . . .

"One Race," "One Nation"?

The "island-country theory" and the "rice monoculture theory" stem from a view of "Japan" as having been from ancient times a "unified state" peopled by one highly homogeneous race.

The "original Japanese," who are different in character from neighboring peoples and have been living in the Japanese archipelago since the Jōmon period, are our ancestors. The culture and way of life centering on rice-cultivation spread from Western Japan during the Yayoi period and was widely adopted by these people. From this emerged the state with the name "Japan," headed by the emperor. Despite various vicissitudes, this country Japan (*Nihonkoku*) has continued to the present, and the Japanese people (*Nihonjin*) who comprise it have undergone a distinct historical development without suffering any major invasion or conquest by neighboring peoples. . . .

Yet this "common knowledge" is no more than a fantasy based to a considerable degree on distortions. In particular, it is a historical fabrication which has almost entirely purged the unique society—including the Ainu—which existed in Hokkaido and northern Tōhoku; it also ignores the formation and development of the Ryūkyū kingdom in the Okinawan islands. Furthermore, it embodies a perspective that entirely overlooks the numerous attempts to establish a state separate from that of Kinai (Yamato), attempts that were made not only on the main islands of the archipelago—Honshū, Shikoku, Kyūshū—territories which constituted the main reach of Nihonkoku ("Japan")—but also in regions like northern Kyūshū and the Tōhoku–Kantō region in the Northeast of the country. Indeed, the situation that obtained in these regions indicates the coexistence of several separate states. . . .

. . . These considerations, however, cannot, I believe, alter the fact that a difference between East and West Japan (taking the division along the central structural line [the geological fold that runs down the center of Japan's main island]) has existed throughout history, perhaps from as early as Neolithic times. . . . This means that even in the early Yayoi period in Western Japan and the Jōmon period in Eastern Japan, two discrete societies existed side by side. . . .

In Western Japan there were [areas], which although differing among themselves maintained links with the Korean peninsula and the Chinese mainland, but may be regarded as a distinct region . . . and "Okinawa," which was an independent region maintaining its own communications beyond the Japanese archipelago. At the same time, a network of sea communications grew up between the people living along the Japan Sea, the Seto Inland Sea, and the Pacific coast. They maintained links with the regions listed above, and probably also expanded their networks beyond the Japanese archipelago. . . .

Suffice it to say that the argument that from Jōmon times there has been in Japan a "single race" and a "single state" is a baseless fabrication. An appreciation of this makes any simplistic linear periodization of the Japanese archipelago problematic, to say the least. It is also obvious that, historically, views of the emperor and likewise of "Japan" have been far from homogeneous throughout the Japanese archipelago.

[Amino, "Deconstructing 'Japan,'" trans. McCormack, pp. 122–25, 132–34]

ARANO YASUNORI AND COLLEAGUES

The project of rethinking Japanese history in the context of Asia generated considerable dynamism and revision of received notions of national history. Scholars breached the lines drawn in universities since the 1890s among Japanese, Asian, and Western history and proposed regional and transnational approaches. They intervened in the once sacrosanct ideological precincts surrounding the origin of the emperor and the Japanese people to connect them to Korea. They showed that definitions of Asia changed over time and that conventional periodizations of Japanese history had to be revised to include larger regional developments like the decline of the China-centered tribute system. They also challenged the idea of the closed-off country (*sakoku*) so long associated with Tokugawa Japan. Arano Yasunori (b. 1946) proposed instead the dual concept of, first, a "Japan-centered order of civilized and barbarian," which replaced the earlier Sinocentric order and had four gates open to the world (Ezo, Satsuma, Tsushima, and Nagasaki), and, second, the "ban on going abroad," which placed trade and travel in the control of the shogunal state. Neither, he argued, was designed to close off the country, but to keep its commerce with Asia and the world under state control.[6]

As coeditors of the series *The History of Japan in Asia (Ajia no naka no Nihonshi)*, Arano and his colleagues introduced the imperatives of replacing Japan in Asia in terms of the political context and scholarly approaches typical of the 1990s.

THE HISTORY OF JAPAN IN ASIA
(*AJIA NO NAKA NO NIHONSHI*)

Japanese behavior seems always to return to the pattern of "Escape from Asia, Enter Europe" [in Fukuzawa Yukichi's famous formulation]. On the other hand, the tendency to concentrate Japanese identity in the singular Emperor remains strong. One cannot underestimate the potential of the combination of these two tendencies to lead Japanese once again into nationalism and discrimination against [the rest of] Asia.

Now that we realize that even the firmest of national boundaries are not immutable, it is essential to break free of the mode of thinking that puts national

---

6. Arano, *Kinsei Nihon to higashi Ajia.*

interest above all else and to envision instead a free and multidimensional exchange among different peoples (*minzoku*) and regions (*chiiki*). In this we must not regard Asia with condescension or single out one or two countries as models but move toward proper relations based on dispassionate and independent views. Toward this end we must trace the historical development of Japan's relations with Asia in both directions: "Japan in Asia" (e.g., the characteristics and roles of Japan in Asia, Japanese who advanced into Asia) and "Asia in Japan" (e.g., Asian characteristics within Japanese society and Asians who became part of Japanese society). This history is necessary if we are to ascertain the legacies that still affect Japanese views of Asia. In this series of volumes, we concentrate on the premodern period. With contemporary historiographical concerns in mind, we situate our basic point of view in three contexts:

I. Ethnos

Japanese must now overcome their tendency to assume that "nation equals emperor" and instead establish themselves first as an ethnic subject and then engage in independent and equal interchange with other ethnicities (*minzoku*). We have to apply a different logic to rethink those peoples who were forced as subordinates to collude with the state on the basis of the illusion of the homogeneous nation-state. Then we must reconstruct the aspects of exchange, fusion, and opposition between Japanese and other ethnicities. Rather than use the concept of ethnicity (*minzoku*) that is premised on the existence of the "nation-state," we take the term "ethnos" from cultural anthropology because it is relatively free of the framework of the state and the limitations of a particular historical period.

II. Region

We do not regard the connections between Japan and Asia solely in terms of international relations. Instead we use the framework of a regional space that transcended national borders, which allows for a concrete grasp of the diverse exchanges carried out by such people as monks, pirates, and merchants. We approach the "region" in terms of national subregions with distinctive characteristics (e.g., Kyūshū and its relations with the China Sea rim region). We also examine how moments of interethnic exchange and fusion existed beyond the control of the state and what kinds of conflict such exchanges engendered within states.

III. Comparison

Conventional methods of "comparative history" have tended either to attribute Japan's backwardness to some abstract "Asian characteristics" or to emphasize the inevitability of Japan's "modernization" in terms of its resemblance to

Europe. This bias reflected Japan's "Escape from Asia" (*datsua*) orientation. In contrast, there have been only meager achievements in studies comparing Japan with Asian countries, except in such areas as early institutional history (e.g., the *ritsuryō* system). On the basis of objective comparison and mindful of mutual connections, we seek a historical grasp of the commonalities and differences between Asian nations and ethnic societies and those of Japan and the inter-relations that determined them.

[Arano et al., eds., *Ajia to Nihon*, vol. 1 of *Ajia no naka no Nihonshi*, pp. ii–iii; CG]

BIBLIOGRAPHY

SERIES AND COLLECTIONS ABBREVIATION

NKST   *Nihon kindai shisō taikei*. 24 vols. Tokyo: Iwanami shoten, 1988–1992.

PRIMARY AND SECONDARY SOURCES

Allén, Sture. *Nobel Lectures in Literature, 1991–1995*. Singapore: World Scientific, 1997.

Allinson, Gary D. *The Columbia Guide to Modern Japanese History*. New York: Columbia University Press, 1999.

Amino, Yoshihiko. "Deconstructing 'Japan': From *Nihonron no shiza*" [1990]. Translated by Gavan McCormack. *East Asian History*, no. 3 (1992): 121–42.

Aoki Yayoi. *Feminizumu to ekorojī*. Tokyo: Shinhyōron, 1988.

Arano Yasunori. *Kinsei Nihon to higashi Ajia*. Tokyo: Tōkyō daigaku shuppankai, 1988.

Arano Yasunori, Ishii Masatoshi, and Murai Shōsuke, eds. *Ajia to Nihon*. Vol. 1 of *Ajia no naka no Nihonshi*. Tokyo: Tōkyō daigaku shuppankai, 1992.

Arita Hachirō. "The International Situation and Japan's Position" [radio address, June 29, 1940]. *Tokyo Gazette* 4 (August 1940).

Asukai Masamichi. *Meiji taitei*. Tokyo: Chikuma shobō, 1989.

Banno Junji. *Democracy in Pre-War Japan: Concepts of Government, 1871–1937: Collected Essays*. Translated by Andrew Fraser. New York: Routledge, 2001.

Beauchamp, Edward R., ed. *Learning to Be Japanese: Selected Readings on Japanese Society and Education*. Hamden, Conn.: Linnet Books, 1978.

Beckmann, George M. *The Making of the Meiji Constitution: The Oligarchs and the Constitutional Development of Japan, 1868–1891*. Lawrence: University Press of Kansas, 1957.

Bitō Masahide. *Edo jidai to wa nani ka?* Tokyo: Iwanami shoten, 1992.

Braisted, William R. *Meiroku Zasshi: Journal of the Japanese Enlightenment*. Cambridge, Mass.: Harvard University Press, 1976.

Buckley, Sandra, ed. *Broken Silence: Voices of Japanese Feminism*. Berkeley: University of California Press, 1997.

Ch'oe, Yŏngho, Peter H. Lee, and Wm. Theodore de Bary, eds. *Sources of Korean Tradition*. Vol. 2. New York: Columbia University Press, 2000.

Craig, Albert. *Chōshū in the Meiji Restoration*. Cambridge, Mass.: Harvard University Press, 1961.

Crump, John. *The Origins of Socialist Thought in Japan*. New York: St. Martin's Press, 1983.

Dai Saigō zenshū. Edited by Ōkawa Nobuyoshi. 3 vols. Tokyo: Dai Saigō zenshū kankōkai, 1926–1927.

Dajōkan. "Gakusei ni tsuki Ōseidasaresho." Edited by Yamazumi Masami. In *NKST*, vol. 6.

de Bary, Wm. Theodore, and Irene Bloom, eds. *Sources of Chinese Tradition*. 2nd ed. Vol. 1. New York: Columbia University Press, 1999.

Deguchi Nao. *Ōmoto shin'yu*. In *Ōmoto shiryō shūsei*, vol. 1. Edited by Ikeda Akira. Tokyo: San'ichi shobō, 1982.

Deguchi Onisaburō. *Michi no shiori*. Kyoto: Tenseisha, 1904.

Deguchi Onisaburō. *Reikai monogatari*. 81 vols. Ayabe: Ōmoto, 1921–1934.

Dennett, Raymond, and Katherine D. Durance, eds. *Documents on American Foreign Relations*. Vol. 9, 1951. Boston: World Peace Foundation, 1953.

Department of State. *Foreign Relations of the United States, 1948*. Vol. 6, *The Far East and Australasia*. Washington, D.C.: Government Printing Office, 1974.

Devine, Richard. "The Way of the King: An Early Meiji Essay on Government." *Monumenta Nipponica* 34 (1979): 49–72.

Dilworth, David A., and Valdo H. Viglielmo, eds. *Sourcebook for Modern Japanese Philosophy: Selected Documents*. Westport, Conn.: Greenwood Press, 1998.

Documents on International Affairs [annual]. Oxford: Oxford University Press, 1929–1973.

Dulles, John Foster. "Free or Captive World?" *Nippon Times*, June 23, 1950.

Economic Planning Agency (Keizai kikakuchō). *Economic White Paper, 1956*. Tokyo: Keizai kikakuchō, 1956.

Economic Planning Agency (Keizai kikakuchō). *Kokumin seikatsu hakusho*. Tokyo: Nihon keizai shinbunsha, 1960.

Economic Planning Agency (Keizai kikakuchō). *New Long-Range Economic Plan of Japan (1961–1970): Doubling National Income Plan*. Tokyo: Japan Times, 1961.

Endō Shūsaku. *Endō Shūsaku bungaku zenshū*. 15 vols. Tokyo: Shinchōsha, 2000.

Endō Shūsaku. "Watashi no nyūshin." In Endō Shūsaku, *Watashi ni totte kami to wa*. Tokyo: Kōbunsha bunko, 1988.

Fujiwara Akira. *Nankin jiken o dō miru ka*. Tokyo: Aoki shoten, 1998.

Fukuda Hideko. *Warawa no hanshōgai.* Tokyo: Iwanami shoten, 1958.

Fukuzawa Yukichi. *An Encouragement of Learning.* Translated by David A. Dilworth and Umeyo Hirano. Tokyo: Sophia University Press, 1969.

Fukuzawa Yukichi. *An Outline of a Theory of Civilization.* Translated by David A. Dilworth and G. Cameron Hurst. Tokyo: Sophia University, 1973.

Gluck, Carol. *Japan's Modern Myths: Ideology in the Late Meiji Period.* Princeton, N.J.: Princeton University Press, 1985.

Gondō Seikei (Seikyō). *Jichi minpan.* Tokyo: Heibonsha, 1927.

Hall, Ivan Parker. *Mori Arinori.* Harvard East Asian Series 68. Cambridge, Mass.: Harvard University Press, 1973.

Hall, Robert King, and John Owen Gauntlett. *Kokutai no hongi.* Cambridge, Mass.: Harvard University Press, 1949.

Hane, Mikiso, trans. and ed. *Reflections on the Way to the Gallows: Rebel Women in Prewar Japan.* Berkeley: University of California Press, 1988.

Hardacre, Helen. "Creating State Shintō: The Great Promulgation Campaign and the New Religions." *Journal of Japanese Studies* 12 (1986): 29–63.

Hardacre, Helen. *Shintō and the State, 1868–1988.* Princeton, N.J.: Princeton University Press, 1989.

Hardacre, Helen. "The Shintō Priesthood in Early Meiji Japan: Preliminary Inquiries." *History of Religions* 27 (1988): 294–320.

Hayakawa Kiyoji. *Tokutomi Sohō.* Tokyo: Ōzorasha, 1968.

Heisig, James W., and John C. Maraldo. *Rude Awakenings: Zen, the Kyoto School, and the Question of Nationalism.* Honolulu: University of Hawai'i Press, 1994.

Henny, Sue, and Jean-Pierre Lehmann, eds. *Themes and Theories in Modern Japanese History: Essays in Memory of Richard Storry.* London: Athlone, 1988.

Hijiya-Kirschnereit, Irmela, ed. *Canon and Identity: Japanese Modernization Reconsidered: Transcultural Perspectives.* Berlin: Deutsches Institut für Japanstudien, 2000.

Holtom, Daniel C. *Modern Japan and Shintō Nationalism: A Study of Present-Day Trends in Japanese Religions.* 1943. Reprint. New York: Paragon, 1963.

Holtom, Daniel C. *The National Faith of Japan.* New York: Dutton, 1938.

Hōrei zensho. 1867–1871.

Ienaga Saburō. *Ichi rekishigakusha no ayumi: kyōkasho saiban ni itaru made.* Tokyo: Sanseidō, 1967. [*Japan's Past, Japan's Future: One Historian's Odyssey.* Translated and introduced by Richard H. Minear. Lanham, Md.: Rowman & Littlefield, 2001.]

Ienaga Saburō. *Ienaga Saburō kyōkasho saiban.* Tokyo: Nihon hyōronsha, 1998.

Ienaga Saburō. *Minobe Tatsukichi no shisō shiteki kenkyū.* Tokyo: Iwanami shoten, 1964.

Ienaga Saburō. *The Pacific War, 1931–1945: A Critical Perspective on Japan's Role in World War II* [1968]. Translated by Frank Baldwin. New York: Pantheon Books, 1978.

Ifa (Iha) Fuyū. *Koryūkyū.* Naha: Okinawa kōronsha, 1911.

Ike, Nobutaka. *Japan's Decision for War: Records of the 1941 Policy Conferences.* Stanford, Calif.: Stanford University Press, 1967.

Ikeda Akira, ed. *Ōmoto shiryō shūsei.* 3 vols. Tokyo: San'ichi shobō, 1982.

International Military Tribunal for the Far East (IMTFE). International Prosecution Section. Document 487B, exhibit 1290; document 2402B, exhibit 1336.

Irokawa, Daikichi. *The Culture of the Meiji Period.* Translation edited by Marius B. Jansen. Princeton, N.J.: Princeton University Press, 1985.

Irokawa Daikichi. *Meiji no bunka.* Tokyo: Iwanami shoten, 1970.

Ishibashi Tanzan. *Ishibashi Tanzan chosakushū.* 4 vols. Tokyo: Tōyō keizai shinpōsha, 1996.

Ishibashi Tanzan. *Ishibashi Tanzan hyōron senshū.* Tokyo: Tōyō keizai shinpōsha, 1990.

Ishibashi Tanzan. *Ishibashi Tanzan hyōronshū.* Edited by Matsuo Takayoshi. Tokyo: Iwanami shoten, 1984.

Ishihara Kanji. *Ishihara Kanji shiryō: Kokubō ronsaku.* Edited by Tsunoda Jun. In *Meiji hyakunenshi sōsho,* vol. 18. Tokyo: Hara shobō, 1967.

Ishii Takashi. *Boshin sensō ron.* Tokyo: Yoshikawa kōbunkan, 1984.

Ishikawa Kaoru. *What Is Total Quality Control? The Japanese Way.* Translated by David J. Lu. Englewood Cliffs, N.J.: Prentice-Hall, 1985.

Ishimure Michiko, ed. *Waga shimin: Minamata byō tōsō.* Tokyo: Gendai hyōronsha, 1972.

Ishin Sūden. *Shintei honkō kokushi nikki.* 7 vols. Tokyo: Zoku gunsho ruijū kanseikai, 1966–1971.

Ishiwara Kanji. *See* Ishihara Kanji.

Ishizaka Kei. *Tadashii sensō.* Tokyo: Shūeisha, 1991.

Itagaki Taisuke, ed. *Jiyūtō shi.* In *Aoki bunko.* 4 vols. Tokyo: Aoki shoten, 1955.

Itō Hirobumi. *Itō Hirobumi den.* Edited by Shunpo kō tsuishōkai. 3 vols. Tokyo: Hara shobō, 1970.

Itō Hirobumi, trans. *Itō Miyoji Commentaries on the Constitution of the Empire of Japan.* Tokyo: Igirisu-hōritsu gakkō, 1889.

Iwakura Kō. *Iwakura Kō jikki.* Edited by Tada Kōmon. 3 vols. Tokyo: Hara shobō, 1968.

Iwakura Tomomi. "Dōjo shokei o imashimuru ikensho." In *Iwakura Tomomi kankei monjo,* vol. 1. Edited by Ōtsuka Takematsu. Tokyo: Nihon shiseki kyōkai, 1927.

Iwakura Tomomi. *Iwakura Tomomi kankei monjo.* Edited by Nihon shiseki kyōkai. 8 vols. Tokyo: University of Tokyo Press, 1968.

Iwasaki Hideshige. *Sakamoto Ryōma kankei monjo.* Tokyo: Nihon shiseki kyōkai, 1926.

Jennison, Rebecca. "Narrative Strategies in Shikin's 'The Broken Ring.'" *Journal of Kyoto Seika University,* no. 3 (1992): 28–35.

Jones, F. C. *Japan's New Order in East Asia: Its Rise and Fall, 1937–45.* Oxford: Oxford University Press, 1954.

Kagawa Toyohiko. *Before the Dawn* [1920]. Translated by I. Fukumoto and T. Satchell. New York: Doran, 1924.

Kamei Katsuichirō. *Nijisseiki Nihon no risōzō.* 1954. Reprint. Tokyo: Mikasa shobō, 1965.

Kaneko Fumiko. *The Prison Memoirs of a Japanese Woman.* Translated by Jean Inglis. Armonk, N.Y.: Sharpe, 1991.

Kano Masanao. *Kaisei suru rekishigaku: Jimeisei no kaitai no naka de.* Tokyo: Azekura shobō, 1998.

Katayama Sen and Nishikawa Kōjirō. *Nihon nō rōdō undō.* Tokyo: Iwanami shoten, 1952.

Katō Genchi. A *Study of Shintō, the Religion of the Japanese Nation*. Tokyo: Zaidan hōjin Meiji seitoku kinen gakkai, 1926.

Katō Shūichi et al. *Kido Takayoshi: Fukai kyōiku no shinbō ni tsuite kengen shoan*. In *NKST*, vol. 6.

Kawakami Hajime. *Gokuchū zeigo*. Kyoto: Kawahara shoten, 1949.

Kawakami Hajime. *Jijoden*. 5 vols. Tokyo: Iwanami shoten, 1952–1953.

Keene, Donald. *Emperor of Japan: Meiji and His World, 1852–1912*. New York: Columbia University Press, 2002.

Kido Takayoshi (Kōin). "Futsū kyōiku no shinkō ni tsuki kengen shōan." In *Kyōiku no taikei*. Edited by Yamazumi Masami. In *NKST*, vol. 6.

Kido Takayoshi. *Kido Takayoshi monjo*. Edited by Tsumaki Chūta. 8 vols. Tokyo: Nihon shiseki kyōkai, 1929–1931.

Kido Takayoshi. *Kido Takayoshi nikki*. Edited by Tsumaki Chūta. 3 vols. In *Nihon shiseki kyōkai sōsho*, vols. 74–76. Edited by Nihon shiseki kyōkai. Tokyo: University of Tokyo Press, 1967.

Kido Takayoshi. *Shōgiku Kido-kō den*. Edited by Kido-kō denki hensanjo. 2 vols. 1927. Reprint. Tokyo: Matsuno shoten, 1996.

Kikuchi Dairoku. *Japanese Education: Lectures Delivered in the University of London*. London: Murray, 1909.

Kita Ikki. *Nihon kaizō hōan taikō*. Tokyo: Minzoku mondai kenkyū-jo, 1953.

Kiyosawa Kiyoshi. *Gaiseika to shite no Ōkubo Toshimichi*. Tokyo: Chūō kōronsha, 1942.

Kiyosawa Kiyoshi. *Gendai Nihon ron*. Tokyo: Chikuma shobō, 1935.

Kobayashi Yoshinori. *Sensōron*. Tokyo: Gentōsha, 1998.

Kodansha Encyclopedia of Japan. 9 vols. Tokyo: Kodansha, 1983.

Konoe Fumimaro. "Against a Pacifism Centered on England and America." *Japan Echo*, November 1918, pp. 12–14. Reprinted in *Japan Echo* 22 (1995): 51–55. ["Ei-Bei hon'i no heiwashugi o haisu." *Nihon oyobi nihonjin*, December 15, 1918, pp. 23–26.]

Kōsaka Masaaki, ed., and David Abosch, trans. and adapter. *Japanese Thought in the Meiji Era*. Vol. 9 of *Japanese Culture in the Meiji Era*. Tokyo: Pan-Pacific Press, 1958.

Kōtoku Shūsui. "Waga shisō no henka." *Heimin shinbun*, February 5, 1907.

Kume Kunitake. *Kume Kunitake rekishi chosakushū*. 6 vols. Tokyo: Yoshikawa kōbun-kan, 1988–1991.

Kume Kunitake. "Shigaku kōshō no hei." In *Kume Kunitake rekishi chosakushū*, vol. 3. Tokyo: Yoshikawa kōbunkan, 1988.

Kume Kunitake. *Tokumei zenken taishi Bei-Ō kairan jikki*. 5 vols. 1878. Reprint. Tokyo: Iwanami shoten, 1977–1982.

Kurihara Sadako. *Black Eggs*. Translated by Richard H. Minear. Ann Arbor: Center for Japanese Studies, University of Michigan, 1994.

"Kyōgaku taishi." In *Kyōiku no taikei*. Edited by Yamazumi Masami. In *NKST*, vol. 6.

"Kyōkasho no sentaku ni wa kanshō no usuki o nozomu" [editorial]. *Kyōiku jiron*, February 25, 1886.

Lanman, Charles. *Leading Men of Japan*. Boston: Lothrop, 1883.

Lincicome, Mark E. *Principle, Praxis, and the Politics of Educational Reform in Meiji Japan*. Honolulu: University of Hawai'i Press, 1995.

Makiguchi Tsunesaburō. "Shūkyō to kagaku, dōtoku oyobi kyōiku to no kankei." In *Makiguchi Tsunesaburō zenshū*. Edited by Ikeda Daisaku. 5 vols. Tokyo: Tōzai tetsugaku shoin, 1965.

Maruyama Masao. "8/15 and 5/19." *Chūō kōron*, August 1960, pp. 51–54.

Maruyama Masao. *Gendai seiji no shisō to kōdō zōhoban*. Tokyo: Miraisha, 1964.

Maruyama Masao. "Kindai Nihon no chishikijin." In Maruyama Masao, *Kōei no ichi kara: "Gendai seiji no shisō to kōdō" tsuiho*. Tokyo: Miraisha, 1982.

Maruyama Masao. "The Logic and Psychology of Ultranationalism." In Maruyama Masao, *Thought and Behavior in Modern Japanese Politics*. Edited by Ivan Morris. New York: Oxford University Press, 1969.

Matsushita Keiichi. "Taishū tennōsei ron." *Chūō kōron*, April 1959, pp. 30–47.

Mayo, Marlene J. "The Iwakura Embassy and the Unequal Treaties, 1871–1873." Ph.D. diss., Columbia University, 1961.

McLaren, W. W. "Japanese Government Documents." *Transactions of the Asiatic Society of Japan* 42, pt. 1 (1914).

McLaren, W. W. *Japanese Government Documents*. Bethesda, Md.: University Publications of America, 1979.

Meiji boshin. Compiled by Bunmei kyōkai. Tokyo: Bunmei kyōkai, 1928.

Meiji nyūsu jiten. Mainichi komyunikeshon shuppanbu. Edited by Edamatsu Shigeyuki, Sugiura Tadashi, and Yagi Kōsuke. 9 vols. Tokyo: *Mainichi* komyunikeshonzu, 1983–1986.

Meiji tennō ki. Compiled by Kunaichō. 13 vols. Tokyo: Yoshikawa kōbunkan, 1968–1977.

Miki. *See* Nakayama Miki.

Miller, Frank O. *Minobe Tatsukichi: Interpreter of Constitutionalism in Japan*. Berkeley: University of California Press, 1965.

Ministry of Education. *The Way of Subjects*. Reprinted in Otto D. Tolischus, *Tokyo Record*. New York: Reynal and Hitchcock, 1943.

Minobe Tatsukichi. *Chikujō kenpō seigi*. Tokyo: Yūhikaku, 1927.

Minobe Tatsukichi. *Gikai seiji no kentō*. Tokyo: Hyōronsha, 1934.

Minobe Tatsukichi. *Kenpō kōwa*. Tokyo: Yūhikaku, 1913.

Minobe Tatsukichi. *Nihon kenpō*. 3rd ed. Tokyo: Yūhikaku, 1924.

Mishima Yukio. *Mishima Yukio hyōron zenshū*. 4 vols. Tokyo: Shinchōsha, 1989.

Mori Arinori. "Gakusei yōryō." In *Kyōiku no taikei*. Edited by Yamazumi Masami. In *NKST*, vol. 6.

Mori Arinori. "Saitamaken jinjō shihan gakkō ni okeru enzetsu" [speech delivered at the Saitama Prefectural Elementary Teachers School, December 19, 1885]. In *Kyōiku no taikei*. Edited by Yamazumi Masami. In *NKST*, vol. 6.

Morita, Akio. *Made in Japan: Akio Morita and Sony*. New York: Dutton, 1986.

Morito Tatsuo. "Heiwa kokka no kensetsu." *Kaizō* 27, January 1946. ["The Construction of a Peaceful Nation." *Contemporary Japan* 15 (January–April 1946): 109–17.]

Motoyama, Yukihiko. *Proliferating Talent: Essays on Politics, Thought, and Education in the Meiji Era*. Edited by J. S. A. Elisonas and Richard Rubinger. Honolulu: University of Hawai'i Press, 1997.

Nakae Chōmin. *A Discourse by Three Drunkards on Government*. Translated by Nobuko Tsukui. Edited by Nobuko Tsukui and Jeffrey Hammon. New York: Weatherhill, 1984.

Nakamura Keiu [Masanao]. "Kokin tōzai itchi dōtoku no setsu." *Tōkyō gakushikaiin zasshi*, April 14, 1890. In *Meiji keimō shisō shū*. Edited by Ōkubo Toshiaki. Vol. 3 of *Meiji bungaku zenshū*. Tokyo: Chikuma shobō, 1967.

Nakamura Masanori. "Meiji ishin kenkyū no konnichiteki imi." *Asahi shinbun* [evening edition], April 4, 1989.

Nakasone Yasuhiro. "The Problems of Japanese Democracy" [speech delivered at Harvard University, July 30, 1953]. In Nakasone Yasuhiro, *Nihon no shuchō*. Tokyo: Keizai ōrai sha, 1954.

Nakayama Miki. *Mikagura-uta*. Tenri: Tenrikyō Church Headquarters, 1990.

Nakayama Miki. *Ofudesaki, The Tip of the Writing Brush: English, Japanese, and Romanization*. Multivolume ed. Tenri: Tenrikyō Church Headquarters, 1998.

Nikkan gappō hishi. 2 vols. Tokyo: Kokuryūkai shuppanbu, 1930.

Nishida Kitarō. *Nihon bunka no mondai*. Vol. 60 of *Iwanami shinsho*. Tokyo: Iwanami shoten, 1940.

Nishida Kitarō. *Nihon bunka no mondai*. In *Nishida Kitarō zenshū*, vol. 12. Tokyo: Iwanami shoten, 1978–1980.

Noro Eitarō. *Nihon shihonshugi hattatsushi*. Tokyo: Tetsuto shoin, 1930.

Notehelfer, Fred G. "Japan's First Pollution Incident." *Journal of Japanese Studies* 1 (1975): 351–83.

Ōe Kenzaburō. *Hiroshima Notes*. Translated by Toshi Yonezawa and David Swain. Tokyo: YMCA Press, 1981.

Ōe Kenzaburō. "Japan, the Ambiguous, and Myself" [Nobel Prize lecture, December 7, 1994]. In *Nobel Lectures in Literature, 1991–1995*. Edited by Sture Allén. Singapore: World Scientific, 1997.

Ōe Kenzaburō. "A Portrait of the Postwar Generation." *Japan Quarterly* 12 (1965): 347–51.

Okakura, Kakuzō. *The Book of Tea*. New York: Fox, Duffield, 1906.

Okakura, Kakuzō. *The Ideals of the East, with Special Reference to the Art of Japan*. New York: Dutton, 1904.

Ōkuma Shigenobu. *Fifty Years of New Japan*. 2 vols. London: Smith, Elder, 1909.

Ōkurashō zaiseishitsu. *Shōwa zaisei shi shūsen kara kōwa made, eibun shiryō*. Vol. 20 of *Shōwa zaiseishi shūsen kara kōwa made*. Tokyo: Tōyō keizai shinpōsha, 1984.

Orii Hyūga. *Rōmu kanri 20 nen*. Tokyo: Tōyō keizai shinpōsha, 1973.

Ōsugi Sakae. *The Autobiography of Ōsugi Sakae* [1930]. Translated and introduced by Byron K. Marshall. Berkeley: University of California Press, 1992.

Ozaki Yukio, with Joseph Ernest DeBecker. *The Voice of Japanese Democracy: Being an Essay on Constitutional Loyalty*. Yokohama: Kelly and Walsh, 1918.

Passin, Herbert. *Society and Education in Japan*. New York: Teachers College Press and the East Asian Institute, Columbia University, 1965.

Peace Problems Discussion Group. "Kōwa mondai ni tsuite no heiwa mondai kondan kai seimei." *Sekai*, no. 51 (March 1950).

Pierson, John D. *Tokutomi Sohō, 1863–1957: A Journalist for Modern Japan*. Princeton, N.J.: Princeton University Press, 1980.

Pittau, Joseph, S.J. "Inoue Kowashi, 1843–1895, and the Formation of Modern Japan." In *Learning to Be Japanese: Selected Readings on Japanese Society and Education*. Edited by Edward R. Beauchamp. Hamden, Conn.: Linnet Books, 1978.

Rikugunshō. *Kokubō no hongi to sono kyōka no teishō*. Tokyo: Shinbunhan, 1934.

Rubin, Jay. "Sōseki on Individualism: "Watakushi no kojin shugi." *Monumenta Nipponica* 34 (1979): 21–48.

Ryū Shintarō. *Nihon keizai no saihensei*. Tokyo: Chūō kōronsha, 1940.

Saigō Takamori. *Saigō Takamori monjo*. In *Nihon shiseki kyōkai sōsho*, vol. 102. Edited by Nihon shiseki kyōkai. Tokyo: University of Tokyo Press, 1967.

Sano Manabu and Nabeyama Sadachika. "Kyōdō hikoku dōshi ni tsuguru sho." *Kaizō*, July 1933.

Satow, Ernest. *A Diplomat in Japan*. Oxford: Oxford University Press, 1968.

Shiba Ryōtarō. *Tōge*. Tokyo: Shinchōsha, 1968.

Shigeno Yasutsugu. "Shigaku ni jūji suru mono wa sono kokoro shikō shihei narazaru bekarazu." *Shigakkai zasshi*, December 15, 1889.

Shikin. *See* Shimizu Toyoko.

Shimazu, Naoko. *Japan, Race, and Equality: The Racial Equality Proposal of 1919*. New York: Routledge, 1998.

Shimizu Toyoko. *Shikin zenshū*. Edited by Kozai Yoshishige. Tokyo: Sōdo bunka, 1983.

Shinobu Seizaburō. *Taishō seiji shi*. 4 vols. Tokyo: Kawade shobō, 1951–1952.

Shinshūkyō jiten. Edited by Inoue Nobutaka et al. Tokyo: Yoshikawa kōbunkan, 1990.

Sievers, Sharon Lee. *Flowers in Salt: The Beginnings of Feminist Consciousness in Modern Japan*. Stanford, Calif.: Stanford University Press, 1983.

Smith, Thomas. "Japan's Aristocratic Revolution." *Yale Review* 50 (1961): 370–83.

Special Survey Committee, Ministry of Foreign Affairs. *Postwar Reconstruction of the Japanese Economy*. Compiled by Ōkita Saburō. Tokyo: University of Tokyo Press, 1992.

Stanley, Thomas A. *Ōsugi Sakae: Anarchist in Taishō Japan: The Creativity of the Ego*. Cambridge, Mass.: Council on East Asian Studies, Harvard University, 1982.

Supreme Commander for Allied Powers (SCAP), Civil Information and Education Section. *Education in the New Japan*. 2 vols. Tokyo: General Headquarters, Civil Information and Education Section, Education Division, 1948.

Supreme Commander for Allied Powers (SCAP), Government Section. *Political Reorientation of Japan: September 1945 to September 1948*. 2 vols. Washington, D.C.: Government Printing Office, 1949.

Supreme Commander for Allied Powers (SCAP), Government Section. Report, January 30, 1951, "Opposition Representatives Interpellate PM on Treaty" (January 29, 1951). Reel 25, 0238, Justin Williams Papers, Gordon W. Prange Collection, University of Maryland Libraries, College Park.

Taguchi Ukichi. *Nihon kaika shōshi*. 1955. Reprint. Tokyo: Kōdansha, 1981.

Takamure Itsue. *Josei no rekishi* [1954–1958]. In *Takamure Itsue zenshū*, vol. 4. Tokyo: Rironsha, 1965–1966.

Tanabe Hajime. *Philosophy as Metanoetics*. Translated by Takeuchi Yoshinori et al. Berkeley: University of California Press, 1986.

Tanaka Kakuei. *Building a New Japan: A Plan for Remodeling the Japanese Archipelago*. Tokyo: Simul Press, 1973.

Tanaka Kōtarō. *Shinri to heiwa o motomete*. Tokyo: Dai Nihon yūbenkai Kōdansha, 1950.

Tenrikyō Church Headquarters. *The Life of Oyasama, Foundress of Tenrikyō*. 2nd ed. Tenri: Tenri jihōsha, 1991.

Tenrikyō Overseas Mission Department. *Selections from the Osashizu*. Tenri: Tenri jihōsha, 1990.

Tiedemann, Arthur E. *Modern Japan: A Brief History*. Rev. ed. New York: Van Nostrand Reinhold, 1962.

Toda Jōsei. "Seimeiron." In Kodaira Yoshihei, *Shakubuku kyōten*. Tokyo: Sōka gakkai, 1954.

Tōjō Hideki. "Address to Greater East Asia Conference." *Contemporary Japan* 12 (November 1943): 1343–47.

Tokutomi Sohō. "Jishuteki gaikō no igi." *Kokumin no tomo*, February 8, 1896.

Tokutomi Sohō. *Jiyū dōtoku oyobi jukyōshugi*. Kumamoto, 1884.

Tokutomi Sohō. In *Ōsaka mainichi shinbun*, February 25, 1933.

Tokutomi Sohō. In *Ōsaka mainichi shinbun*, November 4, 1941.

Tokutomi Sohō. *Senji gaigen*. Tokyo, 1937.

Tokutomi Sohō. *Shōrai no Nihon* [1886]. [*The Future Japan*. Translated by Vinh Sinh, with Hiroki Matsuzawa and Nicholas Wickenden. Edmonton: University of Alberta Press, 1989.]

Tokutomi Sohō. *Shōwa ishin ron*. Tokyo, 1927.

Tolischus, Otto D. *Tokyo Record*. New York: Reynal and Hitchcock, 1943.

Toriumi Yasushi et al. *Gendai no Nihonshi* [1994]. In International Society for Educational Information, *High School*. Vol. 2 of *Japan in Modern History*. Tokyo: International Society for Educational Information, 1995.

Tosaka Jun. *Nihon ideorogī ron*. Tokyo: Hakuyōsha, 1938.

Toynbee, Arnold, and Daisaku Ikeda. *Choose Life: A Dialogue*. Edited by Richard L. Gage. Oxford: Oxford University Press, 1976.

Tsunoda, Ryusaku, Wm. Theodore de Bary, and Donald Keene, eds. *Sources of Japanese Tradition*. 1st ed. Vol. 2. New York: Columbia University Press, 1958.

Ubukata Toshirō. "Kenpō happu to Nisshin sensō." In Tsurumi Shunsuke, *Jiyanarizumu no shisō*, Tokyo: Chikuma shobō, 1965.

Uchida Yoshihiko et al., eds. *Marukushizumu* I. Vol. 20 of *Gendai Nihon shisō taikei*. Tokyo: Chikuma shobō, 1966.

Uchimura Kanzō. *Uchimura Kanzō zenshū*. 20 vols. Tokyo: Iwanami shoten, 1932–1933.

Umetani Noboru. *Meiji zenki seijishi no kenkyū*. Tokyo: Miraisha, 1978.

Uno Kōzō. Shihonron *no kakushin*. Vol. 4 of *Uno Kōzō chosakushū*. Tokyo: Iwanami shoten, 1973–1974.

Watanabe Ikujirō. *Ōkuma Shigenobu, shin Nihon no kensetsusha*. Tokyo: Shōrindō shoten, 1943.

Watsuji Tetsurō. *A Climate: A Philosophical Study*. Translated by Geoffrey Bownas. Tokyo: Japanese Committee for UNESCO, 1961.

Wilson, George M. *Patriots and Redeemers in Japan: Motives in the Meiji Restoration*. Chicago: University of Chicago Press, 1992.

Woodward, William P. *The Allied Occupation of Japan 1945–1952 and Japanese Religions*. Leiden: Brill, 1972.

Yada Giichi. "Sayonara chūryū ishiki." *Asahi shinbun*, November 9, 1997.

Yagiri Tomeo, ed. *Meiji shigakkai zasshi: Nihon rekishi shiryō taisei* [*Shigakkai zasshi* (1889)]. Tokyo: Nihon sheru shuppan, 1976.

Yamada Moritarō. *Nihon shihon-shugi bunseki*. 1934. Reprint. Tokyo: Iwanami bunko, 1992.

Yamamoto Yoshihiko. *Kindai Nihon shihonshugi: Rekishi kara gendai*. Kyoto: Minerva, 2002.

Yamamoto Yoshihiko. *Kiyosawa Kiyoshi hyōronshū*. Tokyo: Iwanami shoten, 2002.

Yamamuro Sōbun. *Kinkaikin o chūshin to seru wagakuni keizai oyobi kin'yū*. In *Keizaigaku zenshū*, vol. 46. Tokyo: Kaizōsha, 1931.

Yamamuro Sōbun. *Waga kuni keizai oyobi kin'yū*.

Yanagi Muneyoshi. "Chōsen to sono geijutsu." In *Yanagi Muneyoshi senshū*, vol. 4. Tokyo: Shunjūsha, 1954.

Yanagita Kunio. *Minkan denshōron* [1934]. Tokyo: Daisan shokan, 1986.

Yokota Kisaburō. "Shakai to gaikō." In *Shakai shichō*, vol. 1. Tokyo: Hōsei daigaku shuppan kyoku, 1991.

Yoshida, Shigeru. *The Yoshida Memoirs: The Story of Japan in Crisis*. Translated by Kenichi Yoshida. Boston: Houghton Mifflin, 1962.

Yoshimi, Yoshiaki. *Comfort Women: Sexual Slavery in the Japanese Military During World War II*. Translated by Suzanne O'Brien. New York: Columbia University Press, 2000.

Yoshimoto Takaaki. "Gisei no shūen." In Tanigawa Gan et al., *Minshushugi no shinwa*. Tokyo: Gendai no shichōsha, 1966. Reprinted in *Yoshimoto Takaaki zenchosaku shū*. Tokyo: Keisō shobō, 1969.

Yoshino Sakuzō. *Minpon shugi ron*. Vol. 1 of *Yoshino Sakuzō hakushi minshu shugi ron*. Tokyo: Shin kigensha, 1948.

PERIODICALS AND NEWSPAPERS

Asahi
Chūō kōron
Contemporary Japan
Heimin shinbun
Japan Echo
Japan Quarterly
Jiji shinpō
Kaizō
Kokumin no tomo
Kyōiku jiron
Mainichi
Monumenta Nipponica
Nihon oyobi nihonjin
Nippon Times
Ōsaka mainichi shinbun
Rekishigaku kenkyū

Sekai
Shakai shichō
Tokio Times
Tokyo gakushikaiin zasshi
Tokyo Gazette
Tōkyō nichi nichi shinbun
Tokyo Times
Yale Review
Yomiuri shinbun

INDEX

OTHER WORKS IN THE

COLUMBIA ASIAN STUDIES SERIES

Reflections on Things at Hand: The Neo-Confucian Anthology, comp. Chu Hsi and Lü Tsu-ch'ien, tr. Wing-tsit Chan 1967

The Platform Sutra of the Sixth Patriarch, tr. Philip B. Yampolsky. Also in paperback ed. 1967

Essays in Idleness: The Tsurezuregusa of Kenkō, tr. Donald Keene. Also in paperback ed. 1967

The Pillow Book of Sei Shōnagon, tr. Ivan Morris, 2 vols. 1967

Two Plays of Ancient India: The Little Clay Cart and the Minister's Seal, tr. J. A. B. van Buitenen 1968

The Complete Works of Chuang Tzu, tr. Burton Watson 1968

The Romance of the Western Chamber (Hsi Hsiang chi), tr. S. I. Hsiung. Also in paperback ed. 1968

The Manyōshū, Nippon Gakujutsu Shinkōkai edition. Paperback ed. only. 1969

Records of the Historian: Chapters from the Shih chi of Ssu-ma Ch'ien, tr. Burton Watson. Paperback ed. only. 1969

Cold Mountain: 100 Poems by the T'ang Poet Han-shan, tr. Burton Watson. Also in paperback ed. 1970

Twenty Plays of the Nō Theatre, ed. Donald Keene. Also in paperback ed. 1970

Chūshingura: The Treasury of Loyal Retainers, tr. Donald Keene. Also in paperback ed. 1971; rev. ed. 1997

The Zen Master Hakuin: Selected Writings, tr. Philip B. Yampolsky 1971

Chinese Rhyme-Prose: Poems in the Fu Form from the Han and Six Dynasties Periods, tr. Burton Watson. Also in paperback ed. 1971

Kūkai: Major Works, tr. Yoshito S. Hakeda. Also in paperback ed. 1972

The Old Man Who Does as He Pleases: Selections from the Poetry and Prose of Lu Yu, tr. Burton Watson 1973

The Lion's Roar of Queen Śrīmālā, tr. Alex and Hideko Wayman 1974

Courtier and Commoner in Ancient China: Selections from the History of the Former Han by Pan Ku, tr. Burton Watson. Also in paperback ed. 1974

Japanese Literature in Chinese, vol. 1: Poetry and Prose in Chinese by Japanese Writers of the Early Period, tr. Burton Watson 1975

Japanese Literature in Chinese, vol. 2: Poetry and Prose in Chinese by Japanese Writers of the Later Period, tr. Burton Watson 1976

Scripture of the Lotus Blossom of the Fine Dharma, tr. Leon Hurvitz. Also in paperback ed. 1976

Love Song of the Dark Lord: Jayadeva's Gītagovinda, tr. Barbara Stoler Miller. Also in paperback ed. Cloth ed. includes critical text of the Sanskrit. 1977; rev. ed. 1997

Ryōkan: Zen Monk-Poet of Japan, tr. Burton Watson 1977

Calming the Mind and Discerning the Real: From the Lam rim chen mo of Tsoṇ-kha-pa, tr. Alex Wayman 1978

The Hermit and the Love-Thief: Sanskrit Poems of Bhartrihari and Bilhaṇa, tr. Barbara Stoler Miller 1978

The Lute: Kao Ming's P'i-p'a chi, tr. Jean Mulligan. Also in paperback ed. 1980

A Chronicle of Gods and Sovereigns: Jinnō Shōtōki of Kitabatake Chikafusa, tr. H. Paul Varley 1980

Among the Flowers: The Hua-chien chi, tr. Lois Fusek 1982

Grass Hill: Poems and Prose by the Japanese Monk Gensei, tr. Burton Watson 1983

Doctors, Diviners, and Magicians of Ancient China: Biographies of Fang-shih, tr. Kenneth J. DeWoskin. Also in paperback ed. 1983

Theater of Memory: The Plays of Kālidāsa, ed. Barbara Stoler Miller. Also in paperback ed. 1984

The Columbia Book of Chinese Poetry: From Early Times to the Thirteenth Century, ed. and tr. Burton Watson. Also in paperback ed. 1984

Poems of Love and War: From the Eight Anthologies and the Ten Long Poems of Classical Tamil, tr. A. K. Ramanujan. Also in paperback ed. 1985

The Bhagavad Gita: Krishna's Counsel in Time of War, tr. Barbara Stoler Miller 1986

The Columbia Book of Later Chinese Poetry, ed. and tr. Jonathan Chaves. Also in paperback ed. 1986

The Tso Chuan: Selections from China's Oldest Narrative History, tr. Burton Watson 1989

Waiting for the Wind: Thirty-six Poets of Japan's Late Medieval Age, tr. Steven Carter 1989

Selected Writings of Nichiren, ed. Philip B. Yampolsky 1990

Saigyō, Poems of a Mountain Home, tr. Burton Watson 1990

The Book of Lieh Tzu: A Classic of the Tao, tr. A. C. Graham. Morningside ed. 1990

The Tale of an Anklet: An Epic of South India—The Cilappatikāram of Iḷaṅkō Aṭikaḷ, tr. R. Parthasarathy 1993

Waiting for the Dawn: A Plan for the Prince, tr. and introduction by Wm. Theodore de Bary 1993

Yoshitsune and the Thousand Cherry Trees: A Masterpiece of the Eighteenth-Century Japanese Puppet Theater, tr., annotated, and with introduction by Stanleigh H. Jones, Jr. 1993

The Lotus Sutra, tr. Burton Watson. Also in paperback ed. 1993

The Classic of Changes: A New Translation of the I Ching as Interpreted by Wang Bi, tr. Richard John Lynn 1994

Beyond Spring: Tz'u Poems of the Sung Dynasty, tr. Julie Landau 1994

The Columbia Anthology of Traditional Chinese Literature, ed. Victor H. Mair 1994

Scenes for Mandarins: The Elite Theater of the Ming, tr. Cyril Birch 1995

Letters of Nichiren, ed. Philip B. Yampolsky; tr. Burton Watson et al. 1996

Unforgotten Dreams: Poems by the Zen Monk Shōtetsu, tr. Steven D. Carter 1997

The Vimalakirti Sutra, tr. Burton Watson 1997

Japanese and Chinese Poems to Sing: The Wakan rōei shū, tr. J. Thomas Rimer and Jonathan Chaves 1997

Breeze Through Bamboo: Kanshi of Ema Saikō, tr. Hiroaki Sato 1998

A Tower for the Summer Heat, Li Yu, tr. Patrick Hanan 1998

Traditional Japanese Theater: An Anthology of Plays, Karen Brazell 1998

The Original Analects: Sayings of Confucius and His Successors (0479–0249), E. Bruce Brooks and A. Taeko Brooks 1998

The Classic of the Way and Virtue: A New Translation of the Tao-te ching of Laozi as Interpreted by Wang Bi, tr. Richard John Lynn 1999

The Four Hundred Songs of War and Wisdom: An Anthology of Poems from Classical Tamil, The Puṛanāṉūṛu, ed. and tr. George L. Hart and Hank Heifetz 1999

Original Tao: Inward Training (Nei-yeh) *and the Foundations of Taoist Mysticism*, by Harold D. Roth 1999

Lao Tzu's Tao Te Ching: A Translation of the Startling New Documents Found at Guodian, by Robert G. Henricks 2000

The Shorter Columbia Anthology of Traditional Chinese Literature, ed. Victor H. Mair 2000

Mistress and Maid (Jiaohongji), by Meng Chengshun, tr. Cyril Birch 2001

Chikamatsu: Five Late Plays, tr. and ed. C. Andrew Gerstle 2001

The Essential Lotus: Selections from the Lotus Sutra, tr. Burton Watson 2002

Early Modern Japanese Literature: An Anthology, 1600–1900, ed. Haruo Shirane 2002

The Sound of the Kiss, or The Story That Must Never Be Told: Pingali Suranna's Ka-lapurnodayamu, tr. Vecheru Narayana Rao and David Shulman 2003

The Selected Poems of Du Fu, tr. Burton Watson 2003

Far Beyond the Field: Haiku by Japanese Women, tr. Makoto Ueda 2003

Just Living: Poems and Prose by the Japanese Monk Tonna, ed. and tr. Steven D. Carter 2003

Han Feizi: Basic Writings, tr. Burton Watson 2003

Mozi: Basic Writings, tr. Burton Watson 2003

Xunzi: Basic Writings, tr. Burton Watson 2003

Zhuangzi: Basic Writings, tr. Burton Watson 2003

The Awakening of Faith, Attributed to Aśvaghosha, tr. Yoshito S. Hakeda, introduction by Ryuichi Abe 2005

The Tales of the Heike, tr. Burton Watson, ed. Haruo Shirane 2006

Tales of Moonlight and Rain, Ueda Akinari, tr. and introduction by Anthony H. Chambers 2007

MODERN ASIAN LITERATURE

Modern Japanese Drama: An Anthology, ed. and tr. Ted. Takaya. Also in paperback ed. 1979

Mask and Sword: Two Plays for the Contemporary Japanese Theater, by Yamazaki Masakazu, tr. J. Thomas Rimer 1980

Yokomitsu Riichi, Modernist, Dennis Keene 1980

Nepali Visions, Nepali Dreams: The Poetry of Laxmiprasad Devkota, tr. David Rubin 1980

Literature of the Hundred Flowers, vol. 1: Criticism and Polemics, ed. Hualing Nieh 1981

Literature of the Hundred Flowers, vol. 2: Poetry and Fiction, ed. Hualing Nieh 1981

Modern Chinese Stories and Novellas, 1919–1949, ed. Joseph S. M. Lau, C. T. Hsia, and Leo Ou-fan Lee. Also in paperback ed. 1984

A View by the Sea, by Yasuoka Shōtarō, tr. Kären Wigen Lewis 1984

Other Worlds: Arishima Takeo and the Bounds of Modern Japanese Fiction, by Paul Anderer 1984

Selected Poems of Sō Chōngju, tr. with introduction by David R. McCann 1989

The Sting of Life: Four Contemporary Japanese Novelists, by Van C. Gessel 1989

Stories of Osaka Life, by Oda Sakunosuke, tr. Burton Watson 1990

The Bodhisattva, or Samantabhadra, by Ishikawa Jun, tr. with introduction by William Jefferson Tyler 1990

The Travels of Lao Ts'an, by Liu T'ieh-yün, tr. Harold Shadick. Morningside ed. 1990

Three Plays by Kōbō Abe, tr. with introduction by Donald Keene 1993

The Columbia Anthology of Modern Chinese Literature, ed. Joseph S. M. Lau and Howard Goldblatt 1995

Modern Japanese Tanka, ed. and tr. Makoto Ueda 1996

Masaoka Shiki: Selected Poems, ed. and tr. Burton Watson 1997

Writing Women in Modern China: An Anthology of Women's Literature from the Early Twentieth Century, ed. and tr. Amy D. Dooling and Kristina M. Torgeson 1998

American Stories, by Nagai Kafū, tr. Mitsuko Iriye 2000

The Paper Door and Other Stories, by Shiga Naoya, tr. Lane Dunlop 2001

Grass for My Pillow, by Saiichi Maruya, tr. Dennis Keene 2002

For All My Walking: Free-Verse Haiku of Taneda Santōka, with Excerpts from His Diaries, tr. Burton Watson 2003

The Columbia Anthology of Modern Japanese Literature, vol. 1: *From Restoration to Occupation, 1868–1945,* ed. J. Thomas Rimer and Van C. Gessel, vol. 1, 2005

STUDIES IN ASIAN CULTURE

The Ōnin War: History of Its Origins and Background, with a Selective Translation of the Chronicle of Ōnin, by H. Paul Varley 1967

Chinese Government in Ming Times: Seven Studies, ed. Charles O. Hucker 1969

The Actors' Analects (Yakusha Rongo), ed. and tr. Charles J. Dunn and Bungō Torigoe 1969

Self and Society in Ming Thought, by Wm. Theodore de Bary and the Conference on Ming Thought. Also in paperback ed. 1970

A History of Islamic Philosophy, by Majid Fakhry, 2d ed. 1983

Phantasies of a Love Thief: The Caurapañcāśikā Attributed to Bilhaṇa, by Barbara Stoler Miller 1971

Iqbal: Poet-Philosopher of Pakistan, ed. Hafeez Malik 1971

The Golden Tradition: An Anthology of Urdu Poetry, ed. and tr. Ahmed Ali. Also in paperback ed. 1973

Conquerors and Confucians: Aspects of Political Change in Late Yüan China, by John W. Dardess 1973

The Unfolding of Neo-Confucianism, by Wm. Theodore de Bary and the Conference on Seventeenth-Century Chinese Thought. Also in paperback ed. 1975

To Acquire Wisdom: The Way of Wang Yang-ming, by Julia Ching 1976

Gods, Priests, and Warriors: The Bhṛgus of the Mahābhārata, by Robert P. Goldman 1977

Mei Yao-ch'en and the Development of Early Sung Poetry, by Jonathan Chaves 1976

The Legend of Semimaru, Blind Musician of Japan, by Susan Matisoff 1977

Sir Sayyid Ahmad Khan and Muslim Modernization in India and Pakistan, by Hafeez Malik 1980

The Khilafat Movement: Religious Symbolism and Political Mobilization in India, by Gail Minault 1982

The World of K'ung Shang-jen: A Man of Letters in Early Ch'ing China, by Richard Strassberg 1983

The Lotus Boat: The Origins of Chinese Tz'u Poetry in T'ang Popular Culture, by Marsha L. Wagner 1984

Expressions of Self in Chinese Literature, ed. Robert E. Hegel and Richard C. Hessney 1985

Songs for the Bride: Women's Voices and Wedding Rites of Rural India, by W. G. Archer; ed. Barbara Stoler Miller and Mildred Archer 1986

The Confucian Kingship in Korea: Yŏngjo and the Politics of Sagacity, by JaHyun Kim Haboush 1988

COMPANIONS TO ASIAN STUDIES

Approaches to the Oriental Classics, ed. Wm. Theodore de Bary 1959

Early Chinese Literature, by Burton Watson. Also in paperback ed. 1962

Approaches to Asian Civilizations, ed. Wm. Theodore de Bary and Ainslie T. Embree 1964

The Classic Chinese Novel: A Critical Introduction, by C. T. Hsia. Also in paperback ed. 1968

Chinese Lyricism: Shih Poetry from the Second to the Twelfth Century, tr. Burton Watson. Also in paperback ed. 1971

A Syllabus of Indian Civilization, by Leonard A. Gordon and Barbara Stoler Miller 1971

Twentieth-Century Chinese Stories, ed. C. T. Hsia and Joseph S. M. Lau. Also in paperback ed. 1971

A Syllabus of Chinese Civilization, by J. Mason Gentzler, 2d ed. 1972

A Syllabus of Japanese Civilization, by H. Paul Varley, 2d ed. 1972

An Introduction to Chinese Civilization, ed. John Meskill, with the assistance of J. Mason Gentzler 1973

An Introduction to Japanese Civilization, ed. Arthur E. Tiedemann 1974

Ukifune: Love in the Tale of Genji, ed. Andrew Pekarik 1982

The Pleasures of Japanese Literature, by Donald Keene 1988

A Guide to Oriental Classics, ed. Wm. Theodore de Bary and Ainslie T. Embree; 3d edition ed. Amy Vladeck Heinrich, 2 vols. 1989

INTRODUCTION TO ASIAN CIVILIZATIONS
Wm. Theodore de Bary, General Editor

Sources of Japanese Tradition, 1958; paperback ed., 2 vols., 1964. 2d ed., vol. 1, 2001, compiled by Wm. Theodore de Bary, Donald Keene, George Tanabe, and Paul Varley; vol. 2, 2005, compiled by Wm. Theodore de Bary, Carol Gluck, and Arthur E. Tiedemann

Sources of Indian Tradition, 1958; paperback ed., 2 vols., 1964. 2d ed., 2 vols., 1988

Sources of Chinese Tradition, 1960, paperback ed., 2 vols., 1964. 2d ed., vol. 1, 1999, compiled by Wm. Theodore de Bary and Irene Bloom; vol. 2, 2000, compiled by Wm. Theodore de Bary and Richard Lufrano

Sources of Korean Tradition, 1997; 2 vols., vol. 1, 1997, compiled by Peter H. Lee and
Wm. Theodore de Bary; vol. 2, 2001, compiled by Yŏnghu Ch'oe, Peter H. Lee,
and Wm. Theodore de Bary

NEO-CONFUCIAN STUDIES

*Instructions for Practical Living and Other Neo-Confucian Writings by Wang Yang-
ming*, tr. Wing-tsit Chan 1963

Reflections on Things at Hand: The Neo-Confucian Anthology, comp. Chu Hsi and
Lü Tsu-ch'ien, tr. Wing-tsit Chan 1967

Self and Society in Ming Thought, by Wm. Theodore de Bary and the Conference on
Ming Thought. Also in paperback ed. 1970

The Unfolding of Neo-Confucianism, by Wm. Theodore de Bary and the Conference
on Seventeenth-Century Chinese Thought. Also in paperback ed. 1975

Principle and Practicality: Essays in Neo-Confucianism and Practical Learning, ed.
Wm. Theodore de Bary and Irene Bloom. Also in paperback ed. 1979

The Syncretic Religion of Lin Chao-en, by Judith A. Berling 1980

The Renewal of Buddhism in China: Chu-hung and the Late Ming Synthesis, by Chün-
fang Yü 1981

Neo-Confucian Orthodoxy and the Learning of the Mind-and-Heart, by Wm. Theodore
de Bary 1981

Yüan Thought: Chinese Thought and Religion Under the Mongols, ed. Hok-lam Chan
and Wm. Theodore de Bary 1982

The Liberal Tradition in China, by Wm. Theodore de Bary 1983

The Development and Decline of Chinese Cosmology, by John B. Henderson 1984

The Rise of Neo-Confucianism in Korea, by Wm. Theodore de Bary and JaHyun Kim
Haboush 1985

Chiao Hung and the Restructuring of Neo-Confucianism in Late Ming, by Edward T.
Ch'ien 1985

Neo-Confucian Terms Explained: Pei-hsi tzu-i, by Ch'en Ch'un, ed. and tr. Wing-tsit
Chan 1986

Knowledge Painfully Acquired: K'un-chih chi, by Lo Ch'in-shun, ed. and tr. Irene
Bloom 1987

To Become a Sage: The Ten Diagrams on Sage Learning, by Yi T'oegye, ed. and tr.
Michael C. Kalton 1988

The Message of the Mind in Neo-Confucian Thought, by Wm. Theodore de Bary 1989